Brief Contents

i

ELEVENTH EDITION

Strategies for Successful Writing

A Rhetoric, Research Guide, Reader, and Handbook

James A. Reinking

Robert von der Osten

New!
2016
MLA
Updates

PEARSON

Boston   Columbus   Indianapolis   New York   San Francisco
Amsterdam   Cape Town   Dubai   London   Madrid   Milan   Munich   Paris   Montréal   Toronto
Delhi   Mexico City   São Paulo   Sydney   Hong Kong   Seoul   Singapore   Taipei   Tokyo

Vice President and Editor-in-Chief: Joseph Opiela
Program Manager: Anne Shure
Development Editor: Steven Rigolosi
Product Marketing Manager: Ali Arnold
Field Marketing Manager: Mark Robinson
Digital Editor: Tracy Cunningham
Media Producer: Marisa Massaro
Content Specialist: Laura Olson

Project Manager: Shannon Kobran
Project Coordination, Text Design, and Electronic Page Makeup: Lumina Datamatics, Inc.
Design Lead: Heather Scott
Cover Designer: Studio Montage
Senior Manufacturing Buyer: Roy L. Pickering, Jr.
Printer/Binder: LSC Communications/Crawfordsville
Cover Printer: Lehigh-Phoenix Color/Hagerstown

Acknowledgments of third-party content appear on pages 645–648, which constitute an extension of this copyright page.

Library of Congress Cataloging-in-Publication Data

Reinking, James A., author.
    Strategies for successful writing: a rhetoric, research guide, reader, and handbook / James A. Reinking,
Robert Von Der Osten.—Eleventh Edition.
        pages cm
    Includes bibliographical references and index.
    ISBN 978-0-13-411924-3—ISBN 0-13-411924-X
    1. English language–Rhetoric–Handbooks, manuals, etc.   2. English language–Grammar–Handbooks, manuals, etc.
3. Report writing–Handbooks, manuals, etc.   4. College readers.   I. Von der Osten, Robert, author.   II. Title.
    PE1408.R426 2016
    808'.0427–dc23
                                                                                    2015035527

2 17

www.pearsonhighered.com

Student Edition ISBN-13: 978-0-13-467874-0
Student Edition ISBN-10:   0-13-467874-5

A la Carte ISBN-13: 978-0-13-471377-9
A la Carte ISBN-10:   0-13-471377-X

Contents

Verbals Not in Phrases   Participles, gerunds, and infinitives can function as nouns, adjectives, or adverbs, even when they are not parts of phrases.

> That *sunbathing* woman is a well-known model. (participle as adjective)
> *Dancing* is fine exercise. (gerund)
> The children want *to play*. (infinitive as noun)
> If you're looking for a job, Sally is the person *to see*. (infinitive as adjective)
> I'm prepared *to resign*. (infinitive as adverb)

Testing a Phrase's Function

To determine whether a phrase is functioning as noun, adjective, or adverb, try a substitution test; if a common noun (something, someone, or it), adjective or adjective phrase, or adverb fits, that demonstrates the function of the phrase.

> *Walking at a brisk pace* is excellent exercise. (gerund phrase)
> *Something* is excellent exercise. (noun phrase)
> I am prepared *to finish the job*. (infinitive phrase)
> I am prepared *completely*. (adverb phrase)
> He was a man *of unusual craftiness*. (prepositional phrase)
> He was a *crafty* man. (adjective phrase)

EXERCISE   *Identify the italicized phrases as prepositional, participial, gerund, or infinitive and indicate whether each is used as a noun, an adjective, or an adverb.*   MyWritingLab

1. *Sleeping in late* can be one of the great pleasures of a holiday.
2. The students waited *for 10 minutes* before they left.
3. *Racing around the corner*, Tim crashed into another student and sent her sprawling.
4. The employees were afraid that there was a plan *to lay off a third of the workforce.*
5. Our guest speaker has written a book about *kayaking around New Zealand.*
6. Most high school students cannot wait *to graduate.*
7. David broke his leg *skiing in Colorado.*

Clauses

A clause is a word group that includes a subject and a predicate. An *independent clause*, sometimes called a main clause, expresses a complete thought and can function as a simple sentence. A *subordinate clause*, or dependent clause, cannot stand by itself. Subordinate clauses may serve as nouns, adjectives, or adverbs.

Noun Clauses   A noun clause can serve in any of the ways that ordinary nouns can.

> *What the neighbor told John* proved to be incorrect. (noun clause as subject)
> The woman asked *when the bus left for Spokane*. (noun clause as direct object)

cl

I'll give a reward to *whoever returns my billfold.* (noun clause as object of preposition *to*)

Noun clauses normally begin with relative pronouns such as *who, what, which, that,* or *whatever* or interrogative pronouns such as *when, why, where, how,* or *whether.*

The complementizer *that* is sometimes omitted from the beginning of a clause that acts as a direct object.

Dr. Kant thinks *(that) he knows everything.*

Adjective Clauses   Like ordinary adjectives, adjective clauses, often called *relative clauses,* modify nouns and noun substitutes.

Give me one reason *why you feel the way you do.* (Adjective clause modifies noun.)

I'll hire anyone *that Dr. Stone recommends.* (Adjective clause modifies pronoun.)

Generally, adjective clauses begin with relative pronouns such as *who, whom, whose, what, which,* or *that* or relative adverbs such as *where, why, after,* or *before.*

Sometimes the word that introduces the clause can be omitted.

The chair *(that) we ordered last month* has just arrived. (pronoun *that* omitted but understood)

The man *(whom) we were talking to* is a movie producer. (pronoun *whom* omitted but understood)

An adjective clause may be restrictive and distinguish whatever it modifies from others in the same class, or it may be nonrestrictive and provide more information about whatever it modifies.

Flora wiped up the cereal *that the baby had spilled.* (restrictive clause)

Harriet Thomas, *who was born in Alaska,* now lives in Hawaii. (nonrestrictive clause)

As these examples show, restrictive clauses are not set off with commas, but nonrestrictive clauses are. See page 624 for further information.

Adverb Clauses   These clauses modify verbs, adjectives, adverbs, and sentences, answering the same questions that ordinary adverbs do.

You may go *whenever you wish.* (Adverb clause modifies verb.)

Sandra looked paler *than I had ever seen her look.* (Adverb clause modifies adjective.)

Darryl shouted loudly *so that the rescue party could hear him.* (Adverb clause modifies adverb.)

Unless everyone cooperates, this plan will never succeed. (Adverb clause modifies whole sentence.)

The word or word group that introduces an adverb clause is always a subordinating conjunction. Common subordinate clauses that introduce adverb

clauses include words that suggest when (*after, before, since, when, while*), where (*where, wherever*), why (*as, because, since, so that, now that*), under what condition (*although, if, once, provided that, though*), and extent (*than*).

Occasionally in an adverb clause, the omission of one or more words won't hurt its meaning. Such a construction is called an *elliptical clause.*

While (he was) making a sandwich, Garth hummed softly. (*he was* omitted but understood)

Unlike noun and adjective clauses, adverb clauses can often be moved about in their sentences.

Garth hummed softly *while (he was) making a sandwich.*

EXERCISE *Identify the italicized clauses as noun, adjective, or adverb.*   My WritingLab

1. Brad pulled a muscle in his back *while he was lifting weights.*
2. The astronauts *who landed on the moon* should still be household names.
3. Some astronomers suggested *that Pluto should not be considered a planet.*
4. Jody Singleton was touched by the cards *her students sent her.*
5. *Although coffee shops would seem like the quintessential small business,* some companies have turned America's coffee habit into multimillion dollar chains.

Coordination and Subordination

Coordination and subordination are ways to rank ideas in sentences. Coordination makes ideas equal; subordination makes them unequal. To understand coordination and subordination, you need to know about four kinds of sentences: simple, compound, complex, and compound–complex.

Simple Sentences   A simple sentence has one subject and one predicate. Some simple sentences consist merely of a single noun and a single verb.

Millicent shouted.

Others include elements such as compound subjects, compound verbs, direct objects, indirect objects, and subject complements.

Jim and Sue have bought a car. (*compound subject, direct object*)
Lucrezia Borgia smiled and mixed her guests a cocktail. (*compound verb, indirect object, direct object*)
Autumn is a sad season. (*subject, complement*)

Compound Sentences   A compound sentence contains two or more independent clauses, each holding the same (coordinate) rank, using a coordinating conjunction, conjunctive adverb, or semicolon.

Coordinating conjunction: Name the baby Huey, *or* I'll cut you out of my will.
The audience was young, friendly, and responsive, *so* it cheered for each speaker.

Conjunctive adverb: Today, many young women do not rush into marriage and motherhood; *instead*, they spend several years establishing careers.

Semicolon: Be sure to read this Hemingway novel; it suggests how to cope gracefully with pressure.

As the preceding sentences show, compound sentences allow writers to express simple relationships among simple ideas. However, such sentences have one important limitation: It is impossible to highlight one particular idea. To do this, we need complex sentences.

Complex Sentences   A complex sentence has one independent clause and one or more dependent clauses. Relegating an idea to a dependent clause shows that the writer wishes it to receive less emphasis than the idea in the main clause. In the following examples, the dependent clauses are italicized.

> *After the dance was over*, Arthur collapsed on the sofa.
> *Once they had reached the lakeshore*, the campers found a level spot *where they could pitch their tent.*

Unlike compound sentences, complex ones allow writers to vary the emphasis of ideas.

> *While I watered the grass*, I discussed stock options with Liz.
> I watered the grass *while I discussed stock options with Liz.*

The first sentence emphasizes the talk with Liz, the second watering the lawn.

Compound–Complex Sentences   This type of sentence features two or more independent clauses and one or more dependent clauses. Here are two examples with the dependent clauses italicized:

> Ms. Harris works as an investment manager, and Mr. Williams, *who lives next door to her*, owns a jewelry store.
> *If you are to communicate properly*, your thoughts must be clear and correct; thoughts are wasted *when language is muddled.*

MyWritingLab   **EXERCISE**   *Label the independent and dependent clauses in the sentences below. Then identify each sentence as simple, compound, complex, or compound–complex.*

1. A career in broadcasting requires good verbal skills, an extensive wardrobe, and a pleasant smile.
2. Because its bag was too full, the vacuum cleaner backfired, leaving the room dirtier than it had been.
3. Leave your boots in the back hall, please.
4. When Tom arrived home, his roommate asked him where he had really gone; six hours seemed too long a time to spend in the library.
5. My orange tree blossomed last week; however, the grapefruit trees have withered, probably because of the freeze last month.

Editing to Correct Sentence Errors

frag

Accepted usage improves the smoothness of your prose, makes your writing easier to understand, and demonstrates that you are a careful communicator.

When you've finished revising the first draft of a piece of writing, edit it with a critic's eye to ensure that you eliminate errors. Circle sentences or parts of them that are faulty or suspect. Then check your circled items against this section of the Handbook, which deals with the most common errors in college writing.

Visit MyWritingLab **to complete the writing assignments in this chapter and for more resources on editing.**

Revising Sentence Fragments

A sentence fragment is a group of words that fails to qualify as a sentence but is capitalized and punctuated as if it were a sentence. To be a sentence, a word group must (1) have a subject and a verb and (2) make sense by itself. The first of the following examples has a subject and a verb; the second does not. Neither makes sense by itself.

If you want to remain.

His answer to the question.

Methods of Revision   Eliminating a sentence fragment is not hard. Careful reading often shows that the fragment goes with the sentence that comes just before or just after it. And sometimes two successive fragments can be joined. Note how we've corrected the fragments (italicized) in the following pairs:

Faulty	*Having been warned about the storm.* We decided to stay home.
Revision	Having been warned about the storm, we decided to stay home.
Faulty	Sally went to work. *Although she felt sick.*
Revision	Sally went to work although she felt sick.
Faulty	*That bronze clock on the mantel. Once belonged to my grandmother.*
Revision	That bronze clock on the mantel once belonged to my grandmother.

Joining a fragment to a sentence or to another fragment works only if the problem is simply one of a mistake in punctuation. If the fragment stems from an improperly developed thought, revise the thought into correct sentence form.

Intentional Fragments   Fragments are commonly used in conversation and the writing that reproduces it. Professional writers also use fragments to gain special emphasis or create special effects. In Chapter 6, pages 109–110 discuss these applications.

MyWritingLab   **EXERCISE** *Five main clauses paired with fragments are shown below. In each case, identify the sentence (S) and the fragment (F) and then eliminate the fragment.*

ro cs

1. There are many ways for businesses to remind customers of appointments. One of them, texting.
2. Mary Ann thought she was completely finished writing her research report. But then realized it would be better with visuals throughout.
3. In order to get tickets to the concert. We had to stand in line for hours.
4. After we finish studying for our math test. We plan to go out for pizza.
5. Our professor banned computers from his classroom. Because too many students were paying attention to Facebook instead of his lecture.

Connected Discourse Exercise

Identify and correct the sentence fragments in the following letter:

My recent bill included $254 in charges for text messages. I do not understand these charges. Since my plan includes unlimited text messaging. In fact, the bill includes a charge for that very service. In addition, many of these text messages are unsolicited and come from companies selling products I don't want. Including several text messages from your company reminding me of your services. One company I contacted admitted that they got my name from a list they purchased from you. Without my granting permission for such a release. Because I pride myself on paying my bills on time. I am submitting payment for all but the $254. However, I expect you to appropriately adjust my bill. And fix this problem for future billing cycles.

Sincerely,

Texted Out.

Revising Run-On Sentences and Comma Splices

A run-on, or fused, sentence occurs when one sentence runs into another without anything to mark their junction. A comma splice occurs when only a comma marks the junction. These errors lead your readers to think that you are hasty or careless. Here are some examples:

Run-on sentence   Rick refused to attend the movie he said he hated horror shows.

Comma splice   Perry watched the road carefully, he still missed his turn.

Testing for Errors   To check out a possible comma splice or fused sentence, read what precedes and follows the comma or suspected junction and see whether the two parts can stand alone as sentences. If *both parts* can stand alone, there is an error. Otherwise, there is not.

Darryl is a real troublemaker, someday he'll find himself in serious difficulty.

Examination of the parts preceding and following the comma shows that each is a complete sentence:

Darryl is a real troublemaker.
Someday he'll find himself in serious difficulty.

The writer has therefore committed a comma splice that needs correction.

ro cs

Methods of Revision   You can correct run-on sentences and comma splices in several ways.

1. Create two separate sentences.
   Revision   Violets are blooming now. My lawn is covered with them.
   Revision   Rick refused to attend the movie. He said he hated horror shows.

2. Join the sentences with a semicolon.
   Revision   Violets are blooming now; my yard is covered with them.
   Revision   Rick refused to attend the movie; he said he hated horror shows.

3. Join the sentences with a comma and a coordinating conjunction *(and, but, or, nor, for, yet, so)*.
   Revision   Laura failed to set her alarm, *so* she was late for work.
   Revision   Perry watched the road carefully, *but* he still missed his turn.

4. Join the sentences with a semicolon and a conjunctive adverb (see page 587).
   Revision   Laura failed to set her alarm; *consequently*, she was late for work.
   Revision   Violets are blooming now; *in fact*, my yard is covered with them.

5. Introduce one of the sentences with a subordinating conjunction (see page 587).
   Revision   *Bec*ause Laura failed to set her alarm, she was late for work.
   Revision   Janet worked on her term paper *while* her friend studied for a calculus test.

As our examples show, you can often correct an error in several ways.

EXERCISE   *Indicate whether each item is correct (C), is a run-on sentence (RO), or contains a comma splice (CS) and then correct the faulty items.*

MyWritingLab

1. Our computers have not been replaced for five years, they have trouble running some of the new software.
2. Ellen worked very hard on her report she really earned her A.

3. The research on the effect of television violence on children remains inconclusive, but still most of us would think that excessive exposure to images of violence would be harmful.
4. Alternative forms of punishment such as home incarceration have proven very effective, nevertheless prison is still the standard punishment for most nonviolent crimes.
5. Many of us own compact digital cameras as a result we take many more pictures of everyday events.

Connected Discourse Exercise

sv agr

Identify and correct the comma splices and run-on sentences in the following message:

Text Message from the Cell Phone Company.

Thank you for your recent bill payment of eighty-five dollars, our records show that you still owe an additional $254. Given the significant volume of your text messaging, this is clearly a service that is valuable to you. You might consider paying an increased fee for unlimited text messaging this fee is significantly less than you are currently paying with a charge for each text message. We appreciate the permission you granted us to share your names with other companies. We have shared your name with a number of companies, you should be receiving even more text messages for new products and sales. This is another reason to change to our unlimited text-messaging plan for only $50 a month. You may pay the remaining $254 online using your credit card, this will allow you to continue to receive a service you so clearly value.

Creating Subject–Verb Agreement

A verb should agree in number with its subject. Singular verbs should have singular subjects, and plural verbs should have plural subjects.

Correct   My *boss is* a grouch. (singular subject and verb)

Correct   The *apartments have* two bedrooms. (plural subject and verb)

Ordinarily, matching subjects and verbs causes no problems. The following special situations, however, can create difficulties.

Subject and Verb Separated by a Word Group   Sometimes a word group that includes one or more nouns comes between the subject and the verb. When this happens, match the verb with its subject, not a noun in the word group.

Correct   Our *basket* of sandwiches *is* missing.

Correct   Several *books* required for my paper *are* not in the library.

Correct   The old *bus*, crammed with passengers, *was* unable to reach the top of the hill.

Two Singular Subjects   Most singular subjects joined by *and* take a plural verb.

Correct   The *couch* and *chair were* upholstered in blue velvet.

Sentences like the one above almost never cause problems. With subjects like *restoring cars* and *racing motorcycles*, however, singular verbs are often mistakenly used.

Faulty   *Restoring cars* and *racing motorcycles consumes* most of Frank's time.

Revision   *Restoring cars* and *racing motorcycles consume* most of Frank's time.

When *each* or *every* precedes the subjects, use a *singular* verb in place of a plural.

Correct   Every *book* and *magazine was* badly water-stained.

Singular subjects joined by *or, either—or,* or *neither—nor* also take singular verbs.

Correct   A *pear* or an *apple is* a good afternoon snack.

Correct   Neither *rain* nor *snow slows* our letter carrier.

Finally, use a singular verb when two singular subjects joined by *and* name the same person, place, or thing.

Correct   My *cousin* and business *partner is* retiring next month.

Cousin and *partner* refer to the same person.

One Singular and One Plural Subject   When one singular subject and one plural subject are joined by *or, either—or,* or *neither—nor,* match the verb with the closer of the two.

Correct   Neither *John* nor his *parents were* at home.

Correct   Neither his *parents* nor *John was* at home.

As these examples show, the sentences are usually smoother when the plural subject follows the singular.

Collective Nouns as Subjects   Collective nouns (*assembly, class, committee, family, herd, majority, tribe,* and the like) are singular in form but stand for groups or collections of people or things. Ordinarily, collective nouns are considered to be singular and therefore take singular verbs.

Correct   The *class is* writing a test.

Correct   The *herd was* clustered around the water hole.

Sometimes, though, a collective noun refers to the separate individuals making up the grouping, and then it requires a plural verb.

Correct   The *jury are* in dispute about the verdict.

Sentences in Which the Verb Comes Ahead of the Subject   Sentences that begin with words such as *here, there, how, what,* and *where* fall into this category. With such sentences, the verb must agree with the subject that follows it.

Correct   Here *is* my *house.*

Correct   Where *are* my *shoes?*

Correct   There *is* just one *way* to solve this problem.

Correct   There *go* my *chances* for a promotion.

MyWritingLab   **EXERCISE**   *Choose the correct verb form from the pair in parentheses.*

sv agr

1. The library, along with many of the books, (*was, were*) severely damaged by the storm.
2. Congress (*retains, retain*) the right to control the country's purse strings.
3. A house with two baths and four bedrooms (*is, are*) for sale in my neighborhood.
4. What (*does, do*) these new printers cost?
5. Each of the logo designs (*offer, offers*) a lot of advantages for branding.
6. Either the floor-to-ceiling bookshelf or two of the shorter bookshelves (*has, have*) enough room for all my books.
7. Dr. Findley and his teaching assistant (*provides, provide*) review sessions each Monday after class.
8. There (*is, are*) a few advantages to carefully planning your work schedule.
9. Neither the players nor the coach (*understands, understand*) why the team keeps winning despite the inexperience of the players.
10. Every flask, test tube, and chemical sample (*has, have*) to be returned to the supply office.

Connected Discourse Exercise

Identify and correct the subject–verb agreement errors in the following e-mail:

To: Cell Phone Service

From: Texted Out

Re: Phone Bill ID 754 657 8934 265

One of the phone representatives handling my case have seriously misunderstood my previous letter. My records show that I have paid for unlimited text messaging for the last three years; yet, I am still being charged a fee for individual text messages. Either your records or your billing system are faulty. Worse, each of the text messages listed are from a company that purchased my name from you without my permission. Your team of representatives are the worst that I have ever seen. This charge, along with any additional individual text messaging charges, need to be dropped from my bill immediately. If this problem, as well as the unwanted text messages, are not corrected immediately, I will have to change my cell phone provider.

Achieving Pronoun–Antecedent Agreement

The antecedent of a pronoun is the noun or pronoun to which it refers. Just as subjects should agree with their verbs, pronouns should agree with their antecedents: singular antecedents require singular pronouns, and plural antecedents require plural pronouns. Ordinarily, you will have no trouble matching antecedents and pronouns. The situations that follow, however, can cause problems.

Indefinite Pronouns as Antecedents   Indefinite pronouns include words like *each, either, neither, any, everybody, somebody, and nobody.* Whenever an indefinite pronoun is used as an antecedent, the pronoun that refers to it should be singular.

pa agr

Faulty	*Neither* of the actors had learned *their* lines.
Revision	*Neither* of the actors had learned *his* lines.

As the revised example shows, this rule applies even when the pronoun is followed by a plural noun.

When the gender of the antecedent is unknown, you may follow it with *his or her*, or if this results in awkwardness, rewrite the sentence in the plural.

Correct	*Anyone* who has studied *his or her* assignments properly should do well on the test.
Correct	*Those* who have studied *their* assignments properly should do well on the test.

Occasionally, a ridiculous result occurs when a singular pronoun refers to an indefinite pronoun that is obviously plural in meaning. When this happens, rewrite the sentence to eliminate the problem.

Faulty	*Everybody* complained that the graduation ceremony had lasted too long, but I didn't believe *him*.
Revision	Everybody complained that the graduation ceremony had lasted too long, but I didn't agree.

Two Singular Antecedents   Two or more antecedents joined by *and* ordinarily call for a plural pronoun.

Correct	Her briefcase and umbrella were missing from *their* usual place on the hall table.

When *each* or *every* precedes the antecedent, use a singular pronoun.

Incorrect	Every college and university must do *their* best to provide adequate student counseling.
Correct	Every college and university must do *its* best to provide adequate student counseling.

Singular antecedents joined by *or*, *either—or*, or *neither—nor* call for singular pronouns.

> *Correct*   Neither Carol nor Irene had paid *her* rent for the month.

Applying this rule can sometimes yield an awkward sentence. When this happens, rewrite the sentence to avoid the problem.

> *Faulty*   Neither James nor Sally has finished *his or her* term project.
>
> *Revision*   James and Sally have not finished *their* term projects.

Singular antecedents joined by *and* that refer to the same person, place, or thing use a singular pronoun.

> *Correct*   My *cousin* and business *partner is* retiring to *her* condo in Florida next month.

pa agr

Singular and Plural Antecedents   If one singular and one plural antecedent are joined by *or*, *either—or*, or *neither—nor*, the pronoun agrees with the closer one.

> *Correct*   Either Terrence James or the Parkinsons will let us use *their* lawn mower.
>
> *Correct*   Either the Parkinsons or Terrence James will let us use *his* lawn mower.

Sentences of this sort are generally smoother when the plural subject follows the singular.

Collective Nouns as Antecedents   When a collective noun is considered a single unit, the pronoun that refers to it should be singular.

> *Correct*   The *troop* of scouts made *its* way slowly through the woods.

When the collective noun refers to the separate individuals in the group, use a plural pronoun.

> *Correct*   The *staff* lost *their* jobs when the factory closed.

MyWritingLab   **EXERCISE**   *Choose the right pronoun from the pair in parentheses.*

1. Neither of the dancers brought (*her, their*) pointe shoes.
2. Professor Widwick required every assignment and paper to have (*its, their*) assignment number in the upper-left corner.
3. After weeks of deliberation, the jury finally reached (*its, their*) decision.
4. Maria and Tim completed (*his or her, their*) project by the deadline.
5. Either Jasmine Stoutler or her assistants will send you (*her, their*) contact information.
6. Everybody has been assigned (*his or her, their*) own log-on name and password.
7. Every one of the women in our police force has proved that (*she, they*) can handle the duties of an officer.

Connected Discourse Exercise

Identify and correct the pronoun–antecedent agreement errors in the following e-mail:

To: Texted Out

From: Your Cell Phone Service

Re: Phone Bill ID 754 657 8934 265

Our team appreciates your kind compliments about their hard work. Your phone representatives do the best they can to meet your needs. Any of our representatives would have been glad to do their part to explain your bill. You owe $254 for the text messages you received from numerous companies and an additional $50 in late fees. Today every customer and business does their best to reduce costs. You can reduce your costs by either paying for unlimited texting or by limiting the number of texts messages you receive. Either your local phone retailer or one of our many representatives would be glad to offer you their assistance in promptly resolving this matter before we have to discontinue your service.

pr ref

Using Effective Pronoun Reference

Any pronoun except an indefinite pronoun should refer to just one noun or noun substitute—its antecedent. Reference problems result when the pronoun has two or more antecedents, a hidden antecedent, or no antecedent. These errors can cause mix-ups in meaning as well as ridiculous sentences.

More Than One Antecedent The following sentences lack clarity because their pronouns have two possible antecedents rather than just one:

Faulty   Take the screens off the windows and wash *them.*

Faulty   Harry told Will that *he* was putting on weight.

The reader can't tell whether the screens or the windows should be washed or who is putting on weight.

Sometimes we see a sentence like this one:

Faulty   If the boys don't eat all the Popsicles, put *them* in the freezer.

In this case, we know it's the Popsicles that should be stored, but the use of *them* creates an amusing sentence.

Correct these faults by replacing the pronoun with a noun or by rephrasing the sentence.

Revision   Wash the windows after you have taken off the screens.

Revision   Take off the screens so that you can wash the windows.

Revision   Harry told Will, "I am (you are) putting on weight."

Revision   Put any uneaten Popsicles in the freezer.

Hidden Antecedent An antecedent is hidden if it takes the form of an adjective rather than a noun.

Faulty The movie theater is closed today, so we can't see *one*.

Faulty As I passed the tiger's cage, it lunged at me.

To correct this fault, replace the pronoun with the noun used as an adjective or switch the positions of the pronoun and the noun and make any needed changes in their forms.

Revision The theater is closed today, so we can't see a movie.

Revision As I passed its cage, the tiger lunged at me.

No Antecedent A no-antecedent sentence lacks any noun to which the pronoun can refer. Sentences of this sort occur frequently in everyday conversation but should be avoided in formal writing. The examples below illustrate this error:

Faulty The lecture was boring, but *they* took notes anyway.

Faulty On the news program, *it* told about a new crisis in the Persian Gulf.

To set matters right, substitute a suitable noun for the pronoun or reword the sentence.

Revision The lecture was boring, but the students took notes anyway.

Revision The news program told about a new crisis in the Persian Gulf.

Sometimes *this, that, it, or which* will refer to a whole idea rather than a single noun. This usage is acceptable provided the writer's meaning is obvious, as in this example:

Correct The instructor spoke very softly, *which* meant we had difficulty hearing him.

Problems occur, however, when the reader can't figure out which of two or more ideas the pronoun refers to.

Faulty Ginny called Sally two hours after the agreed-upon time and postponed their shopping trip one day. *This* irritated Sally very much.

What caused Sally to be irritated—the late call, the postponement of the trip, or both? Again, rewording or adding a clarifying word will correct the problem.

Revision Ginny called Sally two hours after the agreed-upon time and postponed their shopping trip one day. *This tardiness* irritated Sally very much.

Revision Ginny called Sally two hours after the agreed-upon time and postponed their shopping trip one day. Ginny's *change of plans* irritated Sally very much.

The first of these examples illustrates the addition of a clarifying word; the second illustrates rewriting.

EXERCISE *Indicate whether each sentence is correct (C) or contains a faulty pronoun reference (F) and then correct the faulty sentences.*   MyWritingLab

1. When the supervisor walked by the water cooler, they stopped talking.
2. I like trout fishing because it is very relaxing.
3. Since I knew that our employees found their chairs uncomfortable, I replaced them with new ones.
4. In the report, it suggested that we needed to be more attentive to employee suggestions.
5. Janine asked Caroline if she could rewrite her paper for her English class.

Connected Discourse Exercise

Identify and correct any faulty pronoun references in the following e-mail:

To: Cell Phone Service

From: Texted Out

Re: Phone Bill ID 754 657 8934 265

Given the erroneous charge for my phone service, I expect you to discontinue it immediately. Despite my attempts to resolve this problem with the company, they were unhelpful. As a result, I intend to change to a different carrier who promises a better one. I will also not pay it and will take legal action if you attempt to harm my credit rating. The mistake in the billing was yours, not mine, and I stand ready to prove it in court.

Managing Shifts in Person

Pronouns can be in the first person, second person, or third person. *First-person* pronouns identify people who are talking or writing about themselves (I). *Second-person* pronouns identify people being addressed directly (you), and *third-person* pronouns identify persons or things that are being written or spoken about (he). See page 575 for a list of pronouns with persons and cases.

All nouns are in the third person. As you revise, be alert for unwarranted shifts from one person to another.

Faulty	I liked *my* British vacation better than *my* vacation in France and Italy because *you* didn't have language problems.
Revision	I liked *my* British vacation better than *my* vacation in France and Italy because *I* didn't have language problems.
Faulty	Holidays are important to *everyone*. They boost *your* spirits and provide a break from *our* daily routine.
Revision	Holidays are important to *everyone*. They boost *one's* spirits and provide a break from *one's* daily routine.

shft

As these examples show, the shift can occur within a single sentence or when the writer moves from one sentence to another.

Some shifts in person, however, are warranted. Read the following correct sentence:

> *Correct*   *I* want *you* to deliver these flowers to Ms. Willoughby by three o'clock. *She* needs them for a party.

Here the speaker identifies himself or herself (*I*) while speaking directly to a listener *(you)* about someone else *(she)*. In this case, shifts are needed to get the message across.

shft   MyWritingLab   **EXERCISE**   *Indicate whether the sentence is correct (C) or contains an unwarranted shift in person (S). Correct faulty sentences.*

1. After the teacher collected our essays, she told the students that she would return the graded papers on Wednesday.
2. For someone to be successful in today's marketplace, you need to have adequate technical skills.
3. If you each will bring the results of your assigned research to the next meeting, we will be ready to begin working on our collaborative report.
4. Anyone who would like to purchase the discounted Caribbean cruise tickets should place your order by May 15.
5. We enjoy living in the Grand Rapids area very much; you have access to theater, sporting events, and fine dining.
6. If you would like to learn to kayak, novices can usually get free lessons from the people who sell kayaks.
7. In our attempt to determine whether there has been an increase in tornado activity over the last 20 years, the researchers collected data on storm sightings and damage reports.

Connected Discourse Exercise

Identify and correct the unwarranted shifts in person in the following e-mail:

To: Texted Out

From: Cell Phone Service

Re: Contract Violation ID 754 657 8945 265

We are sorry to hear that you have decided to violate your contract. One has a responsibility to his contract, which is the customer's agreement with our company to pay for your services. In the small print at the bottom of the agreement you signed, one will notice that in case of cancellation of the contract they are required to pay $1,000 in cancellation fees. We will, however, allow one to reconsider canceling the service. To keep their service in place, one only needs to pay $154 for text messages and $100 in late fees. We value you as a customer, which is why we work hard to meet ones wireless needs.

Using the Right Pronoun Case

Case means the changes in form that a personal pronoun (see page 575) undergoes to show its function in a sentence. English has three cases: the *subjective (I)*, the *nonsubjective* (objective) (*me*), and the *possessive (my/mine)*.

The subjective case is used for subjects and subject complements, the nonsubjective for direct objects, indirect objects, and objects of prepositions. The possessive case shows ownership and is also used with gerunds.

The following pointers will help you select the proper pronoun as you revise.

case

We and Us Preceding Nouns   Nouns that serve as subjects take the pronoun *we*. Other nouns take the pronoun *us*.

Correct	*We* tourists will fly home tomorrow. (*We* accompanies the subject.)
Correct	The guide showed *us* tourists through the cathedral. (*Us* accompanies a nonsubject.)

If you can't decide which pronoun is right, mentally omit the noun and read the sentence to yourself, first with one pronoun and then with the other. Your ear will indicate the correct form.

My mother made (*we, us*) children vanilla pudding for dessert.

Omitting *children* shows immediately that *us* is the right choice.

Correct	My mother made *us* children vanilla pudding for dessert.

Pronouns Paired with Nouns   When such a combination serves as the subject of a sentence or accompanies the subject, use the subject form of the pronoun. When the combination plays a nonsubject role, use the nonsubject form of the pronoun.

Correct	Arlene and *I* plan to join the Peace Corps. (*I* is part of the compound subject.)
Correct	Two people, Mary and *I*, will represent our school at the meeting. (*I* is part of a compound element accompanying the subject.)
Correct	The superintendent told Kevin and *him* that they would be promoted soon. (*Him* is part of a compound nonsubject.)
Correct	The project was difficult for Jeffrey and *him* to complete. (*Him* is part of a compound nonsubject.)

Again, mentally omitting the noun from the combination will tell you which pronoun is correct.

Who and Whom in Dependent Clauses   Use *who* for the subjects of dependent clauses; otherwise, use *whom*.

Correct   The Mallarys prefer friends *who are interested in the theater.* (*Who* is the subject of the clause.)

Correct   Barton is a man *whom very few people like.* (*Whom* is not the subject of the clause.)

A simple test will help you decide between *who* and *whom.* First, mentally isolate the dependent clause. Next, block out the pronoun in question and then insert *he* (or *she*) and *him* (or *her*) at the appropriate spot in the remaining part of the clause. If *he* (or *she*) sounds better, *who* is right. If *him* (or *her*) sounds better, *whom* is right. Let's use this test on the sentence below:

The woman *who(m) Scott is dating* works as a mechanical engineer. Scott is dating (*she, her*).

Clearly, *her* is correct; therefore, *whom* is the proper form.

Correct   The woman *whom Scott is dating* works as a mechanical engineer.

Pronouns as Subject Complements   In formal writing, pronouns that serve as subject complements (see pages 572–573) always take the subject form.

Correct   It is *I.*

Correct   It was *she* who bought the old Parker mansion.

This rule, however, is often ignored in informal writing.

It's her.

That's *him* standing over by the door.

Comparisons Using *Than* or *As . . . As*   Comparisons of this kind often make no direct statement about the second item of comparison. When the second naming word is a pronoun, you may have trouble choosing the right one.

Harriet is less outgoing than (*they, them*).
My parents' divorce saddened my sister as much as (*I, me*).

Not to worry. Expand the sentence by mentally supplying the missing material. Then try the sentence with each pronoun and see which sounds right.

Harriet is less outgoing than (*they, them*) are.
My parents' divorce saddened my sister as much as it did (*I, me*).

Obviously, *they* is the right choice for the first sentence, and *me* is the right choice for the second one.

Correct   Harriet is less outgoing than *they* are.

Correct   My parents' divorce saddened my sister as much as it did *me.*

Pronouns Preceding Gerunds   Use the possessive form of a pronoun that precedes a gerund (see page 590) to emphasize the action.

> I dislike *their* leaving without saying goodbye.
>
> Ted can't understand *her* quitting such a good job.

When the pronoun precedes a participle (see pages 589–590), it should be in the nonsubject case to emphasize the actor.

> Jennifer caught *them* listening to records instead of studying.

In this example, Jennifer caught the listeners, not the listening.

If you have trouble deciding between the nonsubject and possessive forms of a pronoun, ask yourself whether you want to emphasize the action or the actor; then proceed accordingly.

case

EXERCISE   *Choose the right form of the pronoun for each of the following sentences. For the purpose of this exercise, assume that there would have been the appropriate pronoun antecedent in the sentence preceding the one that is shown.*   MyWritingLab

1. No one is as pleased as (*I, me*) by John's recent promotion to assistant vice president.
2. There is no excuse for (*him, his*) yelling at us in public.
3. The newspaper's editor praised Marge and (*I, me*) for our coauthored article on women in the military.
4. Megan is one student (*who, whom*) I believe really understands the importance of writing well.
5. (*We, Us*) Americans pride ourselves on our individuality.
6. The manager politely suggested that Marie and (*I, me*) should re-check the data from the survey.
7. Rilke is the poet (*who, whom*) I like best.
8. The adventure company asked (*we, us*) participants in the zipline plunge to sign a waiver.

Connected Discourse Exercise

Identify and correct the pronoun case errors in the following paragraph:

Between my best friend and I, there has always been a competition to see whom could participate in the most extreme sports. My friend took up extreme snow-boarding, and him and some other nuts raced down a mountain just ahead of an avalanche. I didn't think I could try anything as crazy as him. However, someone who I had climbed mountains with gave me a chance to go hang gliding off the Grand Canyon. I jumped at the chance, literally, and broke both legs and four ribs. Who do you think won the competition?

time

Creating Consistency in Showing Time

Inconsistencies occur when a writer shifts from the past tense to the present or vice versa without a corresponding shift in the time of the events being described. The following paragraph contains an uncalled-for shift from the present tense to the past:

> As *The Most Dangerous Game* opens, Sanger Rainsford, a famous hunter and author, and his old friend Whitney are standing on the deck of a yacht and discussing a mysterious island as the ship passes near it. Then, after everyone else has gone to bed, Rainsford manages to fall overboard. He swims to the island and ends up at a chateau owned by General Zaroff, a refugee from the Communist takeover in Russia. Zaroff, bored with hunting animals, has turned to hunting humans on his desert island. Inevitably, Rainsford is turned out into the jungle to be hunted down. There were [shift to past tense] actually four hunts over a three-day period, and at the end of the last one, Rainsford jumped into the sea, swam across a cove to the chateau, and killed Zaroff in the general's own bedroom. Afterward he sleeps [shift back to present tense] and decides "he had never slept in a better bed."

The sentence with the unwarranted shift in tense should read as follows:

> There are actually four hunts over a three-day period, and at the end of the last one, Rainsford jumps into the sea, swims across a cove to the chateau, and kills Zaroff in the general's own bedroom.

The time shift in the quotation part of the final sentence is justified because the sleeping has occurred before Rainsford's thoughts about it.

MyWritingLab   **EXERCISE** *Indicate whether each sentence is correct (C) or contains an unwarranted shift (S) in tense. Then correct the faulty sentences.*

1. A thin wisp of smoke drifts from under the hood, and then the engine burst into flames.
2. Jason took on many projects but finishes few of them.
3. As Charlie laid pieces of the model on the table, his wife picks them up.
4. David is building his own house but found it harder work than he anticipated.
5. While Robert applies the adhesive, David carefully positioned the floor tiles.

Connected Discourse Exercise

Identify and correct any inconsistencies in showing time in the following passage:

There is no better time to go swimming than at night. The summer after I had graduated from high school, I worked for a landscaping company. After a sweaty day mowing lawns and digging up gardens, all of us who worked there would jump into the back of Dick's old pickup and rattle out to Woods Lake. It is just dark as we

arrive. The moon is beautiful, reflected in that black mirror set in a frame of hills. We stumble down a small, sandy hill to the beach, where we strip off our dusty jeans and sweaty shirts before plunging into the cool reflection of stars.

Using Adjectives and Adverbs Effectively

Inexperienced writers often use adjectives when they should use adverbs and also confuse the comparative and superlative forms of these parts of speech when making comparisons.

Misusing Adjectives for Adverbs   Although most adjectives can be misused as adverbs, the following seven, listed with the corresponding adverbs, cause the most difficulty.

mis
adj/adv

Adjectives	Adverbs
awful	awfully
bad	badly
considerable	considerably
good	well
most	almost
real	really
sure	surely

The following sentences show typical errors:

Faulty   Bryan did *good* in his first golf lesson. (*good* mistakenly used to modify verb *did*)

Faulty   *Most* every graduate from our auto service program receives several job offers. (*most* mistakenly used to modify adjective *every*)

Faulty   The speech was delivered *real* well. (*real* mistakenly used to modify adverb *well*)

Because adverbs modify verbs, adjectives, and other adverbs (see pages 585–586), and adjectives modify nouns and noun substitutes (see pages 583–584), the above sentences clearly require adverbs.

Revision   Bryan did *well* in his first golf lesson.

Revision   *Almost* every graduate from our auto service program receives several job offers.

Revision   The speech was delivered *really* well.

In one notable case, an adverb is commonly misused as an adjective.

Faulty   I feel *badly* about providing the wrong phone number. (*Badly* is mistakenly used as a subject complement.)

Revision   I feel *bad* about providing the wrong phone number.

If you can't decide whether a sentence requires an adjective or an adverb, determine the part of speech of the word being modified and proceed accordingly.

Confusing the Comparative and Superlative Forms in Comparisons

The comparative form of adjectives and adverbs is used to compare two things, the superlative form to compare three or more things. Adjectives with fewer than three syllables generally add *-er* to make the comparative form and *-est* to make the superlative form (tall, tall*er*, tall*est*). Adjectives with three or more syllables generally add *more* to make the comparative and *most* to make the superlative (enchanting, *more* enchanting, *most* enchanting), as do most adverbs of two or more syllables (loudly, *more* loudly, *most* loudly).

When making comparisons, beginning writers sometimes mistakenly use double comparatives or double superlatives.

Faulty   Harry is *more taller* than James. (double comparative)

Faulty   The Chrysler Building has the *most splendidest* lobby I've ever seen. (double superlative)

The correct versions read as follows:

Revision   Harry is *taller* than James.

Revision   The Chrysler Building has the *most splendid* lobby I've ever seen.

In addition, writers may erroneously use the superlative form, rather than the comparative form, to compare two things.

Faulty   Barry is the *richest* of the two brothers.

Faulty   Jeremy is the *most talented* of those two singers.

Here are the sentences correctly written:

Revision   Barry is the *richer* of the two brothers.

Revision   Jeremy is the *more talented* of those two singers.

Reserve the superlative form for comparing three or more items.

Correct   Barry is the *richest* of the three brothers.

Correct   Jeremy is the *most talented* of those four singers.

MyWritingLab   **EXERCISE** *For each of the following sentences, choose the proper word from the pair in parentheses:*

1. The milk in the refrigerator tastes (*bad, badly*).
2. Old science fiction movies can be (*real, really*) funny to watch because of the clumsy special effects and stilted dialogue.
3. Steve did (*good, well*) on his history project.
4. The Vandorns have the (*prettiest, most prettiest*) house in the development.
5. Terry hurt his knees (*bad, badly*) playing football.

6. The Mustang is the (*less, least*) expensive of the two sports cars you are considering.

7. (*Most, Almost*) all of our employees make use of the day care facility we provide on the premises.

Connected Discourse Exercise

Identify and correct the adjective–adverb errors in the following paragraph:

Roller Derby is back; and our team, the Crushers, is the better team in the league. We play to win, so we play real fierce, ready to crush the opposition. That is how we got our name. Our blockers show no mercy, smashing others to the rink so that our wild skating jammer can streak past for points. Seeing members of the other team sprawled helpless on the rink is a most wonderfulest feeling. It is an experience that we can sure plan on enjoying in future matches.

Placing Modifiers Correctly

A misplaced modifier is a word or word group that is improperly separated from the word it modifies. When separation of this type occurs, the sentence often sounds awkward, ridiculous, or confusing.

Usually, you can correct this error by moving the modifier next to the word it is intended to modify. Occasionally, you'll also need to alter some of the phrasing.

Faulty	There is a bicycle in the basement *with chrome fenders.* (The basement appears to have chrome fenders.)
Faulty	David received a phone call from his uncle *that infuriated him.* (The uncle appears to have infuriated David.)
Revision	There is a bicycle *with chrome fenders* in the basement.
Revision	David received an *infuriating* phone call from his uncle. (Note the change in wording.)

In shifting the modifier, don't inadvertently create another faulty sentence.

Faulty	Fritz bought a magazine with an article about Michael Jackson *at the corner newsstand.* (The article appears to tell about Jackson's visit to the corner newsstand.)
Faulty	Fritz bought a magazine *at the corner newsstand* with an article about Michael Jackson. (The corner newsstand appears to have an article about Jackson.)
Revision	*At the corner newsstand,* Fritz bought a magazine with an article about Michael Jackson.

mm

dm

As you revise, watch also for squinting modifiers—that is, modifiers positioned so that the reader doesn't know whether they are supposed to modify what comes ahead of them or what follows them.

Faulty　　The man who was rowing the boat *frantically* waved toward the onlookers on the beach.

Is the man rowing frantically or waving frantically? Correct this kind of error by repositioning the modifier so that the ambiguity disappears.

Revision　　The man who was *frantically* rowing the boat waved toward the onlookers on the beach.

Revision　　The man who was rowing the boat waved *frantically* toward the onlookers on the beach.

MyWritingLab　**EXERCISE** *Indicate whether each sentence is correct (C) or contains a misplaced modifier (MM). Correct faulty sentences.*

1. Jason handed his report to his teacher neatly tucked into a binder.
2. The girl driving past the school wildly waved at her friends.
3. The dancers practiced Swan Lake for a month before the performance.
4. I tossed the rainbow trout to my brother still hooked firmly in the mouth.
5. Our residents have 24-hour access to nurses who are specially trained to work with the elderly.
6. We watched a video about the causes of homicide in our sociology class.
7. Jasmine found an apartment near the university with a great view of the lake.

Revising Dangling Modifiers

A dangling modifier is a phrase or clause that lacks clear connection to the word or words it is intended to modify. As a result, sentences are inaccurate, often comical. Typically, the modifier leads off the sentence, although it can also come at the end.

Sometimes the error occurs because the sentence fails to specify who or what is modified. At other times, the separation is too great between the modifier and what it modifies.

Faulty　　*Walking in the meadow*, wildflowers surrounded us. (The wildflowers appear to be walking in the meadow.)

Faulty　　Dinner was served *after saying grace*. (The dinner appears to have said grace.)

Faulty　　*Fatigued by the violent exercise*, the cool shower was very relaxing. (The cool shower appears to have been fatigued.)

The first of these sentences is faulty because the modifier is positioned too far away from *us*. The other two are faulty because they do not identify who said grace or found the shower relaxing.

You can correct dangling modifiers in two basic ways. First, leave the modifier unchanged and rewrite the main part of the sentence so that it begins with the term actually modified. Second, rewrite the modifier so that it has its own subject and verb, thereby eliminating the inaccuracy.

Revision   *Walking in the meadow,* we were surrounded by wildflowers. (The main part of the sentence has been rewritten.)

Revision   *As we walked in the meadow,* wildflowers surrounded us. (The modifier has been rewritten.)

Revision   *Dinner was served after we had said grace.* (The modifier has been rewritten.)

Revision   *Fatigued by the violent exercise,* Ted found the cool shower very relaxing. (The main part of the sentence has been rewritten.)

Revision   *Because Ted was fatigued by the violent exercise,* the cool shower was very relaxing. (The modifier has been rewritten.)

Ordinarily, either part of the sentence can be rewritten, but sometimes only one part can.

EXERCISE *Indicate whether each sentence is correct (C) or contains a dangling modifier (DM). Correct faulty sentences.*   MyWritingLab

1. After listening to a tape of Orson Welles' radio broadcast of *The War of the Worlds,* I understood why many who tuned into the middle of the broadcast panicked.
2. The baseball game will start after singing *The Star-Spangled Banner.*
3. Looking at the night sky, a million stars seemed to smile down on us.
4. Having scored 100 percent on the pretest, the teacher placed two students in the next level math class.
5. Picasso was known to leave customers waiting for several days, painting furiously.
6. John cataloged his CD collection, listing each CD in a database.
7. Rushing over the banks, Main Street was soon under three feet of water.

Maintaining Parallelism

Nonparallelism results when equivalent ideas follow different grammatical forms. One common kind of nonparallelism occurs with words or word groups in pairs or in a series.

Faulty   Althea enjoys *jogging, biking,* and *to swim.*

Faulty   The superintendent praised the workers *for their productivity* and *because they had an excellent safety record.*

Faulty   The banner was *old, faded,* and *it had a rip.*

Note how rewriting the sentences in parallel form improves their smoothness.

Revision   Althea enjoys *jogging, biking,* and *swimming.*

Revision   The superintendent praised the workers for *their productivity* and *their excellent safety record.*

Revision   The banner was *old, faded,* and *ripped.*

Nonparallelism also occurs when correlative conjunctions *(either—or, neither—nor, both—and,* and *not only—but also)* are followed by unlike elements.

Faulty   That sound *either* <u>was a thunderclap</u> *or* <u>an explosion.</u>

Faulty   The basement was *not only* <u>poorly lighted</u> *but also* <u>it had a foul smell.</u>

Ordinarily, repositioning one of the correlative conjunctions will solve the problem. Sometimes, however, one of the grammatical elements must be rewritten.

Revision   That sound was *either* <u>a thunderclap</u> *or* <u>an explosion.</u> (*Either* has been repositioned.)

Revision   The basement was *not only* <u>poorly lighted</u> *but also* <u>foul smelling.</u> (The element following *but also* has been rewritten.)

MyWritingLab   **EXERCISE**   *Indicate whether each sentence is correct (C) or nonparallel (NP). Correct faulty sentences.*

1. The cause of the fire either was faulty wiring or an overloaded outlet.
2. After graduation, Marci will be moving to Chicago and work for a large public relations firm.
3. For spring break, Steve and his friends plan to visit either New Orleans or Orlando.
4. A good candidate for social work enjoys talking with people, helps solve problems, and seeing projects through to their conclusion.
5. This course will involve reading a number of short stories, and you will need to turn in weekly journal responses.

Revising Faulty Comparisons

A faulty comparison results if you (1) mention one of the items being compared but not the other, (2) omit words needed to clarify the relationship, or (3) compare different sorts of items. Advertisers often offend in the first way.

Faulty   Irish tape has better adhesion.

With what other tape is Irish tape being compared? Scotch tape? All other transparent tape? Mentioning the second term of a comparison eliminates reader guesswork.

Revision   Irish tape has better adhesion than any other transparent tape.

Two clarifying words, *other* and *else,* are frequently omitted from comparisons, creating illogical sentences.

Faulty	Sergeant McNabb is more conscientious than any officer in his precinct.
Faulty	Stretch French is taller than anyone on his basketball team.

The first sentence is illogical because McNabb is one of the officers in his precinct and therefore cannot be more conscientious than any officer in the precinct. Similarly, because French is a member of his basketball team, he can't be taller than anyone on his team. Adding *other* to the first sentence and *else* to the second corrects matters.

Revision	Sergeant McNabb is more conscientious than any *other* officer in his precinct.
Revision	Stretch French is taller than anyone *else* on his basketball team.

Comparing unlike items is perhaps the most common kind of comparison error. Here are two examples:

Faulty	The cities in California are larger than North Dakota.
Faulty	The cover of this book is much more durable than the other book.

The first sentence compares the cities of California with a state, while the second compares the cover of a book with a whole book. Correction consists of rewriting each sentence so that it compares like items.

Revision	The cities in California are larger than *those in* North Dakota.
Revision	The cover of this book is much more durable than *that of* the other book.

Connected Discourse Exercise

Identify and correct the misplaced modifiers, dangling modifiers, nonparallelism, and faulty comparisons in the following memorandum:

TO: Roger's Electronics Employees

FROM: Tim Colton, Sales Vice President

RE: Cell Phone Sales

I have received a report on our cell phone sales from our store manager that greatly disturbs me. Our cell phone sales still significantly lag the national average. Our sales numbers are even lower than Tidley Market. As an electronics store, we make our greatest profits from cell phone sales, signing up customers for wireless plans, and extended warranties. Working harder, cell phone sales should at least double next month. You must ask each customer if they are interested in a new cell phone with a wireless plan, regardless of the purchase. There is a sheet next to each

register with the updated plan information. I look forward to a much better sales report next month.

MyWritingLab   **EXERCISE**   *Indicate whether each sentence is correct (C) or contains a faulty comparison (FC). Correct the faulty comparison.*

1. *Death of a Salesman* is performed more often than any American play.
2. This quarter's earning report shows significantly greater net profits.
3. The Sunday brunch at the 1913 room is much more elegant than the Eatery.
4. In contrast to your car, I usually get 40 miles to the gallon.
5. The winters in North Dakota are much worse than Maine.

comp

Editing to Correct Faulty Punctuation and Mechanics

Punctuation marks indicate relationships among different sentence elements, clarifying the meaning of written material.

This part of the Handbook covers the fundamentals of punctuation and mechanics. Review it carefully when you edit your final draft.

Visit MyWritingLab **to complete the writing assignments in this chapter and for more resources on punctuation and mechanics.**

Apostrophes

Apostrophes (') show possession, mark contractions, and indicate plurals that are singled out for special attention.

Possession   Possessive apostrophes usually show ownership *(Mary's cat)*. Sometimes, though, they identify the works of creative people *(Hemingway's novels)* or indicate an extent of time or distance *(one hour's time, one mile's distance)*.

Possessive apostrophes are used with nouns and with pronouns like *someone, no one, everybody, each other,* and *one another.* The possessive form is easily recognized because it can be converted to a prepositional phrase beginning with *of.*

The collar of the dog
The intention of the corporation

To show possession with pronouns like those above, singular nouns, and plural nouns that do not end in an *s,* add an apostrophe followed by an *s.*

Someone's car is blocking our drive. (possessive of pronoun *someone*)

The *manager's* reorganization plan will take effect next week. (possessive of singular noun *manager*)

The *women's* lounge is being redecorated. (possessive of plural noun *women*)

Sentences that make comparisons sometimes include two possessives, the second coming at the very end. In such cases, be sure to use an apostrophe with the second possessive.

Birmingham's football team is much better than *Central's.*

With singular nouns that end in *s,* the possessive is sometimes formed by merely adding an apostrophe at the end *(James' helmet).* The preferred usage, however, is *'s (James's helmet)* unless the addition of the *s* would make it awkward to pronounce the word.

Moses's followers entered the Promised Land. (awkward pronunciation of *Moses's*)

Moses' followers entered the Promised Land. (nonawkward pronunciation of *Moses'*)

Plural nouns ending in *s* form the possessive by adding only an apostrophe at the end.

All the *ladies'* coats are on sale today. (possessive of plural noun *ladies*)

The *workers'* lockers were moved. (possessive of plural noun *workers*)

To show joint ownership by two or more persons, use the possessive form for the last-named person only. To show individual ownership, use the possessive form for each person's name.

Ronald and *Joan's* boat badly needed overhauling. (joint ownership) *Laura's* and *Alice's* term projects are almost completed. (individual ownership)

Hyphenated nouns form the possessive by adding *'s* to the last word.

My *mother-in-law's* house is next to mine.

Never use an apostrophe with the possessive pronouns *his, hers, whose, its, ours, yours, theirs.*

This desk is *his;* the other one is *hers.* (no apostrophes needed)

Contractions   Contractions of words or numbers omit one or more letters or numerals. An apostrophe shows exactly where the omission occurs.

Wasn't that a disappointing concert? (contraction of *was not*)

Around here, people still talk about the blizzard of, *'79.* (contraction of *1979*)

Don't confuse the contraction *it's,* meaning *it is* or *it has,* with the possessive pronoun *its,* which should never have an apostrophe. If you're puzzled by an *its* that you've written, try this test. Expand the *its* to *it is* or *it has* and see whether the sentence still makes sense. If it does, the *its* is a contraction and needs the apostrophe. If the result is nonsense, the *its* is a possessive pronoun and does not get an apostrophe. Here are some examples:

Its awfully muggy today. (incorrect)

Its been an exciting trip. (incorrect)

Every dog has *its* day. (correct)

The first example makes sense when the *its* is expanded to *it is*.

> *It is* awfully muggy today. It's awfully muggy today. (apostrophe required)

The second makes sense when the *its* is expanded to *it has*.

> *It has* been an exciting trip. It's been an exciting trip. (apostrophe required)

The last sentence, however, turns into nonsense when the *its* is expanded.

> Every dog has *it is* day.

> Every dog has *it has* day.

In this case, the *its* is a possessive pronoun and requires no apostrophe.

> Every dog has *its* day.

Plurals To improve clarity, the plurals of letters, numbers, symbols, and words being singled out for special attention are written with apostrophes.

> Mind your *p*'s and *q*'s. (plurals of letters)

> Your *5*'s and *6*'s are hard to tell apart. (plurals of numbers)

> The formula was sprinkled with Φ's and σ's. (plurals of symbols)

> Don't use so many *however*'s and *therefore*'s in your writing. (plurals of words)

Apostrophes can be used, though they are not needed, to form the plurals of abbreviations.

> How many *CD*'s (or *CDs*) do you own? (plurals of abbreviation for *compact discs*)

When no danger of confusion exists, an *s* alone will suffice.

> During the late *1960s*, many university students demanded changes in academic life.

EXERCISE *Supply apostrophes where necessary to correct the following sentences:*   MyWritingLab

1. A good manager is ready to listen to anyones suggestions on how to improve the workplace.
2. Given the developing line of severe thunderstorms, were concerned about the possibility of tornadoes.
3. The police officer spotted someones car keys clutched in the victims hand.
4. This months sales figures were much better than last months.
5. Cindys computer program was much more efficient than her peers programs.
6. There are two *Rs* and two *Ss* in the word "embarrassment."
7. Lets determine what caused the schools mainframe computer to fail before we panic.

Connected Discourse Exercise

Supply, delete, or relocate apostrophes as necessary in the following paragraph:

Its very important to understand todays media environment. The three major network's market share has decreased significantly over the year's as the number of cable channels increased. Now as people turn to services like

Hulu and Netflix, the Internet's impact on entertainment consumption has become almost as great as televisions. The Internet provides viewers' with the programs they want when and where they want them. With the numerous wireless devices, it's portability makes the Internet services especially attractive to younger audience. Television has been a staple in many American homes since the 1950's; the question is whether television as we know it has a place in our future.

Commas

Since commas (,) occur more frequently than any other mark of punctuation, it's vital that you learn to use them correctly.

Commas separate or set off independent clauses, items in a series, coordinate adjectives, introductory elements, places and dates, nonrestrictive expressions, and parenthetical expressions.

Independent Clauses When you link two independent clauses with a coordinating conjunction (*and, but, or, nor, for, yet,* or *so*), put a comma in front of the conjunction.

> Arthur is majoring in engineering, *but* he has decided to work for a clothing store following graduation.

> The water looked inviting, *so* Darlene decided to go for a swim.

Don't confuse a sentence that has a compound predicate (see page 572) with a sentence that consists of two independent clauses.

> Tom watered the garden and mowed the lawn. (single sentence with compound predicate)

> Tom watered the garden, *and* Betty mowed the lawn. (sentence with two independent clauses)

Here's a simple test. Read what follows the comma. Unless that part can stand alone as a sentence, don't use a comma.

Items in a Series A series consists of three or more words, phrases, or clauses following on one another's heels. Whenever you write a series, separate its items with commas.

> *Sarah, Paul,* and *Mary* are earning A's in advanced algebra. (words in a series)

> Nancy strode *across the parking lot, through the revolving door,* and *into the elevator.* (phrases in a series)

> The stockholders' report said *that the company had enjoyed record profits during the last year, that it had expanded its work force by 20 percent,* and *that it would soon start marketing several new products.* (clauses in a series)

comma

Coordinate Adjectives   Use commas to separate coordinate adjectives—those that modify the same noun or noun substitute and can be reversed without altering the meaning of the sentence.

> Andrea proved to be an efficient, cooperative employee.

> Andrea proved to be a cooperative, efficient employee.

When reversing the word order wrecks the meaning of the sentence, the adjectives are not coordinate and should be written without a comma.

> Many new brands of videocassette recorders have come on the market lately.

Reversing the adjectives *many* and *new* would turn this sentence into nonsense. Therefore, no comma should be used.

Introductory Elements   Use commas to separate introductory elements—words, phrases, and clauses—from the rest of the sentence. When an introductory element is short and the sentence will not be misread, you can omit the comma.

> *Correct*   After bathing, Jack felt refreshed.
> *Correct*   Soon I will be changing jobs.
> *Correct*   Soon, I will be changing jobs.
> *Correct*   When Sarah smiles her ears wiggle.
> *Correct*   When Sarah smiles, her ears wiggle.

The first example needs a comma; otherwise, the reader might become temporarily confused.

> After bathing Jack . . .

Always use commas after introductory elements of six or more words.

> *Correct*   Whenever I hear the opening measure of Beethoven's *Fifth Symphony*, I get goose bumps.

Places and Dates   Places include mailing addresses and geographical locations. The following sentences show where commas are used:

> Sherry Delaney lives at 651 Daniel Street, Memphis, Tennessee 38118.

> I will go to Calais, France, next week.

> Morristown, Oklahoma, is my birthplace.

Note that commas appear after the street designation and the names of cities, countries, and states, except when the name of the state is followed by a zip code.

> Dates are punctuated as shown in the following example:

> On Sunday, June 9, 1991, Elaine received a degree in environmental science.

Here, commas follow the day of the week, the day of the month, and the year.

comma

With dates that include only the month and the year, commas are optional.

Correct   In July 1989 James played chess for the first time.

Correct   In July, 1989, James played chess for the first time.

Nonrestrictive Expressions   A nonrestrictive expression supplies added information about whatever it modifies. This information, however, is *nonessential* and does not affect the basic meaning of the sentence. The two sentences below include nonrestrictive expressions:

Senator Conwell, *the senior senator from this state,* faces a tough campaign for reelection.

My dog, *frightened by the thunder,* hid under my bed while the storm raged.

If we delete the phrase *the senior senator from this state* from the first sentence, we still know that Senator Conwell faces a tough reelection battle. Likewise, if we delete *frightened by the thunder* from the second sentence, we still know that the dog hid during the storm.

Restrictive expressions, which are written *without commas,* distinguish whatever they modify from other persons, places, or things in the same category. Unlike nonrestrictive expressions, they are almost always *essential* sentence elements. Omitting a restrictive expression alters the meaning of the sentence, and the result is often nonsense.

Any person *caught stealing from this store* will be prosecuted.

Dropping the italicized part of this sentence leaves us with the absurd statement that any person, not just those caught stealing, faces prosecution.

Parenthetical Expressions   A parenthetical expression is a word or a word group that links one sentence to another or adds information or emphasis to the sentence in which it appears. Parenthetical expressions include the following demonstrated by example:

Myra Hobbes, *our representative in Seattle,* is being transferred to Spokane next month. (clarifying phrase)

I think, *Jill,* that you'd make a wonderful teacher. (name of person addressed directly)

Tell me, *Captain,* when the cruise ship is scheduled to sail. (title of person addressed directly)

Harley Kendall, *Ph.D.,* will be this year's commencement speaker. (degree title following name)

Alvin realizes, *doesn't he,* that he stands almost no chance of being accepted at West Point? (echo question)

Mathematics, *not home economics,* was Tammy's favorite high school subject. ("not" phrase)

The road, *muddy and rutted,* proved impassable. (adjectives following word they modify)

Punctuating Conjunctive Adverbs Writers often mistakenly punctuate conjunctive adverbs with commas and create, as a result, a comma splice.

> Floridians do not have the heating bills of their Northern neighbors, however, they do have extensive air-conditioning bills.

Conjunctive adverbs actually do not join sentences and can actually be moved, revealing the underlying comma splice.

> Floridians do not have the heating bills of their Northern neighbors, they do, however, have extensive air-conditioning bills.

To fix such comma splices, join the sentences with a semicolon or punctuate with a period and start a new sentence.

> Floridians do not have the heating bills of their Northern neighbors; however, they do have extensive air-conditioning bills.

> Floridians do not have the heating bills of their Northern neighbors. They do, however, have extensive air-conditioning bills.

EXERCISE *Supply commas as necessary to correct the following sentences:*   MyWritingLab

1. Let us know Ms. Granger when you would like to enjoy your free stay at Rolling Hills Resort.
2. The landscapers killed the existing grass rototilled the ground added new topsoil and sprayed the prepared ground with hydroseed.
3. If you are interested in making a tax-deductible donation to the Stratford Festival please write Carla Darma treasurer at 165 University Avenue Suite 700 Toronto Ontario Canada M5H 3B8.
4. Waking up at four A.M. on the first day of online registration Tammy had time to brew some coffee before hitting her computer.
5. A number of students persisted in texting during the class hour so Professor Capstain had to ban cell phones during her lectures.
6. Tim Badgett's classes ran through Wednesday May 20 2015 but he was supposed to start in his new position in Lexington KY on Monday April 6.
7. Before eating raccoons carefully wash their paws.

Connected Discourse Exercise

Add or delete commas as necessary in the following letter:

Grendel College Alumni

While it as only been a few years since you graduated from Grendel you have already joined a long history of proud capable Grendel graduates who have forged successful futures. That is why we are inviting you to join your fellow graduates, at a special alumni recognition weekend to be held from 6 PM Friday March 22 to 6 PM Sunday March 24 here in Bliss Michigan.

We would like you to join Dr. Jasmine Kleften our current president, and members of the board for a special dinner on Friday evening. After the gourmet meal served by dining services there will be a wine and cheese reception where you can reunite with your old friends and favorite faculty members. On Saturday there will

be a breakfast buffet a home football game and a jazz concert on the quad. Sunday after a delightful brunch we would like to give you a tour of the campus, to show you many of the developments that are underway. In the afternoon you will have an opportunity to meet many of our current brilliant students, and attend a poster session that showcases their work.

No we are not going to ask you for money, however, if you feel at the end of the visit that you wish to make a contribution our Jim Beowulf Vice President for University Advancement will be available to speak with you. We want you back to visit us, because you are an important part of our family. Just send back the confirmation card with your signature and we will make all of the arrangements.

Semicolons

The main use of the semicolon (;) is to separate independent clauses, which may or may not be connected with a conjunctive adverb (see pages 587–588). Other uses include separating

- two or more series of items
- items containing commas in a single series
- independent clauses that contain commas and are connected with a coordinating conjunction.

Independent Clauses   The examples that follow show the use of semicolons to separate independent clauses.

> The fabric in this dress is terrible; its designer must have been asleep at the swatch. (no conjunctive adverb)

> Steve refused to write a term paper; *therefore*, he failed the course. (conjunctive adverb *therefore* joining independent clauses)

Conjunctive adverbs can occur within, rather than between, independent clauses. When they do, set them off with commas.

> Marsha felt very confident. Jane, *on the other hand*, was nervous and uncertain. (conjunctive adverb within independent clause)

To determine whether a pair of commas or a semicolon and comma are required, read what comes before and after the conjunctive adverb. Unless both sets of words can stand alone as sentences, use commas.

Two or More Series of Items   With sentences that have two or more series of items, writers often separate the series with semicolons in order to lessen the chances of misreading.

> My duties as secretary include typing letters, memos, and purchase orders; sorting, opening, and delivering mail; and making plane and hotel reservations for traveling executives.

The semicolons provide greater clarity than commas would.

Comma-Containing Items within a Series   When commas accompany one or more of the items in a series, it's often better to separate the items with semicolons instead of commas.

> The meal included veal, which was cooked to perfection; asparagus, my favorite vegetable; and brown rice, prepared with a touch of curry.

Once again, semicolons provide greater clarity than additional commas.

Independent Clauses with Commas and a Coordinating Conjunction
Ordinarily, a comma is used to separate independent clauses joined by a coordinating conjunction. When one or more of the clauses have commas, however, a semicolon provides clearer separation.

> The long black limousine pulled up to the curb; and Jerry, shaking with excitement, watched the President alight from it.

The semicolon makes it easier to see the two main clauses.

EXERCISE   *Supply semicolons wherever they are necessary or desirable in the following sentences. You may have to substitute semicolons for commas. If a sentence is correct, write C.*

MyWritingLab

1. When he visits the main office, Mr. Harmon would like to meet with the vice president of marketing, Carol Chaffe, the personnel director, Carl Hart, and the vice president of finance, Mary Angelo.
2. Social media has invaded the standard network news channels; indeed, television news even reports on celebrity tweets.
3. Thomas Piketty, a French economist, has written what many consider an important book on the inequality of wealth, but, despite its supposed importance, few people, including economists, have actually read the entire work.
4. The Southwest once again is experiencing a severe drought, this increases the chances of deadly forest fires.
5. The reading for the course was eclectic, including *The Invisible Man*, a science fiction novel, *Shane*, a western, and *Antigone*, a classic Greek play.
6. Computers can crash at any time, therefore, it is important to back up your data frequently.
7. Attempting to flee the frigid North Dakota winters, Dan Silver applied for positions in Louisville, Kentucky, Dallas, Texas, Tampa, Florida, and Atlanta, Georgia.

Connected Discourse Exercise

Add and delete semicolons as appropriate in the following letter. You may have to substitute semicolons for commas.

To: All Students
From: John Bits; IT Manager
Re: Improving Our Online Learning Environment

As many of you have pointed out, there have been a number of problems with GrendelUP, our online learning platform, and those problems, President Kleften agrees, have been severe enough to warrant a new system.

You deserve a system that offers consistent, reliable service, is compatible with recent Java Script, allows you to easily view Internet links, and makes it possible for you to review your grades, without changing systems. We believe that you should have an opportunity to have a say in the system we select, therefore, you are invited to attend the demonstration sessions for the possible replacements.

We hope you will attend one or all of these sessions, the system we select should reflect your needs as students.

Periods, Question Marks, and Exclamation Points

Since periods, question marks, and exclamation points signal the ends of sentences, they are sometimes called *end marks*. In addition, periods and question marks function in several other ways.

Periods   Periods (.) end sentences that state facts or opinions, give instructions, make requests that are not in the form of questions, and ask indirect questions—those that have been rephrased in the form of a statement.

Linda works as a hotel manager. (Sentence states fact.)

Please move away from the door. (Sentence makes request.)

I wonder whether Ruthie will be at the theater tonight. (Sentence asks indirect question.)

Periods also follow common abbreviations as well as a person's initials.

Mr.	Dr.	A.D.	lb.
Ms.	Sr.	A.M.	St.
Jr.	B.C.	P.M.	Corp.

Mark J. Valentini, Ph.D., has consented to head the new commission on traffic safety.

Writers today often omit periods after abbreviations for the names of organizations or government agencies, as the following examples show:

ABC	AFL-CIO	FHA	IRS	USAF
ACLU	FBI	GM	NAM	

Dr. Angela Fish has accepted the position as the CEO of BioMed Corp and will help make the company a leader in bioengineering technology.

An up-to-date college dictionary will indicate whether a certain abbreviation should be written without periods.

.?!

Periods also precede decimal fractions and separate numerals standing for dollars and cents.

0.81 percent	$5.29
3.79 percent	$0.88

Question Marks   A question mark (?) ends a whole or a partial sentence that asks a direct question (one that repeats the exact words of the person who asked it).

Do you know how to operate this movie projector? (whole sentence asking a direct question)

Has Cinderella scrubbed the floor? Swept the hearth? Washed the dishes? (sentence and sentence parts asking direct questions)

Dr. Baker—wasn't she your boss once?—has just received a promotion to sales manager. (interrupting element asking a direct question)

The minister inquired, "Do you take this woman to be your lawful wedded wife?" (quotation asking a direct question)

A question mark may be used to indicate uncertainty.

Jane Seymour (1509?–1537), third wife of Henry VIII, was a lady in waiting to his first two wives.

Exclamation Points   Exclamation points (!) are used to express strong emotion or especially forceful commands.

Darcy! I never expected to see you again!

Sam! Turn that radio down immediately!

Help! Save me!

Use exclamation points sparingly; otherwise, they will quickly lose their force.

EXERCISE   *Supply periods, question marks, or exclamation points wherever they are necessary. You may have to change existing punctuation marks. If a sentence is correct, write C.*

MyWritingLab

1. Be sure to proofread your paper before you submit it for a grade.
2. Sigmund Freud—isn't he now generally dismissed by many psychologists—really established the concept of the unconscious.
3. Stan was glad to see that with his bookstore bill at $17832, he finally managed to pay less than the two hundred dollars his parents allotted for his textbooks.
4. When you got your new cell phone plan, did you identify the coverage area, determine how much data transfers cost, and ensure that you had unlimited texting.
5. B. F. Skinner – is he still studied in psychology classes—argued that there was no such thing as free will and that all our policies should reflect that psychological fact.
6. Ouch, tuition has gone up another twelve percent.
7. Has Dr Stevens read the research on the most recent anti-clotting medication.

Connected Discourse Exercise

Add, change, or remove end marks as necessary. You may want to do some slight rewording.

Are you worried about being audited by the I.R.S. Stop worrying. Dr Carl Sly, a C.P.A. with a PhD in Accounting, will be available next Friday afternoon in the Chomsky room to answer all of your questions. Many often ask, "does using a tax preparation program protect you." No. Tax preparation software doesn't keep you from an audit. Only the kind of knowledge Carl Sly provides can make certain you avoid costly hours answering an audit! Learn how to itemize safely, how to avoid the dreaded alternative minimum tax, and how to even take off for home improvements?

Colons, Dashes, Parentheses, and Brackets

Colons, dashes, parentheses, and brackets separate and enclose, thereby clarifying relationships among the various parts of a sentence.

: – ( ) [ ]

Colon   Colons (:) introduce explanations and anticipated lists following words that could stand alone as a complete sentence.

His aim in life is grandiose: to corner the market in wheat. (explanation)

Three students have been selected to attend the conference: Lucille Perkins, Dan Blakely, and Frank Napolis. (list)

Three factors can cause financial problems for farmers: (1) high interest rates, (2) falling land values, and (3) a strong dollar, which makes it difficult to sell crops abroad. (numbered list)

The first of the following sentences is incorrect because the words preceding the colon can't stand alone as a sentence:

Faulty   The tools needed for this job include: a hacksaw, a file, and a drill.

Revision   The tools needed for this job include a hacksaw, a file, and a drill.

Colons also frequently introduce formal quotations that extend beyond a single sentence.

The speaker stepped to the lectern and said: "I am here to ask for your assistance. Today several African nations face a food crisis because drought has ruined their harvests. Unless we provide help quickly, thousands of people will die of starvation."

In such situations, the material preceding the quotation need not be a complete sentence.

Colons also separate hours from minutes (8:20 A.M.), salutations of business letters from the body of the letters (Dear Ms. Stanley:), titles of publications from subtitles (*The Careful Writer: A Guide to English Usage*), numbers indicating ratios (a 3:2:2 ratio), and chapter from verse in biblical references (Luke 6:20–49).

Dashes   Like colons, dashes (—) set off appositives, lists, and explanations but are used in less formal writing. A dash emphasizes the material it sets off.

> Only one candidate showed up at the political rally—Jerry Manders. (appositive)

> The closet held only three garments—an out-at-the-elbows sports coat, a pair of blue jeans, and a tattered shirt. (list)

> I know what little Billy's problem is—a soiled diaper. (explanation)

Dashes set off material that interrupts the flow of thought within a sentence.

> Her new car—didn't she get it just three months ago?—has broken down twice.

Similarly, dashes are used to mark an interrupted segment of dialogue.

> "I'd like to live in England when I retire."

> "In England? But what will your wife—?"

> "My wife likes the idea and can hardly wait for us to make the move."

Dashes set off parenthetical elements containing commas, and a dash can set off comments that follow a list.

> The comedian—short, fat, and squeaky-voiced—soon had everyone roaring with laughter. (parenthetical element with commas)

> A brag, a blow, a tank of air—that's what Senator Conwell is. (comment following a list)

Type a dash as two unspaced hyphens and leave no space between it and the words on either side of it.

Parentheses   Parentheses () are used to enclose numbers or letters that designate the items in a formal list and to set off incidental material within sentences. Except in the kind of list shown in the first example below, a comma does not usually precede a parenthesis.

> Each paper should contain (1) an introduction, (2) several paragraphs developing the thesis statement, and (3) a conclusion.

> Some occupations (computer programming, for example) may be overcrowded in 10 years.

If the material in parentheses appears within a sentence, don't use a capital letter or period, even if the material is itself a complete sentence.

> The growth of genetic engineering (one cannot foresee its consequences) worries some people today.

If the material in parentheses is written as a separate sentence, however, then punctuate it as you would a separate sentence.

> Paula's angry outburst surprised everyone. (She had seemed such a placid person.)

If the material in parentheses comes at the end of a sentence, put the final punctuation after the closing parenthesis.

> This company was founded by Willard Manley (1876–1951).

> In contrast to dashes, parentheses de-emphasize the material they enclose.

Brackets   In quoted material, brackets [] enclose words or phrases that have been added to make the message clearer. They are also used with the word *sic* (Latin for "thus") to point out errors in quoted material.

> "This particular company [Zorn Enterprises, Inc.] pioneered in the safe disposal of toxic wastes," the report noted. (The bracketed name is added to the original.)

> "[John Chafin's] expertise in science has made him a popular figure on the lecture circuit," his friend stated. (The bracketed name replaces *his* in the original.)

> "The principle [sic] cause of lung cancer is cigarette smoking," the article declared. (the word *principal* is misspelled "principle" in the original.)

To call attention to an error, follow it immediately with the bracketed *sic*. The reader will then know that the blame rests with the original writer, not with you.

MyWritingLab   **EXERCISE**   *Supply colons, dashes, parentheses, and* brackets wherever *they are necessary.*

1. Many former Presidents Millard Fillmore, for example have been largely forgotten by most Americans.
2. Our international sales have outperformed domestic sales by an 83 ratio.
3. The newspaper headline read, "Piece sic deal broken."
4. Among our social ills, one condition seems to be the source of many other problems poverty.
5. The new library better considered an information center will have over 50 computers with full Internet capability.
6. Our city area offers many advantages to businesses a skilled workforce, a well-developed infrastructure, and low taxes.
7. Mozart, Miles Davis, The Talking Heads his tastes certainly are eclectic.

Connected Discourse Exercise

Supply any necessary or appropriate colons, dashes, parentheses, and brackets in the following paragraph.

America's entitlement programs Medicare, Medicaid, and Social Security offer a serious challenge to our future budget. The recipients mostly the

elderly, the poor, and the disabled are ones few would like to see harmed. However, with the national debt increasing to nearly 90% of GDP Gross Domestic Product, there are only a few option increase taxes a lot, cut spending deeply, or do some of both. As one pundit put it, "we ain't sic going to be able to have our cake for free and eat it too." There are only tough choices ahead of us. Let's hope we have the political will to make those choices.

Quotation Marks

Quotation marks (" ") set off direct quotations, titles of short written or broadcast works, subdivisions of books, and expressions singled out for special attention.

Direct Quotations   A direct quotation repeats a speaker's or writer's exact words.

> "Tell me about the movie," said Debbie. "If you liked it, I may go myself."

> The placement director said, "The recruiter for Procter and Gamble will be on campus next Thursday to interview students for marketing jobs." (spoken comment)

> "The U.S. trade deficit is expected to reach record levels this year," the *Wall Street Journal* noted. (written comment)

> Jackie said the party was "a total flop."

As these sentences show, a comma or period that follows a direct quotation goes inside the quotation marks. When a quotation is a sentence fragment, the comma preceding it is omitted.

When an expression like "he said" interrupts a quoted sentence, use commas to set off the expression. When the expression comes between two complete quoted sentences, use a period after the expression and capitalize the first word of the second sentence.

> "Hop in," said Jim. "Let me give you a ride to school."

> "Thank you," replied Kelly, opening the car door and sliding into the front seat.

> "I can't remember," said Jim, "when we've had a worse winter."

Titles of Short Works and Subdivisions of Books   These short works include magazine articles, essays, short stories, chapters of books, one-act plays, short poems, songs, and television and radio episodes.

> The article was titled "The Real Conservatism." (article)

> Last night I read John Cheever's "The Enormous Radio," "Torch Song," and "The Swimmer." (short stories)

> Many John Denver fans consider "Take Me Home, Country Roads" to be his greatest piece of music. (song)

The unsuccessful TV show *Pursued* ended its brief run with a segment titled "Checkmate." (TV episode)

Here, as with direct quotations, a comma or period that follows a title goes inside the quotation marks.

Expressions Singled Out for Special Attention

Writers who wish to call the reader's attention to a word or symbol sometimes put it within quotation marks.

The algebraic formula included a "π," a "Θ," and a "Δ."

"Bonnets" and "lifts" are British terms for car hoods and elevators.

More frequently, however, these expressions are printed in italics (pages 642–643).
Again, any commas and periods that follow expressions set off by quotation marks go inside the marks.

Quotation Marks within Quotation Marks

When a direct quotation or the title of a shorter work appears within a direct quotation, use single quotation marks (' ').

"I heard the boss telling the foreman, 'Everyone will receive a Christmas bonus,'" John said.

The instructor told the class, "For tomorrow, read Ernest Hemingway's 'The Killers.'"

Note that the period goes inside of both the single and double quotation marks.

Positioning of Semicolons, Colons, and Question Marks

Position semicolons and colons that come at the end of quoted material after, not before, the quotation marks.

Marcia calls Francine "that greasy grind"; however, I think Marcia is simply jealous of Francine's abilities.

There are two reasons why I like "Babylon Revisited": the characters are interesting and the writing is excellent.

When a question mark accompanies a quotation, put it outside the quotation marks if the whole sentence rather than the quotation asks the question.

Why did Cedric suddenly shout, "This party is a big bore"?

Put the question mark inside the quotation marks if the quotation, but not the whole sentence, asks a question or if the quotation asks one question and the whole sentence asks another.

Marie asked, "What college is your brother planning to attend?" (The quoted material, not the whole sentence, asks the question.)

Whatever possessed him to ask, "What is the most shameful thing you ever did?" (The whole sentence and the quoted material ask separate questions.)

EXERCISE   *Supply properly positioned quotation marks wherever they are necessary.*   MyWritingLab

1. Some linguists think that the quintessential American ok may have come from the African waka.
2. My favorite piece of jazz music is St. James Infirmary.
3. What did Yeats mean by the line in his famous poem The Second Coming, Things fall apart, the center cannot hold?
4. Carl Thomas described the performance as extremely intense.
5. I managed to read Faulkner's short story The Bear, Jennifer sighed, but I don't really know what I want to say about it in my paper for English.
6. In response to the Great Depression, Franklin Roosevelt declared The only thing we have to fear is fear itself; however, many families who had lost their homes and couldn't even earn enough for food really did have something to fear.
7. In his closing argument, the defense attorney asked the jury, How would any one of us act if accused of a crime we knew we didn't commit?

Connected Discourse Exercise

Use quotation marks correctly in the following paragraph:

Mr. Silver recently lectured our class on Stephen Crane's The Bride Comes to Yellow Sky. One thing we shouldn't forget, Mr. Silver insisted, is that the town is deliberately named Yellow Sky. What is the significance of Crane's choice of the words Yellow Sky? Mr. Silver pointed out a number of possible associations, including cowardice, the setting sun, the open expanse of the West, freedom, the sand in the concluding passage. The story, Mr. Silver stated, is drenched in color words. For example, he pointed out, in the first three paragraphs alone Crane mentions vast flats of green grass, brick-colored hands, new black clothes, and a dress of blue cashmere.

Hyphens

Hyphens (-) are used to join compound adjectives and nouns, compound numbers and word-number combinations, and certain prefixes and suffixes to the words with which they appear. In addition, hyphens help prevent misreadings and awkward combinations of letters or syllables and are used to split words between two lines.

Compound Adjectives   Hyphens are often used to join separate words that function as single adjectives and come before nouns. Typical examples follow:

Howard is a very *self-contained* person.

The *greenish-yellow* cloud of chlorine gas drifted toward the village.

Betty's *devil-may-care* attitude will land her in trouble someday.

When the first word of the compound is an adverb ending in -*ly* or when the compound adjective follows the noun it modifies, no hyphen is used.

The *badly* burned crash victim was rushed to the hospital.

The color of the chlorine gas was *greenish yellow.*

When two or more compound adjectives modify the same last term, the sentence will flow more smoothly if that term appears just once, after the last item in the series. The hyphens accompanying the earlier terms in the series are kept, however.

> Many seventeenth-, eighteenth-, and nineteenth-century costumes are on display in this museum.

Compound Nouns   Hyphenated nouns include such expressions as the following:

secretary-treasurer	good-for-nothing
sister-in-law	man-about-town

Here is a sentence with hyphenated nouns:

> Denton is *editor-in-chief* of the largest newspaper in this state.

Compound Numbers and Word-Number Combinations   Hyphens are used to separate two-word numbers from twenty-one to ninety-nine and fractions that have been written out.

> Marcy has worked *twenty-one* years for this company.

> *One-fourth* of my income goes for rent.

Similarly, hyphens are used to separate numerals from units of measurement that follow them.

> This chemical is shipped in *50-gallon* drums.

Prefixes and Suffixes   A prefix is a word or set of letters that precedes a word and alters its meaning. A suffix is similar but comes at the end of the word. Although most prefixes are not hyphenated, the prefixes *self-* and *all-* do get hyphens, as does the suffix *-elect.* Also the prefix *ex-* is hyphenated when it accompanies a noun.

> This stove has a *self-cleaning* oven.

> Let Claire Voyant, the *all-knowing* soothsayer, read your future in her crystal ball.

> Ethel is the *chairperson-elect* of the club.

> Several *ex-teachers* work in this department.

A prefix used before a capitalized term is always hyphenated.

> The *ex-FBI* agent gave an interesting talk on the operations of that agency.

Preventing Misreadings and Awkward Combinations of Letters and Syllables   Hyphens help prevent misreadings of certain words and also break up awkward combinations of letters and syllables between certain prefixes and suffixes and their core words.

The doctor *re-treated* the wound with a new antibiotic. (The hyphen prevents the misreading *retreated*.)

The company plans to *de-emphasize* sales of agricultural chemicals. (The hyphen prevents the awkward repetition of the letter *e* in *deemphasize*.)

Between Syllables   Whenever you have to split a word between two lines, place a hyphen at the end of the first line to show the division. The word is always broken, and the hyphen inserted, between syllables. (Any good dictionary shows the syllable divisions of each word it includes.) Never divide a one-syllable word or leave two letters to be placed on the second line, even if those two letters constitute a syllable.

EXERCISE   *Supply hyphens wherever they are necessary. If the sentence is correct, write C.*   MyWritingLab

1. The piece of music ended with bird like sounds made by the entire woodwind section.
2. In this brokerage firm we follow sound investment strategies rather than chase after will o' the wisp schemes.
3. It can be sobering for the president elect to learn the full requirements of the job.
4. The union negotiators were forced to retreat from their initial demands.
5. One fifth of the shipment of fresh tomatoes turned out to be spoiled.
6. The classical radio station can be received by anyone within a 100 mile radius of its broadcasting tower.
7. In this class, we will study nineteenth and twentieth century American authors.
8. Emerson thought that it was important for people to be self reliant.
9. Once the power came back on, I had to recreate the file.
10. The Gundersons have been married for thirty five years.

Capitalization

Capitalize the first word in any sentence, the pronoun *I*, proper nouns and adjectives, titles used with names, and the significant words in literary and artistic titles.

Proper Nouns   A proper noun names one particular person, group of persons, place, or thing. Such nouns include the following:

Persons	Days, months, and holidays
Organizations	Trademarks
Racial, political, and religious groups	Languages
Countries, states, cities, and streets	Ships and aircraft
Companies and buildings	Abbreviations for academic degrees
Geographical locations and features	Sacred writings and pronouns standing for God and Jesus
	Titles used in place of names

The sentences below show the capitalization of proper nouns:

> *Sigmund* works for the *National Psychoanalytical Institute*, an organization that has done much to advance the science of psychiatry.

> How much does this roll of *Saran Wrap* cost?

> *Gwen Greene* moved to *Paris, France*, when her father became the consul there.

> On *Friday, December* 10, 1993, *Michael Jordan* visited our city.

> *Larry* has a master of arts degree, and his sister has a *Ph.D.*

> My father works for the *Ford Motor Company*, but I work for *Daimler Chrysler*.

Do not capitalize words like *institute, college, company,* or *avenue* unless they form part of a proper name. Likewise, do not capitalize the names of courses unless they start a sentence, are accompanied by a course number, or designate a language.

> I have a 95 average in *Economics* 112 but only a 73 average in sociology.

> Harry plans to take intermediate *German* in his junior year.

> Do you plan to attend *Drew College* or some other college?

Proper Adjectives   Adjectives created from proper nouns are called proper adjectives. Like the nouns themselves, they should be capitalized.

> Lolita Martinez, our class valedictorian, is of *Mexican* ancestry. (*Mexican* is derived from the proper noun *Mexico*.)

Abbreviations   As a general rule, capitalize abbreviations only if the words they stand for are capitalized.

> Milton DeWitt works for the *IRS*. (*IRS* is capitalized because *Internal Revenue Service* would be.)

> The flask holds 1,500 *ml* of liquid. (The abbreviation *ml* is not capitalized because *milliliters* would not be.)

A few abbreviations are capitalized even though all or some of the words they stand for aren't. Examples include TV (television) and VCR (videocassette recorder).

Personal Titles   Capitalize a personal title if it precedes a name or is used in place of a name. Otherwise, do not capitalize.

> The division is under the command of *General* Arnold Schafer.

> Tell me, *Doctor*, do I need an operation?

> The *dean* of our engineering division is Dr. Alma Haskins.

cap

Many writers capitalize titles of high rank when they are used in place of names.

>   The *President* will sign this bill tomorrow.

>   The *president* will sign this bill tomorrow.

Either usage is acceptable.

Titles of Literary and Artistic Works   When citing the titles of publications, pieces of writing, movies, television programs, paintings, sculptures, and the like, capitalize the first and last words and all other words except *a, an, the,* coordinating conjunctions, and one-syllable prepositions.

>   Last week I played *Gone with the Wind* on my VCR and read Christopher Isherwood's *Goodbye to Berlin.* (the preposition *with,* the article *the,* and the preposition *to* are not capitalized.)

>   John is reading a book called *The Movies of Abbott and Costello.* (The preposition *of* and the coordinating conjunction *and* are not capitalized. *The* is capitalized because it is the first word of the title.)

>   Although I'm no TV addict, I used to watch every episode of *Murder, She Wrote.* (All of the words in the title are capitalized.)

Note that the titles of literary and artistic works are italicized.

EXERCISE   *Identify any word or abbreviation that should be capitalized in the following*   MyWritingLab **ab**
sentences:

1. Every friday at 1:00 P.M. the computer support team meets to review the problems that occurred during the previous week.
2. Any student of mexican history will soon see how radically different that history has been from american history.
3. Though many consider it a liberal organization, the aclu has actually protected the right to free speech of many extremely conservative groups.
4. Many students in the rotc choose to take history 321: american military history to satisfy their humanities requirement.
5. Your request for a leave of absence cannot be approved by professor Murphy.
6. Students of roman literature should be familiar with ovid's *metamorphoses.*
7. During World War II, dr. Johnson served on the u.s. submarine eel.

Abbreviations

Items that are abbreviated include certain personal titles, names of organizations and agencies, Latin terms, and specific and technical terms.

Personal Titles   Abbreviate *Mister, Doctor,* and similar titles when they come just ahead of a name, and *Junior, Senior,* and degree titles when they follow names.

>   Will *Mr.* Harry Babbitt please come to the front desk?

Arthur Compton, *Sr.*, is a well-known historian; his son, Arthur Compton, *Jr.*, is a television producer.

This article on marital discord was written by Irma Quarles, *Ph.D.*

Names of Organizations and Agencies   Many organizations and agencies are known primarily by their initials rather than their full names. Several examples follow:

AAA   CIA   FHA   NATO   UNESCO
CARE   FBI   IBM   NBC

Latin Terms   Certain Latin terms are always abbreviated; others are abbreviated when used with dates or times.

e.g. (*exempli gratia:* for example)

i.e. (*id est:* that is)

etc. (*et cetera:* and [the] others)

vs. or v. (*versus:* against)

A.D. (*anno Domini:* in the year of our Lord)

A.M. or A.M. (*ante meridiem:* before noon)

P.M. or P.M. (*post meridiem:* after noon)

The play starts at 8 P.M.

Many writers (*e.g.*, Dylan Thomas and Truman Capote) have had serious problems with alcohol.

ab

Scientific and Technical Terms   For brevity's sake, scientists and technicians abbreviate terms of measurement that repeatedly occur. Terms that the reader would not know are written out the first time they are used, and they are accompanied by their abbreviation in parentheses. Unfamiliar organizations and agencies that are mentioned repeatedly are handled in like manner.

The viscosity of the fluid measured 15 centistokes (cs) at room temperature.

Common practice calls for writing such abbreviations without periods unless they duplicate the spelling of some word.

Standard dictionaries list common abbreviations. When you don't recognize one, look it up. Use abbreviations sparingly in essays. If you're unsure about what is appropriate, don't abbreviate.

MyWritingLab   **EXERCISE**   *Supply abbreviations wherever they are necessary or are customarily used.*

1. We are pleased that Mister Jones has decided to join our firm.
2. Dissolve 1 gram of NaCl in 20 milliliters of water.
3. The freezing point of water at sea level is 32° Fahrenheit (0° Celsius).
4. Since its start, the National Broadcasting Company has been strongly committed to its news programming.
5. Doctor Baxter has been doing extensive research on nanotechnology, supported by a National Science Foundation grant.
6. Carl Thorton, Junior, will offer a workshop on how to save for retirement.
7. Many composers who are now seen as giants of classical music (*exempli gratia*, Mozart and Beethoven) died paupers.

Numbers

Some instructors ask their students to use figures for numbers larger than ninety-nine and to spell out smaller numbers.

Boise is *100* miles from here.

Boise is *ninety-nine* miles from here.

Other instructors prefer that students switch to figures beginning with the number ten.

My son will be *nine* years old on his next birthday.

My son will be *10* years old on his next birthday.

With either practice, the following exceptions apply.

Numbers in a Series   Write all numbers in a series the same way regardless of their size.

Gatsby has *64* suits, *110* shirts, and *214* ties.

In just one hour the emergency room personnel handled *two* stabbings, *five* shootings, and *sixteen* fractures.

We have *150* salespeople, *51* engineers, and *7* laboratory technicians.

Dates   Use figures for dates that include the year.

February *14, 1985* or 14 February 1985 (not February 14th, 1985)

When the date includes the day but not the year, you may use figures or spell out the number.

June 9

June ninth

the ninth of June

Page Numbers and Addresses   Use figures for page numbers and street numbers in addresses.

Check the graph on page *415*.

I live at *111* Cornelia Street, and my office is at *620* Fifth Avenue.

Numbers Beginning Sentences   Spell out any number that begins a sentence. If this requires three or more words, rephrase the sentence so that the number comes after the opening and numerals can be used.

The year *1989* was a good year for this wine.

Sixty thousand fans jammed the stadium.

num

An army of *265,000* troops assaulted the city. (If this number began the sentence, five words—an excessive number—would be needed to write it out.)

Decimals, Percentages, Times   Use figures for decimals and percentages as well as for expressions of time that are accompanied by A.M. or P.M.

The shaft has a *0.37*-inch diameter.

Last year the value of my house jumped *25* percent.

The plane leaves here at *9:50* A.M. and reaches New Orleans at *2:30* P.M.

One Number Following Another   When a number-containing term that denotes a unit of weight or measurement comes immediately after another number, spell out the first number, if smaller than 100, and use numerals for the second one. If the first number is larger than 100, use numerals for it and spell out the second one.

We ordered *six 30-*gallon drums of solvent for the project.

The supplier shipped us *600 thirty-*gallon drums by mistake.

MyWritingLab   **EXERCISE**   *Identify any miswriting of numbers in the following sentences and rewrite these numbers correctly:*

ital

1. The supermarket ordered five hundred five-pound bags of sugar.
2. The holes that the automated system drilled in the brackets were off by two hundredths of an inch.
3. The first memo warning the company of the problem was dated May fifteenth, 1993.
4. 8,000 people usually subscribe to our symphony orchestra series.
5. There are a number of serious editing errors on page thirty-nine of the report.
6. Over the last year, sales have increased by twenty-three percent.
7. We found that only 3 computers needed to be upgraded.

Italics

Italics are used for the titles of longer publications, the names of vehicles and vessels, foreign words and phrases, and expressions singled out for special attention. Use underlining to represent italics when hand writing or typing papers.

Titles of Longer Publications and Artistic Works   These items may include the following:

books	record albums	long musical works and poems
magazines	paintings	plays
newspapers	movies	sculptures

As noted on pages 633–634, quotation marks are used for the titles of articles, short stories, short poems, one-act plays, and other brief pieces of writing.

Last night I finished F. Scott Fitzgerald's *The Great Gatsby* and read two articles in *The New Yorker.* (book, magazine)

Michelangelo's *David* is surely one of the world's greatest sculptures. (sculpture)

The *Detroit Free Press* had praise for the revival of Tennessee Williams's play *The Glass Menagerie.* (newspaper, play)

Stephen Vincent Benét's poem *John Brown's Body* won a Pulitzer Prize in 1929. (book-length poem)

Do not use italics when naming the Bible and its parts or other religious works such as the Torah and Koran.

Joanna's favorite book of the Bible is the Book of Ecclesiastes, part of the Old Testament.

Names of Vehicles and Vessels   Names of particular airplanes, ships, trains, and spacecraft are italicized.

The plane in which Charles Lindbergh flew over the Atlantic Ocean was named *The Spirit of St. Louis.*

Foreign Expressions   Use italics to identify foreign words and phrases that have not yet made their way into the English language.

The writer has a terribly pessimistic *weltanschauung.* (philosophy of life)

This season, long skirts are the *dernier cri.* (the latest thing)

When such expressions become completely assimilated, the italics are dropped. Most dictionaries use an asterisk (*), a dagger (†), or other symbol to identify expressions that need italicizing.

Expressions Singled Out for Special Attention   These include words, letters, numerals, and symbols.

The Greek letter *pi* is written π.

I can't tell whether this letter is meant to be an *a* or an *o* or this number a *7* or a *9.*

In England, the word *lorry* means truck.

As noted on pages 633–634, quotation marks sometimes replace italics for this purpose.

EXERCISE   *Supply italics wherever they are necessary.*   MyWritingLab

1. The British often use the word lift to refer to an elevator.
2. Arthur Miller's Death of a Salesman is considered by many critics to be the great American tragedy.

3. Given the quality of the movie version, it takes a considerable amount of courage to produce a stage version of the musical West Side Story.
4. The delight many people take in the discomfort of characters in situation comedies suggests that all of us may be subject to some schadenfreude.
5. The USS Enterprise was the first nuclear aircraft carrier.
6. I have always fantasized about taking a ride on the Orient Express, which figured so prominently in a mystery by Agatha Christie.
7. There has been a very conscious effort to make Scientific American available to a larger segment of the reading public.

Connected Discourse Exercise

Use hyphens, capitalization, abbreviations, numbers, and italics properly in the following passage:

Because I can speak Russian fluently, I was recruited by the central intelligence agency while still at Boston college. I suspected that it was professor Hogsbottom, a Political Science teacher, who had suggested that they consider me. After all, he had been a General during World War II and still had connections with the intelligence community. It turned out that my brother in law was responsible; he was an ex FBI agent. Soon I was an american spy located, of all places, in England. Who would suspect that we had to spy on the english? For 3 years I posed as a british aristocrat who was a general bon vivant and man about town. I went by the alias of Mister Henry Higgins, Junior. Everyone, of course, wanted to know if I had seen My Fair Lady. Personally I thought the whole thing was a monty python type of joke until I found a position in the british secret service. Who could have believed the british kept so many secrets from their american allies? For twenty one years I spied on the british without anyone suspecting that I was an all american boy. I did find out recently, however, that because of my fluent russian they had suspected me of being a russian spy and had been feeding me false information all along.

ital

Credits

Photo Credits

Cover/common art: Bekulnis/Shutterstock; **p. 143:** Rubberball/Corbis; **p. 161:** Rubberball/Corbis; **p. 177:** Paul McKinnon /Alamy; **p. 193:** Ariel Skelley/Corbis; **p. 206:** Elena Schweitzer/Shutterstock; **p. 222:** © Fly Fernandez/Corbis; **p. 236:** Eleanor /Corbis; **p. 251:** The International Astronomical Union; **p. 268:** Jeffrey Markowitz/Sygma/Corbis; **p. 283:** Image Source/Getty; **p. 348:** Software copyright Innovative Interfaces, Inc.; **p. 349:** Software copyright Innovative Interfaces, Inc.; **p. 350 (top):** Software copyright Innovative Interfaces, Inc.; **p. 350 (bottom):** Software copyright Innovative Interfaces, Inc.; **p. 353:** Used with permission of Ferris State University; **p. 354 (top):** Used with permission of Ferris State University; **p. 354 (bottom):** From Gale. Infotrac Search Screen for General Reference Center Gold. © 2015, a part of Cengage Learning, Inc. Reproduced by permission. www. cengage.com/permissions. Also used by permission of Ferris State University.; **p. 356:** Used by permission of Ferris State University.; **p. 480:** Aurin/Shutterstock.

Text Credits

Chapter 1

pp. 4-5: Halavage, Marianne: "Turn Down Your iPod Volume (Or Go Deaf)." Used by permission of the author.

Chapter 2

pp. 32-33, 33, 34-35: Gross, Amy: "The Appeal of the Androgynous Man," *Mademoiselle*, 1976. Reprinted with permission of the author.

Chapter 5

p. 87: Davies, Paul C.W.: Excerpt from *What We Believe But Cannot Prove*, Edited by John Brockman. Copyright (c) 2006 by John Brockman. Introduction copyright (c) 2006 by Ian McEwan. Reprinted by permission of HarperCollins Publishers.

p. 87: Davies, Paul C.W.: Excerpt from *What We Believe But Cannot Prove: Today's Leading Thinkers on Science in the Age of Certainty*. Reprinted with permission of Brockman, Inc.

p. 87: Gimlett, John: *Theatre of Fish: Travels Through Newfoundland and Labrador*, ©1996 Random House.

p. 87: Fadiman, Anne: *Ex Libris: Confessions of a Common Reader*, ©2000, Farrar, Straus & Giroux.

p. 88: Tratey, M.D., John J.: *A User's Guide to the Brain*, ©2002, Random House.

p. 88: Lovesey, John: "A Myth Is As Good As a Mile," *Sports Illustrated*, February 15, 1965.

p. 89: Otis, Laura: *Literature and Science in the Nineteenth Century*, ©2009, Oxford University Press.

p. 92: Turk, Jon: *Cold Oceans: Adventures in Kayaks, Rowboat, and Dogsled*, ©1998, HarperCollins.

p. 93: Strayer, David L., Frank A. Drews, and Dennis J. Crouch: *A Comparison of the Cell Phone Driver and the Drunk Driver, Human Factors*, Summer 2006.

p. 96: Machlowitz, Mary: "Workaholism: What's Wrong with Being Married to Your Work?" *Working Woman*, May 1978. Reprinted with permission of the author.

pp. 96-97: Becker, Carl: *Freedom and Responsibility in the American Way of Life*, ©1955, Random House.

p. 97: Jordan, Eileen Herbert: "My Affair with the One-Armed Bandit," *Modern Maturity*, July/August 1995.

p. 98: Parker, Jo Goodwin: "What Is Poverty?" from George Henderson, *America's Other Children: Public Schools Outside Suburbia*, ©1971, University of Oklahoma Press.

p. 99: "Controlling Phobias Through Behavior Modification," *USA Today*, August 1978.

p. 100: Billington, Ray Allen: "The Frontier Disappears," *Westward Expansion: A History of the American Frontier*, ©2001, University of New Mexico Press.

p. 100: Engel, Marian: "Women Also Have Dark Hearts," *New York Times Book Review*, November 24, 1974.

p. 100: Perry, Nancy: "Saving the Schools: How Business Can Help," *Fortune*, December 1987.

pp. 100-101: Rowe Karlyn, Kathleen: *Unruly Girls Unrepentant Mothers: Redefining Feminism on Screen,* ©2011 University of Texas Press.

p. 101: Callahan, Maureen: "Lady Gaga Gives 50 Percent of Her Earnings to Her Father," *New York Post,* November 20, 2011.

p. 101: Bettelheim, Bruno: "Joey: A Mechanical Boy," *Scientific American,* March 1959.

p. 102: Jordan, Jr., Vernon E.: *The New Negativism,* September 15, 1978.

p. 103: Fixx, James: "What Running Can't Do for You," *The Complete Book of Running,* ©1977, Random House.

p. 103: Booth, Stephanie: "A Slew of Suspects," *Psychology Today,* November 1, 2011.

p. 103: Hobsbawm, Eric: *On History,* ©1988, The New Press.

p. 104: Page, Max; Sigrid Miller Pollin: "Proposal for a Landscape of Learning," *Serpents in the Garden: Liaisons with Culture & Sex,* edited by Alexander Cockburn; Jeffrey St. Clair, ©2004, AK Press.

p. 104: Lemke, J. L.: "Metamedia Literacy: Transforming Meanings and Media," *Handbook of Literacy and Technology: Transformations in a Post-Typographic World,* D. Reinking, L. Labbo, M. McKenna, & R. Kiefer (Eds.), ©1998, Erlbaum.

Chapter 6

p. 109: Waggoner, John: "Is Today's Economic Crisis Another Great Depression," *USA Today,* November 4, 2008.

p. 109: Deems Taylor: "The Monster," *Of Men and Music,* ©1937, Simon and Schuster.

p. 109: Kingsolver, Barbara: *High Tide in Tucson: Essays from Now or Never,* ©2003, HarperCollins.

p. 113: Carson, Rachel: Excerpt from *Silent Spring.* Copyright © 1962 by Rachel Carson, renewed 1990 by Roger Christie.

p. 115: King, Jr., Martin Luther: "Pilgrimage to Nonviolence." September 1, 1958

Chapter 7

pp. 120-121: Didion, Joan: "On Self Respect," *Slouching Toward Bethlehem,* ©1990, Farrar, Straus & Giroux.

p. 121: Manchester, William: *A World Lit Only by Fire: The Medieval Mind and the Renaissance: Portrait of an Age,* ©1993, Little Brown.

p. 123: By permission. From *Merriam-Webster's Collegiate® Dictionary,* 11th Edition ©2015 by Merriam-Webster, Inc. (www.Merriam-Webster.com).

p. 126: By permission. From *Merriam-Webster's Collegiate® Dictionary,* 11th Edition ©2015 by Merriam-Webster, Inc. (www.Merriam-Webster.com).

p. 126: Middleton, Thomas H.: "The Magic Power of Words," *Saturday Review,* December 11, 1976.

p. 128: Levitin, Daniel J.: *This is Your Brain on Music: The Science of a Human Obsession,* ©2007, Penguin.

p. 129: "Neurotransmitters," *Encyclopedia of Mental Disorders,* Elsevier Science.

p. 129: Russel, Bertrand: *The ABC of Relativity,* ©1925, Harper & Bros.

pp. 129-130: Denes, Magda: *In Necessity and Sorrow: Life and Death in an Abortion Hospital,* ©1976, Basic Books.

p. 130: Wolfe, Tom: *The Pump House Gang,* ©1968, Farrar Straus and Giroux.

p. 132: Jackson, Bruce: "Who Goes to Prison: Caste and Careerism in Crime," *Atlantic Monthly,* January 1966.

p. 132: Mannes, Marya: "Wasteland," *More in Anger: Some Opinions, Uncesored and Unteleprompted of Marya Mannes,* ©1958, Lippincott.

p. 132: Allen, RT: "The Porcupine," *Maclean's Magazine,* August 15, 1952.

p. 133: Claiborne, Robert: "Future Schlock," *The National.*

p. 133: St. Clair, Jeffrey: "Seduced by a Legend," *Serpents in the Garden: Liaisons with Culture & Sex,* edited by Alexander Cockburn; Jeffrey St. Clair, ©2004, AK Press.

pp. 134-135: Kearns Goodwin, Doris: *Lyndon Johnson and the American Dream: The Most Revealing Portrait of a President and Presidential Power Ever Written,* ©1991, St. Martins Press.

p. 136: Irving, Washington: "The Spectre Bridegroom," *The Sketch Book,* ©1875, J.B. Lippincott & Co.

p. 138: Brown, Claude: *Manchild in the Promised Land,* ©2011, Touchstone.

Chapter 8

p. 145: Fairlie, Harry: "A Victim Fights Back," *Washington Post,* April 30, 1978.

p. 145: Hersey, John: Hiroshima, ©1989, Random House, Inc.

p. 145: London, Jack: *The Sea Wolf,* 1904.

p. 146: Thoreau, Henry David: *A Week on the Concord and Merrimac Rivers,* 1849.

p. 147: Kingsolver, Barbara: *High Tide in Tucson: Essays from Now or Never,* ©2003, HarperCollins.

pp. 153-156: Coggin, Brittany: "Joy Through Tears." Used by permission of the author.

Chapter 9

p. 163: Dick-Read, Robert: *Sanamu: Adventures in Search of African Art,* ©1964, Penguin Group.

pp. 163-164: Twain, Mark: *Autobiography,* ©1917, Harper.

pp. 164-165: Conrad, Joseph: *Lord Jim,* ©1920, Doubleday.

p. 165: Kluger, Marilyn: "A Time of Plenty," *Gourmet Magazine.*

pp. 165-166: Becker, Jasper: *The Chinese: An insider's look at the issues which affect and shape China today,* ©2000, Oxford University Press.

Chapter 10

p. 180: Miller, Don Ethan: "A State of Grace: Understanding the Martial Arts," *Atlantic Monthly,* March 1981.

p. 180: Thomas, Lewis: *The Lives of a Cell: Notes of a Biology Watcher,* ©1995, Penguin Group.

p. 187: Frank, Adam: "Winds of Change," *Discover Magazine,* June 1, 1994.

Index

A

Abbreviations, 638, 639–40
Abstract terms, 252–53, 254, 258, 266
Abstract words, 120–21
Accept/except, 120
"Accidental Discoveries" (Krock), 490–94
Action, role of, in narration, 145–46
Action verbs, 578
Active voice, 115, 116
Addresses, 641
Adjective clauses, 592
Adjectives, 583–85
   common, 583
   comparison with, 584
   compound, 635–36
   confusing the comparative
      and superlative forms in
      comparisons, 612
   coordinate, 623
   determiners, 584–85
   misusing, 611–12
   proper, 583
   using, 611–13
Advanced search, 355–56
The Adventures of Huckleberry Finn
   (Twain), 127
Adverb clauses, 592–93
Adverbs, 585–86
   comparison with, 585–86
   confusing the comparative
      and superlative forms in
      comparisons, 612
   conjunctive, 587–88, 625
   formation of, 585
   misusing, 611–12
   using, 611–13
Agencies, 640
Alternating pattern in organizing
   comparison, 226
Altman, Robert, 320, 325
Ambiguity, 137, 332

The American Economic Review, 562–63
American Heritage, 514
The American Heritage Dictionary, 124
American Psychological Association
   (APA) system
   for authors identified in text, 427–28
   for authors with same last name, 424
   for indirect citations, 427
   for in-text citations, 423–26
   for preparing research paper,
      414–15
   for quotations, 426–28
   separate works by same author, 425
   student research paper, 428–34
   for two sources for same citation, 425
   for unsigned references, 425–26
America Online, 393
Analogy
   in argument, 280–81
   in comparison, 226–27
   faulty, 287
   thinking critically about, 227–28
Anecdotes in introduction, 98, 100
Angelou, Maya, 9
Annotated bibliography, 360
Antecedents
   collective nouns as, 602
   hidden, 604
   indefinite pronouns as, 601
   more than one, 603
   singular, 601–2
Antigone, 323
APA. *See* American Psychological
   Association (APA) system
Apostrophes, 619–22
   contractions, 620–21
   plurals, 621
   possession, 619–20
Appeal
   to the crowd, 288
   emotional, 281–82
   rational, 271–75

The Appeal of the Androgynous Man
   (Gross), 28, 30–32, 33, 34–35
Applied Science and Technology Index, 355
Appositives
   defined, 573
   nonrestrictive, 573
   restrictive, 573
"Are Video Games Now More
      Sophisticated than Cinema?"
   (Graham), 519–22
Arguing off the point, 287–88
Argument *ad hominem,* 288
Argumentation
   concept of critical thinking, 11
Argument paper, 343
Arguments, 268–308
   analogy in, 280–81
   critical synthesis with sources, 306–7
      critically evaluating the sources,
         306–7
      planning and drafting the synthesis,
         307
      prewriting for synthesis, 306
      purposes for synthesis, 306
   defined, 269
   dialogue, effective technique, 293
   for different purposes, 294–95
   directing, to readers, 295
   discussion questions, 305
   drafting, 295–99
   emotional appeal in, 281–82
   ethical appeal in, 283–84
   ethical issues in, 290–91
   exploratory, 285
   extra-high-voltage electric transmission
      line, 272
   framing, 270–71
   making with visuals, 283
   organization and, 92
   pattern for, 299
   planning, 294–95
   prewriting the, 291

Editing Symbols

Symbol	Problem	Page
ab	improper abbreviation	639–640
agr pa	faulty agreement of pronoun and antecedent	601–603
agr sv	faulty agreement of subject and verb	598–600
V or apos	missing or misused apostrophe	619–622
awk	awkward phrasing	
bib	faulty bibliographic form	386–427
cap	capital letter needed	637–639
case	wrong case	607–609
cl	cliché	138–139
↑ or com	missing or misused comma	622–626
cs	comma splice	596–598
comp	faulty comparison	616–618
dm	dangling modifier	614–615
… or ellip	missing or misused ellipsis	367–368
frag	sentence fragment	595–596
ital	missing or misused italics	642–644
lc	lowercase (small) letter needed	637–639
// or lev	wrong level of usage	126–130
log	faulty logic	
mm	misplaced modifier	613–614
num	use numerals	641–642
nsu	nonstandard usage new paragraph needed	

Symbol	Problem	Page
no	new paragraph not needed	
⊙	period needed	628–629
// or para	nonparallelism	615–616
? or ques	missing or misused question mark	629
"/" or quot	missing or misused quotation marks	633–635
ref	unclear reference of pronoun to antecedent	603–605
ro	run-on sentence	596–598
; or sem	missing or misused semicolon	626–628
sp	spelling error	
shift p	shift in person	605–606
shift t	shift in tense	610–611
sq	squinting modifier	613–614
t or tense	wrong tense	580–582
trans	poor transition	
vb	wrong verb form	
wdy	wordiness	136–137
ww	wrong word	
ℱ	delete (omit)	
^	material omitted	
⦸	meaning unclear or word illegible	

Reader   455

Rhetorical Table of Contents

Education and Learning

Popular Culture and the Arts

Science and Technology

Diversity in Our Lives

Language Use and Abuse

Struggling with Ethical Issues

Handbook 571

Sentence Elements

Editing to Correct Sentence Errors

Editing to Correct Faulty Punctuation and Mechanics

Preface

The eleventh edition of *Strategies for Successful Writing: A Rhetoric, Research Guide, Reader, and Handbook* is a comprehensive textbook that offers ample material for a full-year composition course. Instructors teaching a one-term course can make selections from Chapters 1 to 18, from whatever types of specialized writing suit the needs of their students, and from appropriate essays in the Reader.

Because we strongly believe that an effective composition textbook should address the student directly, we have aimed for a style that is conversational yet clear and concise. We believe that our style invites students into the book, lessens their apprehensions about writing, and provides a model for their own prose. This style complements our strong student-based approach to writing, and together they help create a text that genuinely meets students' needs.

Changes in the Eleventh Edition

The enthusiastic response to the ten previous editions both by teachers and students has been very gratifying. The eleventh edition retains the many popular features of the previous editions and incorporates a number of improvements suggested by users and reviewers that should considerably enhance the utility of the text. Among the changes the following are noteworthy.

- **Critical thinking** is now a centerpiece of the text. Chapter 1 introduces students to critical thinking and how to use this text to develop their critical-thinking skills. Chapter 2 stresses critical thinking in reading; Chapters 3 and 4 identify the role of critical thinking in the writing process. Chapter 19 on the research process emphasizes critical thinking, and critical-thinking questions also appear throughout the Reader. Sharpened **Critical Synthesis** sections appear at the end of each modes-based chapter (Chapters 8–16), helping students integrate source material regardless of which type of rhetorical strategy they are using. The section includes guidelines for prewriting, evaluating sources, planning, and drafting a source-based paper for each of the writing strategies. Each modes-based chapter also includes a section on thinking critically about the mode.

- **Chapter 16 on Argument** has been reorganized to be easier to follow. It features a strengthened section on emotional appeal, enhanced coverage of thinking critically, and prominently located material on visual rhetoric.
- The **Reader** has been enhanced. Nearly half of the professional selections in the Reader have been replaced with essays from a variety of media in a range of styles on current topics, social media, immigration, citizen videos of police activity, education, and more. A new preface has been added to enhance student access to the Reader. Each modes-based section of the reader now has one selection identified as using multiple strategies with an explanation of how and why those strategies are used.
- **The multimedia approach** has been extended through the entire text, providing opportunities for students to write about many forms of media and to write for different media.
- **New MLA and APA sample student essays** address current topics (contagious disease and reality TV). **New case studies in Chapter 19 (The Research Paper)** reflect the new MLA research paper.
- **MLA and APA documentation chapters have been updated** to ensure that the most current rules are presented. The chapters have been expanded to include the documentation rules for social media. Updated discussion of research methods now emphasizes electronic research, including refining online searches and evaluating sources, more accurately reflecting how students conduct research today (Chapter 20).
- **The Writing About Literature chapter** has been revised to include writing about film and television, updated critical approaches, a new section on writing explications, and a new student sample essay.
- The emphasis on **visual rhetoric** has been strengthened. Additional revisions have been made to make the text more visually accessible and to model the best practices of visual rhetoric. **Multimedia Writing Assignments** in the rhetoric ask students to write about texts and visuals found in different types of media.
- In an effort to **keep the text streamlined and affordable**, the separate chapter on writing with multiple strategies and the section of the reader on the same topic have been integrated into the reader. In addition, the **handbook** has been streamlined while retaining its usability.

Classic Pedagogy

In addition to the new features discussed above, the eleventh edition continues the tried-and-true pedagogy of previous editions.

- Color highlighting of key passages in sample texts identifies different writing strategies in action.
- Graphic organizers in the form of flowcharts provide guidelines for developing essays.
- Sample Student Essays are annotated to draw students' attention to writers' strategies.
- Learning objectives frame each chapter's content to guide both instructors and students to the goals of the chapter.

- The text provides short, relevant, and engaging samples of the principles being discussed.
- Connected Discourse exercises remain a hallmark of the handbook, but many have been revised so that the topics of the exercises are more current.

The Rhetoric

The Rhetoric consists of 18 chapters, grouped into four parts. The first part includes four chapters. Chapter 1 introduces students to the purposes of writing; the need for audience awareness, which includes a discussion of discourse communities; and the qualities of good writing. Chapter 2 offers suggestions for effective and critical reading and thinking. Chapter 3 looks at planning and drafting stages. Chapter 4 takes students through the various revision stages, starting with a systematic procedure for revising the whole essay and then moving to pointers for revising its component parts. Sets of checklists pose key questions for students to consider. Chapters 3 and 4 are unified by an unfolding case history that includes the first draft of a student paper, the initial revision marked with changes, and the final version. Notes in the margin highlight key features of the finished paper. Students can relate the sequence of events to their own projects as they work through the various stages. Both chapters offer suggestions for using word-processing programs, and Chapter 4 explains peer evaluation of drafts, collaborative writing, and maintaining and reviewing a portfolio.

In the second part, we shift from full-length essays to the elements that make them up. Chapter 5 first discusses paragraph unity; it then takes up the topic sentence, adequate development, organization, coherence, and finally introductory, transitional, and concluding paragraphs. Throughout this chapter, as elsewhere, carefully selected examples and exercises form an integral part of the instruction.

Chapter 6 focuses on strategies for creating effective sentences. Such strategies as coordinating and subordinating ideas and using parallelism help students to increase the versatility of their writing. The concluding section offers practical advice on crafting and arranging sentences so that they work together harmoniously. Some instructors may wish to discuss the chapters on paragraphs and sentences in connection with revision.

Chapter 7, designed to help students improve their writing style, deals with words and their effects. We distinguish between abstract and concrete words as well as between specific and general terms, and we also discuss the dictionary and thesaurus. Levels of diction—formal, informal, and technical—and how to use them are explained, as are tone, various types of figurative language, and irony. The chapter concludes by pointing out how to recognize and avoid wordiness, euphemisms, clichés, mixed metaphors, and sexist language.

The nine chapters in the third part (Chapters 8–16) feature the various strategies, or modes, used to develop papers. These strategies, which follow a general progression from less to more complex, are presented as natural ways of thinking, as problem-solving strategies, and therefore as effective ways of organizing writing. One chapter is devoted to each strategy. Each chapter includes (among other relevant topics) a section on thinking critically about the mode, considering the ethics of writing in that mode, and critical synthesis of sources.

The discussion in each chapter follows a similar approach: first explaining the key elements of the strategy; next pointing out typical classroom and on-the-job applications to show students its practicality; and then providing specific planning, drafting, and revising guidelines. Practical heuristic questions are also posed. A complete student essay, accompanied by questions, follows the discussion section. These essays represent realistic, achievable goals and spur student confidence, while the questions reinforce the general principles of good writing and underscore the points we make in our discussions. Twenty carefully chosen writing suggestions follow the questions in most chapters. All chapters conclude with a section titled "Critical Synthesis with Sources." These sections explain and illustrate how students can advance their writing purpose by synthesizing material from various sources. Synthesis, of course, helps students develop and hone their critical reading and thinking skills. Furthermore, *Teaching Composition with Strategies for Successful Writing* includes suggestions for using the Reader essays and writing strategies to build assignments around themes.

The fourth and final part of the Rhetoric concentrates on two specialized types of college and on-the-job writing. Chapter 17 offers practical advice on studying for exams, assessing test questions, and writing essay answers. To facilitate student comprehension, we analyze both good and poor answers to the same exam question and provide an exercise that requires students to perform similar analyses. Chapter 18 has been expanded to focus on writing about literature, film, and television. The chapter focuses on plot, point of view, character, setting, symbols, irony, theme, and other elements that students will most likely be asked to write about. For each element, we first present basic features and then offer writing guidelines. Diverse examples illustrate these elements. The chapter distinguishes writing an explication, a review, and a literary analysis. The chapter ends with sections that detail the development of a student paper and explain how to include the views of others when writing about literature.

The Research Guide

The Research Guide consists of four chapters. Chapter 19 is a thorough and practical guide to writing library research papers. A sample pacing schedule not only encourages students to plan their work and meet their deadlines but also enables them to track their progress. As in Chapters 3 and 4, a progressive case history gradually evolves into an annotated student paper. The chapter also includes a detailed account of how to handle a variety of quotations and avoid plagiarism.

Chapter 20 details and illustrates the correct formats for bibliographical references and in-text citations for the MLA style and Chapter 21 does the same for the APA systems of documentation. Guidelines are based on the 2009 edition of the *Publication Manual of the American Psychological Association* and current online updates as well as the 2016 edition of *MLA Handbook*. Our detailed treatment in Chapters 19, 20, and 21 should make supplemental handouts or a separate research-paper guide unnecessary.

Chapter 22 offers an in-depth discussion of interview, questionnaire, and direct-observation reports. After pointing out the nature, usefulness, and requirements of primary research, we explain how to plan and write each report, concluding with an annotated student model that illustrates the guidelines.

The Reader

The Reader, sequenced to follow the order of the strategies presented in the Rhetoric, expands the utility of the text by providing a collection of 30 carefully selected professional models that illustrate the various writing strategies and display a wide variety of style, tone, and subject matter and from a wide range of sources. These essays, together with the nine student models that accompany the various strategy chapters, should make a separate reader unnecessary.

Supplementing the chapter on reading strategies, the Reader comes with reading suggestions for each strategy that detail how to read the essays of a given type, how to read essays critically, and how to read the essays as a writer.

Each essay clearly illustrates the designated pattern, each has been thoroughly class-tested for student interest, and each provides a springboard for a stimulating discussion. In making our selections we have aimed for balance and variety:

1. Some are popular classics by acknowledged prose masters; some, anthologized for the first time, are by fresh, new writers.
2. Some are straightforward and simple, some challenging and complex.
3. Some adopt a humorous, lighthearted approach; some a serious, thoughtful one.
4. Some take a liberal stance, some a conservative one; and some address ethnic, gender, and cultural diversity.
5. A few are rather lengthy; most are relatively brief.

The first essay in each strategy section is annotated in the margin to show which features of the strategy are included. These annotations not only facilitate student understanding but also help link the Rhetoric and Reader into an organic whole. A brief biographical note about the author precedes each selection, and stimulating questions designed to enhance student understanding of structure and strategy follow it. In addition, a segment titled "Toward Key Insights" poses one or more broad-based questions prompted by the essay's content. Answering these questions, either in discussion or writing, should help students gain a deeper understanding of important issues. Finally, we include a writing assignment suggested by the essay's topic. The final selection for each strategy identifies the ways in which multiple strategies are employed in the essay.

The Handbook

The comprehensive Handbook, which features tab indexing on each page for easy access to all material, consists of three parts: "Sentence Elements," "Editing to Correct Sentence Errors," and "Editing to Correct Faulty

Punctuation and Mechanics." Explanations skirt unneeded grammatical terminology and are reinforced by sets of sentence exercises. We also include connected-discourse exercises—unfolding narratives that engage and retain student interest and therefore facilitate learning—in the "Sentence Errors" and "Punctuation and Mechanics" sections. Extra sets of 20-item exercises that parallel those in the Handbook are available in the downloadable Instructor's Manual (ISBN 0134119398) to instructors who adopt the book. Instructors can use the Handbook either as a reference guide or as a basis for class discussion.

Supplements

MyWritingLab

MyWritingLab is an online homework, tutorial, and assessment program that provides engaging experiences for teaching and learning. Flexible and easily customizable, *MyWritingLab* helps improve students' writing through context-based learning. Whether through self-study or instructor-led learning, *MyWritingLab* supports and complements course work

Writing at the Center. With the new composing space and Review Plan, *MyWritingLab* unites instructor comments and feedback on student writing with targeted remediation via rich multimedia activities, allowing students to learn from and through their own writing.

Writing Help for Varying Skill Levels. For students who enter the course underprepared, *MyWritingLab* identifies those who lack prerequisite skills for composition-level topics, and provides personalized remediation.

Proven Results. No matter how *MyWritingLab* is used, instructors have access to powerful gradebook reports, which provide visual analytics that give insight to course performance at the student, section, or even program level.

A Deeper Connection Between Print and Media. The *MyWritingLab* logo (**MyWritingLab**) is used throughout the book to indicate exercises and writing activities that can be completed and submitted through *MyWritingLab* (appropriate results flow directly to the Instructor Gradebook).

Additional Prompts to Support Accelerated Learners. The major writing assignments in each chapter are supplemented by two prewriting prompts and the readings throughout the book are complemented by prereading prompts to support learners who can benefit from extra help.

Revel for *Strategies for Successful Writing*

Designed for the way today's composition students read, think, and learn

In English, reading is never the endgame. Instead—whether in a textbook, an exemplar essay, or a source—it begins a conversation that plays out in writing.

REVEL complements the written word with a variety of writing opportunities, brief assessments, model documents, and rich annotation tools to deepen students' understanding of their reading. By providing regular opportunities to write and new ways to interact with their reading, REVEL engages students and sets them up to be more successful readers and writers—in and out of class.

Video and Rich Multimedia Content
Videos, audio recordings, animations, and multimedia instruction encourage students to engage with the text in a more meaningful way.

Interactive Readings and Exercises
Students explore reading assignments through interactive texts. Robust annotation tools allow students to take notes, and low-stakes assessments and writing exercises enable students to engage meaningfully with the text outside of the classroom.

Integrated Writing Assignments
Minimal-stakes, low-stakes, and high-stakes writing tasks allow students multiple opportunities to interact with the ideas presented in the reading assignments, ensuring that they come to class better prepared.

Teaching Composition with *Strategies for Successful Writing*

The Teaching Composition with *Strategies for Successful Writing*, Eleventh Edition (ISBN 0134119398), supplement offers various suggestions for preparing for and teaching first-year composition, constructing a syllabus, teaching critical thinking, crafting assignments, conducting a conference, using multimedia in the classroom, and grading both holistically and with rubrics. Also provided are a sample syllabus for a sequence of two 15-week semesters, numerous guidelines for responding to student writing, and a detailed set of grading standards. This new edition has added for each chapter teaching strategies, classroom activities, suggested readings, alternate exercises, and answers to the chapter exercises.

Online Resources for Instructors and Students
eTextbooks

Students can subscribe to *Strategies for Successful Writing*. The format of the eText allows students to search the text, bookmark passages, save their own notes, and print reading assignments that incorporate lecture notes.

Acknowledgments

Like all textbook writers, we are indebted to many people. Our colleagues at Ferris State University and elsewhere, too numerous to mention, have assisted us in several ways: critiquing the manuscript; testing approaches, essays, and exercises in their classrooms; and suggesting writing models for the text.

We would like to thank all those faculty members who forwarded student work to be considered for the 9th and 10th editions and that have been continued in the 11th. These essays are powerful evidence of the effective teaching of all of the contributors and their tremendous impact on student lives: David Burlingame, Heald College; Sandra Cusak, Heald College & Reedley College; Ruth Dalton, Montgomery College; Linda Gary, Tyler Junior College; Vicki Holmes, University of Nevada Las Vegas; Theresa Mlinarcik, Macomb Community College; Emily Moorer, Hinds Community College; Carol Osborne, Coastal Carolina University; Roseann Shansky, Ferris State University; Efstathia Siegel, Montgomery College; and Geraldine Yap, Cosumnes River College.

In addition, we thank our reviewers, whose many suggestions have greatly improved our text: Linda Brender, Macomb Community College; Amber Brooks, Georgia Perimeter College; Joann Bruckwicki, Tyler Junior College; Jim Brueggeman, Western Technical College; Kimberley Carter, Virginia College; Tammy L. Cherry, Florida State College at Jacksonville; Scott Contor, Oakland Community College; Edwin Cummings, Bryant and Stratton College; Sonia Delgado-Tall, Kennedy-King College; Lisa Eutsey, Diné College; Tammy M. Forbes, Patrick Henry Community College; Anthony Gancarski, Virginia College; Suzanne Martens, Grand Rapids Community College; Arch Mayfield, Wayland Baptist University; Robin McGinnis, Daymar College Bowling Green; Summerlin Page, Central Carolina Community College; Sarah Peters, Collin College; Philip Poulter, Texas State Technical College; Jim Richey, Tyler Junior College; Nancy M. Risch, Caldwell Community College; Kevin Sanders, University of Arkansas–Pine Bluff; Andrea Serna, National American University; Marianne Trale, Community College of Allegheny County; and Josh Woods, Kaskaskia College.

Special thanks are also due to the outstanding team at Pearson, whose editorial expertise, genial guidance, and promotional efforts have been vital to this project: Phil Miller, former President of Humanities and Social Sciences Division, who first saw the potential in our approach; Joe Opiela, Vice President and Editor-in-Chief for English; Steven Rigolosi, Development Editor; Anne Shure, Program Manager; Shannon Kobran, Project Manager; and Ali Arnold, whose marketing expertise will help our book find its way.

Special thanks goes to Kyra Hunting and Elyse Glass, who have provided the personal support that has made both the work of teaching as well as the editing of this book possible.

J.A.R.

R.v.d.O.

To the Student

No matter what career you choose, your ability to communicate clearly and effectively will directly affect your success. In the classroom, your instructor will often evaluate your mastery of a subject by the papers and examinations you write. Prospective employers will make judgments about your qualifications and decide whether to offer you an interview on the basis of your job application letter and résumé. On the job, you will be expected to write clear, accurate reports, memorandums, and letters.

There is nothing mysterious about successful writing. It does not require a special talent, nor does it depend on inspiration. It is simply a skill, and like any other skill, it involves procedures that can be learned. Once you understand them and the more you practice, the easier writing becomes.

Strategies for Successful Writing will help you become a successful writer. And after you graduate it can serve as a useful on-the-job reference. The first, third, and fourth chapters explore the fundamentals of writing and the general steps in planning, drafting, and revising papers. Chapter 2 will help you read more effectively for college and show you how to read like a writer. The next three chapters zero in on paragraphs, sentences, and writing style. The next nine explain the basic writing strategies you can use for most writing projects. The final six turn to specialized writing—essay examinations, papers about literature, library research papers, and papers based on your own original research results. The book concludes with a Reader and, if you are using the complete version of the text, a Handbook.

From time to time you have probably had the unpleasant experience of using textbooks that seemed to be written for instructors rather than students. In preparing this book, we have tried never to forget that you are buying, reading, and using it. As a result, we have written the text with your needs in mind. The book uses simple, everyday language and presents directions in an easy-to-follow format. The chapters on writing strategies provide examples of student essays that supplement the professional essays in the Reader. These student examples represent realistic, achievable goals. When you compare them to the professional examples, you'll see that students can indeed do excellent work. We are confident that by learning to apply the principles in this text, you will write well too.

Here's wishing you success!

J.A.R.
R.v.d.O.

Rhetoric

CHAPTER 1

Writing: A First Look

In this chapter, you will learn how to:

1.1 Establish the purpose for your writing.

1.2 Determine the audience for your writing.

1.3 Identify the qualities of good writing.

1.4 Employ techniques to think critically about your writing.

1.5 Apply writing techniques for multimedia.

1.6 Write ethically and avoid plagiarism.

Visit MyWritingLab **to complete the writing assignments in this chapter and for more resources on writing.**

Why write? Aren't texting, e-mail, voice mail, and cellular phones dooming ordinary writing? Not long ago, some people thought and said so, but events haven't supported those predictions. In fact, much electronic media, such as blogging and tweeting, have increased the amount of writing people do. Although devices such as cell phones have made some writing unnecessary, the written word still flourishes both on campus and in the world of work.

Writing offers very real advantages to both writers and readers:

- It gives writers time to reflect on and research what they want to communicate and then lets them shape and reshape the material to their satisfaction.
- It makes communication more precise and effective.
- It provides a permanent record of thoughts, actions, and decisions.
- It saves the reader's time; we absorb information more swiftly when we read it than when we hear it.

What kind of writing will people expect you to do?

- At college you may be asked to write lab reports, project proposals, research papers, essay exams, or marketing plans.
- Job hunting requires application letters.
- On the job, you might describe the advantages of new computer equipment, report on a conference you attend, explain a new procedure, suggest a new security system, or present a marketing plan.

- Personally, you may need to defend a medical reimbursement, request a refund for a faulty product, or find a solution to a personal problem.

Here is the raw truth: the ability to write will help you earn better grades, land the job you want, and advance in your career. Writing will help you create the future you want in a competitive world.

When we write, it is often in response to a situation that shapes the purpose and audience of our writing. We rarely write in isolation, but instead write to others who have an interest in our message.

The Purposes of Writing

Whenever you write, some clear purpose should guide your efforts. If you don't know why you're writing, neither will your reader. Fulfilling an assignment doesn't qualify as a real writing purpose. Faced with a close deadline for a research paper or report, you may tell yourself, "I'm doing this because I have to." An authentic purpose requires you to answer this question: What do I want this piece of writing to do for both my reader and me?

1.1

Establish the purpose for your writing.

Purpose, as you might expect, grows out of the writing situation. You explore the consequences of the greenhouse effect in a report for your science instructor. You write an editorial for the college newspaper to air your frustration over inadequate campus parking. You propose that your organization replace an outdated piece of equipment with a state-of-the-art model.

Following are four common *general writing purposes*, two or more of which often join forces in a single piece:

To Inform   We all have our areas of expertise and often share that information with each other. A student in computer science could post a blog on a class instructional site on how to create a Web page. A medical researcher shares her research in her publications with other doctors and other research professionals.

To Persuade   You probably have strong views on many issues, and these feelings may sometimes impel you to try swaying your reader. In a letter to the editor, you might attack a proposal to establish a nearby chemical waste dump. Or, alarmed by a sharp jump in state unemployment, you might write to your state senator and argue for a new job-training program.

To Express Yourself   When you text a friend, you choose words and phrases to show off who you are. By your topic, word choice, example, or turn of phrase, you display a bit of yourself whether in e-mails, journals, poetry, essays, or fiction.

To Entertain   Some writing merely entertains; some writing couples entertainment with a more serious purpose. A lighthearted approach can help your reader absorb dull or difficult material.

More Specific Purposes

Besides having one or more *general purposes*, each writing project has its own *specific purpose*. Consider the difference in the papers you could write about solar homes. You might explain how readers could build one, argue that readers should buy one, express the advantages of solar homes to urge Congress to enact a tax credit for them, or satirize the solar home craze so that readers might reevaluate their plans to buy one.

Having a specific purpose assists you at every stage of the writing process. It helps you define your audience; select the details, language, and approach that best suit their needs; and avoid going off in directions that won't interest them. The following example from the Internet has a clear and specific purpose.

Turn Down Your iPod Volume (or Go Deaf)

Marianne Halavage

1   I have had a Walkman, CD Walkman or iPod surgically attached to my ears via headphones since about the age of about five (anatomically strange. But true).

2   So chances are that I'm a case in point for the recent LA Times article. It says that one in every five teens has at least a slight hearing loss. Many experts think the culprit is the use of headphones to listen to portable music.

3   LA Times said:

> *Most teens think they are invulnerable and for most of them, the hearing loss is not readily perceptible so they are not aware of the damage. But the bottom line is, "Once there, the damage is irreversible," said Dr. Gary C. Curhan of Brigham and Women's Hospital.*

4   Irreversible, you HEAR him. Gone. NEVER to return.

5   The idea of losing my hearing, even a little bit, terrifies me. Struggling to hear my music: my first love, my passion and my therapist; unable to hear my family and friends. I don't even want to think about it.

6   But for my hearing's sake in the future, I will. I'm 28, long out of teenie-dom, so no doubt some damage has been done. But I will, from now on, keep the volume on my iPod at an ear-friendly level, as the experts advise:

> *"The message is, we've got to stop what we are doing," said Dr. Tommie Robinson Jr., president of the American Speech-Language-Hearing Assn. "We have to step back and say: OK, turn down the volume on iPods and earbuds and MP3 players. Wear ear protection at rock concerts or when you are exposed to loud noises for long periods of time," like when using a lawn mower.*

7   Um, not so sure that many teens will take to wearing ear protection at concerts. They'd probably rather lose their hearing than have their pals laugh at them for looking a bit naff in it.

8   But, no ear protection now, hearing aid later...

9   Suddenly ear protection never sounded so good.

To grab her reader in a busy Internet environment, Marianne Halavage announces her purpose boldly in her title. The remainder of the paragraphs provide, alternately, statements by authority arguing that listening to loud music is likely to result in hearing loss with her own personal reaction where she identifies with her audience. The last two single-sentence paragraphs provide the reader with a stark choice and reaffirm the essay's purpose.

Now examine this paragraph, which does *not* have a specific purpose:

> Imagine people so glued to their computers that they forget to eat or sleep and even miss work. It is like a strange version of a zombie movie. What could have eaten their brains? Video games can be addictive as players struggle to get to the next level. Still, this negative effect is exaggerated. But there are a number of qualities that make a video game player want to keep coming back to the game and any good game designer needs to know those qualities.

Is the paper for game addicts to get them to quit, a humorous analogy, or a serious recommendation to game designers? Once the writer decides on a purpose, the paragraph can be focused.

> The stereotype of gamers is that they are so glued to their computers that they forget to eat, sleep, or work. While this is a gross exaggeration, game designers do want their players to be hooked on their games. There are in fact a number of qualities that make video players want to keep returning to a favorite game, and any good game designer needs to know those qualities.

The Audience for Your Writing

Everything you write is aimed at some audience—a person or group you want to reach. The ultimate purpose of all writing is to have an effect on a reader (even if that reader is you), and therefore purpose and audience are closely linked. You would write differently about your college experience to a young relative, your best friend, your parents, your advisor, or a future employer.

1.2

Determine the audience for your writing.

- School is fun and I am learning a lot—to a young relative to reassure
- I went to the greatest party—to your best friend to entertain
- I am working hard—to your parents to persuade them to send extra support
- I have learned many things that will help me contribute to your company—to an employer to persuade him or her to consider you for a job

It is important to recognize that writing, even texting, is very different from face-to-face conversations.

Face-to-Face	Writing
You can observe body language and vary what you are saying in response.	You don't get to see how people are responding.
You can respond to immediate questions.	It would be hard for people to get questions to you.
There is little record of what you say.	Readers can reread your text.

Once written work has left your hands, it's on its own. You can't call it back to clear up a misunderstanding or adjust your tone. What this means is that as a writer, you need to be able to anticipate your readers' needs and responses.

Establishing rapport with your audience is easy when you're writing for your friends or someone else you know a great deal about. You can then judge the likely response to what you say. Often, though, you'll be writing for people you know only casually or not at all: employers, customers, fellow citizens, and the like. In such situations, you'll need to assess your audience before starting to write and/or later in the writing process.

A good way to size up your readers is to develop an audience profile. This profile will emerge gradually as you answer the following questions:

1. What are the educational level, age, social class, and economic status of the audience I want to reach?
2. Why will this audience read my writing? To gain information? Learn my views on a controversial issue? Enjoy my creative flair? Be entertained?
3. What attitudes, needs, and expectations do they have?
4. How are they likely to respond to what I say? Can I expect them to be neutral? Opposed? Friendly?
5. How much do they know about my topic? (Your answer here will help you gauge whether you're saying too little or too much.)
6. What kind of language will communicate with them most effectively? (See "Selecting the Best Level of Diction" in Chapter 7.)

College writing assignments sometimes ask you to envision a reader who is intelligent but lacking specialized knowledge, receptive but unwilling to put up with boring or trite material. Or perhaps you'll be assigned, or choose, to write for a certain age group or readers with particular interests. At other times, you'll be asked to write for a specialized audience—one with some expertise in your topic. This difference will affect what you say to each audience and how you say it.

The Effect of Audience on Your Writing

Let's see how audience can shape a paper. Suppose you are explaining how to take a certain type of X-ray.

If your audience is a group of lay readers who have never had an X-ray, you might

- Avoid technical language.
- Compare an X-ray to a photograph.
- Explain the basic process, including the positioning of patient and equipment.
- Comment on the safety and reliability of the procedure.
- Indicate how much time it would take.

If, however, you were writing for radiology students, you might

- Consistently use the technical language appropriate for this audience.
- Emphasize exposure factors, film size, and required view.
- Provide a detailed explanation of the procedure, including how to position patients for different kinds of X-rays.
- Address your readers as colleagues who want precise information.

Audience shapes all types of writing in a similar fashion, even your personal writing. Assume you've recently become engaged, and to share your news you write two e-mails: one to your minister or rabbi and the other to your best friend back home. You can imagine the differences in details, language, and general tone of each e-mail. Further, think how inappropriate it would be if you accidentally sent the e-mail intended for one to the other. Without doubt, different readers call for different approaches.

Discourse Communities

Professionals often write as members of specific communities. For example, biologists with similar interests often exchange information about their research. The members of a community share goals, values, concerns, background information, and expectations, and this fact in turn affects how they write. Because such writing is closely tied to the interests of the community, professional articles often start with a section linking their content to previous research projects and articles. Often custom dictates what information must be included, the pattern of organization, and the style the paper should follow. Throughout college, you will discover that part of learning to write is becoming familiar with the values and customs of different discourse communities. To do this, you'll need to read carefully in your major field, acquainting yourself with its current issues and concerns and learning how to write about them. As you start reading in any professional area, ask yourself these questions:

1. What are the major concerns and questions in this field?
2. What seems to be common knowledge?
3. To what works do writers regularly refer?
4. How do those in the field go about answering questions?
5. What methods do they follow?
6. Which kinds of knowledge are acceptable? Which are not?
7. What values seem to guide the field?

8. What kinds of information must writers include in papers?
9. How are different writing projects organized?
10. What conventions do writers follow?

We all, of course, belong to many different communities. Furthermore, a community can involve competing groups, conflicting values, differing kinds of writing projects, and varying approaches to writing. But as part of your growth as a writer and professional, you'll need to understand the goals and rules of any community you enter.

Writing Assignment

Interview faculty in a career area or field you hope to enter. Ask them the ten questions above and write a short paper or a blog summarizing the results of your interview.

MyWritingLab   **EXERCISE**   *The following two excerpts deal with the same subject—nanotechnology—but each explanation is geared to a different audience. Read the passages carefully; then answer the following questions:*

1. **What audience does each author address? How do you know?**
2. **Identify ways in which each author appeals to a specific audience.**

A. Nanotechnology is the creation of functional materials, devices and systems through control of matter on the nanometer length scale (1–100 nanometers) and exploitation of novel phenomena and properties (physical, chemical, biological, mechanical, electrical …) at that length scale. For comparison, 10 nanometers is 1,000 times smaller than the diameter of a human hair. A scientific and technical revolution has just begun based upon the ability to systematically organize and manipulate matter at nanoscale. Payoff is anticipated within the next 10–15 years.

CNT Center for Nanotechnology

B. Today's manufacturing methods are very crude at the molecular level. Casting, grinding milling and even lithography move atoms in great thundering statistical herds.

It's like trying to make things out of LEGO blocks with boxing gloves on your hands. Yes, you can push the LEGO blocks into great heaps and pile them up, but you can't really snap them together the way you'd like.

In the future, nanotechnology (more specifically, *molecular nanotechnology* or MNT) will let us take off the boxing gloves. We'll be able to snap together the fundamental building blocks of nature easily, inexpensively, and in most of the ways permitted by the laws of nature. This will let us continue the revolution in computer hardware to its ultimate limits: molecular computers made from molecular logic gates connected by molecular wires. This new pollution free manufacturing technology will also let us inexpensively fabricate a cornucopia of new products that are remarkably light, strong, smart, and durable.

Dr. Ralph Merkle, *Nanotechnology*

Just as you would not dial a telephone number at random and then expect to carry on a meaningful conversation, so you should not expect to communicate effectively without a specific audience in mind.

One other note: As you shape your paper, it is important that the writing please you as well as your audience—that is, satisfy your sense of what good writing is and what the writing task requires. You are, after all, your own first reader.

The Qualities of Good Writing

Good writing is essential if you want your ideas to be taken seriously. Just as you would have trouble listening to someone with his shirt on backward and wearing two different kinds of shoes, most readers dismiss out of hand writing that is disorganized, poorly worded, or marred by errors in grammar and spelling. In a world where most people are drowning under an information overload, few have the time or inclination to hunt through bad writing to search for quality ideas. Employers discard job seekers with poorly worded cover letters; badly written proposals are rejected; and few bother to read poorly written articles.

1.3

Identify the qualities of good writing.

Three qualities—fresh thinking, a sense of style including the use of correct grammar and punctuations, and effective organization—help to ensure that a piece of prose will meet your reader's expectations.

Fresh Thinking   You don't have to astound your readers with something never before discussed in print. Unique ideas and information are rare. You can, however, freshen your writing by exploring personal insights and perceptions. Think about the role of general education. One student who works on cars for fun might consider the way education functions as a toolbox, while another student who is interested in change might consider the way students are transformed by education. Keep the expression of your ideas credible, however; far-fetched notions spawn skepticism.

Sense of Style   Readers don't expect you to display the stylistic flair of Maya Angelou. Indeed, such writing would impair the neutral tone needed in certain kinds of writing, such as technical reports and legal documents. Readers do, however, expect you to write in a clear style. And if you strengthen it with vivid, forceful words, readers will absorb your points with even greater interest. Readers also expect you to use standard grammar, spelling, and punctuation. The chapters ahead show you how to use language in ways that project your views and personality. Chapters 6 and 7, in particular, will help you develop a sense of style, as will the many readings throughout the book.

Effective Organization   All writing should be organized so it is easy to follow. A paper should have a beginning, a middle, and an end, that is, an introduction, a body, and a conclusion. The introduction sparks interest and acquaints the reader with what is to come. The body delivers the main message and exhibits a clear connection between ideas so that the reader can easily follow your thoughts. The conclusion ends the discussion so the reader feels satisfied rather than suddenly cut off. Overall, your paper should follow a pattern that is suited to its content and will guide the reader. Organizational patterns, or strategies of development, are the subject of Chapters 8-17. Chapter 5 discusses introductions and conclusions.

Freshness, style, and organization are weighted differently in different kinds of writing. For example, a writer who drafts a proposal to pave a city's streets will probably attach less importance to fresh thinking than to clear writing and careful organization. On the other hand, fresh thinking can be very important in a description of an autumn forest scene. You will learn more about these qualities throughout this book.

Writing and Critical Thinking

Good writing is connected to effective critical thinking. The more effectively a writer thinks about a topic or issue, the more likely it is that what he or she has to say will be worthwhile and credible. Writing the first thing that comes to mind can be a good way to get ideas, but it doesn't guarantee that the ideas are good ones.

What is "critical thinking"? That's really a tough question that could be a paper topic. Much of your college experience will help you think critically. Here are a few strategies you can use:

- **Question assumptions and claims fiercely** "Why do you think that?" and "How do you know that is true?" are good questions. There is much we take for granted. Do we know that electric cars or hybrids are more environment-friendly than gas-powered cars? Does or doesn't an increase in the minimum wage cost jobs?

- **Test the evidence ruthlessly** The evidence once seemed to suggest that the sun revolved around the earth. We see that the sun moves and the earth certainly feels stable beneath our feet. Someone (Copernicus) was bright enough to test the evidence and look at other evidence. He proved that, contrary to common sense, it is the earth that revolves around the sun, which makes it seem that the sun moves.

- **Imagine alternatives and be fearlessly ready to think differently** The Copernicus story is an example of someone imagining an alternative to the common point of view. Today we might imagine alternatives for higher education. What, some might ask, would happen if instead of earning degrees, students earned knowledge and skill badges (for example, one in writing competency) that they could take to an employer? Could higher education be porous and online with students/employees acquiring the skills and knowledge they need when they need it, instead of a sequence of courses over a four-year period?

While the goal of this text is to help you improve your writing skill, each chapter on writing strategies (Chapters 8-16) introduces important critical-thinking concepts.

- **Narratives** How are narratives constructed, and how could they be told differently from different points of view? Consider how a parent and teen might tell the tale of the same violation of a curfew.

- **Description** How could something be described differently or from a different vantage point? A delicious meal could be described as "oozing" and "squishy" in ways that would make the food seem disgusting.

- **Process** How else could something be done or are there other ways for something to happen? If you outline your steps for studying, consider how someone else might outline a very different process for studying.

- **Illustration** We make a point through examples. What happens if we turn to other examples? Examples that focus on struggling students can be used to make the case that college courses are difficult. But surely there are examples of students who find only some parts of their coursework difficult and even examples of students who find their coursework easy.

- **Classification** To learn how we classify is to learn how we could classify things differently. We can ask how things are classified and experiment with alternative classifications. Thinking of colleges, we often think of administrators, teachers, and students. What if we classified instead by the degree of involvement in campus life: very involved, somewhat involved, and minimally involved?

- **Comparison** Often things look as they do based on comparison. How would they look different if we change the comparison? Football may look like a violent sport in comparison to baseball. How does it look when compared to rugby or hockey?

- **Cause and Effect** Can we consider other causes or effects beyond those that immediately come to mind? Often a new president or governor sees improvements in the economy during the first six months of his or her term. Some give these politicians credit for the improvement, but their policies may not have even been put into effect. What really caused the improvement?

- **Definition** In what other ways can we define something? How we define things shapes how we think about them. What, after all, is a "family"? At one time, we might have assumed that a family is a biological unit of father and mother with their biological children. Now there are many more definitions of family and much dispute about the term, as there is about terms like "marriage." Critical thinking requires thinking about how concepts are defined and alternate ways of defining them.

- **Argumentation** What reasons and evidence can be used logically and effectively to support a claim and how? Chapter 16 on argument offers good strategies for questioning assumptions, assessing the evidence, evaluating sources of evidence, critically examining the relationship between evidence and claims, and testing the logic of arguments.

As you work to develop each strategy, consider how the strategy offers ways for you to think critically about ideas and the world.

Writing in a Multimedia World

1.5

Apply writing techniques for multimedia.

At college and on the job, you will e-mail, text message, tweet, blog, and write text for Web pages. The processes and principles in this book apply to any media for which you may write. Regardless of the media, you need to employ effective writing processes, consider your purpose and audience, and employ effective organizational strategies. If you are texting your boss to let him know why you will be late to work, you know you will have to be polite and clear about the reasons you are delayed. Clearly, "Dude, traffic-jam," won't do. If you are creating a Web site that presents your restaurant, you are likely to write a description of the restaurant, revising the text several times to make it as effective as possible. If you are writing a blog on your favorite rock group, you might identify what has caused them to be successful or compare them with other groups. Throughout college, instructors may encourage you to use other media to complete assignments. Almost every career will expect you to know a wide range of communication media. What follows are a few points you might consider.

E-mail While in college, you will e-mail faculty and advisors. E-mail has the advantage of giving both you and your reader a written record of the exchange. If you ask a faculty member for permission to vary an assignment, it might be better to ask using an e-mail. A conversation will soon fade from each of your memories. However, an e-mail provides you with a written record of your request and, hopefully, the permission you received.

Though e-mail is often informal, you should still follow good writing practices when writing e-mail. The following e-mail to a professor is clearly too informal and incomplete. It also establishes the wrong tone.

Prof,

Sorry missed class. Car trouble. I'll turn my paper in Monday when I see ya, OK.

Thanks tons.

Who is writing the message? Was the car trouble sufficient for an extension on the paper? Is the person simply using the car trouble to stall for extra time? Why didn't she jump the car or get a ride to campus? The informal tone makes it seem that the student does not take the class or the professor seriously.

A more formal communication sensitive to the situation and the audience would be much better.

Professor von der Osten

I am very sorry I missed class today. I live in Cadillac, an hour's drive from campus; unfortunately, this morning my car would not start because the distributor is broken. This is my first absence, and I notice from the syllabus we are allowed five unexcused absences. If you wish, I can bring in the estimate from the garage. I have e-mailed Tim Sullivan for notes from today's class.

Attached you will find a copy of the paper due today, Friday, September 25. Thank you for allowing us to submit our papers electronically in case of an emergency. I will also bring in a hard copy on Monday in case that would assist you.

I look forward to seeing you in class on Monday.

Susan Miller

ENGL 150: 9:00 A.M.

This more complete e-mail recognizes the formality of the situation, uses an appropriate form of address, provides a clearer explanation, indicates a serious attitude about the work in question, takes clear steps to meet the demands of the situation, and clearly identifies the writer in a way that recognized the reader may have many classes and students.

Your e-mail, like all writing, should be appropriate to the situation and the audience. An e-mail in response to a formal situation or to an important audience should be appropriately formal and serious. Since you and your readers are busy, try to write clearly and completely so that follow-up exchanges are unnecessary. Use a subject line that clearly identifies what the e-mail is about. Avoid abbreviations, slang, emoticons, or other informal devices except with close friends. Be sure to clearly identify who you are, your position, and why you are writing; not all e-mail addresses clearly identify the writer. Most important of all, remember that your e-mail can be forwarded to other readers, so make sure your messages reflect well on you.

EXERCISE *Below are sample e-mails one of the authors received in a single semester. In each case, indicate what the problem with the e-mail is and how could it be written to be more effective for the audience.*

MyWritingLab

1. Here. (The only message on an e-mail that submitted an attached paper)
2. Hey teach, Sorry I won't be in class. Family trouble. (A student with excessive absences)
3. Do you mind writing a letter of recommendation for me? The position I am applying for is attached. (A colleague looking for another job)
4. Can I drop my chemistry class? The teacher sucks. (An e-mail from an advisee to her advisor)
5. I really don't understand this assignment. Can I do it differently? I have got lots of ideas. (From a student beginning a class assignment)

Text Messaging   Text messaging has some dangers. It is easy to respond too quickly to a question and so provide an incomplete answer. Because messages are necessarily short, they can often be incomplete or lack the necessary context.

Since people text from their phones, it is easy to be excessively informal or make careless mistakes in spelling or grammar.

As with all writing, you should know your audience and person. If you are writing to your BFF, you can LOL ☺. If you are writing to someone you don't know well or with whom you have a professional relationship, avoid abbreviations and symbols. Crafting a short message can be harder than writing a longer text since it takes skill to be clear and concise. The short text message "Go ahead with 3 copies to Madison" will be confusing unless the context is clear. If you can't assume the context, and many people are too busy to recall the assumed details, you need to be more complete. "Please send 3 copies each of the editions of FemSpec from 4.1 to 10.2 to our Madison address, 324 Blakemore Road, Madison, WI 43432." A complete message may require more typing, but it will save time in the long run.

Twitter   There are some fields, such as media studies or business, where you may be required to follow a Twitter account for an industry or area. Twitter is simply a system for sharing short messages of 140 characters. Most tweets are not very consequential. However, if you are writing or responding to a tweet, the goal is to have an interesting message in a very few words. Wordiness is out. You must assume some context. *Bring four copies of writing assignment 1 rough draft to class Monday for peer response.*

MyWritingLab   **EXERCISE** *Rewrite the following messages so that they would be suitable as a tweet.*

1. Katherine Briggs has done it again and in *River Marked* produced another compelling Mercy Thompson story with magic, mystery, and romance. She is on her honeymoon with husband, a werewolf, but their getaway doesn't last long as she ends up in a battle for her life with a river monster that threatens humankind. (Create a tweet for Katherine Briggs fans.)
2. This semester our online registration system will allow interested students to sign up for two semesters instead of just one, locking in their schedule for not just the Fall but also the Spring semester. Students are not required to schedule the second semester. If they do so, they will have to do an online drop and add process to change schedules. However, students who do not register for two semesters may find the classes they want closed for the Spring semester. (Create a tweet that could go to students.)

Blogs   Sometimes it seems as if almost everyone has a blog. There is nothing fancy about a "blog," a term which is simply a blending of the words Web Log. A blog is a Web-based statement of the writer's idea, a Web essay. Many learning platforms allow you to blog to share your ideas with your class. Some teachers have students create blogs using a common blog-based program, such as WordPress or Blogger, which are very easy to use.

Blogs let you make an argument, share an enthusiasm, review a movie, and more. A blog needs to follow many of the strategies of writing explained in this text. However, in addition a blog lets you link your blog to other blogs or sites that might relate to or develop an idea; it also allows you to use images or video files. Ideally blogs are the length of a single page, though they can be longer. In a blog you are competing on a very busy Internet, so it is very important to grab your reader's attention quickly and have something interesting to say with vivid language.

Writing for a Web Page   Increasingly students applying for jobs provide on their resume an address to their Web pages. A Web page lets them post more information about their experience, show samples of their work, and shape the kind of professional impression that they make. Employers often look for the Web site of applicants because it not only lets them have more information about a job candidate but demonstrates whether or not the prospective employee has initiative and the necessary skills. In many careers, writing for a Web page can be a regular responsibility. A nurse might write for a hospital Web page on standard post-operative care. An engineer may write technical information about the company's product line. To help you get ready for your Web-based future, a number of college courses have students work on a Web-based project.

Web pages need to be attractive, easy to use, clear, and meet the needs of multiple users. Web design is an important skill beyond the scope of this book, but following are a few key ideas you should know.

- Keep the information clear and simple.
- Recognize that you need to grab and hold your reader's attention, so you need to make it immediately clear what information the Web site is providing.
- Use hypertext strategies. That means you can provide a simpler statement to meet the needs of most audiences and then provide links from key words to additional information for the reader who is seeking more.
- Make it easy for the reader to process information. Where appropriate, you should use visual strategies such as headings, subheadings, and bullets to guide your reader. Use pictures or other visuals that clearly make your point and make the site attractive.

Because Web pages are public documents, you want to make certain that your document is very well proofread.

Creating Presentations   In your college career, you will need to create a variety of presentations using software like PowerPoint, Keynote, or Prezi. There are lots of links online about how to create effective presentations. Below are some of the key principles.

- Use the same format or design for all of your slides and keep the design simple. People are easily distracted.
- Keep individual slides simple. Don't put on a slide everything you are going to say. Instead focus on the key phrase, image, or graphic that you want your audience to remember.

- Don't clutter the slide with lots of images that will distract the viewers.
- When a gripping image or graphic will make your point, use the image or graphic.

Using Graphics and Text   Increasingly, writers combine graphics with text to make their point. There are books that use a comic style to explain complex philosophical ideas. Graphic novels are an art form that many take seriously. New computer programs make it easy to create an illustrated storyboard with text to make your point or use pictures and add text.

Writing for such a graphic form requires several distinct techniques:

1. The images need to clearly make the point or support the point.
2. The writing needs to be very clear and concise.
3. Shorter sentences and precise vocabulary are needed to make certain that the reader doesn't get confused.
4. The graphic needs to fit the available space without overrunning the text.

Writing and Ethics

1.6

Write ethically and avoid plagiarism.

Think for a minute about how you would react to the following situation. You decide to vacation at a resort after reading a brochure that stressed its white-sand beach, scenic trails, fine dining, and peaceful atmosphere. When you arrive, you find the beach overgrown with weeds, the trails littered, and view unappealing, and the restaurant a greasy-spoon cafeteria. Worse, whenever you go outside, swarms of vicious black flies attack you. Wouldn't you feel cheated? Closer to home, think how you'd react if you decided to attend a college because of its distinguished faculty members only to discover upon arrival that they rarely teach on campus. The college counts on their reputations to attract students even though they are usually unavailable. Hasn't the college done something unethical?

As these examples show, good writing is also ethical writing. Like you, readers expect that what they read will be dependable information. Few, if any, would bother with a piece of writing that they realized was intended to deceive. A good test of the ethics of your writing is whether you would read your own work and act on the basis of it. Would you feel comfortable with it, or would you feel cheated, manipulated, deceived, or harmed in some way? By learning and practicing the principles of ethical writing, you will help ensure that your writing meets the standards that your readers expect.

The Principles of Ethical Writing

- **Truthful**   Writing perceived as truthful should *be* truthful. Granted, a writer may use humorous exaggeration to make us laugh, and some sales pitches may stretch the truth a bit in order to entice buyers. ("Try Nu-Glo toothpaste and add sparkle to your life.") But most readers recognize and discount such embellishments which, unlike major distortions, harm nobody. Deliberate, serious falsehoods, however, may harm not only the reader but sometimes the writer as well. Angered by the misrepresentations in the vacation brochure, you would certainly warn your friends against the resort and might even take some legal action against it.

- **Complete**   Writing meant to be perceived as truthful should tell the whole truth, omitting nothing the reader needs to know in order to make informed decisions. The text should not be deliberately incomplete so as to mislead. Suppose that a university's recruitment brochures stress that 97 percent of its students get jobs upon graduation. What the brochures don't say is that only 55 percent of the jobs are in the graduates' chosen fields despite strong employer demand for graduates in those areas. Clearly these brochures are deceptive, perhaps attracting students who would otherwise choose schools with better placement records.

- **Clear**   Writing should be clear to the reader. All of us know the frustration of trying to read a crucial regulation that is impossible to comprehend. A person who writes instructions so unclear that they result in harmful mistakes is partially responsible for the consequences. Readers have a right to expect understandable, accurate information. Thus, it would be deceptive for a group of state legislators to call a proposed bill the Public Education Enhancement Act when it would in fact bar teachers from belonging to unions.

- **No Harm**   Writing should not be intended to harm the reader. Certainly it is fair to point out the advantages of a product or service that readers might not need. Most people understand the nature of this type of advertising. But think how unethical it would be for a writer to encourage readers to follow a diet that the writer knew was not only ineffective but harmful. Think of the harm a writer might cause by attempting, deliberately, to persuade readers to try crack cocaine.

Plagiarism

Often our writing draws on the work of others. We get information from an article, summarize what they have to say, perhaps paraphrase their wording, or use quotes that really help make a point. There are techniques for using information from sources discussed, which you should review if you are drawing information from sources. Still, pivotal to ethics in writing is avoiding plagiarism. When you turn in a piece of writing, you designate it as your own work in your own words. If you have taken material from sources (including the Internet) without using the proper documentation, even if it is in your own words, it is plagiarism, an unacceptable practice for any writer. If you use another writer's language, even in part, without using quotation marks, you are also engaging in plagiarism. Most faculty members check carefully for plagiarism and many automatically fail a paper for academic dishonesty. Some even give the student an F for the entire course.

Why is this an important issue?

1. Other people have worked hard to develop ideas, do research, and write effectively. They deserve credit for their work when someone else uses it; it is their property. The authors of this text, for example, pay fees to use the essays of others. You would probably not like it if others used material from your papers without giving you credit.
2. Proper documentation strengthens your work since the source, often written by an expert, can add credibility to your claims if properly recognized.
3. If you take some material from a source and use it in your paper without documentation or quotation, you are falsely presenting another writer's work as your own. It is not much different from cheating and simply presenting an entire paper purchased from the Internet as your own work.
4. You are in the process of being trained in college to be professionals. Professionals need to be ethical. You wouldn't want someone to take credit for the computer program you wrote, charge you for repairs they didn't make, or write you a ticket for a traffic violation you didn't commit. Journalists have been fired, politicians have lost elections, and companies have been sued because they have been involved in plagiarism.
5. You certainly cannot develop as a writer if your writing isn't mostly your own work.

How can you avoid plagiarism and the failing grade that often comes with it?

1. Be committed to honesty. You should make certain your writing is your own work.
2. If an assignment does not ask you to use sources but you believe information from sources would be useful, talk to your teacher. There may be a reason that you are not asked to use sources. If sources are acceptable, you may be asked to follow a specific procedure for that assignment, such as turning in copies of your sources.
3. Be meticulous in documenting your sources, even if the material is in your own words, and in quoting and documenting any language that comes from another writer, even if it is only part of a sentence.
4. Carefully double-check to make certain that all the content in your text is your own and that if you used a source at all, it is documented.
5. Carefully double-check to make certain that all of your text uses your own language and that if you did use another writer's language, you used quotation marks.
6. If you are not sure about whether documentation or quotation marks are necessary, check with your teacher.
7. Make clear decisions about what counts as common knowledge. No one is expected to document what a reasonably educated person would know: that George Washington was our first president, that water consists

of H_2O, or that the Supreme Court rules on constitutional issues. As you proceed in college, your stock of common knowledge will grow. Yet, be careful that you don't sweep too many things under the common knowledge rug. One good rule of thumb is that if you didn't know it before you read the source, you probably should not count it as common knowledge and should document the information.

You must make a conscious effort to avoid plagiarism. Ignorance and carelessness are rarely accepted as an excuse by professors trying hard to make certain that students are graded fairly and no one gets credit for work that is not their own. If you follow the guidelines in this text and ask your teacher for help when you are confused, you will easily avoid the embarrassment and the often dire consequences of being accused of plagiarism.

A First Look at Your Writing

Know your discourse community.

- Read works in a community and talk to participants to discover shared questions.
- Determine what counts as knowledge.
- Look at sample writing to determine conventions.

Know your purpose.

- Decide if you are going to inform, persuade, express yourself, entertain.
- Identify the specific purpose.

Know your audience.

- List what you think your reader already knows.
- Identify the reasons they will read your writing.
- Try to read as your audience to anticipate their response.

Apply principles of good writing.

- Write with fresh thinking that offers your own slant. Being honest about your observations will help.
- Write with a clear style in your own voice; don't overly inflate your language.
- Use the techniques in this text to create effective organization.

Make certain your writing is ethical!

- Write in a way that is truthful, unslanted, complete, clear, and helpful, rather than harmful.
- Make your writing your own, and avoid plagiarism.

2

Strategies for Successful and Critical Reading

In this chapter, you will learn how to:

2.1 Read for different purposes.

2.2 Employ different strategies for a first and second reading.

2.3 Overcome reading challenges.

2.4 Read critically by employing critical-thinking skills.

2.5 Use reading techniques to develop your writing.

2.6 Write a summary.

2.7 Write a critique.

Visit MyWritingLab **to complete the writing assignments in this chapter and for more resources on critical reading.**

Good writing requires good reading. You get ideas, information, a feel for language, and ideas for writing from what you read. As a writer, you are a part of a knowledge community that learns from reading and responds to the texts of others. Effective reading is not the passive process that many people imagine. On the contrary, it requires the ongoing interaction of your mind and the printed page. Bringing your knowledge and experience to bear on a piece of writing can help you assess its events, ideas, and conclusions. For example, an understanding of marriage, love, and conflict, as well as experience with divorce, can help readers comprehend an essay that explores divorce. As you read, you must also understand each point that's made, consider how the various parts fit together, and try to anticipate the direction the writing will take. Successful reading requires work. Fortunately, you can follow specific strategies to help yourself read better.

Orienting Your Reading

Different purposes require different approaches to reading. When reading for pleasure, you can relax and proceed at your own pace, slowing down to savor a section you especially enjoy, speeding up when you encounter less interesting

2.1

Read for different purposes.

material, and breaking off when you wish. Reading for information, for solid understanding, or to critique an argument calls for a more methodical approach. Sometimes, you read specifically for material or arguments that you can use in your own writing. Following are some useful questions to guide your reading:

- **Why am I reading this material?** Is it for long-term use, as a reference for a project, or as a building block to understanding more material?
- **How well do I need to know the material in the article?** Can you look back to the article as a reference? Is there only one main point you need to know? Are you going to be tested on much of the material in depth?
- **Is some material in the article more important to me than other material?** Sometimes in doing research you may be looking for a specific bit of information that is only a paragraph in a long article. If so, you can skim for the information. In most things you read, some sections are more important than others. Often you can read to get the main points of the article and not focus on all the details. Sometimes, of course, you need to know the material in depth.
- **What will I need to do with the material from the article?** If you are looking for ideas for your own writing, you might read quickly. If you will be responsible for writing a critique of the article, you will need to read carefully and critically.
- **What kind of reading does the material suggest?** The significance, the difficulty, and the nature of the writing all can influence how you read. An easy humorous narrative can be read in a more leisurely fashion. A careful argument on an important issue merits careful attention to the main points and the evidence and may even require you to outline the argument.

MyWritingLab   **EXERCISE** *Look briefly at "The Appeal of the Androgynous Man" on page 30. Identify three purposes you could have for reading this essay. Identify how these purposes would affect how you would read the essay and what you would look for in the essay.*

Strategies for Reading and Rereading

2.2

Employ different strategies for a first and second reading.

You don't just jump in your car and take off. Usually you take a few minutes to think about where you want to go. Sometimes you even have to check your route. The same is true of effective reading. Because of the challenging nature of most college-level reading assignments, you should plan on more than one reading.

A First Reading

A good first reading should orient you to the material.

Orient Yourself to the Background of the Essay Before you begin, scan any accompanying biographical sketch and try to determine the writer's expertise and views on the topic. Catherine Steiner Adair's practice as a clinical psychologist as well as her role as a research associate in Harvard's Department of Psychiatry give credibility to her claims about the impact of digital technology in the selection "The Revolution in the Living Room" (in the Reader). Sometimes there is material by the author or the editor on the writing of the essay. Professional essays often start with an abstract that provides a brief summary of the article. At this point you may want to judge the credibility of the source.

Use the Title as a Clue   Most titles identify the topic and often the viewpoint as well. Thus, "If You're Happy and You Know It, Must I Know, Too?" (in the Reader) suggests that the author seems to be somewhat skeptical of the need to show our feelings, in this case through emoticons. Some titles signal the writer's primary strategy, whether it is a comparison, definition, or argument. "Grant and Lee: A Study in Contrasts" (in the Reader) is clearly a comparison.

Skim to Get the Gist of the Article   Sometimes you can just read the introductory and concluding paragraphs and the topic sentences (often the first or last sentences of paragraphs). Other times you will need to read the whole essay quickly. Try to gain an idea of the essay's main thrust, the key ideas that support it, and the ways that they are organized. In your first reading, you can skim the more difficult sections without trying to understand them fully.

Make Connections with What You Have Read   When you've finished skimming the essay, and before you reread the essay, think about what you've learned and then, either by saying it to yourself or jotting it down, express it *in your own words*. You can hardly be said to understand what you've read, and you will be less likely to remember it, until you can state its essence in your own words. Go back and underline the thesis statement (a statement of the main point of the essay) or, if one is not included, try to formulate one in your own words. Try to identify the strategy used by the writer. Also, stop and identify what you already know about the topic and your connection to the issue. You will read more effectively if you can connect what you read to your own knowledge and interests. Jot down questions that the first reading has raised in your mind. Try to identify the strategies used by the writer; if any were effective, write those strategies down for your own possible use.

EXERCISE **Reading Activities**   MyWritingLab

1. Identify what you can about the background of the article, "The Appeal of the Androgynous Man," from the statement about the author.
2. Write what you expect based on the title.
3. Skim the essay and then write down what you identify as the main points of the essay. Identify the essay's thesis. Jot down at least two questions you have.

The Second Reading and Beyond

If the material was difficult or you need to know it well, a second or even third reading may be necessary. On the second reading, which will take more time than the first, you carefully absorb the writer's ideas.

Read Carefully and Actively Read at a pace suitable to the material. Underline significant topic sentences as well as other key sentences and ideas or facts that you find important, but keep in mind that underlining in itself doesn't ensure comprehension. Restating the ideas in your own words is more effective. Depending on your purposes, you may want to write down the main points in your own words or jot down the ideas in the margins. As you proceed, examine the supporting sentences to see how well they back up the main idea. Keep an eye out for how the essay fits together.

Consider Reading as a Kind of Conversation with the Text Develop the habit of asking questions about facts, reasons, and ideas—practically anything in the essay. Jot your queries and their answers in the margins. (On page 30, you can see how a student interacted with the first page of Amy Gross's essay, "The Appeal of the Androgynous Man.") Good writers anticipate your questions and answer them; and because you have posed the questions yourself, you are more likely to see the connections in the text. If the author hasn't answered your questions, there may be problems with the work. It can help to keep a reading log in a notebook or as a computer file where you jot down your ideas as you are reading. Your notes or questions on your reading can be the basis for a writing project, or they can offer material you can use in a later research paper.

Master Unfamiliar Words At times, unfamiliar words can hinder your grasp of the material. Whenever you encounter a new word, circle it, use context to help gauge its meaning, check the dictionary for the exact meaning, and then record it in the margins or some other convenient place. If the writing is peppered with words you don't know, you may have to read the whole piece to figure out its general drift; then, look up key words, and finally reread the material. A word list from your reading can help you enhance the vocabulary in your writing. Sometimes unfamiliar vocabulary, such as "derivatives," is part of the professional vocabulary you will need to know to discuss the issues involved.

Take Conscious Steps to Understand Difficult Material When the ideas of a single section prove difficult, restate the points of those sections you do understand. Then experiment by stating in your own words different interpretations of the problem section and see which one best fits the writing as a whole.

Sometimes large sections or entire texts are extremely difficult. Following are several strategies you can use to help yourself:

- State the ideas that are easier for you to understand and use them as keys to unlock meanings that are difficult but not unintelligible. Save the most difficult sections until last. Don't think you have to understand everything completely. Some works take a lifetime to fully understand.
- Discuss a difficult essay with others who are reading it.
- Read simpler material on the topic.
- Go to your teacher for help. He or she may help you find background material that will make the selection easier.

Pull the Entire Essay Together   Whenever you finish a major section of a lengthy essay, express your sense of what it means. Speak it out loud or write it down. If you have trouble seeing the connections between ideas, try visually representing them. You might make an outline that states the main points followed by subpoints. For a comparison, you might create a table with the main points of the comparison side by side. You can make a drawing connecting the main ideas in a network, list the steps in an instruction, or write out the main facts.

To strengthen your grasp of material, you'll need to remember for some time, try restating its main points a couple of days after the second reading. Sometimes it is helpful to explain the material to a sympathetic listener. If anything has become hazy or slipped your mind, reread the appropriate section(s). If you really must know the material, try making up your own test and giving it to yourself. Writing in your own words about what an essay meant can give you ideas for an essay that develops the reading, contradicts it, or takes a part of it and launches in a new direction.

Mastering Reading Problems

Many factors are important to effective reading. If your environment is too noisy, you are too tired, or you have something on your mind, you can have trouble reading. Do your reading at the time of day when you are most alert. Be sure you are in an environment that lets you concentrate and that is well lit. Try to be rested and comfortable. If you get tired, take a break for a specific time period; perhaps go for a short walk. If something else is bothering you, try to resolve the distraction or put it out of your mind. If you find the material uninteresting, try to find a connection between the topic and your interests and goals; read more actively. Of course, all these principles apply to your writing as well.

In turn, this broadened perspective can supply you with writing ideas.

2.3

Overcome reading challenges.

- Write down new perspectives, insights, or ways of viewing the world.
- Keep a reading/writing journal where you summarize what you've read and jot down writing ideas.
- Take down specific ideas, facts, and even quotes that you might use.
- Always note the source so you can document it properly to avoid plagiarism.

Such a rich treasure trove will provide a powerful resource for writing ideas, writing strategies, and material to strengthen your essays.

If you have extensive problems reading for college, you can get help. Most colleges have courses in reading and tutors. College often requires a lot of reading, so take the steps necessary to be the most effective reader possible.

EXERCISE   **Reading Activities**   MyWritingLab

1. Read "The Appeal of the Androgynous Man" a second time, continuing to write your own questions and notes in the margin.

2. Create a table with two columns comparing the all-man and the androgynous man.
3. Identify three words that you might find relatively new and find their definitions from the context and a dictionary.
4. Try explaining the article to a friend or your roommate.

Reading to Critique: Reading Critically

2.4

Read critically by employing critical-thinking skills.

In college you usually read not only to understand but also to evaluate what you read. Your instructors will want to know what you think about what you've read. Often you'll be asked whether you agree or disagree with a piece of writing. Sometimes you will be asked to write an explicit critique of what you read.

Merely because information and ideas are in print does not mean that they are true or acceptable. An essay, for example, might include faulty logic, unreasonable ideas, suspect facts, or unreliable authorities. Don't hesitate to dispute the writer's information.

- Does it match your experience?
- What biases or points of view might guide the writing?
- What assumptions is the writer making?
  - Do the pieces of evidence support the claim?
  - Do the ideas appear reasonable?
- What other positions are possible?
- Are there other pieces of evidence or other works that contradict these claims?
- Do the ideas connect in a logical way?

Knowledge of the principles of argumentation and various reasoning fallacies can help you critique a piece of writing. These issues are discussed in the chapter on argumentation.

MyWritingLab   **EXERCISE**   **Reading Activities**

Prepare your critique of "The Appeal of the Androgynous Man" by doing the following:

1. Identify where and how the claims don't match your experience.
2. Indicate where the evidence does not support the claims.
3. Indicate at least a few places where the ideas do not appear reasonable.
4. Identify any evidence that seems to contradict the author's claims.
5. Evaluate whether the ideas connect in a logical way.

Reading Assignments Carefully

Many students could get better grades by simply reading their assignments more carefully. In assignments, professors often indicate possible topics, suggest readers, identify the kinds of information that should and **should not** be included, set expectations on style and format, and establish procedures for the assignment such as the due date. You should read the assignment several times. Carefully note any specifications on topic, audience, organizational strategy, or style and format. Be sure to jot down procedures, such as due dates, in an assignment log or your calendar. Do not make assumptions. If you are not clear about a part of the assignment, ask your instructor.

The following is a very specific assignment; read it over carefully to determine what it requires.

Objective Description Short Assignment (50 points)

Typed final draft following the class format guide is due in class September 12. This assignment page should be turned in with your completed description:

The corner of Perry and State Street, near the Starr building has been the scene of a terrible accident. The insurance company has asked you to write a brief objective description (approximately two pages double spaced) of the intersection for a report for possible use in court. Your description should not try to take a position about the relative danger of the intersection but rather provide as clear a picture as possible of the situation. The description should include the arrangement of the streets including the number of lanes, the businesses located immediately around the intersection, traffic and pedestrian flow, and the timing of the lights and the effect of that timing on traffic.

Checklist:

The description should:
1. Provide the general location of the intersection.
2. Indicate their traffic function—i.e., major route from 131 into downtown Big Rapids.
3. Describe the actual roads.
4. Identify the businesses and their locations.
5. Describe traffic and pedestrian flow.
6. Detail the timing of the lights.
7. Maintain objective language.
8. Use clear, nontechnical language.

The assignment specifies the topic (a specific intersection), an audience (a court of law and an insurance company), key elements that are required as part of the description, a general style of writing (objective without taking a stance), and procedures including a deadline and format constraints. Clearly a short paper about the accident would not be acceptable since the assigned topic is the actual structure of the intersection. A style of writing that stressed the "horribly short lights that force students to scurry across like mice in front of a cat" would lose points since it takes a position and is not objective. Any description that left out any of the required elements (such as the timing of the lights) would also lose points.

Reading as a Writer

2.5

Use reading techniques to develop your writing.

All of us who write can use reading as a springboard for improving our writing. You can do several things to make your reading especially useful.

As you read, the views of others, the experiences they relate, and the information they present often deepen your understanding of yourself, your relationships, and your surroundings. In turn, this broadened perspective can supply you with writing ideas. When possibilities surface, be sure to record them. Some writers keep a reading journal in which they summarize what they've read and jot down writing ideas that come to mind. In addition, you can take down specific ideas, facts, and perhaps even a few particularly telling quotations that you discover. You may want to incorporate this material into your writing at a later time. Carefully record the source so that you can document it properly in order to avoid plagiarism.

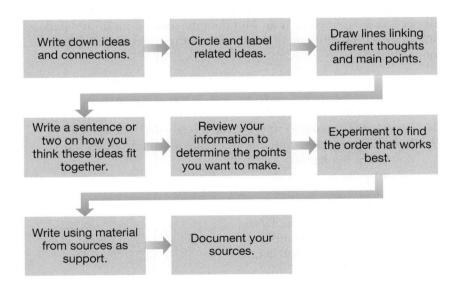

When you read various sources that explore the same topic or related topics, you may notice connections among their ideas. Let's see how you might use synthesis in writing an actual essay. Suppose you've read Amy Gross's "The Appeal of the Androgynous Man," "Sound and Fury" by Dan Greenburg, and Chris Lee's "Invasion of the Bodybuilders" (in the Reader).

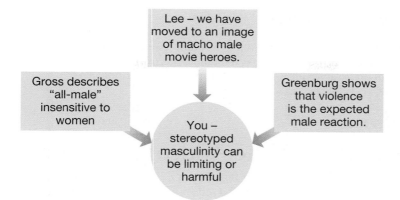

How do you use this to write an essay?

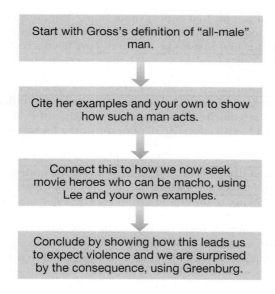

All of these ideas and examples could help you build an essay that points out how men can sometimes become desensitized or trapped, even victimized, by living according to stereotypes of masculinity. If you will be writing a paper that synthesizes material from various sources, review how to document your sources properly.

Because writers solve problems, you'll want to pay attention to the techniques and strategies that other writers use. If you find an introduction, an organizational pattern, a transition, a certain description, or a comparison unusually engaging, study the writer's technique. Perhaps you can use it yourself. Similarly, observe when a piece of writing fails and try to determine why.

MyWritingLab   **EXERCISE**   **Reading Activities**

1. Identify at least two strategies that the author used that you would find useful.
2. Identify at least two phrases that you found effective.
3. Identify at least two ideas that could spark your own writing.

AMY GROSS

both male and
female in one

The Appeal of the Androgynous Man

Amy Gross, a native of Brooklyn, New York, earned a sociology degree at Connecticut College. Upon graduation, she entered the world of fashion publishing and has held writing or editorial positions at various magazines, including Talk, Mademoiselle, Good Housekeeping, Elle, *and* Mirabella. *She is the newly appointed editor-in-chief of* O, the Oprah Magazine. *In our selection, which first appeared in* Mademoiselle, *Gross compares androgynous men favorably to macho "all-men."*

Does she favor androgynous men? What kind of appeal?

She will give a woman's perspective. She writes for and edits women's magazines.

Seems like she is going to talk about the advantages of androgynous men as compared to other men. Sees them as better.

Attempt to counter stereotype? Can't androgynous men also be effeminate?

Suggests "all-men" men reject behaviors and interests they consider feminine, but isn't she stereotyping? Are all these men like this? She seems to be exaggerating.

1   James Dean was my first androgynous man.[1] I figured I could talk to him. He was anguished and I was 12, so we had a lot in common. With only a few exceptions, all the men I have liked or loved have been a certain kind of man: a kind who doesn't play football or watch the games on Sunday, who doesn't tell dirty jokes featuring broads or chicks, who is not contemptuous of conversations that are philosophically speculative, introspective, or otherwise foolish according to the other kind of man. He is more self-amused, less inflated, more quirky, vulnerable and responsive than the other sort (the other sort, I'm visualizing as the guys on TV who advertise deodorant in the locker room). He is more like me than the other sort. He is what social scientists and feminists would call androgynous: having the characteristics of both male and female.

2   Now the first thing I want you to know about the androgynous man is that he is neither effeminate nor hermaphroditic. All his primary and secondary sexual characteristics are in order and I would say he's all-man, but that is just what he is not. He is more than all-man.   both male and female sex in one

3   The merely all-man man, for one thing, never walks to the grocery store unless the little woman is away visiting her mother with the kids, or is in the hospital having a kid, or there is no little woman. All-men men don't know how to shop in a grocery store unless it is to buy a 6-pack and some pretzels. Their ideas of nutrition expand beyond a 6-pack and pretzels only to take in steak, potatoes, scotch or rye whiskey, and maybe a wad of cake or apple pie. All-men men have absolutely no taste in food, art, books, movies, theatre, dance, how to live, what are good questions, what is funny, or anything else I care about. It's not exactly that the all-man's man is an uncouth illiterate. He may be educated, well-mannered, and on a first-name basis with fine wines. One all-man man I knew was a handsome individual who gave the impression of being gentle, affectionate, and sensitive. He sat and ate dinner one night while I was doing something endearingly feminine at the sink. At one point, he mutely held up his glass to indicate in a primitive, even ape-like, way his need for a refill. This was in 1967, before Women's Liberation. Even so, I was disturbed. Not enough to break the glass over his handsome head, not even enough to mutely indicate the

[1]James Dean (1931–1955) was a 1950s film star who gained fame for his portrayals of restless, defiant young men.

whereabouts of the refrigerator, but enough to remember that moment in all its revelatory clarity. No androgynous man would ever brutishly expect to be waited on without even a "please." (With a "please," maybe.)

4   The brute happened to be a doctor—not a hard hat—and, to all appearances, couth. But he had bought the whole superman package, complete with that fragile beast, the male ego. The androgynous man arrives with a male ego too, but his is not as imperialistic. It doesn't invade every area of his life and person. Most activities and thoughts have nothing to do with masculinity or femininity. The androgynous man knows this. The all-man man doesn't. He must keep a constant guard against anything even vaguely feminine (i.e., "sissy") rising up in him. It must be a terrible strain.

5   Male chauvinism is an irritation, but the real problem I have with the all-man man is that it's hard for me to talk to him. He's alien to me, and for this I'm at least half to blame. As his interests have not carried him into the sissy, mine have never taken me very far into the typically masculine terrains of sports, business and finance, politics, cars, boats and machines. But blame or no blame, the reality is that it is almost as difficult for me to connect with him as it would be to link up with an Arab shepherd or Bolivian sandalmaker. There's a similar culture gap.

6   It seems to me that the most masculine men usually end up with the most feminine women. Maybe they like extreme polarity. I like polarity myself, but the poles have to be within earshot. As I've implied, I'm very big on talking. I fall in love for at least three hours with anyone who engages me in a real conversation. I'd rather a man point out a paragraph in a book—wanting to share it with me—than bring me flowers. I'd rather a man ask what I think than tell me I look pretty. (Women who are very pretty and accustomed to hearing that they are pretty may feel differently.) My experience is that all-men men read books I don't want to see paragraphs of, and don't really give a damn what I or any woman would think about most issues so long as she looks pretty. They have a very limited use for women. I suspect they don't really like us. The androgynous man likes women as much or as little as he likes anyone.

7   Another difference between the all-man man and the androgynous man is that the first is not a star in the creativity department. If your image of the creative male accessorizes him with a beret, smock and artist's palette, you will not believe the all-man man has been seriously short-changed. But if you allow as how creativity is a talent for freedom, associated with imagination, wit, empathy, unpredictability, and receptivity to new impressions and connections, then you will certainly pity the dull, thick-skinned, rigid fellow in whom creativity sets no fires.

8   Nor is the all-man man so hot when it comes to sensitivity. He may be true-blue in the trenches, but if you are troubled, you'd be wasting your time trying to milk comfort from the all-man man.

9   This is not blind prejudice. It is enlightened prejudice. My biases were confirmed recently by a psychologist named Sandra Lipsetz Bem, a professor at Stanford University. She brought to attention the fact that high masculinity in males (and high femininity in females) has been "consistently correlated with lower overall intelligence and lower creativity." Another psychologist, Donald W. MacKinnon, director of the Institute of Personality Assessment and Research at the University of California in Berkeley, found that "creative males give more expression to the feminine side of their nature than do less creative men.... [They] score relatively high on femininity, and this despite the fact that, as a group, they do not present an effeminate appearance or give

evidence of increased homosexual interests or experiences. Their elevated scores on femininity indicate rather an openness to their feelings and emotions, a sensitive intellect and understanding self-awareness and wide-ranging interests including many which in the American culture are thought of as more feminine...."

10   Dr. Bem ran a series of experiments on college students who had been categorized as masculine, feminine, or androgynous. In three tests of the degree of nurturance—warmth and caring—the masculine men scored painfully low (painfully for anyone stuck with a masculine man, that is). In one of those experiments, all the students were asked to listen to a "troubled talker"—a person who was not neurotic but simply lonely, supposedly new in town and feeling like an outsider. The masculine men were the least supportive, responsive or humane. "They lacked the ability to express warmth, playfulness and concern," Bem concluded. (She's giving them the benefit of the doubt. It's possible the masculine men didn't express those qualities because they didn't possess them.)

11   The androgynous man, on the other hand, having been run through the same carnival of tests, "performs spectacularly. He shuns no behavior just because our culture happens to label it as female and his competence crosses both the instrumental [getting the job done, the problem solved] and the expressive [showing a concern for the welfare of others, the harmony of the group] domains. Thus, he stands firm in his opinion, he cuddles kittens and bounces babies and he has a sympathetic ear for someone in distress."

12   Well, a great mind, a sensitive and warm personality are fine in their place, but you are perhaps skeptical of the gut appeal of the androgynous man. As a friend, maybe, you'd like an androgynous man. For a sexual partner, though, you'd prefer a jock. There's no arguing chemistry, but consider the jock for a moment. He competes on the field, whatever his field is, and bed is just one more field to him: another opportunity to perform, another fray. Sensuality is for him candy to be doled out as lure. It is a ration whose flow is cut off at the exact point when it has served its purpose—namely, to elicit your willingness to work out on the field with him.

13   Highly masculine men need to believe their sexual appetite is far greater than a woman's (than a nice woman's). To them, females must be seduced: Seduction is a euphemism for a power play, a con job. It pits man against woman (or woman against man). The jock believes he must win you over, incite your body to rebel against your better judgment: in other words—conquer you.

14   The androgynous man is not your opponent but your teammate. He does not seduce: he invites. Sensuality is a pleasure for him. He's not quite so goal-oriented. And to conclude, I think I need only remind you here of his greater imagination, his wit and empathy, his unpredictability, and his receptivity to new impressions and connections.

Writing a Summary

2.6

Write a summary.

Often in college you will be asked to write about what you read. This culminates in the research paper. However, sometimes you will have to write shorter summaries and critiques.

A summary states the main points of an essay in your own words. It is a useful way to learn what you read. It is also how you share what you read. Instructors sometimes have students read different books and articles and share the results. Many readers summarize their favorite books online as a service to others searching for something good to read. Businesses and professionals will have employees summarize articles to share with their colleagues. The art of summarizing is the backbone of research writing.

A good summary lets someone who hasn't read the essay understand what it says. A summary can be one or more paragraphs. It should

- provide a context for the essay,
- introduce the author of the essay,
- and state the thesis (these first three elements often form the introduction of a multiparagraph summary),
- then state the main points of the essay (sometimes but not always based on the topic sentences), and
- conclude by pulling the essay together.

To prepare to write a summary, follow the steps in effective reading:

- Underline the main points of the essay.
- Write in the margins or a separate sheet of paper those main points in your own words.
- Decide the order that would make sense for your reader.
- Prepare a brief outline.
- Use your own words; if you use the author's words, quote, and document to avoid plagiarism.
- Don't insert your own views, since a summary is about the author's position.

A Sample Single Paragraph Summary of "The Appeal of the Androgynous Man"

What kind of man should appeal to women? According to Amy Gross, the editor-in-chief of *O* magazine, in "The Appeal of the Androgynous Man," her ideal is and the ideal of women should be the "androgynous man," a man who shares the personality characteristics of both male and female. To make her point, Amy Gross contrasts the all-man man and the androgynous man. She believes that the all-man man does not share in activities like shopping, has no taste in the arts, is imperialistic, resists anything feminine, and is interested in only exclusively male topics. Worse, she points to studies that show that more masculine men are less creative. Further, she argues that the all-man tends to see women as something to conquer rather than as partners. The androgynous man, by comparison, is very different. He does not resist things that are feminine and so shares in domestic activities, is comfortable with the arts, and can share interests with women. He is shown by studies to be more creative. Further, according to Gross, "The androgynous man is not your opponent but your teammate." As a result, she concludes that the androgynous man has the qualities that women should really look for in a man.

Writing a Critique

2.7

Write a critique.

Often you will be asked to give your views on an essay, indicating where you agree and disagree with the author's position. A faculty member may ask students to critically respond to an article. Employers may want your response to someone else's report or a professional article affecting your field. In general, writing a critique is a vital part of building an argument or a critical research paper. Remember you can always agree with part of what a person says and disagree with other parts. A critique combines a summary of the article with your thoughtful reaction. Most critiques consist of several paragraphs. A critique usually includes the following:

- A context for the essay
- An introduction to the author
- A statement of the essay's thesis
- The thesis for your critique
- A summary of the essay
- A statement of the points with which you agree
- A statement with reasons and evidence for your disagreement
- A conclusion

You are well prepared to write a critique if you follow the steps for reading effectively and reading critically.

- In addition to the summarizing comments, jot down whether you agree or disagree and why.
- It may be helpful to create a table that lists the major claims of the essay and your response, including whether you agree or disagree and why, including reasons or facts you have at your disposal.
- Determine an organizational pattern that works.
- Write your draft and revise.

A Sample Multiparagraph Critique of "The Appeal of the Androgynous Man"

1   What kind of man should appeal to women? According to Amy Gross, the editor-in-chief of *O* magazine, in "The Appeal of the Androgynous Man," her ideal is and the ideal of women should be the "androgynous man," a man who shares the personality characteristics of both male and female. But matters are not so simple. Amy Gross falsely divides men into two stereotyped categories. In fact, real men are much more complex.

2   To make her point, Amy Gross contrasts the all-man man and the androgynous man. She believes that the all-man man does not share in activities like shopping, has no taste in the arts, is imperialistic, resists anything feminine, and is interested in only exclusively male topics. Worse, she points to studies that show that more masculine men are less creative. Further, she argues that the all-man tends to see women as something to conquer rather than as partners. The androgynous man, by comparison, is very different. He

does not resist things that are feminine and so shares in domestic activities, is comfortable with the arts, and can share interests with women. He is shown by studies to be more creative. Further, according to Gross, "The androgynous man is not your opponent but your teammate." As a result, she concludes that the androgynous man has the qualities that women should really look for in a man.

3   She is right that if the all-man male were like she said, he would truly be undesirable. No woman should want a partner who takes her for granted, doesn't share her interests, or treats her simply as someone to conquer. But is that really what men are like? My brother plays football and loves to watch it on television. He also hunts and fishes. But that isn't all he does. He plays with kittens, loves to cook, plays the guitar and sings, and secretly likes "chick flicks." As far as I can tell, he treats his girlfriend well. He seems genuinely concerned about her, will spend hours shopping with her, goes to events that interest her, and generally seems sensitive to her needs. Is he an "all-man" or an "androgynous man"? Equally a man can write poetry, love Jane Austen, cook gourmet meals, and still take women for granted. From what I have read, Pablo Picasso treated women dreadfully, even if he was a great artist. Was he an "all-man" man or an "androgynous man"?

4   Ms. Gross seems to present evidence from psychological studies that show that more masculine men are less creative than more feminine men. Maybe so, but she doesn't give us the evidence we need to make up our own minds. How did they actually measure masculinity and femininity? How many people were tested? What did they count as creativity? Personally I have my doubts. Writers such as Ernest Hemingway and Norman Mailer were pretty masculine men and yet were still very creative. I know a lot of men who have feminine characteristics who aren't any more creative than the average person.

5   The mistake Ms. Gross makes is that she believes that women should select types of men. They shouldn't. Women date, love, and marry individual men. As a result, a woman should really be concerned about whether the man shares her interests, treats her well, has qualities she can love, and will be faithful. Where the man fits on Ms. Gross's little chart is far less important than the kind of man he is, regardless of whether he is "androgynous."

Successful Reading

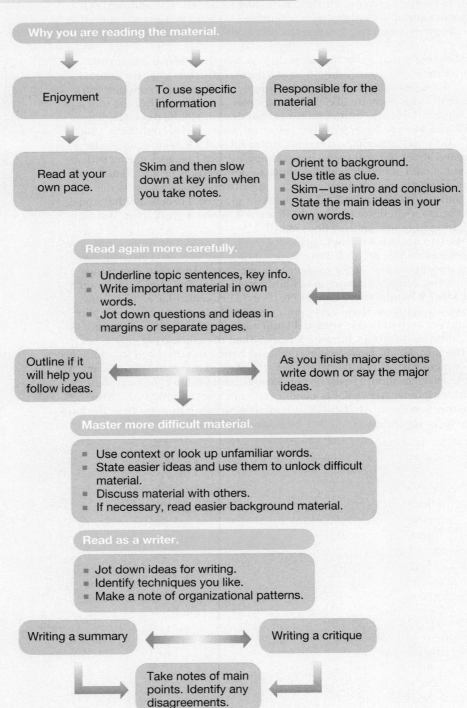

Why you are reading the material.

- Enjoyment
- To use specific information
- Responsible for the material

- Read at your own pace.
- Skim and then slow down at key info when you take notes.
- Orient to background.
- Use title as clue.
- Skim—use intro and conclusion.
- State the main ideas in your own words.

Read again more carefully.

- Underline topic sentences, key info.
- Write important material in own words.
- Jot down questions and ideas in margins or separate pages.

Outline if it will help you follow ideas.   As you finish major sections write down or say the major ideas.

Master more difficult material.

- Use context or look up unfamiliar words.
- State easier ideas and use them to unlock difficult material.
- Discuss material with others.
- If necessary, read easier background material.

Read as a writer.

- Jot down ideas for writing.
- Identify techniques you like.
- Make a note of organizational patterns.

Writing a summary   Writing a critique

Take notes of main points. Identify any disagreements.

CHAPTER 3

Planning and Drafting Your Paper: Exploration

In this chapter, you will learn how to:

3.1 Analyze the assignment to understand its goals.

3.2 Use different strategies to find and develop a topic.

3.3 Gather information to support your topic.

3.4 Think critically about your topic.

3.5 Organize and outline your paper.

3.6 Develop an effective thesis statement.

3.7 Write a first draft of your paper.

Visit MyWritingLab **to complete the writing assignments in this chapter and for more resources on planning and drafting.**

Many students believe that good essays are dashed off in a burst of inspiration by born writers. Some boast that they cranked out A papers in an hour. Perhaps. But for most of us, writing is a process that takes time and work. It is also a messy process. Don't confuse your planning and drafting with a final version. If your grammar and spell check slow you down, turn them off until you are revising a later draft or proofreading your work.

Writing is a flexible process. No approach works for every writer. Some writers establish their purpose and draft a plan for carrying it out at the start of every project. Others begin with a tentative purpose or plan and discover their final direction as they write.

Regardless of how it unfolds, the writing process consists of the following stages. Advancing through each stage will guide you if you have no plan or if you've run into snags with your approach. Once you're familiar with these stages, you can combine or rearrange them as needed.

- Understanding the assignment
- Zeroing in on a topic
- Gathering information
- Organizing the information
- Developing a thesis statement
- Writing the first draft

Types of Writers

Planners	Explorers
Start with a focused idea. Usually have a clear plan. Tend to develop existing plan.	Discover ideas while writing. Often follow out inspirations. Can develop tangents. Usually write more than final.
Can write like an outline. May tend to underdevelop. Can miss possible ideas.	Can go off on tangents. May initially lack obvious organization. Usually have more than needed.
Can benefit from additional brainstorming. May need additional development. May need to explore ideas outside plan.	May need to plan after drafting. Might need several revisions. Might need to refocus and cut.

Understanding the Assignment

3.1

Analyze the assignment to understand its goals.

Instructors differ in how they approach writing assignments. Some specify the topic; some give you several topics to choose from; and still others offer you a free choice. Likewise, some instructors dictate the length and format of the essay, whereas others don't. Whatever the case, be sure you understand the assignment before you go any further.

Think of it this way: If your boss asked you to report on ways of improving the working conditions in your office and you turned in a report on improving worker benefits, would you expect the boss's approval? Following directions is crucial, so ask your instructor to clear up any questions you might have about the assignment. Don't be timid; it's much better to ask for directions than to receive a low grade for failing to follow them.

Once you understand the assignment, consider the project *yours*. If you are asked to describe a favorite vacation spot for a local newspaper, here is your chance to inform others about a place that is special to you. By asking yourself what the assignment allows you to accomplish, you can find your own purpose.

Zeroing in on a Topic

A subject is a broad discussion area: sports, college life, culture, and the like. A topic is one small segment of a subject, such as testing athletes for drug use, Nirvana College's academic probation policy, or texting. If you choose your own topic, pick one that is narrow enough so that you can develop it properly. Avoid sprawling, slippery issues that lead to a string of trite generalities.

3.2

Use different strategies to find and develop a topic.

In addition, choose a familiar topic or one you can learn enough about in the time available. Avoid overworked topics such as arguments about the death penalty or the legal drinking age, which generally repeat the same old points. Instead, select a topic that lets you draw upon your unique experiences and insights and offer a fresh perspective to your reader.

Strategies for Finding a Topic

Whenever your instructor assigns a general subject, you'll need to stake out a limited topic suitable for your paper. If you're lucky, the right one will come to mind immediately. More often, though, you'll need to resort to some special strategy. Following are six proven strategies that many writers use. Not all of them will work for everyone, so experiment to find those that produce a topic for you.

Tapping Your Personal Resources   Over the years, you've packed your mind with memories of family gatherings, school activities, movies, concerts, plays, parties, jobs, books you've read, TV programs, dates, discussions, arguments, and so on. All these experiences can provide suitable topics. Suppose you've been asked to write about some aspect of education. Recalling the difficulties you had last term at registration, you might argue for better registration procedures. Or if you're a hopeless TV addict who must write on some advertising topic, why not analyze TV advertising techniques?

Anything you've read in magazines or journals, newspapers, novels, short stories, or textbooks can also trigger a topic. Dan Greenburg's "Sound and Fury" (in The Reader), in which a potentially explosive situation is defused, might suggest a paper on some dangerous encounter in your past. An article reviewing the career of a well-known politician might stir thoughts of a friend's experience in running for the student council.

EXERCISE   *Select five of the subjects listed below. Tapping your personal resources, name one topic suggested by each. For each topic, list three questions that you might answer in a paper.*

MyWritingLab

Life on a city street	Some aspect of nature
A particular field of work	Contemporary forms of dancing
Some branch of the federal bureaucracy	Youth gangs
Concern for some aspect of the environment	Fashions in clothing

Saving money	Trendiness
Home ownership	Human rights
Schools in your town	Public transportation
Leisure activities	Childhood fears
Trends in technology	A new scientific discovery
A best-selling book	A religious experience

Keeping a Journal   Many writers record their experiences in a journal. A journal provides a number of possible writing topics as well as valuable writing practice.

In a journal you have the freedom to explore thoughts, feelings, responses, attitudes, and beliefs without reservation and without concern for "doing it right." *You* control the content and length of the entry. Furthermore, depending on your instructor's preference, you usually don't have to worry about correct spelling or grammar. Journal writing does not represent a finished product but rather an exploration.

A few simple guidelines ensure effective journal entries:

1. Write on the computer or in any kind of notebook that appeals to you; the content, not the package, is the important thing.
2. Write on a regular basis—at least five times a week, if possible. In any event don't write by fits and starts, cramming two weeks of entries into one sitting.
3. Write for 10–20 minutes, longer if you have more to say. Don't aim for uniform entry length, such as three paragraphs or a page and a half. Simply explore your reactions to the happenings in your life or to what you have read, heard in class, or seen on television. The length will take care of itself.
4. If you have multiple pages of journals in your word processor, you can use Find to search key words to discover related ideas.

Let's examine a typical journal entry by Sam, a first-year composition student.

Last week went back to my hometown for the first time since my family moved away and while there dropped by the street where I spent my first twelve years. Visit left me feeling very depressed. Family home still there, but its paint peeling and front porch sagging. Sign next to the porch said house now occupied by Acme Realtors. While we lived there, front yard lush green and bordered by beds of irises. Now an oil-spattered parking lot. All the other houses on our side of the street gone, replaced by a row of dumpy buildings housing dry cleaner, bowling alley, hamburger joint, shoe repair shop, laundromat. All of them dingy and rundown looking, even though only a few years old.

Other side of the street in no better shape. Directly across from our house a used-car dealership with rows of junky looking cars. No trace left of the Little League park that used to be there. Had lots of fun playing baseball and learned meaning of sportsmanship. To left of the dealership my old grade school, now boarded and abandoned. Wonder about my fifth-grade teacher Mrs. Wynick. Is she still teaching? Still able to make learning a game, not a chore? Other side of dealership the worst sight of all. Grimy looking plant of some sort pouring foul smelling smoke into the air from a discolored stack. Smoke made me cough.

   Don't think I'll revisit my old street again.

This journal entry could spawn several essays. Sam might explore the causes of residential deterioration, define sportsmanship, explain how Mrs. Wynick made learning a game, or argue for stricter pollution control laws.

EXERCISE   *Write journal entries over the next week or two for some of the following items that interest you. If you have trouble finding a suitable topic for a paper, review the entries for possibilities.*   MyWritingLab

Encounters with technology	Developing relationships
Single or married life	Parents
Financial or occupational considerations	Ideas gained through reading

Sorting Out a Subject   All of us sort things. We do it whenever we tackle the laundry, clear away a sink full of dishes, or tidy up a basement or garage. Sorting out a subject is similar. First, we break our broad subject into categories and subcategories and then allow our minds to roam over the different items and see what topics we can turn up. The chart on page 42 shows what one student found when she explored the general topic of Internet communication. It is easy to create a table in your software program or use graphic visuals that help you highlight relationships.

 As you'll discover for yourself, some subjects yield more topics than others; some, no topics at all.

EXERCISE   *Select two of the following subjects and then subdivide those two into five topics.*   MyWritingLab

Advertising	Movies	The space program
Dwellings	Occupations	Sports
Fashions	Popular music	Television programs
Magazines	Social classes	Vacations

Results of Sorting out the Subject of Internet Communication					
Personal		Community		Large Community of Followers	
Texting	Chat	Discussion Boards	Facebook	Blogs	Tweeting
The reasons texting is replacing E-mail The style of texting The extent to which texting influences language use The dangers of texting and driving; the effects of texting on attention.	The growing use of chat for online support. The role of Chat in higher education and online classes. The comparison of online chat and phone calls.	Fan Boards Professional Discussion Boards Discussion Boards in the classroom Frequently Asked Questions The problem of civility in discussion boards The growing use of discussion boards with online news media	Why FB became so popular. The challenges of keeping FB profitable. Effects FB has on the social relations of college students.	Political Blogs Corporate Blogs Personal Blogs How to write a successful blog The way blog may keep us in our personal information bubble. The extent to which blogs give average citizens a political voice.	Celebrity tweets Political tweets Tweeting Friends Product Tweets The ways tweeting is increasingly used in political campaigns. The ways tweets are used to manage a celebrity's image. A classification of the different kinds of people who tweet and follow tweets.

Asking Questions   Often, working your way through these basic questions will lead you to a manageable topic:

1. Can I define my subject?
2. Does it break into categories?
3. If so, what comparisons can I make among these categories?
4. If my subject is divided into parts, how do they work together?
5. Does my subject have uses? What are they?
6. What are some examples of my subject?
7. What are the causes or origins of my subject?
8. What impact has my subject had?

Let's convert these general questions into specific questions about telescopes, a broad general subject:

1. What is a telescope?
2. What are the different kinds of telescopes?
3. How are they alike? How do they differ?
4. What are the parts of each kind of telescope, and how do they work together?
5. What are telescopes used for?
6. What are some well-known telescopes?
7. Who invented the telescope?
8. What impact have telescopes had on human life and knowledge?

Each of these questions offers a starting point for a suitably focused essay. Question 3 might launch a paper comparing reflecting and refracting telescopes; question 6 might be answered in a paper about the Hubble Space Telescope and the problems with it.

EXERCISE *Select two of the following subjects. Create general questions and then convert them into specific questions. Finally, suggest two essay topics for each of your two subjects.*   MyWritingLab

Astrology	Games	Shopping malls
Books	Microorganisms	Stars
Colleges	Plays	Television
Emotions	Religions	Warships

Freewriting   The freewriting strategy snares thoughts as they race through your mind, yielding a set of sentences that you then look over for writing ideas. To begin, turn your pen loose and write for about five minutes on your general subject. Put down everything that comes into your head, without worrying about grammar, spelling, or punctuation. What you produce is for your eyes alone. If the thought flow becomes blocked, write "I'm stuck, I'm stuck …" until you break the mental logjam. When your writing time is up, go through your sentences one by one and extract potential topic material. If you draw a blank, write for another five minutes and look again. A useful strategy is to take key ideas or phrases from your freewriting and then in a separate page or file do additional freewriting on each of those ideas or phrases.

The following example shows the product of one freewriting session. Drew's instructor had assigned a two- or three-page paper on technology; and since Drew is a business major, he considers a more personal technology with which he has experience, the cell phone.

> Technology, huh. What do I know about technology? Cell phones are technology? What about them? There are so many kinds. Razors, Blackberries. I love my new iPhone. It does everything, plays music, lets me text, check out YouTube, e-mail, take pictures and store them. They change people lives. But how? Well, we are always on them talking to friends, to anybody, and parents and teachers never get it. But why do we talk on them so much. Stuck, stuck, stuck. Well, I keep in touch with friends. Some are away at college. My girlfriend is always calling me. We also get lots of stuff done, like checking out my stupid bills.

This example suggests at least three papers. For people shopping for a new cell phone, Drew could identify the advantages of different types. He could write to people who are considering buying an iPhone about the features of the phone. He could write to those perplexed by student behavior to explain why students use cell phones so extensively.

Brainstorming   Brainstorming, a close cousin of freewriting, captures fleeting ideas in words, fragments, and sometimes sentences, rather than in a series of sentences. Brainstorming garners ideas faster than the other strategies do.

But unless you move immediately to the next stage of writing, you may lose track of what some of your fragmentary jottings mean.

To compare the results of freewriting and brainstorming a topic, we've converted our freewriting example into this list, which typifies the results of brainstorming:

Types of Cell Phones	Stores Pictures
Razors	text message
Blackberries	e-mails
iPhones	why people use e-mail
plays music	to coordinate life
view YouTube	to get things done
takes pictures	to keep in touch

MyWritingLab   **EXERCISE** *Return to the five subjects you selected for the exercise on page 39. Freewrite or brainstorm for five minutes on each one and then choose a topic suitable for a two- or three-page essay. State your topic, intended audience, and purpose.*

Narrowing a familiar subject may yield not only a topic but also the main divisions for a paper on it. Drew's freewriting session uncovered several possible cell phone topics as well as a way of approaching each: classifying types of cell phones and writing about the strengths and weaknesses of each or identifying the different features of an iPhone and describing each feature and how it works or explaining each of the reasons college students use cell phones so frequently. Ordinarily, though, the main divisions will emerge only after you have gathered material to develop your topic. Drew, on considering his options, decides he doesn't know enough about types of cell phones and might get carried away when writing about the iPhone. He decides to write about the reasons college students are so attached to their cell phones.

Identifying Your Audience and Purpose

You can identify your purpose and audience at several stages in the writing process. Sometimes both are set by the assignment and guide your selection of a topic. For example, you might be asked to write the college president to recommend improvements in the school's registration system. At other times, you may have to write a draft before you can determine either. Usually, though, the selection of audience and purpose goes hand in hand with determining a topic. Think of the different types of information Drew would gather if he wrote for (1) college students to break them of their cell phone habits, (2) college professors and parents to make cell phone use seem less peculiar, (3) or a sociology professor to demonstrate how common behaviors can be explained through sociological theories.

Considering Your Media

Part of considering your audience and purpose is thinking about the media in which it will be presented. Is your essay going to be part of a blog post, collected with other essays to form a Web page, a separate and distinct paper, a longer e-mail? Understanding the media may help you better decide how formal you want to make your writing, identify what kinds of images or even media clips you might include in your work, and judge how your work might fit with other works around it.

Gathering Information

Once you have a topic, you'll need things to say about it. This supporting material can include facts, ideas, examples, observations, sensory impressions, memories, and the like. Without the proper backup, papers lack force, vividness, and interest and may confuse or mislead readers. The more support you can gather, the easier it will be for you to write a draft. Time spent gathering information is never wasted.

3.3

Gather information to support your topic.

Strategies for Gathering Information

If you are writing on a familiar topic, much of your supporting material may come from your own head. Brainstorming is the best way to retrieve it. With unfamiliar topics, brainstorming won't work. Instead, you'll have to do some background reading. Whatever the topic, familiar or unfamiliar, talking with friends, parents, neighbors, or people knowledgeable about the topic can also produce useful ideas.

Brainstorming   Brainstorming a topic, like brainstorming a subject, yields a set of words, fragments, and occasionally sentences that will furnish ideas for the paper. Drew has decided that he wants to demonstrate to professors and parents that there are good reasons for student cell phone use. He generated the following list through brainstorming:

students open cell phones after class	weather updates
coordinating life	sending e-mails
meeting friends for study sessions	sending pictures by e-mail
arranging a lunch date	holding up a phone at a concert
getting a ride	calling when something funny happens
coordinating a team project	keeping in touch
getting things done	old friends in different colleges
resolving bill disputes	boyfriends or girlfriends
scheduling car repairs	text messaging
finding babysitters	playing music

You can see how some thoughts have led to others. For example, the first jotting, "arranging a lunch date," leads naturally to the next one, "getting a ride." And "keeping in touch" leads to "old friends in different colleges."

Branching is a helpful and convenient extension of brainstorming that allows you to add details to any item on your list. Here's how you might use this technique to approach "cell phone use":

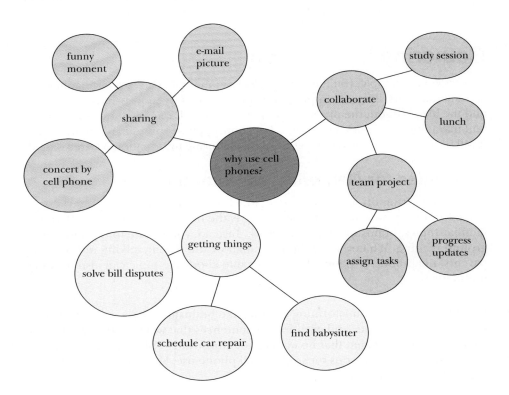

Don't worry if your brainstorming notes look chaotic and if some seem irrelevant. Sometimes the most unlikely material turns out to be the freshest and most interesting. As you organize and write your paper, you'll probably combine, modify, and omit some of the notes, as well as add others. Drew decides from his brainstorming that "playing music," "sending e-mails," and "getting weather updates" are too specific to only a few kinds of cell phones and should not be part of his paper. There are now a number of brainstorming software programs such as the TheBrain and MindMeister that let you brainstorm on your computer on the Web, and even allow you to include images in your brainstorming. You can also use existing graphic programs on your computer.

MyWritingLab   **EXERCISE**   *Prepare a brainstorming sheet of supporting details for one of the topics you developed for the exercise on page 41.*

Reading   When you have to grapple with an unfamiliar topic, look in the library for material to develop it. Once you have a list of references, start searching for the books or articles. Look through each one you find and jot down information that looks useful, either as direct quotations or in your own words.

Whenever you use a direct quotation or rephrased material in your paper, you must give proper credit to the source. If you don't, you are guilty of plagiarism, a serious offense that can result in a failing grade for the course or even expulsion from college.

Talking with Others   You can expand the pool of ideas gained through brainstorming or reading by talking with some of the people around you. Imagine you're writing a paper about a taxpayers' revolt in your state. After checking the leading state newspapers at the library, you find that most of the discontent centers on property taxes. You then decide to supplement what you've read by asking questions about the tax situation in your town.

Your parents and neighbors tell you that property taxes have jumped 50 percent in the last two years. The local tax assessor tells you that assessed valuations have risen sharply and that state law requires property taxes to keep pace. She also notes that this situation is causing some people on fixed incomes to lose their homes. A city council member explains that part of the added revenue is being used to repair city streets, build a new library wing, and buy more fire-fighting equipment. The rest is going to the schools. School officials tell you they're using their extra funds to offer more vocational courses and to expand the program for learning-disabled students. As you can see, asking questions can broaden your perspective and provide information that will help you to write a more worthwhile paper.

Social Media is a powerful tool for getting ideas and information.

- Post your issues and ideas on Facebook to get information and possible reading from friends.
- Conduct a survey using Facebook.
- E-mail friends, family, or even experts.
- Log on to discussion boards on the Internet.

Thinking Critically about Your Topic

As you begin to collect your ideas and information, you should think critically about some of the claims you are considering.

3.4

Think critically about your topic.

- Are you making assumptions that might be questioned? Is Drew exaggerating the usefulness of cell phones, perhaps overgeneralizing from a few incidents?
- How are your biases shaping your thinking? Is Drew's own extensive use of his cell phone forcing him to defend his behavior?
- Are there alternative ways to consider the topic or issue—in Drew's case, the ways the cell phone might shape the interactions, perhaps making them more frequent but less substantive? One useful strategy in

developing a paper is to brainstorm a position different from your own. For Drew that viewpoint might be the ways that cell phones disrupt social relationships and interfere with daily life. He might wish to imagine, in a positive fashion, what college life might be like without cell phones.

- Are there other experiences or evidence that you might wish to consider? Drew might have wished to talk to parents, looked at articles critical of cell phones, and talked to teachers to get a perspective that might challenge his view.

Thinking critically about your topic doesn't mean abandoning your topic. It does mean that you can approach your writing with your ideas tested, alternatives considered, and challenges ready to be addressed. It will make your position and your writing about that position stronger.

Organizing the Information

3.5

Organize and outline your paper.

If you have ever listened to a rambling speaker spill out ideas in no particular order, you probably found it hard to pay attention to the speech, let alone make sense of it. So, too, with disorganized writing. A garbled listing of ideas serves no one; an orderly presentation highlights your ideas and helps communication succeed.

Your topic determines the approach you take. In narrating a personal experience, such as a mishap-riddled vacation, you'd probably trace the events in the order they occurred. In describing a process, say caulking a bathtub, you'd take the reader step by step through the procedure. To describe a hillside view near your home, you might work from left to right. Or you could first paint a word picture of some striking central feature and then fan out in either direction. Other topics dictate other patterns, such as comparison and contrast, cause and effect, and illustration.

You can best organize long pieces of writing, such as library research papers, by following a formal outline. For shorter papers, however, a simple, informal system of *flexible notes* will do nicely.

The Flexible Notes System

To create a set of flexible notes, write each of your key points at the top of a separate page, computer file, or sheet of paper. If you have a thesis statement (see page 51), refer to it for your key points. Next, list under each heading the supporting details that go with that heading. Drop details that don't fit and expand points that need more support. It can be handy to save each new page with a number, such as "topic3," so if you discover that you cut something useful, you can retrieve it. When your points are finished, arrange them in the order you expect to follow in your essay. Your computer allows you to readily pull material from different pages and even files onto a single page. Do not hesitate to cut and paste to try out different organizational patterns. Drew's notes for the cell phone paper look like this:

Coordinating Activities
Meeting friends for a study session
Arranging a lunch date
Getting a ride
Coordinating a team project

Getting Things Done
Resolving bill disputes
Scheduling car repairs
Finding babysitters

Sharing
Sending pictures by e-mail
Holding up phone at concert
Call about something funny happening

Keeping in Touch
Old friends in different colleges
Boyfriends and girlfriends
Text messaging

Since coordinating activities, getting things done, sharing, and keeping in touch are equivalent reasons, this listing arranges them according to their probable importance—starting with the most important reason from the point of view of the audience.

Now you're ready to draft a plan showing how many paragraphs you'll have in each part of the essay and what each paragraph will cover. Sometimes the number of details will suggest one paragraph; other times you'll need a paragraph block—two or more paragraphs. Here's a plan for Drew's cell phone essay:

Coordinating Activities
Meeting for study session
Arranging a lunch date
Getting a ride
Coordinating a team project

Getting Things Done
Resolving bill disputes
Scheduling car repairs
Finding a babysitter

Sharing
Sending pictures by e-mail
Holding up phone at concert
Calling about a funny event

Keeping in Touch
Old friends in different colleges   } By voice
Boyfriends and girlfriends
Text messaging   } By text

These groupings suggest one paragraph about coordinating activities, one about getting things done, one about sharing, and two about keeping in touch.

MyWritingLab   **EXERCISE** *Organize into flexible notes the supporting details that you prepared for the exercise on page 46. Arrange your note pages in a logical sequence and draft a plan showing the number and content of the paragraphs in each section.*

Creating an Outline

With longer essays or if it fits your organizational style, it can be helpful to develop an outline. An outline can show you how to organize and develop your paragraphs. In an outline, you organize your essay into major units using Roman numerals (I, II, III), letters (A, B, C), and numbers to show the structure you will use in the paper. Introductions and conclusions are not usually included in the outline. Most word processing programs have an outline function that lets you easily create an outline. In Word, you simply click on the outline icon in the bottom left of the page. There are two kinds of outlines. A topic outline simply states the main topic to be addressed in a section.

   I. Coordinating Activities
      A. Meeting friends for study sessions
         1. Setting the time
         2. Making certain everyone gets there
      B. Arranging a lunch date
         1. Deciding where everyone is meeting
         2. Arranging a ride to lunch
  II. Getting Things Done
      A. Coordinating a team project
         1. Assign tasks
         2. Monitor progress
      B. Resolving bill disputes
         1. Call during business hours

Topic outlines will quickly let you know if you have enough information for a paragraph. If under one major heading, you only have one letter or under a letter only one number, as in II B, you may need to do more brainstorming.

In a sentence outline, you make full statements or sentences that can often be used in your paper. A sentence outline makes you think about what you really want to say.

   I. Cell phones can be used to coordinate activities that would be otherwise difficult to coordinate given students' busy schedules.

A. Cell phones can help students find out where a study session is being held.
B. Often there is a complex schedule of classes, work, meals, and meetings to organize.
C. Cell phones can let members of a team project keep the project on track.

To develop your outline, you take your brainstorming or notes and mark the major units as I, II, III based on the main ideas they demonstrate. Then you start to develop your outline, identifying the major points for each major heading (I, II, …) and the next major points (A, B, C). You can use your outline as a goad to additional planning as you see the holes. You should rarely have an A without a B or a 1 without a 2.

Developing a Thesis Statement

A thesis statement presents the main idea of a piece of writing, usually in one sentence. The thesis statement points you in a specific direction, helping you to stay on track and out of tempting byways. In addition, it tells your reader what to expect.
    Thesis statements can emerge at several points in the writing process. If an instructor assigns a controversial topic on which you hold strong views, the statement may pop into your head right away. At other times it may develop as you narrow a subject to a topic. Occasionally, you even have to write a preliminary draft to determine your main idea. Usually, though, the thesis statement emerges after you've gathered and examined your supporting information.
    As you examine your information, search for the central point and the key points that back it up; then use these to develop your thesis statement. Converting the topic to a question may help you to uncover backup ideas and write a thesis statement.

3.6

Develop an effective thesis statement.

For example:

Topic: The commercial advantages of computerized data storage systems.

Question: What advantages do computerized data storage systems offer business?

Thesis statement: Computerized data storage systems offer business enormous storage capacity, cheap, instant data transmission almost anywhere, and significantly increased profits.

The thesis statement stems from the specifics the student unearthed while answering the question.
    Following are some key strategies that can help you develop a thesis statement.

- Identify your main topic.
- Review your notes or research and identify the specific, major claims you want to make about your topic.

- Select those claims that will be the focus and organizational structure of the paper. You may need to outline first.
- Combine the major claim or claims with the topic in a statement that represents the main point of your paper.

Requirements of a Good Thesis Statement

Unless intended for a lengthy paper, a thesis statement focuses on just one central point or issue. Suppose you prepare the following thesis statement for a two- or three-page paper:

> Centerville College should reexamine its policies on open admissions, vocational programs, and aid to students.

This sprawling statement would commit you to grapple with three separate issues. At best, you could make only a few general remarks about each one.

To correct matters, consider each issue carefully in light of how much it interests you and how much you know about it. Then make your choice and draft a narrower statement. The following thesis statement would do nicely for a brief paper. It shows clearly that the writer will focus on *just one issue:*

> Because of the rising demand among high school graduates for job-related training, Centerville College should expand its vocational offerings

A good thesis statement also tailors the scope of the issue to the length of the paper. No writer could deal adequately with "Many first-year college students face crucial adjustment problems" in two or three pages. The idea is too broad to yield more than a smattering of poorly supported general statements. Paring it down to "Free time is a responsibility that challenges many first-year college students," however, results in an idea that could probably be developed adequately.

A good thesis statement further provides an accurate forecast of what's to come. If you plan to discuss the effects of overeating, don't say, "Overeating stems from deep-seated psychological factors and the easy availability of convenience foods." Such a statement, incorrectly suggesting that the paper will focus on causes, would only mislead and confuse your reader. On the other hand, "Overeating leads to obesity, which can cause or complicate several serious health problems" accurately represents what's to follow.

Finally, a good thesis statement is precise, often previewing the organization of the paper. Assertions built on fuzzy, catchall words like *fascinating, bad, meaningful,* and *interesting,* or statements like "My paper is about …" tell neither writer nor reader what's going on. To illustrate:

- New York is a fascinating city.
- My paper is about no-fault divorce.
- The United States budget deficit is complex and involves the amount of revenue collected, discretionary and nondiscretionary spending, the long-term prospects of entitlement programs, as well as interest rates and the value of the dollar.
- In this paper I will discuss the dangers of texting.

These examples raise a host of questions. Why does the writer find New York fascinating? Because of its skyscrapers? Its night life? Its theaters? Its restaurants? Its museums? Its shops? Its inhabitants? And what about no-fault divorce? Will the writer attack it, defend it, trace its history, or suggest ways of improving it? To find out, we must journey through the paper, hoping to find our way without a road-map sentence. How can the writer tackle all of these questions concerning the deficit without writing a book? What will actually be the focus? Besides starting with a cliché, we are left to wonder what kinds of danger of texting the writer is going to address.

Now look at the rewritten versions of those faulty thesis statements:

- New York's art museums offer visitors an opportunity to view a wide variety of great paintings.
- Compared to traditional divorce, no-fault divorce is less expensive, promotes fairer settlements, and reflects a more realistic view of the causes of marital breakdown.
- While currently the United States borrows money at historically low rates, the current deficit could easily be made worse by an increase in the rate for U.S. treasuries or a more general increase in interest rates.
- The evidence is clear. Texting while driving is almost as dangerous as drinking and driving.

These statements tell the reader not only what points the writer will make but also the order they will follow.

In brief, your thesis statement should

- Focus on just one central point or issue.
- Narrow the scope of the issue to what is manageable.
- Provide an accurate forecast of what is to come.
- Often preview the organization of the paper.

Your thesis statement should **not**

- Be too vague or general.
- Include more than you can reasonably manage in a paper.
- Suggest a different focus or organization than you follow in your paper.
- Use clichéd and excess wording like "In this paper I will discuss …."

Omission of Thesis Statement

Not all papers have explicit thesis statements. Narratives and descriptions, for example, sometimes merely support some point that is unstated but nevertheless clear, and professional writers sometimes imply their thesis rather than state it openly. Nonetheless, a core idea underlies and controls all effective writing. Usually it is best to state that core idea in a thesis statement.

Changing Your Thesis Statement

Before your paper is in final form, you may need to change your thesis statement several times. If you draft the thesis statement during the narrowing stage, you might change it to reflect what you uncovered while gathering information. Or you might amend it after writing the first draft so that it reflects your additions and deletions. In his first rough draft, Drew thought "In the end this cell phone mania is a necessary part of college life" was an adequate thesis statement. In revising his draft, however, he realized that it was not precise enough to direct his readers. He added a more precise statement that identified the main reasons addressed in his paper to serve as his thesis: "They use cell phones to coordinate the day's activities, to get some business done, to share life's events, and to keep in touch."

Tentative or final, formulated early or late, the thesis statement serves as a beacon that spotlights your purpose.

MyWritingLab   **EXERCISE**

1. **Write a thesis statement for the flexible notes that you developed for the exercise on page 50.**
2. **Reread "Requirements of a Good Thesis Statement" and then explain why each of the following does or does not qualify as an effective thesis statement for a two- or three-page essay.**
   a. My paper discusses the problem of employee absenteeism in American industry.
   b. Living on a small island offers three advantages: isolation from city problems, the opportunity to know your neighbors, and the chance to go fishing whenever you want.
   c. Although I don't know much about running a college, I know that Acme College is not run well.
   d. Increasing federal outlays for education will help us construct needed school buildings and create a better-trained workforce.
   e. Many people, wanting simpler and slower-paced lives, have abandoned high-paying executive positions for lower-paying, less stressful jobs.
   f. Vacationing in Britain is a nice way to spend a summer.
   g. Extending Middletown's intra-city transit system will save consumers money, reduce pollution, and increase city revenues.
   h. Most cable TV companies provide subscribers with several specialized-program channels.
3. **Revise the following five weak thesis statements.**
   a. The first year of college can be hard.
   b. Facebook offers lots of features.
   c. My paper discusses the importance of writing for college students.
   d. Global warming is changing the weather.
   e. In this paper I will talk about how wireless phones do more than ever.

Writing the First Draft

3.7

Write a first draft of your paper.

Now on to the first draft of your essay. The writing should go rather quickly. After all, you have a topic you're qualified to write about, a thesis statement that indicates your purpose, enough information to develop it, and a written plan to follow. But sometimes when you sit down to write, the words won't come, and all you can do is doodle or stare at the blank page. Perhaps the introduction is the problem. Many writers are terrified by the thought of the opening paragraph.

They want to get off to a good start but can't figure out how to begin. If this happens to you, additional brainstorming or freewriting can make you more comfortable and may suggest an opening. Keep in mind that any lead-in you write now can be changed later. If these suggestions don't solve your problem, skip the introduction for the time being. Once you have drafted the body of the paper, an effective opening should come more easily. Always remember how easy it is to revise on a computer, adding material, cutting things that don't work, and moving material around.

Following are some suggestions for writing a first draft:

1. Reread your thesis statement, notes, brainstorming, and written plan. They will start you thinking.
2. Rewrite your thesis statement at the top of your first page to break the ice and build momentum.
3. If it helps, just start writing without worrying about anything but getting ideas down; you can reshape everything later.
4. Write quickly; capture the drift of your thoughts. Concentrate on content and organization, but recognize that you can easily move the organization around later. Don't spend time correcting grammatical or punctuation errors, improving your language or making the writing flow smoothly. You might lose your train of thought and end up doodling or staring again.
5. If you have ideas that may not fit the flow, you can open another page to jot down those ideas so they are not lost and save the page under a different file name. If you don't know what to say about a section, you can mark that place "xxxxx" and fill it in later.
6. If you have ideas while writing for earlier sections, you can either go back and write them or keep a separate page you can open to jot down the additional ideas that come to you.
7. Take breaks at logical dividing points, such as when you finish discussing a key point. Before you start to write again, scan what you've written.

Now for some specific suggestions that will help you with the actual writing:

1. Write your first paragraph, introducing your essay and stating your thesis. If you get stuck here, move on to the rest of the paper.
2. Follow your plan as you write. Begin with your first main point and work on each section in turn.
3. Look over the supporting details listed under the first heading in your flexible notes. Write a topic sentence stating the central idea of the paragraph.
4. Turn the details into sentences; use one or more sentences to explain each one. Add other related details, facts, or examples if they occur to you.
5. When you move from one paragraph to the next, try to provide a transitional word or sentence that connects each paragraph.
6. Write your last paragraph, ending your essay in an appropriate fashion. If you get stuck, set your conclusion aside and return to it later.

Writing a draft isn't always so systematic. If you are inspired, you may want to abandon your plans and simply use your first draft to explore ideas. You can always revise, so don't be overly concerned if you get off track. You might uncover some of your best material during this type of search.

MyWritingLab **EXERCISE** *Using the plan you prepared for the exercise on page 50, write the first draft of an essay.*

Drew now uses his thesis statement and paragraph-by-paragraph plan to write the following draft. Notice that Drew, like many writers, gets off track. That is a common occurrence at this stage and can even be a step in generating new ideas. It isn't something to reject. Drew knows even as he writes that he will need to make significant revisions. We will focus on the revision process and Drew's revisions in the next chapter.

CASE HISTORY — Cell Phone Use Rough Draft

Students check their cell phones almost before they are out of the room. It confuses professors and parents. My parents complain that young people are so wrapped up in their cell conversations that they completely miss the world around them. Why are students such non-stop cell phone users? It looks ridiculous when large numbers of college students wander around talking into their phones, ignoring the people around them. In the end this cell phone mania is a necessary part of college life.

It is hard to imagine how people managed their lives without cell phones since there seems to be so much to get done. Weren't friends going to meet after class for a study session? Where is everybody? Life in college can be crazy. We juggle complex schedules, work, and meals. A quick phone call can organize it all. We arrange study sessions, confirm a lunch date, get a ride, coordinate a team project for class, and maybe even make time for a date.

Students, like everyone else, need to call about possible jobs, resolve disputes over bills, arrange to have their car fixed, find out the results of medical tests, and even, in some cases, find babysitters. Sometimes walking back to the dorm from a night class, students are on the phone simply to feel safer so that if anything happens they can let someone else know and perhaps get help. Cell phones let them get all this done.

Cell phones let us be together at the same time, even if we are in different places. Part of the reason for such widespread cell phone use is that instead of having to wait, a quick phone call has one person getting out of bed while another is getting out of class. Two friends seated at different ends of a stadium can enjoy the blow-by-blow of the action at the same time.

Everyone likes to share. Cell phones let people share. Many phones even let you take a picture and send it by e-mail to a friend. It is because of this practice that cell phones are banned in some locker rooms and why it is dangerous to be caught in an embarrassing situation at a party. You never know what can be e-mailed to your friends or even posted to the Internet. At concerts some in the audience call up friends and then hold up the phone so that they can hear part of a concert. When something really funny is happening, anyone can, with a quick call, share it with someone else who would appreciate the moment. L.O.L. Cell phones allow an instant connection, a voice instant messenger.

Cell phone calls let people reach out and touch each other. Most phone calls are very short. "Hey, what's up"? "What are you doing"? "How are you"? Little information is exchanged. "Nothing much," in fact, is a common answer. What do such phone calls accomplish? They let people keep in touch with each other.

Text messaging is really a very handy way to keep in touch. Even if you can't reach the other person, you can leave a message to let him know that you are thinking about him. Other people keep in touch through MySpace or Facebook, which lets friends know what is going on with each other's lives, even long lost friends. Facebook can even be a great space for sharing since you can post pictures, blog your ideas, identify your favorite group and more. If anything, college students of today can be considered the in-touch generation.

It must have been weird to wait an entire day before bragging to friends and family about getting the only A on a Chemistry test. It is almost impossible to imagine that students managed the complex schedule of their days before cell phones. It should not be surprising that students talk on their cell phones over nothing.

Planning and Drafting Your Paper

Understand the assignment.

- Understand the topic.
- Identify key expectations.
- Make the project yours.

Find your topic.

- Talk with others.
- Keep a journal.
- Sort out the subject into categories.
- Brainstorm.

Identify audience, purpose.

Develop details.

Read, talk to others, and brainstorm.

Organize the information.

- Create labeled flexible notes.
- Develop a rough plan—a list of points in order.
- Write a quick draft to find your focus and pattern.

Develop a focused thesis.

- Focus on just one central point or issue.
- Provide an accurate forecast of what is to come.

Draft to capture your thoughts—expect to revise.

CHAPTER 4

Revising and Editing Your Paper: Courageous Transformations

In this chapter, you will learn how to:

4.1 Approach your writing to effectively revise.

4.2 Use the F.A.C.T. strategy to guide your revision.

4.3 Think critically about your draft.

4.4 Revise at the paragraph and sentence level.

4.5 Write the introduction, conclusion, and title.

4.6 Participate in peer evaluation and use peer responses in your own revision.

4.7 Write collaboratively with others using multimedia.

4.8 Assemble and maintain a portfolio of your writing.

Visit MyWritingLab **to complete the writing assignments in this chapter and for more resources on revising and editing.**

Good writers don't express themselves perfectly on the first try; they revise until their writing is effective.

Just what is revision? Don't confuse it with proofreading or editing, the final stage of the writing process, where you carefully inspect your word choice, spelling, grammar, and punctuation. Revision is much more drastic, often involving an upheaval of your draft as you change its content and organization in order to communicate more effectively.

Most of what you read, including this book, has been altered considerably and improved as the writers progressed through early drafts. This fact shouldn't surprise you. After all, a rough draft is merely a first attempt to jot down some ideas. No matter how well you gather and organize your material, you can't predict the outcome until you've prepared a draft. Sometimes only touch-up changes are required. More often, though, despite your efforts this version will be incomplete, unclear in places, and possibly disorganized. You might even discover an entirely different idea, focus, or approach buried within it. During revision you keep changing things—your focus, approach to the topic, supporting material, and thesis statement—until the results satisfy you.

Inexperienced writers often mistakenly view initial drafts as nearly finished products rather than as experiments to alter, or even scrap, if need be. To revise successfully, you need to control your ego and your fear and become your own first critical reader. Set aside natural feelings of accomplishment ("After all, I've put a great deal of thought into this") and dread ("Actually, I'm afraid of what I'll find if I look too closely"). Instead, recognize that revision offers an opportunity to upgrade your strong features, strengthen your weak ones, or explore entirely new directions.

Preparing to Revise

4.1

Approach your writing to effectively revise.

To distance yourself from your writing and sharpen your critical eye:

- Set your draft aside for at least half a day, longer if possible.
- Write down your purpose and audience for your essay.
- Write down possible alternate directions for your essay.
- Write down any ideas or phrases that have come to you in writing the essay.
- Read your essay at least three times, once for each of the following reasons:
  - To improve the development of the essay as a whole.
  - To strengthen paragraph structure and development.
  - To sharpen sentences and words.

The right attitude is vital to effective revision. Far too many students hastily skim their essays to reassure themselves that "Everything sounds O.K." Avoid such a quick-fix approach. If your draft appears fine on first reading, probe it again with a more critical eye. Try putting yourself in your reader's place. Will your description of a favorite getaway spot be clear to someone who has never seen it? Will your letter home asking for money really convince parents who might think they've already given you too much? Remember: If you aren't critical now in anticipating confusion and objections, then your reader certainly will be later.

When you finish reading your paper for content, make a final, meticulous sweep to search for errors and problems that mar your writing. Use the Personal Revision Checklist on the inside back cover of this book to note your own special weaknesses, perhaps some problem with punctuation or a failure to provide specific support. Later chapters discuss paragraphs, sentences, and words in detail. Check these chapters for more information about the points introduced here.

Considering the Whole Essay

4.2

Use the F.A.C.T. strategy to guide your revision.

If you inspect your draft only sentence by sentence, you can easily overlook alternative directions for your work, gaps in the text, or how the parts work together. A better approach is to step back and view the overall essay rather than its separate parts, asking questions such as "Is there any entirely new direction to take the paper, perhaps following up on a section that works especially well?" "Does the beginning mesh with the end?" "Does the essay wander?" "Has anything been left out?" In this way you can find new approaches and gauge how part and whole relate.

Use the acronym *FACT* to guide this stage of your revision.

F. Ask yourself first whether the whole essay *FITS* together, presenting a central point for a specific audience. Have you delivered what the thesis statement promises? First drafts often include paragraphs, or even large sections, that have little bearing on the main point. Some drafts contain the kernels of several different essays. One section of a draft might be geared to one audience (parents, for example) and another section to an entirely different audience (students, perhaps). As you read each part, verify its connection to your purpose and audience. Don't hesitate to chop out sections that don't fit, redo stray parts so they accord with your central idea, or alter your thesis statement to reflect better your supporting material. Occasionally, you might even expand one small, fertile section of your draft into an entirely new essay.

A. Whenever we write first drafts, we unwittingly leave out essential material. We often produce text based on our own knowledge and assume far too much, leaving large holes and resulting in "writer-based prose." We need to revise these drafts to produce much more complete texts that meet the needs of our readers, resulting in "reader-based prose." As we revise, we need to identify and fill these inevitable gaps. Ask yourself: "Where will the reader need more information or examples to understand my message?" "Where do I need to explain things more fully?" "What major ideas have I left out?" It can be helpful to reread your notes or do some additional brainstorming. *ADD* the appropriate sentences, paragraphs, or even pages.

C. First drafts often contain material that fits the thesis but doesn't contribute to the essay. Writing quickly, we tend to repeat ourselves, include uninteresting or uninformative examples, and crank out whole paragraphs when one clear sentence would suffice. As you revise, *CUT* away this clutter with a free hand. Such paring can be painful, especially if you're left with a skimpy text, but your message will emerge with much greater clarity. As you've probably guessed, revising a draft often requires both adding and cutting.

T. Carefully *TEST* the organization of your essay. The text should flow smoothly from point to point with clear transitions between the various ideas. Test the organization by outlining your major and minor points and then check the results for logic and completeness. Alternatively, read the draft and note its progression. Look for spots where you can clarify connections between words and thus help your readers.

Chapters 8–16 explain nine different writing strategies, each concluding with revision questions geared specifically to that strategy. Use these questions, together with the *FACT* of revision, to help you revise more effectively.

It is crucial that you view revision not as a hasty touch-up job or as a quick sweep through your draft just prior to handing it in. Instead, revision should be an ongoing process that often involves an upheaval of major sections as you see your draft through your reader's eyes and strive to write as well as you can.

Decide if you revise better from the computer screen or using a printout. Sometimes essays look different when read in print and you can benefit from a printed copy of your draft, even if you directly revise your computer version. As you read your own essay, note on a separate sheet of paper or computer page problems to solve, ideas to add, and changes to try. You can insert ideas directly into your draft by using a symbol such as < > or a different color font. Some writers use post-it notes, either a software program on a computer or on actual paper, to paste revision ideas where they apply. If you are revising directly on the computer, you should use the Markup feature of your program and track your changes so that you do not lose them. Always keep a backup copy of everything. Accidentally erasing a file or losing your work to an electrical power surge is not uncommon. In addition, consider saving copies of your earlier drafts either as printouts or on disk; selected parts may prove useful later, and new papers sometimes sprout from old drafts. Regardless of the medium you use, be willing to write three or more versions of the same idea to find out which works best. When you approach the actual essay, make your job easier by using these simple techniques.

1. To delete something, cut it and track the changes or cross it out lightly; you may decide to resurrect it later.
2. If you are revising on a computer, simply insert the new material. You can try two or more versions in the same draft or open a new page to try different options. To add a section of text in a print copy, place a letter (*A, B, C, D*) at the appropriate spot and write the new material on a separate sheet, keyed to the letter. Make changes within sections by crossing out what you don't want and writing the replacement above it or nearby.
3. On the computer, you can simply cut and move sections to rearrange the organization. After you have moved material, you will need to make certain it fits into the new context. The cut and paste feature, when abused, can result in a paper that seems very disjointed. To rearrange the organization on a print copy, draw arrows showing where you want things to go, or cut up your draft and rearrange the sections by taping them on new sheets of paper. Use whatever method works best for you.

When you finish revising your draft, you might want to team up with one or more classmates and read one another's work critically. The fresh eye you bring to the task can uncover shortcomings that would otherwise go unnoticed. Pages 73–79 discuss peer editing in detail.

Drew carefully reconsiders his rough draft, which you read on pages 56–57. As we indicated there, the draft needs extensive work.

FIT. While most of Drew's paper fits his audience and thesis, the material concerning the misuses of the cell phone to e-mail pictures and instant messenger slang like L.O.L. doesn't match his audience or purpose. It is off-track, raises unnecessary suspicion about cell phone use, and is too informal for the audience.

ADD. If Drew really wishes to convince a skeptical audience that student cell phone use is necessary, he needs to make his examples more detailed. The material on using cell phones to be together at the same time and to keep in touch are especially scanty, but each paragraph could be more fully explained with more detailed examples.

CUT. The paragraph on text messaging may fit the topic, but it is different in kind from voice communication. Cutting that paragraph will allow the paper to be more focused on a single type of cell phone use.

TEST. If the paper is going to be organized according to the order of importance to the audience, it would make sense to put a paragraph on sharing after "getting business done" and "keeping in touch" before "together at the same time." A careful review of the flow of the paragraphs shows that the third paragraph lacks a clear transitional topic sentence.

EXERCISE

MyWritingLab

1. *List Drew's other options for revising this draft; indicate the necessary changes if he had decided to write for fellow college students.*
2. *Use the FACT acronym to revise the draft you prepared for the exercise on page 61.*

Thinking Critically about Your Draft

Also consider your draft by thinking critically about your work.

4.3

Think critically about your draft.

- Did you make assumptions you would want to clarify, explain, or change?
- Do your claims really hold up to your experience and evidence or do you need to change your ideas to better match the evidence?
- What alternate claims could someone make and do you want to respond to those alternatives or incorporate them into your essay?
- Do your ideas fit together logically or do you need to rethink your ideas?

CASE HISTORY   **Cell Phone Use Rough Draft Marked Up**

At the end of their class, Students check their cell phones almost before they are out of the room. It confuses professors and parents. Some are greatly confused by this practice and My parents complain that young people are so wrapped up in their cell conversations that they completely miss the world around them. Most wonder Why students are compulsive. such non-stop cell phone users? It looks ridiculous when The large numbers of college students wander around talking into their phones, ignoring the people around them. may seem ridiculous to outsiders. However, In the end this cell phone mania is a necessary part of college life.

There are many reasons students wander around campus talking into the air. They use cell phones to coordinate the day's activities, to get some business done, to share life's events, and to keep in touch.

Continued on next page

Continued from previous page

It is hard to imagine how people managed their lives without cell phones since there seems to be so much to get done. Weren't friends going to meet after class for a study session? Where is everybody? Life in college can be hectic. Students Add(A) crazy. We juggle complex schedules, work, of classes and a social life meals. A quick phone call can organize it all. We arrange study sessions, confirm a lunch date, get a ride, coordinate a team project for class, and maybe even make time for a date.

Add(B) Students, like everyone else, need to call about possible jobs, resolve disputes over bills, arrange to have their cars fixed, find out the results of There is often a lot to get done that has to be squeezed into a busy day. medical tests, and even, in some cases, find babysitters. Sometimes walking back to the dorm from a night class, students are on the phone simply to feel safer so that if anything happens they can let someone else know and perhaps get help. Cell phones let them get all this done, in the time between classes or even while walking back to their dorm, leaving them with more time for other things like studying or going out with friends.

Cell phones let us be together at the same time, even if we are in different places. Part of the reason for such widespread cell phone use is that instead we can be part of the immediate now. of having to wait. A quick phone call has one person getting out of bed while another is getting out of class. Two friends seated at different ends of a Anyone can know what almost anyone else on their call list is doing at any moment. stadium can enjoy the blow by blow of the action at the same time.

Everyone likes to share. Cell phones let people share. Many phones share moments of delight, success, and even failures with others who care. even let you take a picture and send it by e-mail to a friend. It is because of When a baby is expected, the soon to be grandparents this practice that cell phones are banned in some locker rooms and why it can't wait for the call. is dangerous to be caught in an embarrassing situation at a party. You never know what can be e-mailed to your friends or even posted to the internet. At concerts some in the audience call up friends and then hold up the phone so that they can hear part of a concert. When something really funny is happening, anyone can with a quick call share it with someone else who would appreciate the moment. L.O.L. Cell phones allow an instant connection, a voice to let people experience what you are experiencing, whether it is excitement over a success, an instant messenger. idea, the finals of a sporting event, or a newscast.

Add⊙

Cell phone calls let people reach out and touch each other. Most phone calls are very short. "Hey, what's up?" "What are you doing?" "How are you?" Little information is exchanged. "Nothing much," in fact, is a common answer. What do such phone calls accomplish? They let people keep in touch with each other.

~~Text Messaging is really a very handy way to keep in touch. Even if you can't reach the other person, you can leave a message to let you know that you are thinking about them. Other people keep in touch through MySpace or Face Book which lets friends know what is going on with each other's lives, even long lost friends. Face Book can even be a great space for sharing since you can post pictures, blog your ideas, identify your favorite group or more. If anything, college students of today can be considered the in touch generation.~~

Add⒟

It must have been weird to wait an entire day before bragging to friends and family about getting the only A on a Chemistry test. It is almost   Add⒠

incomprehensible

~~impossible~~ that students managed the complex schedule of their days before cell phones. It should not be surprising that students ~~talk~~ are on their cell

all day long. The surprise would be if they kept their cell phones in their pockets and waited.

phones ~~over nothing.~~

A   A quick cell phone call to a friend reveals that the study session was moved to the student center. Does everyone have his or her part ready for the presentation in Speech class at 3:00 P.M.? A flurry of cell phone calls makes certain everyone is ready. Will Collin be able to meet his girlfriend this afternoon? He needs to call to see if she is still free. Where is Jennifer since she said she was picking me up in front of the Science Building?

B   Sometimes cell phone calls get important business done. Heather needs to convince her parents that she really, really needs more money to cover the cost of books. Tim needs to contact his advisor so he can schedule for the next semester.

C   If you got an A on a paper that you thought would get an F, you can quickly spread the celebration to anyone who would echo your joy while

Continued on next page

Continued from previous page

the feeling was still hot. Sometimes a cell phone call can make the sharing very concrete, getting someone to go outside to look at a spectacular meteor shower, getting a friend to change channels so they can see an interview with a favorite rock star, or letting family know about a terrible earthquake in China.

D   Contact is what helps keep people close. Parents like their children to visit. Couples need to make time for each other. When people keep in touch, it lets them know that others care, lets them keep each other as important parts of their lives. Some students call their parents every day keeping the family ties tight, getting the emotional reassurance of those loving connections. Sometimes it seems like couples seem to be holding electronic hands as they walk across campus, with little room for some interloper to break up their relationships. Friends may not be able to see each other since they are going to different colleges, but a simple cell phone lets them each know the others are still friends.

E   What did a student do if a ride didn't show up? How did a couple share the excitement of a concert in the moment or a good joke if they had to wait days? Earlier generations who seem puzzled by the cell phone fever that has hit college campuses might wonder how they might have felt without a phone, having to wait for weeks for the mail or longer for a visit.

CASE HISTORY   Cell Phone Use Second Draft

Clarified room by adding class.

At the end of their class, students check their cell phones almost before they are out of the room. Professors and parents are confused by this practice. Some complain that young people are so wrapped up in their cell conversations that they completely miss the world around them. Most wonder why students are compulsive cell phone users. There are many reasons students wander around campus talking into the air. They use cell phones

Added thesis statement that outlines paper order.

to coordinate the day's activities, to get some business done, to share life's events, and to keep in touch. The large number of college students wandering around talking into their phones, ignoring the people around them, may seem ridiculous to outsiders. However, in the end this cell phone mania is a necessary part of college life.

It is hard to imagine how people managed their life without cell phones since there is so much to coordinate. Weren't friends going to meet after class for a study session? Where is everybody? A quick cell phone call to a friend reveals that the study session was moved to the student center. Does everyone have his or her part ready for the presentation in speech class at 3:00 P.M.? A flurry of cell phone calls makes certain everyone is ready. Will Collin be able to meet his girlfriend this afternoon? He needs to call to see if she is still free. Where is Jennifer since she said she was picking me up in front of the Science Building? Life in college can be hectic as students juggle complex schedules of classes, work, meal times, and a social life. A quick phone call can organize it all; arrange study sessions, confirm a lunch date, arrange a ride, coordinate a team project for class, and maybe even make time for a date.

Sometimes cell phone calls get important business done. Heather needs to convince her parents that she really, really needs more money to cover the cost of books. Tim needs to contact his advisor since he needs to lift his holds so he can schedule for the next semester. Students, like everyone else, need to call about possible jobs, resolve disputes over bills, arrange to have their car fixed, find out the results of medical tests, and even, in some cases, find babysitters. There is often a lot to get done that has to be squeezed into a busy day. Sometimes walking back to the dorm from a night class, students are on the phone simply to feel safer so that if anything happens they can let someone else know and perhaps get help. Cell phones let them get all this done in the time between classes or even while walking back to their dorm, leaving them with more time for other things like studying or going out with friends.

Provided more detailed account of how cell phone use helps. Placed academic material first for audience.

Clarified what was complex.

Added a transitional thesis statement. Added more specific examples to appeal to audience.

Continued on next page

Continued from previous page

Added context that relates to understanding of reader. Moved sharing paragraph up to better order the material. Added more concrete examples appropriate to target audience.

Everyone likes to share moments of delight, success, and even failure with others who care. When a baby is expected, the soon to be grandparents can't wait for the call. Cell phones let people share. Many phones even let you take a picture and send it by e-mail to a friend. At concerts some in the audience call up friends and then hold up the phone so that they can hear part of a concert. When something really funny is happening, anyone can with a quick call share it with someone else who would appreciate the moment. If you got an A on a paper that you thought would get an F, you can quickly spread the celebration to anyone who would echo your joy while the feeling was still hot. Sometimes a cell phone call can make the sharing very concrete, getting someone to go outside to look at a spectacular meteor shower, getting a friend to change channels so they can see an interview with a favorite rock star, or letting family know about a terrible earthquake in China. Cell phones allow an immediate connection to let people experience what you are experiencing, whether it is excitement over a success, an idea, the finals of a sporting event, or a news event.

Added more detailed examples appropriate to target audience.

Cell phone calls let people stay in touch with each other. Most phone calls are very short, over before students have gotten from the classroom to the door of the building. "Hey, what's up?" "What are you doing?" "How are you?" Little information is exchanged and little is really shared. "Nothing much," in fact, is a common response. What do such phone calls accomplish? They let people keep in touch with each other. Contact is what helps keep people close. Parents like their children to visit. Couples need to make time for each other. When people keep in touch, it lets them know that others care, lets them keep each other as important parts of their lives. Some students call their parents every day keeping the family ties tight, getting the emotional reassurance of those loving connections. Sometimes it seems like couples seem to be holding electronic hands as they walk across campus, with little room for some interloper to break up their relationships. Friends

Cut paragraph on text messages and moved insert E earlier.

may not be able to see each other since they are going to different colleges, but a simple cell phone lets them each know the others still are friends.

Part of the reason for such widespread cell phone use is that instead of having to wait, we can be part of the immediate now. A quick phone call has one person getting out of bed while another is getting out of class. Two friends seated at different ends of a stadium can enjoy the blow by blow of the action at the same time. Anyone can know what almost anyone else in their call list is doing at any moment.

It must have been lonely to wait an entire day before bragging to friends and family about getting the only A on a chemistry test. It is almost incomprehensible that students managed the complex schedule of their days before cell phones. What did a student do if a ride didn't show up? How did people share the excitement of a concert in the moment or a good joke if they had to wait days? Earlier generations who seem puzzled by the cell phone fever that has hit college campuses might wonder how they might have felt without a phone, having to wait for weeks for the mail or longer for a visit. It should not be surprising that students pull out their cell phones at the drop of almost anything. The surprise would be if they kept their cell phones in their pockets and waited.

> This paragraph still needs improvement.

Strengthening Paragraphs and Sentences

Once you finish considering the essay as a whole, examine your paragraphs one by one, applying the *FACT* approach that you used for the whole paper.

4.4

Revise at the paragraph and sentence level.

Strengthening Paragraphs

Make sure each paragraph *FITS* the paper's major focus and develops a single central idea. If a paragraph needs more support or examples, *ADD* whatever is necessary. If a paragraph contains ineffective or unhelpful material, *CUT* it. *TEST* the flow of ideas from paragraph to paragraph and clarify connections, both between and within paragraphs, as necessary. Ask the basic questions in the checklist that follows about each paragraph, and make any needed revisions.

REVISION CHECKLIST FOR PARAGRAPHS

- Does the paragraph have one, and only one, central idea?
- Does the central idea help to develop the thesis statement?
- Does each statement within the paragraph help to develop the central idea?
- Does the paragraph need additional explanations, examples, or supporting details?
- Would cutting some material make the paragraph stronger?
- Would reorganization make the ideas easier to follow?
- Can the connections between successive sentences be improved?
- Is each paragraph clearly and smoothly related to those that precede and follow it?

Don't expect to escape making changes. Certain paragraphs may be stripped down or deleted, others beefed up, still others reorganized or repositioned. Chapter 5 contains more information on writing effective paragraphs.

MyWritingLab   **EXERCISE** *Following are three sample paragraphs. Evaluate each according to the Revision Checklist for Paragraphs and suggest any necessary changes.*

1. I can remember so many times when my father had said that he was coming to pick me up for a day or two. I was excited as a young boy could be at the thought of seeing my father. With all the excitement and anticipation raging inside of me, I would wait on the front porch. Minutes would seem like hours as I would wait impatiently.

2. Going to high school for the first time, I couldn't decide if I should try out for the cheerleading team or wait a year. Since I had time and had been on other squads, I decided "why not?" I had nothing to lose but a lot to gain. Tryouts were not as hard as I thought, but I just knew I had to be on the squad. The tryout consisted of learning the routine they made up, making up your own routine, doing splits, and making a chant. Yet although these things were not that hard, I still was not sure whether I would make the team or not. The time came for the judges to make their decisions on who made the squad. Totaling the votes, they handed the results to the coach. She gave her speech that all coaches give. We were all good, but only a few could be picked for the team. As she started to read the names, I got hot. When she called my name, I was more than happy.

3. For hours we had been waiting under the overhang of an abandoned hut. None of us had thought to bring ponchos on our short hike through the woods. Soon it would be dark. Earlier in the day it had been a perfectly clear day. We all agreed that we didn't want to stand here all night in the dark, so we decided to make a dash for it.

Sharpening Sentences and Words

Next, turn your attention to sentences and words. You can improve your writing considerably by finding and correcting sentences that convey the wrong meaning or are stylistically deficient in some way. Consider, for example, the following sentences:

Just Mary was picked to write the report.

Mary was just picked to write the report.

Mary was picked to write just the report.

The first sentence says that no one except Mary will write the report; the second says that she was recently picked for the job; and the third says that she will write nothing else. Clearly, each of these sentences expresses a different meaning.

Now let's look at a second set of sentences:

Personally, I am of the opinion that the results of our membership drive will prove to be pleasing to all of us.

I believe the results of our membership drive will please all of us.

The wordiness of the first sentence slows the reader's pace and makes it harder to grasp the writer's meaning. The second sentence, by contrast, is much easier to grasp.

Like your sentences, your words should convey your thoughts precisely and clearly. Words are, after all, your chief means of communicating with your reader. Examine the first draft and revised version of the following paragraph, which describe the early morning actions of the writer's roommate. The highlighted words identify points of revision.

First Draft

Coffee cup in hand, she moves toward the bathroom. The coffee spills noisily on the tile floor as she reaches for the light switch and turns it on. After looking briefly at the face in the mirror, she walks toward the bathtub.

Revised Version

Coffee cup in hand, she stumbles toward the bathroom. Spilled coffee slaps on the tile floor as she gropes for the light switch and flips it on. After squinting briefly at the face in the mirror, she shuffles toward the bathtub.

Note that the words in the first draft are general and imprecise. Exactly how does she move? With a limp? With a strut? With a spring in her step? And what does "noisily" mean? A thud? A roar? A sharp crack? The reader has no way of knowing. Recognizing this fact, the student revised her paragraph, substituting vivid, specific words. As a result, the reader can visualize the actions more sharply.

Don't confuse vivid, specific words with "jawbreaker words"—those that are complex and pretentious. Words should promote communication, not block it.

Reading your draft aloud will force you to slow down, and you will often hear yourself stumble over problem sections. You'll be more likely to uncover errors such as missing words, excessive repetition, clumsy sentences, and sentence fragments. Be honest in your evaluation; don't read in virtues that aren't there or that exaggerate the writing quality. You can easily try different versions of your sentences and word choice by typing them directly in your document. Sometimes it is helpful to try several different versions on a new page or on a sheet of paper and insert the version that works best.

REVISION CHECKLIST FOR SENTENCES

- What sentences are not clearly expressed or logically constructed?
- What sentences seem awkward, excessively convoluted, or lacking in punch?
- What words require explanation or substitution because the reader may not know them?
- Where does my writing become wordy or use vague terms?
- Where have I carelessly omitted words or mistakenly used the wrong word?

MyWritingLab   **EXERCISE**   *Reread exercise paragraph 1 on page 70 and revise the sentence structure and word choice to create a more effective paragraph.*

Writing the Introduction, Conclusion, and Title

4.5

Write the introduction, conclusion, and title.

If you've put off writing your introduction and conclusion, do it now.

Writing the Introduction and Conclusion

Generally, short papers begin with a single paragraph that includes the previously drafted thesis statement, which sometimes needs to be rephrased so that it meshes smoothly with the rest of the paragraph. The introduction acquaints the reader with your topic; it should clearly signal your intention as well as spark the reader's interest. Pages 98–101 discuss and illustrate effective introductions. Consider drafting two or more versions of an introduction to see which works best.

The conclusion wraps up your discussion. Generally a single paragraph in short papers, a good ending summarizes or supports the paper's main idea. Pages 101–104 discuss and illustrate effective conclusions. Be willing to experiment as well with different conclusions.

Selecting a Title

Most essays require titles. Unless a good title unexpectedly surfaces while you are writing, wait until you finish the paper before choosing one. Since the reader must see the connection between what the title promises and what the essay delivers, a good title must be both accurate and specific.

Titling the essay "Cell Phone Use" would mislead the reader since this would seem to suggest that the essay is on how to use a cell phone. A specific title suggests the essay's focus rather than just its topic. For example, "The Reasons for College Cell Phone Fever" is a clearer and more precise title than simply "Cell Phone Use." The essay is about why cell phones are so extensively used, not about how they are to be used.

To engage your reader's interest, you might try your hand at a clever or catchy title, but don't get so carried away with creativity that you forget to relate the title to the paper's content. Following are some examples of common and clever titles:

Common	"Handling a Hangover"
Clever	"The Morning After"
Common	"Selecting the Proper Neckwear"
Clever	"How to Ring Your Neck"

Use a clever title only if its wit or humor doesn't clash with the overall purpose and tone of the paper.

Peer Evaluation of Drafts

4.6

Participate in peer evaluation and use peer responses in your own revision.

At various points in the writing process, your instructor may ask you and your classmates to read and respond to one another's papers. Peer response often proves useful because even the best writers cannot always predict how their readers will react to their writing. For example, magazine articles designed to reduce the fear of AIDS have, in some cases, increased anxiety about the disease. Furthermore, we often have difficulty seeing the problems with our own drafts because so much hard work has gone into them. What seems clear and effective to us can be confusing or boring to our readers. Comments from our peers can frequently launch a more effective essay.

Just as the responses of others help you, so will your responses help them. You don't have the close, involved relationship with your peers' writing that you do with your own. Therefore, you can gauge their drafts objectively. This type of critical evaluation will eventually heighten your awareness of your own writing's strengths and weaknesses. Knowing how to read your own work critically is one of the most important writing skills you can develop.

Responding to Your Peers' Drafts

Responding to someone else's writing is easier than you might imagine. It's not your job to spell out how to make the draft more effective, how to organize it, what to include, and what language to use. The writer must make these decisions. Your job is to *identify* problems, not *solve* them. You can do that best by responding honestly to the draft.

Some responses are more helpful than others. You don't help the writer by casually observing that the draft "looks O.K." Such a response doesn't point to problem areas; rather it suggests that you didn't read the paper carefully and critically. Wouldn't you inform a friend who was wearing clothes that looked terrible *why* they looked terrible? The same attitude should prevail about writing, something that makes a statement just as clothes do. Nor is a vague comment helpful, such as "The introduction is uninteresting." Point out *why* it is uninteresting.

For instance, you might note that "The introduction doesn't interest me in the paper because it is very technical, and I get lost. I ask myself why I should read on." Following are two more examples of ineffective responses and their more effective counterparts.

Ineffective

The paper was confusing.

Effective

Paragraphs 2, 3, and 4 confused me. You jumped around too much. First, you wrote about your experience on the first day of college, then you went on to how much you enjoyed junior high school, and finally you wrote about what you want to do for a career. I don't see how these ideas relate or why they are in the order that they are.

Ineffective

More examples would help.

Effective

When you indicate that college is a scary place, I get no real idea of why or how. What are the things that you think make college scary? I would like some examples.

Here are some steps to follow when responding to someone else's draft. First, read the essay from beginning to end without interruption. On a separate sheet of paper, indicate what you consider to be the main idea. The writer can then see whether the intended message has come through. Next, identify the biggest problem and the biggest strength. Writers need both negative and positive comments. Finally, reread the paper and write either specific responses to each paragraph or your responses to general questions such as the ones that follow. In either case, don't comment on spelling or grammar unless it really inhibits your reading.

PEER RESPONSE CHECKLIST

- What is the main point of this essay?
- What is the biggest problem?
- What is the biggest strength?
- What material doesn't seem to fit the main point or the audience?
- What questions has the author not answered?
- Where should more details or examples be added? Why?
- At what point does the paper fail to hold my interest? Why?
- Where is the organization confusing?
- Where is the writing unclear or vague?

As you learn the various strategies for successful writing, new concerns will arise. Questions geared to these concerns appear in the revision section that concludes the discussion of each strategy.

An Example of Peer Response in Response to "Cell Phone Use"

What is the main point of this essay?

There are many reasons students use cell phones so extensively, including to coordinate activities, get business done, share with others, keep in touch.

What is the biggest problem?

I didn't really know what was meant by this idea of the immediate now. Where did this idea come from? In what ways do we share the same now. Is this different from keeping in touch?

What is the biggest strength?

The reasons in the paper ring true to my experience, especially with the examples that are used.

What doesn't seem to fit the main point or the audience?

The material on the babysitter doesn't seem to fit or seem likely for most college students. Is walking back to the dorm getting something done? How many students really do that? Doesn't it make you even more vulnerable?

Where should more details or examples be added? Why?

The introduction is kind of boring. An example would make it more real. Also, more details about the paragraph would make it clearer. Isn't the paper missing something about a really important reason which is simply that everyone is doing it?

Where is the writing unclear or vague?

The writing is pretty clear. But some places could be clearer in the intro. Which "some" and "most" do you mean? Some sentences could be tightened up like "Jim needs to contact his advisor. . ." Your pronouns jump around. Sometimes you use "we" and sometimes "students" and "they."

Acting on Your Peers' Responses

Sometimes you need strong nerves to act on a peer response. You can easily become defensive or discount your reader's comments as foolish. Remember, however, that as a writer you are trying to communicate with your readers, and that means taking seriously the problems they identify. Of course, you decide which responses are appropriate, but even an inappropriate criticism sometimes sets off a train of thought that leads to good ideas for revision.

As you read the final version of Drew's paper on cell phones, carefully examine the margin notes, which highlight key features of the revision. Drew added an example to the introduction to make it more interesting, added a section on how the common use of cell phones has an impact, and clarified the paragraph on "the now." He has cut the material on babysitters and walking across campus that his readers found inappropriate. He has tightened his language by sharpening his sentences and his word choice in a few places and using more consistent pronouns.

Changed title to make it more focused.

Added short conversation to make the essay more interesting.

Added sentence with more active verbs to capture scene.

Clarified the "some."

Added trend that is a later paragraph.

Clarified the word "necessary" by expanding idea.

Simplified language. Throughout, language consistently uses student and they, not we.

CASE HISTORY   **The Reasons for College Cell Phone Fever Final Draft**

At the end of their college classes, students check their cell phones almost before they are out of the room.

"Hey, just got out of English."

"What ya goin' to do?"

"Get some coffee and study before Biology. You?"

"Got Intro to Business in ten minutes."

"Well, see ya."

These conversations seem far from necessary. Yet students plow their way from class to class with their cell phones glued to their ears. Professors and parents are confused by this practice. Some parents complain that young people are so wrapped up in their cell conversations that they completely miss the world around them. Many wonder why students are compulsive cell phone users. There are many reasons students wander around campus talking into the air. They use cell phones to coordinate the day's activities, to get business done, to share life's events, and to keep in touch. Part of this trend, undeniably, is that many others are also doing it. The large number of college students who wander around talking into their phones, ignoring the people around them, may seem ridiculous to an outsider. However, in the end this cell phone mania is a reasonable, pleasurable, and vital part of college life.

It is hard to imagine how people managed their lives without cell phones since there is so much to coordinate. Weren't friends going to meet after class for a study session? Where is everybody? A quick call reveals that the study session was moved to the student center. Does everyone have his or her part ready for the presentation in Speech class at 3:00 P.M.? A flurry of calls makes certain everyone is ready. Will Collin be able to meet his girlfriend this afternoon? He needs to call to see if she is still free. Where is Jennifer since she said she was picking me up in front of the Science Building?

College life can be hectic as students juggle classes, work, meal times, and a social life. A quick phone call can organize it all: arrange study sessions, confirm a lunch date, arrange a ride, coordinate a team project for class, and maybe even make time for a date.

Sometimes cell phone calls get important business done. Heather needs to convince her parents that she really, really needs more money to cover the cost of books. Tim needs to ask his adviser to lift his holds so he can schedule next semester's classes. Students, like everyone else, need to call about possible jobs, resolve bill disputes, arrange to have their car repaired and find out medical test results. Cell phones let them get all this done in the time between classes or while walking back to their dorms, leaving them with more time for other things like studying or going out with friends.

Everyone likes to share moments of delight, success, and even failure with others who care. When a baby is expected, the expectant grandparents can't wait for the call. Cell phones let people share. At concerts, some in the audience call up friends and then hold up the phone so that they can hear part of a concert. When something really funny is happening, anyone can with a quick call share it with someone else who would appreciate the moment. If students get an unexpected A, they can quickly spread the celebration to those who would echo their joy. Sometimes a cell phone call can make the sharing very concrete, getting someone to go outside to look at a spectacular meteor shower, getting a friend to change channels to see an interview with a favorite rock star, or letting family know about a terrible earthquake in China. Cell phones allow an immediate connection to let people experience what callers are experiencing, whether it is excitement over a success, a great idea, the finals of a sporting event, or a news event.

Cell phone calls can let people stay in touch with each other. Most phone calls are very short, over before students have gotten from the classroom to the door of the building. "Hey, what's up?" "What are you doing?" "How are you?"

Continued on next page

Changed language to tighten "life in college" to "college life."

Tightened sentence by cutting wordiness.

Tightened language.

Cut the line about walking across campus at night.

Changed pronouns to be consistent.

Cut unnecessary phrase "while the feeling was still hot."

Changed from any idea to a "great idea," more likely to be shared.

Continued from previous page

"Answer" is chosen as a better word than "response."

Little information is exchanged and little is really shared. "Nothing much," in fact, is a common answer. What do such phone calls accomplish? They let people keep in touch with each other. Contact is what helps keep people close. Parents like their children to visit. Couples need to make time for each other. When people keep in touch, it lets them know that others care, lets them keep each other as important parts of their lives. Some students call their parents every day to maintain family ties while getting the emotional reassurance of those loving connections. Couples hold electronic hands as they walk across campus. Friends may not be able to see each other since they are going to different colleges, but a simple cell phone confirms their continued friendship.

Provided a context for the paragraph. Reworded to be clearer.

A sociology professor told her class that she thought that the cell phone "created a virtual society of now." Cell phones create a feeling that all are in it together at the same time, even if in different places. Instead of having to wait to find out what might be happening, students can be part of the same now. A quick phone call has one person getting out of bed while another is getting out of class. Two friends seated at different ends of a stadium can enjoy the blow by blow of the action at the same time. Anyone can know what almost anyone else in their call list is doing at any moment. A clip from a news story on television about cosmetic surgery conveyed this perfectly. A woman is talking on her cell phone while she is undergoing liposuction. "Yeh," she declares, "I am undergoing surgery right now. No, I don't feel much, maybe just a tickle." It is hard to get more immediate than that.

Added a very specific example to make the idea clearer.

Added a specific example.

All of this is made possible because others are doing it. Teenagers are notorious for doing what others are doing. Parents ask, "If your friends jumped off a bridge, would you do it too?" The answer is an embarrassing "yes," especially if the jumpers were attached to bungee cords. It would be embarrassing not to have a cell phone, ideally an Android or an iPhone or whatever is the latest trend. Everyone else seems to be talking while walking. So using cell phones right after class, between classes, during lunch, or at a concert just

Added a phrase to be memorable.

Added specific idea to explain concept.

seems to be normal behavior—and most people want to be normal. Besides, if students are lucky enough to have good friends, their friends are probably calling them; and if friends are calling, it is important to call them back.

It must have been lonely to wait an entire day before bragging to friends and family about getting the only A on a chemistry test. It is almost incomprehensible that students managed their complex schedules before cell phones. What did a student do if a ride didn't show up? How did people share the excitement of a concert in the moment or a good joke if they had to wait days? Earlier generations who seem puzzled by the cell phone fever that has hit college campuses might wonder how they might have felt without a phone, having to wait for weeks for the mail or longer for a visit. It should not be surprising that students pull out their cell phones at the end of class. The surprise would be if they kept their cell phones in their pockets and waited.

ACTING ON PEER RESPONSE CHECKLIST

- Did the readers understand my main point? If not, how can I make it clearer?
- What did they see as the main problem? Can I solve it?
- What strengths did they identify that I can keep?
- What didn't fit that I need to cut or make clearer?
- Which reader's questions should I answer more completely?
- Where should I add details or examples?
- How could I make sections that lose my reader's interest more engaging, or should I cut those sections?
- Why did my readers find some sections confusing? How could I reorganize those sections?
- Where could I rewrite sections to make them clearer?

Proofreading Your Draft

After revising your draft, proofread or edit it to correct errors in grammar, punctuation, and spelling. Effective proofreading is essential since even a few errors quickly detract from the credibility of your work. Since we often overlook our own errors simply because we know what we meant, proofreading can be difficult. Even after you have checked your paper using spell and grammar check, inch through your draft deliberately, moving your finger along slowly under every word. Remember spell check does not catch if you have used the wrong word such as "there" for "their." Grammar check still requires you to make decisions; it does not catch awkward sentences that are grammatical. Ideally follow the above process several times, looking first for errors in grammar, then for sentence errors and problems in punctuation and mechanics, and finally for mistakes in spelling. Be especially alert for problems that have plagued your writing in the past.

Effective proofreading calls for you to assume a detective role and probe for errors that weaken your writing. If you accept the challenge, you will certainly improve the quality of your finished work.

Collaborative Writing

4.7

Write collaboratively with others using multimedia.

In many careers you'll have to work as part of a group to produce a single document. Recognizing this fact, many instructors assign collaborative writing projects. Writing as part of a group offers some advantages and poses some challenges. You can draw on many different perspectives and areas of expertise, split up the work, and enjoy the feedback of a built-in peer group. On the other hand, you must also coordinate several efforts, resolve conflicts over the direction of the project, deal with people who may not do their fair share, and integrate different styles of writing.

Even though you write as part of a group, the final product should read as though it were written by one person. Therefore, take great pains to ensure that the paper doesn't resemble a patchwork quilt. You can help achieve this goal by following the principles of good writing discussed throughout this book. Following are some suggestions for successful collaborative work:

1. Select a leader with strong organizational skills.
2. Make sure each person has every other group member's phone number and e-mail address.
3. Analyze the project and develop a work plan with clearly stated deadlines for each step of the project.
4. Assign tasks on the basis of people's interests and expertise.
5. Schedule regular meetings to gauge each person's progress.
6. Encourage ideas and feedback from all members at each meeting.
7. If each member will develop a part of the paper, submit each one's contribution to the other members of the group for peer evaluation. This can be done electronically.
8. To ensure that the finished product is written in one style and fits together as a whole, give each member's draft to one person and ask him or her to write a complete draft.
9. Allow plenty of time to review the draft so necessary changes can be made.

Collaborative writing provides an opportunity to learn a great deal from other students. Problems can arise, however, if one or more group members don't do their work or skip meetings entirely. This irresponsibility compromises everyone's grade. The group should insist that all members participate, and the leader should immediately contact anyone who misses a meeting. If a serious problem develops despite these efforts, contact your instructor.

Collaboration Using Electronic and Social Media

Many college students and professionals use social media (including e-mail, chat rooms, Facebook, and even text-messaging) to collaborate on writing process. To illustrate:

1. Post a general idea on Facebook so others can add comments on possible topics.
2. E-mail each other information you find, possibly as an attachment in an agreed upon version such as Word.
3. Use a chat room to discuss ideas for the project.
4. Text message your thesis statement to friends to see if it is effective and get feedback.
5. Copy sections of the project into Notes in Facebook or e-mail the sections in an attachment.
6. Share the final document as an attachment.
7. MindMeister and other Web programs allow you to build mind maps and brainstorm with others.
8. Google Docs allows participants to share documents for free and edit them just like a Word document, only online. This is a common tool of most professions.
9. Wikis, such as wikispaces.com or the Wikis spaces that come with many electronic learning environments, provide a common space where writers can post brainstorming, add visuals or information, post entire text online, and edit each other's work. Wikis are especially easy to use.

Whenever you use available media for collaborative writing, it's a good idea to designate a project leader who will ensure that all members participate and who will receive and distribute all materials. Your instructor may request copies of the e-mail exchanges or access to your Web-based collaboration in order to follow your work.

Maintaining and Reviewing a Portfolio

A portfolio is an organized collection of your writing, usually kept in a three-ring binder or folder. It's a good idea to retain all your work for each class, including the assignment sheet, your prewriting, and all your drafts. Organize this material either in the order the papers were completed or by type of assignment.

Why assemble a portfolio? Not only can a portfolio be a source of ideas for future writing, but it also allows you to review the progress of your current papers. In addition, should any confusion arise about a grade or an assignment, the contents of your portfolio can quickly clarify matters.

4.8

Assemble and maintain a portfolio of your writing.

Some instructors will require you to maintain a portfolio. They will probably specify both what is to be included and how it is to be organized. They may use the portfolio to help you gain a better understanding of your strengths and weaknesses. Furthermore, portfolios give your instructor a complete picture of your work. Some departments collect student portfolios to assess their writing program; by reviewing student progress, instructors can determine what adjustments will make the program even more effective. Increasingly, colleges may have you maintain a portfolio using a Web-based program. If your school has you maintain an electronic portfolio, you will receive clear instructions about the process. Do not be afraid to ask questions about this process.

You can review your own portfolio to gain a better understanding of your writing capabilities. Answer these questions as you look over your materials:

1. With what assignments or topics was I most successful? Why?
2. What assignments or topics gave me the most problems? Why?
3. How has my prewriting changed? How can I make it more effective?
4. How has my planning changed? How can I make it more effective?
5. What makes my best writing good? How does this writing differ from my other work?
6. What are the problem areas in my weakest writing? How does this writing differ from my other work?
7. Did I use the checklists in the back of this text to revise my papers? Do I make significant changes on my own, in response to peer evaluation, or in response to my instructor's comments? If not, why not? What kinds of changes do I make? What changes would improve the quality of my work?
8. What organizational patterns have I used? Which ones have been effective? Why? Which ones have given me trouble? Why?
9. What kinds of introductions have I used? What other options do I have?
10. What kinds of grammar or spelling errors mar my writing? (Focus on these errors in future proofreading.)

Revising Your Paper

Prepare to revise.

- Distance yourself from your writing.
- Jot down your initial plans for your writing and ideas that came to mind.
- Talk about your paper with others.
- Read peer response and judge what makes sense.

Revise your whole essay.

- Discover new directions.
- Find what *FITS* and doesn't.
- *ADD* to develop and clarify.
- *CUT* what doesn't help.
- *TEST* the organization and restructure and add transitions.

Revise your paragraphs.

- Read out loud if it is helpful.
- Pay attention to where you stumble and what doesn't sound good.
- Slow down your reading to revise so you don't skim.

- Fit the thesis.
- Focus on central idea.
- Add detail as necessary.
- Cut what doesn't fit.
- Reorganize for easier flow.

Strengthen words and sentences.

- Use more precise and vivid words.
- Make sure sentences mean what you want.
- Cut excess wordiness.

Repeat entire process or parts as needed.

Proofread your paper.

CHAPTER 5

Paragraphs

In this chapter, you will learn how to:

5.1 Create effective paragraphs that have unity.

5.2 Apply different strategies for the placement of topic sentences.

5.3 Write paragraphs that are well developed.

5.4 Use a variety of paragraph organizational patterns.

5.5 Achieve coherence in your paragraphs.

5.6 Write introduction, transition, and conclusion paragraphs using a variety of strategies.

Visit MyWritingLab **to complete the writing assignments in this chapter and for more resources on paragraphs.**

Imagine the difficulty of reading a magazine article or book if you were faced with one solid block of text. How could you sort its ideas or know the best places to pause for thought? Paragraphs help guide readers through longer pieces of writing.

- Some break lengthy discussions of one idea into segments of different emphasis, thus providing rest stops for readers.
- Others consolidate several briefly developed ideas. Yet others begin or end pieces of writing or link major segments together.
- Most paragraphs, though, include a number of sentences that develop and clarify one idea.

Throughout a piece of writing, paragraphs relate to one another and reflect a controlling purpose. To make paragraphs fit together smoothly, you can't just sit down and dash them off. Instead, you first need to reflect on the entire essay, then channel your thoughts toward its different segments. Often you'll have to revise your paragraphs after you've written a draft.

Effective paragraphs are unified, contain a topic sentence, exhibit adequate development, offer clear organization, and exhibit coherence.

Unity

A paragraph with unity develops one, and only one, key controlling idea. To ensure unity, edit out any stray ideas that don't belong and fight the urge to take interesting but irrelevant side trips; they only create confusion about your destination.

5.1

Create effective paragraphs that have unity.

The following paragraph *lacks unity*:

> The Montessori Method for teaching math in the earliest grades builds on the child's natural link to physical objects and concrete learning. Spelling and reading are also taught with special materials. It was the psychologist Piaget who recognized that there were different kinds of cognition from the concrete to the more abstract. Maria Montessori was a pioneer in applying insights into how children actually think to the classroom.

What exactly is this writer trying to say? We can't tell. Each sentence expresses a different, undeveloped idea:

1. The use of concrete materials to teach math.
2. The use of special materials to teach spelling and reading.
3. Piaget's contribution in identifying levels of intelligence.
4. Maria Montessori's contribution to education.

In contrast, the following paragraph develops and clarifies only one central idea, the Montessori Method's use of concrete materials to teach math:

> The Montessori Method for teaching math in the earliest grades builds on the child's natural link to physical objects and concrete learning. Children count out unit beads. When they reach 10 unit beads, they can exchange them for a ten-bar, a line of 10 linked beads. Ten ten-bars can be exchanged for one one-hundred square. By physically placing unit beads, ten-lines, and hundred-squares on a mat, children quickly learn about the units, tens, and hundreds place and how to carry. These concrete tools can also help children learn addition and subtraction. Children lay out a number like 236 on a mat as well as the number 165. They add them together, counting up the five and the six to get eleven and exchanging 10 unit-beads for the ten-bar leaving one unit bead, adding up the now 10 ten-bars and exchanging them for a hundred-square and then reading out the resulting number of 401. While the description of the procedure may sound complicated, the actual process of using these concrete materials to understand addition and carrying is easy for children to grasp.
>
> Diane Honegger, student

Because no unrelated ideas sidetrack the discussion, the paragraph has unity. To check your paragraphs for unity, ask yourself what each one aims to do and whether each sentence helps that aim.

MyWritingLab   **EXERCISE** *After reading the next two paragraphs, answer the questions that follow.*

1. The legend—in Africa—that all elephants over a large geographical area go to a common "graveyard" when they sense death is approaching led many hunters to treat them with special cruelty. Ivory hunters, believing the myth and trying to locate such graveyards, often intentionally wounded an elephant in the hopes of following the suffering beast as it made its way to the place where it wanted to die. The idea was to wound the elephant seriously enough so that it thought it was going to die but not so seriously that it died in a very short time. All too often, the process resulted in a single elephant being shot or speared many times and relentlessly pursued until it either fell dead or was killed when it finally turned and charged its attackers. In any case, no wounded elephant ever led its pursuers to the mythical graveyard with its hoped-for booty of ivory tusks.

   Kris Hurrell, student

2. It is not surprising that the sales figures for CDs keep slumping since it is easier and more convenient to download the music buyers want from the Internet. The online music stores, such as iTunes, are very easy to use with simple instructions for searching for music and making purchases. Music fans can quickly find the performers or albums of their choice, even obscure works, from the convenience of their living room without having to drive from store to store. Then they can buy either the songs or entire albums that interest them. Once downloaded, they can either burn a CD to play on more traditional stereos or copy the music to an mp3 player of some kind. The effects have been devastating on the music retail industry. Major stores such as Tower Records went out of business. Barnes and Noble has cut back on the number of CDs that the chain sells. The shift to online distribution of music has had the added advantage of allowing alternative groups to present their music that they would have had trouble getting made into CDs and distributed through major chains. This also ends the potential impact of major chains such as Wal-Mart on what music is sold.

   Anonymous, student

1. Which of these paragraphs lacks unity? Refer to the paragraphs when answering.
2. How would you improve the paragraph that lacks unity?

The Topic Sentence

5.2

Apply different strategies for the placement of topic sentences.

The topic sentence states the main idea of the paragraph. Think of the topic sentence as a rallying point, with all supporting sentences developing the idea it expresses. A good topic sentence helps you gauge what information belongs in a paragraph, thus ensuring unity. At the same time, it informs your reader about the point you're making.

Placement of the topic sentence varies from paragraph to paragraph, as the following examples show. As you read each, note how supporting information develops the topic sentence, which is highlighted.

Topic Sentence Stated First   Many paragraphs open with the topic sentence. The writer reveals the central idea immediately and then builds from a solid base.

> It has long been my belief that everyone's library contains an Odd Shelf. On this shelf rests a small, mysterious corpus of volume whose subject matter is completely unrelated to the rest of the library, yet which, upon close inspection, reveals a good deal about its owner. George Orwell's Odd Shelf held a collection of bound sets of ladies' magazines from the 1860's, which he liked to read in his bathtub. Philip Larkin had an especially capacious Odd Shelf crammed with pornography, with an emphasis on spanking. Vice Admiral James Stockdale, having heard that Frederick the Great had never embarked on a campaign without his copy of *The Encheiridion*, brought to Vietnam the complete works of Epictetus, whose Stoic philosophy was to sustain him through eight years as a prisoner of war.
>
> Anne Fadiman, *Ex Libris: Confessions of a Common Reader*

Topic Sentence Stated Last   In order to emphasize the support and build gradually to a conclusion, a topic sentence can end the paragraph. This position creates suspense as the reader anticipates the summarizing remark.

> One of the biggest of the Big Questions of existence is, Are (sic) we alone in the universe? Science has provided no convincing evidence one way or the other. It is certainly possible that life began with a bizarre quirk of chemistry, an accident so improbable that it happened only once in the entire observable universe, and we are it. On the other hand, maybe life gets going wherever there are Earthlike planets. We just don't know, (sic) because we have a sample of only one. However, no known scientific principle suggests an inbuilt drive from matter to life. No known law of physics or chemistry favors the emergence of the living state over other states. Physics and chemistry are, as far as we can tell, "life blind."
>
> Paul C. W. Davies, *What We Believe But Cannot Prove*

Topic Sentence Stated First and Last   Some paragraphs lead with the main idea and then restate it, usually in different words, at the end. This technique allows the writer to repeat an especially important idea.

> If schoolchildren ever learn anything about this far-flung place, it is usually no more than the events on Signal Hill. From the ordinary square-mile of granite, the modern world seemed to launch itself. First, Guglielmo Marconi clambered up there in 1901, and received the first radio-waves skittering over the ocean. Then came Alcock and Brown in their preposterous aeroplane, and Charles Lindbergh, en route from New York. But this isn't Newfoundland's story, more the history of passersby. As to what happened in the other 41,999 square miles of Newfoundland, or in Labrador, this is a blank that most children will carry into adulthood.
>
> John Gimlett, *Theater of Fish: Travels Through Newfoundland and Labrador*

Topic Sentence Stated in the Middle   On occasion, the topic sentence falls between one set of sentences that provides background information and a follow-up set that develops the central idea. This arrangement allows the writer to shift the emphasis and at the same time preserve close ties between the two sets.

> Priming people with suggestions can be useful in certain cases. For older folks, it can help them recover real memories. So many elderly people seem unable to "put their finger on" a past experience. But often this is not because the memory has been erased; it's just that the person can't initiate the process of retrieving it. Give such people a beginning—some fact to organize around—and they can then pull all the pieces together. They can remember the word, the name, and the action, and then feel very much relieved. Aging is the most common factor that compromises the memory of us all, and its effects are being studied intensively.
>
> John J. Tratey, M.D., *A User's Guide to the Brain*

Topic Sentence Implied   Some paragraphs, particularly in narrative and descriptive writing, have no topic sentence. Rather, all sentences point toward a main idea that readers must grasp for themselves.

> [Captain Robert Barclay] once went out at 5 in the morning to do a little grouse shooting. He walked at least 30 miles while he potted away, and then after dinner set out on a walk of 60 miles that he accomplished in 11 hours without a halt. Barclay did not sleep after this but went through the following day as if nothing had happened until the afternoon, when he walked 16 miles to a ball. He danced all night, and then in early morning walked home and spent a day partridge shooting. Finally, he did get to bed—but only after a period of two nights and nearly three days had elapsed and he had walked 130 miles.
>
> John Lovesey, "A Myth Is As Good As a Mile"

The details in this paragraph collectively suggest a clear central idea: that Barclay had incredible physical endurance. But writing effective paragraphs without topic sentences challenges even the best writers. Therefore, control most of your paragraphs with clearly expressed topic sentences.

MyWritingLab   **EXERCISE**   *Identify the topic sentences in each of the following paragraphs and explain how you arrived at your decisions. If the topic sentence is implied, state the central idea in your own words.*

1. Last winter, while leafing through the *Guinness Book of World Records*, I came across an item stating that the tallest sunflower ever had been grown by G. E. Hocking, an Englishman. Fired by a competitive urge, I planted a half acre of sunflower seeds. That half acre is now a magnificent 22,000 square feet of green and gold flowers. From the elevated rear deck of my apartment, I can look out over the swaying mass of thick, hairy green stalks and see each stalk thrusting up through the darker heart-shaped leaves below and supporting an ever-bobbing imitation of the sun. In this dwarf forest, some of the flower heads measure almost a foot in diameter. Though almost all my plants are now blooming, none will top the sixteen feet, two inches reached by Hocking's plant. My tallest is just thirteen feet even, but I

don't think that's too bad for the first attempt. Next year, however, will be another matter. I plan to have an automatic watering system to feed my babies.

Joseph Wheeler, student

2. At the most fundamental level, scientific explanation of the world is akin to the process of reading and writing. Whether studying skull structures, geological layers, or bird populations, scientists were deciphering sign systems and interpreting texts. Both the geologist Charles Lyell and the neurobiologist Santiago Ramón y Cajal compared themselves with the linguist Jean François Champollion, who decoded the Egyptian hieroglyphics on the Rosetta stone. Highly conscious of their roles as communicators, scientists did not need critics like Arnold to point out their affinity to ordinary writers. They illustrated it themselves in their own text.

Laura Otis, Literature and Science in the Nineteenth Century

3. The first hostage to be brought off the plane was a dark little man with a bald head and a moustache so thick and black that it obliterated his mouth. Four of the masked terrorists were guarding him closely, each with a heavy rifle held ready for fire. When the group was about fifty feet from the plane, a second hostage, a young woman in flowered slacks and a red blouse, was brought out in clear view by a single terrorist, who held a pistol against the side of her head. Then the first four pushed the dark little man from them and instructed him to kneel on the pavement. They looked at him as they might an insect. But he sat there on his knees, seemingly as indifferent as if he had already taken leave of his body. The shots from the four rifles sounded faintly at the far end of the field where a group of horrified spectators watched the grisly proceedings.

Bradley Willis, student

EXERCISE   My WritingLab

1. Develop one of the following ideas into a topic sentence. Then write a unified paragraph that is built around it.
   a. The career (or job or profession) I want is _____.
   b. The one quality most necessary in my chosen field is _____.
   c. The most difficult aspect of my chosen field is _____.
   d. One good example of the American tendency to waste is _____.
   e. The best (or worst) thing about fast-food restaurants is _____.
   f. The college course I find most useful (or interesting) is _____.
   g. Concentration (or substitute your own term here) is an important part of a successful golf game (or substitute your own sport) _____.
   h. The one place where I feel most at home is _____.
   i. More than anything else, owning a pet (or growing a garden) involves _____.

2. Write a topic sentence that would control a paragraph on each of the following:
   a. Preparations for traveling away from home
   b. Advantages of having your own room
   c. Some landmark of the community in which you live
   d. The price of long-distance telephone calls
   e. Registering for college courses
   f. A cherished memento or souvenir
   g. High school graduation
   h. New Year's resolutions

Adequate Development

5.3

Write paragraphs that are well developed.

Students often ask for guidelines on paragraph length: "Should I aim for fifty to sixty words? Seven to ten sentences? About one-fourth of a page?" The questions are natural, but the approach is wrong. Instead of targeting a particular length, ask yourself what the reader needs to know. Then supply enough information to make your point clearly. Developing a paragraph inadequately is like inviting guests to a party but failing to tell them when and where it will be held. Skimpy paragraphs force readers to fill in the gaps for themselves, a task that can both irritate and stump them. On the other hand, a paragraph stuffed with useless padding dilutes the main idea. In all cases, the reader, the information being presented, and the publication medium determine the proper amount of detail. A newspaper might feature short paragraphs including only key facts, whereas a scientific journal might have lengthy paragraphs that offer detailed development of facts.

The details you supply can include facts, figures, thoughts, observations, steps, lists, examples, and personal experiences. Individually, these bits of information may mean little, but together they clearly illustrate your point. Keep in mind, however, that development isn't an end in itself but instead advances the purpose of the entire essay. Still, less experienced writers often produce underdeveloped paragraphs. Look for places where you can specifically add a clarifying explanation, a detailed example, or a more complete account of an already provided example. You might want to take weak paragraphs and brainstorm for additional details.

Following are two versions of a paragraph, the first inadequately developed:

Underdeveloped Paragraph

Most of the delegates to the Constitutional Convention of 1787 feared too much democracy. As a result, they drafted the Constitution as a document outlining a limited democracy. Indeed, some of the provisions were simply undemocratic. But despite reflecting the delegates' distrust of popular rule, the Constitution did provide a framework in which democracy could evolve.

Adequately Developed Paragraph

Most of the delegates to the Constitutional Convention of 1787 feared too much democracy. As a result, they drafted the Constitution as a document outlining a limited democracy. Indeed, some of the provisions were simply undemocratic: universal suffrage was denied; voting qualifications were left to the states; and women, blacks, and persons without property were denied the federal franchise. Until the passage of the Seventeenth Amendment in 1913, senators were not popularly elected but were chosen by state legislators. But despite reflecting the delegates' distrust of popular rule, the Constitution did provide a framework in which democracy could evolve.

The first paragraph lacks examples of undemocratic provisions, whereas the second one provides the needed information.

Readability also helps set paragraph length. Within a paper, paragraphs signal natural dividing places, allowing the reader to pause and absorb the material presented up to that point. Too little paragraphing overwhelms the reader with long blocks of material. Too much creates a choppy effect that may seem simplistic, even irritating. To counter these problems, writers sometimes use several paragraphs for an idea that needs extended development, or they combine several short paragraphs into one.

EXERCISE

MyWritingLab

1. **Indicate where the ideas in this long block of material divide logically; explain your choices.**

    During the summer following graduation from high school, I could hardly wait to get to college and "be on my own." In my first weeks at State University, however, I found that independence can be tough and painful. I had expected raucous good times and a carefree collegiate life, the sort depicted in old beach movies and suggested by the selective memories of sentimental alumni. Instead, all I felt at first was the burden of increasing responsibilities and the loneliness of "a man without a country." I discovered that being independent of parents who kept at me to do my homework and expected me to accomplish certain household chores did not mean I was free to do as I pleased. On the contrary, living on my own meant that I had to perform for myself all the tasks that the family used to share. Studying became a full-time occupation rather than a nightly duty to be accomplished in an hour or two, and my college instructors made it clear that they would have little sympathy for negligence or even for my inability to do an assignment. But what was more troubling about my early college life than having to do laundry, prepare meals, and complete stacks of homework was the terrifying sense of being entirely alone. I was independent, no longer a part of the world that had seemed to confine me, but I soon realized that confinement had also meant security. I never liked the feeling that people were watching over me, but I knew that my family and friends were also watching out for me—and that's a good feeling to have. At the university no one seemed particularly to be watching, though professors constantly evaluated the quality of my work. I felt estranged from people in those first weeks of college life, desperately needing a confidant but fearful that the new and tenuous friendships I had made would be damaged if I were to confess my fears and problems. It was simply too early for me to feel a part of the university. So there I was, independent in the fullest sense, and thus "a man without a country."

2. **The following short, choppy units are inadequately developed. List some details you could use to expand one of them into a good paragraph.**

    I like living in a small town because the people are so friendly. In addition, I can always get the latest gossip from the local busybody.

    In a big city, people are afraid to get too friendly. Everything is very private, and nobody knows anything about anybody else.

3. **Scan the compositions you have written in other classes for paragraphs that are over- or underdeveloped. Revise any you find.**

Organization

5.4

Use a variety of paragraph organizational patterns.

An effective paragraph unfolds in a clear pattern of organization so that the reader can easily follow the flow of ideas. Usually when you write your first draft, your attempt to organize your thoughts will also organize your paragraphs. Writers do not ordinarily stop to decide on a strategy for each paragraph. But when you revise or are stuck, it's useful to understand the available choices. Here are some options:

1. The strategies discussed in Chapters 8–16
2. Order of climax

The choice you make depends upon your material and purpose in writing.

Writing Strategies   These include all of the following patterns:

- Time sequence (narration)
- Space sequence (description)
- Process analysis
- Illustration
- Classification

- Comparison
- Cause and effect
- Definition
- Argument

Four example paragraphs follow. The first, organized by *time sequence*, traces the sequence of a horrifying failed rescue attempt at sea.

> I once read a story about a sailor who was washed overboard while rounding the Horn on a clipper ship. His shipmates immediately lowered a boat, and a few of them rowed to the rescue while the remainder of the crew dropped sail and brought the ship into the wind. The boat crew plucked the hapless sailor out of the sea, but the small boat broached on a steep breaking wave and capsized. As the men clung to the upturned keel, a flock of albatrosses circled overhead. The lookout on the main ship watched with horror as one of the birds dove, landed on a man's head, and plucked out his eyes. Then a second bird dove, and a third. Another rescue boat was dispatched, but the lines became tangled in the davits as the mother ship drifted downwind. The lost time was fatal. Blinded and bloody, the men in the water untied their life vests and one by one dove to their deaths rather than face the continued assaults.
>
> Jon Turk, *Cold Oceans: Adventures in Kayaks, Rowboat, and Dogsled*

The next paragraph, organized by *space sequence*, describes a ceramic elf, starting from the bottom and working up to the top. Other common spatial arrangements include top to bottom, left to right, right to left, nearby to far away, far away to nearby, clockwise, and counterclockwise.

> The ceramic elf in our family room is quite a character. His reddish-brown slippers, which hang over the mantel shelf, taper to a slender point. Pudgy, yellow-stockinged legs disappear into a wrinkled tunic-style, olive-green jacket, gathered at the waist with a thick, brown belt that fits snugly around his roly-poly belly. His

short, meaty arms hang comfortably, one hand resting on the knapsack at his side and the other clutching the bowl of an old black pipe. An unkempt, snow-white beard, dotted by occasional snarls, trails patriarch-fashion from his lower lip to his belt line. A button nose capped with a smudge of gold dust, mischievous black eyes, and an unruly snatch of hair peeking out from under his burnt-orange stocking cap complete Bartholomew's appearance.

Maria Sanchez, student

Although descriptive paragraphs, like those developed by narration, often lack topic sentences, our example leads off with the central idea.

Here is a paragraph showing *process* development.

Making beer nuts is a quick, simple procedure that provides a delicious evening snack. You'll need six cups of raw peanuts, three cups of sugar, and one-and-one-half cups of water. To begin, combine the sugar and water in a two-quart saucepan and stir to dissolve the sugar. Next, add the peanuts and stir again until all of the peanuts are covered by the sugar-water solution. Leave the pan, uncovered, on a burner set at medium-high heat for ten to twelve minutes, until the sugar crystallizes and coats the peanuts thoroughly. Stay at the stove during the heating process and stir the mixture every two or three minutes to ensure even coating of the nuts. When the peanuts are thoroughly coated, pour them onto an ungreased cookie sheet and bake at 350 degrees for about thirty minutes, stirring and lightly salting at ten-minute intervals. Serve your beer nuts fresh out of the oven or eat them at room temperature.

Kimberlee Walters, student

Again, the topic sentence comes first.

The final example illustrates development by *comparison* and also proceeds from an opening topic sentence.

Taken together, we found that both intoxicated drivers and cell phone drivers performed differently from baseline and that the driving profiles of these two conditions differed. Drivers using a cell phone exhibited a delay in their response to events in the driving scenario and were more likely to be involved in a traffic accident. Drivers in the alcohol condition exhibited a more aggressive driving style, following closer to the vehicle immediately in front of them, necessitating braking with greater force. With respect to traffic safety, the data suggest that the impairments associated with cell phone drivers may be as great as those commonly observed with intoxicated drivers.

David L. Strayer, Frank A. Drews, and Dennis J. Crouch,
A Comparison of the Cell Phone Driver and the Drunk Driver

Order of Climax   Climactic order creates a crescendo pattern, starting with the least emphatic detail and progressing to the most emphatic. The topic sentence can begin or end the paragraph, or it can remain implied. This pattern holds the reader's interest by building suspense. On occasion, writers reverse the order, landing the heaviest punch first; but such paragraphs can trail off, leaving the reader dissatisfied.

Here is a paragraph illustrating climactic order:

> The speaking errors I hear affect me to different degrees. I'm so conditioned to hearing "It don't make any difference" and "There's three ways to solve the problem" that I've almost accepted such usage. However, errors such as "Just between you and I, Arnold loves Edna" and "I'm going back to my room to lay down" still offend my sensibility. When hearing them, I usually just chuckle to myself and walk away. The "Twin I's"—*irrevelant* and *irregardless*—are another matter. More than any other errors, they really grate on my ear. Whenever I hear "that may be true, but it's irrevelant" or "Irregardless of how much I study, I still get C's," I have the urge to correct the speaker. It's really surprising that more people don't clean up their language act.
>
> Valerie Sonntag, student

MyWritingLab   **EXERCISE**   *From a magazine or newspaper article, select four paragraphs that illustrate different patterns of organization. Identify the topic sentence in each case; or if it is implied, state it in your own words. Point out the organization of each paragraph.*

Coherence

5.5

Achieve coherence in your paragraphs.

Coherent writing flows smoothly and easily from one sentence and paragraph to another, clarifying the relationships among ideas and thus allowing the reader to grasp connections. Because incoherent writing fails to do this, it confuses, and sometimes even irritates, the reader.

Here is a paragraph that lacks coherence:

> I woke up late. I had been so tired the night before that I had forgotten to set the alarm. All I could think of was the report I had stayed up until 3 A.M. typing, and how I could possibly get twenty copies ready for next morning's 9 o'clock sales meeting. I panicked and ran out the door. My bus was so crowded I had to stand. Jumping off the bus, I raced back up the street. The meeting was already under way. Mr. Jackson gestured for me to come into the conference room. Inserting the first page of the report into the copier, I set the dial for twenty copies and pressed the print button. The sign started flashing CALL KEY OPERATOR. The machine was out of order. Mr. Jackson asked whether the report was ready. I pointed to the flashing red words. Mr. Jackson nodded grimly without saying anything. He left me alone with the broken machine.

This paragraph has some degree of unity: most of its sentences relate to the writer's disastrous experience with the sales report. Unfortunately, though, its many gaps in logic create rather than answer questions, and in very bumpy prose, at that. Note the gap between the third and fourth sentences. Did the writer jump out of bed and rush right out the door? Of course not, but the reader has no real clue to the actual sequence of events. Another gap occurs between the next two sentences, leaving the reader to wonder why the writer had to race up the street upon leaving the bus. And who is Mr. Jackson? The paragraph never tells, but the reader will want to know.

Now read this rewritten version, additions highlighted:

I woke up late because I had been so tired the night before that I had forgotten to set the alarm. All I could think of was the report I had stayed up until 3 A.M. typing, and how I could possibly get twenty copies ready for next morning's 9 o'clock sales meeting. When I realized it was 8:30, I panicked. Jumping out of bed, I threw on some clothes, grabbed the report, and ran out the door. My bus was so crowded I had to stand and could not see out the window. Two blocks beyond my stop, I realized I should have gotten off. "Stop!" I cried and, jumping off the bus, raced back up the street. When I reached the office, it was 9:15, and the meeting was already under way. Mr. Jackson, the sales manager, saw me and gestured for me to come into the conference room. "One moment," I said as calmly as I could and hurried to the copier. Inserting the first page of the report into it, I set the dial for twenty copies and pressed the print button. Immediately, the sign started flashing CALL KEY OPERATOR. The machine was out of order. The next thing I knew, Mr. Jackson was at my side asking whether the report was ready. I pointed to the flashing red words, and Mr. Jackson nodded grimly without saying anything. Turning on his heel, he walked away and left me alone with the broken machine.

As this example shows, correcting an incoherent paragraph may call for anything from a single word to a whole sentence or more.

Coherence derives from a sufficient supply of supporting details and your firm sense of the way your ideas go together. If you brainstorm your topic thoroughly and think carefully about the relationships between sentences, incoherence isn't likely to haunt your paragraphs.

As you write, and especially when you revise, signal connections to the reader by using *transitions*—devices that link sentences to one another. These are the most common transitional devices:

1. Connecting words and phrases
2. Repeated key words
3. Pronouns and demonstrative adjectives
4. Parallelism

You can use them to furnish links both within and between paragraphs.

Connecting Words and Phrases   Connectors clarify relationships between sentences. The following list groups them according to function:

Showing similarity: in like manner, likewise, moreover, similarly

Showing contrast: at the same time, but, even so, however, in contrast, instead, nevertheless, still, on the contrary, on the other hand, otherwise, yet

Showing results or effects: accordingly, as a result, because, consequently, hence, since, therefore, thus

Adding ideas together: also, besides, first (second, third …), furthermore, in addition, in the first place, likewise, moreover, similarly, too

Drawing conclusions: as a result, finally, in brief, in conclusion, in short, to summarize

Pointing out examples: for example, for instance, to illustrate

Showing emphasis and clarity: above all, after all, again, as a matter of fact, besides, in fact, in other words, indeed, nonetheless, that is

Indicating time: at times, after, afterward, from then on, immediately, later, meanwhile, next, now, once, previously, subsequently, then, until, while

Conceding a point: granted that, of course, to be sure, admittedly

Don't overload your paper with connectors. In well-planned prose, your message flows clearly with only an occasional assist from them.

In the following excerpt, which clarifies the difference between workers and workaholics, the connectors are highlighted:

> My efforts to define workaholism and to distinguish workaholics from other hard workers proved difficult. While workaholics do work hard, not all hard workers are workaholics. Moonlighters, for example, may work 16 hours a day to make ends meet, but most of them will stop working when their financial circumstances permit. Accountants, too, seem to work nonstop, but many slow down after the April 15 tax deadline. Workaholics, on the other hand, always devote more time and thought to their work than their situation demands. Even in the absence of deadlines to meet, mortgages to pay, promotions to earn, or bosses to please, workaholics still work hard. What sets them apart is their attitude toward work, not the number of hours they work.
>
> Marilyn Machlowitz, "Workaholism: What's Wrong with
> Being Married to Your Work?"

MyWritingLab ## Discussion Questions

1. What ideas do each of the highlighted words and phrases connect?
2. What relationship does each show?

Repeated Key Words   Repeating key words, especially those that help convey a paragraph's central idea, can smooth the reader's path. The words may appear in different forms, but their presence keeps the main issues before the reader. In the following paragraph, the repetition of *majority, minority,* and *will* aids coherence, as does the more limited repetition of *government* and *interests.*

> Whatever fine-spun theories we may devise to resolve or obscure the difficulty, there is no use blinking the fact that the will of the majority is not the same thing as the will of all. Majority rule works well only so long as the minority is willing to accept the will of the majority as the will of the nation and let it go at that. Generally speaking, the minority will be willing to let it go at that so long as it feels that its essential interests and rights are not fundamentally different from those of the current majority, and so long as it can, in any case, look forward with confidence to

mustering enough votes within four or six years to become itself the majority and so redress the balance. But if it comes to pass that a large minority feels that it has no such chance, that it is a fixed and permanent minority and that another group or class with rights and interests fundamentally hostile to its own is in permanent control, then government by majority vote ceases in any sense to be government by the will of the people for the good of all, and becomes government by the will of some of the people for their own interests at the expense of the others.

Carl Becker, *Freedom and Responsibility in the American Way of Life*

EXERCISE *Write a paragraph using one of the following sentences as your topic sentence. Insert the missing key word and then repeat it in your paragraph to help link your sentences.*

MyWritingLab

1. _____ is my favorite relative.
2. I wish I had (a, an, some, more) _____.
3. _____ changed my life.
4. _____ is more trouble than it's worth.

5. A visit to _____ always depresses me.
6. Eating _____ is a challenge.
7. I admire _____.

Pronouns and Demonstrative Adjectives   Pronouns stand in for nouns that appear earlier in the sentence or in previous sentences. Mixing pronouns and their nouns throughout the paragraph prevents monotony and promotes clarity. We have highlighted the pronouns in the following excerpt from an article about the writer's first visit to a gambling casino.

There are three of us on this trip, two veterans of Atlantic City and I, a neophyte, all celebrating the fact that we have recently become grandmothers. One of my companions is the canny shopper in our crowd; as a bargain-hunter she knows the ways of the world. I have followed her through discount shops and outlet stores from Manhattan's Lower East Side to the Secaucus, New Jersey, malls …. Without saying a word, she hands me a plastic container of the kind that might hold two pounds of potato salad, and takes one herself. She drags me off to the change booth, where she exchanges bills for tubes of silver, careful not to let me see just how much. I do the same. Then she leads me to a clattering corner, where a neon sign winks on and off, Quartermania. "Let's try to find a couple of machines that only have handles," she says ….

Eileen Herbert Jordan, "My Affair with the One-Armed Bandit"

All the pronouns in the excerpt refer to the writer, her bargain-hunting friend, or the whole group.

Four demonstrative adjectives—*this, that, these,* and *those*—also help hook ideas together. Demonstratives are special adjectives that identify or point out nouns rather than describe them. Here is an example from the Declaration of Independence:

We hold these truths to be self-evident, that all men are created equal, that they are endowed by their Creator with certain unalienable Rights, that among these are Life, Liberty, and the pursuit of Happiness. That to secure these rights, Governments are instituted among Men, deriving their just powers from the consent of the governed. That whenever any Form of Government becomes destructive of these ends, it is the Right of the People to alter or to abolish it, and to institute new Government, laying its foundation on such principles and organizing its power in such form, as to them shall seem most likely to effect their Safety and Happiness.

MyWritingLab **EXERCISE** *In a magazine, newspaper, textbook, or some other written source, find two paragraphs that use pronouns and demonstrative adjectives to increase coherence. Copy the paragraphs, underline the pronouns and demonstrative adjectives, and explain what each refers to.*

Parallelism   Parallelism uses repetition of grammatical form to express a series of equivalent ideas. Besides giving continuity, the repetition adds rhythm and balance to the writing. Note how the following highlighted constructions tie together the unfolding definition of poverty:

Poverty is staying up all night on cold nights to watch the fire, knowing one spark on the newspaper covering the walls means your sleeping children die in flames. In summer, poverty is watching gnats and flies devour your baby's tears when he cries. The screens are torn and you pay so little rent you know they will never be fixed. Poverty means insects in your food, in your nose, in your eyes, and crawling over you when you sleep. Poverty is hoping it never rains because diapers won't dry when it rains and soon you are using newspapers. Poverty is seeing your children forever with runny noses. Paper handkerchiefs cost money and all your rags you need for other things. Even more costly are antihistamines. Poverty is cooking without food and cleaning without soap.

Jo Goodwin Parker, "What Is Poverty?"

Paragraphs with Special Functions: Introductions, Transitions, and Conclusions

5.6

Write introduction, transition, and conclusion paragraphs using a variety of strategies.

Special-function paragraphs include introductions, transitional paragraphs, and conclusions. One-paragraph introductions and conclusions appear in short, multiparagraph essays. Transitional paragraphs occur primarily in long compositions.

Introductions

A good introduction acquaints and coaxes. It announces the essay's topic and may directly state the thesis. In addition, it sets the tone—somber, lighthearted, angry—of what will follow. An amusing anecdote would not be an appropriate opening for a paper about political torture.

With essays, as with people, first impressions are important. If your opening rouses interest, it will draw the reader into the essay and pave the way for your ideas. If, instead, you'd like to try your hand at turning the reader away, search for a beginning that is mechanical, plodding, and dull. Your success will astonish you. Here are some bad openings:

In this paper I intend to…

Wars have always afflicted humankind.

As you may know, having too little time is a problem for many of us.

In the modern world of today…

How would you respond to these openings? Ask yourself that same question about every opening you write.

Gear the length of the introduction to that of the essay. Although longer papers sometimes begin with two or more introductory paragraphs, generally the lead-in for a short essay is a single paragraph. Here are some possibilities for starting an essay. The type you select depends on your purpose, subject, audience, and personality.

A Directly Stated Thesis   This is a common type of opening, orienting the reader to what will follow. After providing some general background, the writer of our example narrows her scope to a thesis that previews the upcoming sections of her essay.

> An increasing number of midlife women are reentering the workforce, pursuing college degrees, and getting more involved in the public arena. Several labels besides "midlife" have been attached to this type of person: the mature woman, the older woman, and, more recently, the re-entry woman. By definition, she is between thirty-five and fifty-five years old and has been away from the business or academic scene anywhere from fifteen to thirty years. The academic community, the media, marketing people, and employers are giving her close scrutiny, and it is apparent that she is having a greater impact on our society than she realizes.
>
> Jo Ann Harris, student

A Definition   This kind of introduction works particularly well in a paper that acquaints the reader with an unfamiliar topic.

> You are completely alone in a large open space and are struck by a terrifying, unreasoning fear. You sweat, your heart beats, you cannot breathe. You fear you may die of a heart attack, although you do not have heart disease. Suppose you decide you will never get yourself in this helpless situation again. You go home and refuse to leave its secure confines. Your family has to support you. You have agoraphobia— a disabling terror of open spaces.
>
> "Controlling Phobias
> Through Behavior Modification"

A Quotation   A beginning quotation, particularly from an authority in the field, can be an effective springboard for the ideas that follow. Make sure any quote you use relates clearly to your topic.

> The director of the census made a dramatic announcement in 1890. The Nation's unsettled area, he revealed, "has been so broken into by isolated bodies of settlement that there can hardly be said to be a frontier line." These words sounded the close of one period of America's history. For three centuries before, men had marched westward, seeking in the forests and plains that lay beyond the settled areas a chance to begin anew. For three centuries they had driven back the wilderness as their conquest of the continent went on. Now, in 1890, they were told that a frontier line separating the settled and unsettled portions of the United States no longer existed. The west was won, and the expansion that had been the most distinctive feature of the country's past was at an end.
>
> Ropropay Allen Billington, "The Frontier Disappears"

An Anecdote or Personal Experience   A well-told personal anecdote or experience can lure readers into the rest of the paper. Like other introductions, this kind should bear on what comes afterward. Engle's anecdote, like the stories she reviews, demonstrates that "women also have dark hearts."

> My mother used to have a little china cream and sugar set that was given to her by a woman who later killed her children with an axe. It sat cheerfully in the china cabinet, as inadequate a symbol as I have ever seen of the dark mysteries within us. Yet at least it was there to remind us that no matter how much Jesus wanted us for a sunbeam, we would still have some day to cope with a deeper reality than common sense could explain. It stood for strange cars not to get into, running shoes to wear when you were out alone at night and the backs of Chinese restaurants you were not supposed to go into.
>
> Marian Engle, review of *The Goddess and Other Women* by Joyce Carol Oates

An Arresting Statement   Sometimes you can jolt the reader into attention, using content, language, or both, particularly if your essay develops an unusual or extreme position.

> It's like Pearl Harbor. The Japanese have invaded, and the U.S. has been caught short. Not on guns and tanks and battleships—those are yesterday's weapons—but on mental might. In a high-tech age where nations increasingly compete on brainpower, American schools are producing an army of illiterates. Companies that cannot hire enough skilled workers now realize they must do something to save the public schools. Not to be charitable, not to promote good public relations, but to survive.
>
> Nancy Perry, "Saving the Schools: How Business Can Help"

Interesting Details   These details pique curiosity and draw the reader into the paper.

> Cher, the pretty sixteen-year-old protagonist of Amy Heckerling's *Clueless* (1995), is a rich dumb blonde who is a mediocre student at best, and is obsessed with the pleasures of fashion, beauty culture, and shopping. A coy daddy's girl, she

pouts and whines when she's frustrated, and her talk is riddled with girly slang. Her universe is filtered entirely through popular culture: she prefers watching cartoons to the news, and she takes pride in the fact that her mother named her after the legendary goddess of pop schlock and excess. (77)

Kathleen Rowe Karlyn, *Unruly Girls Unrepentant Mothers: Redefining Feminism on Screen*

A Question   A provocative question can entice the reader into the essay to find the answer.

How does the biggest pop star on the planet reward herself after she's spent the past year touring the world, performing for President Bill Clinton, opening her own boutique in Barneys, releasing a high-fashion picture book, and prepping for her appearance on "Dick Clark's New Year's Rockin' Eve?"

Maureen Callahan, "Lady Gaga Gives 50 Percent of Her Earnings to Her Father"

EXERCISE   MyWritingLab

1. Explain why each of the preceding introductions interests or does not interest you. Does your response stem from the topic or the way the author introduces it?
2. Find magazine articles with effective introductory paragraphs illustrating at least three different techniques. Write a paragraph explaining why each impresses you.

Transitional Paragraphs

In the midst of a lengthy essay, you may need a short paragraph that announces a shift from one group of ideas to another. Transitional paragraphs summarize previously explained ideas, repeat the thesis, or point to ideas that follow. In our example, Bruno Bettelheim has been discussing a young boy named Joey who has turned into a kind of human machine. After describing Joey's assorted delusions, Bettelheim signals his switch from the delusions to the fears that caused them.

What deep-seated fears and needs underlay Joey's delusional system? We were long in finding out, for Joey's preventions effectively concealed the secret of his autistic behavior. In the meantime we dealt with his peripheral problems one by one.

Bruno Bettelheim, "Joey: 'A Mechanical Boy'"

The following transitional paragraph looks back as well as ahead:

Certainly these three factors—exercise, economy, convenience of shortcuts— help explain the popularity of bicycling today. But a fourth attraction sometimes overrides the others: the lure of the open road.

Mike Bernstein, student

Conclusions

A conclusion rounds out a paper and signals that the discussion has been completed. Not all papers require a separate conclusion; narratives and descriptions, for example, generally end when the writer finishes the story or concludes the impression. But many essays benefit from a conclusion that drives the point home a final time. To be effective, a conclusion must mesh logically and stylistically with what comes earlier. A long, complex paper often ends with a summary of the main points, but any of several other options may be used for shorter papers with easy-to-grasp ideas. Most short essays have single-paragraph conclusions; longer papers may require two or three paragraphs.

Following are some cautions about writing your conclusion:

1. Don't introduce new material. Draw together, round out, but don't take off in a new direction.
2. Don't tack on an ending in desperation when the hour is late and the paper is due tomorrow—the so-called midnight special. Your reader deserves better than "All in all, skiing is a great sport" or "Thus we can see that motorcycle racing isn't for everyone."
3. Don't apologize. Saying that you could have done a better job makes a reader wonder why you didn't.
4. Don't moralize. A preachy conclusion can undermine the position you have established in the rest of your composition.

The following examples illustrate several common types of conclusion.

Restatement of the Thesis   The following conclusion reasserts Jordan's thesis that "a mood of antisocial negativism is creeping through the structure of American life, corroding our ideals, and suffocating the hopes of poor people and minorities."

> There is room for honest differences about each of these key issues, but the new negativism's overt greed and the implicit racism of its loud "No" to minority aspirations indicate that this is a poisonous movement that denies the moral ideals and human values that characterize the best in America's heritage.
>
> Vernon E. Jordan, Jr., "The New Negativism"

A Summary   A summary draws together and reinforces the main points of a paper.

> There are, of course, many other arguments against capital punishment, including its high cost and its failure to deter crime. But I believe the most important points against the death penalty are the possibility of executing an innocent man, the discriminatory manner in which it is applied, and the barbaric methods of carrying it out. In my opinion, capital punishment is, in effect, premeditated murder by society as a whole. As the old saying goes, two wrongs don't make a right.
>
> Diane Trathen, student

A Question   The following paragraph concludes an argument that running should not be elevated to a religion; that its other benefits are sufficient. A final question often prompts the reader to think further on the topic. If your essay is meant to be persuasive, be sure to phrase a concluding question so that the way a reasonable person would answer emphasizes your point of view.

> Aren't those gifts enough? Why ask running for benefits that are plainly beyond its capacity to bestow?
>
> James Fixx, "What Running Can't Do for You"

A Quotation   A quotation can capture the essence of your thought and end the essay with authority.

> If you catch yourself ruminating on why that colleague ignored you in the hall, let it go. "You might never know the reason behind a person's laughter or his look in your direction, so why waste time trying to find an answer?" Freeman says. "Ambiguity is all around us. Don't let it keep you from doing the things you enjoy."
>
> Stephanie Booth, "A Slew of Suspects"

Ironic Twist or Surprising Observation   These approaches prompt the reader to think further about a paper's topic. The following paragraph points out the ironic refusal of the government to confront poverty that exists a mere 10 blocks away from its offices:

> Thus, a stark contrast exists between the two cultures of 14th Street, which appears to be like an earthworm with half of its body crushed by poverty but the other half still alive, wriggling in wealth. The two are alike only in that each communicates little with the other because of the wide disparity between the lives of the people and the conditions of the environments. The devastating irony of the situation on 14th Street lies in the fact that only ten blocks away sit the very government institutions that could alleviate the poverty—the Senate, the House of Representatives, and the White House.

Arresting Statement   A powerfully worded unexpected statement can promote thought about the paper's issue. The final sentence here stops most readers in their tracks.

> Unfortunately, as the situation in large parts of the world at the end of the millennium demonstrates, bad history is not harmless history. The sentences typed on apparently innocuous keyboards may be sentences of death.
>
> Eric Hobsbawm, *On History*

Personal Challenge   A challenge often prompts the reader to take some action.

> And therein lies the challenge. You can't merely puff hard for a few days and then revert to the La-Z-Boy recliner, smugly thinking that you're "in shape." You must sweat and strain and puff regularly, week in and week out. They're your muscles, your lungs, your heart. The only caretaker they have is you.
>
> Monica Duvall, student

Hope or Recommendation   Both a hope and a recommendation may restate points already made in the essay or suggest actions to take in order to arrive at a solution.

> This journey to a tragic past will be inextricably bound up with the uplifting sight of the future. Having reached the formal memorial, the quiet pathways marking the foundations of the Twin Towers, visitors may realize that they have, in fact, just walked alongside the true memorial: the living, human building blocks of a future New York.
>
> Max Page and Sigrid Miller Pollin,
> "Proposal for a Landscape of Learning"

> No one can predict the transformations of twenty-first century society during the information technology revolution. We certainly cannot afford to continue teaching our students only the literacies of the mid-twentieth century, or even to simply lay before them the most advanced and diverse literacies of today. We must help this next generation learn to use these literacies wisely, and hope they will succeed better than we have.
>
> J. L. Lemke, "Metamedia Literacy:
> Transforming Meanings and Media"

MyWritingLab   **EXERCISE**

1. Explain why each of the foregoing conclusions does or does not interest you. Does your response stem from the topic or from the author's handling of it?
2. Copy effective concluding paragraphs, illustrating at least three different techniques, from magazine articles. Then write a paragraph explaining why each impresses you.

Writing Effective Paragraphs

Writing paragraphs.

- Aim for the purpose of the whole paper.
- Use paragraphing to show your paper's organization.
- Focus paragraphs around main ideas.
- Use your writing plan to decide on paragraphs.

Developing your introduction.

- Have a draft thesis statement.
- Choose a strategy based on your audience and purpose.
- Choose a strategy—a definition, a directly stated thesis, a quotation, a personal experience, an arresting statement, a question.

Developing the body paragraphs.

- Build paragraphs around main idea.
- State or imply a topic sentence that provides that main idea.
- Develop main idea with details, explanations, or examples.
- Use a strategy and order for developing each paragraph.
- Provide clear transitions.

Enhancing your paragraphs.

- Check to see if everything in each paragraph fits the topic of the paragraph. Cut or move what doesn't fit.
- Determine if additional details, examples, or explanations are necessary to make your point and add if necessary.
- Make certain that the topic sentence of each paragraph is clear and fits the paragraph.
- Strengthen coherence and cohesion by making certain sentences relate in an order and that repeated words or phrases help show relationships.

Writing a conclusion.

- Aim at pulling the paper together for the reader.
- Determine a strategy based on the paper.
  - Restate thesis in a new way.
  - Offer a summary of paper.
  - Leave the reader with an important question.
  - Offer a personal challenge, hope, or recommendation.
  - Use a telling quotation.
- Check again to determine that the conclusion fits the paper in tone, content, and approach, and does not raise new issues.

CHAPTER 6 Effective Sentences

In this chapter, you will learn how to:

6.1 Write sentences that avoid unnecessary wordiness.

6.2 Write sentences that vary in complexity and length.

6.3 Vary the word order of sentences.

6.4 Vary the positioning of movable modifiers.

6.5 Use parallelism to present equivalent ideas.

6.6 Choose the right verb voice for your sentences.

Visit MyWritingLab **to complete the writing assignments in this chapter and for more resources on sentences.**

Sentences take many forms, some straightforward, others ornate, each with its own stylistic strengths. Becoming familiar with these forms and their uses gives you the option to:

- emphasize or deemphasize an idea
- combine ideas into one sentence or keep them separate in more than one sentence
- make sentences sound formal or informal
- emphasize the actor or the action
- achieve rhythm, variety, and contrast

Effective sentences bring both exactness and flair to your writing. You may wish to read your handbook for review if you are not familiar with the sentence elements or how to identify and correct sentence errors effectively.

Effective sentences are not an accident; they require work. There are several strategies you can employ, including avoiding unnecessary wordiness; varying sentence length, complexity, and word order; using parallelism; and selecting the right verb voice. Usually it's best to work on these different strategies as you revise rather than pause to refine each sentence after you write it.

Avoiding Unnecessary Wordiness

Sometimes in first drafts we write flabby sentences.

6.1

Write sentences that avoid unnecessary wordiness.

- It is my considered opinion that you will make an excellent employee.
- Joan will give a presentation on our latest sales figures to the CEO.
- Mr. Headly, who was my seventh-grade biology teacher, recently was honored for the research he had done over the years with his classes.
- My neighbor's Subaru that was old and rusty still could navigate the winter streets better than most other cars.

Although there may be stylistic reasons for these sentences, such as creating variety or adding a particular emphasis, a writer could sharpen them by reordering the sentence structure and eliminating unnecessary words.

- You will make an excellent employee. (The fact that you write it makes it clear that it is your opinion.)
- Joan will present our latest sales figures to the CEO. (Many times we use verbs as nouns with a filler verb—"have a meeting," "give a talk," "go running." Change these nouns back to verbs and dragging sentences can be energized.)
- Mr. Headly, my seventh-grade biology teacher, recently was honored for the research he had done over the years with his classes. (The rules of English let you delete some redundant phrases, even repeated subjects, to tighten your language.)
- My neighbor's rusty, old Subaru still could navigate the winter streets better than most other cars. (Changing a relative clause to simple adjectives makes this sentence crisper.)

How do most writers do it? Cut out words that seem unnecessary, organize sentences different ways, and let verbs bear the brunt of the burden.

EXERCISE   *Rewrite the sentences to avoid unnecessary wordiness.*

MyWritingLab

1. The principal will give a talk to the parents at the PTA meeting about how important it is for their children to get to school on time.
2. I would like to say that no playwright has ever used language as effectively as Shakespeare.
3. Mozart, who was a musical prodigy, is best known for his operas.
4. The jewelry store sold me a watch that was stolen.
5. The meeting that was scheduled for 3 P.M. was cancelled because Mr. Rushton, the consultant who was giving the presentation about the results on our computer security, was arrested for creating computer viruses that were very destructive.

Varying Sentence Complexity and Length

Sentences that are all the same length yield a repetitive, tedious prose.

6.2

Write sentences that vary in complexity and length.

Janice hated pain. She had her nose pierced. She had her bellybutton pierced. She had her tongue pierced. She wanted to be different. She ended up just like her friends.

This string of simple sentences unnecessarily repeats word phrases and gives the reader a bumpy ride. Combining these sentences results in a smoother and more varied prose style.

> Although Janice hated pain, she had her nose, bellybutton, and tongue pierced in order to be different. She ended up, however, just like her friends.

Simple sentences of one subject and predicate—"The audience was young"—can be combined through coordinate and subordinate conjunctions, as well as the use of relative clause structures and other techniques. The result is not only a smoother style but a combination that more effectively shows the relationship of your ideas.

Coordination   Coordinating conjunctions include *and, but, or, nor, for, yet, and so, and you* can combine clauses or phrases in a way that makes them equal.

- The audience was young, friendly, and responsive; so it cheered for each speaker.
- Either we hang together or we hang separately.
- A tornado ripped through our town but fortunately it spared our house.

Subordination   Subordinate conjunctions such as *because, since, while, before, during, after,* and *instead of* can link dependent clauses to the main independent clause in a way that shows logical relationship.

- Millicent swam 400 laps today **because** she was feeling unusually strong.
- Arthur collapsed on the sofa **after** the dance was over.
- **Once** they had reached the lakeshore, the campers found a level spot **where** they could pitch their tent.

Relative Clauses   Nouns can often be modified by relative clauses, which use a **relative pronoun** that substitutes for a noun and binds ideas together.

- Students **who** work hard usually succeed.
- The books on the history of Crete **that** you ordered have finally arrived.

There are other ways to combine sentences and vary sentence length, including the use of prepositional phrases, participle phrases, and infinitive phrases.

- The crook raced **around** the corner, **down** the alley, **into** the arms **of** the waiting police officers. (prepositional phrases)
- Some people handle a crisis by avoiding it, **ignoring** the problem until someone else solves it. (participle phrase)
- The early settlers moved west **to escape** an unsavory or difficult past, **to forge** a new life, **to realize** dreams. (infinitive phrases)

The point is to find ways to vary your sentences to increase interest and rhythm.

Intentional Fragments   A fragment is a part of a sentence that is capitalized and punctuated as if it were a complete sentence.

Although fragments are seldom used in formal prose, they form the backbone of most conversations. Here's how a typical bit of dialogue might go:

"Where are you going tonight?" (*sentence*)
"To Woodland Mall." (*fragment*)
"What for?" (*fragment*)
"To buy some shoes." (*fragment*)

As with most conversations, the sprinkling of complete sentences makes the fragments clear.

Writers of nonfiction use fragments to create special effects. In the following passage, the fragments focus the reader on the urgency of the situation.

> Failed banks. Panicked markets. Rising unemployment. For students of history, or people of a certain age, it all has an all-too-familiar ring. Is this another Great Depression? Not yet.
>
> John Waggoner, "Is Today's Economic Crisis Another Great Depression"

Before using any fragment, think about your intended effect. Unless only a fragment will serve your needs, don't use one; fragments are likely to be viewed as unintentional—and thus errors—in the work of inexperienced writers.

EXERCISE   *The following passage includes one or more fragments. Identify each and explain its function.*

My WritingLab

> He [Richard Wagner] wrote operas; and no sooner did he have the synopsis of a story, but he would invite—or rather summon—a crowd of his friends to his house and read it aloud to them. Not for criticism. For applause. When the complete poem was written, the friends had to come again, and hear *that* read aloud. Then he would publish the poem, sometimes years before the music that went with it was written.
>
> Deems Taylor, "The Monster"

Working together, these techniques provide varied sentences that create interest. In the following paragraph, the sentences differ considerably in length.

> In a city of half a million I still really look at every face, anticipating recognition, because I grew up in a town where every face meant something to me. I have trouble remembering to lock the doors. Wariness of strangers I learned the hard way. When I was new to the city, I let a man into my house one hot afternoon because he seemed in dire need of a drink of water; when I turned from the kitchen sink I found sharpened steel shoved against my belly. And so I know, I know. But I cultivate suspicion with as much difficulty as I force tomatoes to grow in the drought-stricken hardpan of my strange backyard. No creek runs here, but I'm still listening to secret tides, living as if I belonged to an earlier place: not Kentucky, necessarily, but a welcoming earth and a human family. A forest. A species.
>
> Barbara Kingsolver, *High Tide in Tucson: Essays from Now or Never*

Here Kingsolver uses longer sentences to anticipate her more relaxed sense of the world contrasted with a shorter sentence tied to her experience of the potential of violence. The paragraph ends with two short fragments to focus on those interior spaces.

Varying sentence length can help you emphasize a key idea. If a key point is submerged in a long sentence, highlight it as a separate thought, giving it the recognition it deserves.

Original Version

Employers find mature women to be valuable members of their organizations. They are conscientious, have excellent attendance records, and stay calm when things go awry, but unfortunately many employers exploit them. Despite their desirable qualities, most remain mired in clerical, sales, and elementary teaching positions. On the average they earn two-thirds as much as men.

Revised Version

Employers find mature women to be valuable members of their organizations. They are conscientious, have excellent attendance records, and stay calm when things go awry. Unfortunately, many employers exploit them. Despite their desirable qualities, most remain mired in clerical, sales, and elementary teaching positions. On the average they earn two-thirds as much as men.

MyWritingLab **EXERCISE** *Using coordination and subordination, rewrite the following passages to reduce words and/or improve smoothness.*

1. He played the piano. He played the organ. He played the French horn. He did not play the viola.
2. The weather was icy cold and windy. Lee was wearing only a T-shirt and athletic shorts.
3. Life on Venus may be possible. It will not be the kind of life we know on Earth. Life on Mars may be possible. It will not be the kind of life we know on Earth.
4. He felt his classmates were laughing at his error. He ran out of the room. He vowed never to return to that class.
5. Albert lay in bed. He stared at the ceiling. Albert thought about the previous afternoon. He had asked Kathy to go to dinner with him. She is a pretty, blond-haired woman. She sits at the desk next to his. They work at Hemphill's. She had refused.

Word Order in Independent Clauses

6.3

Vary the word order of sentences.

What other tools do you have to create more interesting prose? One powerful technique is to vary word order in a sentence. Most independent clauses follow a similar arrangement. First comes the subject, then the verb, and finally any other element needed to convey the main message.

Barney blushed. (*subject, verb*)

They built the dog a kennel. (*subject, verb, indirect object, direct object*)

Samantha is an architect. (*subject, verb, subject complement*)

This arrangement puts the emphasis on the subject, right where it's usually wanted.

But the pattern doesn't work in every situation. Occasionally, a writer wants to emphasize some element that follows the verb, create an artistic effect, or give the subject unusual emphasis. Enter inverted order and the expletive construction.

Inverted Order   To invert a sentence, move to the front the element you want to emphasize. Sometimes the rest of the sentence follows in regular subject-then-verb order; sometimes the verb precedes the subject.

Lovable he isn't. (*subject complement, subject, verb*)

This I just don't understand. (*direct object, subject, verb*)

Tall grow the pines in the mountains. (*subject complement, verb, subject*)

Sentences that ask questions typically follow an inverted pattern.

Is this your coat? (*verb, subject, subject complement*)

Will you let the cat out? (*verb, subject, verb, direct object*)

Most of your sentences should follow normal order: Readers expect it and find it easier to read. Don't invert a sentence if the result would sound unnatural. A sentence like "Fools were Brett and Amanda for quitting college" will only hinder communication.

Expletives   An expletive fills a vacancy in a sentence without contributing to the meaning. English has two common expletives, *there* and *it*. Ordinarily, *there* functions as an adverb, *it* as a pronoun, and either can appear anywhere in a sentence. As expletives, however, they alter normal sentence order by beginning sentences and anticipating the real subjects or objects.

Expletives are often used unnecessarily, as in the following example:

There were twenty persons attending the sales meeting.

This sentence errs on two counts: Its subject needs no extra emphasis, and it is very clumsy. Notice the improvement without the expletive and the unneeded words:

Twenty persons attended the sales meeting.

When the subject or object needs highlighting, leading off with an expletive will, by altering normal order, call it more forcefully to the reader's attention.

Normal order:	A fly is in my soup.
	He seeks her happiness.
Expletive construction:	There is a fly in my soup. (*expletive anticipating subject*)
	It is her happiness he seeks. (*expletive anticipating object*)

Once in a while you'll find that something just can't be said unless you use an expletive.

There is no reason for such foolishness.

MyWritingLab   **EXERCISE**   *Indicate which of these sentences follow normal order, which are inverted, and which have expletive constructions. Rewrite so that all will be in normal order.*

1. Dick Lewis is a true friend.
2. It was her car in the ditch.
3. May I go to the movie with you?
4. There are many dead fish on the beach.
5. The instructor gave the class a long reading assignment.
6. The Willetts have bought a new house.
7. It is Marianne's aim to become a lawyer.

Positioning of Movable Modifiers

6.4

Vary the positioning of movable modifiers.

Movable modifiers can appear on either side of the main statement or within it.

Modifiers after Main Statement   Sentences that follow this arrangement, frequently called loose sentences, occur more commonly than either of the others. They mirror conversation, in which a speaker first makes a statement and then adds further thoughts. Often, the main statement has just one modifier.

> Our company will have to file for bankruptcy *because of this year's huge losses.* (*phrase as modifier*)

Or it can head up a whole train of modifiers.

> He burst suddenly into the party, loud, angry, obscene. (*words as modifiers*)

> The family used to gather around the hearth, doing such chores as polishing shoes, mending ripped clothing, reading, chatting, always warmed by one another's presence as much as by the flames. (*words and phrases as modifiers*)

A sentence may contain several layers of modifiers. In the following example, we've indented and numbered to show the different layers.

1. The men struggled to the top of the hill,
   2. thirsty,
   2. drenched in sweat,
   2. and cursing in pain
      3. as their knapsack straps cut into their raw, chafed shoulders
         4. with every step.

In this sentence, the items numbered 2 refer to *men* in the item numbered 1. Item 3 is linked to *cursing* in the preceding item 2, and item 4 is linked to *cut* in item 3.

The modifiers' last arrangement works well for injecting descriptive details into narratives and also for qualifying, explaining, and presenting lists in other kinds of writing.

Modifiers before Main Statement   Sentences that delay the main point until the end are called periodic. In contrast to loose sentences, they lend a formal note to what is said, slowing its pace, adding cadence, and making it more serious.

> *If you can keep your head when everyone around you is panicking, you probably don't understand the situation. (clauses as modifiers)*
>
> *The danger of sideswiping another vehicle, the knowledge that a hidden bump or hole could throw me from the dune buggy,* both of these things added to the thrill of the race. *(noun plus phrase and noun plus clause as modifiers)*
>
> 1. *When the public protests,*
> 2. *confronted with some obvious evidence of the damaging results of pesticide applications,* it is fed little tranquilizing pills of half truth. *(clause and phrase as modifiers)*
>
> Rachel Carson, *Silent Spring*

As shown in the example, periodic sentences can also have layers of modifiers.

Positioning the modifiers before the main point throws the emphasis to the end of the sentence, adding force to the main point. The delay also lets the writer create sentences that, like the first example, carry stings, ironic or humorous, in their tails.

Modifiers within Main Statement   Inserting one or more modifiers into a main statement creates a sentence with *interrupted order*. The material may come between the subject and the verb or between the verb and the rest of the predicate.

> The young girl, wearing a tattered dress and looking anything but well-off herself, gave the beggar a ten-dollar bill. *(phrases between subject and verb)*
>
> The evolutionists, piercing beneath the show of momentary stability, discovered, hidden in rudimentary organs, the discarded rubbish of the past. *(one phrase between subject and verb, another between verb and rest of predicate)*

By stretching out the main idea, inserted modifiers slow the forward pace of the sentence, giving it some of the formality and force of a periodic sentence.

EXERCISE   *Identify each sentence as loose, periodic, or interrupted. Rewrite each as one of the other kinds.*   MyWritingLab

1. Victoria, rejected by family and friends, uncertain where to turn next, finally decided to start a new life in Chicago.
2. When told that she had to have her spleen removed, the woman gasped.

3. The first graders stood in line, talking and giggling, pushing at one another's caps and pencil boxes and kicking one another's shins, unmindful of the drudgery that awaited them within the old schoolhouse.
4. Good health, warm friends a beautiful summer evening—the best things cannot be purchased.
5. A customer, angry and perspiring, stormed up to the claims desk.
6. Stopping just short of the tunnel entrance, the freight train avoided a collision with the crowded commuter train stalled inside.
7. The new kid hammered away at the fading champ, determination in his eyes and glory in his fists.

Using Parallelism

6.5

Use parallelism to present equivalent ideas.

Parallelism presents equivalent ideas in grammatically equivalent form. Dressing them in the same grammatical garb calls attention to their kinship and adds smoothness and polish. The following sentence pairs demonstrate the improvement that parallelism brings:

Nonparallel: James's outfit was wrinkled, mismatched, and *he needed to wash it. (words and independent clause)*

Parallel: James's outfit was *wrinkled, mismatched, and dirty. (words)*

Nonparallel: Oscar likes *reading books, attending plays, and to search for antiques. (different kinds of phrases)*

Parallel: Oscar likes *reading books, attending plays, and searching for antiques. (same kind of phrases)*

Nonparallel: Beth performs her tasks *quickly, willingly, and with accuracy. (words and phrase)*

Parallel: Beth performs her tasks *quickly, willingly, and accurately. (words)*

As the examples show, revising nonparallel sentences smoothes out bumpiness, binds the ideas together more closely, and lends them a more finished look.

Parallelism doesn't always stop with a single sentence. Writers sometimes use it in a series of sentences:

He had never lost his childlike innocence. He had never lost his sense of wonder. He had never lost his sense of joy in nature's simplest gifts.

Balance, a special form of parallelism, positions two grammatically equivalent ideas on opposite sides of some pivot point, such as a word or punctuation mark.

Hope for the best, and prepare for the worst.
Many are called, but few are chosen.
When I'm right, nobody ever notices; when I'm wrong, nobody ever forgets.

Like regular parallel sentences, balanced sentences sometimes come in series:

> The tension in this city is not between white people and Negro people. The tension is, at bottom, between justice and injustice, between the forces of light and the forces of darkness. And if there is a victory, it will be a victory not merely for fifty thousand Negroes, but a victory for justice and the forces of light.
>
> Martin Luther King, Jr., "Pilgrimage to Nonviolence"

Balance works especially well for pitting contrasting or clashing ideas against each other. It sharpens the difference between them while achieving compactness and lending an air of insight to what is said.

EXERCISE   *Identify each sentence as nonparallel, parallel, or balanced; then rewrite each nonparallel sentence to make it parallel.*

MyWritingLab

1. Professor Bartlett enjoys helping students, counseling advisees, and participation in faculty meetings.
2. I can still see Aunt Alva striding into the corral, cornering a cow against a fencepost, try to balance herself on a one-legged milking stool, and butt her head into the cow's belly.
3. The city plans on building a new fishing pier and on dredging the channel of the river.
4. Elton plans on vacationing in New York, but Noreen wants to raft down the Colorado River.
5. You can take the boy out of the country, but you can't take the country out of the boy.
6. Joe's problem is not that he earns too little money but spending it foolishly.
7. The room was dark, gloomy, and everything was dusty.

Choosing the Right Verb Voice

A sentence's verb voice derives from the relationship between the subject and the action. A sentence in the *active voice* has a subject that does something plus a verb that shows action.

6.6

Choose the right verb voice for your sentences.

> The boy hit the target.
>
> The girl painted the garage.

This pattern keeps the key information in the key part of the sentence, making it strong and vigorous and giving the reader a close-up look at the action.

The *passive voice* reverses the subject–action relationship by having the subject receive, rather than perform, the action. It is built around a form of the verb *to be;* for example, *is, are, was,* or *were.* Some sentences identify the actor by using a prepositional phrase; others don't mention the actor at all.

> The target was hit by the boy. (*actor identified*)
>
> The federal debt limit is to be increased. (*actor unidentified*)

Demoting or banishing the actor dilutes the force of the sentence, puts greater distance between the action and the reader, and almost always adds extra words to the message.

Most writers who overuse the passive voice simply don't realize its effects on their writing. Read the following section, written mainly in the passive voice:

> Graft becomes possible when gifts are given to police officers or favors are done for them by persons who expect preferential treatment in return. Gifts of 'many kinds may be received by officers. Often free meals are given to them by the owners of restaurants on their beats. During the Christmas season, they may be given liquor, food, or theater tickets by merchants.

This impersonal, wordy passage plods across the page and therefore lacks any real, persuasive impact. Now note the livelier tone of this rewritten version.

> Graft becomes possible when police officers accept gifts or favors from persons who expect preferential treatment in return. Officers may receive gifts of many kinds. Restaurant owners often provide free meals for officers on the beat. During the Christmas season, merchants may give them liquor, food, or theater tickets.

Don't misunderstand: The passive voice does have its uses. It can mask identities—or at least try to. A child may try to dodge responsibility by saying, "Mother, while you were out, the living room lamp got broken." Less manipulatively, reporters may use it to conceal the identity of a source.

Technical and scientific writing customarily uses the passive voice to explain processes.

> In the production of steel, iron ore is first converted into pig iron by combining it with limestone and coke and then heating the mixture in a blast furnace. Pig iron, however, contains too many impurities to be useful to industry, and as a result must be refined and converted to steel. In the refining process, manganese, silicon, and aluminum are heated with the pig iron in order to degas it; that is, to remove excess oxygen and impurities from it.

Putting such writing in the passive voice provides a desirable objective tone and puts the emphasis where it's most important: on the action, not the actor. On occasion, everyday writing also uses the passive voice.

The garbage is collected once a week, on Monday.

These caves were formed about 10 million years ago.

In the first case, there's no need to tell who collects the garbage; obviously, garbage collectors do. In the second, the writer may not know what caused the formation, and saying "Something formed these caves about 10 million years ago" would sound ridiculous. In both situations, the action, not the actor, is paramount. Unless special circumstances call for the passive voice, however, use the active voice.

MyWritingLab   **EXERCISE** *After determining whether each of the following sentences is in active or passive voice, rewrite the passive sentences as active ones.*

1. Mary's parents gave her a sports car for her sixteenth birthday.
2. Fires were left burning by negligent campers.

3. The new ice arena will be opened by the city in about two weeks.
4. Harry left the open toolbox out in the rain.
5. Corn was introduced to the Pilgrims by friendly American Indians.
6. We have just installed a new computer in our main office.
7. Objections were raised by some members of the legislature to the ratification of the proposed amendment.

Beyond the Single Sentence

Your sentences need to work together to produce the desired effect. Your content and purpose will guide you in determining how your sentences will work together. You will need to vary sentence length, word order, and rhythms to produce your desired effect, but in a way that is not obvious or clumsy. A good place to start is by studying the essays in the Reader to see what kinds of combinations they use—a series of questions that are then answered; long sentences with modifiers that lead to a short sentence that gains emphasis; a series of fragments followed by a long sentence. In your own writing, keep an eye on what kind of sentences you are creating and how those sentences create a pattern.

EXERCISE   *Revise the following passages to improve their style.*   MyWritingLab

1. Andrew Carnegie came to America from Scotland. He worked as a factory hand, a telegrapher, and a railway clerk to support himself. His savings from these jobs were invested in oil and later in the largest steel works in the country. Historians do not agree in their assessments of Carnegie. Some have considered him a cruel taskmaster and others a benevolent benefactor. His contributions to American society, however, cannot be denied. He established public libraries all across the country and spent much time in promoting peace. Good or bad, he ranks as one of our most noteworthy nineteenth-century immigrants.
2. She went to the seashore. She found some seashells. She picked up the seashells. She put the seashells into a basket. She had a whole basketful of seashells. She went home with the basket. She took the shells out of the basket. She put the shells on a dinette table. She brought jeweler's tools to the table. She pierced holes in the shells. She strung the shells on small chains. The chains were gold and silver. She made twenty necklaces. The selling price of the necklaces was $10 a piece. She earned $175 profit. She used her profits to go to the shore again. She could afford to stay for a week this time.

Sentence Strategies

Focus on the sentence.

- When drafting, don't focus excessively on the sentence if doing so interrupts the generation of ideas.
- Focus on sentences during the revision cycle.
- Work to make your sentences as sharp as possible.

Sharpen your sentences.

- Cut unneeded words.
- Reword lengthy phrases. ("The dull speech" instead of "The speech that was dull.")

Create sentence variety.

- Make certain sentences are of different lengths and show logical relationships through coordination, subordination, and relative clauses.
- So that you don't use the same pattern, vary word order by using inverted order, moving modifiers, and varying sentence types.

Strengthen your sentences further.

- Use the right voice. Only use the passive deliberately; otherwise, change passive sentences to an active voice.
- Use patterns in your sentences to build rhythm. It is possible to repeat sentence type and order if it builds a rhythm for an effect.
- Use parallelism within sentences with lists of words or phrases and with multiple sentences.
- Read your paper out loud to see if your paper moves consistently from one paragraph to another.
- Proofread to make certain that your sentences avoid common grammatical and punctuation errors. Avoid sentence fragments unless they are used deliberately and with great care.

CHAPTER 7

Achieving Effective Style and Tone Through Word Choice

In this chapter, you will learn how to:

7.1 Select the kinds of words that will have the most impact in your writing.

7.2 Use the best level of diction and tone for your writing situation.

7.3 Enhance your writing with figurative language and irony.

7.4 Avoid using flawed diction in your writing.

Visit MyWritingLab **to complete the writing assignments in this chapter and for more resources on style and tone.**

You probably don't wear a tuxedo or formal gown to class. It is as much the wrong style for the classroom as shorts and a torn tee shirt are wrong for a business interview. The way we dress, walk, and talk are part of our style for the situations that confront us. The same is true of writing. Writing like "Hey! Wake yourself up, reader. I am giving you truth now" would fit a pop song or informal writing to friends but would horrify teachers or professionals in the workplace. Similarly, a sentence like "It is of the greatest imperative that we deliberate with the greatest care about the matters of profound destiny that should most trouble our conscience" sounds inflated to almost everyone. How do you shape your writing style so it accomplishes what you want? Using effective sentence strategies is part of the story. The other tool you have is your word choice, sometimes called diction. The words you use in the context of your writing can make as much a difference as putting on a tie or a baseball cap.

Selecting the Right Words

Grab a dictionary, or look at the multiple-volume *Oxford English Dictionary*, and you realize how many choices you have for every word you write. You get the most impact by selecting words with the precise meaning you need that also have the right level of abstraction and generality. Reading a lot, studying how words work, and using tools like dictionaries and thesauruses can help you make the best choices. It is a lot to ask, but your writing will get better if you learn to love words and even write in a notebook the ones you would like to use later.

7.1

Select the kinds of words that will have the most impact in your writing.

119

Choosing Words with the Meaning You Want

Danny Ozark, a baseball team manager, infamously said, "It is beyond my apprehension." Such malapropisms, or mistaken uses of a word, are usually funny and we all are guilty of them. Obviously writers need to know what a word means and how it is used before sticking it into their writing.

Such errors occur most often when we reach for large words that we don't fully understand. They also occur with common words as well. Imagine you were told that you were "excepted from the job" for which you applied. What are you to think? *Except* means to "exclude or omit" while the intended word *accept* means "to approve." If you demonstrate your popularity by declaring, "My phone rings *continuously*," the implication is that you never answer your phone since *continuously* means "uninterrupted." What you probably meant was that your phone rang *continually*, which means "frequently or regularly repeated."

Even avoiding mistakes, you need to choose the words that communicate what you intend. Are you a student in "a classroom" or in "a building," at "a school," "a college," "a community college," "a technical institute," "a university," or "an institution of higher education"? If you were in New York City, the important point might be that your English class was held on the 23rd floor of a skyscraper. If you were writing generally about education in America, you would want to discuss "institutions of higher education" because that would cover everything after high school. However, if you were addressing your specific situation, you might need a more precise term such as "a community college," or "liberal arts college." Don't let words master you; choose the one that does what you need.

Deciding on Concrete and Abstract Words

"Live Free or Die." This powerful rallying cry of the American Revolution and the state motto of New Hampshire has punch. It depends on abstract words that name general concepts that don't immediately point to something we can experience with our senses. "Freedom" is pretty abstract, as are words like "love," "patriotism," "conservatism," or even "family." Such words used judiciously can motivate powerful responses; in excess, they can leave writing vague and confusing.

Concrete words evoke precise, vivid mental images and thus help convey a message. A thing is concrete if we can weigh it, hold it, photograph it, smash into it, or borrow it from our neighbors. Abstract terms can create different images for different people. Ask your friends to describe what comes to mind when they think of "joy," "patriotism," "freedom," or other abstract terms. Some may think of "freedom" as a shopping mall, others a church service, others a newspaper free to criticize the president. Concrete terms often add to the precision of our writing and certainly make it juicier.

In the following passage, the concrete diction is highlighted:

> To do without self-respect . . . is to be an unwilling audience of one to an interminable documentary that details one's failings, both real and imagined, with

fresh footage spliced in for every screening. There's the glass you broke in anger, there's the hurt on X's face; watch now, this next scene, the night Y came back from Houston, see how you muff this one. To live without self-respect is to lie awake some night, beyond the reach of warm milk, phenobarbital, and the sleeping hand on the coverlet, counting up the sins of commission and omission, the trusts betrayed, the promises subtly broken, the gifts irrevocably wasted through sloth or cowardice or carelessness. However long we postpone it, we eventually lie down alone in that notoriously uncomfortable bed, the one we make ourselves. Whether or not we sleep in it depends, of course, on whether or not we respect ourselves.

Joan Didion, "On Self-Respect"

Now note how vague and colorless the passage becomes without the concrete diction:

To do without self-respect is to be continuously aware of your failings, both real and imagined. Incidents stay in your mind long after they are over. To live without self-respect means being bothered by intentional or unintentional failings, trusts betrayed, promises subtly broken, and gifts irrevocably wasted through sloth or cowardice or carelessness. However long we postpone it, we eventually must come to terms with who we are. How we respond to this situation depends, of course, on whether or not we respect ourselves.

EXERCISE   *Underline the concrete terms in the following passage:*   MyWritingLab

Gluttony wallowed in its nauseous excess at tables spread in the halls of the mighty. The everyday dinner of a man of rank ran from fifteen to twenty dishes; England's earl of Warwick, who fed as many as five hundred guests at a sitting, used six oxen a day at the evening meal. The oxen were not as succulent as they sound; by tradition, the meat was kept salted in vats against the possibility of a siege, and boiled in a great copper vat. Even so, enormous quantities of it were ingested and digested. On special occasions a whole stag might be roasted in the great fireplace, crisped and larded, then cut up in quarters, doused in a steaming pepper sauce, and served on outsized plates.

William Manchester, *A World Lit Only by Fire: The Medieval Mind*
and the Renaissance: Portrait of an Age

Deciding How Specific or General Words Should Be

If you tell your friends that you are dating "an animal," there are likely to be some titters, both because of the ambiguity and the odd generality of the word choice. When we decide on words, we decide on how concrete or general a word should be. As we move from *Lassie* to *collie* to *dog* to *mammal* and finally to *animal*, we become less and less specific, ending with a term that encompasses every animal on earth. With each step we retain only those features that fit the more general term. Thus, when we move from *collie* to *dog*, we leave out everything that makes collies different from terriers, greyhounds, and other breeds.

Ask yourself how specific you need to be. If, for instance, you're describing a wealthy jet setter, noting that he drives a Ferrari, not just a car, helps establish his character. If, however, you are writing about celebrating Mardi Gras in New Orleans, your readers don't need to know that you drove a rented Ford Focus from the airport.

MyWritingLab   **EXERCISE**

1. **Arrange each set of words from less specific to more specific.**
   a. man, ex-president, human being, George W. Bush, American
   b. Forest Hills Apartments, building, structure, condominium, dwelling

2. **Expand each of the following words into a series of four or more that become progressively more specific. Use 1a or 1b as a pattern.**
   a. activity
   b. event
   c. political party
   d. institution
   e. device
   f. reading matter

Using Dictionaries and Thesauruses

Vocabulary is power, and it is easier than ever to enhance your vocabulary. You can have a word of the day downloaded to your computer or smart phone. Dictionaries and thesauruses are available online. These are powerful tools to strengthen your vocabulary and help you select the most effective word for your writing. Don't overdo it, however. If you look up most words while writing a draft, you will lose your flow; and papers written from a dictionary or thesaurus in a vain attempt to impress the reader often end up comically distorted.

Dictionaries   Dictionaries are storehouses of word meanings, spelling, pronunciation, and even word origins and history. Dictionary makers avoid dictating how words should be used. Instead, they record current and past meanings. When a word gains or loses a meaning or a newly minted word enjoys wide circulation, dictionary makers observe and record. Most users, however, regard dictionaries as authorities on correctness.

Dictionaries supply much more than word meanings. Figure 7.1, an annotated entry from a college-level dictionary, shows what they can provide. Some dictionary entries include idioms, irregular forms of words, usage labels, and supplementary information as well.

Idioms   Idioms express meanings that differ from those of the words that make them up. Here are two examples.

I won't *put up with* any foolishness.
The dowager *gave me the cold shoulder*.

Put up with means "tolerate"; *gave me the cold shoulder* means "snubbed me." Looking up the most prominent word of an unfamiliar idiom may lead you to a listing and a definition.

Spelling, Syllabication. When a word has variant spellings, some dictionaries indicate a preferred version. Alphabetically close variants appear in the same entry. Dots or hyphens separate syllables and tell where to divide a word written on two lines.

Etymology. This term means the origin and development of words. Most college dictionaries limit the entry to the root (original) word and an abbreviation for the original language. The abbreviation key near the front of the dictionary identifies the language.

Pronunciation. Dictionaries indicate preferred as well as secondary pronunciations. Accent marks (') show which syllable gets the primary stress and which the secondary stress, if any. To determine the pronunciation, follow the key at the bottom of the page.

Parts of Speech. Each word is classified by grammatical function. Usually, abbreviations such as *n* (noun), *adj.* (adjective), and *vt.* (transitive verb) identify the part of speech.

man•i•fold \'ma-nə-, fōld\ *adj.* [ME, fr. OE *magnigfeald,* fr. *manig* many + -*feald* –fold] (bef. 12c) **1 a:** marked by diversity or variety **b:** MANY **2:** comprehending or uniting various features: comprehending or uniting various features : MULTIFARIOUS **3:** rightfully so-called for many reasons <a ~ liar> **4:** consisting of or operating many of one kind combined <a ~ bellpull> – *SYN* divers, multifarious, myriad – **man•i•fold•ly** \-, fōl(d)-lē\ *adv* – **man•i•fold•ness** \-, fōl(d)-nəs\ *n*

Additional Word Formations. These are words derived from the one being defined. Their parts of speech are also indicated. Because they have the same basic meaning as the parent word, definitions are omitted.

Meanings. Meanings are grouped by parts of speech. Sometimes usage is briefly illustrated (*manifold* duties). Some dictionaries list meanings in historical order, others according to frequency of use. The front part of the dictionary specifies the arrangement.

Synonyms. These are words close in meaning to the one being defined. Although no synonym carries exactly the same meaning as the original, the two may be interchangeable in some situations.

Figure 7.1   By permission. From *Merriam-Webster's Collegiate® Dictionary*, 11th Edition ©2015 by Merriam-Webster, Inc. (www.Merriam-Webster.com).

Irregular Forms   Any irregular forms are indicated. In *Webster's New World Dictionary*, the entry for the verb *spring* notes that the other forms are *sprang*, *sprung*, and *springing*. This information helps you use correct forms in your writing.

Usage Labels   Usage labels help you determine whether a word suits the circumstances of your writing. Here are the most common labels:

Label	Meaning
Colloquial	Characteristic of informal writing and speaking; should not be considered nonstandard.
Slang	Informal, newly coined words and expressions or old expressions with new meanings.
Obsolete	No longer in use but found in past writing.
Archaic	Still finds restricted use, such as in legal documents; otherwise not appropriate.
Poetic	Used only in poetry and in prose with a poetic tone.
Dialect	Used regularly only in a particular geographical location such as the southeastern United States or the Scottish Lowlands.

Supplementary Information   While focusing primarily on individual words, college-level dictionaries often provide several other kinds of information. They may include a history of the language, lists of standard abbreviations and of colleges and universities, biographical notes on distinguished individuals, and geographical notes on important locations.

Any dictionary is better than none, and often an online dictionary such as *Merriam-Webster's* is most convenient. Many excellent dictionaries, including the *Oxford English Dictionary* and many specialty dictionaries, are available online, though some require a subscription either by the individual or the university. Online dictionaries often offer entertaining ways to explore words, such as an e-mailed word of the day. When the going gets tough, you might need to head to excellent desk-sized dictionaries such as the following:

The American Heritage Dictionary

Funk and Wagnall's Standard College Dictionary

The Random House Dictionary of the English Language

Merriam-Webster's Collegiate Dictionary

Webster's New World Dictionary of the American Language

Unabridged (complete) dictionaries such as *Webster's Third New International Dictionary* and the *Oxford English Dictionary* can be found in college and public libraries. There you'll also find a variety of specialized dictionaries. Your librarian can direct you to dictionaries that list terms in particular fields.

EXERCISE   *Use a good desk dictionary to look up the specified information for each of*   MyWritingLab
the following lists of words:

1. Variant spellings:
airplane	aesthete	gray	tornadoes
color	gaily	theater	usable

2. Syllabication and the syllable that receives the main stress:
Anacrusis	Cadenza	harbinger	misanthrope
baccalaureate	exclamation	ionize	sequester

3. Parts of speech:
before	fair	separate	to
deep	here	then	where

4. Etymology:
Carnival	Icarian	phenomenon	supercilious
Fiduciary	lethargy	sabotage	tawdry

5. Idiomatic phrases:
beat	get	jump	put
eat	high	make	set

6. Synonyms:
attack	ghastly	mercy	plot
distress	keep	object	range

Thesauruses   Thesauruses list synonyms for words but omit the other elements in dictionary entries. There are easy-to-use online thesauruses like Merriam-Webster's that let you simply enter a word and search. Figure 7.2 shows a typical entry. Note that the items are grouped according to parts of speech, and some are cross-indexed.

A thesaurus will help you find a word with just the right shade of meaning or a synonym when you want to avoid repetition. But synonyms are never exactly equal, nor are they always interchangeable. To illustrate, *old* means "in existence or use for a long time"; *antiquated* conveys the notion that something is old-fashioned or outdated. Therefore, use the thesaurus along with the dictionary. Only then can you tell which synonym fits a specific sentence.

Excellent guides to synonyms include the following:

Roget's International Thesaurus
Webster's New Dictionary of Synonyms
Modern Guide to Synonyms and Related Words

formless   *adjective*

1   having no definite or recognizable form <a *formless* mass of clay that the potter transformed into an attractive bowl>

Synonyms amorphous, shapeless, unformed, unshaped, unstructured

Related Words characterless, featureless, nondescript; chaotic, disorganized, incoherent, systemless, unordered, unorganized; dim, fuzzy, hazy, inchoate, indefinite, indeterminate, indistinct, indistinguishable, murky, nebulous, obscure, unclear, undefined, undetermined, vague

Near Antonyms coherent, ordered, orderly, organized; clear, decided, definite, distinct

Antonyms formed, shaped, shapen, structured

2   not composed of matter <from this *formless* void the universe was supposed to have been created>

Synonyms bodiless, ethereal, formless, incorporeal, insubstantial, nonmaterial, nonphysical, spiritual, unbodied, unsubstantial

Related Words metaphysical, psychic (*also* psychical), supernatural; impalpable, insensible, intangible, invisible; airy, diaphanous, gaseous, gossamery, tenuous, thin, vaporous, wispish

Figure 7.2   By permission. From *Merriam-Webster's Collegiate® Dictionary*, 11th Edition ©2015 by Merriam-Webster, Inc. (www.Merriam-Webster.com).

Achieving the Desired Rhetorical Effect

7.2

Use the best level of diction and tone for your writing situation.

What kind of response do you want from your reader based on your writing style? That response generated by the manner of writing rather than the message is the rhetorical effect. Successful writers create a desired effect through the level of their diction and the tone of their writing. In many cases, both diction level and tone are also established by the expectations of the writing community. All developing writers struggle with consistently maintaining the right level of diction. Often your teacher's comments about vocabulary and sentence variety will also be intended to help you maintain the level of diction your readers will expect.

Selecting the Best Level of Diction

What level of diction is best? The answer depends on the writer's audience and purpose as well as the expectations of the discourse community. Think about a safety engineer who investigates a serious industrial accident on which she must write two reports, one for the safety director of the company, who represents a technical audience, and another for the local newspaper, read by a general audience. Although the two accounts would deal with the same matter, clearly they would use very different language: specialized and formal in the first case, everyday and more relaxed in the second. In each case, the language would reflect the background of the audience. As you write, always choose language suited to your audience and purpose.

Edited American English follows the familiar grammatical rules maintained in most formal and academic writing. Generally, everything you write for college courses or on the job should be in edited American English. *Nonstandard English* refers to any version of the language that deviates from these rules. Following is an example from Mark Twain's famous novel *The Adventures of Huckleberry Finn*:

> You don't know about me without you have read a book by the name of *The Adventures of Tom Sawyer*, but that ain't no matter. That book was made by Mr. Mark Twain, and he told the truth, mainly. There was things which he stretched, but mainly he told the truth. That is nothing. I never seen anybody but lied one time or another, without it was Aunt Polly, or the widow, or maybe Mary.

Nonstandard English does have a place in writing. Fiction writers use it to narrate the talk of characters who, if real, would speak that way. Journalists use it to report eyewitness reactions to accidents and crimes, and people who compile oral histories use it to record the recollections of people they interview.

Edited American English includes four levels of usage: formal, informal, formal–informal, and technical. Another commonly recognized category is colloquial language and slang.

Formal Level   The formal level, dignified and serious, is suitable for important political, business, and academic occasions. Its vocabulary is marked by many abstract and multisyllabic words but no slang or contractions. Long sentences and deliberately varied sentence patterns help give it a strong, rhythmic flow. Sentences are often periodic, and many have parallel or balanced structures. (See pages 114–115.) Overall, formal prose impresses the reader as authoritative, stately, and graceful.

The following excerpts from John F. Kennedy's inaugural address illustrate the formal level:

> Now the trumpet summons us again—not as a call to bear arms, though arms we need; not as a call to battle, though embattled we are; but a call to bear the burden of a long twilight struggle, year in and year out, "rejoicing in hope, patient in tribulation," a struggle against the common enemies of man: tyranny, poverty, disease, and war itself.
>
> In the long history of the world, only a few generations have been granted the role of defending freedom in its hour of maximum danger. I do not shrink from this responsibility; I welcome it.

The first sentence opens with parallelism to show contrast: "not as a call to bear arms, though arms we need" and "not as a call to battle, though embattled we are." In the second paragraph, parallelism in the second sentence shows contrast. Except for the second sentence in the second paragraph, all of the sentences are periodic rather than loose. Thus, not until the end of the opening sentence do we learn the nature of the "long twilight struggle" to which "the trumpet summons us." Time and again Kennedy uses elevated diction—polysyllabic words like *embattled, rejoicing, tribulation, tyranny, poverty,* and *generations,* along with shorter abstract words like *hope and freedom.* These carefully controlled sentence patterns, along with this wording, lend rhythmical dignity to the whole passage.

Informal Level   Informal writing resembles orderly, intelligent conversation. Earmarked by relatively ordinary words, loose sentences, and numerous shorter, less varied sentence structures than formal prose, informal writing may include contractions or even slang, and it is more likely than formal writing to use the pronouns *I, me, my, you,* and *yours.* Following is an example:

> There was a distressing story in the paper a few months ago. I wish I'd clipped it out and saved it. As it is, I can only hope I remember it fairly accurately. There was a group of people who wanted a particular dictionary removed from the shelves of the local library because it contained a lot of obscenity. I think they said there were sixty-five or so dirty words in it. Some poor woman who was acting as a spokesman for the group had a list of offending words, which she started to read aloud at a hearing. She managed to read about twenty of them before she started sobbing uncontrollably and couldn't continue.
>
> Thomas H. Middleton, "The Magic Power of Words"

Unlike the Kennedy excerpt, this one has relatively uncomplicated sentences. Three of them—the fourth, sixth, and seventh—are loose rather than periodic. The passage includes two contractions, *I'd* and *couldn't,* one casual expression, *a lot of,* and the pronoun *I.* Most of the words are very short, and none would be out of place in an ordinary conversation.

Formal–Informal Level   As life has become less formal, informal diction has become increasingly widespread. Today many articles and books, even ones on relatively serious topics, mix informal and formal elements. Following is an example:

> A lot of people like really loud music. Concertgoers talk about a special state of consciousness, a sense of thrills and excitement, when the music is really loud—over 115 dB. We don't yet know why this is so. Part of the reason may be related to the fact that loud music saturates the auditory system, causing neurons to fire at their maximum rate. When many, many neurons are maximally firing, this could cause an emergent property, a brain state qualitatively different from when they are firing at normal rates. Still, some people like loud music, and some people don't.
>
> Daniel J. Levitin, *This is Your Brain on Music: The Science of a Human Obsession*

The sentence structure is varied, with most sentences loose. Phrases like "many, many," "really loud music," and "thrills and excitement" suggest a more informal style. Yet phrases like "saturates," "auditory system," and "causing neurons to fire at their maximum rate" indicate a formal and possibly technical diction. The last sentence uses parallel phrases that feel formal but are offset by informal language like "still" and "loud music."

Mixing formal and informal diction can result in some ridiculous sentences, as in the following example. "*The national debt poses extraordinary political challenges for a nation too long used to 'cruising easy street.'* " The slang at the end is jarring and undercuts the seriousness of the rest of the sentence. Mixed levels need to be used carefully.

Technical Level   A specialist writing for others in the same field or for sophisticated nonspecialists writes on the technical level. Technical language uses specialized words that may be unfamiliar to a general audience. Its sentences tend to be long and complex, but unlike formal diction it doesn't lean toward periodic sentences, parallelism, and balance. Read this example on neurotransmitters.

> Once the neurotransmitter is released from the neurotransmitter vesicles of the presynaptic membrane, the normal movement of molecules should be directed to receptor sites located on the postsynaptic membrane. However, in certain disease states, the flow of the neurotransmitter is defective. For example, in depression, the flow of the inhibitory neurotransmitter serotonin is defective, and molecules flow back to their originating site (the presynaptic membrane) instead of to receptors on the postsynaptic membrane that will transmit the impulse to a nearby neuron.
>
> Encyclopedia of Mental Disorders, "Neurotransmitters"

Note the specialized vocabulary—*vesicles, presynaptic membrane, postsynaptic, serotonin, receptors*—as well as the length and complexity of the sentences.

Every field has *jargon*, specialized terms or inside talk that provides convenient shorthand for communication among its members. For an audience of biologists, you may write that two organisms have a *symbiotic relationship*, meaning "mutually beneficial"; for psychology majors, you might use *catalepsy* instead of "a temporary loss of consciousness and feeling, often accompanied by muscular rigidity." As a general rule, use technical terms only if your audience will know their meanings. If you must use unfamiliar words when writing for a general audience, define them the first time they appear.

EXERCISE   *Identify the level of diction in each of the following passages. Support your answers with examples from the passages. Point out slang or colloquial expressions.*   MyWritingLab

1. We may now recapitulate the reasons which have made it necessary to substitute "space-time" for space and time. The old separation of space and time rested upon the belief that there was no ambiguity in saying that two events in distant places happened at the same time; consequently it was thought that we could describe the topography of the universe at a given instant in purely spatial terms. But now that simultaneity has become relative to a particular observer, this is no longer possible.

   Bertrand Russell, *The ABC of Relativity*

2. In some ways I am an exceptionally privileged woman of thirty-seven. I am in the room of a private, legal abortion hospital, where a surgeon, a friend of many years, is waiting for me in the operating room. I am only five weeks pregnant. Last week I walked out of another hospital, unaborted, because I had suddenly changed my mind. I have a husband who cares for me. He yells because my

indecisiveness makes him anxious, but basically he has permitted the final choice to rest in my hands: "It would be very tough, especially for you, and it is absolutely insane, but yes, we could have another baby." I have a mother who cares. I have two young sons, whose small faces are the most moving arguments I have against going through with this abortion. I have a doctorate in psychology which, among other advantages, assures me of the professional courtesy of special passes in hospitals, passes that at this moment enable my husband and my mother to stand in my room at a nonvisiting hour and yell at each other over my head while I sob.

Magda Denes, *In Necessity and Sorrow: Life and Death in an Abortion Hospital*

3. I have just spent two days with Edward T. Hall, an anthropologist, watching thousands of my fellow New Yorkers short-circuiting themselves into hot little twitching death balls with jolts of their own adrenalin. Dr. Hall says it is overcrowding that does it. Overcrowding gets the adrenalin going, and the adrenalin gets them queer, autistic, sadistic, barren, batty, sloppy, hot-in-the-pants, charred-in-the-flankers, leering, puling, numb—the usual in New York, in other words, and God knows where else. Dr. Hall has the theory that overcrowding has already thrown New York into a state of behavioral sink. Behavioral sink is a term from ethology, which is the study of how animals relate to their environment. Among animals, the sink winds up with a "population collapse" or "massive die-off." O rotten Gotham.

Tom Wolfe, *The Pump House Gang*

Establishing the Intended Tone

"That paperback sucked." "That tome was not a real page turner." "The novel lacked engaging characters." These three sentences may have the same evaluation of a novel, but they vary significantly in their tone and the probable impact they will have on readers. Tone reveals the author's attitude toward the topic and the reader. All writing has a tone that stems from the meaning and connotation of words, the sentence patterns, and the rhythm of the prose.

Managing Denotation and Connotation   "PoPo," "fuzz," "cop," "police officer," and "law enforcement officer," all may refer to the person giving you a ticket, but you know that the last two terms might be the better form of address for the situation. The words have the same denotation but differ in their connotation.

The denotation of a word is its direct, essential meaning: what the word always stands for. The word *book*, for example, denotes "a set of printed or blank sheets bound together along one edge to form a volume." This definition is objective and neutral. It does not assign any special value or convey any particular attitude toward the word or what the word stands for. Connotations are the values and emotional associations that accompany a word. When the self-made man snorts "book learnin'" at his better-educated junior partner, he assigns a value and an attitude—that he ranks experience higher than the knowledge gained from books.

Some words—*death*, for instance—almost always carry strong connotations or emotional associations. *Webster's Tenth New Collegiate Dictionary* defines it as "a permanent cessation of all vital functions" or "the end of life," but it means much more. All of us have hopes, fears, and memories about death, feelings that color our responses whenever we hear or read the word. Likewise, we have personal responses to words like *sexy, cheap, radical, politician,* and *mother.* Experience, to a considerable extent, conditions how we think and feel about a word. To an Olympic swimmer who has won a gold medal, *swimming* may stir pleasant memories of the victory and the plaudits that went with it. The victim of a near-drowning, however, might react to the same word with something approaching horror.

Nonetheless, cultural connotations are more important than personal ones. Cultural connotations develop the way individual ones do, but on a much larger scale, growing out of the common experiences of many speakers and writers and changing with usage and circumstances.

Context, the parts of a passage that precede and follow a word, also affects connotation. Note, for instance, the different associations of *dog* in these sentences:

That movie is a real dog.

I sure am putting on the dog!

It's a dog-eat-dog world.

Your dog-in-the-manger attitude makes you very unpopular.

Denotation is sometimes called the language of science and technology; connotation, the language of art. But we need both to communicate effectively. Denotation allows us to convey precise, essential meanings. Connotation adds richness, warmth, and bite.

Objective Tone

An objective tone keeps the writer's personality and opinions out of the message. Following is an example:

> Myopia is a condition of the eye that makes distant vision blurry. In brief, the myopic individual is nearsighted. When the eye is normal, rays of light pass through it and come to focus on the retina, located at the back of the eye. In the myopic eye, however, the rays of light come together a little in front of the retina. As a result, the distant image is not seen clearly.
>
> Janine Neumann, student

This tone suits a popular explanation of a medical condition. The prose is businesslike and authoritative, the sentence patterns uncomplicated, and nothing reveals the person behind the words.

Other Attitudes

Sometimes you write merely to inform, sometimes to persuade. In persuasive writing, let your attitude toward your topic set the tone. Decide how subtle, flamboyant, or formal your writing should be and what special tone—satiric, cynical, serious, mock pompous, bawdy, playful—will win your reader over.

Every essay has combined characteristics that give it a special tone. The following excerpts illustrate some of tone's many dimensions:

> Unless you have led an abnormally isolated adulthood, the chances are excellent that you know many people who have at one time or another committed an act, or consorted with someone who was committing an act, for which they might have been sent to prison. We do not consider most of these people, or ourselves, criminals; the act is one thing, the criminality of it quite something else. Homicide, for example, is in our law not a crime; murder only is proscribed. The difference between the two is the intention, or to be more accurate, society's decision about the nature of that intention.
>
> Bruce Jackson, "Who Goes to Prison: Caste and Careerism in Crime"

Here we have a sophisticated and rather formal tone. Terms like *consorted* and *proscribed*, while exactly suited to Jackson's meaning, do not form part of most people's word kits. The complexity of the first sentence and the varied patterns of the others add to the air of sophistication. The emphatic *quite*, meaning "entirely," is cultivated usage; and along with *society's decision*, it lends the tone a wry touch.

> Cans. Beer cans. Glinting on the verges of a million miles of roadways, lying in scrub, grass, dirt, leaves, sand, mud, but never hidden. Piels, Rheingold, Ballantine, Schaeffer, Schlitz, shining in the sun or picked by moon or the beams of headlights at night; washed by rain or flattened by wheels, but never dulled, never buried, never destroyed. Here is the mark of savages, the testament of wasters, the stain of prosperity.
>
> Who are these men who defile the grassy borders of our roads and lanes, who pollute our ponds, who spoil the purity of our ocean beaches with the empty vessels of their thirst?
>
> Marya Mannes, "Wasteland"

Rhythm and word choice contribute equally to the tone of this passage. The excerpt opens with imagistic sentence fragments that create a panoramic word picture of our littered roadways. Then complete sentences and somber commentary follow. Words and patterns are repeated, mixing the dignified language of epic and religion with common derogatory terms—*testament*, *purity*, and *vessels* set against *savages*, *wasters*, and *defile*—to convey the contradictions *Mannes* deplores. The rhetorical questions, used instead of accusations, add a sense of loftiness to her outrage, helping create a tone both majestic and disdainful.

> *Erethizon dorsatus*, an antisocial character of the Northern U.S. and Canadian forest, commonly called a porcupine, looks like an uncombed head, has a grumpy personality, fights with his tail, hides his head when he's in trouble, attacks backing up, retreats going ahead, and eats toilet seats as if they were Post Toasties. It's a sad commentary on his personality that people are always trying to do him in.
>
> R. T. Allen, "The Porcupine"

The tone of this passage is affectionately humorous. Allen sets this tone by noting the porcupine's tousled appearance, testy personality, and peculiar habits, such as eating outdoor toilet seats (for their salt content, as Allen later explains).

The net effect is to personify porcupines, making them seem like the eccentric reprobate human that others regard with amused toleration.

EXERCISE   *Characterize the tone of each of the following paragraphs. Point out how word choice, sentence structure, rhythm, and other elements contribute to it.*

MyWritingLab

1. America, which leads the world in almost every economic category, leads it above all in the production of schlock. Christmas toys broken before New Year's, wash-n-wear suits that neither wash well nor wear well, appliances that expire a month after the guarantee, Barbie dolls, frozen pizza—these are but a few of the shoddy goods whose main contribution to our civilization, apart from a momentary satisfaction to the purchaser, is to swell the sanitary-fill schlock heaps that are the feces of our Gross (and how!) National Product.

   Robert Claiborne, "Future Schlock"

2. Nelson is known as a blues shouter. But it's a misnomer. "Shouter" gives the impression of a singer who attracts attention by uncontrolled screaming. That's not T99. Nelson brings the whole package. He can be as smooth as Jackie Wilson, as nuanced as his friend Percy Mayfield and urgent as Wynomie Harris. Nelson earned his stripes singing a variety of styles, from straight blues and jump blues to big band and swing to R&B and soul crooner. "It all depended on the audience, man," Nelson told me. "Back then some of those white cats couldn't really understand the blues. You had to sing them something they could relate to."

   Jeffrey St. Clair, "Seduced by a Legend"

Special Stylistic Techniques: Figurative Language and Irony

The style of a piece of writing is its character or personality. Like people, writing can be many things: dull, stuffy, discordant, sedate, lively, flamboyant, eccentric, and so on. Figurative language and irony can contribute to your own distinctive writing style.

7.3

Enhance your writing with figurative language and irony.

Figurative Language

Figurative language uses concrete words in a nonliteral way to create sharply etched sensory images that catch and hold the reader's attention. Besides energizing the writing, figurative language strengthens the reader's grip on the ideas. Five figurative devices are especially important: simile, metaphor, personification, overstatement, and understatement.

Simile and Metaphor   A *simile* directly compares two unlike things by the use of *like* or as. "Todd is as restless as an aspen leaf in a breeze" and "Her smile flicked on and off like a sunbeam flashing momentarily through a cloud bank" are similes. A *metaphor* also compares unlike things, but without using like or as. Some metaphors include a linking verb (*is, are, were,* and so on); others do not. "The moon was a wind-tossed bark" and "The curtain of darkness fell over the land" are both metaphors. Following is an excerpt that contains similes and metaphors:

> The field is a sea of deep, dark green, a sea made up of millions of small blades of grass blended together as one. Each blade is a dark green spear, broad at the bottom and narrowing to a needle point at the tip. Its full length is arched so that, viewed from one end, it looks like a shallow trough with paper-thin sides. On the inner side of this trough, small ridges and shallow valleys run from base to tip. To a finger rubbed across them, they feel like short, bristly hairs.
>
> Daniel Kinney, student

MyWritingLab ## Discussion Questions

1. Locate the similes in this passage and explain how they help the reader.
2. Locate the metaphors and point out how each heightens the sensory impact of the writing.

Writers too often snatch hastily at the first similes and metaphors that come to mind and end up strewing their pages with overused and enfeebled specimens. Johnny is "as blind as a bat," Mary runs around "like a chicken with its head cut off"—and the writing slips into trite gear. Other comparisons link items that are too dissimilar. For example, "The wind whistled through the trees like a herd of galloping horses" would only puzzle a reader.

Personification   This is a special sort of metaphor that assigns human qualities or traits to something nonhuman: a plant, an abstraction, a nonliving thing. Following are some examples:

The vine clung stubbornly to the trunk of the tree.

May fortune smile upon you.

The waves lapped sullenly against the base of the cliff.

Each of these sentences assigns its subject a different emotional quality—stubbornness, friendliness, gloom—each figurative rather than literal: Vines aren't stubborn, fortune doesn't smile, and waves aren't sullen.

Personification sometimes extends beyond a single sentence. To illustrate, the following passage carries a single image through an entire paragraph:

> "I figured when my legislative program passed the Congress," [Lyndon] Johnson said in 1971, "that the Great Society had a real chance to grow into a beautiful woman. And I figured her growth and development would be as natural and inevitable as any small child's. In the first year, as we got the laws on the books, she'd begin to crawl. Then in the second year, as we got more laws on the books, she'd begin to walk, and the year after that, she'd be off and running, all the time growing bigger and healthier and fatter. And when she grew up, I figured she'd be so big and beautiful that the American people couldn't help but fall in love with her, and

once they did, they'd want to keep her around forever, making her a permanent part of American life, more permanent than the New Deal."

Doris Kearns, "Who *Was* Lyndon Baines Johnson?"

Through personification, Johnson expresses affection for his social program.

Personification works best when it is used in moderation and doesn't make outrageous comparisons. Dishes don't run away with spoons except in nursery rhymes.

Overstatement   Overstatement, sometimes called hyperbole, deliberately and drastically exaggerates in order to make a point. An example is "Wilfred is the world's biggest fool."

One of the best examples of sustained overstatement is Mark Twain's essay "Fenimore Cooper's Literary Offences." In it, Twain claims, "In one place in *Deerslayer*, and in the restricted space of two-thirds of a page, Cooper has scored 114 offences against literary art out of a possible 115." Twain also asserts, "There have been daring people in the world who claimed that Cooper could write English, but they are all dead now." Through such exaggerations, Twain mocks the shortcomings of Cooper's novels.

Used sparingly, overstatement is emphatic, adding real force to an event or situation. Writers who consistently exaggerate, however, risk losing their credibility.

Understatement   Understatement makes an assertion in a humble manner without giving something its due, as when a sportscaster calls a team's 23–2 record "pretty fair." By drawing attention to the thing it appears to slight, this soft-spoken approach offers writers an effective strategy. Here is an example:

> To assume that Heidi Mansfield lacks the qualifications for this position is not unwarranted.

Without ever actually calling Mansfield unqualified, the statement suggests that she is. Similarly, when a meat company executive says, "It is not unlikely that beef prices will jump ten cents a pound in the next two months," we might as well count on spending another dime. As these statements show, understatement not infrequently has an ulterior motive.

EXERCISE   *Identify the similes, metaphors, personifications, overstatements, or under-statements in these sentences.*   MyWritingLab

1. The old table greedily sucked up the linseed oil.
2. Russia's social and economic system is a giant staircase that leads nowhere.
3. Stanley has the bile of human meanness by the quart in every vein.
4. Their music sounds like the drumming of an infant's fists against the sides of a crib.
5. You're the world's biggest liar!
6. "Fashion, though folly's child, and guide of fools, Rules e'en the wisest, and in learning rules."
7. Einstein's theories have had some impact on modern science.
8. I'm as tired as a farm horse at sunset.

Irony

Irony occurs when a writer intentionally states one thing but actually means something different or even opposite. A certain point is thus highlighted. The sportswriter who refers to the "ideal conditions" for a tennis tournament when rain has drenched the courts and forced cancellation of matches speaks ironically. Here is a longer example of the same sort of irony:

> The baron, though a small man, had a large soul, and it swelled with satisfaction at the consciousness of being the greatest man in the little world about him. He loved to tell long stories about the dark old warriors whose portraits looked grimly down from the walls around, and he found no listeners equal to those that fed at his expense. He was much given to the marvellous, and a firm believer in all those supernatural tales with which every mountain and valley in Germany abounds. The faith of his guests exceeded even his own; they listened to every tale of wonder with open eyes and mouths, and never failed to be astonished, even though repeated for the hundredth time. Thus lived the Baron Von Landshort, the oracle of his table, the absolute monarch of his little territory, and happy, above all things, in the persuasion that he was the wisest man of the age.
>
> Washington Irving, "The Spectre Bridegroom"

Irving never directly states the baron's shortcomings. Rather, suggestive details such as the swelling of the baron's soul, his belief in the supernatural, and his deception by the sponging guests portray one who, far from being "the wisest man of the age," is pompous, superstitious, and gullible.

Eliminating Flawed Diction

7.4

Avoid using flawed diction in your writing.

"Blah, blah, blah." Wordiness, ambiguity, euphemisms, slang, clichés, mixed metaphors, and sexist language can cause your readers to tune you out. As you revise, search out these common culprits and eliminate them if they are causing trouble.

Wordiness

Wordiness has more than one cause. Some writers try to sound more impressive, some pad an assignment, and some simply don't realize they're doing it. Whatever the reason, the results are the same: ponderous papers that lack punch. To inject vigor, cut out every word that doesn't serve a purpose. If five words are doing the work of one, drop four.

The two major forms of wordiness, deadwood and gobbledygook, often occur together. *Deadwood*, which does nothing but take up space and clutter the writing, is bracketed in the following sentence:

> Responsible parents [of today] neither allow their children [to have] absolute freedom [to do as they please] nor severely restrict their children's activities.

Now read the sentence without the deadwood:

> Responsible parents neither allow their children absolute freedom nor severely restrict their children's activities.

Careful revision has increased the clarity and reduced the words from 23 to 14.

Gobbledygook consists of long, abstract, or technical words that help create unnecessarily long and complex sentences. Some people who write it mistakenly believe it "dignifies" their thoughts. Others want to conceal their meanings by clouding their statements. And some naively think that long words are better than short ones. All of these writers use gobbledygook, but none of their readers appreciates it. Following are some samples of gobbledygook followed by revised versions in plain English:

Original Version	**Revised Version**
The fish exhibited a 100 percent mortality response.	All the fish died.
We have been made cognizant of the fact that the experiment will be terminated in the near future.	We have learned that the experiment will end soon.

Ambiguity

"The teacher carefully read *a paper* while drinking coffee." Is the teacher reading a newspaper or a student paper? It is important to choose words that are precise enough that the reader isn't left to guess your intent. Ambiguity just makes readers work too hard and can lead to misunderstanding. If you suggest that "someone killed off his employees," it sounds like the person needs to be arrested for murder, even if you meant that he fired them.

Euphemisms

Euphemisms take the sting out of something unpleasant or add stature to something humble. Familiar expressions include *pass away* for *die, preowned* for *used,* and *sanitation engineer* for *garbage collector.*

In most cases, the writer simply intends to cushion reality. But euphemisms also have grisly uses. Mobsters don't *beat up* merchants who refuse *protection* (itself a euphemism); they *lean on* them. Hitler didn't talk about exterminating the Jews but about *the final solution to the Jewish problem.* These euphemisms don't just blur reality; they blot out images of horror. Of merchants with broken limbs and bloodied faces. Of cattle cars crammed with men, women, and children en route to death camps. Of barbed wire and gas ovens and starved corpses in the millions.

Any euphemism, however well-intentioned, probably obscures an issue. On occasion you may need one in order to protect the sensitive reader, but usually you will serve readers best by using direct expressions that present reality, not a tidied-up version.

Colloquial Language and Slang

Colloquial originally meant "the language of ordinary conversation between people of a particular region." *Slang*, according to *Webster's Tenth New Collegiate Dictionary*, is "an informal nonstandard vocabulary composed typically of coinages, arbitrarily changed words, and extravagant, forced, or facetious figures of speech." These two categories shade into each other, and even authorities sometimes disagree on whether to label a term *colloquial* or *slang*. The word *bender*, meaning "a drinking spree," seems firmly in the colloquial camp, and *bummer*, a term once used by young people to mean "a bad time," is just as clearly slang. *Break a leg* is theater slang used to wish a performer success. But what about *guy* and *kid?* Once they were slang, but so many people have used them for so long that they have now become colloquial.

Regardless of their labels, colloquial and slang terms are almost never appropriate in formal writing. They sometimes serve a useful purpose in informal writing by creating a special effect or increasing audience appeal. Even so, careful writers use them sparingly. Some readers may not understand some colloquial language, and slang usually becomes dated quickly. The following paragraph uses colloquial and slang expressions successfully:

> . . . When I was just a kid on Eighth Avenue in knee pants [Big Bill] was trying to get himself killed. He was always in some fight with a knife. He was always cutting or trying to cut somebody's throat. He was always getting cut or getting shot. Every Saturday night that he was out there, something happened. If you heard on Sunday morning that somebody had gotten shot or stabbed, you didn't usually ask who did it. You'd ask if Big Bill did it. If he did it, no one paid much attention to it, because he was always doing something like that. They'd say, "Yeah, man. That cat is crazy."
>
> Claude Brown, *Manchild in the Promised Land*

Kid, yeah, and *cat* reflect the speech of Brown's characters and thus add authenticity to his account. Despite the informal diction, Brown uses parallelism in the second, third, and fourth sentences; repetition of "he was always" emphasizes the single-minded self-destructiveness of Big Bill's behavior. However, this is the exception to the rule, and colloquial language and slang need to be avoided in most writing.

Clichés and Mixed Metaphors

Clichés   Clichés are expressions that have become stale from overuse. Rather than respond to experience with their own perceptions, writers sometimes resort to oft-repeated words or phrases that stem from patterned thinking. Dullness follows. Daily conversation abounds with stale expressions because talk is unplanned, but writing allows you time to find invigorating and effective language. Your individual response is what draws the reader's interest, and only fresh thinking will produce that response. The following list of clichés barely "scratches the surface":

acid test	burn the midnight oil	green with envy
almighty dollar	chip off the old block	last but not least
beat a hasty retreat	clear as a bell	nipped in the bud
better late than never	cool as a cucumber	rears its ugly head
black sheep	easier said than done	set the world on fire
blind as a bat	goes without saying	sick as a dog

Mixed Metaphors   Clichéd writing often suffers as well from mixed metaphors—inappropriate combinations that startle or amuse the reader. How would you respond if you came across this example?

> When he opened that can of worms, he bit off more than he could chew.

Can you visualize someone chewing a mouthful of worms? The point is obvious.

Sexist Language

Sexist language can assume several forms. Sometimes it appears as unneeded information that dilutes or even demeans someone's accomplishments. It can occur when the writer uses gender-exclusive pronouns like *he* and *she* inappropriately. And it may attach arbitrary gender labels to persons and groups. All U.S. government agencies, most businesses, and most academic publications prohibit sexist language. Deliberate or accidental, such language has no place in your writing. These guidelines will help you avoid it.

1. Don't unnecessarily mention a person's appearance, spouse, or family.

> *Sexist:*   The cute new loan officer at the Godfather Finance Company is a real hit with customers.
>
> *Sexist:*   Craig Helmond, husband of nationally known cardiologist Dr. Jennifer Helmond, won election to the Beal City Board of Education.
>
> *Sexist:*   After eight years of attending college part time, Angelica Denham, a three-time grandmother, was awarded a bachelor of science degree.
>
> *Nonsexist:*   The efficient new loan officer at the Godfather Finance Company is a real hit with customers.
>
> *Nonsexist:*   Craig Helmond, an accountant at Oakwood Growth Enterprise, won election to the Beal City Board of Education.
>
> *Nonsexist:*   After eight years of attending college part time, Angelica Denham was awarded a bachelor of science degree.

Note how, in each case, the sentence has been rewritten to include only relevant information.

2. Use the pronouns *he, him, his,* and *himself* only when referring to antecedents that are clearly masculine and *she, her, hers,* or *herself* only when their
antecedents are clearly feminine.

Sexist:	Each tourist must carry his passport with him at all times.
Sexist:	If a collector wishes to find an out-of-print book, she should try http://www.bibliofind.com on the Web.

Correct this type of error by substituting plural antecedents and pronouns for the singular ones or by rewriting the sentence to eliminate the
pronouns.

Nonsexist:	Tourists must carry their passports with them at all times.
Nonsexist:	Any collector wishing to find an out-of-print book should try http://www.bibliofind.com on the Web.

3. Don't use occupational labels that imply the positions are held only by
one sex.

Sexist	**Nonsexist**
chairwoman	chair
draftsman	drafter
fireman	fire fighter
policeman	police officer
postman	letter carrier
weatherman	weather reporter

A word of caution here. To avoid sexism, some writers substitute the suffix
-person for *-man* in many job titles (such as *handyperson* for someone who does
odd jobs). Such attempts, however, often create awkward expressions that you
should avoid.

MyWritingLab   **EXERCISE**   *The following sentences are flawed by wordiness, ambiguity, euphemisms, slang, clichés, mixed metaphors, and sexist language. When you have identified the faults, revise the sentences.*

1. The awesome American eagle will never, in the face of foreign threats, pull in its horns or draw back into its shell.
2. Last summer, I was involved in the repair of automobiles.
3. You seem as bright as a button this morning.
4. My mother was called to her heavenly reward last winter.
5. Any student wishing to attend summer school at Burns State College must pay his tuition one week before registration day.

6. My brother is in the process of pursuing a curriculum of industrial chemistry.
7. The ball's in your court, and if you strike out, don't expect me to pick up the pieces.
8. The hot, sultry-voiced clerk quickly finished the order.
9. Winning first prize for her essay was a real feather in Peggy's cap.
10. Our company plans to confer retirement on 200 employees by year's end.

Achieving Effective Style and Tone

Based on your topic, readers, purpose, and discourse community select the style that is most appropriate.

- Formal—for serious, professional communication.
  - More abstract and multisyllabic words, longer and more structured sentences, though varied.
- Informal—for lighter topics or more familiar communication.
  - More conversational with ordinary words, looser sentences, some contractions and even colloquial expressions.
- Technical—for specifically technical fields and audiences.
  - Uses specialized vocabulary for the field, longer and more complex sentences.

Choose the right words.

- Check words you don't know well in the dictionary.
- Use the thesaurus to find alternate word choices.
- Determine if your word choices are the right level of concrete/abstract. Most writers need to change more abstract words to concrete words and more general words to specific words.

Eliminate flawed diction.

- Cut unnecessary words and tighten wordy phrases.
- Test for and eliminate ambiguity.
- Rewrite euphemisms unless the phrases are needed.
- Eliminate slang unless required for a deliberate effect.
- Rework clichés and mixed metaphors.
- Reword any sexist language.

CHAPTER 8 Narration: Relating Events

In this chapter, you will learn how to:

8.1 Use narrative as a writing strategy.

8.2 Develop and organize your narrative with action, conflict, and point of view.

8.3 Brainstorm the key events of your narrative.

8.4 Integrate dialogue into your narrative.

8.5 Think critically about your narrative.

8.6 Write so that your narrative is ethical.

8.7 Prewrite, plan, draft, and revise your narrative.

8.8 Critically synthesize material from sources to create your narrative.

Visit MyWritingLab **to complete the writing assignments in this chapter and for more resources on narration.**

Rubberball/Corbis

Clicking off the evening news and padding toward bed, Heloise suddenly glimpsed, out of the corner of her eye, a shadow stretching across the living room floor from under the drawn curtains.

"Wh—who's there?"

No response.

Edging backward toward the table where she left her cell phone, her eyes riveted on the shadow, she stammered, "I—I don't have any money."

Still no answer.

She reached for her phone and started to call 911. Just then . . .

If you want to know more, the above *narrative* has worked. A narrative relates a series of events, whether real such as histories, biographies, or news stories, or imaginary as in short stories and novels. Everyone responds to narratives and shares stories. We gossip about friends, share odd events that happen to us, or report on a story we heard on the news.

Many classroom and on-the-job writing situations call for narratives.

- Your English instructor might ask you to trace the development of a literary character.
- Your history instructor might have you recap the events leading to a major war.
- Your psychology instructor could ask you to report on society's changing attitudes toward the treatment of depression.
- A police officer may record the events leading to an arrest.
- A nurse will have to report on the deteriorating conditions of a patient.
- A manager might prepare a history of an employee work problem.

The Purpose of a Narrative

8.1

Use narrative as a writing strategy.

A narrative, like any other kind of writing, makes a point or has a purpose. The point can either be stated or left unstated, but it always shapes the writing.

Some narratives simply tell what happened or establish an interesting or useful fact. The reporter who writes about a heated city council meeting or a lively congressional committee hearing usually wants only to set facts before the public.

Most narratives, however, go beyond merely reciting events. Writers of history and biography delve into the motives underlying the events and lives they portray, while narratives of personal experience offer lessons and insights. In the following conclusion to a narrative about an encounter with a would-be mugger, the writer offers an observation on self-respect.

I kept my self-respect, even at the cost of dirtying my fists with violence, and I feel that I understand the Irish and the Cypriots, the Israelis and the Palestinians, all those who seem to us to fight senseless wars for senseless reasons, better than before. For what respect does one keep for oneself if one isn't in the last resort ready to fight and say, "You punk!"?

Harry Fairlie, "A Victim Fights Back"

Action, Conflict, and Point of View

Three key elements of any narrative are action, conflict, and point of view.

8.2

Develop and organize your narrative with action, conflict, and point of view.

Action

Action plays a central role in any narrative. Other writing often only suggests action, leaving readers to imagine it for themselves:

A hundred thousand people were killed by the atomic bomb, and these six were among the survivors. They still wonder why they lived when so many others died. Each of them counts many small items of chance or volition—a step taken in time, a decision to go indoors, catching one streetcar instead of the next—that spared him. And now each knows that in the act of survival he lived a dozen lives and saw more death than he ever thought he would see. At the time, none of them knew anything.

John Hersey, *Hiroshima*

This passage suggests a great deal of action—the flash of an exploding bomb, the collapse of buildings, screaming people fleeing the scorching devastation—but *it does not present the action.* Narration, however, recreates action:

Three yards away from Johnson he was, and sitting down. Nine feet! And yet he left the chair in full leap, without first gaining a standing position. He left the chair, just as he sat in it, squarely, springing from the sitting position like a wild animal, a tiger, and like a tiger covered the intervening space. It was an avalanche of fury that Johnson strove vainly to fend off. He threw one arm down to protect the stomach, the other arm up to protect the head; but Wolf Larsen's fist dove midway between, on the chest, with a crushing, resounding impact. Johnson's breath, suddenly expelled, shot from his mouth and as suddenly checked, with the force, audible expiration of a man wielding an axe. He almost fell backward, and swayed from side to side in an effort to recover his balance.

Jack London, *The Sea Wolf* (p. 79)

London does not just suggest. He provides us with a vivid account of the action that lets us see all the details of the fight, including Wolf Larsen's leap.

A few words of caution are in order here. Action entails not only exotic events such as the theft of mass-destruction weapons, then the ransom demand, the recovery of the weapons and the pursuit of the villains. A wide variety of more normal events also qualify as action: a long, patient wait that comes to nothing; an unexpected kiss after some friendly assistance; a disappointing gift that signals a failed relationship. Furthermore, the narrative action must all relate to the main point—not merely chronicle a series of events.

Conflict

The events in our world are often shaped by conflicts that need to be resolved. It should not be surprising then that conflict and its resolution, if any, are crucial to a narrative since they motivate and often structure the action.

Read the following student paragraph and note how common sense (highlighted in yellow) and fear (highlighted in blue) struggle within the writer, who has experienced a sharp, stabbing pain in his side:

> Common sense and fear waged war in my mind. The first argued that a pain so intense was nothing to fool with, that it might indicate a serious or even life-threatening condition. Dr. Montz would be able to identify the problem and deal with it before it worsened. But what if it was already serious? What if I needed emergency surgery? I didn't want anyone cutting into me. "Now wait a minute," I said. "It's probably nothing serious. Most aches and pains aren't. I'll see the doctor, maybe get some pills, and the problem will clear up overnight. But what if he finds something major, and I have to spend the night in the hospital getting ready for surgery or recovering from it? I think I'll just ignore the pain."
>
> Luis Rodriguez, Student

Point of View

Narrative writers may adopt either a first-person or third-person point of view. In first-person narratives, one of the participants tells what happened, whereas with third-person narration the storyteller stays completely out of the tale. Narratives you write about yourself use the first person, as do autobiographies. Biographies and histories use the third person, and fiction embraces both points of view.

In first-person narration, pronouns such as *I, me, mine, we,* and *ours* identify the storyteller. With the third person, the narrator remains unmentioned, and the characters are identified by nouns and such pronouns as *he, she, him,* and *her.* The following two paragraphs illustrate the difference, using highlighting to draw your attention to the use of first or third person:

First-Person Narration

Long before daylight we ranged abroad, hatchet in hand, in search of fuel, and made the yet slumbering and dreaming wood resound with our blows. Then with our fire we burned up a portion of the loitering night, while the kettle sang its homely strain to the morning star. We tramped about the shore, waked all the muskrats, and scared up the bittern and birds that were asleep upon their roosts; we hauled up and upset our boat and washed it and rinsed out the clay, talking aloud as if it were broad day, until at length, by three o'clock, we had completed our preparations and were ready to pursue our voyage as usual; so, shaking the clay from our feet, we pushed into the fog.

Henry David Thoreau, *A Week on the Concord and Merrimac Rivers*

Third-Person Narration

In the depths of the city walk the assorted human creatures who do not suspect the fate that hangs over them. A young woman sweeps happily from store to store, pushing a baby carriage along. Businessmen stride purposefully into their office buildings. A young man sulks down the sidewalks of his tenement, and an old woman tugs her shopping basket across a busy thoroughfare. The old woman is not happy: she has seen better days. Days of parks and fountains, of roses and grass, still stir in her memory. Reaching the other side, she stops and strains her neck upward, past the doorways, past the rows and rows of mirror glass, until her eyes rest on the brilliant blue sky so far away. She looks intently at the sky for a few minutes, noting every cloud that rolls past. And the jet plane. She follows the plane with her deep-socketed eyes and for some unexplainable reason suspects danger. She brings her gaze back to earth and walks away as the jet releases a large cloud of brownish-yellow gas. The gas hangs ominously in the air for a while, as if wanting to give humankind just a few more seconds. Then the cloud slowly descends to the surface, dissipating as it goes. By the time it reaches the glittering megalopolis, it is a colorless, odorless blanket of death.

Richard Latta, student

EXERCISE *Identify the point of view in each of the following excerpts:*

MyWritingLab

1. The bus screeched to a stop, and Pat stepped out of it and onto the sidewalk. Night enveloped the city, and a slight drizzle fell around her as she made her way to Al's office. Turning the corner, she stepped into the dark entryway.

   The receptionist had gone home, so she proceeded directly to the office. She knocked on the door and entered. Al, standing behind his desk and looking out the window, turned toward her with a startled look on his face.

   Jennifer Webber, student

2. In the darkness before dawn I stood on the precipice of a wilderness. Inches in front of my toes, a lava cliff dropped away into the mammoth bowl of Haleakala, the world's largest dormant volcano. Behind me lay a long green slope where clouds rolled up from the sea, great tumbleweeds of vapor, passing through the pastures and eucalyptus forests of upland Maui to the volcano's crest, then spilling over its edge into the abyss.

   Barbara Kingsolver, *High Tide in Tucson: Essays from Now or Never*

Key Events

Any narrative includes many separate events, enough to swamp your narrative boat if you try to pack them all in. Suppose you wish to write about your recent

8.3

Brainstorm the key events of your narrative.

attack of appendicitis in order to make a point about heeding early warnings of an oncoming illness. Your list of events might look like this:

Awakened	Ate lunch	Was rushed to hospital
Showered	Ate breakfast	
Experienced acute but passing pain in abdomen	Opened garage door	Entered building
	Started car	Greeted fellow employees
	Drove to work	
Dressed	Parked in employee lot	Began morning's work
Took coffee break		
Visited bathroom	Returned to work	Felt nauseated
Experienced more prolonged pain in abdomen	Began afternoon's work	Met with boss
		Underwent diagnostic tests
Walked to cafeteria	Collapsed at work	Had emergency operation

A narrative that included all, or even most, of these events would be bloated and ineffective. To avoid this outcome, identify and build your narrative around its key events—those that bear directly on your purpose. Include just enough secondary events to keep the narrative flowing smoothly. Here's how you might present the first attack of pain:

> My first sign of trouble came shortly after I stepped out of the shower. I had just finished toweling when a sharp pain in my lower right side sent me staggering into the bedroom, where I collapsed onto an easy chair in the corner. Biting my lip to hide my groans, I sat twisting in agony as the pain gradually ebbed, leaving me gray faced, sweat drenched, and shaken. What, I asked myself, had been the trouble? Was it ulcers? Was it a gallbladder attack? Did I have stomach cancer?

This passage convinces, not just tells, the reader that an attack has occurred. Its details vividly convey the nature of the attack as well as the reactions of the victim. As in any good narrative, the reader shares the experience of the writer, and the two communicate.

Dialogue

8.4

Integrate dialogue into your narrative.

Dialogue, or conversation, animates narratives, enlivening the action and drawing the reader into the story. Written conversation, however, doesn't duplicate real talk. In speaking with friends, we repeat ourselves, throw in irrelevant comments, use slang, lose our train of thought, and overuse expressions like *you know*, *uh*, and *well*. Dialogue that reproduced real talk would weaken any narrative.

Good dialogue resembles real conversation without copying it. It features simple words and short sentences while avoiding the over-repetition of phrases like *she said* and *he replied*. If the conversation unfolds smoothly, the speaker's identity will be clear. To heighten the sense of reality, the writer may use an occasional sentence fragment, slang expression, or pause, as in this passage:

> They both looked at the rapids cascading down the mountainside.
>
> "Dare you," Drew challenged, leaning against his river kayak.
>
> Tom studied the river. "We've run worse. I think." He paused. "But I don't remember when."
>
> Drew punched him in the arm. "Dude, that's why it's called an extreme sport. Extreme broken bones."
>
> Tom tapped his helmet and picked up his kayak. "I am inventing extreme portaging, and the rad idea of staying alive," he shouted over his shoulder, as he started down the trail around the falls.

Note the use of the slang expressions "dude" and "rad," as well as a sentence fragment ("Extreme broken bones") as pauses in the conversation covered by descriptions like "Tom studied the river" and "Tom tapped his helmet and picked up his kayak." These strategies lend an air of realism to Drew and Tom's words.

In addition to making your dialogue realistic, be sure that you punctuate it correctly. Following are some key guidelines:

- Each shift from one speaker to another requires a new paragraph.
- When an expression like *he said* interrupts a single quoted sentence, set it off with commas.
- When such an expression comes between two complete sentence, put a period after the expression and capitalize the first word of the second sentence. "I know it looks bad," she said. "But I didn't mean to blow up the lab."
- Put commas, periods, and other punctuation marks that come at the end of a direct quote inside of the quotation marks. "What do you want from me?"

Thinking Critically About Narratives

When you read a narrative work or write a narrative of your own, there are some key critical questions you should ask.

8.5

Think critically about your narrative.

- Who is telling the narrative and how is that viewpoint biasing or shaping the narrative?
- How would the narrative look if told from another point of view?
- What has the narrative overemphasized, or what might the narrative have left out that might have shaped or skewed the narrative?
- If more context were included or the narrative covered more of the events involved, how might these choices change the narrative and the reader's view of the situation?

Ethical Issues

8.6

Write so that your narrative is ethical.

Think of your response if you were surfing the Internet and came across a narrative about your first date that used your actual name and cast you in an unfavorable light. At the very least you would find it embarrassing. As you mull over any narrative you write, you'll want to think about several ethical issues, especially if you're depicting an actual event.

- Am I providing a truthful account that participants will recognize and accept? Deliberate falsification of someone's behavior that tarnishes that person's reputation is libel and could result in legal action.
- Would the narrative expose any participants to possible danger if it became public? Do I need to change any names to protect people from potential harm? Say your narrative includes someone who cooperates behind the scenes with authorities to help solve a case. You should probably give that person a fictitious name.
- Does the narrative encourage unethical or illegal behavior? For example, extolling the delights of smoking marijuana for a teenage audience is clearly unethical.

These guidelines don't rule out exaggerated, humorous, or painfully truthful narratives. As with any writing, however, narratives can impact the lives of people; as ethical writers we need to consider the possible consequences of our work.

Writing a Narrative

8.7

Prewrite, plan, draft, and revise your narrative.

Most of the narratives you write for your composition class will relate a personal experience and therefore use the first person. On occasion, though, you may write about someone else and therefore use the third person. In either case make sure the experience you pick illustrates some point. A paper that indicates only how you violated a friend's confidence may meander along to little purpose. But if that paper is shaped by some point you wish to make—for instance, that you gained insight into the obligations of friendship—the topic can be worthwhile.

Prewriting the Narrative

To get started, do some guided brainstorming, asking yourself these questions:

FINDING YOUR TOPIC
- What experience in my life or that of someone I know interests me?
- Is there an event in my community or history that I would like to relate?
- Who was involved and what parts did they play?
- What main point would you want to make about this event in one or two sentences?

When you have pinpointed a topic, use further brainstorming to generate supporting material. Here are some suggestions:

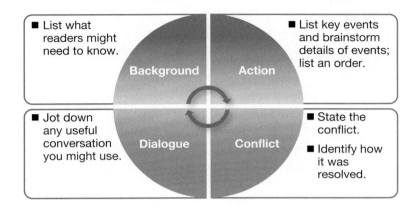

Planning and Drafting the Narrative

Before you start to write, develop a plot outline showing the significant events of your narrative.

For each one, jot down what you saw, heard, or did, and what you thought or felt.

To create a **thesis statement**, ask yourself what was the important lesson from the event. As Brittany Coggin thought about her grandmother, she realized that the most important lesson she taught was the value of the love of the family. The thesis statement, in turn, helps you select the events and details that matter, in Coggin's case, the way the grandmother interacted with her family, even while dying.

Following are suggestions for organizing your narrative:

Introduction
- Sets the stage for what follows.
- Possibly tells when and where the action occurred.
- Provides useful background information.
- Notes the incident that started events.
- States main point here or in the conclusion.

Body
- Moves action forward to turning point.
- Establishes conflict.
- Provides sequence of main events.
- Usually resolves conflict.
- Uses time signals such as "now," "next," "finally," "when I returned" to help reader.
- Uses dialogue.

Conclusion
- Ties up loose ends.
- Gives a sense of completion.
- May include a reflective summary of events, note your reactions, offer a surprise twist, or discuss aftermath.

Revising the Narrative

As you revise, follow the guidelines in Chapter 4. With narratives, it is especially useful to brainstorm details for the events in the narrative or try jotting down additional dialogue. Sometimes it is useful to briefly freewrite about the narrative from someone else's point of view. In addition, ask yourself these questions:

- Have I made the point, stated or unstated, that I intended? What events or wording could strengthen that point?
- What background is missing that the reader might need to better follow the narrative?
- What action does not relate to the main point or could be cut to make the sequence of events stronger?
- How could the order of events or transitions be made clearer?
- What could make the conflict clearer and stronger for the reader?
- What events have been left out that are important to the purpose of the narrative? What details would make the narrative more powerful and interesting? Have time indicators been used where needed, but not excessively?
- Does the point of view work for the reader? Are there any places where it changes and is confusing?

- Where is more dialogue necessary, where does it get in the way, and where does it seem artificial and uninteresting?
- Where could paragraphs be better focused or developed?
- Where could you strengthen the word choice by using concrete verbs and enhance sentence structure?
- What could be done to make the conclusion better provide an interesting resolution to the narration?
- Is the narrative ethical or are there sections that cause misgivings?

STUDENT ESSAY OF **NARRATION**

Joy Through the Tears

Brittany Coggin

1   When I was growing up, there was a plaque in my grandmother's kitchen that read, "Don't get too busy making a living that you forget to make a life." My grandmother certainly followed this precept. Family was the most important thing in the world to her, and my family and I knew that we were loved.

2   As a child, I spent most days with my grandmommy while my mother was finishing school. My days were filled with baking cookies, playing games, reading stories, and making our famous mud pies. Grandmommy made time for all of this while working and taking care of all the daily chores around the house. When my mother would arrive to pick me up, it was no surprise for her to walk into the house and see Grandmommy and me prancing through the house banging pans while singing "Jingle Bells," with bright red buckets on our heads. We even called ourselves the "bucket heads."

3   My grandmother was a remarkable woman. I have always thought of her as the "center" of my family because she was. Grandmommy held high standards for her children and grandchildren, but she held even higher standards for herself. There was never a time that we did not know where she stood on an issue or where we stood with her. She had a way of holding us accountable while still leaving us in no doubt of her love for us. Although I can recall many times that I disappointed her, there was never a time that my grandmother ever disappointed me. If I thought I was in trouble and might get spanked, I usually was and did. If I thought she would be proud of me, she was. Honesty and integrity were very important to her, and she had both in abundance.

Continued on next page

Establishes first-person point of view. Uses quote to define main character. States thesis of narrative

Establishes context of relationship with grandmother with specific examples to define character

Provides additional context to define relationship and character

Continued from previous page

Identifies initial conflict

4   <u>Tragedy usually strikes when we least expect it. Nothing could have prepared me for what happened with my grandmother.</u> She was the larger-than-life force who kept our family focused. If ever there was a problem, we took it to Grandmommy, knowing she would be able to point us in the right direction.

Presents event 1 in sequence with detailed accounts

5   <u>The first sign that there was a problem was when she began having excruciating pain in her legs.</u> Her doctor thought it could be neuropathy or nerve damage because she had shingles when she was young. The doctor then sent her to a specialist, who could find nothing wrong. The following months were filled with specialist after specialist who prescribed pain medication after pain medication but could never diagnose the problem. The second clue that there was actually more to the story began when my grandmother complained that every time she ate, it felt as if her chest was on fire, and she would experience a lot of pressure in her chest. Once again, specialist after specialist could find nothing wrong. By this point, my grandmother's weight went from 125 pounds to 85 pounds. Despite the weight loss, our family doctor told her that he could find nothing wrong with her. He told her to take Tylenol and to "go home and live her life."

Presents next major event that intensifies the conflict with the mention of "cancer"

6   <u>Two weeks later, she was so weak that she fell down the porch steps of our family's farmhouse.</u> We rushed her to the hospital in Henderson, Texas. She had broken her ankle, wrist, and both of her hips when she fell. While in the hospital, the doctor ordered a "swallow study" to be completed. My aunt, who is a speech pathologist, knew the speech pathologist doing the study. She asked her to go down lower into the esophagus and to use contrast. That was when we found out that my grandmother's esophagus had completely closed and the opening into the stomach was blocked. Everything she swallowed, including any medication that was prescribed, had gathered at the end of her esophagus. By this time, she was much too weak to have the procedure to open the esophagus. Her doctor sent her to Tyler to have a procedure to remove all of the material in her esophagus and to try alternatives to surgery. During this time, the doctor finally ordered a scan, which revealed that she had lung cancer and that the cancer had metastasized to the bone.

Describes the narrator's first-person reaction, how the writer reacted to the news

7   <u>This news was shocking to all of us. I had the surreal feeling that I was dreaming and that at any moment, I would wake up and my world would be as it had always been. Instead, the reality was that my world would never be the same again.</u> Grandmommy was devastated but ready

to fight. My mom stayed with her the first night in the hospital because she had to have three rounds of chemotherapy the first night. Mom said that after each round, she and Grandmommy "high-fived." That's my Grandmommy!

8   During this time, amazingly, it was my grandmother who gave us the strength to handle each day. Mom started graduate school that summer, so I would stay with Grandmommy while she was at school. Each day, Grandmommy seemed to lose the use of something. I found that I could handle more than I ever thought possible. I had to learn how to feed her and administer medication through a feeding tube. All I could think about was how I could not possibly do this. It was just too much and too hard. After a while, it became second nature. I can remember putting her false teeth in without thinking twice about it. When she lost all of her hair, we would play with hats and headbands. I would give her a make-over every time she had a doctor's appointment. Even when she began to lose the use of her hands, she cooked dinner for my mother. Grand-mommy was disappointed with how it came out, but my mom said those were the best salmon patties she had ever eaten. That dinner was a labor of love because every step in the process involved immense pain.

9   While this was a time of loss, it was also a time of happiness. The time I was able to spend with my grandmother drew us closer. Each moment I spent with her seemed suspended in time. Every word, facial expression, and hug became an everlasting memory. Sometimes it seemed that my whole family was in so much pain, and no one could reach out to help each other. My grandmother loved each of us so much, so she reached out to help each family member. Her love enveloped each of us, and it kept us believing that she would get better. I know that love is not tangible, but during this time, Grandmommy could look at me, and I could feel how much she loved me. In the midst of her suffering, she gave me love and comfort. In a sense, she helped prepare me for what was to come.

10   In December 2005, my grandfather was taking Grandmommy to her doctor's appointment. After getting in the car, she collapsed and then became unconscious. I rushed to meet my family at the emergency room. When I got there, Grandmommy had regained consciousness but was not getting enough oxygen. My mother explained to her that she had pneumonia, and the doctors wanted to put her on a breathing machine until she got over it. Mom asked her to squeeze her hand if that was okay.

Continued on next page

Continues sequence of events to reconfirm the positive family-centered nature of the grandmother. Demonstrates transformation of the writer's role

Develops paragraph 8, showing relationship tied to the main point concerning family love

Event that brings events to crisis point. Confirms the relationship

Continued from previous page

Though Grandmommy could not speak, she squeezed my mom's hand to tell her to let the doctors go ahead with the procedure. She then went into a coma that lasted a week.

11   When she awoke, she was terrified. The doctors said that she had a severe staph infection. This scared her because her father died of a staph infection. Doctors told us she would not be able to live without the breathing machine. Grandmommy had signed an advance directive requesting that she not be allowed to live with such suffering. The days following were miserable. I did not want to lose the one person who truly understood me, but we could not let her suffer. Even without the use of her body, her mind remained alert. We would stand around the bed in her room, and she would look past us with the most beautiful smile on her face. She mouthed that she was tired, and we knew it was time. The following morning, the doctor took her off the breathing machine, and she died with her family around her.

12   My grandmother lost her battle with cancer in December 2005. While I still mourn her loss, I feel honored to have known her. Grandmommy's life will always serve as an example of how to live a life that needs no apology. She taught me that love is everlasting and that people are more important than material things. Because of her, I am stronger than I ever thought possible. I am blessed to have had this remarkable woman as my grandmother.

Side note: Culminates sequence of events with death and reconfirms importance of family

MyWritingLab   Discussion Questions

1. Identify the point of view of the narrative. Why is that choice of point of view important to this particular narrative?
2. What context did the writer provide before the central conflict of her grandmother's illness? What was the role of this context information?
3. Narratives depend on very specific details. What details best helped develop the character of the writer's grandmother? Why were those details effective?
4. What is the main point of this narrative? What other possible conflicts or themes might the reader have focused on? How would the narrative have to be rewritten to make that point?
5. This narrative uses very little dialogue. Would the narrative have been improved by dialogue? Where could dialogue have been added effectively?

SUGGESTIONS FOR WRITING

Writing: Narration

1. Write a personal narrative about an experience that
   a. Altered either your opinion of a friend or acquaintance or your views about some important matter.
   b. Taught you a lesson or something about human nature.
   c. Acquainted you with some previously unrecognized facet of your character or personality.
   d. Brought about a significant change in your way of life.

   Keep in mind all the key narrative elements: purpose, action, conflict, point of view, key events, and dialogue.

2. A *maxim* is a concise statement of a generally recognized truth. Noting the key elements above, write a first-person or third-person narrative that illustrates one of the following maxims or another that your instructor approves:
   a. A little learning is a dangerous thing.
   b. The more things change, the more they stay the same.
   c. Don't judge a book by its cover.
   d. The road to hell is paved with good intentions.
   e. Pride goeth before a fall.
   f. Sometimes too much of a good thing can be wonderful.
   g. Sometimes good intentions have unexpected consequences.

3. Write a third-person narrative based on the following activities:
   a. Interview someone who works in a career area that interests you. Ask them about how they got involved in that area and write a narrative reporting the results.
   b. Find out about the history of a place that you know well and write a narrative about how the place changed.
   c. Interview someone in your class about an important event that made them who they are and write a narrative about that person.
   d. Talk to a small business owner in your area or a leader of a nonprofit group to find out how it got started in your area and write a narrative about that business or group.

Multimedia Writing

1. Examine the photo at the start of the chapter (page 143). Write a narrative that results in photo picture or follows from this picture.

2. Collect photos from an event you were involved with or from your life and write a narrative that makes sense of the photos. Include the photos either in the Word document or in a blog post to illustrate the narrative.

Critical Synthesis with Sources: Narration

8.8

Critically synthesize material from sources to create your narrative.

Purposes of Synthesis   Sometimes writers create narratives by weaving together information from different sources. When developing a narrative about some childhood experience, you might supplement your own recollections by asking relatives and friends to supply details that you've forgotten or clear up points that have become hazy. A police officer investigating an accident questions witnesses, examines physical evidence, and uses the findings to draft an accurate report. A historian writing a biography draws upon public documents, newspaper accounts, diaries, notes of other investigators, and—depending on when the subject lived—other material such as newsreels, TV clips, and interviews in order to create a balanced portrait.

Integrating material from several sources into a coherent piece of writing is called **synthesis**. When you synthesize, you reflect on ideas you have found in various sources, establish on your own the connections among those ideas, and then determine how the ideas and connections can advance the purpose of your writing. Thus, synthesis features independent thinking in which *you* evaluate, select, and use the material of others—which, of course, must be properly documented—to further your own purpose. Although synthesis can be challenging and does call for judgment on your part, following an effective procedure can help ensure success.

Prewriting for Your Synthesis   Start by jotting down the main points of information from your sources and identifying where those points agree. Sometimes accounts of the same event differ. A friend's memory of your childhood experience may differ markedly from your own. A police officer may find that two witnesses disagree about how an accident happened. A historian may discover that public documents and newspapers offer different motives for an action by a biographical subject. When you encounter this type of contradiction, you'll need to weigh each position carefully in order to determine the most believable account.

Critically Evaluating Your Sources   Narratives can be one sided or exclude vital information. You should test the narratives of your sources to determine whether they present multiple perspectives on the issue, seem complete enough, or consistent enough with the narratives of other sources. You may wish to deliberately seek out sources representing different perspectives on an event. Test your sources to make certain they are credible.

Planning and Drafting Your Synthesis   As in developing any narrative, arrange your material in a pattern that helps make your point. Let's say, for example, that you're narrating the history of a suburban housing development for low-income families built on land that was formerly owned by a nearby chemical plant and later was found to be contaminated by toxic chemicals. Company officials admit that wastes were buried there but insist that the chemicals were properly contained and posed absolutely no health threat. After stating the company's position, you present the findings of government investigators who analyzed soil samples from the site. These findings revealed that the containers were corroded and leaking and that the wastes included chemicals that attack the nervous system, as well as highly toxic herbicides designed for chemical warfare operations. You conclude that the company is responsible for the serious health problems that now plague the people living in the housing development. Note how the strategy of presenting the company's position early in the narrative lends added force to the point that shapes your writing—company accountability for the health of the housing development's residents.

Getting Started

MyWritingLab

1. Review a number of articles in your school or local newspaper to develop a sense of journalistic style. Then interview several people about a recent event on campus or at the place you live, and write a narrative that reports the event and draws on the interviews.

2. Take notes from several newspaper accounts of an important or controversial event, and write an account of the event that includes your notes.

Writing a Narrative

Prewriting the narrative.

- Identify topic if assigned or brainstorm personal experiences or observations for ideas.
- Check to make sure that the topic is ethical and not likely to encourage unethical or harmful behaviors.
- Talk to others to get ideas, more information, and new perspectives.
- Read for information if needed.
- Brainstorm background information, actions, key conflicts, and possible dialogue.

Planning the narrative.

- Let main point guide you.
- Identify the key conflict.
- List sequence of events (plot outline).
- Identify point of view: first or third.
- Identify needed context.
- Would the narrative harm any person mentioned if it becomes public?

Drafting the narrative.

- Introduction sets context, provides background, initiates action, and may state main point.
- Body develops action in sequence of key events—signals transitions in time.
- Conclusion pulls together narrative and may restate main point.
- Is the account being written truthfully and fairly?

Revising the narrative.

- Did you make your main point?
- Does the action fit the main point?
- Are any key events missing?
- Is the point of view appropriate?
- Does the dialogue ring true?

Repeat the process as necessary.

Proofread.

CHAPTER 9 Description: Presenting Impressions

In this chapter, you will learn how to:

9.1 Use description as a writing strategy.

9.2 Use sensory perceptions to create a dominant impression.

9.3 Determine a vantage point for your description.

9.4 Select and arrange the details of your description.

9.5 Think critically about your description.

9.6 Write so that your description is ethical.

9.7 Prewrite, plan, draft, and revise your description.

9.8 Critically synthesize source materials to create your description.

Visit MyWritingLab **to complete the writing assignments in this chapter and for more resources on description.**

Rubberball/Corbis

The afternoon was perfect. Stretched out on a chaise lounge by the pool, Carla could feel the heat from the sun sinking into her skin. She could still taste the cool, tangy blend of sweet and bitter of fresh lemonade. In the distance, she could hear the afternoon buzz of lawnmowers. The air barely moved, as if the earth were holding its breath. She had sunk a little more deeply into a heat-basking doze when she was startled by a loud boom from the pool followed by an icy splash of water over her legs. She sat up, eyes wide open, to see her brother emerging from the pool, grinning, water dripping from his hair.

You are there. Seeing, hearing, touching, tasting. This is a *description* of an afternoon in the suburbs. Effective description creates sharply etched word pictures of objects, persons, scenes, events, or situations. Sensory impressions—sight, sound, taste, smell, and touch—form the backbone of descriptive writing. Often, they build toward one dominant impression that the writer wants to evoke, an impression that can convey emotions such as shock we experience in response to a description of an abused child.

Many occasions call for description.

- In a lab report for your chemistry class, you might have to describe the odor or appearance of a chemical substance.
- For an art class, you might need to describe a painting.
- For a brochure prepared for your hospitality management class, you might need to describe a banquet room.
- A realtor might write a glowing description of a house for an advertisement.
- A nurse might describe the postoperative status of a surgical incision in her notes on a patient's recovery.

The Purpose of Description

9.1

Use description as a writing strategy.

Sometimes description stands alone; sometimes it enriches other writing. It appears in histories and biographies, fiction and poetry, journalism and advertising, and even in technical writing. Some descriptions merely create images and mood, as when a writer paints a word picture of a boggy, fog-shrouded moor. But description can also stimulate understanding or lead to action. A historian may juxtapose the splendor of French court life with the wretchedness of a Paris slum to help explain the French Revolution. And everyone knows the persuasive power of advertising's descriptive enticements.

Description will provide effective backup for the writing you do in your composition classes, helping you to drive home your points vividly.

Sensory and Dominant Impressions

Precise sensory impressions begin with close observation. If you can reexamine your subject, do it. If not, recall it; then capture its features with appropriate words. When you can't find the right words, try a comparison. Does it smell like a rotten egg? A ripe cantaloupe? Burning rubber? Does it sound like a high sigh? A soft rustle? To come across, the comparison must be accurate and familiar. If the reader has never smelled a rotten egg, the point is lost.

9.2

Use sensory perceptions to create a dominant impression.

Following is a passage marked by particularly vivid sight impressions:

> After our meal we went for a stroll across the plateau. The day was already drawing to a close as we sat down upon a ledge of rock near the lip of the western precipice. From where we sat, as though perched high upon a cloud, we looked out into a gigantic void. Far below, the stream we had crossed that afternoon was a pencil-thin trickle of silver barely visible in the gloaming. Across it, on the other side, the red hills rose one upon another in gentle folds, fading into the distance where the purple thumblike mountains of Adua and Yeha stretched against the sky like a twisting serpent. As we sat, the sun sank fast, and the heavens in the western sky began to glow. It was a coppery fire at first, the orange streaked with aquamarine; but rapidly the firmament expanded into an explosion of red and orange that burst across the sky sending tongues of flame through the feathery clouds to the very limits of the heavens. When the flames had reached their zenith, a great quantity of storks came flying from the south. They circled above us once, their slender bodies sleek and black against the orange sky. Then, gathering together, they flew off into the setting sun, leaving us alone in peace to contemplate. One of the monks who sat with us, hushed by the intensity of the moment, muttered a prayer. The sun died beyond the hills; and the fire withdrew.
>
> Robert Dick-Read, *Sanamu: Adventures in Search of African Art*

At first, the western sky glows with "a coppery fire," which then expands into "an explosion of red and orange" that sends "tongues of flame" heavenward and then withdraws as the sun disappears. Comparisons strengthen the visual impression: the "pencil-thin" stream, the "thumblike" mountains stretching across the sky "like a twisting serpent." The familiar pencil, thumb, and serpent help us to visualize the unfamiliar landscape.

Most descriptions blend several sense impressions rather than focusing on just one. In the following excerpt, Mark Twain, reminiscing about his uncle's farm, includes all five. As you read it, note which impressions are most effective.

> As I have said, I spent some part of every year at the farm until I was twelve or thirteen years old. The life which I led there with my cousins was full of charm, and so is the memory of it yet. I can call back the solemn twilight and mystery of the deep woods, the earthy smells, the faint odors of the wild flowers, the sheen of rain-washed foliage, the rattling clatter of drops when the wind shook the trees, the far-off hammering of woodpeckers and the muffled drumming of wood pheasants in the remoteness of the forest, the snapshot glimpses of disturbed wild creatures scurrying through the grass—I can call it all back and make it as real as it ever was, and as blessed. I can call back the prairie, and its loneliness and peace, and a vast hawk hanging motionless in the sky, with his wings spread wide and the blue of the

vault showing through the fringe of their end feathers. I can see the woods in their autumn dress, the oaks purple, the hickories washed with gold, the maples and the sumacs luminous with crimson fires, and I can hear the rustle made by the fallen leaves as we plowed through them. I can see the blue clusters of wild grapes hanging among the foliage of the saplings, and I remember the taste of them and the smell. I know how the wild blackberries looked, and how they tasted, and the same with the pawpaws, the hazelnuts, and the persimmons; and I can feel the thumping rain, upon my head, of hickory nuts and walnuts when we were out in the frosty dawn to scramble for them with the pigs, and the gusts of wind loosed them and sent them down. I know the stain of blackberries, and how pretty it is, and I know the stain of walnut hulls, and how little it minds soap and water, also what grudged experience it had of either of them. I know the taste of maple sap, and when to gather it, and how to arrange the troughs and the delivery tubes, and how to boil down the juice, and how to hook the sugar after it is made, also how much better hooked sugar tastes than any that is honestly come by, let bigots say what they will.

Mark Twain, *Autobiography*

MyWritingLab   **EXERCISE**   *Spend some time in an environment such as one of the following. Concentrate on one sense at a time. Begin by observing what you see; then jot down the precise impressions you receive. Now do the same for impressions of touch, taste, smell, and sound.*

1. The woods in the early morning
2. A city intersection
3. A restaurant or cafeteria
4. A scenic spot under a full moon
5. A storm

6. A pool or other recreation area
7. A crowded classroom or hallway
8. A construction site
9. A park or playground
10. A holiday gathering

Dominant Impression

Skillful writers select and express sensory perceptions in order to create a *dominant impression*—an overall mood or feeling such as joy, anger, terror, or distaste. This impression may be identified or left unnamed for the reader to deduce. Whatever the choice, a verbal picture of a storm about to strike, for example, might be crafted to evoke feelings of fear by describing sinister masses of clouds, cannon salvos of thunder, blinding lightning flashes, and viciously swirling wind-caught dust.

The following paragraph establishes a sense of security as the dominant impression:

A marvelous stillness pervaded the world, and the stars together with the serenity of their rays seemed to shed upon the earth the assurance of everlasting security. The young moon recurved, and shining low in the west, was like a slender shaving thrown up from a bar of gold, and the Arabian Sea, smooth and cool to the eye like a sheet of ice, extended its perfect level to the perfect circle of a dark horizon. The propeller turned without a check, as though its beat had been part of the scheme of a safe universe; and on each side of the Patna two folds of water, permanent and somber on the unwrinkled shimmer, enclosed within their straight and diverging ridges a few white swirls of foam bursting in a low hiss, a few wavelets, a few ripples, a few undulations that, left behind, agitated the surface of the sea for an instant after the passage of the ship, subsided splashing gently, calmed down at last into the circular stillness of water and sky with the black speck of the moving hull remaining everlastingly in its centre.

Joseph Conrad, Lord Jim

EXERCISE   *Select one of the following topics and write a paragraph that evokes a dominant impression. Omit details that run counter to your aim.*

MyWritingLab

1. A multi-alarm fire
2. A repair facility (automobile, appliance, and so on)
3. A laboratory
4. Some aspect of summer in a particular
5. A religious service
6. A doctor's or dentist's office
7. A dark street
8. A parade or other celebration
9. Some landmark on your college campus
10 A municipal night court or small-claims court

Vantage Point

You may write a description from either a fixed or a moving vantage point. A fixed observer remains in one place and reports only what can be perceived from there. Here is how Marilyn Kluger describes the Thanksgiving morning sounds she remembers hearing from her bed as a child:

9.3

Determine a vantage point for your description.

> On the last Thursday in November, I could stay in bed only until the night chill left the house, hearing first the clash of the heavy grates in the huge black iron range, with its flowery scrolls and nickled decorations, as Mother shook down the ashes. Then, in their proper sequence, came the sounds of the fire being made— the rustle of newspaper, the snap of kindling, the rush of smoke up the chimney when Mother opened the damper, slid the regulator wide open, and struck a match to the kerosene-soaked corncobs that started a quick hot fire. I listened for the bang of the cast-iron lid dropping back into place and for the tick of the stovepipes as fierce flames sent up their heat, then the sound of the lid being lifted again as Mother fed more dry wood and lumps of coal to the greedy new fire. The duties of the kitchen on Thanksgiving were a thousand-fold, and I could tell that Mother was bustling about with a quicker step than usual.
>
> Marilyn Kluger, "A Time of Plenty"

A moving observer views things from a number of positions, signaling changes in location with phrases such as "moving through the turnstile" and "as I walked around the corner." In the following section, Jasper Becker explicitly changes our position from the air to the ground to show us a different perspective on the Chinese countryside.

> For all its poverty, the Loess Plateau has a stark grandeur about it. From the air one sees the vast badlands of treeless gullies and waterless rivers branching out in an endless intricate pattern. Through it all the Yellow River carves its way with slow and lazy strength, like a giant serpent. On the ground, a drive to northern Shanxi,

Identifies our first perspective

Descriptions consistent with vantage point

Identifies the change in vantage point
Identifies direction of motion
Offers description consistent with shifting vantage point
Identifies and provides description from new vantage point

where the silt-laden river forms the border with inner Mongolia, takes one through a landscape which might be on Mars. The riverbeds are dry. The hills are barren. The villages are silent. Some homes consist of nothing more than a door and window facing a tunnel carved into the hillside. Elsewhere people live in villages closed in behind tall fortress-like walls of thick mud, part of a network of fortified settlements built to resist recurrent invasions by horsemen from Mongolia.

  We stop at Zijinshan, a collection of villages built in the shadow of 30-foot-high Ming dynasty watchtowers, part of a massive early warning defense system. From here the ground drops away down steep gullies to the Yellow River, which lies hidden a thousand feet below. Across the river is Mongol territory.

Jasper Becker, *The Chinese*

Whatever your vantage point, fixed or moving, report only what would be apparent to someone on the scene. If you describe how a distant mountain looks from a balcony, don't suddenly leap to a description of a mountain flower; you couldn't see it from your vantage point.

MyWritingLab   **EXERCISE**

1. **Writing as a fixed observer, describe in a paragraph your impressions of one of the following. Be sure to indicate your vantage point.**
   a. A post office lobby two weeks before Christmas
   b. The scene following a traffic accident
   c. A classroom when the bell rings
   d. A campus lounge
   e. An office

2. **Writing as a moving observer, describe in a paragraph or two your impressions as you do one of the following things. Clearly signal your movements to the reader.**
   a. Walk from one class to another
   b. Shop in a supermarket or clothing store
   c. Walk from your home to the corner
   d. Water-ski
   e. Go through a ticket line and enter a theater, auditorium, or sports arena

Selection and Arrangement of Details

Select and arrange the details of your description.

Good description requires an attention to detail.

Selection of Details

Effective description depends as much on exclusion as on inclusion. Don't try to pack every possible detail into your paper by providing an inventory of, for example, a room's contents or a natural setting's elements. Such an approach shows only that you can see, not write. Instead, select details that deliberately point toward the mood or feeling you intend to create. Read the following student description:

  At night, a restful stillness falls over the suburbs. . . . Everyone has vanished inside the carefully maintained homes that line the winding streets. The children have gone to bed, leaving the occasional motionless wagon or tricycle in the driveway. A light gleams in some bedroom windows. TV sets silently flicker a tranquil blue in a few living rooms. The street lamps curve protectively over the empty streets and sidewalks. The stillness is only disturbed by the brief, familiar bark of a neighbor's dog, quickly hushed, intensifying in its wake the silence that holds sway with the dark.

Kim Granger, student

This writer evokes a sense of stillness by noting "the occasional motionless wagon or tricycle," that "TV sets silently flicker a tranquil blue," that "the street lamps curve protectively," that the dog is "quickly hushed." She ignores the car that cruises homeward, stereo booming; the husband and wife screaming at each other; the caterwauling catfight. Mentioning these things would detract from the desired mood.

Arrangement of Details

Description, like any other writing, must have a clear pattern of organization to guide the reader and help you fulfill your purpose. Often some spatial arrangement works nicely. You might, for example, move systematically from top to bottom, left to right, front to back, nearby to far away, or the reverse of these patterns. To describe Saturday afternoon at the football game, you might:

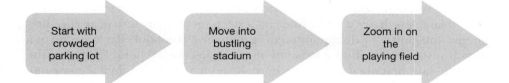

For other purposes, you might start with some central feature, then branch out to things around it. To capture the center of a mall, you might:

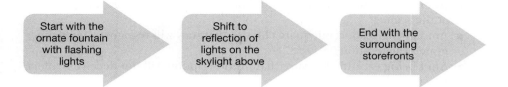

Sometimes when a writer writes about change, a time sequence makes sense. A writer might portray the changes in a woodland setting as follows:

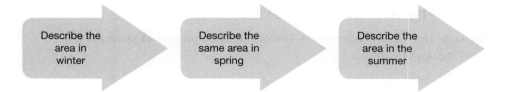

Thinking Critically About Descriptions

9.5

Think critically about your description.

When you read a description or write your own, here are some questions you should ask yourself. One thing we know from studies in criminal justice is that eyewitness accounts are not as reliable as we would like to think.

1. How is the writer or your vantage point shaping what you perceive? A stranger walking past a classroom will see very different things than a student who is in the class for an extended period of time.
2. How might the writer's or your interests shape what you are perceiving? A person seeking to develop land might overlook the wetland and its wildlife and focus instead on the land's development potential.
3. What details have been overemphasized or left out of the description, and how might this emphasis or omission unreasonably bias the account or be misleading?
4. What other vantage points, interests, or ways of exploring the thing being described would allow for an effective alternative description?

Ethical Issues

9.6

Write so that your description is ethical.

Imagine a police description of an auto accident that misstated the length of a car's skid marks or failed to note the icy patches of road at the scene. It might cost a blameless driver a heavy fine and a steep increase in auto insurance premiums. Imagine your disappointment and anger if you booked a weekend at a distant resort only to find it situated on an algae-covered pond instead of the beautiful lake described in the brochure. Imagine your irritation if a going-out-of-business sale described as "fabulous" turned out to offer only 10 percent price reductions. Clearly, inaccurate descriptions can create a wide range of undesirable consequences. Ask and answer these questions about your description.

- Am I making my observations carefully, accurately, and fairly?
- Am I writing so that readers would find my writing credible if they were at the scene?
- Am I giving readers adequate clues so that they will recognize any deliberate exaggeration?
- Am I being careful to ensure that my description will not deceive readers in a harmful way?

You have an ethical obligation to present a reasonably accurate portrayal of your topic.

Writing a Description

9.7

Prewrite, plan, draft, and revise your description.

To write an effective description, follow the usual process of prewriting, drafting, and revising.

Prewriting the Description

If you're choosing your own topic:

FINDING YOUR TOPIC

- Select something with which you are familiar.
- Review your journal for ideas.
- Talk to friends or post on Facebook to determine what readers may want to know about.
- Look through old photos of trips you have taken, at art, movies, or other points of interest.

To help gather and organize support for your topic,

DEVELOPING YOUR DESCRIPTION

- Determine what you want your description to do: Create an impression or persuade a reader to act.
- Identify the interest of your readers—perhaps talk to others.
- Brainstorm additional details, possibly employing different vantage points.
- Link sensory impressions to details with key words.
- Connect details with the dominant impression you want to make.
- Map the order of your description.

After brainstorming a list of potential details, you might use branching to start accumulating sensory impressions. This illustrates how student writer Kim Swiger used branching to obtain and group the sensory impressions for a paragraph describing the sounds of her kitchen at breakfast time. Note that her grouping provided Swiger with the pattern used to organize her paragraph. Thus, the paragraph begins with stove-related sounds, moves to sounds associated with coffee-making and cooking, and ends with the sounds of mixing orange juice.

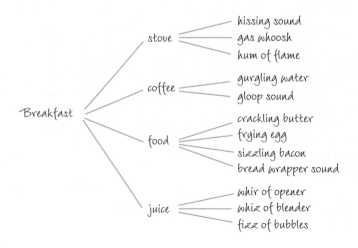

Planning and Drafting the Description

To formulate a **thesis statement**, focus on the dominant impression or what you think the description shows. "Suburban developments, often a joke on TV shows, instead are beautiful parks that can nourish the soul." "In only a few years, a once vibrant community became a visual wasteland." Here is how to organize your paper.

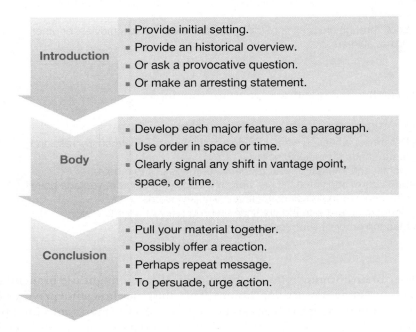

Introduction
- Provide initial setting.
- Provide an historical overview.
- Or ask a provocative question.
- Or make an arresting statement.

Body
- Develop each major feature as a paragraph.
- Use order in space or time.
- Clearly signal any shift in vantage point, space, or time.

Conclusion
- Pull your material together.
- Possibly offer a reaction.
- Perhaps repeat message.
- To persuade, urge action.

As you write, aim for vivid, original language. We've all encountered writers who tell us that raindrops "pitter-patter," clouds are "fleecy white," and the sun is "a ball of fire." Such stale, worn-out language does nothing to sharpen our vision of the rain, the clouds, or the sun. The Swiger paragraph avoids this pitfall.

> Sure signs of a new day are the sounds in the kitchen as breakfast is prepared. The high sigh of the gas just before it whooshes into flame and settles into a whispering hum blends with the gurgling of the water for the morning coffee. Soon the gloop, gloop, gloop of the coffee sets up a perky beat. Then in mingles the crackle of creamy butter on a hot skillet and the shush of an egg added to the pan. Ribbons of bacon start to sizzle in the spitting grease. The soft rustle of plastic as bread is removed from its wrapper contributes to the medley. The can opener whirs, and the orange juice concentrate drops with a splat into the blender, which whizzes together the orange cylinder and splashed-in water. For minutes after the blender stops, bubbles of various sizes fizz.
>
> Kim Burson Swiger, student

You are there in the kitchen, hearing the carefully selected and freshly described sounds.

A word of caution about making your writing vivid. Some students are tempted to enhance their descriptions by stringing together a chain of adjectives without considering the effect on a reader. Think how you'd react if told that

> A dented, cylindrical, silver-gray, foul-smelling, overloaded trash can sat in the alley.

As you can see, more than the garbage can is overloaded here. Resist the temptation to inject similar sentences into your description. Carefully examine your adjectives and eliminate those that don't advance your purpose.

Revising the Description

As you revise, apply the guidelines in Chapter 4 and ask the following questions:

- What sections of the description can better tie to your purpose and audience?
- Where could additional sensory details add to the description?
- What additional features could be added to make the impression stronger?
- What details should be added or cut to strengthen the dominant impression?
- Where might the vantage point be confusing?
- How could the order for the details be made clearer for the reader or more effectively signaled?
- Where could paragraphs be more focused or developed?
- Is the essay ethical, honest, fair, and not harmful?

SAMPLE

STUDENT ESSAY OF DESCRIPTION

My Serenity

Rachel Harvey

1   The building blends in with the landscape, its faint yellow tin siding disguising it from passersby on the road. As the icicles split-splop from the entryway overhang, one devious droplet sneaks into my shirt to roll down my neck. As I step into the barn, I am bombarded with the musty smell of clay dirt, sawdust, and sweet hay. The air here is more inviting than outside; it beckons me as an old friend would. I know my welcoming committee is in full swing when I hear a faint meow and a series of whinnies rising up out of the stalls. A large black-and-white barn cat, appropriately named Sylvester for his markings and ability to catch birds, stares at me with his intense yellow eyes. My boots sink into the soft dirt

Establishes context—moves from outside to inside with details. Includes visual and sound

Continued on next page

Continued from previous page

as I wade my way over to the worn, wooden stalls and stoop to pet the oversized feline. I stop at Dynamite Kid's stall to pay him a visit.

Focuses on horse. Continues moving vantage point with writer. Uses multiple senses including sight, sound, feeling, and smell and writer's emotional reaction

2   Kid stands a beautiful five feet two inches tall, with his white blond mane and tail and sleek white coat dappled with gray. As I approach him, he starts to dance, or at least a horse's version of dancing. His front legs splayed wide and rocking his weight from side to side, he resembles a flagpole in a gusty storm. I find myself giggling because he thinks I'm going to feed him; he always dances for his food. I slip into his stall and his petal-soft lips scour my hand for his treat. His teeth sound as if they're cutting bolts as he pulverizes the pea-green pellet into bits. I nuzzle up to his soft neck and inhale his aroma. The musk of a horse is unforgettable because it's natural but so unique. This scent brings some of my most treasured memories back. Here I can forget about my ten-page paper that's due Friday and about the fight my significant other and I just had.

Focuses on horse. Continues moving vantage point with writer. Uses multiple senses including sight, sound, feeling, and smell and writer's emotional reaction

3   Everything seeps away from my mind as I snatch a stiff-bristled brush and start grooming him, plumes of dust rising off his back. Here it's only Kid, me, and the rustles and sighs of the other horses in their stalls. Twenty minutes later, once I've lunged and tied him, I head to the tack room to find Kid's equipment. I step into a room full of worn leather, colorful nylon, and jangling metal. I sort out his equipment: a burgundy leather bridle with a jointed bit, matching reins, and chocolate saddle trimmed with burgundy suede. The feel of chafed leather in my hand is a familiar one, both comforting and exciting. I slip the bridle over Kid's head and force the bit between his teeth. He mauls it, trying to get comfortable with the feel and taste of the harsh metal. I heft the heavy woolen saddle blanket and awkward saddle over his back to his withers and cinch it down. After some fine tuning and other adjustments, I'm sitting five foot two taller and making my way out toward the woods.

At the end identifies change of vantage point

Starts with clear change of vantage point and writer's emotional reaction

Follows sequence of writer's movements in time and space

4   On top of Kid, I feel as if nothing can touch me. The rich smell of wet, rotting wood and melting snow waft over me as I pick my way through the trees. The dull colors of the landscape contrast with the white snow that is slowly but surely disappearing. The first robins are back: I can't see them, but their fluttering voices reveal their presence. Red squirrels are starting to venture out to harvest their stores of nuts, their red fur a sharp distinction from their surroundings. I steer Kid through a small depression. His feet squish into the ground, and I realize a small creek has

revived. As I breathe deeply, I inhale the spring breeze picking its way over the fields. Here, spring is a timid but gay being; she will take her time in showing herself, but what she shows is wonderful and can enrapture the most stubborn of souls. I stop and close my eyes.

5   Surrounded by the countryside, I have a sense of peace and tranquility. I try my hardest to stow away this emotion, this feeling of completeness. Nature has always been able to capture my mind and whisk it away from my problems, giving me a temporary relief from the pressures of life. Kid snorts impatiently underneath me. He's eager to continue exploring, but I'm content to just stay here. After a few minutes of serenity, my cell phone blares out an excerpt of a song from George Strait, its noise a searing intrusion, and my head is violently ripped from its retreat. It's my boyfriend. I choose not to answer, trying to prolong my escape, but the spell is broken. I turn Kid back toward the barn and reality.

Uses personification, giving inanimate objects the quality of life

Clearly locates setting in countryside and emotional reaction of writer that defines dominant impression of essay

Ends with a contrast between the quiet place and cell phone to end description by a return to the starting place

Discussion Questions

MyWritingLab

1. Identify details that appeal to each of the senses. Describe the dominant impression these details produce.
2. How is this description organized? Given the purpose of the essay, how effective is this pattern?
3. Where does the writer indicate movement in time and space? Does she keep the reader clearly located?
4. How effectively does the description of the phone call in the conclusion contrast with the rest of the description?

SUGGESTIONS FOR WRITING

MyWritingLab

Writing: Description

Choose one of the following topics or another that your instructor approves for a properly focused essay of description. Create a dominant impression by using carefully chosen, well-organized details observed from an appropriate vantage point. Try to write so that the reader actually experiences your description.

1. An art work or art installation
2. An exercise class or recreation center
3. An amusement park, a miniature or full-sized golf course, or some other type of recreational facility

4. A coffee shop
5. A construction site, a chemistry lab result, or injury
6. A fast-food restaurant
7. An outdoor place of special importance to you
8. A NASCAR race
9. A scene of environmental damage or any natural environment
10. A historical building or site

Multimedia Writing

1. Write a description of the photo at the start of the chapter that would give a reader a good sense of the scene without seeing the photo. Another option would be to write a description that compares a picture of the witness with the drawing.
2. Write a description of a scene or still from a movie or an arresting graphic image. If possible, include the still or the image in your paper and/or include the actual film clip, film still, or graphic image in a blog entry.
3. Imagine that you have been hired by a company that creates audio descriptions for the blind. Create a short description of a scene from a movie that could be used as a voice-over for a blind listener. If your school has the technology and you have the training, you might record your voice-over on the actual film clip.

Critical Synthesis with Sources: Description

9.8

Critically synthesize source materials to create your description.

Purposes of Synthesis   Most of us know that any two people are likely to see and describe the same object, place, or event differently. A motorist whose car broke down in the desert would note the impossible distances, the barrenness, the absence of human life, the blazing sun. A biologist who was well-supplied with food and water would see a rich ecosystem with a wide variety of plant life and an interesting population of insects and animals. Each would produce a different description that served a different purpose. The motorist would emphasize the grueling heat and desolation to establish the danger of the situation. The biologist would provide a detailed description of the plants, insects, and animals to advance scientific understanding of the area.

Prewriting for Your Synthesis   As a writer, you may occasionally need to synthesize information supplied by others when creating your own description. Suppose that you're writing a paper about the old growth forests of Oregon. You may read a naturalist's description of the ancient, rare species of trees and how the forest provides a habitat for much unique wildlife. You might also read a lumber industry study indicating that the trees are an important economic resource. You might even uncover an account by an early explorer that captures the emotions aroused by the discovery of the forest.

Critically Evaluating Your Sources   Descriptions can be slanted, sometimes in ways that can misrepresent a problem. An account of logging may exclude the new growth in the areas harvested. As you read the descriptions of others, you may want to see how consistent they are with the works of others or your own experience. Where a description seems exaggerated, implausible, or too deliberately slanted to the author's point, you may want to verify it against the work of others. Check to determine what interests might influence the writer and whether the writer has the experience and expertise to be credible.

Planning and Drafting Your Synthesis   Armed with these and other descriptions, you could create a composite picture that captures all the different perspectives. You might start by offering the views of the Native American forest dwellers, and then detail the towering majesty of the trees and the abundance of game as reported by early explorers. Next, you might turn to the accounts of early farmers, who regarded the forest as an obstacle to be cleared away, and continue by presenting the view of the forest as a lumber resource, perhaps including a description of a depleted lumbering site. To end the paper, you might note how contemporary conservationists view what remains of the forest. Collectively, this information would offer a stark portrayal of the near-total destruction of a splendid natural resource and by implication argue for preserving what is left. While this kind of writing task seems daunting, you can simplify it if you take up one perspective at a time.

Revising Your Synthesis   Because different people are likely to see and describe the same object, place, or event differently, it's important to look critically at any description you consider for your paper. When you finish reading, ask yourself what features might have been omitted and what another slant on the material might have yielded. To illustrate, in "Once More to the Lake" E. B. White describes early morning fishing as follows: "We went fishing the first morning. I felt the same damp moss covering the worms in the bait can, and saw the dragonfly alight on the tip of my rod as it hovered a few inches from the surface of the water." If White had found fishing repugnant, he could just as easily have described the worms squiggling in the can as if they were afraid of the hook, the slimy feel of his hands after baiting the hook, the swarm of mosquitoes around his face, and the tangle in his line. Clearly, description demands choices. Different impressions and varying emphases can be selected. And like any other writer, you should carefully consider the details and slant of any description you write.

Getting Started

MyWritingLab

1. Select a famous U.S. landmark, such as the Grand Canyon, and read several writers' descriptions of it. After taking notes, write a description that includes their differing perspectives.
2. Rewrite a different version of "When the Full Moon Shines Its Magic over Monument Valley" (in The Reader) to create a different emphasis.
3. Interview several students to learn their impressions of your campus and weave those impressions into a descriptive essay.

Writing a Description

Prewriting the description.

- Read assignment and select familiar topic.
- Identify your purpose for your description.
- Identify and analyze audience.
- Observe subject of the paper carefully, if possible.
- Make certain your observations are complete and fair.
- Identify the dominant impressions.
- Brainstorm details, possibly using branching.
- Check to be sure your description is ethical and will not harm the reader or others.

Planning the description.

Select an organizational structure:
- Space
- Time
- Importance

Drafting the description.

- Introduction—ease your reader into your paper.
- Identify your thesis.
- Develop each major feature in one or more paragraphs.
- Use vivid, detailed language.
- Be sure you ethically represent the scene.

Repeat the process as necessary.

Revising the description.

- Read description critically, collect reader response, re-observe if possible.
- Be consistent with impression.
- Add details as needed.
- Cut details that don't fit.
- Test organization, and make consistent with transitions.
- Review again whether the description is credible.

Proofread.

CHAPTER 10

Process Analysis: Explaining How

In this chapter, you will learn how to:

10.1 Use process analysis as a writing strategy.

10.2 Distinguish between processes that readers will or won't perform.

10.3 Write a process in an electronic exchange such as e-mail or instant messaging.

10.4 Think critically about processes.

10.5 Write so that your process analysis is ethical.

10.6 Prewrite, plan, and draft your process analyses for readers who will perform them.

10.7 Prewrite, plan, and draft your process analyses for readers who won't perform them.

10.8 Revise your process analysis.

10.9 Critically synthesize source materials to create your process analysis.

Visit MyWritingLab **to complete the writing assignments in this chapter and for more resources on process analysis.**

Paul McKinnon/Alamy

Drat, you can't get your course software to run at all. After getting out of your browser and trying all over again, you call your school's technical support. The person on the help desk walks you through several steps. She has you check to see if your browser is up to date and compatible with the software. Next, she has you run a diagnostic to determine if you have the appropriate, up-to-date software, including something called Java. You discover that your Java Script is not up to date. The technician then talks you through the steps of going to the Web site, identifying the version appropriate for your computer, downloading the software, and finally eliminating older versions of Java. You try again.

As we pursue our affairs, we perform processes almost constantly, ranging from such daily rituals as brewing a pot of coffee to taking a picture, burning a CD, preparing for a date, or replacing a light switch. Often we share our special technique for doing something—for example, making chicken cacciatore—by passing it on to a friend.

Many popular publications feature *process analyses* that help readers to sew zippers in garments, build catamarans, live within their means, and improve their work technique.

The Purpose of Process Analysis

10.1

Use process analysis as a writing strategy.

A process analysis helps readers understand how to do something or the stages of an observed process. Process analysis frequently helps you meet the writing demands of your courses and future careers.

- For political science, you may need to explain how your state governor won nomination.
- For biology, you may need to explain how bees find their way back to the hive.
- You may need to explain how to analyze a chemical compound, take fingerprints, or prepare a slide for a lab test.
- As a lab manager, you may have to explain the process of a new technique.
- An IT specialist may need to explain to employees how to use new software.
- A nurse may need to provide home care instructions for diabetes patients.

As these examples show, a process can be technical, nontechnical, historical, scientific, or natural, and it can have audiences with very different levels of expertise.

Kinds of Process Analysis Papers

Process papers fall into two categories: those intended for readers who will perform the process and those intended to explain the process for nonperformers. Papers in either category can range from highly technical and sophisticated to nonspecialized and simple.

10.2

Distinguish between processes that readers will or won't perform.

Processes for Readers Who Will Perform Them   The audience for these papers may be technical and professional personnel who need the information to carry out a work-related task or individuals who want to perform the process for themselves.

A how-to-do-it paper must include everything the reader needs to know in order to ensure a successful outcome. Its directions take the form of polite commands, often addressing readers directly as "you." This approach helps involve readers in the explanation and emphasizes that the directions must, not merely should, be followed. Here is an illustration:

> To prepare a bacterial smear for staining, first use an inoculating loop to place a drop of distilled water on a clean glass microscope slide.
>
> Next, pass the loop and the opening of the tube containing the bacterial culture to be examined through a Bunsen burner flame to sterilize them.
>
> From the tube, remove a small bit of culture with the loop and rub the loop in the drop of water on the slide until the water covers an area one and one-half inches long and approximately the width of the slide.
>
> Next, reflame the opening of the culture tube to prevent contamination of the culture, and then plug it shut.
>
> Allow the smear to air dry, and then pass the slide, smear side up, through the flame of the burner until it is warm to the touch. The dried smear should have a cloudy, milky-white appearance.

Warning of possible risk

Feedback on what will be seen with a successful completion

Darryl Williams, student

Often each separate step is represented as a step in separate paragraphs or a numbered list to make it easier for the reader to see the separate actions that need to be completed. In a process, each step must be signaled by key words that let the reader know a shift took place. The key words are highlighted above in yellow. Also, it is important to provide readers with warnings when there are risks, either from the procedure or in making a mistake, as well as feedback that will let them know if they have been successful, noted above.

Processes for Readers Who Won't Perform Them   These papers may tell how some process is or was performed or how it occurs or occurred. A paper might, for instance, detail the stages of grief, the procedure involved in an operation, the role of speech in the development of children's thinking, or the sequence involved in shutting down a nuclear reactor. These papers serve many purposes—for example, to satisfy popular curiosity; to point out the importance, difficulty, or danger of a process; or to cast a process in a favorable or unfavorable light. Even though the writers of such papers often explain their topic in considerable detail, they do not intend to provide enough information for readers to carry out the process.

Papers of this sort present the needed information without using polite commands. Sometimes a noun, a pronoun like *I, we, he, she,* or *it,* or a noun–pronoun combination identifies the performer(s). At other times, the performer remains unidentified. Three examples follow, using highlight to identify the performer.

Pronouns Identify Performer

Thus, when I now approach a stack of three two-inch cinder blocks to attempt a breaking feat, I do not set myself to "try hard," or to summon up all my strength. Instead I relax, sinking my awareness into my belly and legs, feeling my connection with the ground. I breathe deeply, mentally directing the breath through my torso, legs, and arms. . . . When I make my final approach to the bricks, if I regard them at all they seem light, airy, and friendly; they do not have the insistent inner drive in them that I do.

> Don Ethan Miller, "A State of Grace:
> Understanding the Martial Arts"

Noun–Pronoun Combination Identifies Performers

Termites are even more extraordinary in the way they seem to accumulate intelligence as they gather together. Two or three termites in a chamber will begin to pick up pellets and move them from place to place, but nothing comes of it; nothing is built. As more join in, they seem to reach a critical mass, a quorum, and the thinking begins. They place pellets atop pellets, then throw up columns and beautiful, curving, symmetrical arches, and the crystalline architecture of vaulted chambers is created.

> Lewis Thomas, "Societies as Organisms"

Performer Unidentified

The analyzer was adjusted so the scale read zero and was connected to the short sampling tube, which had previously been inserted into the smokestack. The sample was taken by depressing the bulb the requisite number of times, and the results were then read and recorded. The procedure was repeated, this time using the long sampling tube and sampling through the fire door.

> Charles Finnie, student

MyWritingLab **EXERCISE**

1. Examine your favorite newspaper, magazine, or Web pages for examples of process analysis. Bring them to class for group discussion of which kind each represents and the writer's purpose.
2. Examine science textbooks and professional journals for more complex examples of process analysis. Bring your examples to class and discuss how they differ from simple instructions.

Writing Process Analysis in Electronic Communications

Instructions are often provided through e-mail or instant messaging. A technical support person might use instant messaging, for example, to walk a computer user through the process of completing a task such as saving a Web page as a PDF file. Such situations can present in a challenge in writing about process.

10.3

Write a process in an electronic exchange such as e-mail or instant messaging.

Start by establishing the reader's context.	Jim, are you using a Mac or PC? Which browser are you using?
Provide focused explanations that are responsive to the reader's immediate situation.	Jim, do you have the Web page you want to copy open? If not, please open it now.
Provide step-by-step instructions, with opportunity for feedback tied to the reader's situation. If possible, offer visuals that will help.	(Having determined that Jim uses a Mac and Safari) On the top tool bar, next to the word Safari, click on File. When that window opens, select Print, not Save. A box should pop open with your printer and in the lower left, you should see a small box labeled PDF with an arrow. Do you see that?
[We will not complete the instructions here, but you would end by confirming that the reader has completed the task and has no remaining problems.]	Jim, can you now open the PDF file you saved, which is now on your desktop? Do you have any remaining questions? Can I help you with anything else?

Thinking Critically About Process

Processes may seem straightforward and beyond question, but consider how a dispute over the way a process like fracking (a method of extracting natural gas from the earth) works can lead to political dispute.

10.4

Think critically about processes.

1. Who is providing an account of the process, what are his or her purposes and interests, how might these influence the way the process is presented? For example, someone who opposes fracking might downplay the safety measures used in the process; a proponent of the process might not mention some of the more harmful results of the process.
2. What other ways might the process be explained or completed? Sometimes, for example, a process may provide many complicated steps for doing something when simpler processes are available.
3. What consequences of the process may occur that have not been identified?

Ethical Issues

10.5

Write so that your process analysis is ethical.

Unclear, misleading, incomplete, or erroneous instructions written for someone to follow can spawn a wide range of unwanted consequences. Often frustration and lost time are the only results. Sometimes, though, the fallout is more serious, as in the case of a lab explosion. And in extreme cases, the outcome can be catastrophic, as when an accident occurs in a nuclear power plant. As writers, we have an ethical obligation to write clear and complete instructions. To help you do this, ask and answer the following questions when you're writing a process that the reader will perform.

- Am I using clear and unambiguous language so that the reader will not encounter unnecessary frustration and inconvenience?
- Am I clearly indicating any requirements such as time needed or additional supplies that will have to be purchased?
- Am I clearly warning readers about any possible harm they could face?

Writing a Process Analysis for Readers Who Will Perform the Process

10.6

Prewrite, plan, and draft your process analyses for readers who will perform them.

As always, when the choice is yours, select a familiar topic. If you're not the outdoor type and prefer a Holiday Inn to the north woods, don't try to explain how to plan a campout. Muddled, inaccurate, and inadequate information will result. On the other hand, if you've pitched many a tent, you might want to share your technique with your readers.

FINDING YOUR TOPIC

- Use the strategies in Chapter 3.
- Select a familiar topic, not something you don't know well.
- List the things you know how to do or have observed.
- Decide why the readers may find the process interesting or useful.
- Decide if you want to provide directions for the reader to follow, explain the process, or explain how others perform it.
- Test to see if it can be explained within the assigned length.

Prewriting for the Process Analysis To develop a process for readers to follow:

DEVELOPING YOUR PROCESS

- Brainstorm the steps and details in the steps.
- Check to make certain you didn't miss a step.
- Identify the reasons for each action.
- Test each action to determine if any warning is necessary to keep readers safe.
- Build a chart like the one below.
- Review the chart and add needed material.
- Group-related actions to form steps, the major subdivision of the procedure.

Planning and Drafting the Process Analysis When you have your answers, record them in a chart similar to this one:

Action	Reason for Action	Warning
First action	First reason	First warning
Second action	Second reason	Second warning

Sometimes a reason will be so obvious that no mention is necessary, and many actions won't require warnings. When you've completed the chart, review it carefully and supply any missing information. If necessary, make a revised chart.

Once you've listed the actions, group-related ones to form steps, or the major subdivisions of the procedure. The following actions constitute the first step—getting the fire going—of a paper explaining how to grill hamburgers:

remove grill rack	light briquets
stack charcoal briquets	spread out briquets

EXERCISE

MyWritingLab

1. **Develop a complete list of the actions involved in one of the following processes; then arrange them in an appropriate order.**
   a. Registering for class at your college
   b. Assembling or repairing some common household device
   c. Carrying out a process related to sports
   d. Breaking a bad habit
   e. Installing new software from the internet

2. **Examine your course material, favorite how-to Web sites, or instructions you have around the home for examples of process analysis. Bring them to class for group discussion of how they illustrate step-by-step directions.**

The **thesis statement** for a process paper identifies the key process that is being explained and a key point you may want to make about that process. "CPR is easy to perform and can save lives." "Grilling hamburgers outdoors is a simple process." "Geothermal energy is simply a way of using the temperature of the earth to heat or cool a building through very basic techniques."

Introduction
- Identify the process and arouse interest.
- Possibly note importance, usefulness or ease of process.
- Indicate the list of items needed for the work.
- Note any special conditions required for a successful outcome.

The paper explaining how to grill hamburgers might begin as follows:

> Grilling hamburgers on an outdoor charcoal grill is a simple process that almost anyone can master. Before starting, you will need a clean grill, charcoal briquets, charcoal lighter fluid and matches, hamburger meat, a plate, a spatula, and some water to put out any flames caused by fat drippings. The sizzling, tasty patties you will have when you finish are a treat that almost everyone will enjoy.

MyWritingLab ## Discussion Question

How does the writer try to induce the reader to perform the process?

Use the body of the paper to:

The Body

- Describe the process in detail.
- Present each step in a distinct paragraph clearly and accurately.
- If two steps must be performed simultaneously, tell the reader at the start of the first step.
- In some places, offer feedback to let readers know what to expect if they completed the instructions properly. This lets them know if they are on track.
- Note the reason for each action unless it is obvious.
- Flag with a warning any step that is difficult, dangerous, or in need of special care.
- Check to make certain you included everything readers need.

Let's see how the first step of the hamburger-grilling paper might unfold:

> The first step is to get the fire going. Remove the grill rack and stack about twenty charcoal briquets in a pyramid shape in the center of the grill. Stacking allows the briquets to burn off one another and thus produces a hotter fire.
>
> Next, squirt charcoal lighter fluid over the briquets. Wait about five minutes so that the fluid has time to soak into the charcoal. Then toss in a lighted match. The flame will burn for a few minutes before it goes out. When this happens, allow the briquets to sit for another 15 minutes so that the charcoal can start to burn.
>
> Once the burning starts, do not squirt on any more lighter fluid. A flame could quickly follow the stream back into the can, causing it to explode.
>
> As the briquets begin to turn from pitch black to ash white, spread them out with a stick so that they barely touch one another. Air can then circulate and produce a hot, even fire, the type that makes grilling a success.

Discussion Questions

1. At what points has the writer provided reasons for doing things?
2. Where has the writer included a warning?

Some processes can unfold in *only one order*. When you shoot a free throw in basketball, for example, you step up to the line and receive the ball before lining up the shot, and you line up the shot before releasing the ball. Other processes can be carried out in an *order of choice*. When you grill hamburgers, you can make the patties either before or after you light the charcoal. If you have an option, use the order that has worked best for you.

Conclusion	■ Provide a few brief remarks on the process.
	■ With longer processes, summarize the steps.
	■ Evaluate the result of the process.

The paper on hamburger grilling notes the results.

> Once the patties are cooked the way you like them, remove them from the grill and place them on buns. Now you are ready to enjoy a mouthwatering treat that you will long remember.
>
> E. M. Pryzblyo, student

Writing a Process Analysis for Readers Who Will Not Perform the Process

Are you writing about a process for a reader who will not perform the process? Use the following steps.

10.7

Prewrite, plan, and draft your process analyses for readers who won't perform them.

Prewriting the Process Analysis Like how-to-do-it processes, those intended for nondoers require you to determine the steps—or for natural processes, the stages—that are involved and the function of each before you start to write.

	DEVELOPING YOUR PROCESS
■ Brainstorm steps, or with natural processes, stages.	
■ Since readers won't perform the process, identify your purpose or why readers would be interested.	
■ Identify steps that fit that purpose.	

Planning and Drafting the Process Analysis If you're trying to persuade readers that the use of rabbits in tests of the effects of cosmetics should be discontinued, the choices you make in developing your steps should reflect that purpose, including some of the painful consequences for the animal.

The thesis statement for a process that won't be performed by the reader often identifies the process and either the main point or the reasons for the reader to know the process. "Children acquire the rules of English in a consistent pattern. Knowing this natural process lets caregivers distinguish normal from less common developmental events."

To arouse your reader's interest:

Introduction	▪ Offer an historical overview. ▪ Or offer a brief summary of the whole process. ▪ Or explain its importance.

The following introduction to an essay on the aging of the stars provides a brief historical perspective:

> Peering through their still-crude telescopes, eighteenth-century astronomers discovered a new kind of object in the night sky that appeared neither as the pinprick of light from a distant star nor as the clearly defined disk of a planet but rather as a mottled, cloudy disk. They christened these objects planetary nebulas, or planetary clouds. . . . Modern astronomers recognize planetary nebulas as the fossil wreckage of dying stars ripped apart by powerful winds . . . .

Because the reader will not perform the process:

Body	▪ The reader will not perform the process, so supply enough details for the understanding that fits your process. ▪ Show the function of each stage and how it fits the overall process. ▪ Present each stage in a distinct paragraph with clear transitions.

The following excerpt points out the changes that occur as a young star, a red giant, begins the aging process:

> As the bloated star ages, this extended outer atmosphere cools and contracts, then soaks up more energy from the star and again puffs out: with each successive cycle of expansion and contraction the atmosphere puffs out a little farther. Like a massive piston, these pulsations drive the red giant's atmosphere into space in a dense wind that blows with speeds up to 15 miles per second. In as little as 10,000 years some red giants lose an entire sun's worth of matter this way. Eventually this slow wind strips the star down close to its fusion core.

Conclusion
- Provide some perspective.
- Evaluate the results.
- Assess its importance.
- Point out further consequences.

The ending of the essay on star aging illustrates the last option:

> The cloud of unanswered questions surrounding planetaries should not obscure the real insight astronomers have recently gained into the extraordinary death of ordinary stars. In a particularly happy marriage of theory and observation, astronomers have discovered our own sun's fate. With the interacting stellar winds model, they can confidently predict the weather about 5 billion years from now; very hot, with *really* strong gusts from the east.
>
> Adam Frank, "Winds of Change"

Revising the Process Analysis

To revise, follow the guidelines in Chapter 4 and the following suggestions:

10.8

Revise your process analysis.

- Have I written consistently for someone who will perform the process or who will merely understand it?
- If my paper is intended for those who will perform a process, have I included every necessary action, offered reasons where necessary, and provided necessary warnings? Brainstorm briefly to determine additional details that might be necessary.
- Test the process by following the instructions to see if they work or help readers understand the process.
- Are my steps in the appropriate order? Would any other order be more helpful?
- Is my paper ethical?

SAMPLE

STUDENT ESSAY OF **PROCESS ANALYSIS**

Basic Songwriting Techniques

Hannah Hill

Tyler Junior College

Faculty Member: Dr. Linda Gary

1   When listening to a song, one always wonders where the idea of the song comes from. What was the singer thinking, and what provoked him or her to write such a song? Songwriting is a simple technique that

Establishes reader point of interest. Establishes thesis with main points discussed in paper

Continued on next page

Continued from previous page

anyone can do if they put their hearts into it. Songs are stories put to music through the process of emotion, thought, and rhythm.

2   Emotional feelings are important when composing a good song. Start by finding a comfortable place to relax and to think freely. Perhaps a favorite room or an outdoor getaway could rid the mind of distractions. Once settled and comfortable, begin jotting down notes. Focus on feelings and emotions that are current to life or thoughts from the past that weigh heavily on the mind. For example, express how a certain situation feels or affects day-to-day life. Make it either dominantly positive or negative, but avoid mixing the emotions. Allow the mysterious secrets to flow freely. Do not be afraid to let go. Expression of the heart and mind is the most coveted form of music because it is so real. "To take an emotion and make it mean something, take other people into the feeling" is famous country singer/songwriter Kenny Chesney's initial form of songwriting ("Kenny Chesney" T14). He puts his true life on the line to create amazing music for country fans to enjoy. Ultimately, personal experience will always draw the listener in with the passion that comes from loving to write and listen to music.

Explains parts of how to connect to emotional feelings

Offers concrete practices and clearly marks steps

3   After putting feelings into words, a clear thought process helps to organize and put these emotions into a clear composition. Don't worry about rhyme scheme yet until all the ideas are put down and arranged. Processing through the jotted notes of life will add organization. This assembling will, in turn, add clarity of understanding for the listener. Add description and detail that brings insight of the writer out to the listener. Although life experience is the best writing utensil, it is not the only one. Add fantasy or exaggeration to liven up and add spice. Be overly emotional in certain and pertinent areas. The most important situation should show the most drama to the listener. It is common for depressing lyrics to be favored over upbeat ones. For instance, twists and turns are always more interesting than perfectly happy endings. Always remember, less is more. Take out the unnecessary, so there's not an overload of information. Leave mystery to be interpreted by the listener.

Offers transition to next step

Foreshadows next step, rhyme, and indicates that the next step should be delayed

Offers sequences for ordering and developing initial idea

4   After modifying thoughts and before moving onto rhyme, put all information in an organized structure. Assembling begins with determining the order of the writing. Pick out the writing and separate it into sections. The first paragraph part becomes the introduction or verse one. Next is the chorus, which will repeat in between each verse. Add the

Offers transition to next step

second section, which becomes verse two, and repeat the chorus. If necessary, add a bridge, which is the part that intertwines but differs from the rest of the song. Then repeat the chorus one more time. Organization puts an intellectual tweak on mainstream emotions on which the song is based.

5   Finally, thoughts and feelings are translated into a potential rhythmic pattern. This is where the mainstream thinking turns into a complete thought. The story is then formed into a poetic framework. Manipulate words and sentences to contrast the feelings in the most exciting way. Be sure to avoid clichés, but add interest and uniqueness. Determine a pattern of rhyme as one would in poetry. Rhyming every other line is the most popular style of rhyme, but this is where the exotic twist of the writer can step in. However, avoid overrhyming and nonsense rhyming. Make certain that the rhyme has a reasonable flow. Form the song around individuality. This distinguishing and poetic step perfects the complete thought and finishes the writing step of song formation.

6   Writing songs can be a subtle attempt to make a statement. Songwriting is an emotional release that can be personal to both writer and listener for many different reasons. Writing of any kind should be emotionally sincere and can be very therapeutic for both writer and reader. Honest writing is always the easiest and best procedure. A passionate realization can openly interpret thoughts and feelings in an indescribable way. So get out there, write, and discover the hidden truth.

Work Cited

"Kenny Chesney: Here Comes His Life." *The Cincinnati Post*, 8 July 2004, p. T14.

Margin annotations:

Offers concrete actions. Uses verbs at start of sentence to indicate action

Offers transition to next step, rhythm

Offers concrete strategies that might be completed in multiple orders

Conclusion summarizes the center of the process—emotional release

Ends by encouraging reader to act

Discussion Questions

MyWritingLab

1. What is the purpose of this process essay? How does this purpose influence how the process is explained?
2. Identify the key steps the writer recommends for writing a song.
3. Identify places where the writer offers clear warnings.
4. There are many possible ways to write a song, yet the writer only suggests one approach. What are the advantages and disadvantages of this approach?
5. What changes could the writer provide to make this essay even more effective?

MyWritingLab   ## SUGGESTIONS FOR WRITING

Writing: Process Analysis

Write a process analysis on one of the following topics or one approved by your instructor. The paper may provide instructions for the reader to follow, tell how a process is performed, or describe how a process develops. Prepare a complete list of steps, arrange them in an appropriate order, and follow them as you write the body of your essay.

1. Observing or researching a natural process, such as erosion or a storm
2. Explaining the stages in a technical process such as paper production
3. Outlining the stages in a student's adjustment to college
4. Using a particular computer program or social media, such as Twitter
5. Registering for classes online
6. Carrying out a process related to your hobby
7. Studying for an examination
8. Performing a process required by your job or one of your classes
9. Throwing a successful party
10. Pledging a fraternity or sorority

Multimedia Writing

1. Research glass blowing. Using the photo at the start of the chapter, write a step-by-step process for blowing a simple glass bowl.
2. Write a process analysis of something that you know how to do. Include labeled pictures or screen shots if your process focuses on something using a computer. Insert these pictures or screen shots into your document or blog.
3. Either record a video of a process or find a process-based video online. Then write a detailed account of the steps in that process. For example, if you have a recording of someone diving incorrectly and ending up doing a belly flop, you could explain the process followed in the video, including what went wrong and what the person needed to do to dive correctly.

Critical Synthesis with Sources: Process Analysis

10.9

Critically synthesize source materials to create your process analysis.

Purposes for Synthesis   Is there only one way to study effectively, develop a marketing campaign, or cope with a demanding supervisor? No, of course not. As you've already learned, not all processes unfold in a single, predetermined order. As Chapter 1 makes clear, writers can approach generating a draft or revising in many different ways. A detailed account of the processes might need to synthesize several different approaches.

Prewriting for Synthesis   Sometimes the same writing occasion may allow for differing procedures so you may need to take notes on multiple kinds of writing people do. If you're writing an essay for your English class, you might brainstorm for ideas, develop a detailed outline, rough out a bare-bones draft, and add details as you revise. In talking to other students with the same assignment, you might find that they prefer to write a much longer draft and then whittle it down. Still other students might do very little brainstorming or outlining but a great deal of revising, often making major changes over several drafts. Research papers present a more complex challenge, requiring that the student find and read source material, take notes, and document sources properly. Whatever your topic, you should collect information on the different processes employed.

Critically Evaluating Your Sources   Some important processes have been disputed in print, and if you wanted to investigate them you would need to consult written sources rather than talk to others. Informed disagreements exist about how the human species originated, how language developed, and how children mature. Police officers debate the best way to handle drunks, and management experts determine the best way to motivate employees. When you investigate such controversies, determine which view is supported by the best evidence and seems most reasonable. Test your sources to make certain they are credible. You should be suspicious of an unusual account that most people don't agree with posted on an obscure Web site. Then, as a writer, you can present the accounts in an appropriate order and perhaps indicate which one you think merits acceptance.

Planning and Drafting Your Synthesis   If you decided to synthesize your findings about student writing practices, you would, of course, need to organize your material in some fashion. Perhaps you might focus on the differences that distinguish one writing occasion from another. You could develop each occasion in a separate section by presenting the practices followed by most students while ignoring variations. A second possibility would be to report different practices used for the same writing occasion, first considering the most common practice and then describing the variations. The result might be likened to a cookbook that gives different recipes for the same dish.

Getting Started   MyWritingLab

1. Interview several students about the stages they experienced in a developing friendship and write a paper that discusses these stages. Note any discrepancies in the accounts provided by different students.
2. Research the writing process as presented in several first-year composition textbooks; after pointing out how they differ, indicate which process you prefer and why.
3. Research a controversial process, such as the extinction of the dinosaurs. After presenting different theories about the process, explain which one seems most plausible and why.

Writing a Process Analysis

Prewriting the process analysis.

- Select a topic you know well.
- Brainstorm a list of any materials, all steps, and any reasons for the steps, any warnings, and any useful feedback.

Planning the process analysis.

- Write out a sequence of steps in their order and double-check them for accuracy.
- Create a table with each step, any reasons, any feedback if available, and any warnings if necessary.

Drafting a process analysis for readers who will perform the action.	**Drafting a process analysis for readers who will not perform the action.**
<ul><li>Use the polite implied "you" command.</li><li>Provide an introduction that explains the context for the process.</li><li>Identify the necessary materials.</li><li>Provide steps in sequence with reasons.</li><li>Offer warnings where needed.</li><li>Give periodic feedback so the reader knows if the work is successful.</li><li>Employ clear and unambiguous language.</li></ul>	<ul><li>Use pronouns, identified performer, or performer unidentified.</li><li>Provide an introduction that engages the reader.</li><li>Provide steps in the process and explain the reasons that they happen.</li><li>Let the reader know the function of each step and stage and how it fits the overall process.</li></ul>

Revising a process analysis.

- Have you rechecked each step, received peer feedback, and revised until satisfactory?
- Have you written consistently for whether the person is performing the action or just understanding it?
- Have you explained all steps, the purpose, and any dangers to ensure the safety and success of the reader?
- Are your steps in the appropriate order?

Repeat the process as necessary.

Proofread.

CHAPTER 11

Illustration: Making Yourself Clear

In this chapter, you will learn how to:

11.1 Use illustration as a writing strategy.

11.2 Select appropriate examples for your illustration.

11.3 Determine the best number of examples to use.

11.4 Organize the examples of your illustration.

11.5 Think critically about illustrations.

11.6 Write so that your illustration is ethical.

11.7 Prewrite, plan, draft, and revise your illustration.

11.8 Critically synthesize source materials to create your illustration.

Visit MyWritingLab **to complete the writing assignments in this chapter and for more resources on illustration.**

Ariel Skelley/Corbis

"Many intelligent people lack common sense. Take Dr. Brandon . . ."

"Predicting the weather is far from an exact science. Two winters ago, a surprise snowstorm . . ."

People often use examples (*illustrations*) to clarify general statements.

Ordinary conversations teem with "for example," and "for instance," often in response to a puzzled look. A local character, Hank Cassidy, might serve as the perfect example of a "good old boy," or Chicago's Water Tower Place illustrates a vertical shopping mall.

The Purpose of Illustration

11.1

Use illustration as a writing strategy.

Illustration is not limited to concrete items. Teachers, researchers, and writers often present an abstract principle or natural law, then supply concrete examples that bring it down to earth. An economics instructor might illustrate compound interest by an example showing how much $100 that is earning 5 percent interest would appreciate in 10 years. Examples can also persuade, as when advertisers trot out typical satisfied users of their products to induce us to buy.

Many classroom and job-related writing projects benefit from illustration.

- A paper for a management class can demonstrate effective management techniques by using examples of successful managers.
- A political science paper defining democracy would benefit from examples of several different types of democratic government.
- A literature paper on irony would want to use examples from stories and poems.
- A high school principal writing for a larger counseling staff would use examples of students who needed help and couldn't get it.
- A nurse who advocates for a new method for distributing medication would provide examples of where the current system failed patients.
- A marketing professional arguing for an increased use of social media would use examples of companies that used social media successfully.

Just like you, readers respond to concrete, vivid examples. The concrete is always easier to grasp than the abstract, and examples add flavor and clarity to what might otherwise be flat and vague.

Selecting Appropriate Examples

Make sure that your examples stay on target. For instance, if you're making the point that the lyrics in a rock group's latest album are not in good taste, don't inject comments on the fast lifestyle of one of its members. Instead, provide examples of lyrics that support your claim, chosen from different songs in the album to head off objections that your examples aren't representative.

Furthermore, see that your examples display all the chief features of whatever you're illustrating. Don't offer a country as an example of a democracy if, despite an election, there is only one party on the ballot and the results are all rigged. Consider the following appropriate student example of someone suffering from depression.

> Carl wasn't just sad. Nothing really bad had happened in his life. But he had lost all interest in his past favorite activities. His skateboard had been discarded in a corner of his room. He no longer bothered to play his video games. Simple things like getting tickets to a rock concert seemed to be too much effort for him. Some days he stayed in bed and missed his classes. Often he irritably snapped at anyone who talked with him. Friends could easily see the difference in him when he shuffled to the dining room, his head down. Without a doubt, Carl was depressed.

This short example meets many of the key characteristics of depression: a lack of interest in normal activities, a sense that ordinary things aren't worth the effort, an inability to attend to ordinary responsibilities, and irritability.

11.2

Select appropriate examples for your illustration.

Number of Examples

How many examples will you need? One long one, several fairly brief ones, or a large number of very short ones? Look to your topic for the answer.

11.3

Determine the best number of examples to use.

One Long Example: Topics where traits are combined in a single object

- The qualities of a successful nurse
- The challenges of running a small business
- The excitement of participating in a political campaign.

Several Examples: Historical trends or broader, more general claims

- To show that parents have been raising children more permissively over the last half century, a minimum of three examples are called for: one family from 1955, a second from about 1985, and another from the present.
- To demonstrate the different attitudes of Chinese and American students toward school work, examples would need to include several different children from each culture.

A Large Series of Examples: Very general or very important claims

- To demonstrate that slang arises from many subcultures, examples of many slang words and cultures would be required.
- To demonstrate that individuals abuse Medicare, a writer would need to use many examples to avoid the impression that the practice is not widespread.

MyWritingLab **EXERCISE**

1. **Choose one of the following topic sentences. Select an appropriate example and write the rest of the paragraph.**
   a. Sometimes a minor incident drastically changes a person's life.
   b. _____'s name exactly suits (her/his) personality.
   c. Not all education happens in a classroom.
   d. I learned the value of _____ the hard way.

2. **Explain why you would use one extended illustration, several shorter ones, or a whole series of examples to develop each of the following statements. Suggest appropriate illustrations.**
   a. Many parents think for their children.
   b. The ideal pet is small, quiet, and affectionate.
   c. Different college students view their responsibilities differently.
   d. The hotels in your city or a city near you run the gamut from sumptuous to seedy.
   e. Modern English includes any number of words taken directly from foreign languages.

Organizing the Examples

11.4

Organize the examples of your illustration.

Your organizational strategy will depend on your topic and the number of examples.

A single extended example

- Often follows a narrative, following events in a time sequence such as the busy workday of a small business owner.
- Provides the details spatially or in order of importance, as in an account of the damage that can be done by a tornado.

Multiple examples that try to show degrees of something or change.

- Often in order from least to most or the reverse. Types of sales clerks may go from an example of a hostile clerk, to a pleasant one, to a highly considerate and helpful person.
- Trends offer examples in time. How phones get smarter may go from early rotary dials, to touch phones with Caller ID, to today's smart phones.

A large number of examples

- May be grouped in categories that are arranged in order, such that slang might be organized by words that originate from music, surfing, or teenagers.
- May also be organized by time or by degrees of a quality, as in a paper on the changing ways we work may include multiple examples of different kinds of workers from different time periods.

Sometimes any arrangement will work equally well. Suppose you're showing that Americans are taking various precautions to ward off heart attacks. Although you might move from a person who exercises to one who diets and finally to one who practices relaxation techniques, no special order is preferable.

Large numbers of examples might first be grouped into categories and the categories then arranged in a suitable order. For example, the expressions from the world of gambling could be grouped according to types of gambling: cards, dice, horse racing, and the like. Depending upon the specific categories, one arrangement may or may not be preferable to another.

Thinking Critically About Illustrations

Because illustrations always select some examples and exclude other possible examples, they can easily be skewed and need to be carefully questioned.

11.5
Think critically about illustrations.

1. What interests and biases might the writer have, even if that writer is you, and how could that bias have affected the examples that were selected and highlighted?
2. What other examples might have been identified and how would those other examples confirm or contradict the claims and impressions of the illustration?
3. What do the examples emphasize and how might a different emphasis lead to different impressions or conclusions?

Ethical Issues

In writing an illustration, we try to show readers something truthful about our understanding of the world. They wouldn't read what we've written if they suspected we were unusually careless in our thinking or knew we were trying to deceive them. Deception may stem from prejudice, which causes people to distort examples. For instance, parents trying to talk their teenager out of a career in acting will probably cite only examples of failed or struggling performers who have miserable lives, and they will fail to mention many successful performers. Such a distortion isn't fair to the acting profession or the teenager. Some distortions can be outright lies. In the past debate about welfare, some commentators wrote about people who lived like millionaires while on welfare. It turned out the examples were falsified, and no real instances of such massive abuse could be found. To avoid ethical pitfalls, ask and answer the following questions:

11.6
Write so that your illustration is ethical.

- Am I giving adequate thought to the point I'll make and the examples I'll use?
- Are the examples supporting my point truthful, or are they slanted to deceive the reader?
- Could my illustrations have harmful consequences? Do they stereotype an individual or group? Do they harm someone's reputation unjustly?
- Will my examples promote desirable or undesirable behavior?

Writing an Illustration

Assertions, unfamiliar topics, abstract principles, natural laws—as we've seen, all of these can form the foundation for your paper. If you have a choice, you should experience little difficulty finding something suitable. After all, you've observed and experienced many things—for example, how people can be TV junkies and the ways students manage the stresses of college life. As always, the strategies in Chapter 3 can help generate some possibilities, along with these strategies.

11.7
Prewrite, plan, draft, and revise your illustration.

Prewriting for the Illustration

To prewrite for your illustration:

FINDING YOUR TOPIC
- Keep a journal noticing basic patterns or trends you have observed or read about.
- Brainstorm a list of observations you have made about the world.
- Write down some main points you want to make.
- Think about what impact you would want your paper to have on readers.
- Decide if you need one extended example or multiple examples.

Once you have your topic, you can easily develop your illustration.

DEVELOPING YOUR ILLUSTRATION
- Brainstorm a list of examples.
- Brainstorm supporting details for each example.
- Decide which examples and details would be best for your audience.
- Review and add examples and details as necessary.
- Create a chart or use branching as below.

Once you've picked your topic, ask yourself, "What example(s) will work best with my audience?" Then brainstorm each one for supporting details. Use a chart patterned after the one below to help you.

Example 1	Example 2	Example 3
First supporting detail	First supporting detail	First supporting detail
Second supporting detail	Second supporting detail	Second supporting detail

Brainstorming on the difficulty of running a small store:

Drafting the Illustration

A **thesis statement** for an illustration usually states the main point that the rest of the essay demonstrates by example and sometimes adds to the importance the illustration has for readers. The original topic selection will give you a clue for your thesis.

Introduction
- Introduce topic and give the reader a reason to read paper.
- Possibly create an arresting or unexpected statement. "Americans work harder than employees of any other country."
- Or indicate the stake a reader has in the essay. "Every student can learn from those who have been successful."

Body
- Present the examples that achieve your purpose.
- Use an order for examples that fit your topic.
- Often there are separate paragraphs for each example. An essay on how phones got smarter might have a paragraph for each phone type you discuss.

Conclusion
- Summarize the examples and re-emphasize the main point.
- Or issue a warning or challenge, as might follow from a paper on binge drinking.
- Or offer a hope or recommendation, as in a paper on how to become the employee of the future.
- Or discuss broader implications, as in a paper on how people have thrown off repressive governments.

Revising the Illustration

Think about the following suggestions and questions as well as the general guidelines in Chapter 4 as you revise your paper.

- What idea am I trying to present to my reader? Have I chosen the examples that best demonstrate that idea?
- What additional examples or details could make my paper more engaging for my reader?
- What details or choice phrase could make my examples more interesting?
- Do any examples or details fail to fit my main point and distract from the paper and so should be cut?

- How could I organize my paper with transitions or arrange the order of examples that would make my paper easier to read?
- Where could I better focus or develop my paragraphs around key examples?
- Is my paper ethical, with honest examples that are fairly selected?

SAMPLE

STUDENT ESSAY OF **ILLUSTRATION**

If It Is Worth Doing. . . .

Janice Carlton

Offers main point of illustration and clarifies that claim. Indicates reason idea is important

1   Everyone should keep a slogan in his or her back pocket to pull out at difficult times. Mine may seem a bit ridiculous, but I have found it to be a life saver: "If it is worth doing, it is worth doing badly." This slogan turns my parent's phrase—If it is worth doing, it is worth doing well—completely upside down. To be clear, I am not suggesting that anyone should deliberately do things badly. No one wants to be operated on by a surgeon whose hand shakes. Hopefully, accountants know their subject and offer sound advice. Still, some activities are so worth doing that the fact that we might do them badly is no reason not to take up the task. Far too often we are tempted to give up art because our paintings are bad, avoid writing because our spelling is poor, or avoid helping a friend build a pole barn because we might make mistakes. My slogan reminds me that my possible failure is no reason to avoid a worthwhile project.

Offers a clear thesis in last sentence

Offers first example

Indicates importance of singing to reader

2   Consider singing for a moment. Singing can be tremendous fun. A good song can lift the heart. Singing with others can offer a delightful sense of sharing. My only problem is that I have a terrible voice. It cracks, soars when it should sink, and rises when it should drop. Usually, I hit the right pitch, but sometimes I have to wiggle into it as though it were a pair of excessively tight jeans. My more musically gifted friends usually cringe when they hear me sing and mutter something under their breath about "the tone deaf." Should I stop singing just because I do it badly? To me, I sound like a great rock singer, at least when I sing in the shower. Sometimes I sing while I walk from class to class, and I feel, as a result, that I am in an exciting musical. I can even sing with my friends, who only insist that I sing a little more quietly and try, try, try to stay on

tune. Probably it would be unfair of me to log in hours at a karaoke bar, and I usually keep from singing around those who tend to stuff their fingers in their ears. But <u>with some reasonable precautions, the fact that I</u> <u>sing badly should not prevent me from enjoying the obvious pleasures of</u> <u>singing.</u>

3   <u>Writing poetry is another practice that is worth doing even if we do it</u> <u>badly.</u> What makes poetry worth writing? Writing poetry involves taking time out of the rush of life to reflect on what you're feeling, to perceive more clearly, to hunt for the right word. When it works, you feel like everything in your life has come together.

> As I raced through the forest,
> I stopped to smell a flower,
> a violet, perhaps, a purple pause
> Between home and grandmother's house.
> The flower didn't have any smell,
> But that didn't matter any.
> For a moment, I contemplated
> The breath of a flower,
> And avoided, in the process,
> Meeting any unexpected wolves.

<u>This poem isn't very good, I admit. No one would want to publish it.</u> Most readers may not understand how, feeling like Little Red Riding Hood, I rush from place to place to avoid meeting stray wolves. None of that is the point. When writing the poem, I felt in touch with my life while savoring a creative joy. <u>There is no reason to let anything get in the way of</u> <u>such a delight, not even the poor quality of the resulting poem.</u>

4   Of course, it is easy to sing in the shower and write poetry no one ever sees, even if the results, to put it mildly, stink. <u>What about where</u> <u>others are involved? Imagine my predicament when my big brother</u> <u>called and asked me if I would help him put up a pole barn. "Me,"</u> <u>I pleaded, "I'm all thumbs."</u> And I meant it, but somehow he needed my help, so despite my complete lack of construction experience, I chanted my mantra three times and said "yes." <u>For a day I held up beams, sawed</u> <u>boards (sometimes off the measured line), and hammered in nails (bend-</u> <u>ing more than a few).</u> But I did help my brother. He said that he couldn't have done it without me; and while he probably could have built the

Ends by tying example to main point

Offers second example

Provides detail to illustrate point

Ends by tying example to main point

Offers a third example that expands the point by extending consequences

Uses narrative organization

Continued on next page

Continued from previous page

Ends by detailing benefit

barn without me, it would have been harder for him. Besides, working side by side for a day, we got to reconnect in ways that I hadn't thought possible. I also learned some construction skills. Without being willing to help badly, I would have missed a tremendous opportunity.

Offers a fourth example that is the most serious yet in narrative

5   There are times when doing something badly is significantly better than doing nothing at all. Our local newspaper featured a story about a hiker who was miles from anywhere on the trail when he came across another hiker who was choking on his lunch. What could he do? He couldn't run for help. He was out of his cell phone region. And he didn't know CPR. What he did know was that the man in front of him was starting to turn blue. He pounded the man on the back, but that didn't work. Finally, in desperation he pushed down underneath the man's rib cage. The pressure popped something out of his windpipe and he started breathing again. The point of the article was the importance of learning CPR, the Heimlich maneuver, and other lifesaving skills. The hiker, of course, knew none of those skills and could have done tremendous damage, perhaps breaking the victim's ribs. Clearly, it would be worthwhile to be expert at lifesaving skills. But what should the hiker have done? If he had just stood there

Ends with important consequence of principle

paralyzed by his lack of expertise, the man would have choked to death. Fortunately, he seems to have believed in my slogan and did what was worth doing, saving a life, even if he did it badly.

Conclusion. Reiterates general point

Challenges the reader

6   There are lots of pressure in our culture to "leave it to the experts." We can listen to CDs instead of sing ourselves. We can call towing services that are glad to change our flats for us. We can watch soccer instead of play it. With so many skilled people, it is easy to be embarrassed by our own lack of expertise and abandon everything except what we do well. Unfortunately, our lives would be significantly poorer for such a surrender. Instead, we would be better off adapting the adage that "if it is worth doing, it is worth doing badly" and step up to the plate at a softball game, grab a sketch pad and draw what we see, write a poem, sing, cook a meal for a friend. In the end, we have nothing to lose but our false pride.

MyWritingLab

Discussion Questions

1. What is the writer trying to illustrate?
2. How is this particular illustration developed?
3. Why did the writer include a poem in her essay?
4. What does the paragraph on the use of CPR add to the essay?
5. In the last paragraph, why does the writer use the pronoun "we"?

SUGGESTIONS FOR WRITING

Writing: Illustration

Use one of the following ideas or another that your instructor approves for your illustration essay. Select appropriate examples, determine how many you will use, and decide how you will organize them.

1. Incivility has or has not become quite common in public places.
2. New communication technologies help keep friends in close touch or help keep us separate.
3. _____ is the secret of success for many athletes (or use any other field or occupation).
4. Video games can take over people's lives or create friendships or be educational.
5. Actions can have unintended consequences.
6. "Doing your own thing" does not always work out for the best.
7. _____ makes college difficult for students.
8. Today's college student is _____.
9. Sometimes we need to take risks.
10. Wanting more than we need can be destructive.

Multimedia Writing

1. Write a short paper explaining how the photo at the start of the chapter (p. 193) illustrates either a challenge with the economy or merely a personal crisis.
2. Write an illustration paper on a concern of yours, such as the impact of littering on a community. Include pictures or other images to support your claim. If you are preparing a blog entry, you could use audio clips or video clips to support the point that you are illustrating, such as how hard it is to hear the words in certain songs.
3. Create a script that illustrates a main point you want to make, such as the way houses in a development seem to be very similar, and then create a video with voice-over, using your script to make your point. As an alternative, you could edit preexisting video clips to help support the points you make in your voice-over.

Critical Synthesis with Sources: Illustration

Purposes of Synthesis   When we write an illustration paper, we don't always draw our examples from personal experience. As we reflect on a topic, we may talk with other people and read various source materials to broaden our understanding. We explore differing perspectives and determine the connections between them en route to arriving at our own views and insights, which are best when they are more inclusive.

11.8

Critically synthesize source materials to create your illustration.

Prewriting for Synthesis   Take, for instance, the topic of racism in America. You would want to read many different accounts by those who have experienced racism, as well as accounts of those who have experienced little racism. Reading essays or blogs, drawing upon your own observations, and perhaps questioning other students could lead you to an important insight: for example, that racism can have personal effects that are very different from the more widely discussed kinds of institutional discrimination. You might then synthesize others' illustrations and your own to produce a paper that presents this insight.

Critically Evaluating Your Sources Sometimes illustrations don't reflect reality. An author trying to make the point that many college students are irresponsible might offer examples of students who skip classes, fail to hand in assignments, and party constantly. These examples, however, overlook the many students who hold part-time jobs while taking a full load of classes, participate in professional organizations, and function successfully as spouses, and even parents, while earning good grades. Because published material can paint an inaccurate picture, develop the habit of judging the examples you read in the light of what your knowledge, further investigation, and other sources reveal. Critical thinking is one of the most important skills a writer can cultivate.

Planning and Drafting Your Synthesis Whether you draw on material from informal resources, conversations, or notes from reading, the process for planning and drafting your synthesis follows a familiar pattern. Determine how many examples you will use to illustrate your point. Check to be sure those points fit. Determine an appropriate order for them and build paragraphs around your key point. For example, if you were trying to illustrate how video games interfere with studying, you might start a paragraph with data from a source followed by your own personal observations. Sometimes in representing conflicting viewpoints, you may want to organize the paper based on those viewpoints leading to the position you support the most. You will need to clearly shift any changes in the point you want to make with effective transitions.

MyWritingLab ## Getting Started

1. Search online for articles about or examples of the ways social media has been harmful or helpful to people in their careers.
2. Read several issues of a magazine such as *Sports Illustrated* or *Working Woman* and determine what the articles suggest about American life. Then write an essay that illustrates your conclusions and incorporates relevant material from the articles.
3. "Accidental Discoveries" illustrates the way people make unexpected discoveries. Do your own research on how students and others make discoveries and write your own essay that supports or disagrees with the account in "Accidental Discoveries."

Writing an Illustration

Prewriting the illustration.

- Identify and write the key concept or observation to illustrate by reading, talking to others, or jotting down your own observations.
- Identify your purpose.
- Identify your audience.
- Brainstorm examples and supporting details.
- Select the most effective examples.
- Determine if the illustration could have harmful consequences or promote undesirable behavior.

Planning the illustration.

- Decide on the examples to use.
- Decide on an organizational strategy such as order of time, order of climax (least to greatest or the reverse), or by categories.
- Create a rough outline.
- Make certain to give adequate thought to the point you want to make and your examples.

Drafting the illustration.

- Introduction engages the reader and establishes the topic.
- Body provides examples with detail following order.
- Chosen examples are truthful and not slanted.
- Specific, concrete language is used to make the examples vivid.
- Conclusion reestablishes the main point.

Repeat the process as necessary.

Revising the illustration.

- Collect peer responses and reread the illustration critically.
- Check fit to the main point.
- Add examples or details.
- Cut what doesn't work.
- Test organization.
- Test for ethics.

Proofread.

CHAPTER **12** # Classification: Grouping into Categories

In this chapter, you will learn how to:

12.1 Use classification as a writing strategy.

12.2 Select categories for classification.

12.3 Determine the best number of categories.

12.4 Develop categories with specific details.

12.5 Think critically about classification.

12.6 Write so that your classification is ethical.

12.7 Prewrite, plan, draft, and revise your classification.

12.8 Critically synthesize source materials to create your classification.

Visit MyWritingLab **to complete the writing assignments in this chapter and for more resources on classification.**

Elena Schweitzer/Shutterstock

Help Wanted, Situations Wanted, Real Estate, Personal. Do these terms look familiar? They do if you've ever scanned the classified ads of the newspaper or online. Ads are grouped into categories, and each category is then subdivided. The people who assemble this layout are *classifying*. Figure 12.1 shows the main divisions of a typical classified ad section and provides a further breakdown of one of them.

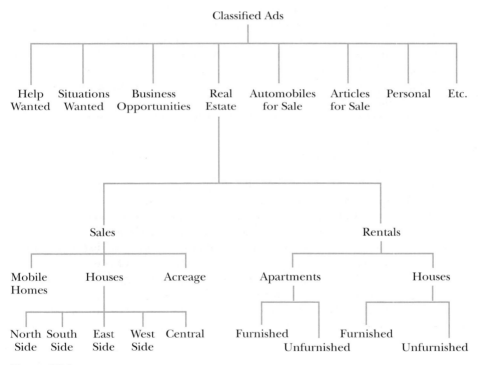

Figure 12.1

As this figure indicates, grouping allows the people who handle ads to divide entries according to a logical scheme and helps readers find what they are looking for. Imagine the difficulty of checking the real estate ads if all the entries were run in the order that the ads were placed.

The Purpose of Classification

Our minds naturally sort information into categories. Within a few weeks after their birth, infants can tell the faces of family members from those of outsiders. Toddlers learn to distinguish between cats, dogs, and rabbits. In both cases the

12.1

Use classification as a writing strategy.

classification rests solely on physical differences. As we mature we start classifying in more abstract ways, and by adulthood we are constantly sorting things into categories: dates or mates, eating places, oddballs, friends, investments, jobs, or political views.

Classification also helps writers and readers come to grips with large or complex topics. It breaks a broad topic into categories according to some specific principle, presents the distinctive features of each category, and shows how the features vary among categories. Segmenting the topic simplifies the discussion by presenting the information in small, neatly sorted piles rather than in one jumbled and confusing heap.

Furthermore, classification helps people make choices. Identifying which groups of consumers—students, accountants, small-business owners—are most likely to buy some new product allows the manufacturer to advertise in appropriate media. Knowing the engine size, maneuverability, seating capacity, and gas mileage of typical subcompact, compact, and intermediate-size cars helps customers decide which one to buy. Examining the features of term, whole-life, and endowment insurance enables prospective buyers to select the policy that best suits their needs.

Because classification plays such an important part in our lives, it is a useful writing tool in many situations.

- For an accounting class, you might categorize accounting procedures for retail businesses.
- For a computer class, you may classify computer languages and then specify appropriate applications for each grouping.
- For an industrial hygiene class, you might categorize types of respiratory protective equipment and indicate when each type is used.
- On the job, a state health department employee may prepare a brochure grouping illegal drugs into categories based on their effects.
- A financial advisor might write a customer letter categorizing investments according to their degree of risk.
- An employee at Amazon might list new books under categories that interest readers.

Selecting Categories

12.2

Select categories for classification.

People classify in different ways for different purposes, which generally reflect their interests. A clothing designer might classify people according to their fashion sense, a representative of the National Organization for Women according to their views on women's rights, and the Secretary of Labor according to their occupations. A college's director of housing might classify students according to their type of residence, the dean of students according to their behavior problems, and the financial aid officer according to their sources of income.

When you write a classification paper, choose a principle of classification that's suited not only to your purpose but also to your audience. To illustrate, if you're writing for students, don't classify instructors according to their manner of dress, body build, or car they drive. These breakdowns probably wouldn't interest most students and certainly wouldn't serve their needs. Instead, develop a more useful principle of classification—perhaps by teaching styles, concern for students, or grading policies.

Sometimes it's helpful or necessary to divide one or more categories into subcategories. If you do, use just one principle of classification for each level. Both levels in Figure 12.2 meet this test because each reflects a single principle: place of origin for the first, number of cylinders for the second.

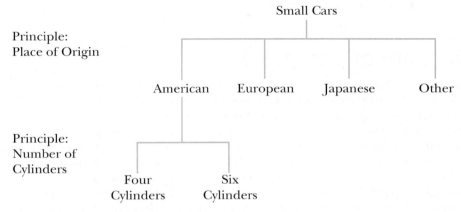

Figure 12.2

Now examine Figure 12.3. This classification is *improper* because it groups cars in two ways—by place of origin and by kind—making it possible for one car to end up in two categories. For example, the German Porsche is both a European car and a sports car. When categories overlap in this way, confusion reigns and nothing is clarified.

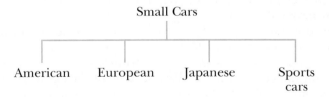

Figure 12.3

EXERCISE   MyWritingLab

1. **How would each of the following people be most likely to classify the families in Anytown, USA?**
    a. The bishop of the Roman Catholic diocese in which the city is located
    b. The state senator who represents the city
    c. A field worker for the NAACP
    d. The director of the local credit bureau

2. **The following lists contain overlapping categories. Identify the inconsistent item in each list and explain why it is faulty.**

Nurses	Pictures	Electorate in Midville
Surgical nurses	Oil paintings	Republicans
Psychiatric nurses	Magazine illustrations	Democrats
Emergency room nurses	Lithographs	Nonvoters
Terminal care nurses	Watercolors	Independents
Night nurses	Etchings	

Number of Categories

12.3

Determine the best number of categories.

Some classification papers discuss every category included in the topic. Others discuss only selected categories. Circumstances and purpose dictate the scope of the discussion. Suppose you work for the commerce department of your state and are asked to write a report that classifies the major nonservice industries in a certain city and assess their strengths and weaknesses. Your investigation shows that food processing, furniture making, and the production of auto parts account for more than 95 percent of nonservice jobs. Two minor industries, printing and toy making, provide the rest of the jobs. Given these circumstances, you'd probably focus on the first three industries, mentioning the others only in passing. But if printing and toy making were significant industries, they too would require detailed discussion.

Developing Categories

12.4

Develop categories with specific details.

Develop every category you include with specific, informative details that provide a clear picture of each one and help the reader grasp the distinctions and relationships among them.

Consider the student example on video games at the end of this chapter. The student does not just identify interactive simulation games as a type of game. She explains how these games are distinctive and provides a detailed example of how the games must be played. "One of the earliest of these games was an arcade game called *Dance Dance Revolution*. It requires players to match on a dance pad the moves they are instructed to do on the screen. . . . The success of this game prompted many others like *Karaoke Revolution* in which players sing popular songs into a microphone for points and *Guitar Hero* and *Donkey Konga* where players play on controllers that emulate a guitar and a set of bongos." By developing the paragraph with different examples of how interactive games are played, she builds a better understanding of that distinctive kind of game.

Thinking Critically About Classification

The categories we employ can have a significant impact. Imagine the consequences if colleges were to classify students by IQ. The effects on admissions, registration, and advising might be chilling. We need to think critically about the categories that we and others use.

12.5

Think critically about classification.

1. How were the categories developed and by whom? A film category like "chick flick" implies "a film for women" and refers to a movie created for a specific market, but it also stereotypes the audience and creates a bias about the film.
2. What other categories or systems of categorization could be used? Scholars of science fiction may resist making a distinction between "science fiction" and "fantasy" and instead use the category of "speculative fiction" to emphasize common elements rather than differences.
3. How is the category system guiding our perceptions? Could we think differently about the topic? Classifying *Star Wars* as science fiction might cause us not to recognize the way the film includes elements of fantasy, adventure, comedy, and "chick flicks."

Ethical Issues

Classification can seem quite innocent, and yet it can cause great harm. In India, an entire group numbering millions of people was once classified as "untouchables," and so members of this group were denied the jobs and rights of other citizens. Although political progress has considerably improved the lot of these people, discrimination still hobbles their lives. In this country, many high school students have suffered the sting of being classified as "nerds" or "geeks." Clearly you'll have to evaluate the appropriateness and consequences of your classification scheme. To avoid problems, ask and answer these questions:

12.6

Write so that your classification is ethical.

- Is my classification called for by the situation? It may be appropriate to classify students in a school environment according to their reading skills, but classifying factory workers in this fashion may well be inappropriate and unfair to the people involved.
- Have I avoided the use of damaging classifications? We resent stereotyping because it unjustly reduces us to some distorted general idea. No one is simply a "hillbilly" or a "jock."
- Have I applied my classification without resorting to overgeneralization? In a paper classifying student drinkers, it would be a mistake, and even harmful, to imply that all college students drink excessively.
- Could my classification promote harmful behavior? When classifying the behavior patterns of young urban dwellers, it would be unethical to present favorably the lifestyle of a group that uses hard drugs and engages in disruptive behavior at sporting events.

We are ethically responsible for the classification systems that we use in our writing. Always examine the one you use for suitability, fairness, and potential harm.

Writing a Classification

12.7

Prewrite, plan, draft, and revise your classification.

Many topics that interest you are potential candidates for classification. If you're selecting your own topic, you might explain different kinds of rock music to novices, take a humorous look at types of teachers, or, in a more serious vein, identify types of discrimination.

Rewriting for the Classification

FINDING YOUR TOPIC

- Brainstorm areas where you and others make decisions or distinguish between types of things.
- Keep notes on places where people you know make choices.
- Branch from brainstorming why people might be interested in classification of topic.
- Test topic by seeing if you can identify three or more distinct categories.

DEVELOPING YOUR CLASSIFICATION

- List the reasons readers may use classification.
- List real examples of the topic and organize into categories.
- Develop a table like the one below identifying the different categories and the features that distinguish the category.
- Brainstorm examples and details for each category.

Planning and Drafting the Classification

Once you have your details, create an outline or a second map of categories that distinguishes features and details in the order that you want to present them.

Category 1	Category 2	Category 3
First distinguishing feature	First distinguishing feature	First distinguishing feature
Second distinguishing feature	Second distinguishing feature	Second distinguishing feature

A **thesis statement** for classification often, though not always, identifies the reason for the reader to know the classification and the major categories that will be discussed. For example: "The ecofriendly consumer needs to decide between fully electric, hybrid, flex-fuel, and fuel-efficient vehicles, each with its own advantages and challenges." To develop your thesis statement, review your brainstorming on how readers would use your classification and the major categories.

Introduction

- Capture your reader's attention by identifying the reader's interest, as in selecting among a complex range of cell phones.
- Or stress the importance of the topic, as in the types of pollutants affecting our atmosphere.
- Or offer a personal experience that is interesting, as in taking a class with a teacher whose teaching style was wrong for you but right for your friend.
- Provide a thesis that clearly identifies the reason for the paper, the fundamental topic, and major categories.

Body

- Organize the paper by categories in the order that makes sense to you (most common to least common; most fuel efficient to least fuel efficient).
- Clearly signal the shifts from category to category, not with common words like "next" but phrases that show your logic. "Though using traditional fuel rather than electricity, the hybrid."
- Follow a pattern in the paragraphs such as major characteristics of the category.

Conclusion

- Summarize the categories the reader may make with key features, possibly with recommendations.
- Or provide some expectation, like the long-term success of hybrids and flex-fuel vehicles over all electric cars.
- Or offer ways of responding to different categories, such as types of teachers.

Revising the Classification

Revise your paper by following the guidelines in Chapter 4 as well as by employing these questions and strategies:

- How could the purpose and audience for the classification be clearer?
- Where do the categories or how they are presented not fit the audience and purpose and therefore need to be cut or redirected?
- What categories, if any, have been forgotten? Apply the paper yourself to the real world and test to see if it works and then brainstorm.
- Do any of your categories overlap? If so, consider redefining your category or cutting some that don't fit.
- Have you chosen an appropriate number of categories?
- Where could the categories be developed with additional details or examples?

- Are the categories and details arranged in an effective order that will be clear to the reader? Try changing the order in an outline or on computer to see if another order works better.
- Where do paragraphs lack focus or development? Brainstorm to develop or organize paragraphs so there is a clear focus.
- Where could the transitions be made clearer, signaling the actual logic of the order rather than using stock words like "first" or "second."
- Is the project of categorizing or the way the categories are presented ethical?

SAMPLE

STUDENT ESSAY FOR **CLASSIFICATION**

Types of Video Games for Children
Kyra Glass

Identifies reason for reader's interest

1   Gift-giving for children and grandchildren has been getting increasingly difficult as the number of options increase. Today dolls and toy cars and board games just aren't going to cut it. Many children are used to interactive toys and toys with electronic components. Most children don't think of Monopoly or tag when they hear the word *game*; to them games are played on a television or a computer screen. Indeed, video game consoles in homes with children have become almost as ubiquitous household appliances as televisions. Most parents and grandparents are familiar with demands for *the* hot new game, but buying video games for their loved ones can be overwhelming. Many adults never had video games growing up, or if they did, video games meant *Pac Man*, *Donkey Kong*, or two plumbers named Mario and Luigi. Although these gaming

Identifies reader's concern that motivates purpose of essay

icons are still available, many parents and grandparents are concerned that they are far outnumbered by extremely violent or gruesome video games that they don't want their children playing. Those buying for young gamers may feel that they are stuck, that they will either be unable to buy a game or will end up with a hack-and-slash game that is too violent for younger children. In reality, there is a wide variety of fun and family-friendly games that parents or grandparents can feel good about buying for their young gaming enthusiasts. The easiest way to pick safe games is to check the ratings printed on them; anything that is rated E (for everyone) is safe for children of any age to play; anything rated E 10+ may have some mild cartoon violence but is usually acceptable for most families as well. Games that are rated Teen (T) or Mature (M) are not a good bet for younger children, and parents should research these games before giving them to their children. But checking the ratings is only the first step. There are many different categories of games with options that are appropriate for younger players: interactive simulation games, adventure/role-playing games, party games, and sports games.

2   One of the most common types of games for children or adults is adventure/role-playing games. In these games, players take on the persona of a character (or several characters) and work their way through a narrative as that character. Although there are many games of this type that aren't appropriate for younger children, a number of age-appropriate games do fall into this category. The key to finding adventure/role-playing games that are appropriate for younger players is in looking at what story the game tells and who the main characters are. A large number of games in this category are based on characters with which children are already familiar. Some of these are based on both live-action and animated children's movies. *A Series of Unfortunate Events* and *The Incredibles* inspired games of the same name, and a whole series of games based on the popular Harry Potter books and movies have been produced. Many of these games based on movies let the players go through an enhanced version of the plot of the movies or books, letting children interact with their favorite stories. Other games are based on TV cartoons like *Jimmy Neutron, Kim Possible*, and *SpongeBob SquarePants*, to name only a few. These games often retain the characters and themes of the shows while inventing a new narrative for players to go through in the game. Many of these games, including *Kingdom Hearts* for Play Station 2 or *Nicktoons Unite!* for GameCube, combine many characters owned by the same company such as Disney or Nickelodeon. However, there are also adventure/role-playing games with well-known and beloved characters from other children's video games. The familiar kid-friendly Mario has a role-playing game called *Paper Mario* and an adventure game called *Super Mario Sunshine*, while older children might enjoy *Sonic the Hedgehog's* cousin in the adventure game *Shadow the Hedgehog*. When trying to choose an adventure or simulation game for a child, often the best place to start is by picking one of the child's favorite stories or characters from movies, cartoons, and games and seeing if there is a game that features them. It is surprising how often the answer is "yes."

Continued on next page

States thesis

Transition clearly identifies first category and logic for organization

Identifies distinguishing characteristic

Provides criteria for decision based on reader's interest

Provides examples with details tied to purpose of selecting a game as a gift

Provides criteria for making a choice

Continued from previous page

Provides transition
to next category

Provides
distinguishing
criteria

3   In general, the category of sports games is a pretty safe choice when picking games for children. Sports games emulate a version of a sports competition or event for the player's participation. Many different types of games fall into this category: racing games are included here, as are games based on team sports like basketball or football, extreme sports like skateboarding or motorbike racing, and individual sports like skiing or golf. Although there are some sports games that aren't appropriate for children, shoppers can usually find a game rated E for everyone in nearly any category of sports. However, although most sports games are appropriate for children, there are also, on every platform, sports games that are made especially for children to play. These games, like the adventure/role-playing games, keep the best aspects of their genre but draw on characters and environments that are familiar to children. Disney's *Extreme Skate Adventure*, on all three platforms, is a skateboarding game that allows children to create their own character or play as a familiar Disney character. They can then skate in environments from *Toy Story 2*, *The Lion King*, and *Tarzan*. Because this game is tailored to children, it allows them to pick objects such as mirrors or frying pans as well as skateboards. This is part of a series of Disney sports games including *Soccer*, *Football*, and *Basketball*, all on GameCube, and *Golf*, on Playstation 2. The ever-present Mario also has his own series of sports games for children, including *Mario Kart* racing games; *Super Mario Strikers*, a racing game; and games based on baseball, tennis, and golf. These sports franchises might be good for younger players because they are often easier to play and use familiar characters, while Madden, Fifa, or NBA sports games from Electronic Arts may be better choices for older children.

Offers examples
with detail of the
categories

Offers examples
with detail of the
categories

Identifies how
category fits gift-
giving purpose

Provides transition
to next category and
value of category to
reader

Identifies distinguish-
ing characteristics

Provides examples
with details

4   Interactive simulation games are an excellent choice for families because they are capable of getting children off the couch, something that many parents worry about with TV and video games. Interactive simulation games give players a hands-on experience that is as close as possible to what their character is doing in the game. One of the earliest of these games was an arcade game called *Dance Dance Revolution*. It requires players to match on a dance pad the moves they are instructed to do on the screen. Versions of this game are now available on the three main game consoles: X-Box, Playstation 2, and GameCube. The success of this game prompted many others like *Karaoke Revolution*, in which players sing popular songs into a microphone for points, and *Guitar Hero*

and *Donkey Konga*, where players play on controllers that emulate a guitar or set of bongos. Most interactive simulation games require special controllers or accessories to play, and one of these accessories, the Eye Toy for Playstation 2, might change the way children think about "sitting" in front of the TV and playing video games. Eye Toy uses a USB camera so the player's body becomes the controller. Games using Eye Toy respond to the movement of the player's body to interact with the game play on screen. Eye Toy was originally packaged with the game *Play*, which featured 12 mini games that used this body motion for everything from dancing to kung fu. Since then, Eye Toy has come out with a variety of interactive games including *Play 2*, *Operation Spy*, and *AntiGrav*, as well as workout-minded games such as *Eye Toy Groove* and *Kinetic*. Interactive simulation games are the perfect choice for parents and grandparents who want to see their children physically active while having a good time.

5   Along with the concern that children spend too much time in front of the TV or on the couch, another common complaint parents have about video games is that unlike board games, they don't always encourage siblings or families to play together. That is why party games are such a great option for parents who want to be able to play along with their children and are interested in making video game time part of family time. Party games usually involve up to four players in competition and are short enough to play a round in one sitting. Most of them are made up of a series of many mini-games (short and simple games or puzzles) that are easy to learn. Most, although not all, of these party games are styled after board games and are turn-based. A few, like *Monopoly Party*, are exactly like popular board games in video game form. Like adventure games, most party games are based on well-known children's characters. Some of these family-friendly party games are *Disney Party*, *Nickelodeon Party Blast*, *Muppets Party Cruise*, *Shrek*, *Super Party*, and *Wario Ware Inc*. These games range across a variety of console platforms, and all feature well-known characters from movies, television, and children's games. However, perhaps the best-known game in this category is the *Mario Party* series; for Game Cube, there are *Mario Parties 4 through 7*. All these games are different and feature an extensive number of levels and mini-games for families to play together.

Provides distinguishing reason for selecting category

Transition to category, indicating the value of the category

Identifies distinguishing characteristics

Provides examples with details

Re-stresses the value for the category

Continued on next page

Continued from previous page

Reasserts the purpose of the essay for the reader

Recalls some categories with indication of value of choice

Identifies categories not discussed

Offers challenge to the reader

6   There are clearly many options for parents and grandparents who want to allow their children to enjoy the same electronic entertainment as their peers while still making sure that they are playing games that are appropriate for them. Buyers can choose from a variety of sports and adventure games that allow children to play as their favorite cartoon characters from movies like Harry Potter to video game icons like Mario or Sonic. Sports games in general are usually good choices for children, but Disney and Mario series can be easier and more fun for younger children. Interactive simulation games get children on their feet dancing, singing, and moving their body to win the game. Party games allow family members to play together in board-game-like formats filled with mini-games. This account of video games is, of course, not all-inclusive, and there are other categories of games, including puzzle games, arcade games, and strategy games, that can be appropriate for children as well. The most important thing for any parent or grandparent to realize is that not all video games are the same. Becoming active in how children spend their play time and helping them choose the games that are appropriate for their age and their personality can help to make sure that they are playing games that are both fun for them and good for the family.

MyWritingLab   ## Discussion Questions

1. This classification paper is written to help parents or grandparents select video games for children. How do the purpose and audience of the paper influence how it was written?
2. How does the writer organize each classification section? Is this approach effective?
3. Why does the writer point out the advantage of each kind of video game? Is this appropriate for a classification?
4. In the concluding paragraph the writer indicates that there are other kinds of video games that are not discussed in the paper. How does this affect the credibility and overall effectiveness of the paper?
5. Transitions can be a difficult part of any classification. How would you evaluate the effectiveness of this writer's transitions?

MyWritingLab   ## SUGGESTIONS FOR WRITING

Writing: Classification

Write a classification paper on one of the topics below or one approved by your instructor. Determine your purpose and audience, select appropriate categories, decide how many you'll discuss, develop them with specific details, and arrange them in an effective order.

1. College teachers, college pressures, or college students
2. Kinds of extreme sports, sports, or sports fans
3. Action movies, romantic comedies, or video games
4. Reasons for surfing the Internet or types of Web pages
5. Television reality shows, sitcoms, or crime shows
6. Careers in your field of interest
7. Dates, friends, enemies, or another social relationship
8. Types of medical treatment or kinds of alternative medicines
9. Leaders or leadership styles

Multimedia Writing

1. Study the photo at the start of the chapter (p. 206). Write a classification of the different food groups demonstrated by the photo as text to accompany this image on a Web page.
2. Collect images or photos of something you might want to classify–for example, different ways to dress like a hipster, different kinds of instructional devices used in classrooms, different kinds of superheroes—and then write a classification essay that incorporates those images or photos as support.
3. Write a classification essay and use charts or diagrams to visually support or represent your classification. (Include those graphics in your essay.)
4. In a blog post, create a classification of something visual or auditory (for example, types of YouTube presentations, kinds of fashion blogs, or styles of hip-hop). As appropriate, include links or audio files as examples in your blog entry.

Critical Synthesis with Sources: Classification

Purposes for Synthesis   Classification provides an effective tool for organizing material into categories. But you won't always rely exclusively on your own knowledge or experience to determine or develop categories. At times you'll supplement what you bring to a writing assignment with information gained through outside reading because we often work from the range of categories others have used (for example, different systems of classifying foods).

12.8

Critically synthesize source materials to create your classification.

Prewriting for Synthesis   Suppose that for an introductory business course, you're asked to prepare a paper that explores major types of investments. You realize that some research will be necessary. After consulting a number of books and magazines, you conclude that stocks, bonds, and real estate represent the three main categories of investments and that each category can be divided into several subcategories. Bonds, for example, can be grouped according to issuer: corporate, municipal, and U.S. Treasury securities.

At this point, you recognize that the strategy of classification would work well for this assignment. Reading further, you learn about the financial risks, rewards, and tax consequences associated with ownership. For example, U.S. Treasury securities offer the greatest safety, while corporate and municipal bonds, as well as stocks and real estate, entail varying degrees of risk depending on the financial condition of the issuer and the state of the economy. Similarly, the income from the different categories and subcategories of investments is subject to different kinds and levels of taxation. Thus, income from municipal bonds is generally tax free; income from U.S. Treasury securities is exempt from state and local taxes, and income from other kinds of investments does not enjoy such exemptions.

Critically Evaluating Your Sources   Before using the material of others in your writing, examine its merits. Do some sources seem more convincing than others? Why? Do any recommendations stem from self-interest? For example, a writer who seems overly enthusiastic about one type of investment may be associated with an organization that markets it. Are any sources overloaded with material irrelevant to your purpose? Which sources offer the most detail? Which come from the most reliable professional sources? Asking and answering questions such as these will help you write a more informed paper.

Planning and Drafting Your Synthesis   After assimilating the information you've gathered, you could synthesize the views expressed in your sources as well as your own ideas about investments. You might organize your categories and subcategories according to probable degree of risk, starting with the least risky investment and ending with the most risky. For your conclusion you might offer purchase recommendations for different groups of investors, such as young workers, wealthy older investors, and retirees.

MyWritingLab   Getting Started

1. Examine the Reader essays on our relationship to nature and then write a paper that draws upon these sources and classifies their content into different ways to relate to or respond to nature.
2. Read several authors' views on diversity and then write a paper that draws on these sources and classifies their content into different stances toward diversity, using examples from the works for support.
3. Reflect on the Reader essays that you've studied and then write a paper that presents an appropriate classification system for them, perhaps based on the writers' levels of diction, tone, or reliance on authorities.

Writing a Classification

Prewriting the classification.

- Identify subject for classification.
- Establish purpose for classification.
- Identify audience.
- Brainstorm key categories appropriate to purpose.
- Create a table of categories and brainstorm distinguishing features and details.
- If multiple levels of categories, create a category tree.
- Test categories to make certain they are complete and not overlapping.
- Check to see if your classification is fair to the situation.
- Check to see if your classification could encourage harmful behavior.

Planning the classification.

- Select the organizational strategy:
  - From most important to least.
  - From least to most important.
  - By key topic.
- Use the table to organize.
- Ensure that your classifications avoid excessive or distorting generalizations.

Drafting the classification.

- Introduction: engage reader, identify reason for classification, establish topic.
- Body: explain and exemplify each category in order.
- Conclusion: vary.

Revising the classification.

- Gather peer feedback; test hard to see if a category is missing; try other categories.
- Make sure the classification fits the purpose.
- Determine if categories overlap.
- Add necessary details or categories.
- Cut categories that don't fit or help.
- Test the organization.
- Test for ethics.

Repeat the process as needed.

Proofread.

CHAPTER **13** # Comparison: Showing Relationships

In this chapter, you will learn how to:

13.1 Use comparison as a writing strategy.

13.2 Select items for comparison.

13.3 Use details to develop a comparison.

13.4 Use different patterns to organize a comparison.

13.5 Use analogies in your comparison.

13.6 Think critically about comparisons and analogies.

13.7 Write so that your comparison is ethical.

13.8 Prewrite, plan, draft, and revise your comparison.

13.9 Critically synthesize source materials to create your comparison.

Visit MyWritingLab **to complete the writing assignments in this chapter and for more resources on comparison.**

©Fly Fernandez/Corbis

Which candidate for senator should get my vote, Ken Conwell or Jerry Mander?
Let me know whether this new shipment of nylon thread meets specs.
Doesn't this song remind you of Faith Hill?
How does high school in Australia stack up against high school in this country?

Everyone makes *comparisons*, not just once in a while but day after day. When we compare, we examine two or more items for likenesses, differences, or both.

The Purpose of Comparison

13.1
Use comparison as a writing strategy.

Comparison often helps us choose between alternatives. Some issues are trivial: whether to play FIAA 15 or Madden NFL 15, whether to order pizza or a sub sandwich. But comparison also influences our more important decisions. We weigh majoring in chemistry against majoring in finance, buying against renting, or working for Microsoft against working for IBM.

Comparison also acquaints us with unfamiliar things. To help American readers understand the English sport of rugby, a sportswriter might compare its field, team, rules, and scoring system with those for football. To teach students about France's government, a political science textbook might discuss the makeup and election of its parliament and the method of picking its president and premier, using our own government as a backdrop.

Both your classes and your job will call for comparison writing.

- Your humanities instructor may have you compare a short story and its movie adaptation to explain the adaptation process.
- Your psychology instructor may want you to compare two types of psychosis and assess the legal and medical ramifications of each.
- Your health administration instructor may have you compare two different types of elder care facilities to determine the best choice for different individuals.
- An office manager may compare different types of cell phone services to determine which is best for the company's work force.
- A nurse assesses the condition of a patient before and after a new medicine is given.
- An insurance agent points out the features of two insurance policies to highlight the advantages of one.

Selecting Items for Comparison

13.2
Select items for comparison.

Any items you compare must share some common ground. For example, you could compare two golfers on driving ability, putting ability, and sand play, or two cars on appearance, gas mileage, and warranty; however, you can't meaningfully compare a golfer with a car, any more than you could compare guacamole with Guadalajara or chicken with charcoal. There's simply no basis for comparison.

Any valid comparison, on the other hand, presents many possibilities. Suppose you head the music department of a large store and have two excellent salespeople working for you. The manager of the store asks you to prepare a one- or two-page report that compares their qualifications for managing the music department in a new branch store. Assessing their abilities becomes the guiding purpose that motivates and controls the writing. On the spot you can rule out points such as eye color, hairstyle, and religion, which have no bearing on job performance. Instead, you must decide what managerial traits the job will require and the extent to which each candidate possesses them. Your thinking might result in a list like this:

Points of Similarity or Difference	Pat	Mike
1. Ability to deal with customers, sales skills	Excellent	Excellent
2. Effort: regular attendance, hard work on the job	Excellent	Excellent
3. Leadership qualities	Excellent	Good
4. Knowledge of ordering and accounting procedures	Good	Fair
5. Musical knowledge	Excellent	Good

This list tells you which points to emphasize and suggests Pat as the candidate to recommend. You might briefly mention similarities (points 1 and 2) in an introductory paragraph, but the report would focus on differences (points 3, 4, and 5) since you're distinguishing between two employees.

MyWritingLab   **EXERCISE**   *Say you want to compare two good restaurants in order to recommend one of them. List the points of similarity and difference that you might discuss. Differences should predominate because you will base your decision on them.*

Developing a Comparison

13.3

Use details to develop a comparison.

Successful comparisons rest upon ample, well-chosen details that show just how the items under consideration are alike and different. Such support helps the reader grasp your meaning. Read the following student paragraphs and note how the concrete details convey the striking differences between south and north 14th Street:

On 14th Street running south from P Street are opulent department stores, such as Woodward and Lothrop and Julius Garfinkle, and small but expensive clothing stores with richly dressed mannequins in the windows. Modern skyscraping office buildings harbor banks and travel bureaus on the ground floors and insurance companies and corporation headquarters in the upper stories. Dotting the concretescape are high-priced movie theaters, gourmet restaurants, multilevel parking garages, bookstores, and candy-novelty-gift shops, all catering to the prosperous population of the city. This section of 14th Street is relatively clean: The city maintenance crews must clean up after only a nine-to-five populace and the Saturday crowds of shoppers. The pervading mood of the area is one of bustling wealth during the day and, in the night, calm.

Crossing P Street toward the north, one notes a gradual but disturbing change in the scenery of 14th Street. Two architectural features assault the eyes and automatically register as tokens of trouble: the floodlights that leave no alley or doorway in shadows and the riot screens that cage in the store windows. The buildings are old, condemned, decaying monoliths, each occupying an entire city block. Liquor stores, drugstores, dusty television repair shops, seedy pornographic bookstores that display photographs of naked bodies with the genital areas blacked out by strips of tape, discount stores smelling perpetually of stale chocolate and cold popcorn, and cluttered pawnshops—businesses such as these occupy the street level. Each is separated from the adjoining stores by a littered entranceway that leads up a decaying wooden stairway to the next two floors. All the buildings are three stories tall; all have most of their windows broken and blocked with boards or newspapers; and all reek of liquor, urine, and unidentifiable rot. And so the general atmosphere of this end of 14th Street is one of poverty and decay.

Vivid details depict with stark clarity the economic differences between the two areas.

Organizing a Comparison

You can use either of two basic patterns to organize a comparison paper: block or alternating. The paper may deal with similarities, differences, or some combination of them.

13.4

Use different patterns to organize a comparison.

The Block Pattern

The block pattern first presents all of the points of comparison for one item and then all of the points of comparison for the other. Following is the comparison of the two salespeople, Pat and Mike, outlined according to the block pattern:

  I. Introduction: mentions similarities in sales skills and effort but recommends Pat for promotion.
 II. Specific points about Mike
     A. Leadership qualities
     B. Knowledge of ordering and accounting procedures
     C. Musical knowledge
III. Specific points about Pat
     A. Leadership qualities
     B. Knowledge of ordering and accounting procedures
     C. Musical knowledge
 IV. Conclusion: reasserts that Pat should be promoted.

The block pattern works best with short papers or ones that include only a few points of comparison. The reader can easily remember all the points in the first block while reading the second.

The Alternating Pattern

The alternating pattern presents a point about one item, then follows immediately with a corresponding point about the other. Organized in this way, the Pat-and-Mike paper would look like this:

I. Introduction: mentions similarities in sales skills and effort but recommends Pat for promotion.
II. Leadership qualities
   A. Mike's qualities
   B. Pat's qualities
III. Knowledge of ordering and accounting procedures
   A. Mike's knowledge
   B. Pat's knowledge
IV. Musical knowledge
   A. Mike's knowledge
   B. Pat's knowledge
V. Conclusion: reasserts that Pat should be promoted.

For longer papers that include many points of comparison, use the alternating method. Discussing each point in one place highlights similarities and differences; your reader doesn't have to pause and reread in order to grasp them. The alternating plan also works well for short papers.

Once you select your pattern, arrange your points of comparison in an appropriate order. Take up closely related points one after the other. Depending on your purpose, you might work from similarities to differences or the reverse. Often, a good writing strategy is to move from the least significant to the most significant point so that you conclude with punch.

MyWritingLab   **EXERCISE** *Using the points of comparison you selected for the exercise on page 224, prepare outlines for a paper organized according to the block pattern and then the alternating pattern.*

Using Analogy

13.5

Use analogies in your comparison.

An *analogy*, a special type of comparison, calls attention to one or more similarities underlying two kinds of an item that seem to have nothing in common. While some analogies stand alone, most clarify concepts in other kinds of writing. Whatever their role, they follow the same organizational pattern as ordinary comparisons.

An analogy often explains something unfamiliar by likening it to something familiar. Following is an example:

The atmosphere of Earth acts like any window in serving two very important functions. It lets light in, and it permits us to look out. It also serves as a shield to keep out dangerous or uncomfortable things. A normal glazed window lets us keep our houses warm by keeping out cold air, and it prevents rain, dirt, and unwelcome insects and animals from coming in. . . . Earth's atmospheric window also helps to keep our planet at a comfortable temperature by holding back radiated heat and protecting us from dangerous levels of ultraviolet light.

Lester del Rey, *The Mysterious Sky*

Conversely, an analogy sometimes highlights the unfamiliar in order to help illuminate the familiar. The following paragraph discusses the qualities and obligations of an unfamiliar person, the mountain guide, to shed light on a familiar practice—teaching:

The mountain guide, like the true teacher, has a quiet authority. He or she engenders trust and confidence so that one is willing to join the endeavor. The guide accepts his leadership role, yet recognizes that success (measured by the heights that are scaled) depends upon the close cooperation and active participation of each member of the group. He has crossed the terrain before and is familiar with the landmarks, but each trip is new and generates its own anxiety and excitement. Essential skills must be mastered; if they are lacking, disaster looms. The situation demands keen focus and rapt attention: slackness, misjudgment, or laziness can abort the venture.

Nancy K. Hill, "Scaling the Heights: The Teacher as Mountaineer"

When you develop an analogy, keep these points in mind:

1. Your readers must be well acquainted with the familiar item. If they aren't, the point is lost.
2. The items must have significant similarities. You could develop a meaningful analogy between a kidney and a filter or between cancer and anarchy but not between a fiddle and a flapjack or a laser and limburger cheese.
3. The analogy must truly illuminate. Overly obvious analogies, such as one comparing a battle to an argument, offer few or no revealing insights.
4. Overextended analogies can tax the reader's endurance. A multipage analogy between a heart and a pump would likely overwhelm the reader with all its talk of valves, hoses, pressures, and pumping.

Thinking Critically About Comparisons and Analogies

13.6

Think critically about comparisons and analogies.

Comparisons can easily be misleading. If we compare the average students at most universities with the best students at the best institutions, the ordinary student will not seem very good; but that would not be good reason to conclude that average college students are as poor as the comparison makes them seem. We can be good without being the very best. When we read comparisons and analogies, we need to be carefully critical.

1. What purposes seem to guide the comparison or analogy? A comparison of a clear-cut (logged) forest with a pristine wilderness may be seeking to criticize the logging industry. In other words, the writer's feelings about environmental conservation will guide the comparison.

2. What has been left out of the comparison? The description of the clear-cut land may leave out a description of the forested area after reclamation efforts or may not reveal that the forest was heavily damaged by a fire.

3. Could other comparisons be made here? For example, the writer might compare a managed logging job with a free-for-all logged area to provide a different picture of logging and the timber industry.

4. How might the analogy mislead us? For a while, some writers used an analogy comparing the human brain with a computer, which treated our thinking as a form of calculation. This analogy, however, might not be appropriate because brain cells work very differently from silicon chips.

Ethical Issues

13.7

Write so that your comparison is ethical.

Although an old adage declares that "comparisons are odious," most people embrace comparisons except when they are unfair. Unfortunately, this situation occurs all too often. For example, advertisers commonly magnify trivial drawbacks in competitive products while exaggerating the benefits of their own merchandise. Politicians run attack ads that distort their opponents' views and demean the opponents' character. And when scientific theories clash, supporters of one view have been known to alter their findings in order to undermine the other position. Your readers expect any comparison to meet certain ethical standards. Ask and answer these questions to help ensure that those you write measure up.

- Am I avoiding skewing one or both of my items in order to ensure a particular outcome?
- Are the items I'm comparing properly matched? It would be unethical to compare a student essay to a professional one in order to demonstrate the inadequacy of the former.
- If I'm using an analogy, is it appropriate? Comparing immigration officials to Nazi storm troopers is ethically odious: It trivializes the suffering and deaths of millions of Nazi victims and taints the officials with a terrible label.

Writing a Comparison

13.8

Prewrite, plan, draft, and revise your comparison.

Don't write merely to fulfill an assignment; if you do, your paper will likely ramble aimlessly and fail to deliver a specific message. Instead, build your paper around a clear sense of purpose. Do you want to show the superiority of one product or method over another? Do you want to show how sitcoms today differ from those twenty years ago? Purpose governs the details you choose and the organization you follow.

Prewriting the Comparison

- Brainstorm major areas of interest: movies, TV shows, teaching styles.
- Brainstorm basic areas of comparison, or narrowing: "the representation of fathers on TV in the 1950s and now."
- Identify your purpose for the comparison, such as to show progress or help consumers make a choice.
- Identify what audience would be interested in your comparison.

FINDING YOUR TOPIC

- If possible, re-observe or use items to be compared and take notes of similarities and differences.
- Brainstorm or create a chart of the major similarities and differences of the items being compared.
- Branch or chart the details and examples.
- Decide what points of comparison you will use based on audience and purpose.
- Create a chart or create an outline that establishes an order for your comparison.

DEVELOPING YOUR COMPARISON

Planning and Drafting the Comparison

When you decide upon an order, copy the points of comparison and the details, arranged in the order you will follow, into a chart like the one below.

Item A	Item B
First point of comparison	First point of comparison
First detail	First detail
Second detail	Second detail
Second point of comparison	Second point of comparison

A **thesis statement** for a comparison often stresses the major point or two of comparison and relates that point to the reader's interests. "While earthquakes in the East may be more infrequent and less severe than those in California, they may be more widely felt because they tend to be shallower and are not dampened by additional faults." To develop your thesis, review your brainstorming to identify the main points of comparisons that will interest your reader and consider why those points are important.

Introduction
- Connect to reader's interest, identifying reader's interest in making a choice or reasons for understanding something unfamiliar.
- Identify items being compared and main points of comparison.
- Sometimes preview the key points of comparison in the order they will be presented in the paper.

Body
- Based on purpose, number of points you will make, and length, select organizational pattern: block or alternating.
- If explaining something unfamiliar, start with something familiar.
- If trying to demonstrate superiority of an item, go from less to more desirable.
- Follow a consistent pattern throughout.
- Provide details or examples to develop points of comparison.

Conclusion
- Possibly end with a recommendation, like whether to buy Mac or PC.
- Or make a prediction, such as the growing popularity of rugby at colleges.
- Or stress the major point of the comparison and its importance: "Why the East Coast also needs to be prepared for earthquakes."
- Do not summarize all similarities and differences for a short paper. You may provide such a summary on a much longer paper.

Revising the Comparison

Revise your paper in light of the general guidelines in Chapter 4 and the questions and suggestions that follow:

- What could help strengthen the achievement of the paper's purpose, whether to choose between alternatives or acquaint the reader with something unfamiliar?
- For something unfamiliar, where could the unfamiliar features be made clearer by a stronger comparison with something familiar?
- Where could the paper be better directed to the audience? Cut or revise material not appropriate to the audience and purpose.
- What additional points of similarity and difference might be included? Brainstorm.

- Where would additional details or examples strengthen the paper? Brainstorm or use branching.
- Does the organization of the paper not fit the purpose and audience? Where doesn't the paper follow a consistent pattern? Experiment with reorganization.
- Where could the transitions be strengthened to better show the shifts in points of comparison?
- Where do paragraphs lose focus or try to deal with too many points of comparison?
- Where, if anywhere, does the paper unfairly distort the comparison unethically?

SAMPLE

STUDENT ESSAY OF **COMPARISON**

Differences between Korean and English

Sunho Lee

1   As the world undergoes globalization, English is given a great deal of weight as an official language; as a result, many people have been trying to learn English. The Korean people have also been making efforts to acquire the language; however, learning is troublesome for Korean students because English and Korean have a lot of differences. Three major differences between English and Korean give people from Korea special difficulty in learning English: accent, tense, and articles.

2   Accent is one of the obvious differences that frustrate Korean people who try to become skilled at English. For instance, *impact* can be a noun or a verb, depending on how it is stressed. When people who speak English emphasize the first syllable, *impact* is a noun. If people who use English stress the second syllable, *impact* is a verb. The Korean tongue does not use accents in this way and spells noun and verb forms completely differently. Thus distinguishing parts of speech by accent is not something familiar to Korean learners.

3   The second difference is tense, especially the present perfect tense. The present perfect tense describes actions or states that begin in the past, continue into the present, and might continue into the future. This kind of tense does not exist in Korean grammar. For example, the meanings of "I worked out" and "I have worked out" are slightly dissimilar. Of course, Korean students can interpret both meanings, yet when

Continued on next page

Establishes point of topic

Identifies major items to be compared and ordered

Identifies key points of comparison and reasons for the discussion of those points

Identifies first major point of comparison and reason for discussion

Identifies differences with example

Identifies second point of difference

Explains difference with example

Continued from previous page

people who are used to speaking Korean use the present perfect tense in English, they have trouble because past and present perfect are not distinguished in the Korean language.

Identifies final difference to be discussed

Explains difference with examples

4   The last noticeable difference between Korean and English is the use of articles: definite and indefinite. "Ducks like to swim," "There is a duck in my bathtub," and "The duck quacked all night" are good examples. Each *ducks* or *duck* is different in these examples, but a Korean learner cannot easily see the difference between the usages. One English instructor said, "When I speak English, a bird flies to me and gives me some tips about what article I should use in this situation." This means that even native English speakers cannot define exactly how to use articles. To be sure, English grammar has some rules about how to use articles, but the number of exceptions is more than the regulations. The Korean language does not have articles; in addition, before Korean students learn English, they do not know what an article is exactly. Accordingly, for someone learning English using articles precisely is very complicated.

Explains importance of difference

Reaffirms importance of difference

5   All languages have differences. Thus for a second language learner, studying English is very hard, and it is challenging to overcome the variations between the two languages. It is especially difficult because of the differences in stress, the present perfect tense, and articles. Although these features of English are not easy to understand and use, if Koreans who struggle to use English fluently study constantly, they can finally conquer English.

Challenges Korean readers

MyWritingLab   ## Discussion Questions

1.   This writer decided to use a point-by-point rather than a block comparison. Was this the right decision? Why?
2.   While the writer provides clear examples in English, there are no matching examples in Korean. Is this the right choice for this communication situation? Why or why not?
3.   What is the audience and purpose for this essay? Does it achieve its purpose?
4.   What are some of the effective organizational strategies of this essay?
5.   What are the advantages and disadvantages that would result if the writer had looked at additional differences between English and Korean?

SUGGESTIONS FOR WRITING

MyWritingLab

Writing: Comparison

1. Write a properly focused comparison essay on one of the topics below or another that your instructor approves. Determine the points you will discuss and how you will develop and arrange them. Emphasize similarities, differences, or both.

    a. The representation of women, fathers, teenagers, or some other group in a 1950s or 1960s sitcom and in a similar contemporary sitcom

    b. Male and female styles of conversation

    c. The playing styles of two NBA or WNBA superstars

    d. Online and traditional classes

    e. The effectiveness of two pieces of writing or Web pages

    f. Two or more products being considered for purchase

    g. Two or more video games or types of video games

2. Develop an analogy based on one of the following sets of items or another set that your instructor approves. Proceed as you would for any other comparison.

    a. Writing and gardening or mountain climbing and spelunking

    b. A teacher and a merchant, coach, or prison guard

    c. Developing an idea and building a house or exploring new territory (or another idea)

    d. Succeeding at school and winning a military campaign or a sporting event or other activity

    e. Your mind and a battleground, a cluttered attic, an airport, or another point of analogy

    f. Reading a book and exploring a new place or hunting for treasure

Multimedia Writing

1. Write a comparison of the two women in the photo at the beginning of the chapter (p. 222) to make a point about what the women might reveal about different ways of life or different parts of the same culture.

2. Write a comparison on a topic of interest to you (or on a topic suggested in this chapter) and then use a graphic, chart, or table to visually represent the comparison you are making.

3. Compare two related movies or TV shows. You might focus on a character, (such as the most recent and a previous Doctor Who) or on the opening scenes of two series. Write a comparison to be posted on a television or movie review blog for interested viewers. If you are creating a blog, use links to actual video clips that reveal what you are comparing.

Critical Synthesis with Sources: Comparison

Purposes of Synthesis   Although you rely on your own knowledge or findings to develop many comparisons, in some cases you'll synthesize material from other sources. We often don't know enough about a product, a service, our brains, or our bodies to develop a reasonable comparison without research.

13.9

Critically synthesize source materials to create your comparison.

Prewriting for Synthesis Let's say that your business management instructor has asked you to prepare a report on the management styles of two high-profile chief executive officers (CEOs) at Fortune 500 companies that manufacture the same kinds of products. You realize that you'll need to do some reading in business periodicals like *Forbes, Fortune,* and the *Wall Street Journal* in order to complete this assignment. Your sources reveal that the first CEO favors a highly centralized managerial structure with strict limits on what can be done by all employees except top executives. The company has pursued foreign markets by establishing factories overseas and has aggressively attempted to merge with or acquire its domestic competitors. The second CEO has established a decentralized managerial structure that allows managers at various levels of the company to make key decisions. The company has also established a strong foreign presence, but it has done so primarily by entering into joint ventures with foreign firms. Most of its domestic expansion has resulted from the construction of new plants rather than from mergers or takeovers. Both CEOs have borrowed heavily to finance their companies' expansion.

Critically Evaluating Your Sources After you've read the views expressed by your sources, examine them critically. Does any of the information about the two CEOs seem slanted so that it appears to misrepresent their management styles? For example, do any of the writers seem to exaggerate the positive or negative features of centralized or decentralized management? Do appropriate examples support the writers' contentions? Does any relevant information appear to be missing? Does any source contain material that isn't related to your purpose? Judging the works of others in this fashion will help you write a better report.

Planning and Drafting Your Synthesis The three differences and one similarity between CEOs are your points of comparison, which you can organize using either the block or alternating pattern. You could make a chart with each of the key points of comparison in order with information from your sources. When you write your rough draft, you will want to decide in advance whether you want an unbiased comparison or whether you will lead to a preference. If the latter, your introduction might focus on the challenges of determining a more effective management style; your paragraphs would compare the styles point by point that lead to an emphasis on the qualities of the one you favor. You might conclude by indicating why you prefer one of the two management styles.

MyWritingLab Getting Started

1. Read "Going Nuclear" by Patrick Moore and "Ten Reasons Why New Nuclear Was a Mistake—Even before Fukushima" by Alexis Rowell (in the Reader) and then compare the views of these two writers on the feasibility and safety of nuclear power.
2. Read several reviews of the same movie and then compare what the critics have written.
3. Write a criticism of a comparison you read recently that you thought was unreasonable.

Writing a Comparison

Prewriting the comparison.

- Identify items for comparison, purpose, and audience.
- Make observations of objects to compare if possible.
- Brainstorm or create a branching tree of details for comparison.
- Check to make certain that the items being compared are properly matched.

Planning the comparison.

- Create a table laying out points of comparison and details.
- Determine pattern: block or point by point.
- Create a rough outline.
- Test to determine whether points are complete, meet the purpose, and are not skewed.

Drafting the comparison.

- Introduction establishes purpose for comparison and main point.
- Body develops each point of comparison with detail using pattern.
- Conclusion may vary but reaffirms the main point.

Revising the comparison.

- Gather peer responses, talk over the topic, and reexamine items being compared.
- Check to make certain everything fits the purpose.
- Add additional similarities or differences as needed.
- Cut points that don't fit.
- Test organization, especially transitions.

Repeat the process as needed.

Proofread.

CHAPTER **14** **Cause and Effect: Explaining Why**

In this chapter, you will learn how to:

14.1 Use cause and effect as a writing strategy.

14.2 Select an organizational pattern for your causal analysis.

14.3 Avoid making reasoning errors about cause and effect.

14.4 Think critically about cause and effect.

14.5 Write so that your causal analysis is ethical.

14.6 Prewrite, plan, draft, and revise your causal analysis.

14.7 Critically synthesize source materials to create your cause-and-effect essay.

Visit MyWritingLab **to complete the writing assignments in this chapter and for more resources on cause and effect.**

Eleanor/Corbis

Cause and effect are inseparably linked and together make up *causation*. Cause probes the reasons why actions, events, attitudes, and conditions exist. Effect examines their consequences. Causation is important to us because it can explain historical events, natural happenings, and the actions and attitudes of individuals and groups. It can help us anticipate the consequences of personal actions, natural phenomena, or government policies.

The Purpose of Cause and Effect

14.1

Use cause and effect as a writing strategy.

Everyone asks and answers questions of causation. Scott wonders why Sue *really* broke off their relationship, and Jennifer speculates on the consequences of changing her major. People wonder why child abuse and homelessness are on the rise, and millions worry about the effects of corporate cost cutting and violence in our schools.

Inevitably, therefore, you will need to write papers and reports that employ causation.

- For a history class, you might write on the causes of the American Revolution.
- For a criminal justice class, you might write about the consequences of white-collar crime.
- For an ornamental horticulture course, you might examine the effects of different fertilizers on plant growth.
- An employer may want a report on why a certain product malfunctions.
- A transportation professional might analyze the consequences if a community redesigns its traffic pattern.
- A public health professional might seek the causes of food poisoning.

Patterns in Causal Analysis

14.2

Select an organizational pattern for your causal analysis.

Several organizational patterns are possible for a causal analysis. Sometimes, a single cause produces several effects. For instance, poor language skills prevent some college students from keeping up with required reading, taking adequate notes, writing competent papers, and completing essay exams. To explore such a single cause-multiple effect relationship, construct outlines similar to the following two:

I. Introduction: identifies cause
II. Body
   A. Effect number 1
   B. Effect number 2
   C. Effect number 3
III. Conclusion

I. Poor language skills
II. Body
   A. Can't keep up with required reading
   B. Can't take adequate notes
   C. Can't write competent papers or exams
III. Conclusion

Alternatively, you might discuss the cause after the effects are presented.

On the other hand, several causes may join forces to produce one effect. Zinc production in the United States, for example, decreased because it can be produced more cheaply abroad than it can here, it has been replaced on cars by plastics and lighter metals, and it cannot be recycled. Here's how you might organize a typical multiple cause-single effect paper:

I. Introduction: identifies effect	I. Decrease in U.S. zinc production
II. Body	II. Body
A. Cause number 1	A. Produced more cheaply abroad
B. Cause number 2	B. Replaced on cars by plastics, lighter metals
C. Cause number 3	C. Cannot be recycled
III. Conclusion	III. Conclusion

Sometimes discussion of the effect follows the presentation of causes.

At times a set of events forms a causal chain, with each event the effect of the preceding one and the cause of the following one. For example, a student sleeps late and so misses breakfast and ends up hungry and distracted, which in turn results in a poor performance on an exam. Interrupting the chain at any point halts the sequence. Such chains can be likened to a row of upright dominoes that fall one after the other when the first one is pushed. Belief in a domino theory—which held that if one nation in Southeast Asia fell to the communists all would, one after the other—helped bring about the U.S. entry into the Vietnam War. Causal chains can also help explain how devices function and how some social changes proceed. The following outlines typify the arrangement of a paper explaining a causal chain:

I. Introduction	I. Introduction
II. Body	II. Body
A. Cause	A. Sleep late
B. Effect	B. Miss breakfast
C. Cause	C. Become hungry and distracted
D. Effect	D. Perform poorly on exam
III. Conclusion	III. Conclusion

Papers of this kind resemble process analyses, but process is concerned with *how* the events occur, cause and effect with *why*.

In many situations the sequence of causes and effects is too complex to fit the image of a chain. Suppose you are driving to a movie on a rainy night. You approach an intersection screened by bushes and, because you have the right-of-way, start across. Suddenly a car without its headlights on looms directly in your path. You hit the brakes but skid on the slippery pavement and crash into the other car, crumpling its left fender and damaging your own bumper. Later, as you think about the episode, you begin to sense its complexities.

Obviously, the *immediate cause* of the accident was the other driver's failure to heed the stop sign. But other causes also played roles: the bushes and unlit headlights that kept you from seeing the other car sooner; the starts and stops, speedups and slowdowns that brought the two cars to the intersection at the same time; the wet pavement you skidded on; and the movie that brought you out in the first place.

You also realize that the effects of the accident go beyond the fender and bumper damage. After the accident, a police officer ticketed the other driver. As a result of the delay, you missed the movie. Further, the accident unnerved you so badly that you couldn't attend classes the next day and therefore missed an important writing assignment. Because of a bad driving record, the other driver lost his license for 60 days. Clearly, the effects of this accident rival the causes in complexity.

Here's how you might organize a multiple cause-multiple effect essay:

Introduction	The accident
Body	Body
I. Causes	I. Causes of the accident
A. Cause number 1	A. Driver ran stop sign
B. Cause number 2	B. Bushes and unlit headlights impaired vision
C. Cause number 3	C. Wet pavement caused skidding
II. Effects	II. Effects of the accident
A. Effect number 1	A. Missed the movie
B. Effect number 2	B. Unnerved so missed classes next day
C. Effect number 3	C. Other driver lost license
Conclusion	Conclusion

In some situations, however, you might first present the effects, and then turn to the causes.

EXERCISE   MyWritingLab

1. **Read the following selection and then arrange the events in a causal chain:**

   Although some folk societies still exist today, similar human groups began the slow process of evolving into more complex societies many millennia ago, through settlement in villages and through advances in technology and organizational structure. This gave rise to the second level of organization: civilized preindustrial, or "feudal," society. Here, there is a surplus of food because of the selective cultivation of grains—and also because of the practice of animal husbandry. The food surplus permits both the specialization of labor and the kind of class structure that can, for instance, provide the leadership and command the manpower to develop and maintain extensive irrigation systems (which, in turn, makes possible further increases in the food supply). . . .

   Gideon Sjöberg, "The Origin and Development of Cities"

2. **Trace the possible effects of the following occurrences:**
   a. You pick out a salad at the cafeteria and sit down to eat. Suddenly you notice a large green worm on one of the lettuce leaves.
   b. As you leave your composition classroom, you trip and break your arm.
   c. Your boss has warned you not to be late to work again. You are driving to work with 10 minutes to spare when you get a flat tire.

Reasoning Errors in Causal Analysis

Ignoring Multiple Causes

14.3

Avoid making reasoning errors about cause and effect.

An effect rarely stems from a single cause. The person who believes that permissive parents have caused an upsurge of venereal disease or the one who blames television violence for the climbing numbers of emotionally disturbed children oversimplifies the situation. Permissiveness and violence perhaps did contribute to these conditions. Without much doubt, however, numerous other factors also played important parts.

Mistaking Chronology for Causation

Don't assume that just because one event followed another that the first necessarily caused the second. This kind of faulty thinking feeds many popular superstitions. Jake walks under a ladder, later stubs his toe, and thinks that his path caused his pain. Sue breaks a mirror just before Al breaks their engagement; then she blames the cracked mirror. Don't misunderstand: One event *may* cause the next; but before you go on record with your conclusion, make sure that you're not dealing with mere chronology.

Confusing Causes with Effects

Young children sometimes declare that the moving trees make the wind blow. Similarly, some adults may think that Pam and Paul married because they fell in love, when in reality economic necessity mandated the vows, and love came later. Scan your evidence carefully in order to avoid such faulty assertions.

MyWritingLab   **EXERCISE**

1. **Which of the following statements point toward papers that will focus on causes? Which point toward papers that will focus on effects? Explain your answers**.
   a. Most of the problems that plague newly married couples are the direct outgrowth of timidity and pride.
   b. The Marshall Plan was designed to aid the economic recovery of Europe after World War II.
   c. The smoke from burning poison ivy can bring on a skin rash and lung irritation.
   d. Popularity in high school stems largely from good looks, a pleasing personality, participation in school activities, the right friends, and frequent dates.

2. **Identify which of the following paragraphs deals with causes and which with effects. List the causes and effects.**
   a. Color filters offer three advantages in black-and-white photography. First, a particular color will be lightened by a filter of the same color. For example, in a photograph of a red rose in a dark blue vase, both will appear almost the same shade of gray if no filter is used. However, when photographed through a red filter, the rose will appear much lighter than the vase; and through a blue filter the vase will appear much lighter than the rose. This effect can be useful in emphasizing or muting certain objects in a photograph. Second, a particular color filter will darken its complementary color in the scene. Consequently, any

orange object will appear darker than normal if a blue filter is used. Finally, color filters can reduce or increase atmospheric haze. For example, in a distant aerial shot there will often be so much haze that distant detail is obscured. To eliminate haze almost entirely, the photographer can use a deep red filter. On the other hand, if more haze is desired in order to achieve an artistic effect, varying shades of blue filters can be used.

Timothy Kelly, student

b. Overeating, which has become a national pastime for millions of Americans, has several roots. For example, parents who are concerned that their children get enough to eat during the growing years overfeed them and thereby establish a lifetime overeating habit. The child who is constantly praised for cleaning up his plate experiences a sort of gratification later on as he cleans up all too many plates. The easy availability of so much food is a constant temptation for many people, especially the types of food served at fast-food restaurants and merchandised in the frozen food departments of supermarkets. Equally tempting are all the snack foods constantly advertised on TV. But many people don't need temptation from the outside; their overeating arises from such psychological factors as nervousness, boredom, loneliness, insecurity, an overall discontent with life, or an aversion to exercise. Thus, overeating can actually be a symptom of psychological surrender to, or withdrawal from, the complexities and competition of modern life.

Kenneth Reichow, student

Thinking Critically About Cause and Effect

Cause and effect are often confused. A person is elected president and the economy starts to improve. Many give the new president credit for the improving economy even though the cause may be his or her predecessor's policies finally paying off. Below are a few questions you should ask about any causal analysis you read or write.

14.4

Think critically about cause and effect.

1. How adequate is the evidence in support of the attributed causes or effects? Does contrary evidence exist? Often the evidence for causes and effects surrounding controversial issues (such climate change or autism) can be very complex. There has been an increase in fracking; and in some areas in which fracking takes place there has been an increase in earthquakes. But did the fracking cause the earthquakes?
2. What other causes might explain the situation or event? Are the wrong effects emphasized? The earthquakes mentioned above might have been caused by fracking, or they may have been caused by other factors. When many people argued in favor of prohibiting people from countries with Ebola outbreaks from entering the United States, some argued that the actual effect of the prohibition would be individuals entering the United States by lying about their country of origin or health status.
3. Could there be a misunderstanding about the time sequence, the cause, and the effect? That fact that fracking preceded an earthquake doesn't mean that the fracking caused the earthquake (or that it didn't).

Ethical Issues

14.5

Write so that your causal
analysis is ethical.

Causation is not immune from abuse, either accidental or deliberate. Imagine the consequences of an article that touts a new herbal remedy but fails to mention several potentially serious side effects that could harm many users. Think about the possible strain on your relationship with a friend if she unjustly suspected you of starting a vicious rumor about her. Writing cause-and-effect papers creates an ethical responsibility. Asking and answering these questions will help you meet that obligation.

- Am I trying to uncover all of the causes that might result in a particular outcome? A report blaming poor instruction alone for a high student failure rate in a certain town's public schools almost certainly overlooks such factors as oversized classes, inadequate facilities, and poor home environments.
- Have I carefully weighed the importance of the causes I've uncovered? If a few, but not most, of the classes in the problem school system are oversized, then the report should not stress their significance.
- Have I tried to uncover and discuss every important effect, even one that might damage a case I'm trying to make? A report emphasizing the beneficial effects of jogging would be dangerously negligent if it failed to note the potential for injury.
- What would be the consequences if people act on my analysis?

Careful evaluation of causes and effects not only fulfills your writing obligation but also your ethical one.

Writing a Causal Analysis

14.6

Prewrite, plan, draft,
and revise your causal
analysis.

Because you have probably speculated about the causes and effects of several campus, local, state, or national problems, writing this type of paper should pose no great difficulty.

Prewriting the Cause-and-Effect Essay

FINDING YOUR TOPIC

- Brainstorm events or circumstances in your life that you might explain for an audience or whose effect could be of interest, such as "why I dropped out of high school," or "the effects of counseling on my life."
- Keep notes of social trends or news events that are of interest, such as the rapid growth of the Tea Party movement. You might read or watch the news to get ideas.
- Note topics that may be of interest and broad appeal, such as why people become addicted to video games.

- Identify your audience and purpose for your paper. What do you want to accomplish and why would people be interested?
- Decide whether you would be better off focusing on causes, effects, or both.
- Brainstorm causes and/or effects. Research examples and details.
- For causes, identify how significant each cause is, what role it played in producing the effect, and whether it is part of a chain.
- For effects, identify the importance of the evidence and how the cause produced the effects.

DEVELOPING YOUR CAUSE AND EFFECT

Planning and Drafting a Cause-and-Effect Essay

Use a chart like the one below or an outline or a cognitive map with detail to organize your paper.

To tabulate causes, use an arrangement like this one:

Cause	Contribution to Effect
First cause	Specific contribution
Second cause	Specific contribution

For effects, use this chart:

Effect	Importance
First effect	Why important
Second effect	Why important

A **thesis statement** for a cause and effect often identifies the event to be explained or the effects to be considered, explains the importance of understanding the causes or effects, and sometimes offers a summary of the major causes or effects. "The debt crisis in Greece which may damage the world economy was not only caused by excessive public spending and the failure of many to pay taxes, but also the factors that produced a noncompetitive environment for business." To aid in forming your thesis statement, identify the reasons you think the topic is important and the major causes or effects you need to discuss. Your thesis statement can be a question that the paper answers and often signals whether the paper concerns causes, effects, or both.

To prepare for a focus on causes, you might use the words *cause, reason,* or *stem from,* or you might ask why something has occurred. To signal a paper on effects, you might use *effect, fallout,* or *impact,* or you might ask what has happened since something took place. Read these examples:

Signals causes: Midville's recent decrease in street crime stems primarily from its expanded educational program, growing job opportunities for young people, and the falling rate of drug addiction.

Signals effects: Since my marriage to Rita, how has my social life changed?

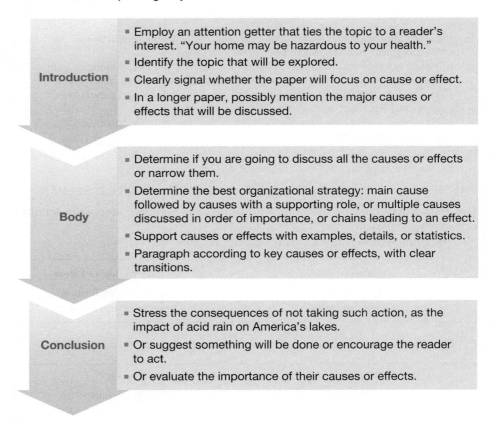

Introduction
- Employ an attention getter that ties the topic to a reader's interest. "Your home may be hazardous to your health."
- Identify the topic that will be explored.
- Clearly signal whether the paper will focus on cause or effect.
- In a longer paper, possibly mention the major causes or effects that will be discussed.

Body
- Determine if you are going to discuss all the causes or effects or narrow them.
- Determine the best organizational strategy: main cause followed by causes with a supporting role, or multiple causes discussed in order of importance, or chains leading to an effect.
- Support causes or effects with examples, details, or statistics.
- Paragraph according to key causes or effects, with clear transitions.

Conclusion
- Stress the consequences of not taking such action, as the impact of acid rain on America's lakes.
- Or suggest something will be done or encourage the reader to act.
- Or evaluate the importance of their causes or effects.

As you write, don't restrict yourself to a bare-bones discussion of causes and effects. If, for instance, you're exploring the student parking problem on your campus, you might describe the jammed lots or point out that students often miss class because they have to drive around and look for spots. Similarly, don't simply assert that the administration's insensitivity contributes to the problem. Instead, cite examples of the college's refusal to answer letters about the situation or to discuss it. To provide statistical evidence of the problem's seriousness, you might note the small number of lots, the limited spaces in each, and the approximate number of student cars on campus.

It's important to remember, however, that you're not just listing causes and effects; you're showing the reader their connection. Let's see how one student handled this connection. After you've read "Why Students Drop Out of College," the student essay that follows, carefully reexamine paragraph 3. Note how the sentence beginning "In many schools" and the two following it show precisely how poor study habits develop. Note further how the sentence beginning "This laxity produces" and the three following it show precisely how such poor habits result in "a flood of low grades and failure." Armed with this information, readers are better able to avoid poor study habits and their consequences.

Revising the Cause-and-Effect Analysis

Follow the guidelines in Chapter 4 and answer these questions and suggestions as you revise your causal analysis:

- How could the paper better achieve its purpose or reach its audience?
- Does the focus on causes, effects, or both accomplish the goal of the paper?
- Does the paper address the important causes and effects necessary for its purpose? Brainstorm or do additional research.
- Does the paper address the right relationships? Check brainstorming to determine if the paper needs to address a causal chain, an immediate cause with several supporting causes, or multiple causes and effects.
- Are there any mistakes in reasoning? Test to see that other causes aren't neglected, chronology is not mistaken for causation, and causes are not confused with effects.
- Where could the order and relationship between causes and effects be clearer or placed in a better order?
- Where could the discussion be supported with better explanation, details, examples, or statistics?
- Where could the paragraphs be better focused or developed? Too many causes or effects in a paragraph can be confusing.
- Where could the transitions be made clearer?
- Does the paper accurately represent the causes or effects and their relationships without distortion in an ethical manner?

SAMPLE

STUDENT ESSAY OF **CAUSE AND EFFECT**

Why Students Drop Out of College

Diann Fisher

1   Each fall a new crop of first-year college students, wavering between high hopes for the future and intense anxiety about their new status, scan college maps searching for their classrooms. They have been told repeatedly that college is the key to a well-paying job, and they certainly don't want to support themselves by flipping hamburgers or working at some other dead-end job. So, notebooks at the ready, they await what college

Continued on next page

Identifies importance of topic and area of concern

Continued from previous page

Identifies primary
question and
main causes to be
discussed

has in store. Unfortunately many of them—indeed, over 30 percent—will not return after the first year. Why do so many students leave? There are several reasons. Some find the academic program too hard, some lack the proper study habits or motivation, others fall victim to the temptations of the college environment, and a large group leave for personal reasons.

Transition identifies
first major cause

Provides detail
of related causes
producing lack of
preparation

2   Not surprisingly, the academic shortcomings of college students have strong links to high school. In the past, a high school student who lacked the ability or desire to take a college-preparatory course could settle for a diploma in general studies and afterward find a job with decent pay. Now that possibility scarcely exists, so many poorly prepared students feel compelled to try college. Getting accepted by some schools isn't difficult. Once in, though, the student who has taken nothing beyond general mathematics, English, and science faces serious trouble when confronted with college algebra, first-year composition, and biological or physical science. Most colleges do offer remedial courses and other assistance that may help some weaker students to survive. In spite of everything, however, many others find themselves facing ever-worsening grade-point averages and either fail or just give up.

Offers qualification,
but links major cause
with effect

Transition to second
cause

Provides details that
lead to poor study
habits

3   Like academic shortcomings, poor study habits have their roots in high school, where even average students can often breeze through with a minimum of effort. In many schools, outside assignments are rare and so easy that they require little time or thought to complete. To accommodate slower students, teachers frequently repeat material so many times that slightly better students can grasp it without opening their books. And when papers are late, teachers often don't mark them down. This laxity produces students who can't or don't want to study, students totally unprepared for the rigorous demands of college. There, courses may require several hours of study each week in order to be passed with even a C. In many programs, outside assignments are commonplace and demanding. Instructors expect students to grasp material after one explanation, and many won't accept late papers at all. Students who don't quickly develop disciplined study habits face a flood of low grades and failure.

Explains relationship
between cause and
result

Provides transition
to next cause

Details related
sequence of events
that result in effect

4   Poor student motivation aggravates faulty study habits. Students who thought high school was boring find even less allure in the more challenging college offerings. Lacking any commitment to do well, they shrug off assigned papers, skip classes, and avoid doing required reading. Over time, classes gradually shrink as more and more students stay away. With final exams upon them, some return in a last-ditch effort to

salvage a passing grade, but by then it is too late. Eventually, repetition of this scenario forces the students out.

5   The wide range of freedoms offered by the college environment can overwhelm even well-prepared newcomers. While students are in high school, parents are on hand to make them study, push them off to class, and send them to bed at a reasonable hour. Once away from home and parents, however, far too many students become caught up in a constant round of parties, dates, bull sessions, and other distractions that seem more fascinating than schoolwork. Again, if such behavior persists, poor grades and failure result.

6   Personal reasons also take a heavy toll on students who might otherwise complete their programs successfully. Often money problems are at fault. For example, a student may lose a scholarship or grant, fail to obtain needed work, or find that the family can no longer afford to help out. Some students succumb to homesickness; some are forced out by an illness, injury, or death in the family; and yet others become ill or injure themselves and leave to recuperate. Finally, a considerable number become disillusioned with their programs or the size, location, or atmosphere of their schools and decide not to return.

7   What happens to the students who drop out? Some re-enroll in college later, often in less demanding two- and four-year schools that offer a better chance of academic success. Of the remainder, the great bulk find civilian jobs or enlist in the armed forces. Most, whatever their choice, go on to lead productive, useful lives. In the meantime, campus newcomers need to know about the dangers that tripped up so many of their predecessors and make every effort to avoid them.

Margin notes:

Offers a transition to the next cause

Provides supporting details

Links cause to result under discussion

Offers transition to final cause discussed

Provides supporting examples

Identifies effects of item under consideration

Challenges the reader

Discussion Questions

MyWritingLab

1. Identify the thesis statement in this essay.
2. Trace the causal chain that makes up paragraph 2.
3. What is the function of the first sentence in paragraph 3?
4. In which paragraphs does the writer discuss causes? Effects?

SUGGESTIONS FOR WRITING

MyWritingLab

Writing: Cause and Effect

Use one of the following topics, or another that your instructor approves, to develop a causal analysis. Determine which causes and/or effects to consider. Scrutinize your analysis for errors in reasoning, settle on an organization, and write the essay.

1. Reasons why relationships fail
2. The effect of some friend, acquaintance, public figure, or writer on your life
3. Why you are a _____ major
4. Causes, effects, or both of the popularity of Facebook, Twitter, Snapchat, or some other popular form of social media
5. Causes or effects of school violence, bullying, or college drinking or drug use
6. Causes, effects, or both of widespread cell phone use
7. Causes or effects of sleep deprivation
8. Effects of a recent Supreme Court decision or change in public policy
9. The effects of environmental concerns on our way of life
10. Causes or effects of procrastination

Multimedia Writing

1. Suppose you work as a traffic-accident analyst for the police department. Write a report that provides a plausible account for the court of how two cars could end up as shown in the photo at the beginning of this chapter (p. 236). Your explanation should be something that could be used in court.
2. Take pictures or videos of something that merits explaining—for example, the pattern of stream erosion, the buckling of a sidewalk by tree roots, or the formation of a thunderhead. Write an essay that either indicates the causes of the phenomenon or the observed effects. Include pictures with the essay. If you are writing a blog, include the images and/or video clips in the blog.
3. Search the Internet to find videos on the impact of some natural or human-caused phenomenon (flooding, fire, war). Based on these clips, create a blog that explains the effects you found most compelling and important. Include the clips with your blog entry.
4. Write a cause or effect paper based on the writing suggestions above (or on a topic of your choice), but use graphics or charts to show the connections you highlight in the essay.

Critical Synthesis with Sources: Cause and Effect

14.7

Critically synthesize source materials to create your cause-and-effect essay.

Purposes for Synthesis   Although nearly everyone recognizes the role of causation in human affairs, differences of opinion often surface about the causes and effects of important matters. What lies behind the widespread incivility in the United States today? Why are women more likely than men to leave management jobs? How do video games affect children? Obviously, such questions lack simple answers; as a result investigators, even when they agree on the causes and effects involved, often debate their relative importance. Any reasonable paper therefore needs to evaluate different perspectives on the matter and the full range of evidence.

Prewriting for Synthesis   Suppose your women's studies instructor has asked you to investigate the departure of women from managerial positions. A library search reveals several articles on this topic as well as a number of reasons for resigning. Some women leave because they find it harder to advance than men do, and as a result they seldom attain senior positions. Others leave because they receive lower salaries than their male counterparts. Still others leave because of the stifling effects of corporate rigidity, unrealistic expectations, the demands of raising a family, or possibly diminished chances of marriage. Although most articles cite these causes, their relative importance is debatable. One writer, for example, emphasizes family concerns by discussing them last and at greatest length. Another puts the chief blame on obstacles to upward mobility—the existence of a "glass ceiling" that blocks women from upper-level positions along with an "old-boy network" of entrenched executives that parcels out jobs among its members.

Critically Evaluating Your Sources   Once you've finished your research, you're ready to synthesize the views of your sources as well as your own views. Before you start to write, though, take some time to consider carefully each cause and effect you've uncovered. Obviously you should ground your paper on well-supported and widely acknowledged causes and effects, but you might also include more speculative ones as long as you clearly indicate their secondary nature. To illustrate, one writer, while mentioning corporate rigidity as a reason that women leave management jobs, clearly labels this explanation as a theory and backs it with a single example. As you examine your material, ask yourself these critical questions as well as any others that occur to you: Does any writer exhibit obvious bias? Do the studies cited include a sufficient number of examples to be meaningful? Do the statistics appear reliable, or are some out of date, irrelevant, or skimpy? Have the writers avoided the reasoning errors discussed on page 240? How credible is the source? What biases might the writer bring to the subject? Whenever you find a flaw, note where the problem lies so that you can discuss it in your writing if you choose. Such discussions often clear up common misconceptions.

Planning and Developing Your Synthesis   There are various possibilities for organizing your paper. If your sources substantially agree on the most important cause, you might begin with that one and then take up the others. A second possibility, the order-of-climax arrangement, reverses the procedure by starting with secondary causes and ending with the most significant one. You can use the same options for organizing effects. When no clear consensus exists about the relative importance of the different causes and effects, there is no best arrangement of the material.

Getting Started
MyWritingLab

1. Read three articles on the causes of a major social problem, such as domestic violence, and incorporate those causes and your own views in a paper.
2. Read two articles that disagree about the effects of a proposed government program, such as oil and gas drilling on public land, and write a paper that incorporates the writers' views and presents your own conclusions.
3. Write an essay that corrects a common misconception about the causes or effects of a matter about which you feel strongly. Possibilities might include the causes of homelessness or the impact of capital punishment on murder rates in different states.

Writing a Causal Analysis

Prewriting the cause and effect analysis.

- Identify key topic based on assignment or personal interest.
- Identify audience and purpose.
- Decide if you are more interested in causes or effects.
- Brainstorm and take notes on causes and effects based on reading, observations, and talking with others.
- Test your causes and effects to make certain that you are not:
  - Missing causes or effects
  - Ignoring multiple causes
  - Mistaking correlation for causation
  - Confusing cause and effect
- Have you carefully uncovered all the appropriate causes and effects and weighed their importance fairly?
- Have you considered the consequence if people act on your analysis?

Planning the cause and effect analysis.

- Identify the most appropriate pattern: effects of a single cause, or a single event, a chain of effects or causes or effects of an event.
- Create a table that organizes causes or effects and provides the details you will stress.
- Create a rough outline, or plan, of the pattern of causes and effects.

Drafting the cause and effect analysis.

- Introduction introduces topic, reasons for analysis, and focuses on cause or effect.
- Body provides causes or effects with details and reasons, shows connections, and follows pattern.
- Conclusion may specify consequences, warn readers, or evaluate importance of cause or effect.
- Check to determine whether you are discussing every important cause or effect, even if it might damage a case you are trying to make.

Revising the cause and effect analysis.

- Does the focus on cause or effect fit the purpose and facts?
- Add missing cause or effect, detail, or evidence.
- Cut parts that don't fit.
- Evaluate accuracy of account and pattern.
- Test organization to make it clear to reader.

Repeat process as necessary.

Proofread.

CHAPTER 15

Definition: Establishing Boundaries

In this chapter, you will learn how to:

15.1 Use definition as a writing strategy.

15.2 Develop synonyms and essential definitions.

15.3 Avoid common pitfalls of definition.

15.4 Employ various writing strategies to create extended definitions.

15.5 Think critically about definitions.

15.6 Write so that your definition is ethical.

15.7 Prewrite, plan, draft, and revise your extended definition.

15.8 Critically synthesize source materials to create your definition.

Visit MyWritingLab **to complete the writing assignments in this chapter and for more resources on definition.**

The International Astronomical Union

That movie was egregious.

Once the bandage is off the wound, swab the proud flesh with the disinfectant.

Speaking on statewide television, Governor Blaine called his opponent a left-winger.

Do you have questions? You're not alone. Many people would question the sentences above: "What does *egregious* mean?" "How can flesh be *proud?*" "What does the governor mean by *left-winger?* What specific policies does the opponent support that warrant this label?" To avoid puzzling and provoking your own readers, you'll often need to explain the meaning of some term. The term may be unfamiliar (*egregious*), used in an unfamiliar sense (*proud flesh*), or mean different things to different people (*left-winger*). Whenever you clarify the meaning of some term, you are *defining.*

The Purpose of Definition

15.1

Use definition as a writing strategy.

Humans are instinctively curious. We start asking about meanings as soon as we can talk, and we continue to seek, as well as supply, definitions all through life.

- In school, instructors expect us to explain all sorts of literary, historical, scientific, technical, and social terms.
- On the job, a member of a company's human resources department might prepare a brochure that explains the meaning of such terms as *corporate responsibility* and *product stewardship* for new employees.
- An accountant might define *statistical sampling inventory* in a report calling for a change in the inventory system.
- A special education teacher might write a memo explaining *learning disabled* to the rest of the staff.

When you define, you identify the features that distinguish a term, thereby putting a fence around it, establishing its boundaries, and separating it from all others. Knowing these features enables both you and your reader to use the term appropriately.

Sometimes a word, phrase, or sentence will settle a definition question. To clear up the mystery of "proud flesh," all you'd need to do is insert the parenthetical phrase "(excessively swollen and grainy)" after the word *proud.* But when you're dealing with new terms—*information superhighway* and *virtual reality* are examples—brief definitions won't provide the reader with enough information for proper understanding.

Abstract terms—those standing for things we can't see, touch, or otherwise detect with our five senses—often require extended definitions. It's impossible to capture the essence of *democracy* or *hatred* or *bravery* in a single sentence: The terms are too complex, and people have too many differing ideas about what they mean. The same holds true for some concrete terms—those standing for actions and things we can perceive with our five senses. Some people, for instance, limit the term *drug pusher* to full-time sellers of hard drugs like cocaine and heroin. Others, at the opposite extreme, extend the term to full- and part-time sellers of any illegal drug. Writing an argument recommending life sentences for convicted drug pushers would require you to tell just what you mean by the term so that the reader would have solid grounds for judging your position.

Types of Definitions

Three types of definition—synonyms, essential definitions, and extended definitions—serve writers' needs. Although the first two seldom require more than a word or a sentence, an extended definition can run to several pages. The three types, however, are related, and synonyms and essential definitions both furnish starting points for extended definitions.

15.2

Develop synonyms and essential definitions.

Synonyms

Synonyms are words with very nearly the same meanings. *Lissome* is synonymous with *lithe* or *nimble*, and *condign* is a synonym of *worthy* and *suitable*. Synonyms let writers clarify meanings of unfamiliar words without using cumbersome explanations. To clarify the term *expostulation* in a quoted passage, all you'd have to do is add the word *objection*, in brackets, after it. Because synonyms are not identical twins, using them puts a slightly different shade of meaning on a message. For example, to "protest" and to "object" are certainly similar in many ways. Yet the claim that we "object" to the establishment of a nuclear waste site in our area fails to capture the active and sustained commitment implied in our willingness to "protest" against such a site.

Essential Definitions

An essential definition does three things: (1) names the item being defined, (2) places it in a broad category, and (3) distinguishes it from other items in that category. Following are three examples:

Item Being Defined	Broad Category	Distinguishing Features
A howdah	is a covered seat	for riding on the back of an elephant or camel.
A voiceprint	is a graphical record	of a person's voice characteristics.
To parboil	is to boil meat, vegetables, or fruits	until they are partially cooked.

Writing a good essential definition requires careful thought. Suppose your instructor has asked you to write an essential definition of one of the terms listed in an exercise, and you choose vacuum cleaner. Coming up with a broad category presents no problem: A vacuum cleaner is a household appliance. The hard part is pinpointing the distinguishing features. The purpose of a vacuum cleaner is to clean floors, carpets, and upholstery. You soon realize, however, that these features alone do not separate vacuum cleaners from other appliances. After all, carpet sweepers also clean floors, and whisk brooms clean upholstery. What then does distinguish vacuum cleaners? After a little thought, you realize that, unlike the other items, a vacuum cleaner works by suction. You then write the following definition:

> A vacuum cleaner is a household appliance that uses suction to clean floors, carpets, and upholstery.

The same careful attention is necessary to establish the distinguishing features of any essential definition.

Limitations of Essential Definitions   Essential definitions have certain built-in limitations. Because of their brevity, they often can't do full justice to abstract terms such as *cowardice, love, jealousy, or power*. Problems also arise with terms that have several settled meanings. To explain jam adequately, you'd need at least three essential definitions: (1) a closely packed crowd, (2) preserves, and (3) a difficult situation. But despite these limitations, an essential definition can be useful by itself or as part of a longer definition.

Pitfalls in Preparing Essential Definitions

15.3

Avoid common pitfalls of definition.

When you prepare an essential definition, guard against these flaws:

Circular definition. Don't define a term by repeating it or changing its form slightly. Saying that a psychiatrist is "a physician who practices psychiatry" will only frustrate someone who's never heard of psychiatry. Repress circularity and provide the proper insight by choosing terms the reader can relate to; for example, "A psychiatrist is a physician who diagnoses and treats mental disorders."

Overly broad definition. Shy away from definitions that embrace too much territory. If you define a skunk as "an animal that has a bushy tail and black fur with white markings," your definition is not precise. Many cats and dogs also fit this description. But if you add "and that ejects a foul-smelling secretion when threatened," you will clear the air.

Overly narrow definition. Don't hem in your definition too closely. "A kitchen blender is a bladed electrical appliance used to chop foods" illustrates this error. Blenders perform other operations, too. To correct the error, add the missing information: "A kitchen blender is a bladed electrical appliance used to chop, mix, whip, or otherwise process foods."

Omission of main category. Avoid using "is where" or "is when" instead of naming the main category. Here is an example of this error: "A bistro is where food and wine are served." The reader will not know exactly what sort of thing (a bar? a party?) a *bistro* is. Note the improvement when the broad category is named: "A bistro is a small restaurant where both food and wine are served."

EXERCISE

MyWritingLab

1. **Identify the broad category and the distinguishing traits in each of these essential definitions:**
   a. Gangue is useless rock accompanying valuable minerals in a deposit.
   b. A catbird is a small American songbird with a slate-colored body, a black cap, and a catlike cry.
   c. A soldier is a man or woman serving in an army.
   d. Myelin is a white, fatty substance that forms a sheath around some nerve fibers.
   e. A gargoyle is a waterspout carved in the likeness of a grotesque animal or imaginary creature and projecting from the gutter of a building.
   f. A magnum is a wine bottle that holds about two-fifths of a gallon.

2. **Indicate which of the following statements are acceptable essential definitions. Explain what is wrong with those that are not. Correct them.**
   a. A scalpel is a small knife that has a sharp blade used for surgery and anatomical dissections.
   b. A puritan is a person with puritanical beliefs.
   c. A kraal is where South African tribes keep large domestic animals.
   d. A rifle is a firearm that has a grooved barrel and is used for hunting large game.
   e. A motorcycle is a two-wheeled vehicle used mainly for human transportation.
   f. Fainting is when a person loses consciousness owing to inadequate flow of blood to the brain.

3. **Write an essential definition for each of the following terms:**
   a. groupie
   b. happy hour
   c. hit man
   d. jock
   e. pushover
   f. hard grader

Extended Definitions

Sometimes it's necessary to go beyond an essential definition and write a paragraph or whole paper explaining a term. New technical, social, and economic terms often require extended definitions. To illustrate, a computer scientist might need to define *data integrity* so that computer operators understand the importance of maintaining it. Terms with differing meanings also frequently require extended definitions. To let voters know just what he means by *left-winger*, Governor Blaine might detail the kinds of legislation his opponent favors and opposes.

Extended definitions are not merely academic exercises; they are fundamental to your career and your life. A police officer needs to have a clear understanding of what counts as *reasonable grounds for search and seizure*; an engineer

15.4

Employ various writing strategies to create extended definitions.

must comprehend the meaning of *stress*; a nuclear medical technologist had better have a solid grasp of *radiation*. And all of us are concerned with the definition of our basic rights as citizens.

Extended definitions are montages of other methods of development—narration, description, process analysis, illustration, classification, comparison, and cause and effect. Often, they also define by negation: explaining what a term *does not* mean. The following paragraphs show how one writer handled an extended definition of *sudden infant death syndrome*. The student began by presenting a case history (illustration), which also incorporated an essential definition and two synonyms.

> Jane and Dick Smith were proud, new parents of an eight-pound, ten-ounce baby girl named Jenny. One summer night, Jane put Jenny to bed at 8:00. When she went to check on her at 3:00 A.M., Jane found Jenny dead. The baby had given no cry of pain, shown no sign of trouble. Even the doctor did not know why she had died, for she was healthy and strong. The autopsy report confirmed the doctor's suspicion—the infant was a victim of "sudden infant death syndrome," also known as SIDS or crib death. SIDS is the sudden and unexplainable death of an apparently healthy, sleeping infant. It is the number-one cause of death in infants after the first week of life and as a result has been the subject of numerous research studies.

MyWritingLab ## Discussion Questions

1. What synonyms does the writer use?
2. Which sentence presents an essential definition?

In the next paragraph, the writer turned to negation, pointing out some of the things that researchers have ruled out about SIDS.

> Although researchers do not know what SIDS is, they do know what it is not. They know it cannot be predicted; it strikes like a thief in the night. Crib deaths occur in seconds, with no sound of pain, and they always happen when the child is sleeping. Suffocation is not the cause, nor is aspiration or regurgitation. Researchers have found no correlation between the incidence of SIDS and the mother's use of birth control pills or tobacco or the presence of fluoride in water. Since it is not hereditary or contagious, only a slim chance exists that SIDS will strike twice in the same family.

Finally, the student explored several proposed causes of SIDS as well as how parents may react to the loss of their child.

> As might be expected, researchers have offered many theories concerning the cause of crib death. Dr. R. C. Reisinger, a National Cancer Institute scientist, has linked crib deaths to the growth of a common bacterium, *E. coli*, in the intestines of newborn babies. The organisms multiply in the intestines, manufacturing a toxin that is absorbed by the intestinal wall and passes into the bloodstream. Breast milk stops the growth of the organism, whereas cow's milk permits it. Therefore, Dr. Reisinger believes, bottle-fed babies run a higher risk of crib death than other babies. . . .

Trudy Stelter. student

Thinking Critically About Definitions

Definitions are often extremely contested because they have real consequences. Is a "marriage" only between a man and a woman, or is it an arrangement between two consenting adults? What counts as a "living wage"? When reading or thinking about definitions, you should consider the following questions.

15.5

Think critically about definitions.

1. Does the person writing a definition have an agenda or bias that is guiding the definition and its use? For example, if the word "protest" is defined under a broader term such as "civil disturbance" or "riot," the new definition may warrant arrests.
2. What does the definition include, what does it exclude, and is the result acceptable? Does the definition seem justified by circumstances? Some have suggested that the law be changed so that those babies born in the United States to illegal immigrants are not defined as "U.S. citizens." This change in definition would have significant impact.
3. What are some of the implications of the definition? If "freedom" is defined as unconstrained action, then any and all laws are a limit on freedom. But if freedom is defined as self-determination, the formation of laws in a democracy and living under those laws are consistent with freedom.
4. What other definitions are possible? As the above example shows, there are many possible definitions of "freedom" with very different implications for how we conceive of our lives and our relationships with others.

Ethical Issues

How we define can have devastating consequences. For centuries, the practice of defining Africans as "subhuman" helped justify the slave trade and slavery. During the 1930s and early 1940s, labeling Jews as "vermin" was used to fuel the attempt to exterminate them both in Nazi Germany and much of Western Europe. Even in the absence of malice, definition can have far-reaching effects, both good and bad. For instance, a change in the federal definition of "poverty" can increase or decrease by millions the number of individuals and households eligible for benefits such as Medicaid. Although the consequences of your writing won't approach those of the above examples, you'll nevertheless need to think about possible ethical implications. Addressing the following questions will help you do this.

15.6

Write so that your definition is ethical.

- Have I carefully evaluated all of the features of my definition? In clarifying what constitutes "excessive force" by the police, it would be unfair to include the reasonable means necessary to subdue a highly dangerous suspect.
- Have I slanted my definition to reflect some prejudice? Let's say a writer opposed to casino gambling is defining "gambling addicts." The paper should focus on those who spend an excessive amount of time in casinos,

bet and often lose large sums of money, and in so doing neglect family, financial, and personal obligations. It would be unfair to include those who visit casinos occasionally and strictly limit their losses.

- Have I avoided unnecessary connotations that might be harmful? A definition of teenagers that overemphasized their swift changes in mood might be unfair, perhaps even harmful, since it may influence the reactions of readers.

Writing an Extended Definition

15.7

Prewrite, plan, draft, and revise your extended definition.

If you choose your own topic, pick an abstract term or one that is concrete but unfamiliar to your reader. Why, for instance, define *table* when the discussion would likely bore the reader? On the other hand, a paper explaining *computer virus* might well prove interesting and informative.

Prewriting the Extended Definition

FINDING YOUR TOPIC

- Brainstorm key words or phrases that interest you or you have disputed.
- Write down terms you have read that are points of contention.
- Identify a term you know about or that interests you.
- Determine what purpose would be served by defining the term. Clarify a specialized concept? Persuade the reader to adopt an attitude toward it? Discuss some neglected facet? Show what it means to you.
- Jot down ideas about audiences that would be interested in this term.

DEVELOPING YOUR DEFINITION

- Select clear examples of what you wish to define, such as the United States as an example of democracy.
- Brainstorm major identifying characteristics, such as majority rule, free elections, and separately elected chief executive.
- Test these characteristics against other legitimate examples, such as Britain, which is a democracy but lacks a separately elected chief executive.
- Test your characteristics against clear counterexamples, such as the People's Republic of China, which the definition shouldn't fit.
- Chart the method you will use and brainstorm details.

Planning and Drafting the Extended Definition

Each method has its own set of special strengths, as the following list shows:

Narration. Tracing the history of a new development or the changing meaning of a term: the birth of the Internet

Description. Pointing out interesting or important features of a device, an event, or an individual: a blizzard

Process. Explaining what a device does or how it is used, how a procedure is carried out, or how a natural event takes place: an earthquake

Illustration. Tracing changes in meaning and defining abstract terms by providing examples: tyranny

Classification. Pointing out the different categories into which an item or an event can be grouped: types of romantic comedies

Comparison. Distinguishing between an unfamiliar and a familiar item: terrorist distinguished from soldier

Cause and effect. Explaining the origins and consequences of events, conditions, problems, and attitudes: disease defined by cause

Negation. Placing limitations on conditions and events and correcting popular misconceptions: why liberty isn't anarchy

Don't hesitate to use a method for some purpose not mentioned here.

The example that follows is for a paper using a chart to develop four methods of development.

Narration	Classification	Process	Negation
Beginning American Democracy	Types of democracy	Election process	Not democracies
Forming a constitutional committee	Parliamentary democracy: England	Initial exploration	Single party states: Old Soviet Union
Drafting a constitution	Independent presidency: U.S.	Fund raising	Controlled elections: Egypt

The **thesis statements** for extended definitions often focus on the reason the readers may be interested in a term or concept combined with a major defining characteristic. "Many politicians claim the libertarian mantle, but few really accept the core idea that government and laws should be drastically limited." Look to your major defining characteristic and the reason in your brainstorming on why this term is important for ideas for your thesis.

Definition papers can begin in various ways. In writing the body of the paper, present the methods of development in whatever order seems most appropriate. A paper defining *drag racing* might first describe the hectic scene as the cars line up for a race, then classify the different categories of vehicles, and finally explain the steps in a race. One defining *intellectual* might start by showing the differences between intellectuals and scholars, then name several prominent intellectuals and note how their insights have altered our thinking, and conclude by trying to explain why many Americans hold intellectuals in low regard.

Introduction
- If no agreed upon definition (as in "conservatism"), maybe note different views and then your own.
- If the term reflects a new development (as in "the cloud"), possibly mention how it came to be.
- A definition of a colloquial or slang word (chutzpah), but other topics as well, can start with an example that grabs the reader.
- Sometimes a short dictionary definition can be useful, but this can often create a stale beginning.

Body
- Have a clear, logical order for your reader.
- Select the strategies you use based on your purpose and audience. Don't use strategies just to use them.
- Develop each part of the definition with examples and details that will make it concrete for your reader.
- Provide clear transitions for your reader.

Conclusion
- If defining some undesirable condition (such as sudden infant death syndrome), maybe express hope for a speedy solution.
- Or if reporting a new development, discuss its impact.
- Or if defining a socially important term (such as "post-racial"), you might call for a certain action.
- Or if the paper is longer, summarize main points.

Revising the Extended Definition

Use the general guidelines in Chapter 4 and these specific questions and suggestions as you revise your extended definition:

- Where could the paper better fit your audience and purpose? If your definition of "drought" is to show the social impact and encourage action, you may need to strengthen your personal examples.
- If an essential definition was used, does it avoid the pitfalls?
- What other defining characteristics may be missing? Look for some additional examples and brainstorm.
- Where are additional examples and details necessary to make the definition clear and vivid for readers? Try brainstorming tied to specific paragraphs.
- What other strategies might have helped clarify the definition? Was any strategy unhelpful? Try writing some additional approaches on a separate page.

- Where could the organization of the paper be made more effective?
- Where could transitions be strengthened to more clearly signal shifts in focus to the reader?
- Where could paragraphs be more specifically focused? It can be helpful to label each paragraph to see what it is intended to contribute to the paper.
- Has the paper avoided being slanted by prejudice or presenting harmful and unnecessary connotations so that the paper is ethical?

SAMPLE

STUDENT ESSAY OF **DEFINITION**

Vigilante Justice

Heather Hornbrook

1   Criminal justice systems, as a whole, rarely function in the best way possible. Like most things in life, they are flawed, and have been throughout time. People realize this, and in some instances, they decide to do something about it. Some try to change the system itself, while others decide to take aspects of the law into their own hands. The latter group is often called "vigilantes," going around delivering their own particular brand of justice. Various groups may go so far as acting as their own little police force, acting as judge, jury, and executioner. Others simply provide extra support where the regular police force cannot due to a lack of numbers, crisis in other areas which demand more attention, lack of interest, et cetera. A common question concerning this is, "How far is too far?" What brand of vigilante justice is justified, and which brand is not?

2   Andrew Karmen, in *The Encyclopedia of Crime and Justice*, states that the term "vigilante" is of Spanish origin, meaning "watchman" or "guard." The Latin root *vigil* means "awake" or "observant." By this meaning alone, a vigilante is someone observes and keeps watch for danger, and guards against it. Vigilantism in the United States originated in the frontier, where the first settlers in the area had no established criminal justice system. Due to the lack of law enforcement individuals, jails, and other staples of the law in the immediate area, citizens would at times dole out their own justice. Doing so was simply easier than heading into the nearest town with a sheriff or marshal,

Provides context for term being defined

Identifies initial broad definition

Identifies possible range for term

Raises moral questions concerning extent of application

Uses source to define history of the term to assist in definition

Continued on next page

Continued from previous page

Provides historical
examples to explain
the term and why
vigilante justice was
needed

which might take days or even weeks depending on the distance to travel, and the means of travel available. Some men—it was a very rare occurrence for women to take part in acts vigilantism in the Old West— would gather and form vigilance committees, and then fight against the perils that faced the community as a whole, or individual families, properties, and more; however, some of these perils were real, while others were strictly imagined or grossly exaggerated. The first recorded instance of American vigilantism was in South Carolina in 1767. A group of frontiersmen called themselves the Regulators, and began a two-year endeavor to combat desperadoes and plunderers in the area (Karmen).

Provides one kind of
example

3   Despite the creation of a national criminal justice system, vigilantism still persists today. A significant amount of vigilantism occurs in revenge killings by criminals, such as drive-by shootings, turf wars, and so on. Criminals cannot take their grievances to the police; otherwise, they would incriminate themselves, so instead of reporting it they take care of the situation on their own terms, often through violent means. The opposition may retaliate, and the cycle continues. Despite the large number of instances, vigilantism is not limited to criminals. Overenthusiastic

Provides additional
example

neighbors, who may have never even received a parking ticket, may burn down crack houses, or the houses of former child molesters and rapists, all to protect their neighborhood. Teenagers attack the homeless to drive them away, and groups may attack known or even suspected criminals, such as robbers and rapists, before the police arrive (Karmen). These people may think they are helping, but may tend to cause more harm than good by acting irrationally and attacking people undeserving of such treatment.

Uses source to
provide a contrasting
example of
vigilantism

4   Not all acts of vigilantism are violent, or as extreme as some tend to be. Some groups are actually making a difference. In Logan Hill's article, "The Second Coming of Cyberangels," he discusses how Cyberangels has become WiredSafety, and is helping crack down on child pornography. Guardian Angels founder, Curtis Sliwa, asked lawyer Parry Aftab to direct the Cyberangels site for a brief time. She agreed to do so, and on her first tip she found fifty images of children having sexual intercourse with adults. After that case, she told Sliwa that she would run the site. She completely redid the site, changed the name, and made its appearance less foreboding and more friendly; however, that

doesn't mean the group is not doing its job. They work with the U.S. Customs Department to help stop child pornographers, and also assist the Federal Bureau of Investigation. Since that first case, Aftab has helped hundreds of parents, with both the troubling cases and even how to ensure their child is safe while on the Internet with books such as *A Parent's Guide to the Internet* (Hill).

5   In her article, "Are You Authorized to Defend Yourself?" Wendy McElroy discusses a situation in the UK that caused instances of vigilantism throughout. Mobs began descending upon unsuspecting neighborhoods, and the residents fought back to protect their businesses and homes. These individuals did what they had to because there were no police around. Some want to criticize these people, while others are heralding them as heroes (McElroy). This shows that vigilantism is a fine line between right and wrong. A single action may tip the scale either way, making the difference on whether or not the vigilantes will be praised or condemned.

6   In some instances, vigilantism is unnecessary. The vigilantes go far beyond what would be considered appropriate behavior, such as bombing crack houses, instead of calling the authorities to come in and properly handle the situation. However, if there is a lack of police officials in the area, and the danger is immediate, people should be allowed to fight back and defend themselves to the best of their abilities. Groups such as WiredSafety are truly making a difference, and are providing aid to police forces, which they may desperately need. Vigilantism can be helpful when cooperating with law enforcement officials, not in spite of them. Vigilantism will most likely continue to be a controversial subject, but it is definitely one that needs to be addressed.

Provides another example that raises questions about the value of vigilantism

Conclusion pulls together a distinction between justified and unjustified vigilantism

Works Cited

Hill, Logan. "Second Coming of Cyberangels." *Wired*, archive.wired.com/culture/lifestyle/news/2000/03/35279.

Karmen, Andrew. "Vigilantism." *Encyclopedia of Crime and Justice*, www.encyclopedia.com/topic/Vigilantism.aspx.

McElroy, Wendy. "Are You Authorized to Defend Yourself?" *Mises Institute*, 18 Aug. 2011, mises.org/library/are-you-authorized-defend-yourself.

MyWritingLab ## Discussion Questions

1. How would you summarize the definition in this essay of "vigilantism"? What would you identify as the most direct statement of the definition?
2. Why might the writer have chosen to explain the history of the term? What does this history contribute to the definition?
3. What are the advantages of treating "vigilantism" as a matter of different degrees?
4. How effective are the examples in giving the reader a better understanding of "vigilantism"?
5. What does the conclusion accomplish?
6. Given this definition, how would the author see neighborhood watches that would patrol a neighborhood and contact the police regarding suspicious activity, possibly actively intervening to prevent a home invasion?

MyWritingLab ## SUGGESTIONS FOR WRITING

Writing: Definition

Write a properly focused extended definition using one of the following suggestions or one approved by your instructor. The term you define may be new, misused, or misunderstood or may have a disputed meaning. Develop the essay by any combination of writing strategies.

1. Integrity
2. Green technologies
3. Stress
4. Human genome
5. Extreme sports, performance art, improvisation, or any other activity
6. Feminist
7. Hate crimes
8. Family values, the Christian Right, Liberal, or any other broad political term
9. Some term from your job or chosen career
10. Rap, hip-hop, jazz, country, and western, or some other musical genre

Multimedia Writing

1. Collect some images and data available regarding the planets in the solar system, including "Pluto." Based on research, and using your images, define what counts as a planet and use your definition to indicate whether or not Pluto should count as a planet.
2. Collect photographic examples of something you might wish to define (such as "hipsters" or a type of street art). Write a definition that uses those images as part of the definition. If you are creating a blog, you might include video clips that help support your definition.
3. Create a visual representation of something you want to define, using pictures, audio examples, video clips, or other types of multimedia. Based on your visual representation or definition, write a corresponding definition.

Critical Synthesis with Sources: Definition

Purposes for Synthesis   Definitions are always social creations. The way various people and communities understand and use any word determines its definition. As a result, writers who use complex words such *as justice, love, and charisma* to convey a message may need to consult a number of sources to determine how others have used the words. With this research in mind, writers can stake out their own meanings of those words.

15.8

Critically synthesize source materials to create your definition.

Prewriting for Synthesis   If you were writing a paper defining *dance* for a humanities class, you would probably find several conflicting meanings of the term. Frank Thiess, writing in *The Dance as an Artwork*, defines dance as the use of the body for expressive gesture. But as you mull over that definition, you realize that it is both too broad and too narrow. While some forms of dance, such as ballet, feature expressive gesture, so does pantomime or even a shaken fist; and neither of these qualifies as dance. A square dance clearly qualifies, but does it represent expressive gesture? Susanne Langer, in *Philosophy in a New Key*, defines dance as "a play of Powers made visible," pointing to the way dancers seem to be moved by forces beyond themselves. You recognize that this definition may apply to religious dance forms, that dancers sometimes appear swept away by the music, and that you yourself have experienced a feeling of power when dancing. Nevertheless, upon reflection you decide that often it's the dancer's skill that attracts us, and rarely do we dance to reveal invisible powers. Finally, you discover that Francis Sparshott, in *The Theory of the Arts*, defines dance as a rhythmical, patterned motion that transforms people's sense of their own existence according to the dance they do. As you evaluate Sparshott's contention, you decide that it has considerable merit, although you aren't convinced that every dance transforms our sense of existence.

Critically Evaluating Your Sources   Carrying out this type of project requires you to look critically at the definitions of others. Do they accurately reflect the examples you know about? Do they describe examples that do not fit the definition? Are any parts of the definition questionable? Does the writer have the expertise to be credible on the topic? Once you've answered these questions, you can then draw on the appropriate elements of the definitions to formulate your own.

Planning and Drafting Your Synthesis   When you think about the kinds of dance you know and the various definitions you have uncovered, you conclude that each of these writers, like the blind men who felt different parts of an elephant and tried to describe it, is only partly correct. For your humanities paper, you decide to synthesize the different definitions. You might explain that all dance involves a rhythmical, patterned movement of the body for its own sake. Sometimes such movement can transform our sense of existence, as in trance dances or even waltzes. Other dances, such as story ballets, use rhythmical movements as expressive gestures that tell stories or convey emotions. Still other dances may suggest the manifestation of powers beyond the dances themselves. You proceed to explain each of these features with details drawn from both your sources and personal experience.

You might organize such a paper by developing each definition in a separate section, first presenting it in detail and then pointing out its strengths and weaknesses. In the final section, you could offer your own definition and support it with your reasoning and suitable examples.

MyWritingLab   ## Getting Started

1. Read the essay "The Revolution in the Living Room" (p. 498) and then other articles either on childhood or the family to write a definition of either *childhood* or *family*.
2. Identify a term that seems related to political controversy, such as "marriage," "voter rights," or "secure borders." Research the topic and then write a definition that accounts for the differing positions. Or, as an alternative, write an essay explaining how the disputes depend on different definitions of the term.
3. Do some research about an abstract term like *bravery, democracy*, or *paternalism,* consulting at least three sources. Use the sources to develop your own definition of the term.

Writing an Extended Definition

Prewriting the definition.

- Identify your topic, audience, and purpose.
- Read about the term, talk to others, and observe its use.
- Brainstorm distinguishing characteristics, examples, and characteristics that are excluded.
- Test your defining features against ordinary usage to determine if they are too broad or narrow.
- Evaluate all the features of the definition.

Planning the definition.

- Create a table or chart of your definition with key characteristics, examples, and conclusions.
- Identify useful strategies for the definition: narration, description, process, illustration, cause-effect, negation.
- Create a plan of organization; organization may reflect strategies used or may be arranged by key defining characteristics.
- Check to be sure that the definition isn't being slanted to reflect prejudice.

Drafting the definition.

- Introduction introduces term, reason for definition, and dominant characteristic.
- Body presents distinctive defining characteristics.
- Conclusion may summarize main point, call for action, predict an outcome, or stress importance.
- Check that unnecessary harmful connotations are avoided.

Repeat the process as needed.

Revising the definition.

- Check to see if the definition is too general, too narrow, or uses circular definitions.
- Do defining characteristics fit?
- Add needed traits or examples.
- Cut unneeded elements.
- Test to make certain definition is complete and follows a clear pattern.

Proofread.

16 Argument: Convincing Others

In this chapter, you will learn how to:

Visit MyWritingLab **to complete the writing assignments in this chapter and for more resources on argument.**

Jeffrey Markowitz/Sygma/Corbis

"What did you think of that movie?"

"Great!"

"What do you mean, *great*? I thought the acting was awkward and the story completely unbelievable."

"That's about what I'd expect from you. You wouldn't know a good movie if it walked up and bit you."

"Oh yeah? What makes you think you're such a great. . . ?"

Argument or *quarrel*? Many people would ask, "What's the difference?" To them, the two terms convey the same meaning, both calling to mind two angry people, shouting and trading insults. In writing, however, *argument* means something quite different.

The Purpose of Argument

In writing, an *argument* is a paper, grounded on logical, structured evidence, that attempts to convince the reader to accept a claim, take some action, or do both. Argument is also a process during which you explore an issue fully, considering different perspectives, assumptions, reasons, and evidence to reach your own informed position.

16.1

Use argument as a writing strategy.

The ability to argue effectively will help you succeed both in class and on the job.

- A business instructor may ask students to defend a particular management style.
- A political science instructor may want you to support or oppose limiting the number of terms that members of a legislature can serve.
- A special education instructor may have students make a written case for increased funding for exceptional students.
- In the workplace, a computer programmer may argue that the company should change its account-keeping program.
- An automotive service manager may call for new diagnostic equipment.
- A hospital administrator may argue for a better system to track patient care.

Arguments don't always involve disagreements. Some simply support a previously established decision or course of action, as when a department manager sends her boss a memo justifying some new procedure that she implemented. Others try to establish some common ground, just as you might do when you and your date weigh the pros and cons of two films and pick one to see.

When preparing to write an argument, you need to be aware that certain kinds of topics just aren't arguable. There's no point, for instance, in trying to tackle questions of personal preference or taste. (Is red prettier than blue?) Such contests quickly turn into "it is," "it isn't" exchanges that establish nothing.

Questions of simple fact (Was Eisenhower first elected president in 1952?) don't qualify either. Bickering will never settle these issues; reference books quickly will. We turn to argument when there is room for disagreement.

When you write an argument, you don't simply sit down and dash off your views as though they came prefabricated. Instead, argument represents an opportunity to think things through, to gradually, and often tentatively, come to some conclusions, and then, in stages, begin to draft your position with the support you have discovered. You should try to keep an open mind as you formulate and then express your views. And remember, you rarely start from scratch. Instead, you join a conversation where ideas and evidence have already been exchanged. As a result, you need to be thoughtful and informed.

The most successful arguments rest on a firm foundation of solid, logical support. In addition, many arguments include emotion because it can play an important part in swaying reader opinion. Furthermore, writers often make ethical appeals by projecting favorable images of themselves since readers form conclusions based on their judgments of the writer.

Framing the Argument

16.2

Frame an argument effectively.

Before you argue about something, it is helpful to be clear about what you are arguing. On any topic, there are many different ways to frame the issue. Some have framed the very emotional abortion debate around a woman's right to choose and have control over her own body while others have focused on the life of the fetus as an *unborn child*.

Any issue may be framed in a number of different ways. The frame then influences what reasons, evidence, and appeals make the most sense. The issue of the cost of higher education might be framed in terms of whether college is worth the cost, whether the burden of student loans hurts the economy, whether the loans are too much for students to bear, or whether the cost of higher education could be reduced by restructuring colleges and universities. Any of these different approaches will lead to different arguments and possibly different conclusions. The cost of education looks very different when framed as an investment in future earnings or framed as a debt that students will have to carry after graduation. The first frame might look at the average debt and compare it with the gains in earnings over a lifetime, showing that a loan is an investment that brings substantial rewards. The second frame would look at how student loans become a burden for graduates, how loans eat into earnings after graduation, and how loans may delay things like buying a home.

Frames are built on assumptions. We build our arguments, reason, and collect evidence based on assumptions. Many decide to go to college based on the assumption that it results in better job prospects and higher earnings. The evidence bears this assumption out. But what if we made different assumptions about education? Some have questioned the basic assumption of higher earnings by showing how learning a trade like plumbing or electrical work can have long-term payoffs as well. Others may show the advantages of joining the military, testing the assumption that college should be everyone's first choice.

Others may look to different educational systems entirely, such as Germany's, and ask what would happen if we had more educational and training options. When we think about issues or make arguments, we need to test our assumptions before proceeding.

The Rational Appeal

In society, and certainly in professional circles, you are usually expected to reach your conclusions on the basis of good reasons and appropriate evidence. Reasons are the key points or general ideas you'll use to defend your conclusions. If, for instance, you support the Keystone pipeline to ship Canadian tar sands oil, one reason might be the initial jobs created while building the pipeline. If you oppose the pipeline, one reason may be the environmental harm an oil spill might cause.

To convince readers, your reasons must be substantiated by evidence. If you favor the pipeline, you could to report how economists calculated the number of jobs created. If you're against the pipeline, you might detail the number of spills from other pipelines and the damage caused by these accidents.

When you appeal to reason in an argument, then, you present your reasons and evidence in such a way that if your readers are also reasonable they will likely agree with you, or at least see your position as plausible. That assumes, of course, that you and your readers start from some common ground about the principles you share and what you count as evidence. Evidence falls into several categories: established truths, opinions of authorities, primary source information, statistical findings, and personal experience. The strongest arguments usually combine several kinds of evidence.

16.3

Critically evaluate and use different kinds of claims and evidence.

Established Truths

These are facts that no one can seriously dispute. Following are some examples:

Historical fact: The First Amendment to the United States Constitution prohibits Congress from abridging freedom of the press.

Scientific fact: The layer of ozone in the earth's upper atmosphere protects us from the sun's harmful ultraviolet radiation.

Geographical fact: The western part of the United States has tremendous reserves of coal.

Established truths aren't arguable themselves but do provide strong backup for argumentative propositions. For example, citing the abundant coal supply in the western regions could support an argument that the United States should return to coal to supply its energy needs.

Most such "truths" are often repeated across a number of reputable sources, including standard encyclopedias and textbooks. Some established truths, the result of careful observations and thinking over many years, basically amount to enlightened common sense. The notion that everyone possesses a unique combination of interests, abilities, and personality characteristics illustrates this kind of truth. Few people would seriously question it.

Opinions of Authorities

An authority is a recognized expert in some field. Authoritative opinions play a powerful role in winning readers over to your side. The views of metropolitan police chiefs and criminologists could support your position on ways to control urban crime. Researchers who have investigated the effects of air pollution could help you argue for stricter smog-control laws. Whatever your argument, don't settle for less than heavyweight authorities, and, when possible, indicate their credentials to your reader. This information makes their statements more persuasive. For example, "Ann Marie Forsythe, a certified public accountant and vice-president of North American operations for Touche Ross Accounting, believes that the president's tax cut proposal will actually result in a tax increase for most Americans." You should, of course, also cite the source of your information. Follow your instructor's guidelines.

The following paragraph, from an article arguing that extra-high-voltage electric transmission lines pose a health hazard, illustrates the use of authority:

> Robert Becker, a physician and director of the Orthopedic–Biophysics Laboratory at the Syracuse, New York, Veterans Administration Hospital–Upstate Medical Center, has been researching the effects of low-frequency electric fields (60 Hz) for fifteen years. Testifying at health and safety hearings for proposed lines in New York, he said that exposure to the fields can produce physiological and functional changes in humans—anything from increased irritability and fatigue to raised cholesterol levels, hypertension and ulcers. Studies of rats exposed to low-level electric fields showed tumor growths and abnormalities in development. Dr. Becker believes we are performing unauthorized medical experiments by exposing people to the electromagnetic fields surrounding the transmission lines.
>
> Kelly Davis, "Health and High Voltage: 765 KV Lines"

Beware of biased opinions. The agribusiness executive who favors farm price supports or the labor leader who opposes any restrictions on picketing may be writing merely to guard old privileges or garner new ones. Unless the opinion can stand especially close scrutiny, don't put it in your paper; it will just weaken your case with perceptive readers.

Because authorities don't always see eye to eye, their views lack the finality of established truths. Furthermore, their opinions will convince only if the audience accepts the authority *as* authoritative. Although advertisers successfully present football stars as authorities on shaving cream and credit cards, most people would not accept their views on the safety of nuclear energy.

Primary Source Information

You'll need to support certain types of argument with primary source information—documents or other materials produced by individuals directly involved with the issue or conclusions you reached by carrying out an investigation yourself. To argue whether the United States should have dropped the atom bomb on Japan to end World War II, for example, you would want to examine the autobiographies of those involved in making the decision and perhaps even the documents that prompted it. To take a position on the violence mentioned in some gangster rap,

Identifies professional role that confirms authority

Identifies credible institutions

Documents length of work in the field that makes him an expert

Ties claims to specific research

you would want to analyze the actual lyrics in a number of songs. To make a claim about the press coverage of the first Persian Gulf War, you would want to read the newspaper and magazine accounts of correspondents who were on the scene. To convince readers to adopt your solution for the homeless problem, you might want to visit a homeless shelter or interview (in a safe place) some homeless people. This type of information can help you reach sound conclusions and build strong support for your position. Most college libraries contain a significant amount of primary source materials.. Sometimes you may need to look more directly to the actual material in the world. If you want to make claims about the relative number of female and male characters in animation, you would possibly have to view the episodes yourself and count or use a source like Website details of the characters and voices in the animated series and use that to count characters. Document the sources you use according to your instructor's guidelines.

Statistical Findings

Statistics—data showing how much, how many, or how often—can also buttress your argument. Most statistics come from books, magazines, newspapers, handbooks, encyclopedias, and reports, but you can use data from your own investigations as well. *Statistical Abstract of the United States* is a good source of authoritative statistics on many topics.

Because statistics are often misused, many people distrust them, so any you offer must be reliable. First, make sure your sample isn't too small. Don't use a one-day traffic count to argue for a traffic light at a certain intersection. City Hall might counter by contending that the results are atypical. To make your case, you'd need to count traffic for perhaps two or three weeks. Take care not to push statistical claims too far. You may know that two-thirds of Tarrytown's factories pollute the air excessively, but don't argue that the same figures probably apply to your town. There's simply no carryover. Keep alert for biased statistics; they can cause as serious a credibility gap as biased opinions. Generally, recent data are better than old data, but either must come from a reliable source. Older information from the *New York Times* would probably be more accurate than current data from some publication that trades on sensationalism. Note how the following writer uses statistics in discussing America's aging population and its impact on the federal budget:

> . . . In 1955 defense spending and veterans benefits accounted for almost 70 percent of federal outlays. By 1995 their share was 19 percent. In the same period social security and Medicare (which didn't exist until 1965) went from 6 percent to 34 percent of the budget. Under present trends, their share would rise to 39 percent by 2005, projects the Congressional Budget Office. . . . Between 2010 and 2020, the older-than-65 population will rise by about a third; in the next decade, it will rise almost another third. Today, about one in eight Americans is older than 65; by 2030, the proportion is projected to be one in five. The older-than-85 population will rise even faster.
>
> Robert J. Samuelson, "Getting Serious"

Again, follow your instructor's guidelines when documenting your sources.

Personal Experience

Sometimes personal experience can deliver an argumentative message more forcefully than any other kind of evidence. Suppose that two years ago a speeder ran into your car and almost killed you. Today you're arguing for stiffer laws against speeding. Chances are you'll rely mainly on expert opinions and on statistics showing the number of people killed and injured each year in speeding accidents. However, describing the crash, the slow, pain-filled weeks in the hospital, and the months spent hobbling around on crutches may well provide the persuasive nudge that wins your reader over.

Often the experiences and observations of others, gathered from books, magazines, or interviews, can support your position. If you argue against chemical waste dumps, the personal stories of people who lived near them and suffered the consequences—filthy ooze in the basement, children with birth defects, family members who developed a rare form of cancer—can sway your reader.

Despite its usefulness, personal experience generally reinforces but does not replace other kinds of evidence. Unless it has other support, readers may reject it as atypical or trivial.

Evaluation of Evidence

Once you have gathered the appropriate type(s) of evidence, certain standards govern the evaluation and use of that evidence. That a piece of information is in some way connected to your topic does not make it good evidence or qualify it for inclusion in your paper. Readers won't be convinced that trains are dangerous merely because you were in a train wreck. You should not reach a conclusion based on such flimsy evidence either. In order to reach a reasonable conclusion and defend a position with suitable evidence, you should apply the following principles.

Evaluation Criteria	Explanation
How credible are the sources of the information? How reliable is the evidence?	Not all sources are created equal. U.S. Census data about population change is more credible than a local newspaper's estimate, though both may be more valid than your own estimate.
How much confirming evidence is there?	With evidence, more is better. One scientific study on the efficacy of high-protein diets would be good, but several would be better. One authority who claims that global warming is a reality becomes more credible when confirmed by several other authorities.
How much contradictory evidence is there?	If several scientific studies or authorities point to the efficacy of high-protein diets and several other studies find such diets harmful, clearly you would need to weigh the evidence more carefully.
How well established is the evidence?	Extremely established evidence, such as the evidence for atoms, becomes the basis for textbooks and is assumed in most other research. This evidence is usually unquestionable, although it also can be overturned.

Evaluation Criteria	Explanation
How well does the evidence actually support or fit the claim?	The fact that most Americans are immigrants or descendents of immigrants has no bearing on whether the country is admitting too many or too few immigrants. To make a case for or against some policy on immigration, the evidence would have to focus on its good or bad results.
What does the evidence actually allow you to conclude?	The evidence shouldn't lead you to reach an exaggerated conclusion. Studies showing that television violence causes children to play more aggressively do not warrant the conclusion that it causes children to kill others.

Sometimes unwarranted conclusions result because a writer fails to take competing claims and evidence into consideration. For example, evidence shows that children in Head Start programs do better than others during the first three years of school. Other evidence, however, shows that in later years these students do not do significantly better. Yet other evidence shows that they are more likely to stay in school and less likely to get into trouble. Clearly, you shouldn't argue that Head Start ensures continuing success at all grade levels. You would need to weigh the credibility, quantity, reliability, and applicability of the available evidence to reach and defend a more limited conclusion.

Reasoning Strategies

An argument, then, consists of a conclusion you want to support, your reasons for that conclusion, and the evidence that supports your reasons. But how are reasons and evidence fitted together? Rational appeals include three reasoning strategies: induction, deduction, and analogy.

16.4

Construct effective inductive and deductive arguments, and use analogy.

Induction

An argument from induction occurs when a general claim is supported by specific evidence, whether direct observations, statistical data, or scientific studies. Most of our conclusions are supported inductively. When we conclude that a movie is worth watching because our friends liked it, when we decide a college program is effective because most students in it get jobs, or even when we support a scientific hypothesis based on formal experimentation, we are basing a conclusion on bits of evidence. We need to be thoughtful in reaching such conclusions. Are our friends like us and trustworthy? Are the jobs that students get good jobs? All the principles for evaluating evidence apply.

Induction makes our conclusions probable but rarely proves them. To prove something by induction, we must check every bit of evidence and often that's just not practical or possible. The greater the number of observations and the larger the populations surveyed, the more strongly the conclusion is supported. Obviously then, just a few observations makes the evidence very weak. If you ask 10 of 15,000 students whether they like the meal plan, you cannot conclude much if eight of the students liked the plan. These students may just be atypical.

All inductive evidence only makes supported conclusions likely. It is important to measure the strength of the supporting evidence.

You have several options for organizing an inductive argument.

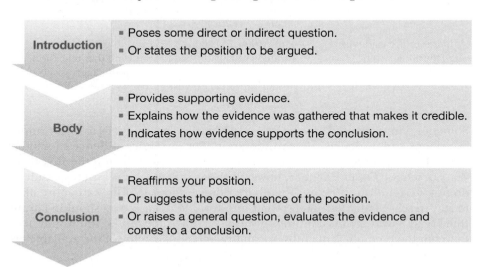

Introduction
- Poses some direct or indirect question.
- Or states the position to be argued.

Body
- Provides supporting evidence.
- Explains how the evidence was gathered that makes it credible.
- Indicates how evidence supports the conclusion.

Conclusion
- Reaffirms your position.
- Or suggests the consequence of the position.
- Or raises a general question, evaluates the evidence and comes to a conclusion.

The following short example illustrates inductive argument.

States claim to be proven

Identifies justification of study

Provides results of evidence that supports major claim

Offers a second study to strengthen support

States results that support claim

Provides qualification to support credibility

Connects evidence clearly as support for claim

Systematic phonics, the method of reading instruction that shows children how to sound out letters, is an effective method of teaching word reading in the first three grades. A large study, sponsored by the federal government in the 1970s, compared how effective different instructional methods were in helping disadvantaged children. The direct instruction program resulted in children, otherwise expected to fall below the norm, to meet or be close to the national standard for reading (Stebbins et al., 1977). Another study compared the effect of the whole-language instruction, embedded phonics, and direct code instruction on 285 students in a district with a high risk of reading failure. The university researchers found that the children taught by direct instruction improved in word reading much faster than students in the other groups. In fact, most taught with the whole-language approach had no measurable gains in word reading, even if they did have a more positive attitude towards reading (Stahl et al., 1994). While these studies may not fully demonstrate that systematic phonics is the best method for teaching reading, the fact that in experiments students taught with direct code instruction demonstrated greater gains in word reading than those taught by other methods at least shows that systematic phonics can help students make gains in word reading.

Marjorie Hawkins, student

When writing an induction argument, in addition to presenting the available evidence, there are two other important things you should do. It is helpful to demonstrate the credibility of your evidence. Here, the student writer identified that the first study was large and sponsored by the federal government and gave the exact number of subjects in the second study, as well as the information that the researchers were from a university.

Also, if possible, try to show how the evidence fits the conclusion you want to reach. The author, above, made certain her claims were not overstated by being clear about what she was not stating and then directly tied the research studies to her conclusion.

Deduction

Deduction is a process of argumentation that demonstrates how a specific conclusion follows logically from some initial premises about which people might agree. For example, to convince a friend to study harder, you begin with the assumption that a profitable career requires a good education; proceed to argue that for a good education students must study diligently; and conclude that, as a result, your friend should spend more time with the books. Politicians who assert that we all want to act in ways beneficial to future generations, then point out how the policies they favor will ensure that outcome, argue deductively.

As with induction, you have several options when organizing a deductive argument.

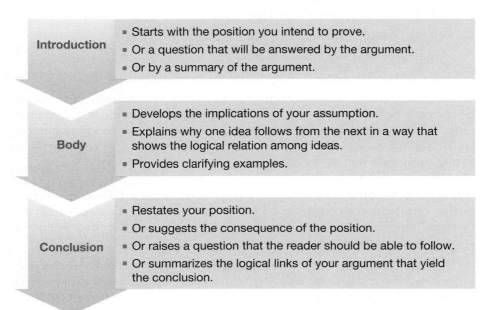

Introduction
- Starts with the position you intend to prove.
- Or a question that will be answered by the argument.
- Or by a summary of the argument.

Body
- Develops the implications of your assumption.
- Explains why one idea follows from the next in a way that shows the logical relation among ideas.
- Provides clarifying examples.

Conclusion
- Restates your position.
- Or suggests the consequence of the position.
- Or raises a question that the reader should be able to follow.
- Or summarizes the logical links of your argument that yield the conclusion.

Here is a short example of deductive argument:

States the point to be argued

The recent spot-checks of our rooms by the dorm's head advisor are an unacceptable invasion of privacy. This practice should stop immediately.

Establishes basic agreed-upon assumption

The United States Constitution prohibits searches by police officers unless these officers have adequate reason. That is why the police need a search warrant before they can search any home. If they fail to obtain one, a case that ends up in court will likely be thrown out. Our right to privacy, then, can't be violated without due cause.

States the chain of logical relationships

Attempts to draw a parallel to lead the reader to the logical conclusion

If the police can't search our homes without good reason, why should our head advisor spot-check our rooms for signs of wrongdoing?

Sammy Borchardt, student

When arguing from deduction, you need to make clear how your conclusions do actually follow from the agreed-upon premises. Those premises may also be questionable and need support, whether by induction or by demonstrating their deductive relationship to other strongly held ideas.

Syllogisms: Deduction Must Follow Logically

Conclusions in an argument should follow logically from their premises. Some conclusions follow a form known as a **categorical syllogism**, a set of three statements that follow a fixed pattern to ensure sound reasoning. The first statement, called the *major premise*, names a category of things and says that all or none of them share a certain characteristic. The *minor premise* notes that a thing or group of things belongs to that category. The *conclusion* states that the thing or group shares the characteristics of the category.

Major premise: All humans make mistakes.
Minor premise: Doctors are human.
Conclusion: Doctors make mistakes.

Sometimes syllogisms appear in stripped-down form, with one of the premises or the conclusion omitted. The following example omits the major premise: "Because Wilma is a civil engineer, she has a strong background in mathematics." Obviously the missing major premise is as follows: "All civil engineers have strong backgrounds in mathematics."

Syllogistic Argument at Work A syllogism can occur anywhere in an essay: in the introduction to set the stage for the evidence, at various places in the body, even in the conclusion in order to pull the argument together. Following is an example that uses a syllogism in the introduction:

In 1966, when the Astrodome was completed in Houston, Texas, the managers concluded that it would be impossible to grow grass indoors. To solve their problem, they decided to install a ruglike synthetic playing surface that was fittingly called Astroturf. In the ensuing years, many other sports facilities have installed synthetic turf. Unfortunately, this development has been accompanied by a sharp rise in the number and severity of injuries suffered by athletes—a rise clearly linked to the surface they play upon. Obviously, anything that poses a threat to player safety is undesirable. Because synthetic turf does this, it is undesirable and should be replaced by grass.

Denny Witham, student

To support his position, the writer then goes on to note that turf, unlike grass, often becomes excessively hot, tiring players and increasing their chances of injury; that seams can open up between sections of turf and lead to tripping and falling; that players can run faster on artificial turf and thus collide more violently; and that the extreme hardness of the turf leads to torn ligaments and tissues when players slam their toes into it.

Avoiding Misuse of Syllogisms   Whenever using a syllogism in a deductive argument, care must be taken.

First, any of the premises may be disputable. In the above example, one might question whether synthetic turf does or doesn't pose a threat to player safety. Much of the rest of the paper would need to prove that this premise is true.

Second, you need to be sure the logic works. We all make mistakes in deduction. If you look outside and see that the sidewalk is wet and conclude it rained, you may be surprised to learn that the wet sidewalk was really a result of your neighbor's sprinkler. Your argument went something like the following:

> If it rains, the sidewalk will get wet.
>
> The sidewalk is wet.
>
> Therefore, it rained.

You could have reasonably concluded from a rainstorm that the sidewalk would be wet, but a wet sidewalk does not allow you to conclude rain.

Third, you might end up abusing the form of the syllogism. Consider this example:

> College students study different subject matter.
>
> Jason studies different subject matter.
>
> Therefore, Jason is a college student.

If we had known that Jason was a college student, we could conclude that he had the characteristic of studying. But his studying doesn't prove he is a college student. He could be a professor, someone just interested in a topic, or an employed professional keeping up to date in his field.

Reductio ad Absurdum

A common and powerful form of deduction called *reductio ad absurdum* ("to reduce to absurdity") is used to question a position by showing that its consequences are problematic if carried to their logical end. To counter the position that the government should impose no restrictions on the public's right to bear arms, you might point out that, carried to its logical extreme, such a policy would allow individuals to own bazookas, cannons, and nuclear bombs. This absurd result makes it clear that certain restrictions should apply to our right to bear arms. The question then becomes where we should draw the ownership line.

MyWritingLab   **EXERCISE**   *Which of these syllogisms is satisfactory, which have false major premises, and which is faulty because the last two statements reverse the proper order?*

1. All singers are happy people.
    Mary Harper is a singer.
    Therefore, Mary Harper is a happy person.
2. All cowards fear danger.
    "Chicken" Cacciatore is a coward.
    Therefore, "Chicken" Cacciatore fears danger.
3. All cats like meat.
    Towser likes meat.
    Therefore, Towser is a cat.
4. No salesperson would ever misrepresent a product to a customer.
    Sabrina is a salesperson.
    Therefore, Sabrina would never misrepresent a product to a customer.

Analogy in Argument

An analogy compares two unlike situations or things. Arguers often use analogies to contend that because two items share one or more likenesses, they are also alike in other ways. Familiar analogies assume that humans respond to chemicals as rats do and that success in school predicts success on the job. You have used analogy if you ever pressed your parents for more adult privileges, such as a later curfew, by arguing that you were like an adult in many ways.

Because its conclusions about one thing rest upon observations about some different thing, analogy is the weakest form of rational appeal. Analogies never prove anything. But they often help explain and show probability and therefore are quite persuasive.

For an analogy to be useful, it must feature significant similarities that bear directly on the issue. In addition, it must account for any significant differences between the two items. It is often helpful to test an analogy by listing the similarities and differences. Here's an effective analogy, used to back an argument that a liberal education is the best kind to help us cope successfully with life:

Establishes basis of
analogy

> Suppose it were perfectly certain that the life and fortune of every one of us would, one day or other, depend upon his winning or losing a game of chess. Don't you think that we should all consider it to be a primary duty to learn at least the names and the moves of the pieces; to have a notion of a gambit, and a keen eye for all the means of giving and getting out of check? Do you not think that we should look with a disapprobation amounting to scorn, upon the father who allowed his son, or the state which allowed its members, to grow up without knowing a pawn from a knight?

Yet it is a very plain and elementary truth, that the life, the fortune, and the happiness of every one of us, and, more or less, of those who are connected with us, do depend upon our knowing something of the rules of a game infinitely more difficult and complicated than chess. It is a game which has been played for untold ages, every man and woman of us being one of the two players in a game of his or her own. The chessboard is the world, the pieces are the phenomena of the universe, the rules of the game are what we call the laws of Nature. The player on the other side is hidden from us. We know that his play is always fair, just, and patient. But also we know, to our cost, that he never overlooks a mistake, or makes the smallest allowance for ignorance. To the man who plays well, the highest stakes are paid, with that sort of overflowing generosity with which the strong shows delight in strength. And one who plays ill is checkmated—without haste, but without remorse. . . .

> Finishes defining analogy by indicating how life is like a game

> Details the comparison of life and chess

Well, what I mean by Education is learning the rules of this mighty game. In other words, education is the instruction of the intellect in the law of Nature, under which name I include not merely things and their forces, but men and their ways; and the fashioning of the affections and of the will into an earnest and loving desire to move in harmony with those laws. For me, education means neither more nor less than this. Anything which professes to call itself education must be tried by this standard, and if it fails to stand the test, I will not call it education, whatever may be the force of authority, or of numbers, upon the other side.

> Completes the argument by demonstrating the rules that need to be learned and how that is an education

Thomas Henry Huxley, "A Liberal Education and Where to Find It"

To develop an argument by analogy, brainstorm the two items being compared for significant similarities and prepare a chart that matches them up. The greater the number and closeness of these similarities, the better the argument by analogy.

The Emotional Appeal

Although effective argument relies mainly on reason, an emotional appeal can lend powerful reinforcement. Indeed, emotion can win the hearts and the help of people who would otherwise passively accept a logical argument but take no action. Organizations raise funds to fight famine with television ads that feature skeletal, swollen-bellied children. Still other groups use emotion-charged stories and pictures to solicit support for environmental protection, to combat various diseases, and so on. Advertisers use emotion to play upon our hopes, fears, and vanities in order to sell mouthwash, cars, clothes, and other products. Politicians paint themselves as God-fearing, honest toilers for the public good while lambasting their opponents as the uncaring tools of special interests. In evaluating or writing an argument, ask yourself whether the facts warrant the emotion. Is the condition of destitute children truly cause for pity that requires financial action? Is any politician unwaveringly good, any other irredeemably bad?

16.5

Use effective emotional appeals to persuade.

The following passage, from a student argument favoring assisted suicide for the terminally ill, draws on the strategies of narration and description to create an appropriate use of emotions to demonstrate the painfully debilitating nature of terminal illnesses.

<table>
<tr>
<td>

Description indicates dependency and weakness

Contrast shows change in quality of life

Identifies degradation

Shows narrator's love, which makes subsequent argument more credible

</td>
<td>

When I visited Grandpa for the last time, he seemed imprinted on the hospital bed, a motionless, skeleton-like figure tethered by an array of tubes to the droning, beeping machine at his bedside. The eyes that had once sparkled with delight as he bounced grandchildren on his knee now stared blankly at the ceiling, seemingly ready to burst from their sockets. His mouth, frozen in an open grimace, emitted raspy, irregular noises as he fought to breathe. Spittle leaked from one corner of his mouth and dribbled onto the sheet. A ripe stench from the diaper around his middle hung about the bedside, masking the medicinal sickroom smells. As I stood by the bedside, my mind flashed back to the irrepressible man I once knew, and tears flooded my eyes. Bending forward, I planted a soft kiss on his forehead, whispered "I love you, Gramps," and walked slowly away.

</td>
</tr>
</table>

Dylan Brandt Chafin, student

To develop an effective emotional appeal, identify the stories, scenes, or events of the topic that arouse the strongest emotional response within you. Do some thinking about the types of words that will best convey the emotion you feel. Then write the section so that it builds to the kind of emotional conclusion that will help your argument.

There are many specific models to help guide an emotional appeal. One of the most common, frequently used in advertisements, is the hierarchy of needs identified by Abraham Maslow, an American psychologist. Next is a table identifying the hierarchy of needs and how they might play a role in an emotional appeal concerning climate change.

Need	**Appeal**
Self-actualization	When writers claim that you can use and extend your talents to make a difference, they are appealing to your engagement in your own personal development.
Status, self-esteem	When writers appeal to your discerning taste or superior intellect, as in arguing that those who value science recognize the danger of climate change, the writers are appealing to status or self-esteem.
Love and belonging	Those forming an argument may suggest that you can belong to a serious group of concerned citizens, thus appealing to your sense of belonging.
Safety and security	The writer can appeal to your need for safety and security by suggesting the risks raised by climate change and severe weather.
Physical need (food, clothing, shelter)	A writer might attempt appeal to your physical needs by showing how climate change could threaten food production or how severe weather might destroy homes.

Making Arguments with Visuals

Because visuals often make a point powerfully and emotionally, you can often use visual aids to make an emotional appeal, to make your point with oomph. The following image makes a quick point about lectures.

16.6

Use visual aids to support arguments.

Lectures don't always promote learning.

   Photographs and cartoons, accompanied by a few pithy phrases, can make powerful arguments. A photo of a river clogged with litter makes a strong environmental point. A cartoon showing a rich person picking the pocket of a poor person quickly presents a political argument. A short caption like "Your latte could have fed five children today" concisely appeals to our sense of charity. While these short arguments are rarely appropriate in a college setting, where reasons and evidence are carefully weighed, they are part of how we communicate to persuade. However, short, visual arguments can be part of a larger essay to effectively emphasize key points. For visual arguments to be effective, the image needs to be easily understood, directly illustrate the point, and have emotional punch.

The Ethical Appeal

Before logic can do its work, the audience must be willing to consider the argument. If a writer's tone offends the audience, perhaps by being arrogant or mean-spirited, the reasoning will fail to penetrate. But if the writer comes across as pleasant, fair-minded, and decent, gaining reader support is much easier. The image that the writer projects is called the *ethical appeal.*

16.7

Use effective ethical appeals to persuade.

If you write with a genuine concern for your topic, a commitment to the truth, and a sincere respect for others, you will probably come across reasonably well. When you finish writing, check to see that an occasional snide comment or bitter remark didn't slip unnoticed onto the page. In the following introductory paragraph, from an essay arguing that many universities violate the Constitution by imposing campus rules that restrict freedom of speech, the student establishes an appealing ethical image:

> Most of us would agree that educated people should not indulge in name-calling and stereotyping in their speaking and writing. To do so is an essential mark of irrational prejudice. Nevertheless, such speaking and writing are protected by the United States Constitution, which prohibits anyone from abridging freedom of expression. Today, many colleges and universities, in a well-meaning attempt to shield particular groups from unwelcome or insensitive words, are subverting this prohibition. Former Supreme Court Justice William Brennan, noted for his liberal views, has stated, "If there is a bedrock principle underlying the First Amendment, it is that the government may not prohibit the expression of an idea simply because society finds the idea offensive or disagreeable."
>
> Linda Kimrey, student

The writer opposes on constitutional grounds any attempts to ban the expression of two forms of "irrational prejudice." Nevertheless, she characterizes these attempts as "well-meaning" and acknowledges that they are prompted by worthy motives. As a result, she emerges as fair-minded, decent, sensitive, and concerned, an image she maintains throughout the essay.

Marginal notes (left column):

Concedes how others feel, projecting a fair-minded approach

Suggests a founding support for position other than prejudice

Indicates understanding for the position she opposes

Uses an authority the reader is likely to acknowledge to present her position to show sympathy with the opponent's "experts"

Other Types of Arguments: Rogerian and Exploratory Arguments

16.8

Understand Rogerian and exploratory argument.

Rogerian Arguments

If you're arguing an emotionally charged issue such as gun control or federally funded abortions for the poor, you may want to use *Rogerian argument*. Named for psychologist Carl Rogers, this type of argument attempts to reduce the antagonism that people with opposing views might feel toward your position. To succeed, you must show that you understand and respect the opposing position as well as acknowledge its good points. You try to establish some common point of agreement, then show how the conclusion you want really follows from the reader's own values and assumptions without compromising your own. If you want stricter gun-control laws, for example, you might begin by acknowledging that the Constitution grants citizens the right to bear arms and that you believe anyone with legitimate uses for guns—hunters, target shooters, those who feel a need for a gun in their home for protection, and the like—should have access to them.

Moving on, you might point out that gun owners and those who agree with the Second Amendment support the proper, safe use of firearms and are concerned about firearm abuse. You might then possibly agree with the premise that people, rather than guns themselves, kill people, and for that reason, no one wants criminals to have guns. Finally, you might demonstrate that requiring computer background checks before issuing handgun permits would deprive criminals of such weapons while protecting the constitutional right to bear arms.

Exploratory Argument

You do not always have to write an argument to forcefully convince someone. In an *exploratory argument*, you write to share with your reader how you came to your conclusion. This form of discussion allows you to indicate your doubts about your own position, explain why certain reasons and evidence have weight for you, include personal reasons that influenced you, and address alternative positions and arguments that may tempt you. The goal in such an argument is really to provide the readers with your thinking on the matter; if they are convinced along the way, so much the better. Below is a short excerpt of what a section of an answer to an argument against a ban on semiautomatic weapons might look like.

> While the authors of the Bill of Rights may have intended the Second Amendment to allow all citizens the right to bear arms, the amendment was drafted in a very different period of our history, which would seem to raise some questions about its current application. We had just won a revolutionary war that had depended on a citizen army. Americans faced real threats from the native population and other armed groups and states were protective of their own state militias. Their weapons were different as well. Citizens mostly owned a muzzle-loading musket that was slow and cumbersome to use, as well as inaccurate. It would seem that understanding the intent of these authors would require us to understand the historical period shaping their vision, a period when a well-ordered militia seemed essential. What would they make, then, of our current situation where the threat we face is almost always from fellow citizens and the power of today's guns would have been unimaginable?

Tentative question to explore

Note the exploratory and tentative nature of question

Exploratory essays do not need to be informal or personal. An academic paper that considers the political influences on television programming may make little use of the personal pronoun and yet still explain tentative ideas and show connections in an exploratory rather than strictly argumentative fashion. Sometimes it can be useful to write out an exploratory essay to find your position before you craft a more focused argument.

Ferreting Out Fallacies

Fallacies are lapses in logic that reflect upon your ability to think clearly, and therefore they weaken your argument. The fallacies described below are among the most common. Correct any you find in your own arguments, and call

16.9

Recognize and avoid logical fallacies.

attention to those used by the opposition. Fallacies fall into three general categories: fallacies of evidence, fallacies of logical order, and fallacies that are faulty forms of emotional appeal.

Fallacies of Evidence

Hasty Generalization   Hasty generalization results when someone bases a conclusion on too little evidence. The student who tries to see an instructor during one of her office hours, finds her out, and goes away muttering, "She's never there when she should be" is guilty of hasty generalization. Perhaps the instructor was delayed by another student, attended a special department meeting, or went home ill. Even if she merely went shopping, that's not a good reason for saying she always shirks her responsibility. Several more unsuccessful office visits would be needed to make such a charge stick.

Card Stacking   In card stacking, the writer presents only part of the available evidence on a topic, deliberately omitting essential information that would alter the picture considerably. For instance: "College students have a very easy life; they attend classes for only twelve to sixteen hours a week." This statement ignores the many hours that students must spend studying, doing homework and/or research, writing papers, and the like.

Stereotyping   A person who commits this fallacy attaches one or more supposed characteristics to a group or one of its members. Typical stereotypes include "Latins make better lovers," "Blondes have more fun," and "Teenagers are lousy drivers." Stereotyping racial, religious, ethnic, or nationality groups can destroy an argument. The images are often malicious and always offensive to fair-minded readers.

Fallacies of Logical Order

Non Sequitur   From the Latin "It does not follow," the *non sequitur* fallacy draws unwarranted conclusions from seemingly ample evidence. Consider this example: "Bill's been out almost every night for the last two weeks. Who is she?" These evening excursions, however numerous, point to no particular conclusion. Bill may be studying in the library, participating in campus organizations, taking night classes, or walking. Of course, he *could* be charmed by a new date, but that conclusion requires other evidence.

Post Hoc, Ergo Propter Hoc   The Latin meaning, "after this, therefore because of this," refers to the fallacy of assuming that because one event follows another, the first caused the second. Such shoddy thinking underlies many popular superstitions ("If a black cat crosses your path, you'll have bad luck") and many connections that cannot be substantiated ("I always catch cold during spring break"). Sometimes one event does cause another: A sudden thunderclap might startle a person into dropping a dish. At other times, coincidence is the only connection. Careful thinking will usually lay farfetched causal notions to rest.

Either/or Fallacy   The either/or fallacy asserts that only two choices exist when, in fact, several options are possible. A salesperson who wants you to buy snow tires may claim, "Either buy these tires or plan on getting stuck a lot this winter." But are you really that boxed in? You might drive only on main roads that are plowed immediately after every snowstorm. You could use public transportation when it snows. You could buy radial tires for year-round use. If very little snow falls, you might not need special tires at all.

Not all either/or statements are fallacies. The instructor who checks a student's record and then issues a warning, "Make at least a *C* on your final or you'll fail the course," is not guilty of a reasoning error. No other alternatives exist. Most situations, however, offer more than two choices.

Begging the Question/Circular Argument   A person who begs the question asserts the truth of some unproved statement. Here is an example: "Vitamin A is harmful to your health, and all bottles should carry a warning label. If enough of us write the Food and Drug Administration, we can get the labeling we need." But how do we know vitamin A does harm users? No evidence is offered. People lacking principles often use this fallacy to hit opponents below the belt: "We shouldn't allow a right-wing sympathizer like Mary Dailey to represent us in Congress." Despite a lack of suitable evidence, voters often accept such faulty logic and vote for the other candidate.

Faulty Analogy   This is the error of assuming that two circumstances or things are similar in all important respects, when in fact they are not. Here's an example: Harvey Thompson, high school football coach, tells his players, "Vince Lombardi won two Super Bowls by insisting on perfect execution of plays and enforcing strict disciplinary measures. We're going to win the conference championship by following the same methods." Thompson assumes that because he and Lombardi are coaches, he can duplicate Lombardi's achievements by using Lombardi's methods. Several important differences, however, mark the two situations:

1. Lombardi had very talented players, obtained through the player draft or trades; Thompson can choose only from the students in his high school.
2. Lombardi's players were paid professionals who very likely were motivated, at least in part, by the financial rewards that came from winning the Super Bowl; Thompson's players are amateurs.
3. "Perfect execution of plays" is probably easier to attain on the professional level than in high school because of the players' experience.
4. Despite Lombardi's rigid disciplinary measures, very few of his players quit, perhaps because they were under contract. Could Thompson expect his players, who are essentially volunteers, to accept the kind of verbal and physical rigors Lombardi was famous for?

Arguing Off the Point   The writer who argues off the point, which is sometimes called "ignoring the question" or "a red herring," sidetracks an issue by introducing irrelevant information. To illustrate: "The Ford Thunderbolt is a much better value than the Honda Harmony. Anyway, far too many foreign cars are coming into the country. As a result, thousands of autoworkers have lost their jobs and had to take lower-paying jobs. Many Americans strongly oppose this state of affairs." The writer sets out to convince us that the American car is superior in value but then abruptly shifts to the plight of downsized autoworkers—a trend that has no bearing on the argument.

Fallacies That Are Faulty Forms of Emotional Appeal

The Argument Ad Hominem The Latin term *to the man* designates an argument that attacks an individual rather than that individual's opinions or qualifications. Note this example: "Sam Bernhard doesn't deserve promotion to personnel manager. His divorce was a disgrace, and he's always writing letters to the editor. The company should find someone more suitable." This attack completely skirts the real issue—whether Sam's job performance entitles him to the promotion. Unless his personal conduct has caused his work to suffer, it should not enter into the decision.

Appeal to the Crowd An appeal of this sort arouses an emotional response by playing on the irrational fears and prejudices of the audience. Terms like *communists, fascists, bleeding hearts, right-winger, welfare chiselers*, and *law and order* are tossed about freely to sway the audience for or against something. Consider:

> The streets of our country are in turmoil. The universities are filled with students rebelling and rioting. Communists are seeking to destroy our country. Russia is threatening us with her might, and the public is in danger. Yes, danger from within and without. We need law and order. Yes, without law and order our nation cannot survive. Elect us, and we shall by law and order be respected among the nations of the world. Without law and order our republic shall fall.

Tapping the emotions of the crowd can sway large groups and win acceptance for positions that rational thinking would reject. Think what Adolf Hitler, the author of the foregoing excerpt, brought about in Germany.

Guilt by Association This fallacy points out some similarity or connection between one person or group and another. It tags the first with the sins, real or imagined, of the second. The following excerpt from a letter protesting a speaker at a lecture series illustrates this technique:

> The next slated speaker, Dr. Sylvester Crampton, was for years a member of the Economic Information Committee. This foundation has very strong ties with other ultra-rightwing groups, some of which have been labeled fascistic. When he speaks next Thursday, whose brand of Americanism will he be selling?

MyWritingLab   **EXERCISE** *Identify and explain the fallacies in the following examples. Remember that understanding the faulty reasoning is more important than merely naming the fallacy.*

1. After slicing a Golden Glow orange, Nancy discovers that it is rotten. "I'll never buy another Golden Glow product," she declares emphatically.
2. A campaigning politician states that unless the federal government appropriates funds to help people living in poverty, they will all starve.
3. A husband and wife see an X-rated movie called *Swinging Wives*. A week later the husband discovers that his wife, while supposedly attending an evening class, has been unfaithful to him. He blames the movie for her infidelity.
4. "Look at those two motorcycle riders trying to pick a fight. All those cycle bums are troublemakers."
5. "Bill really loves to eat. Some day he'll have a serious weight problem."
6. "Because no-fault divorce is responsible for today's skyrocketing divorce rate, it should be abolished."
7. "This is the best-looking picture in the exhibit; it's so much more attractive than the others."
8. "I do not support this school millage proposal. It's sponsored by James McAndrews, who's about the most ill-tempered, quarrelsome person I've ever met. I'd never favor anything he supports."
9. "My position on social and economic issues is easy to state. I am against wooly-brained do-gooders and big-spending, pie-in-the-sky social programs that have brought us to the brink of social disaster. I stand four square behind our free-enterprise system, which has given us a standard of living the whole world envies; and if elected, I will defend it with everything at my command."
10. "I am against the proposed ban on smoking in public places. As long as I don't inhale and I limit my habit to 10 cigarettes a day, my health won't suffer."
11. "Life today has become far too frenzied and stressful. It was much better a century ago."

Thinking Critically About Arguments

You find your own position by critically thinking through the arguments and positions of others. Drawing on the material in this chapter gives you good critical tools for assessing arguments. Below are some additional suggestions for critically evaluating arguments.

16.10

Think critically about argument.

- Determine the assumptions the writer is making. Test to see if things look different if you make other assumptions. Often in evaluating the value of higher education, we assume that only the current educational options are available. What would happen if we developed other training models that are linked more closely with employment?
- Test each claim to see if it needs to be supported by evidence. People often make claims without support. Some claim that higher education enriches a person's life. You would want to see what evidence they provided to support this claim.
- Using the principles of evidence discussed on pages 265–269, test to determine how well the evidence supports the claim. Is there evidence that contradicts the claim? How strong is the evidence? Are the sources for the evidence good ones? How closely related is the evidence to the claim? For example, the data clearly show that those with a college degree earn

more. Many use these data to support the value of a college education. However, does salary information show all the valuable aspects of education? How much of college graduates' salaries is a result of the degree itself? Because many who go to college are already ambitious and have supportive families, how might these factors contribute to their higher salaries?

- Test to see if the argument follows logically. Someone might argue that a college education is likely to make individuals more successful. The writer might further show that many of today's jobs require a higher education and therefore argue that education should be affordable to all and that tuition must be decreased. While the conclusion may or may not be reasonable, it doesn't necessarily follow from the premises. Perhaps paying for college makes students value it more and make more of an effort. Perhaps the results of lowering costs (increased taxes for public support or reduced teacher salaries) may be worse than the impact of the current costs.

- Test the argument to see if it falls into the dangerous area of reductio ad absurdum. Some now argue that we need fewer students in college and more students in the trades. They go so far as to argue that it is a mistake to go to college, so students shouldn't go to college. Think of the consequences of this type of argument.

- Look hard for any of the fallacies. For example, the choice of either going to college (assuming a four-year institution) or not is a false either/or. One could attend to a community college, take online courses while working, or alternate college and work.

- Check to make sure the argument doesn't attempt to sway people with unreasonable emotional appeals. Some top four-year institutions make an appeal to status. Status needs may be important for some, but they are not necessarily important for everyone.

Even if you agree with an argument or a position, it is good to test it hard. Act at first as if you disagree and try hard to make other assumptions, counter the evidence, and point out flaws in the logic.

Ethical Issues

16.11

Write so that your argument is ethical.

When writing an argument we attempt to alter attitudes or spark some action. These objectives create an ethical responsibility for both the quality and the possible consequences of our arguments. Suppose a doctor writing a nationally syndicated advice column recommends an over-the-counter herbal product but fails to disclose that it may cause a serious reaction in users who also take a certain prescription drug. Clearly this writer has acted irresponsibly and risks legal action if some readers suffer harm. Asking and answering the following questions will help you avoid any breach of ethics.

- Have I carefully considered the issue I'm arguing and the stance I'm taking? Since you're trying to convince readers to adopt your views, you'll need either to make sure they are credible or make very clear that your position is tentative or dependent on certain conditions.

- Am I fair to other positions on the issue? Careless or deliberate distortion of opposing views is ethically dishonest and could raise questions about your credibility.
- Are my reasons and evidence legitimate? Presenting flawed reasons as if they were credible or falsifying evidence are attempts to deceive the reader.
- Do I use fallacies or other types of faulty thinking to manipulate the reader unfairly?
- What consequences could follow if readers adopt my position? Say a writer strongly opposes genetically modified foods and advocates disrupting installations that help develop them. If some who agree act on the recommendation, innocent people could be injured.

Writing an Argument

Some instructors assign argumentative topics, and some leave the choice of topic to you.

16.12

Prewrite, plan, draft, and revise your argument.

Prewriting the Argument

- Take notes on current disputes on television, the radio, and other media.
- Write down the major issues you and others find yourselves discussing or posting about on Facebook.
- Select from class notes issues that are raised and that interest you.

FINDING YOUR TOPIC

Focusing Your Question

As you explore your topic you should be prepared to focus your question. You may begin to examine whether you should support or oppose gun control, but you will soon begin to discover there are hundreds of related, narrower questions. Does the right to carry concealed weapons reduce crime? How should the Second Amendment be interpreted? Should guns be registered? Does the Brady Bill work? Do background checks deter criminals from purchasing guns? Should there be a ban on automatic and semiautomatic weapons? You may discover that one of your related questions is more than enough of a subject.

Exploring Your Topic

You never really start an argument with a blank page. There is almost always an ongoing conversation about the issue. Before you enter a conversation, it helps to be informed. You can do research by reading. If your paper is based on sources, you may want to review information about proper documentation. You may want to talk to others to get their views on the matter. Or you might make your own formal or informal observations.

Some students approach an argument with such strong attitudes that they ignore evidence that contradicts their thinking. Don't make this mistake. Instead, maintain an open mind as you research your issue, and then, after careful thought, choose the position you'll take. Often, several possible positions exist. On the question of whether individuals should have the right to carry handguns, the positions might include: (1) banning the right to carry handguns by anyone except law enforcement officers and military personnel, (2) allowing anyone who legitimately owns a handgun to carry that weapon without a permit, (3) or allowing citizens to carry concealed weapons but only with a permit granted after training and a background check. Even if you don't shift your position, knowing the opposition's strengths allows you to counter or neutralize it, and thus enhance your argument. Suppose you favor the first position. You need to know that several state constitutions grant citizens the right to carry handguns without those states collapsing into Wild West shoot-outs. Unless you acknowledge and somehow counter this fact, your case will suffer.

Some find it useful to create a table like the following to sort out the different positions.

Ban Concealed Handguns	Right to Carry Handguns by All Owners	Allow Right to Carry Handguns but Registered and for Justified Purposes
■ People have the right to be protected from potential harm from others. ■ Handguns result in accidental shootings. ■ Could cause increase in emotional killings. ■ Could create increased risk to public safety. ■ Statistics and examples of accidental shootings. ■ Statistics on states with right-to-carry laws. ■ Examples of emotional uses of hand guns. ■ Is the position unconstitutional given the 2010 Supreme Court ruling? ■ Don't criminals carry guns anyway? ■ How often are legitimately owned and carried guns misused?	■ Right to self-protection. ■ Broad interpretation of Second Amendment. ■ Persons could protect self and others. ■ Could reduce crime. ■ People have a constitutional right. ■ Statistics on overall crime rates. ■ Examples of when guns prevented crimes. ■ Statistics comparing right-to-carry states with other states. ■ Authoritative material on the Second Amendment. ■ Aren't there other interpretations of the Second Amendment? ■ Why do police groups often oppose this position?	■ Commonly register cars and other significant property that people then use according to the law. ■ Gun owners need to be held responsible. ■ Guns should not be carried by unstable or dangerous people. ■ Examples and statistics on handguns used in crimes. ■ Examples and statistics on how such restrictions would have had a positive consequence. ■ Who should really get to say who should have handguns? ■ Can't a registration process be misused? ■ Can't criminals or others find illegal ways to get guns and carry them?

Obviously, this table is far from complete, and the writer would need to supply the actual evidence and flesh out the reasons. Still, such a table can be a useful device in sorting out and organizing an argument.

As you investigate the various positions, ask and answer the following questions about each:

- What are the reasons for the various positions?
- What values are at stake, and what conclusions do they imply?
- What shared ideas do we accept, and what can be deduced from those ideas?
- What kinds of evidence support the position?
- If the evidence includes statistics and authoritative opinions, are they reliable or flawed for some reason?
- What are the objections to each position, and how can they be countered?
- If the issue involves taking some action, what might be its consequences?

Another effective technique for developing an argument is to write a dialogue between two or more people that explores the various sides of an issue without trying to arrive at a conclusion. The beginning of such a dialogue on the right to carry handguns might look like the following:

Joe: If people have a right to own a gun for self-protection, as the Supreme Court indicated, they should have a right to carry that gun, not just keep it in the home. How can they use the gun for self-protection if it isn't with them? Besides, allowing them to carry a handgun could act to make criminals think twice. It could surely deter crime.

Doug: It could also lead to public shoot-outs where innocent people could be killed. The United States has the highest murder rate in the industrialized world and the largest number of people owning guns. This is no coincidence. A handgun makes it easy to kill people. Letting people carry a concealed weapon would only make it easier for emotional people to kill each other. Imagine a bar fight with guns.

Leslie: People who legitimately carry concealed weapons don't go around having public shoot-outs. Just owning and carrying a gun doesn't make someone kill. Most legitimate handgun owners who carry a concealed weapon will never use their guns on another human being. Many criminals do, however, kill with illegal weapons, including already banned semiautomatic weapons.

Kyra: Do states where people have a right-to-carry law actually have lower crime rates? I don't think so.

Joe: I didn't say it would always reduce the crime rate. For me the most important issue is that the right-to-carry is the obvious consequence of the Second Amendment.

Writing such a dialogue can help start your mental juices flowing, help you see the issue from many sides, and help you develop effective material for your paper.

DEVELOPING YOUR ARGUMENT

- Research your topic, examining all sides of the issue.
- Create a table with the major options on your position with the available reasons and evidence.
- Create a dialogue that tries to represent different sides of the issue to try out your argument.
- Write down your major reasons and link to evidence and justification for evidence.
- Identify the purpose and audience for your argument and use that to select reasons, evidence, and approach.
- Create a draft outline to help see how the reasons and evidence fit together and brainstorm for possible objections, then answer objections.

Planning an Argument

In planning your argument, consider your purpose and your readers.

Arguments for Different Purposes As you contemplate your position and evidence, consider the purpose of your argument and how that might affect the strategies you choose to employ. Arguments are written for several purposes, each requiring a different approach.

Purpose for argument	Strategy
Demonstrating something is a fact—nursing is hard work, dormitories are poor study places, phonics increases word recognition.	■ Depends on the appropriate evidence— examples, statistics, authoritative claims, personal experience. ■ Nursing is demanding: narrate and describe typical nursing day, cite city hospital nursing supervisors on the job, give statistics of turnover because of stress.
Defend or oppose some policy, action, or project—for example, first-year students should be allowed cars or a company should drug-test employees, adding WiFi to the entire campus.	■ Identify need for policy or action, how it can be met, cost or feasibility of recommendation, and the resulting benefit. ■ For WiFi, the need for students with laptops to connect to the Internet between classes and as part of class projects, the available technology for making a campus and cost, the actual usefulness for students in connecting to course material between class and use in classrooms.

Purpose for argument	**Strategy**
Assert the greater or lesser value of someone or something, as a supervisor ranking candidates for promotion.	■ Indicate what you're trying to prove, criteria or points for evaluation, reasons along with evidence (details, examples, or statistics). ■ May be deductive showing how conclusions follow from agreed-upon values. ■ Candidate may be shown to have more years of experience, greater skills such as more programming languages, more examples of leadership.

Directing Arguments to Readers   With an argument, as with any essay, purpose and audience are closely linked. For example, imagine that your audience is a group of readers who are neutral or opposed to your position; there's no point in preaching to the converted. Take a little time to analyze these readers so that you can tailor your arguments appropriately. Pose these questions as you proceed:

> What are the readers' interests, expectations, and needs concerning this issue?
>
> What evidence is most likely to convince them?
>
> What objections and consequences would probably weigh most heavily with them?
>
> How can I answer the objections?

To convince an audience of farmers that the federal school lunch program needs expanding, you might stress the added income they would gain. For nutritionists, you might note the health benefits that would result, and for school officials, the improved class performance of the students. Even though you are unlikely to convince everyone, it is best to adopt the attitude that most readers are willing to be convinced if your approach is appealing and your evidence is sound.

Drafting the Argument

When you have a good grasp on your position, reasons, evidence, and the approach you want to take, you're ready to draft your paper. Because arguments can be complex, it can be very useful to start by creating an outline of your main reasons, evidence, possible objections to your position, and an answer to those objections. Or you may wish to more informally write out your reasons in order with supporting evidence, possibly even initially labeling them to insure that the reasons are supported.

Reason 1
    Evidence
    Evidence
Reason 2
    Evidence
    Objection
Answer to objection

The more detailed the outline, formal or informal, the easier it will be to draft the paper.

The thesis statement for an argument often indicates which position the writer will take, sometimes including the major reasons for that position. It can declare that something is a fact, support a policy, call for a certain action, or assert that something has greater value than something else. Following are examples:

1. Carron College does not provide adequate recreational facilities for its students. *(Declares something is fact.)*
2. Our company's policy of randomly testing employees for drug use has proved effective and should be continued. *(Supports policy.)*
3. Because the present building is overcrowded and unsafe, the people of Midville should vote funds for a new junior high school. *(Calls for action.)*
4. The new Ford Fire-Eater is superior to the Honda Harmony in performance and economy. *(Asserts value.)*

To formulate your thesis, review your main reasons and focus on the claim you may want to make. Avoid making a claim broader than you want to support. If you believe students need to enhance their computer literacy to be employable, you would over reach if you suggested that students need to become computer *experts*.

Any of the techniques in Chapter 5 can launch your paper.

Introduction
- Jolt your reader, for example by describing a teen paralyzed in a car accident to argue against texting and driving.
- Or start with defining an unfamiliar term, "Why oppose oligarchy?"
- In a longer essay, preview main points.
- In a Rogerian argument, affirm the readers' core beliefs or values.
- In an exploratory essay, you might raise the question you will discuss without taking a position.

After the introduction comes the evidence, arranged in whatever order you think will work best. If one of your points is likely to arouse resistance, hold it back and begin by making points your reader can more easily accept. Argument always goes more smoothly if you first establish some common ground of agreement that recognizes the values of your reader. Where strong resistance is not a factor, you could begin or end with your most compelling piece of evidence.

Body	▪ Define the issue and possible positions. ▪ Present contrary position and its evidence and reasons, offer your contrary reasons and evidence. ▪ Provide your reasons with evidence (often a major reason constitutes a paragraph). ▪ Identify possible objections to your position and answer with reasons and evidence.

The strategies discussed in earlier chapters can help you develop an argument. Some papers incorporate one strategy, while others rely on several. Let's see how you might combine several in an argument against legalized casino gambling.

- You might open with a brief *description* of the frantic way an all-too-typical gambling addict keeps pulling the lever of a slot machine, his eyes riveted on the spinning dials, his palms sweating, as flashing lights and wailing sirens announce winners at other machines.
- Next, you could offer a brief *definition* of gambling fever so that the writer and reader are on common ground, and, to show the dimensions of the problem, *classify* the groups of people who are especially addicted.
- Then, after detailing the negative *effects* of the addiction, you might end by *comparing* gambling addiction with drug addiction, noting that both provide a "high" and both kinds of addict know their habits hurt them.

Whatever strategies you use, make sure that substantiating evidence is embedded in them. To illustrate, in discussing the negative effects of gambling, you might cite statistics that show the extent and nature of the problem. An expert opinion might validate your classification of addicts. Or you might use personal experience to verify gambling's addictive effects.

Besides presenting evidence, use this part of your paper to refute; that is, to point out weaknesses or errors in the opposing position. You might try the following:

- **Point out any evidence that undermines that position.** If one viewpoint holds that drug testing violates cherished privacy rights, you might note that employers already monitor phone calls, check employees' desks, and violate privacy in other ways.
- **Identify faulty assumptions and indicate how they are faulty: they don't lead to the implied conclusion, they lack the effectiveness of an alternative, or they are false or unsupported.** If you oppose drug testing, you could point out problems in the assumption that such tests are necessary to protect the public. Closer supervision of work performance might be a better protection; after all, fatigue, stress, negligence, and

alcohol abuse can all result in serious problems, and they are not detected by drug tests.

■ **Identify problems in the logic of the argument.** Are there missing premises, faulty connections between reasons, or conclusions that don't follow from the premises? The argument against drug testing usually proceeds by asserting that privacy is a fundamental right, that drug testing violates privacy, and that therefore drug testing should not be allowed. There is a missing premise, however: that because privacy is a fundamental right it should never be violated. This premise is, in fact, at the heart of the dispute and therefore cannot be accepted as a reason to disallow drug testing.

You can place refutations throughout the body of the paper or group them together just ahead of the conclusion. Whatever you decide, don't adopt a gloating or sarcastic tone that will alienate a fair-minded reader. Resist the urge to engage in *straw man* tactics—calling attention to imaginary or trivial weaknesses of the opposing side so that you can demolish them. Shrewd readers easily spot such ploys. Finally, don't be afraid to concede secondary or insignificant points to the opposition. Arguments have two or more sides; you can't have all the ammunition on your side. (If you discover you must concede major points, however, consider changing your position.) Following is a sample refutation from a student paper:

Not everyone agrees with workplace drug testing for employees in public

transportation companies, electric utilities, nuclear power plants, and other

industries involving public safety. Critics assert that such tests invade privacy

and therefore violate one of our cherished freedoms. While the examination of

one's urine does entail inspection of something private, such a test is a reason-

able exception because it helps ensure public safety and calm public fears.

Individuals have a right to be protected from the harm that could be caused

by an employee who abuses drugs. An airline pilot's right to privacy should not

supersede the security of hundreds of people who could be injured or killed in

a drug-induced accident. Thus the individual's privacy should be tempered by

concern for the community—a concern that benefits all of us.

Annie Louise Griffith, student

Identifies opponents' objection

Concedes basic objection

Answers with an opposing value or right

Conclude in a manner that will sway the reader to your side.

Conclusion
- Possibly restate your main point and summarize main points.
- Or predict the consequences if your position doesn't prevail.
- Or offer a powerful example or story that clinches your position.
- Or make an emotional appeal for action.
- Look at the strategies in Chapter 5.

There can be more than one pattern for an argument. Following are three examples.

Example 1	Example 2	Example 3
Introduction	Introduction	Introduction
Definition of the issue (optional)	Definition of the issue (optional)	Definition of the issue (optional)
Your reasons and evidence (can be a large number of paragraphs)	Alternative positions and reasons for those positions Objections and contrary evidence and reasons to those positions (can be several paragraphs)	Common objections or questions and answers to both
Objections or questions and answers to both (can be several paragraphs)	Restatement of your position and reasons and evidence for that position. Objections or questions and answers to both	Your reasons and evidence
Conclusion	Conclusion	Conclusion

You are not limited to these patterns. Alternative positions and objections can be discussed and answered within the context of presenting your own reasons. An argument can be built around answering common questions. A Rogerian argument starts by affirming the reader's core values and beliefs and then shows deductively and by supporting evidence how those values and beliefs yield the conclusion you hope to support.

Revising the Argument

Review the guidelines in Chapter 4 and ponder these questions as you revise your argument paper:

- Is my topic controversial? Have I examined all of the main positions? Assessed the evidence supporting each one? Considered the objections to each position and how they can be countered? Weighed the consequences if a position involves taking some action?
- Is the paper aimed at the audience I want to reach? Have I tailored my argument to appeal to that audience?
- Is my evidence sound, adequate, and appropriate to the argument? Are my authorities qualified? Have I established their expertise? Are they biased? Will my audience accept them as authorities? Do my statistics adequately support my position? Have I pushed my statistical claims too far?
- If I've used analogy, are my points of comparison pertinent to the issue? Have I noted any significant differences between the items being compared?
- If I've included an emotional appeal, does it center on those emotions most likely to sway the reader?
- Have I made a conscious effort to present myself in a favorable light?

- Are my ideas logically related?
- Is my evidence effectively structured? Have I adequately refuted opposing arguments? Developed my position with one or more writing strategies?
- Is my argument free of fallacies?
- Have I considered appropriate ethical issues?

SAMPLE

STUDENT ESSAY OF **ARGUMENT**

Bottled Troubled Water

Scott Lemanski

Identifies a general negative trend and uses emotionally charged terms to influence reader

1   A disease has swept over our nation. It's called consumeritis, and its symptoms, among many others, include sluggishness, chronic apathy, alienation, obesity, and a constant, nagging feeling that there is something missing from our lives. We temporarily relieve these symptoms, or at least distract ourselves from them, by seeing or hearing an advertisement, label, or slogan that convinces us that we absolutely need some useless product, then call a toll-free number to place an order or drive over to the local megamart to buy it, along with a few other superfluous items we feel

Ties key topic to negative trend

that we just can't do without. Perhaps the most senseless product with which we've been treating our consumeritis in recent years is that clear, cool, tasteless drink that comes in a plastic container—bottled water. It comes in many attractive shapes and sizes from mountain springs and glaciers all over the world, promising us better health and a convenient way to attain it. The thought of drinking tap water for some people today

Anticipates reader's objection

Raises questions that will guide the argument

Thesis identifies main position and key reasons to be examined

is simply ridiculous because of the commonly held belief that it's just not pure enough. But do we really know how pure our beloved bottled water is? How often do we think about the impact our obsession with bottled water is having on the world or how much we actually benefit from such a product? The harm done to our environment, the waste of our resources, and the potential health risks caused by bottled water's mass production, distribution, and consumption far outweigh its possible benefits.

Identifies consequence of practice

2   Our thirst for bottled water has become seemingly unquenchable, and as it grows, so does its impact on our environment. According to Tony Azios in his article "The Battle over Bottled vs. Tap Water," over 25 billion plastic water bottles per year are sold in the United States. Since 2002, production has increased an average of 9% per year; and since 2003, water has become the highest-selling commercial drink, second only to soft

drinks (Azios). In "The Truth about Tap," Andrew Postman reports that "in 2006, the equivalent of 2 billion half-liter bottles of water were shipped to U.S. ports, creating thousands of tons of global-warming pollution and other air pollution." The transport of bottled water that year from eastern Europe to New York contributed approximately 3,800 tons of global-warming pollution to the atmosphere, while the shipping of 18 million gallons of bottled water from Fiji to California produced about 2,500 tons of such pollution.

3   Given the virtually incomprehensible quantities of bottled water manufactured, transported, bought, and sold, it is no surprise that the waste from it amounts to alarmingly large numbers. In some U.S. states, we are required by law to pay a small deposit when purchasing plastic soda bottles, which works quite well as an incentive to bring them back for recycling. The same is not true for bottled water, although the bottles are recyclable. Postman notes that, "only about 13% of the bottles we use get recycled. In 2005, 2 million tons of plastic water bottles ended up clogging up landfills." Oil, however ultimately damaging to the future of our world it may be, is an ever-increasingly precious resource, now perhaps more than ever, and we're wasting that on bottled water, too. Azios points out that in 2006, "more than 17 million barrels of oil (not including fuel for transportation) were used in plastic bottle production." Even water, arguably our most precious resource, is used in copious amounts in the production. Water is necessary to cool machinery in power plants and molds that form plastic parts, so when taking into account the huge volume of plastic water bottles made every year, it's no wonder that "it takes about 3 liters of water to produce 1 liter of bottled water." It's also no wonder, with all the energy and resources wasted, that we end up paying 2,000 times more for a liter of bottled water than we would a liter of tap water.

4   While it's obvious we are willing to pay entirely too much money for it, are we also willing to gamble our health on bottled water? Since so many different brands of bottled water have words on their labels such as *pure* or *natural*, we are led to believe that drinking bottled water is a choice that will be a benefit to our health. It would be prudent, then, to become educated on some of the risks involved. According to Priscilla Torres in "Bottled Water vs. Tap Water: Think What You Drink," most of the bottles are made of a plastic called polyethylene terepthalate, or PET, which is supposed to be generally safe, but if heated, the plastic could leach chemicals

Continued on next page

Uses statistics in a logical way to suggest negative impact

Identifies next major consequence with logical transition

Uses sources to indicate statistics concerning quantity of waste

Identifies next possible negative consequence

Continued from previous page

Provides causal
analysis of possible
health risk

into the water. There are hazards linked to these chemicals, but "the exact health risks are unknown." Consequently, we are taking a chance with our health if we, for example, leave a bottle in a hot car all day long and later return to drink it. Though a consensus hasn't been reached on the risks of PET chemicals, Torres notes that some findings may be unsettling.

Second causal
argument of health
risk

5   In the meantime, experts have raised a warning flag about a few specific chemicals. Antimony is a potentially toxic material used in making PET. Last year, scientists in Germany found that the longer a bottle of water sits around (in a store, in your home), the more antimony it develops. High concentrations of antimony can cause nausea, vomiting, and diarrhea. In the study, levels found were below those set as safe by the EPA, but it's a topic that needs more research (Torres).

Identifies reader's
objection

Offers alternative to
answer objection

6   Many of us are willing to take our chances with the possible health risks associated with bottled water because, if nothing else, we see it as such a convenient way to obtain the water we need to drink every day. Is it really more convenient to go to the store and spend entirely too much money on a bottle of water than it is to simply fill a glass at home at the faucet? If we want to take it with us while we're out, there are plenty of containers that we can purchase for just such a purpose. Advertisers have cleverly convinced us that somehow it's more convenient to go out of our way to buy what they're selling than it is to take a moment and think about whether we truly need it or not. Do we really need to buy a product such as bottled water?

Identifies next major
objection

Acknowledges
reader's concern
and values

7   Many of us cite the most compelling reason to drink bottled water, besides convenience, is the concern over impurities in the water that comes out of our faucets and drinking fountains. It is a legitimate concern but one that doesn't necessarily have to result in the automatic response of reaching for the bottle. In "Water Quality Information for Consumers: Bottled Water," the Cornell University Cooperative Extension says that tap water can and often does contain contaminants in varying concentrations, such as microorganisms, including pathogens, and sulfur compounds, including metals and metalloids, such as arsenic, lead and iron, just to name a few. However, the regulation of tap water is somewhat more reliable and transparent:

Provides comparison
to answer objection
with authorized data

> Tap water from municipal drinking water treatment plant is regulated by the U.S. Environmental Protection Agency (EPA) . . . for close to a hundred chemicals and characteristics, [while] bottled water sold across state lines is regulated by the U.S. Food and Drug

Administration (FDA). Your supplier must notify the community if there are problems with the water supply. Municipal plants are generally subject to much more frequent testing and inspection and must report test results to the public. ("Water Quality")

Furthermore, since more than 25% of the bottled water comes from a municipal source (Torres), there is a sizable chance that the water in the bottles from which we drink is just as contaminated as the water that comes out of the faucet in our kitchen sink.

8   The fluoridation of tap water is another positive health benefit. Most of us have seen enough television toothpaste commercials go uncontested for long enough to be reasonably confident in fluoride's ability to help prevent tooth decay. Tap water is generally fluoridated, while most bottled water is not, and since many children are drinking more bottled water than tap water, this could explain the current rise in tooth decay among children (Torres).

Offers a contrary reason to objection by identifying benefit of tap water

Provides evidence for position

9   Recently in the *USA Today* article "AP: Drugs Show Up in Americans' Water," it has been reported that quite a few pharmaceuticals, "including antibiotics, anti-convulsants, mood stabilizers and sex hormones have been found in the water supply of at least 41 million Americans" (Donn et al.). Though utilities say their water is safe and that the levels of the drugs found are measured in parts per billion or trillion, "far below the levels of a medical dose . . . [their presence is] heightening worries among scientists of long-term consequences to human health" (Donn et al.). Though these concerns are certainly valid, they still don't warrant turning to bottled water as the solution to the problem. Going back to the point Cornell University made about water regulation, it follows that it is unlikely that bottled water companies are doing the sort of rigorous testing of their water for substances such as pharmaceuticals that could ease our concerns on this matter; and even if they were, would they report it to the public? Also, if over 25% of bottled water comes from municipal sources, what percentage of that percentage might contain such pharmaceuticals?

Further acknowledges concern

Provides evidence and reason to answer objection that bottled water would be better

10   "In general, toxins in drinking water don't exceed EPA limits" (Torres). However, there are steps we can take to inform ourselves of and reduce the risks of tap water contamination. A water quality or consumer confidence report is generally sent out to all customers of local water companies once a year, and it will show if any contaminants have gone over the maximum allowable levels. We can also have our water tested by a state-certified lab. There are also many varieties of

Offers an additional answer to objection to water problem issue

Offers an alternate reason to objection-testing

Continued on next page

Continued from previous page

tap-water filters we can buy to purify the water coming out of our taps, but in order to ensure their effectiveness, they should be "approved by NSF, Underwriters Laboratories, or the Water Quality Association." If after taking all this information into account, you still feel it necessary to replace tap water with bottled water, you can at least look for a brand that comes from a local source, so as to at least limit the environmental impact and waste or resources caused by long-distance mass transport. Also, look for brands with "NSF certification or [those that] belong to the IBWA. Check out the lists at NSF.org or bottledwater.org, or look at the bottle itself" for the NSF logo.

11   In our consumerist society, where so many things are available to us and convenience often seems to be of the greatest importance, it's easy to forget that everything we do in our personal lives has a direct or indirect effect on the rest of the world and our planet. If we go on ignoring growing environmental threats and the resources we're wasting, the consequences will affect us all. No absolute cure has been found for consumeritis, but we can take steps to minimize its impact by taking a little time out from our overly busy lives and trying to think rationally about the implications of something so seemingly harmless as drinking bottled water. The convenience and minimal, if any, health benefits we receive from drinking bottled water don't come close to justifying the harm it causes the earth and perhaps ourselves.

Marginal notes:
Offers an alternative to primary position

Returns to primary interest of effect in conclusion

Confirms main point by comparing benefits to harms

Works Cited

Azios, Tony. "The Battle over Bottled vs. Tap Water." *The Christian Science Monitor*, 17 Jan. 2008, www.csmonitor.com/Environment/2008/0117/p15s03-sten.html.

Donn, Jeff, et al. "AP: Drugs Show Up in Americans' Water." *USA Today*, 12 Sept. 2008, usatoday30.usatoday.com/news/nation/2008-03-10-drugs-tap-water_N.htm.

Postman, Andrew. "The Truth about Tap." *National Resources Defense Council*, 5 Jan. 2016, www.nrdc.org/stories/truth-about-tap.

Torres, Priscilla. "Bottled Water vs. Tap Water: Rethink What You Drink." *Reader's Digest*, www.rd.com/health/diet-weight-loss/rethink-what-you-drink.

"Water Quality Information for Consumers: Bottled Water." *Cornell University Cooperative Extension*, waterquality.cce.cornell.edu/bottled.htm.

Discussion Questions

MyWritingLab

1. This essay tries to convince many readers to give up a common habit. Often readers can be sensitive about such an approach. How does this writer lessen the possible negative impact of his criticism?
2. How does this author's argument appeal to his readers' concerns and values, assuming that many who drink bottled water are concerned about the environment and are health conscious?
3. What types of evidence does the writer use in his argument?
4. Why does the writer in paragraph 10 offer some suggestions for buying bottled water when the entire paper is dedicated to discouraging the practice?
5. In the introduction and the conclusion the writer links buying bottled water with something he calls "consumeritis." Is this strategy effective? Why or why not?

SUGGESTIONS FOR WRITING

MyWritingLab

Writing: Argument

Write a properly focused argument on some topic you feel strongly about. Study all sides of the issue so you can argue effectively and appeal to a particular audience. Support your proposition with logical evidence. Here are some possibilities to consider if your instructor gives you a free choice:

1. Prohibiting the development of private property to save endangered species
2. Prayer in public schools
3. Increasing federal support of developing alternative energy such as solar power
4. Gay marriage
5. Bilingual instruction in schools
6. Allowing or prohibiting guns on college campuses
7. A campus, local, or state issue
8. Immigration reform
9. Monitoring U.S. citizens' phone conversations to detect potential terrorist threats
10. Virtual universities where all classes are conducted on the Internet

Multimedia Writing

1. Does Silence = Death, as the photo at the beginning of the chapter (page 268) suggests? Think about this topic, talk to your friends, and read research, and then write an argument that supports or argues against this image.
2. Visuals can make effective arguments. Collect pictures or cartoons that you think make an argument. For example, a picture of a rich person walking past a homeless person might make a point about the ways we neglect the less fortunate. Then write an argument to the appropriate audience, using the images in your argument.
3. Data can support an argument, and visual representations of the data can make the argument stronger. Research a topic, such as whether growing income inequality is harming our economy, and write a documented report using appropriate data and graphics to make your point.

4. Some of the most powerful arguments on the Internet, including some on income inequality, are done through a video with voice-over. Identify a video on the Internet that makes a powerful argument. Write a short paper analyzing the argument and what makes that argument effective. If your training and the class permits, you might create a short video argument. For example, if you wish to create an argument that crime procedurals on television falsely represent how crimes are solved with forensics, you might include video clips from shows like *CSI* and contrast those clips with some from the more realistic *Cold Justice*.

Critical Synthesis with Sources: Argument

16.13

Critically synthesize source materials to create your argument.

Purposes for Synthesis   A successful argument, by its very nature, requires critical thinking. This chapter has given you the tools you'll need to test the logic and evaluate the evidence offered in support of argumentative positions. After all, rarely will you generate an idea on your own and then argue for it. Instead, because most important issues have already been debated in print, you'll enter a discussion that's already under way. Sometimes it's on a topic of national interest, such as the desirability of politically correct speech and writing or the need to limit the number of terms elected officials can serve. At other times, the topic may be more localized: Should your state outlaw teacher strikes, your company install new equipment to control air pollution, or your college reduce its sports programs? On any of these issues you begin to form your own view as you read and assess the arguments of other writers.

Prewriting for Synthesis   A good way to take stock of conflicting opinions is to make a chart that summarizes key reasons and evidence on each side of the argument. Here is a segment of a chart that presents opposing viewpoints on whether nuclear power provides a green alternative (based on sources in the reader):

Nuclear Power Is a Green Alternative	Nuclear Power Is Not a Green Alternative
36% of U.S. CO_2 emissions and 10% of global emissions come form 600 coal-fired electric plants. —Patrick Moore	Production of nuclear power includes mining, uranium, building plants, and disposing of waste, producing the same amount of CO_2 as a gas-fired plant. —Alexis Rowell
Wind and solar power are unreliable and unpredictable; they can't replace large plants and natural gas is too expensive. —Patrick Moore	Nuclear power plants cost too much to decommission (73 billion British pounds). They are expensive to insure, require taxpayer subsidies, and will not be available to meet demands, with the earliest new plant only available in Britain by 2020. —Alexis Rowell

Critically Evaluating Your Sources   Even though you investigate the reasons and evidence of others, deciding what position to take and how to support it—that is, establishing your place in the debate—is the real work of synthesis.

This chapter should have helped you focus on how to evaluate the evidence and arguments others make. Also test the sources themselves. Is the source professional and credible? What biases might have influenced the writer? Does the writer have the expertise and draw on appropriate sources?

Planning and Drafting the Synthesis   Therefore, after evaluating your sources, outline the main points you want to make. You can then incorporate material that supports your argument. Let's say that you're considering the issue of global warming. After examining the differing viewpoints, you might conclude that although those who believe that global warming is occurring sometimes overstate their case, those who disagree tend to dismiss important scientific evidence. Because global warming is a serious possibility if not a certainty, you decide to argue for immediate environmental action. You might begin your paper by pointing out the dire consequences that will ensue if global warming becomes a reality, then offer evidence supporting this possibility, acknowledge and answer key opposing viewpoints, and finally offer your recommendations for averting a crisis.

Getting Started   MyWritingLab

1. Read several sources that explore the best solution to the challenges of illegal immigration and then write an argument supporting your own position based on those differing responses.
2. Read several sources that take different positions on how we can meet the energy challenges of the future and write an argument supporting your position on this issue. You may, however, want to focus on specific issues such as the safety or danger of nuclear energy or the feasibility of alternative energy systems.
3. Read several sources that explore the issue of our legal and ethical responsibility for what and how we present ourselves on various social networks and write an argument that takes a position on this issue, drawing on the available sources.

Writing an Argument

Prewriting the argument.

- Identify question or topic you want to explore.
- Read about issue.
- Talk to others.
- Take notes and keep references clear.
- Brainstorm and perhaps create a table of reasons and evidence for and against the position.
- Evaluate the evidence, including the credibility of sources, confirmation of the evidence, contradictory evidence, strength of evidence, and evidence/support for the claims.
- Consider the possible consequences if the readers adopted the position.
- Make certain that all sides of the issue are fairly considered.

Planning and drafting the argument.

- Establish your position and draft thesis statement.
- Establish purpose.
- Identify audience—what key beliefs and attitudes do readers have that you can build on?
- Determine the approaches you are going to use—rational with key reasons and evidence; reduction ad absurdum, Rogerian, emotional appeal, ethical appeal.
- Create a rough draft or outline of the major argument.
- Write so that the argument is fair to all positions on the issue without misrepresenting the views of others.
- Make certain the reasons and evidence are legitimate.

Option for organization.

- Definition of issue.
- Other positions and reasons for those positions.
- Objections and contrary evidence for positions.
- Your position.
- Reasons and evidence.
- Objections to your view.
- Answer to objections.

Option for organization.

- Definition of issue.
- Your reasons and evidence.
- Objections or questions and answers.

Option for organization.

- Definition of issue.
- Common objections and questions.
- Answers.
- Your position.
- Your reasons and evidence.

Revising the argument.

Gather reader responses; read critically as if you oppose your own position. Talk it over with others; check to see if there is another position that makes more sense.

- Do arguments fit audience?
- Add any additional reasons or evidence; answer any outstanding objections.
- Cut reasons, evidence that seem invalid or that don't work.
- Test reason and evidence to ensure validity.
- Test tone to be sure it seems reasonable.
- Test organization so that it is easy to follow with clear transitions.
- Test to make certain that there are no flaws in argument or informal fallacies.

Repeat the process as necessary.

Proofread.

CHAPTER 17   The Essay Examination

In this chapter, you will learn how to:

17.1 Study for an examination.

17.2 Analyze the types of test questions.

17.3 Prepare to write an exam essay by determining what is expected.

17.4 Write an effective essay for an exam.

Visit MyWritingLab **to complete the writing assignments in this chapter and for more resources on essay examinations.**

Instructors use essay examinations to gauge your grasp of ideas, noting how well you apply, analyze, challenge, compare, or otherwise handle them. Facts and figures, on the other hand, are more often tested by objective examinations. Writing essay answers under pressure and with minimal time to rethink and revise differs from writing at home. Instructors expect reasonably complete and coherent answers that are legible. The skills learned in composition class can help you write successful essay exams. A plan, a thesis, specific support, staying on track, and the pointers presented in this chapter—all are grade boosters.

Studying for the Examination

Following are some pointers for studying:

17.1
Study for an examination.

1. Allow adequate preparation time. For a comprehensive test, start reviewing several days in advance. For one that covers a small segment of the course, a day or two should be enough.

2. Reread the key points you've marked in your class notes and textbook. Use them to develop a set of basic concepts.

3. Make up a set of sample questions related to these concepts and do some freewriting to answer them. Even if none of the questions appears on the test, your efforts will ease pretest jitters and supply insights that apply to other questions.

4. Answer your questions by drawing on your concepts and supplying details from your notes and textbook.

Types of Test Questions

17.2

Analyze the types of test questions.

Some instructors favor narrow, highly focused test questions with detailed answering instructions. Others like broad items, perhaps with simple directions. The sample questions below range from very broad to very narrow. Note how when answering them you can often use the writing strategies discussed in Chapters 5–16.

1. Analyze the *influences* of the industrial revolution on European society.
2. Discuss the most important *causes* of the Spanish–American War.
3. Compare and contrast the David statues of Michelangelo and Bernini.
4. Select three different camera shots used in the movie *Titanic*. Identify at least one scene that *illustrates* each shot, then explain how each shot functions by *describing* the relationship between the shot and the action or dialogue.
5. Discuss the stock market plunge of October 27, 1997. Consider the major *factors* involved, such as the liberal lending practices of international banks, the growth in global manufacturing capacity, the severe recessions and monetary turmoil in Pacific Rim countries like Thailand and Malaysia, the concerns of Wall Street, and how these *factors* interacted. Use a thesis statement that signals the points you will discuss.

A highly focused question such as item 5 suggests how to organize and develop the essay. If you know the answer, you can begin writing quickly. In contrast, item 1 forces you to focus and narrow the subject before you respond. Answering this type of item requires careful planning.

Preparing to Write

17.3

Prepare to write an exam essay by determining what is expected.

Effective exam writing requires thoughtful planning. Often students fail to read general directions or to answer what is asked. To avoid penalizing yourself, scan the test items, noting how many must be answered and which ones, if any, are optional. When you have a choice, select the questions you can answer most thoroughly. Pay attention to any suggestions or requirements concerning length (one paragraph, two pages) or relative weight (25 points, 30 minutes, 40 percent), and budget your time accordingly.

The first requirement for most essay tests is to read the question for *key words*. Does the instructor want you to analyze, compare, criticize, defend, describe, discuss, evaluate, illustrate, explain, justify, trace, or summarize? If you are asked to explain how Darwin's theory of evolution affected nineteenth-century thinking, do just that; you won't like your grade if, instead, you summarize the theory. Merely putting ideas on paper, even perceptive ideas, does not substitute for addressing the question.

EXERCISE   *Indicate what each of the following questions calls for. What is required? By*   MyWritingLab
what methods—arguing, describing, or the like—would you develop the answer?

1. Distinguish between mild depression and severe depression. You might focus on the nature, the symptoms, or the potential treatments of each condition.
2. Support or refute the following statement: Because waste incineration generates stack gases and ash that contain high levels of toxic substances, it is not an acceptable solution to waste-disposal problems.
3. Explain how to pressure test a radiator.
4. Briefly relate the events in the Book of Job and then explain the significance of the tale to questions of divine justice. Could the tale be called symbolic? Why or why not?

When you have the essay question clearly in mind, don't immediately start writing. Instead, take a few moments to plan your answer. Following these steps will help you do this:

1. Jot down specific supporting information from your reading lecture notes.
2. Make a rough outline that sketches the main points you'll cover and an effective order for presenting them.
3. Prepare a thesis statement that responds to the question and will control your answer.

Writing an essay exam, like writing an essay, is a front-end-loaded process. Much of the brain work occurs before you put your answer on paper.

Writing the Examination Answer

Here are some guidelines that will help you write a successful exam:

17.4

Write an effective essay for an exam.

1. Position your thesis statement at the beginning of your answer. Make sure each paragraph is controlled by a topic sentence tied to the thesis statement.
2. Don't become excessively concerned about your wording. Focus on content and, if time permits, make stylistic changes later.
3. Fight the impulse to jot down everything you know about the general subject. The grader doesn't want to plow through verbiage to arrive at your answer.

The following essay illustrates these guidelines:

Question:	Discuss the various appeals described by classical rhetoric that an orator can use. Give a brief example of each kind of appeal.
Answer:	Classical rhetoric defines three major appeals—
Thesis statement previews	logical, emotional, and ethical—that orators may
focus and order of answer	use to win support from their audience.
Topic sentence:	Most rhetoricians agree that any argument must be based on logic; that is, it must appeal to the intellect of the listeners. Unless it does,

Example 1:   the orator will fail to convince them. For example, a speaker who is urging the election of a candidate and presents the candidate's voting record is appealing to logic, asking the audience to understand that the voting record predicts how the candidate will continue to vote if

Example 2:   elected. Likewise, a candidate for public office who describes how a tax cut will stimulate the economy and create new jobs is using a logical appeal.

Topic sentence: In addition to logic, emotional appeals are a powerful means of swaying people, especially groups. Though emotional appeals work along with logical appeals, they are quite different because they are directed at the listener's hopes,

Example 1:   fears, and sympathies. The presidential candidate who indicates that a vote for an opponent is a vote to increase government spending and risk a financial crisis is making an emotional

Example 2:   appeal. So, too, is the gubernatorial candidate who asserts that her state's industry can be revitalized and serve as a model for all other states.

Topic sentence: The ethical appeal is more subtle than either of the other two but probably just as important. The orator must strike the audience as a sensible, good person if they are to believe the

Example 1:   message. Sometimes the speaker's logic and also the tone—moderate, sensible, or wise—

Example 2:   will convey sufficient ethical appeal. At other times, a speaker will use statements that are deliberately intended to create ethical appeal. "In developing this program, I will work closely with both houses of the legislature, including the members of both political parties" and "Despite our differences, I believe my opponent to be a decent, honest person" are examples of such statements.

Restatement of thesis: In any speech, all these appeals—logical, emotional, and ethical—work together to convince an audience.

Student Unknown

In contrast, the next two responses to the same question illustrate common faults of examination essays.

Answer A

1   There are three basic appeals that a speaker can make to captivate an audience. These are the ethical appeal, the logical appeal, and the emotional appeal.

2   The first of these—the ethical appeal—includes all the speaker's efforts to be viewed as rational, wise, good, and generous. Needless to say, the ethical appeal is very important. Without it, no one would pay attention to the speaker's argument.

3   The second appeal—logical—is also extremely important. It carries the burden of the argument from speaker to listener and appeals to the intellect of the audience.

4   Emotional appeal—the third and final one—is made to the passions and feelings of the listeners. The significance of such an appeal is obvious.

5   A speaker often uses all three appeals to win an audience over.

Answer A starts with a thesis statement and includes brief definitions of the three appeals; however, it omits any concrete examples and includes no specific details. As a result, the significance of the emotional appeal is not "obvious," as paragraph 4 claims, nor does the answer offer any hints as to why the other appeals are important. This response resembles an outline more than an answer and suggests the student lacked the knowledge to do a good job.

Answer B

1   Orators may make three different kinds of appeals to win favor from an audience: emotional appeal, logical appeal, and ethical appeal.

2   Let's start with emotional appeal because this is the one that is not essential to a speech. Logical and ethical appeals are always included; emotional appeal may be used to help sway an audience, but without logical and ethical appeals no argument is accepted. This simply makes sense: If there is no logic, there is no argument; and if the speaker doesn't come across as an ethical person—someone to be relied upon—then no one will accept the message. But emotional appeal is different. Unemotional arguments may be accepted.

3   Nevertheless, emotional appeal is important. It includes whatever a speaker does to move the feelings of the audience. The speaker asks, "Don't you want to protect your families?" Such an appeal is emotional. A speaker may appeal to the prejudices or biases of listeners. Someone at a Ku Klux Klan rally does that. So does a minister who exhorts people to be "saved." Both speakers address the emotions of the groups they talk to.

4   There is a very fine use of emotional appeal in the "Letter from Birmingham Jail" by Martin Luther King, Jr. At one point King asks his audience of white clergy how they would feel if, like blacks, they had to deny their children treats such as amusement parks and had to fear for the lives of their families, and so on. He also describes the bombings and burnings that blacks are subjected to. All the details move readers emotionally, so that they come to sympathize with blacks who live in fear.

5   Logical appeal, as noted earlier, is crucial. The speaker must seem to have an intelligent plan. The listeners want the plan to meet their needs.

6   The other appeal is the ethical one. It is made when speakers make themselves seem generous, good, and wise.

7   All three appeals can be used in one speech, although the logical and ethical appeals are essential to it.

Although the writer opens with an acceptable thesis statement, this answer shows little evidence of advance planning. Does it make sense to begin in paragraph 2 with an appeal tagged "not essential"? And note how the paragraph drifts from the emotional appeal to the other two types, despite its topic sentence. Paragraphs 3 and 4 do focus on the emotional appeal and ironically, through specific examples, make a good case for its importance. Paragraphs 5 and 6 shortchange logical and ethical appeals by saying next to nothing about them. The essay contradicts itself: If logical and ethical appeals are the essential ones and emotional appeals "not essential," why is more than half of the essay about emotional appeal?

MyWritingLab   **EXERCISE**   *Read the examination questions and answers below. Then respond to the questions that follow the answers.*

A. Question

Living organisms are composed of cells. On the basis of structure, biologists categorize cells into two groups: the prokaryotic cells and the eukaryotic cells. What are the major differences between prokaryotic cells and eukaryotic cells, and in which living organisms are these cells found?

Answer

1   Eukaryotic cells have a true nucleus and their genetic material, the DNA-containing chromosomes, is located within this nucleus, which is surrounded by a nuclear membrane. Prokaryotic cells lack a true nucleus, and their genetic material lies free in the cytoplasm of the cell.

2   Eukaryotic cells are also much more complex than prokaryotic cells. Eukaryotic cells commonly contain organelles such as mitochondria, a Golgi complex, lysosomes, an endoplasmic reticulum, and in photosynthetic cells, chloroplasts. These organelles are typically lacking in the simpler prokaryotic cells.

3   Prokaryotic cells make up the structure of all bacteria and the blue-green algae. These are the simplest of all known cellular organisms. All other cellular organisms, including humans, are composed of eukaryotic cells.

Scott Wybolt, student

a. Does the response answer the question that was asked? Discuss.

B. Question

Analyze the significant relationships between imagination and reality in Coleridge's "This Lime-Tree Bower My Prison." In your answer, you might consider some of the following questions: What is the importance of setting in the poem? Is the speaker's mind a form of setting? How is reality implicitly defined in the poem? How, and through what agencies, can reality be transmitted? What relationship is finally perceived between the spiritual and the concrete? How does friendship or fellow feeling trigger the essential insights revealed in the poem?

Answer

1   Coleridge's "This Lime-Tree Bower My Prison" shows imagination to be a powerful force that can control one's perception of reality and that is, in itself, a kind of reality—perhaps the most important reality. Thus, imagination and reality are more intimately linked and more similar in Coleridge's poem than they are ordinarily thought to be.

2   The relationship between imagination and reality is revealed by the speaker of "Lime-Tree Bower," although he doesn't openly state it. The technique for revelation is dramatic monologue, with the speaker seemingly talking spontaneously as his situation gives rise to a series of thoughts.

3   As the poem begins, the speaker finds himself "trapped" at home in his lime-tree bower, while his friends go on a walk he had hoped to take with them. This situation at first bothers the speaker, causing him to feel imprisoned. As the poem progresses, however, the speaker begins to imagine all the places his friends are visiting on their walk. Though he laments not being with them, he shows excitement as he describes the scenes his friends are viewing: the "roaring dell," the sea, and so on. Thus the speaker recognizes that he is able to participate imaginatively in the walk and, in doing so, to escape his "prison" reality and enter the reality of his friends.

4   The moment of recognition occurs at the beginning of stanza three: "A delight/ Comes sudden on my heart, and I am glad/As I myself was there!" Interestingly, however, this point marks a turn in the speaker's thoughts. Once again he realizes where he actually is—the lime-tree bower. But now he appreciates its beauties. The natural beauties he imagined have taught him to appreciate the beauties of nature right before him. He has learned that there is "No plot so narrow, be but Nature there." The lime-tree bower is no longer a prison but a rich and beautiful, if somewhat small, world.

5   Imagination has again shaped the speaker's perceptions of reality. It controls the perception of circumstances—whether one views a place as a prison or a microcosm of a larger world, with beauties and possibilities in its own right. The use of imagination can teach one about reality, as it has Coleridge's speaker. And, if one surrenders to it completely—as the speaker does when he envisions the world of the walkers—imagination is a delightful reality, as valid as the reality of the place in which one sits.

6   Imagination and reality are merged in "This Lime-Tree Bower My Prison," and though this identification is apparently temporary, one may learn through imagination how to cope with and enjoy reality. Thus, imagination is intimately involved in shaping the perception of reality.

Lori McCue, student

a. Which of the possible approaches suggested in the question does the student select?
b. Which of the other questions does she indirectly answer? Which ones are not addressed?
c. Identify the thesis statement and explain how it controls the answer.
d. Show how the answer demonstrates careful planning.
e. Point out some effective supporting details.

Writing the Examination Answer

Preparing for the examination.

- Ask professor for examples of previous exam questions.
- Review any established class material identifying expectations for essay questions.
- Write your own sample essay questions.
- Review the material you might use to answer possible essay exams.
- Rehearse, possibly in outline form, the answer you would give to possible questions.

Planning your answer to an exam question.

- Read and reread the question carefully.
- Make a specific note of any features required in the answer or any strategies that are expected such as cause/effect, comparison, or argumentation.
- Quickly brainstorm the information you will use in your answer.
- Craft a quick and clear outline and check that it meets the explanation of the question.

Drafting the essay exam.

- **Introduction** introduces topic, hocks the reader, and usually identifies a thesis, but needs to be very clear about how it answers the question.
- **Body** follows an effective organization to answer the exam question. It should be clear how each section meets the exam question. Your exam is likely to be read quickly, so you need to take extra pains to keep your points clear and your examples relevant.
- **Conclusion** very clearly restates the kernel of your answer to the question.
- Check to determine that you have very clear transitions that link to the question.

Revising the essay exam.

You rarely have time for a full revision, but you should still reread your answer from the point of view of the teacher grading the question.

- Check to make certain that you answered all of the question and didn't leave something out. If you did, find a way to insert it.
- Add any example or point of data that would strengthen your answer.
- Cut sentences that don't fit or went off point; be sure to check for inaccuracies or mistakes and cut them.
- Evaluate to make certain that your answer stands out as meeting the question.

You will rarely have time to do another draft.

Proofread.

CHAPTER 18

Writing About Literature, Movies, and Television Shows

In this chapter, you will learn how to:

18.1 Identify the key elements of creative works.

18.2 Analyze and write about plot in creative works.

18.3 Analyze and write about setting in creative works.

18.4 Analyze and write about character in creative works.

18.5 Analyze and write about point of view in creative works.

18.6 Analyze and write about symbols in creative works.

18.7 Analyze and write about themes in creative works.

18.8 Analyze and write about other literary devices: memes, ambiguity, juxtaposition, and irony.

18.9 Write so that your literary analysis is ethical.

18.10 Prewrite, plan, draft, and revise your analysis of literature, movies, or television shows.

18.11 Write a review, explication, or literary analysis.

Visit MyWritingLab **to complete the writing assignments in this chapter and for more resources on writing about literature, movies, and television.**

We read books, go to the movies, and watch TV not only to be entertained but also to understand how other people live, gain insights into our own experience, and grasp the culture in which we live. These stories become part of our world. Who doesn't have at least some idea of Frankenstein's monster, originally a creature in a novel by Mary Shelley but afterward the main character in numerous movies and television shows, including the situation comedy *The Munsters*? Because these narratives are integral to our lives, professors might ask you to write to

- Demonstrate how a short story, play, poem, or movie is constructed;
- Compare different works, including a novel and its film adaptation;
- Explain an important theme;
- Share your own critical review.

Why write about works of culture?

- Sharing your insights enriches your experiences and the experiences of others.
- Careful reading and viewing combined with writing increases your appreciation of the work.
- Writing about creative works sharpens your ability to think critically about your life and the culture that influences you.
- You become a better writer, using the processes and strategies you have learned in this text.

The Elements of Creative Works

18.1

Identify the key elements of creative works.

Most creative works—stories, novels, poems, plays, movies, TV series—share some common elements.

Plot	Setting	Character	Point of view
Symbols	Themes	Memes	Ambiguity
Juxtaposition	Irony		

Plot

18.2

Analyze and write about plot in creative works.

Plot is what grabs most of us. It is the series of events that moves the narrative along.

Plot Factors

Most plots, whether a crime drama on television or a classic short story, follow a standard structure.

- The opening **introduces** the setting and important characters. The introduction sets the stage for what happens.
- One or more **conflicts** develop—person against person or characters against society, nature, fate, or themselves.
- Action builds to a **climax** where something decisive happens.
- The **end** or **denouement** clears up unanswered questions, hints at the future, states a theme, or reestablishes some sort of relationship between two foes.

A number of techniques can be used to develop plots.

- **Foreshadowing** hints at later developments. If we see a large knife during a sustained conflict between characters, we may anticipate the later murder. In the novel *Jacob's Room*, Virginia Woolf hints at the growing conflict in Europe that we recognize as the start of World War I, preventing us from being surprised in the end when the war may have claimed Jacob's life.
- **Flashbacks** interrupt the flow of the plot to explain events that happened before the start of the work. The long-running TV series *Lost* depended

on flashbacks to flesh out the marooned characters' past. In the "Short Happy Life of Francis Macomber," Ernest Hemingway hints that the main character ran from rather than shot a wounded lion; later the story flashes back to show the actual incident.

- **Cutting** is a term used more with regard to movies than literature, but all plots cut from one scene of action to another. No one wants to see every minute, so plots always cut from one crucial event to another. We don't follow every minute of Harry Potter's journey to Hogwarts academy; rather, we move in a sequence from important event to important event.
- **Order** refers to time sequence. Plots can proceed straightforwardly in time, or they can jump back and forth. Many modern stories lack distinct plot order and focus instead on psychological conflicts, abandoning traditional plot structure, perhaps offering a deliberately disorganized sequence to reflect the character's state of mind. In her short story "How I Contemplated the World from the Detroit House of Correction and Began My Life Over Again," Joyce Carol Oates dramatizes her chief character's mental turmoil by presenting the story as a jumbled series of notes for an English composition with labels such as "Events," "Characters," and "Sioux Drive."

Writing About Plot

Unless your instructor asks for a plot summary, don't merely repeat what happens in the story. Instead, help your reader understand what's special about the plot and how it functions. Does it build suspense, mirror a character's confusion, shape a conflict, show how different lives can intersect, or help reveal a theme?

Before starting to write, answer the following questions about plot:

- What are the key events of the story? Do they unfold in conventional fashion or deviate from it in some way and if so, why? To mirror the main character's disordered state of mind? To show that life is chaotic and difficult to understand?
- Does the writer use foreshadowing, flashback, or unusual cuts? If so, for what purpose? Does it build, create, or resolve suspense?
- Is the plot believable and effective, or does it display weakness of some sort: too hard to follow, fails to engage us, fails to create suspense, leaves the conflict unresolved, or depends on unbelievable coincidences?
- Does the plot include any unique features, such as an unexpected twist or an unusual organization?
- Is the plot similar to that of another story or some type of story?
- What plot features could I write about? What examples from the story would support my contentions?

There are multiple ways to organize a paper about plot.

Introduction   Introduce the work you are writing about, indicate the basic idea of the plot, indicate why the plot is worth discussing, and offer your thesis.

The overall plot   Depending on your project, you might need to start with a plot synopsis to orient your reader to your discussion.

Illustration   If you intend to make a broader claim about the work, such as how Robert Altman, a famous movie director, uses third-person point of view to contrast characters, you would support your thesis with examples employing the strategies indicated in Chapter 11 on illustration.

Comparison   You might use the strategies outlined in Chapter 13 to compare plot approaches, such as how two different works use fore-shadowing to produce different results.

Cause and Effect   Sometimes you might employ the strategies of cause and effect—for example, if you are detailing the impact of two very different plots that intersect only at the end of the work.

The movie *Memento* by Christopher Nolan involves a main character who has amnesia and can't retain recent memories. The movie has two sequences. One is in black and white moving forward chronologically in time, and the other is in color moving backward in time to the murder of the character's wife. A paper on the plot might demonstrate how the two sequences come together to provide a resolution for the movie, or it might show how the color sequence follows the character's search for the truth and causes the viewer to experience the character's confusion, highlighting the deliberately confused sequence of events and the disorienting lack of information.

In writing about Diane Glancy's "Aunt Parnetta's Electric Blisters" (page 458), you might want to show how the tight time sequence of events concerning the annoyance with a refrigerator could lead to a pivotal flashback that serves as a personal and spiritual revelation.

MyWritingLab   **EXERCISE**   *In a short story, TV show, or movie with a strong plot line, identify conflicts and climax and explain what the ending accomplishes. Point out any use of foreshadowing or flashback. Explain how the plot is organized and why that organization works or doesn't work.*

Setting

18.3

Analyze and write about setting in creative works.

Plots have to take place somewhere and that location forms the **setting**.

Setting Factors

Setting locates characters in a time, place, and culture so they can think, feel, and act against this background. Writers can generate feelings and moods by describing settings. Sunny spring landscapes signal hope or happiness, dark alleys are foreboding, and thunderstorms suggest violent possibilities. Movies, stories, and poetry all use setting to create mood. A movie that starts with a scene of tight, maze-like winding streets among old, dusty buildings creates an immediate tension, a sense of suspense, a claustrophobia.

Setting can also help reveal a character's personality. The scene of a solitary hero in a Western crossing an open plain with the mountains in the background highlights the character as rugged and independent. In this excerpt from Amy

Tan's novel *The Joy Luck Club*, the size and contents of the wealthy merchant Wu Tsing's house reflect the owner's love of wealthy display:

> As soon as we walked into that big house, I became lost with too many things to see; a curved staircase that wound up and up, a ceiling with faces in every corner, then hallways twisting and turning into one room then another. To my right was a large room, larger than I had ever seen, and it was filled with stiff teakwood furniture: sofas and tables and chairs. And at the other end of this long, long room, I could see doors leading into more rooms, more furniture, then more doors. To my left was a darker room, another sitting room, this one filled with foreign furniture: dark green leather sofas, paintings with hunting dogs, armchairs, and mahogany desks. And as I glanced in these rooms I would see different people. . . .

Settings sometimes function as symbols, reinforcing the workings of the other elements. A broad, slowly flowing river may stand for time or fate, a craggy cliff for strength of character, a blizzard-swept plain for the overwhelming power of nature.

At times, setting provides a clue to some observation about life. At one point in Stephen Crane's story "The Open Boat," the men spot a nearby flock of seagulls sitting comfortably on the turbulent waves. Juxtaposing the complacent gulls and the imperiled men suggests the philosophical point of the story: that the universe is indifferent to human aspirations and struggles.

Shifts in setting often trigger shifts in a character's emotional or psychological state. In changing settings from close, cluttered rooms to an open field near a lake, we might gain a sense of a character's new emotional freedom.

Writing About Setting

Begin your search for a topic by identifying the most prominent settings and then asking these questions about each one:

- What are its key features?
- What does it accomplish? Does it create a mood? Reveal a character? Serve as a symbol? Reinforce the story's point? How does it accomplish these things? If an emotionally barren individual always appears against backdrops of gloomy furnished rooms, cheerless restaurants, and decaying slums, you can assume that the writer is using setting to convey character.
- In what ways does it support or interfere with the story?
- Do the setting and the mood match? What effect is produced?
- Does the setting seem realistic or effective? If not, why not? A novel or movie about the super-rich may linger so lovingly over their extravagant surroundings that the plot lacks force and the characters seem mere puppets.
- What focus would produce an effective paper? What textual or visual evidence would support it?

There are many possible approaches to a paper on setting.

Introduction   Identify the work and its basic themes or concerns, identify and describe the setting you consider relevant, explain its importance, and provide your thesis.

Illustration   Often you may provide detailed examples to show how a setting accomplishes what you claim, such as supporting the theme of humans dwarfed by the power of nature.

Comparison   You might compare different settings in the same work, settings and characters, or settings and our expectations about those settings.

Process   You might use a step-by-step approach to trace how a setting such as the pools in John Cheever's story "The Swimmer" or in the Burt Lancaster movie (of the same title) subtly change over time.

In writing about "Aunt Parnetta's Electric Blisters" (page 458) you might identify how the cramped interior of the characters' humble home contrasts both with the appliance store (which stands for civilization) and the wider and wilder landscape around them. You might use examples to demonstrate how the cramped setting and the cold of a remembered Minnesota illustrate the mental state of the story's main characters. Writing about the classic BBC Masterpiece TV series *Upstairs, Downstairs*, you could examine how the mansion as a setting contrasted the opulent spaces of the upper class with the much more modest spaces for the servants. Or you might identify how the large, sprawling space with lots of rooms creates the very space for the intrigues of the plot.

MyWritingLab   **EXERCISE**

1. What mood does the following description of a room generate? What does it suggest about the situation of the room's inhabitants, two women in an Old Ladies' Home?

   Marian stood enclosed by a bed, a washstand, and a chair; the tiny room had altogether too much furniture. Everything smelled wet—even the bare floor. She held onto the back of the chair, which was wicker and felt soft and damp. . . . How dark it was! The window shade was down, and the only door was shut. Marian looked at the ceiling. . . . It was like being caught in a robbers' cave. . . .

   Eudora Welty, "A Visit of Charity"

2. Identify a setting in a favorite movie or TV show and explain how it establishes a mood, defines the characters, or enables the plot.

Character

18.4

Analyze and write about character in creative works.

What often hooks us in a TV series, a novel, or a movie are the **characters**. Dedicated fans followed the adventures of Harry Potter. Othello, the principal character in a play of the same name by William Shakespeare, has inspired an opera, movie adaptations, and many scholarly papers.

Character Factors

In any medium, characters can play many roles:

■ a *narrator* who tells the story and may or may not be a reliable source of information;

- a *protagonist* who is the main character and main source of action. The protagonist may be good (for example, Harry Potter) or bad (for example, Walter White, the main character in the television series *Breaking Bad*);
- an *antagonist* who is opposed to the protagonist or others. The antagonist is not necessarily bad. For example, the antagonist may be a detective who is trying to stop a serial killer who is the main character;
- support for the action, deliberate distraction, comic relief, or symbol.

The pleasure of any good work is often learning about a character in depth and sometimes having our expectations about a character overturned. Readers struggle across the Harry Potter series to form an opinion about Snape, a teacher at Hogwarts who may or may not be good. Macbeth, the murdering protagonist in a Shakespeare play, in the end acts heroically by accepting his fate and facing it with courage, as summarized in the famous phrase, "Lay on, Macduff." Some characters remain fairly consistent; others change over time. We learn about characters in works in many ways.

- The author, the narrator, or other characters may tell us directly about a character, and these reports may or may not be trustworthy.
- A character may be defined by his or her setting.
- Over the course of a work, we may draw conclusions about characters based on how they act and what they say.

Movies and television shows can offer extensive visual clues about characters, their circumstances, and their actions. The length of time a camera is on a character can signal his or her importance. In literature, writers offer descriptions, offer slices of a character's thoughts, provide detailed background information, or offer more direct commentary.

Writing About Character

In writing about characters, you are attempting to share your insights about what might be distinctive about them, what we could learn from them, or how we might reconsider them. Someone might write about the movie-series character Spiderman to show that he is a psychologically flawed individual rather than just a heroic figure. Someone writing about the Greek play *Antigone* might argue that Creon, who sentences Antigone to death for violating what seems an unjust and arbitrary law, was less the villain we might take him to be.

Start the process by asking yourself these questions:

- What characters offer the potential for a paper?
- What are their most important features, and where are these features revealed?
- Do the characters undergo any changes? If so, how and why do the changes occur?
- Is there something unexpected about any character?
- Are the characters believable, true to life? If not, why?

- Is the character presented in a racist or stereotyped manner, or does the character glorify undesirable behaviors?
- Do any characters show us something distinctive about the human condition or our culture?
- What focus would produce an effective paper?
- What evidence supports the analysis?

Any of the above questions could be the basis of a paper. Writing about F. Scott Fitzgerald's novel *The Great Gatsby* or one of the later movie adaptations, you could argue that Gatsby represents a specific view of the rich and that Gatsby is atypical of the wealthy, describe how the narrator is changed by the course of events, or explain why Daisy is an unfair stereotype of women. The writer could also compare characters in the work (for example, Jay Gatsby and Tom Buchanan).

What you want to say about a character or characters will shape the organization of your paper.

- **Introduction**   Identify the work, the character, his or her place in the work, and your thesis.
- **Plot**   You may provide a plot summary identifying the character's role, or you may need to discuss the plot throughout the paper in relationship to the point you wish to make.
- **Comparison**   If you are comparing characters, or comparing a character with real-world figures, use the strategies explained in Chapter 13.
- **Cause and Effect**   If you are discussing changes in a character, you may use the strategies in Chapter 14, illustrating the characters' initial state of mind or nature, establishing what caused the changes, and illustrating the changes, in the end making some point about those changes.
- **Illustration**   Often in making more general claims about a character (for example, about how Othello is undone by his jealousy or how Batman is driven by the trauma of losing his parents), you need to develop your claim with illustrations that prove your point.

MyWritingLab   **EXERCISE**

1. Write a paragraph making what you consider an important point about a character in a television show or movie, offering the details that will make your point. For example, you might illustrate how Hans Solo in *Star Wars* typifies the reluctant hero.

2. Write a paragraph describing the personality of the character in the following passage:

> The thousand injuries of Fortunato I had borne as I best could, but when he ventured upon insult, I vowed revenge. You, who so well know the nature of my soul, will not suppose, however, that I gave utterance to a threat. *At length* I would be avenged; this was a point definitely settled—but the very definiteness with which it was resolved precluded the idea of risk. I must not only punish, but punish with impunity. A wrong is unredressed when retribution overtakes its redresser. It is equally unredressed when the avenger fails to make himself felt as such to the one who has done the wrong.
>
> Edgar Allan Poe, "The Cask of Amontillado"

Point of View

In front of you is the suspect's car, careening around a corner. Suddenly, the viewpoint changes: The suspect sticks out a gun and fires back toward the screen and the detective's car. Literatures, movies, and television all involve a **point of view** (and sometimes multiple viewpoints) from which the narrative is presented or told.

18.5

Analyze and write about point of view in creative works.

Point of view allows the creator to emphasize a particular point or theme. In *Grendel*, John Gardner writes from the viewpoint of the classic Beowulf monster or antagonist to give readers a new perspective on isolation and the creation of monsters. In the film *Nashville*, director Robert Altman cuts together perspectives on many different characters, revealing how our world is woven out of many different threads and perspectives, which sometimes intersect in unexpected ways.

Point-of-View Factors

The most common points of view are *first person* (the "I" telling the story) and *third person* (told by someone who is not the main character), either *limited* (limited knowledge) or *omniscient* (all-knowing). See the table on the following page for a summary of these viewpoints. Some works combine several of these viewpoints.

Writing About Point of View

For a paper about point of view, ask and answer these questions:

- What point of view is used? Why is it used?
- How does the point of view shape the narrative, such as what is included or excluded?
- How does the point of view directly influence the experience of the reader or viewer?
- Is the point of view suitable for the situation, narrative, or theme? Why or why not?
- If the story uses first-person narration, is the narrator reliable? What evidence supports my answer?
- What focus would produce an effective paper? What evidence would support the discussion?

You need to organize your paper based on what you are trying to accomplish. For example:

- You might write a point-of-view paper exploring the traditional way cop shows are filmed: from the detective's viewpoint. The Canadian TV series *Motive* also provides the murderer's perspective, making the antagonist more sympathetic and more complex.
- You might write a paper using the strategies in Chapter 13, showing how the different perspectives of *Beowulf* and *Grendel*, or *CSI* and *Motive*, explore different themes and characters.

Table 18.1   Point of View: A Summary

	First Person	**Third-Person Limited**	**Third-Person Omniscient**
Perspective of narrator	Told from the perspective of a principal character, as in Jack Kerouac's *On the Road.* Written works often use the pronouns *I, me, mine,* and *my.*	Tells the narrative from a viewpoint outside of the main character. Written works often use the pronouns *he* and *she* to recount the characters' actions.	The narrator, who is sometimes the author, has an overarching view of the situation, events, and characters, including their minds. This approach is very common in fiction (for example, the novels of Jane Austen, including *Pride and Prejudice*).
Influence on presentation and form	Puts the reader or viewer in the scene with immediacy and reveals the world as the character experiences it. For example: "I lurked in the shadows, waiting to turn the tables on my stalker."	Allows the writer or filmmaker the flexibility to move from character to character and scene to scene. Another approach is to provide a more journalistic account that recounts what can be seen or overheard.	Provides the most flexibility in terms of moving from character to character, scene to scene, and even in time, but may require the narrator's voice or a "voice-over" in film and television.
Influence on insight into characters' experiences	Can focus on the narrator's experiences and state of mind, and can show the development or disintegration of that character. In literature, a first-person viewpoint may mean intense access to the narrator's thoughts and feelings. In a narrative technique called *stream of consciousness* or *interior monologue,* the author attempts to give a written account of the character's complicated and sometimes conflicting thought processes.	Can provide the thoughts and experiences of a few or many characters.	Allows for more insight into the circumstances and the characters' lives and thoughts. Can also allow the author or filmmaker to offer commentary.
Specific applications in visual media	In visual media, the first person is established by choosing a main character or characters and filming mostly what they would see from their perspective. Extreme versions of this technique, like that used in *The Blair Witch Project,* use a handheld camera immersed in the scene and a character speaking directly into the camera.	Visual media often use the more objective third-person approach, since the characters' thoughts are generally revealed by dialogue (or sometimes a voice-over). Visual media can switch then from scene to scene and character to character, often to build plot tension.	This approach is less common in visual media and can be accomplished only through extensive voice-over techniques.

- You might employ a cause-and-effect approach to show how a specific viewpoint produces a particular result or impact. For example, Jane Austen's use of omniscience lends itself to a high degree of social commentary and great insights into the characters.
- You might illustrate with examples how a novelist such as Virginia Woolf used first-person stream of consciousness in *Mrs. Dalloway* or how the camera focus produces point of view in *Doctor Who*.

EXERCISE   MyWritingLab

1. Analyze in a paragraph or two, or in a blog post, the use of point of view in your favorite TV show or movie.

2. Read the following two excerpts and answer the questions that follow them:

> Max shook his head no at the mugger, his mouth in a regretful pout.
>
> The teenager lunged at Max's chest with the blade. Instinctively, Max moved one step to his right. He didn't shift far enough. The knife sank into him. Max lowered his head and watched as the metal disappeared into his arm and chest. He felt nothing. With the blade all the way in, the teenager's face was only inches from Max's; he stared at the point of entry, stunned, his mouth sagging open. The mugger's eyes were small and frightened. Max didn't like him. He put his hand on the kid's chest and pushed him away. He didn't want to die looking into scared eyes.
>
> The mugger stumbled back, tripped over his feet and fell.... Max felt the point of the blade in his armpit. He realized he wasn't cut. The stupid kid had stuck the knife in the space below Max's armpit, the gap between his arm and chest. He had torn Max's polo shirt, but missed everything else. For a moment the knife hung there, caught by the fabric. Max raised his arm and the switchblade fell to the ground.
>
> The teenager jumped to his feet and ran away, heading uptown.
>
> Rafael Yglesias, *Fearless*

> "Now!" I cry, aloud or to myself I don't know. Everything has boiled down to this instant. There's nothing in the world except the hand of the gate judge, lowering in slow motion to the catch that contains us. I see each of his fingers clearly, separately, as they fold around the lever, I see the muscles in his forearm harden as he begins to push down.
>
> Wheeling and spinning, tilting and beating, my breath the song, the horse the dance. Time is gone. All the ordinary ways of things, the gettings from here to there, the one and twos, forgot. The crowd is color, the whirl of a spun top. The noises blend into a waving band that flies around us like a ribbon on a string. Beneath me four feet dance, pounding and leaping and turning and stomping. My legs flap like wings. I sail above, first to one side, then the other, remembering more than feeling the slaps of our bodies together. Things happen faster than understanding, faster than ideas. I'm a bird coasting, shot free into the music, spiraling into a place without bones or weight.
>
> Michael Dorris, *A Yellow Boat in Blue Water*

   a. In his third-person narrative, Yglesias depicts the climax of an unsuccessful mugging, entering one character's mind but not the other's. Whose mind does he enter, and how does he convey the other person's mental state?
   b. What does Dorris accomplish by using the first-person point of view?

Symbols

18.6

Analyze and write about symbols in creative works.

Zombies are all the rage in movies, television, and even novels. But what are we to make of them? Are they just the brain-eating living dead, or do they have more meaning? The answer depends on the creative work you are analyzing. In some cases, they have represented the dangers of excessive conformity; in others, the rapacious excesses of capitalism. In Cuban zombie movies, they symbolized the dangers of communism. And in the BBC TV series *In the Flesh* they represent the stigmatized, marginalized survivors of disease, in this case Partially Deceased Syndrome (PDS).

To strengthen and deepen their messages, writers use **symbols**: names, persons, objects, places, colors, or actions that have significance beyond their surface meaning. A symbol may be very obvious—as a name like Mr. Grimm, suggesting the person's character—or quite subtle, as an object such as a stone representing a human quality such as endurance.

Symbol Factors

Some symbols are unique to the work and others conventional. A unique symbol has special significance within a work but not outside it. In the *Hunger Games* novels and movies, the Mockingjay is a symbol of defiance. Conventional symbols, on the other hand, are deeply rooted in culture, and almost everyone knows what they represent. We associate crosses with Christianity and limousines with wealth and power.

Symbols are developed within a work by their associations and use. In Ernest Hemingway's novel *A Farewell to Arms*, rain may fairly be said to symbolize doom because it consistently accompanies disasters, and one of the main characters has visions of herself lying dead in the rain. But if rain is randomly associated with a lakeside resort, a spirited business meeting, a cozy weekend, and the twentieth-anniversary celebration of a happy marriage, the writer probably intends no symbolism.

Writing About Symbols

When you examine the symbols in a literary work, think about these questions:

- What symbols are used, where do they appear, and with what are they associated?
- Are they conventional and, if so, where else do they appear? Or are they unique to this work?
- What do they appear to mean and how are they used in relation to that meaning?
- Do any of them undergo a change in meaning? If so, how and why?
- Which symbol(s) could I discuss effectively?
- What textual evidence would support my interpretation?

To locate symbols, read the literary work carefully, looking for items that seem to have an extended meaning. You might, for example, discover that the cracked walls of a crumbling mansion symbolize some character's disordered mental state or that a voyage symbolizes the human journey from birth to death. Several symbols often mean the same thing; writers frequently use them in sets.

In "Bartleby the Scrivener," for instance, Herman Melville uses windows that look upon walls, a folding screen, and a prison to symbolize Bartleby's alienated condition—that is, his mental separation from those around him.

Sometimes a symbol changes meaning during the course of a work. A woman who regards her lover's large, strong hands as symbols of passion may, following an illness that leaves him a dangerous madman, view them as symbols of danger and brute strength. Note any changes you discover, and suggest what they signify.

For each symbol you discuss, state what you think it means and then support your position with appropriate textual evidence. In writing about "Aunt Parnetta's Electric Blisters," you might argue that the refrigerator symbolizes white people's invasion into Native American culture because the story stresses the whiteness of the refrigerator, where and how it was purchased, its pervasive noise, the way it is treated as an invader that forces Aunt Parnetta outside into a more traditional dwelling, and the contrast of the refrigerator with the natural environment.

EXERCISE

MyWritingLab

1. Identify an additional symbol in "Aunt Parnetta's Electric Blisters" (page 458) and in a paragraph explain the meanings that are suggested by that symbol. Provide evidence that supports this symbolic meaning.

2. Identify a symbol in a TV show or movie. In a paragraph explain the meanings that are suggested by that symbol and provide evidence that points to this symbolic meaning.

Theme

Read a novel and watch a movie and one common response is to wonder what it was about. Many have discussed at length the point of the movie *The Matrix*. Is it about the ways our reality might be constructed, or about our need for heroes, or about the ways our lives have become dominated by the media? What we search for are the **themes**: major ideas presented by the works, observations about our life and world, the insights that often inspire us to read a novel or a poem, or go to a movie. Theme is central to works of literature and other media; and, frequently, all the other elements help develop and support it.

18.7

Analyze and write about themes in creative works.

Theme Factors

On occasion, the writer or a character states the theme directly. Mrs. Alving, the main character in Henrik Ibsen's play *Ghosts*, notes that the dead past plays a powerful and evil role in shaping human lives:

> . . . I am half inclined to think that we are all ghosts, Mr. Manders. It is not only what we have inherited from our fathers and mothers that exists again in us, but all sorts of old dead ideas and all kinds of old dead beliefs and things of that kind. They are not actually alive in us; but there they are dormant, all the same, and we can never be rid of them.

> Henrik Ibsen, *Ghosts*

Ordinarily, though, the theme remains unstated and must be deduced by examining the work's other elements. Movies and television shows rarely state their theme or themes directly, and one of the pleasures of experiencing any work is discussing the themes that might help make sense of the work. Sometimes we can simply try to find the ideas that help pull the work together. However, scholars also often analyze works in relation to theories and important social discussions, such as the way women or minorities are represented, how sexuality is constructed, or the way the work relates to issues of class or the environment. Any social issue can be the starting point for critically examining a work. However, it is important to be attentive to the actual evidence in the work and the historical period in which the work was created.

Writing About Theme

Before you begin writing, freewrite to explore general ideas that make sense of the work. Then ask and answer these questions:

- What are the possible themes of this work? Which of these should I write about? Are they stated or unstated? Are some of the possible themes related?
- If stated, what elements support them, including symbols, characters, plot events, and setting?
- If unstated, what elements create them, including symbols, characters, plot events, and setting?
- Which elements (if any) do not fit the theme, and how might you account for these elements?

Check the comments of the characters and the narrator to see whether they state the themes directly. If they don't, assess the interaction of characters, events, settings, symbols, and other elements to determine them.

The elements of Nathaniel Hawthorne's short story "Young Goodman Brown" work together to yield the primary theme. The story has four characters—Goodman Brown; his wife, Faith; Deacon Gookin; and Goody Cloyse—whose names symbolically suggest that they are completely good. Another symbol, Faith's pink hair ribbon, at first suggests innocence and later its loss. The story relates Brown's nighttime journey into a forest at the edge of a Puritan village and subsequent attendance at a baptismal ceremony for new converts to the Devil. He proceeds into the forest, suggestive of mystery and lawlessness, during a dark night, suggestive of evil, where he meets his guide, the Devil in the guise of his grandfather. As he proceeds, Brown vacillates between reluctance to join the Devil's party and fascination with it. Innocent and ignorant, he is horrified when he finds that the deacon and Goody Cloyse seem to be in league with the Devil. Brown tries to preserve his pure image of his wife, Faith, but her pink ribbon falls out of a tumultuous sky seemingly filled with demons, and Brown sees her at the baptismal ceremony. He shrieks out to her to "resist the wicked one" and is suddenly alone in the woods, not knowing whether she obeyed. The end of the story finds Brown back in his village, unable to view his wife and neighbors as anything but totally evil.

In light of these happenings, it's probably safe to say that the primary theme of the story is somewhat as follows:

> Human beings are a mixture of good and evil, but some individuals can't accept this fact. Once they realize that "good" people are susceptible to sin, they decide that everyone is evil, and they become embittered for life.

Point out any thematic weakness that you find. Including a completely innocent major character in a story written to show that people are mixtures of good and evil would contradict the writer's intention.

You probably realized that a paper on theme is basically an argument. First you present your interpretation and then you present evidence from the work, often deepening the analysis of the theme as you do so. Notice that you would develop the above account of "Young Goodman Brown" in a paper as follows.

Introduction   Identify the work, the writer or creator, a basic overview, and a general statement of the theme.

Symbols of goodness and innocence   Identify the symbols of names that suggest goodness and the ribbon that suggests innocence, including a description of village life.

The forest   Account for how a journey into a forest suggests the protagonist's condition and his moral ambivalence.

Revelation   Discuss the implication of the protagonist seeing his wife in such an environment.

Baptism   Discuss the specific symbolic importance of the baptismal ceremony and the significance of its perversion.

Impact   Using cause and effect, explain the impact of these revelations on the protagonist.

Conclusion   Restate and elaborate on the theme to pull together the argument.

EXERCISE

MyWritingLab

1. Read the short story "Aunt Parnetta's Electric Blisters" (page 458) and identify at least one major theme and the textual evidence that supports that theme.
2. Identify a theme in a TV show or movie you have seen recently; then indicate and explain what evidence supports that theme.

Other Literary Devices: Memes, Ambiguity, Juxtaposition, and Irony

A variety of other literary devices are often the objects of analysis.

18.8

Analyze and write about other literary devices: memes, ambiguity, juxtaposition, and irony.

Memes

Recently attention has been paid to meanings that repeat across a number of works. Some meanings, images, or even fragments of music have staying power; these **memes** are an important part of culture. For example, the original Mary Shelley novel *Frankenstein* has spawned numerous movies, TV shows, Halloween costumes, and phrases like "Frankenfood." It can be important, especially when writing about media, to identify any repeated memes and their roles. Sometimes a paper can be written about a meme and its evolution. For example, a paper might discuss the specific meme of the vampire, exploring how it has remained the same from Bram Stoker's original novel to its newest incarnations on television and in the movies and how it has also changed.

Ambiguity

Many don't like when a novel or movie leaves things unresolved, as in the final scene of *Blade Runner*, which has generated a lot of discussion. **Ambiguity** is an unavoidable part of human life and an essential part of art. It is important to recognize the positive role of ambiguity in a work. A student writing about *Blade Runner* may point out how ambiguity has an important place in the work, with the ending's ambiguity mirroring the protagonist's struggle to reconcile himself to the moral ambiguity of his role in killing replicants (artificially created humans) and raising the possibility that he himself is a replicant.

Juxtaposition

Writers and directors depend heavily on **juxtaposition**, the deliberate parallel contrast of scenes, characters, or events. In the novel *Ragtime*, E. L. Doctorow juxtaposes ornate architectural pieces being delivered from Europe with life in the tenements to make an important point about the injustice of extreme inequalities in wealth and living conditions. In a movie, a director may juxtapose and cut back and forth between the hero and the villain to contrast their moral codes. When you see a clear parallel contrast where the work shifts back and forth between two characters or scenes, you might suspect that the director is using juxtaposition to make a point by the contrast.

Irony

In an episode of the TV series *Murdoch Mysteries*, the detective cleverly follows all the clues to demonstrate that the suspect held in custody and who had confessed was innocent and protecting his brother. The suspect is freed—and then the detective discovers that he had in fact released the real killer and that the brother has been dead for many years. Freeing the guilty killer who had confessed based on the close examination of clues is an example of irony. **Irony** features some discrepancy, some difference between appearance and reality, expectation and outcome. Sometimes a character says one thing but means something else. The critic who, tongue in cheek, says that a clumsy dancer is "poetry in motion" speaks ironically. One of the most famous literary ironies defines O Henry's short story "The Gift of the Magi," where the wife sells her hair to buy a chain for her husband's watch and the husband sells his watch to buy combs for his wife's lovely hair. The revelation of gifts shows an irony that also reaffirms the value of their love and gifts. In writing about irony, it is important to show that the irony is really ironic, demonstrate the irony, and explain the point of the irony.

MyWritingLab   **EXERCISE**   *Identify examples of a meme, ambiguity, juxtaposition, and irony in a short story, poem, movie, or TV show, and then write a paragraph for each explaining the device, what evidence supports your identification, and how it is used in the work.*

Ethical Issues

When you write about literature or other creative works, you need to be aware of certain ethical considerations. Imagine someone reading only part of a short story or viewing only the trailer of a movie and then writing a scathing analysis that suggests he has read or viewed the entire work. Imagine a thematic analysis of a novel that deliberately ignores large sections of the text in order to develop a twisted interpretation about the evils of capitalism. Imagine citing atypical quotations from the heroine of a play that deliberately create a distorted impression of her character. To help fulfill your ethical responsibility, ask and answer the following questions.

18.9

Write so that your literary analysis is ethical.

- Have I read or viewed the entire work carefully?
- Is my interpretation supported by the preponderance of textual evidence? Does it avoid deliberate distortion?
- Have I avoided using quotations that are atypical or taken out of context?
- Is my interpretation fair to the creative work rather than distorting events to promote an agenda?

The Writing Process: Writing About Literature, Movies, and Television

In general, writing about creative works follows the same principles you have employed for other kinds of writing.

18.10

Prewrite, plan, draft, and revise your analysis of literature, movies, or television shows.

- Make sure you understand the assignment.
- Decide on a suitable topic, one that is neither too broad nor too obvious.
- Reread or review the work, taking notes related to the claims that you want to make; but don't neglect material in the work that may contradict your initial position.
- Review your notes to identify a clear thesis.
- Decide on an appropriate organizational approach—comparing characters, arguing for a theme, illustrating the use of setting.
- Create an outline, write a draft, get feedback, revise, and proofread.

Writing a Review, Explication, or Literary Analysis

Many different purposes for writing about creative works will shape your writing. Three of the most common types of writing about creative works are reviews, explication, and literary analysis.

18.11

Write a review, explication, or literary analysis.

Reviews

Reviews are the most common form of writing about literature, movies, or television. You can find reviews almost everywhere, from Rotten Tomatoes to newspapers to blogs. Reviews are our way of sharing our judgment about a work (perhaps by posting a review on Amazon) or finding out how those we trust see the work. A good review offers an overview of the work and some sense of how we might interpret the work. It also evaluates the work, drawing on the elements we have discussed in this chapter as well as techniques such as writing style, acting, or special effects.

The best approach to learning how to write reviews is to read the many reviews online, which is why none are reproduced here. Most reviews follow a common pattern.

Introduction   Identify the work, provide brief background about the work and the author or creator, and provide an overall evaluation of the work as a thesis.

Synopsis   Give an overview of the plot and characters, being careful not to spoil the ending or give away any plot twists.

Balance   No work is all good or bad. Balance the review by detailing some of the work's good features if you are writing a generally negative review (or the reverse if you are writing a generally positive review).

Evaluation   Offer your evaluation of the work based on the work's most important elements. It is important to criticize a work based on its basic aims. For example, it would be unreasonable to criticize a work of science fiction because it lacks realism. Within this constraint, it is still fair to focus on the quality of the characterization, the credibility of the plot, the consistency of the work with the themes, and the overall quality of the writing or filmmaking techniques.

Conclusion   Pull together your recommendation for the reader.

MyWritingLab   **EXERCISE**

1. Write a short analysis of a favorite review that you think is effective, identifying the elements, evidence, and organization of the review.
2. Write a review (possibly as a blog entry) of a story, poem, movie, or TV show.

Explication

Students and scholars of literature are often asked to explicate a difficult work of poetry or a short story. An **explication** explains or clarifies the complex images, rhymes, or plot developments to help readers better understand the work. An explication routinely offers an introduction that provides a context for the essay and a thesis that is the principal point of the explication, presents a detailed account in the order of the work, and then offers a conclusion. Explications can be short (a page or two) or much longer.

The following is the beginning of an explication of the poem by Emily Dickinson called "'Twas like a Maelstrom, with a notch."

Emily Dickinson is a poet who often provides a careful and sensitive poetic account of her emotions. Her poem #414 "'Twas like a Maelstrom, with a notch" is no exception to her complex treatment of the themes of despair and death. Her first stanza to the second line of the second stanza often confuses readers. "'Twas like a Maelstrom, with a notch,/That nearer, every Day,/Kept narrowing its boiling Wheel/ Until the Agony/Toyed coolly with the final inch/Of your delirious Hem–/'"

The first stanza objectifies an emotional state in the form of a "Maelstrom," a classic Gothic element that often represents the unbridled and chaotic forces of nature but also something evil and hostile. But this Maelstrom is already paradoxically with a notch, something that seems small in contrast to the scale of a massive storm, a contrast that Dickinson continues. For the Maelstrom rather than engulfing the poet draws nearer, something incremental, each day. It "narrows" into a "boiling Wheel," somehow smaller as a wheel than a Maelstrom, yet vicious in its boiling, retaining some of the turbulence of the original image. So we can see what seems like massive external events or a terrible emotional event approaches as something smaller, as one may see a mood such as depression coming from far off, threatening in its distant, but smaller, and more personal way when it draws closer.

In her poetry, Emily Dickinson does not use end punctuation (she uses dashes instead) and doesn't always end her lines with a stanza. The approaching storm arrives as an emotional state, "Agony," with the capitalization of the noun suggesting its terrible, single-word, intensity. Yet, maintaining her tension between the massive and the small, the "Agony/Toyed coolly with the final inch/Of your delirious Hem –" What may seem massive, an intense pain, marks its attack on something small and familiar, is like a breeze, disrupting what is intimate and feminine: "an inch of Hem." And what is it to consider that "Hem" as "delirious"? There are dangerous connotations here of the overly wrought feminine, of a kind of hysteria, an excess of emotions.

Even in the start of a poem, Emily Dickinson takes the reader on an inward journey. We are led to understand how what may seem large and overwhelming can in personal ways afflict us, and leave us with a sense of helplessness, of being frozen in doubt. . . .

EXERCISE   *Write an explication of a challenging poem, a difficult section of a short story, or a complex scene from a movie or TV show.*   My WritingLab

Literary Analysis

In college you may be asked to write an analysis of a literary work, a movie, or a TV show. An analysis provides a detailed and developed argument that offers a new insight into a work. In many cases, this analysis is also supported by secondary resources that offer already existing critical views that can inform your own analysis. An analysis creates an argument around the elements discussed in this chapter, often following the suggestions for writing about those elements. For example, a literary analysis may make an argument about the use of symbols in a work, explore how setting becomes a vital part of the meaning of the work (as it does in Westerns), contrast characters, demonstrate the effective use of a technique, or argue for a theme.

What follows is a student's literary analysis of "Aunt Parnetta's Electric Blisters" (page 458), which analyzes the use of the symbol of the "refrigerator" in the story.

STUDENT ESSAY ON **LITERATURE**

**The Refrigerator: A Symbol Between Worlds
in "Aunt Parnetta's Electric Blisters"**

Erin Mueller

Identifies author and work that are the focus of the paper

Thesis statement that also identifies organization of the paper

Topic sentence

Quotes from text as support

Identifies one way refrigerator functions as a symbol

Identifies next symbolic function of the refrigerator as invasion of white civilization

Defines key concept that might be unfamiliar to the reader

Relates this use of the refrigerator to the main thesis

1   Diane Glancy's "Aunt Parnetta's Electric Blisters" defines the conflict between modern technology and Native American culture. Through living qualities, animalistic descriptions, and the concept of "cold," the refrigerator becomes a tangible symbol of the complex relationship between modern technology and Native American culture and the continual modern invasions into Native American lives.

2   From the beginning, the refrigerators that Parnetta and Filo own are treated as more than simple pieces of machinery. After the repairman is unable to fix their old, broken refrigerator, Filo shoots it with his rifle to "take revenge," in order "to stand against civilization" (28). Filo seeks revenge on the broken technology that embodies the hindrance modern society places on the Native American families. After the refrigerator's "death," he applies his knowledge as a medicine man to transcend to the spirit world for the machine's soul. When he could not revive the refrigerator, it is buried in the back yard, like a human body. For the family, this refrigerator is not only an embodiment of the advancements of western civilization, but it is also treated as another living thing, something that actually has a life to save.

3   The dead refrigerator is then replaced by a new one that they buy in town where "the Yellow Hair Custer was there to command [the appliances]" (29). The reference to yellow hair alludes that the technology originates from white man's civilization. The reference to Custer and Little Big Horn becomes more evident once Parnetta and Filo purchase a new fridge; the Native family actually loses to the white civilization by allowing the new refrigerator to enter their home. Despite its mechanical origins, the new refrigerator is "white inside as though cleansed by cedar from the Keetowah fire" (30). Keetowah fire is a Native American ritual used to cleanse living spirits; this suggests that the fridge has a soul to cleanse. The life that both Parnetta and her husband see in the "white man's" technology insinuates that the cold, white box has a spirit, making it as sacred as all living life in Native American culture, and therefore possesses as much importance as Native spirits. Once again the refrigerator functions in the text as a symbol of white civilization that

Continued on next page

invades this Native American home while also being reclaimed within Native American culture, positioning it between two worlds.

4   The life of the refrigerator is also present through animal personification. Once turned on, Aunt Parnetta's refrigerator begins to emit loud grunts and groans like a "giant hog." This technological "beast" frightens Parnetta and keeps her awake at night; her greatest fear is that the "white boar" will come tearing into her room to eat her once she fell asleep. The symbolic use of the white boar continues to incorporate foreign technology into Native culture by bringing mechanics into a wild and natural setting. Because of its terrifying life-like qualities, Parnetta devises ways to avoid being near the fridge, such as sending her grandchildren into the kitchen to grab things for her, performing her daily chores outdoors, and sleeping outside in the teepee. She fears the foreign, technological creature that resides in her home and escapes to the outdoors, finding safety in a Native, machine-less setting. The invasive technology succeeds at pushing her out of her own home, as foreign civilization has done to the Native population for hundreds of years.

5   Though Parnetta tries to separate herself from the refrigerator that invades her home, Parnetta begins appropriating the "white man's" technology into a Native spiritual awakening through the concept of "cold." While lying in bed, she begins to dwell on the machine's invasive coldness. Late at night, Parnetta feels the freezing air around her, and it begins to physically affect her: "the cold place was shriveled to the small, upright triangle in her chest, holding the fish her grandson caught in the river" (31). Parnetta's heart and the refrigerator become the same; the line between machine and humans dissolves as the technology becomes more life-like and Parnetta begins to discover her own mechanical existence. She begins to wonder how different she actually is from the monster in the kitchen: "Maybe she irritated the Great Spirit like the white box irritated her" (32). The refrigerator becomes a source of revelation as its frozen, mechanical interior becomes a symbol of her own spirituality. At the realization of her relation to the coldness of the refrigerator, the Great Spirit saves her from the ice in her veins as he "unplugged her for a minute" and "took his rifle right through her head." For a moment, she recognizes how she has been like the broken refrigerator, living a cold existence until the sparks of the great spirit purify her. Parnetta is able to come to terms with the refrigerator's presence by reflecting on the coldness within herself and realizing her greater connection to the Great Spirit of Native culture.

Continued on next page

Topic sentence identifies new role for the refrigerator

Use of text as support

Links animal personification

Restates symbolic function from the previous paragraph

Topic sentence identifies new symbolic role

Use of text as support

Use of text as support

States final use of the refrigerator as a symbol

Completes narrative to demonstrate use of symbol

6   The refrigerator becomes a symbol of the complex relationship between modern technology and Native American culture by invading the
concepts of Native traditions by possessing Native features of a soul,
expressing characteristics of wild animals, and being a spiritual awakening for Parnetta. In the end, what seems a symbol of white, technological civilization functions as a symbol of inner reflection and spiritual
renewal within Native culture.

Restates the thesis
identifying how it
functioned in the
work

MyWritingLab   **EXERCISE**

1. Write your own analysis of "Aunt Parnetta's Electric Blisters" or another story or
   poem.
2. Write an analysis of a movie or TV show.

Research Guide

Much of your college and workplace writing will require some type of research—obtaining information from one or more sources to help achieve your writing purpose. The nature of your writing task and the demands of the situation determine the format you use and the way you document your sources.

This section of the text explores in detail the research tools and procedures you will use to develop various types of papers and reports. Sometimes you'll draw upon books, magazines, newspapers, and other printed sources, as well as electronic sources, in order to prepare a longer library research paper; at other times you'll do the same for shorter papers. Still other situations call for using primary research—the type in which you develop the information you use—to accomplish your purpose. The four chapters in this section will help you to meet these writing demands.

Chapter 19 explains how to choose a suitable library research topic and then focuses on carrying out the necessary steps to write a research paper and offers guidelines for avoiding plagiarism. The chapter includes a continuing case history that leads to the finished paper in Chapter 20, complete with margin notes that will provide guidance as you prepare your own paper.

Chapters 20 (MLA) and 21 (APA) show how to prepare correct references for your paper's bibliography. They also show the correct formats for references within the body of the paper and explain how to handle quotations.

Chapter 22 explains and illustrates the most common primary research strategies—interviews, questionnaires, and direct observations. In each case, student models, annotated with margin notes, embody the key features of that strategy.

Together, the material in these four chapters should provide all the information you will need to complete writing assignments that require research.

CHAPTER 19

The Research Paper

In this chapter, you will learn how to:

Visit MyWritingLab **to complete the writing assignments in this chapter and for more resources on the research paper.**

"Janice, I need a report on the Chinese economy and its role in solar energy."

"Wait a minute, that sounds like a research paper. I thought that was something for college."

"I don't care what you call it. I need a clear understanding of their growing role in an industry so related to our company."

There are very few decisions we want to make based on just our personal experience, not when there has been a lot of previous study done on most topics.

Whether we are trying to understand how to treat an unusual illness or deciding on the risks of global warming, we turn to the research others have done to formulate our own views. Often when we become knowledgeable about issues and formulate informed conclusions, we share what we have discovered with others.

It is likely that you will be asked to prepare a research paper for your composition class. This assignment calls for you to gather information from a variety of sources and then to focus, organize, and present it in a formal paper that documents your sources. The procedure will familiarize you with the mechanics of documentation, and when you finish you'll have a solid grasp of your topic and pride in your accomplishment. In addition, the experience will help you learn how to meet the research demands of other courses and your job.

Writing a research paper really isn't so formidable. You acquaint yourself with the various resources that will provide easy access to the information you need. Reading what others have written on a topic will give you a chance to draw your own conclusions. And as a writer you can limit your topic so that it doesn't balloon out of control.

Research writing is common both in the classroom and on the job.

- A history professor might require a long report on the causes of the Vietnam War.
- A business instructor might ask you to trace the history of a company, evaluate an advertising campaign, or review the latest styles of management.
- A building trades instructor might call for a short report that compares the effectiveness of several new insulating materials.
- At work, a marketing analyst might report on the development costs, sales potential, and competition for a product the company is considering introducing.
- An engineer might write a journal article that summarizes recent developments in plastic fabrication.
- A physical therapist might prepare a seminar paper that evaluates different exercise programs to follow arthroscopic surgery.

Whatever the writing project, let your purpose guide your research and determine the information you elect to use. When you write, the conclusions you have reached from thinking about what you have read and your purpose in communicating, not your notes, should dictate what you say.

Learning About Your Library

Before starting a library research paper, take time to familiarize yourself with your library. Many college libraries offer guided tours, and almost all of them display floor plans that show where and how the books are grouped. If your library doesn't have tours, browse through it on your own and scan its contents. As you do, note the following features:

19.1

Identify and use your library's resources.

> *Computer Catalog:* The computer catalog allows you to effectively search for the library's books and often most of its other holdings as well. Pages 348–351 discuss computerized catalogs.

Databases: These databases provide organized ways to find articles in magazines and newspapers, and many even provide the full text of the article. Pages 352–357 discuss databases.

Stacks: These are the bookshelves that hold books and bound periodicals (magazines and newspapers). Stacks are either open or closed. Open stacks allow you to go directly to the books you want, take them off the shelf, and check them out. Closed stacks do not allow you direct access to shelved material. Instead, a staff member brings you what you want.

Periodical Area: Here you'll find some current and recent issues of magazines and newspapers. If your topic calls for articles that have appeared within the last few months, you're likely to find them in this area or as an online article.

Microfilm and Microfiche Files: Microfilm is a filmstrip bearing a series of photographically reduced printed pages. Microfiche is a small card with a set of photographically reduced pages mounted on it. A library's older magazine and newspaper collection is on film.

Circulation Desk: Here's where you check materials in and out, renew books you want to keep longer, and pay overdue fines. If you can't find something you want, the desk clerk will tell you whether it's missing, on reserve, or checked out. If it's out, enter a request on the computer or fill out a hold card, and the library will notify you when it is available.

Reserve Area: This area contains books that instructors have had removed from general circulation so students can use them for particular courses. Ordinarily, you can keep these books for only a few hours or overnight.

Interlibrary Loan: Few libraries are large enough to contain all of the major books, government documents, and periodicals. Most have an arrangement for borrowing works from another library. You may be able to request this loan online or confirm the loan and pick up the work at a specific Interlibrary Loan desk. If you will need a resource through interlibrary loan, leave yourself at least three weeks to get the work.

Reference Area: This area houses the library's collection of encyclopedias, periodical indexes, almanacs, handbooks, dictionaries, and other research tools that you'll use as you investigate your topic. You'll also find one or more reference guides, which your librarian can help you use.

Librarian Help Desk: The greatest assets in any library are the librarians who are experts in finding information. They can help you better define your question, use the research tools effectively, and locate the materials you need. Many colleges provide online librarian help as well.

Choosing a Topic

19.2

Select and narrow a research topic and brainstorm to create a research question.

Instructors take different approaches to assigning library research papers. Some want explanatory papers, others want papers that address a two-sided question, and still others allow students a free choice.

- An explanatory paper takes no position but provides information that gives the reader a better grasp of the topic. For example, it may explain the key advantages of solar heating, thereby clearing up popular misconceptions.
- An argument paper, on the other hand, attempts to sway the reader toward one point of view—for instance, that solar heat is commercially feasible.

Some instructors specify not only the type of paper but also the topic. Others restrict students to a general subject area, ask them to pick topics from lists, or give them free choice. If you have little to say in the selection, recognize that you can still make the project effective by committing to the topic and search for what interests you.

Whatever the circumstances, it's a good idea to follow a schedule that establishes completion dates for the various stages of your paper. Such a timetable encourages you to plan your work, clarifies both your progress and the work remaining, and provides an overview of the project. You can use the following sample schedule as a guide, modifying the stages or adding other ones as necessary.

Sample Schedule for a Library Research Paper

Activity	Targeted Completion Date	
Topic Selection	_____	
Working Bibliography	_____	
Research Question and Tentative Thesis	_____	
Note Taking	_____	
Working Outline	_____	
First Draft	_____	
Revised Drafts	_____	_____
Date Due	_____	

Topics to Avoid

If you have free rein to pick your topic, how should you proceed? To begin, rule out certain types of topic.

- Those based entirely on personal experience or opinion such as "The Thrills I Have Enjoyed Waterskiing" or "Colorado Has More [or Less] Scenic Beauty than New Mexico." Such topics can't be supported by library research. Don't hesitate, however, to include personal judgments and conclusions that emerge from your reading.
- Those fully explained in a single source. An explanation of a process, such as cardiopulmonary resuscitation, or the description of a place, such as the Gobi Desert, does not require coordination of materials from various sources. Although you may find several articles on such topics, basically they all contain the same information.
- Those that are brand new. Often it's impossible to find sufficient source material about such topics.

- Those that are overly broad. Don't try to tackle such elephant-sized topics as "The Causes of World War II" or "Recent Medical Advances." Instead, slim them down to something like "How Did Germany's Depression Contribute to the Rise of Hitler?" or "Eye Surgery with Lasers."
- Those that have been worked over and over, such as abortion and the legal drinking age. Why bore your reader with information and arguments that are all too familiar already?

MyWritingLab   **EXERCISE**   *Using the advice on topics to avoid, explain why each of the following would or would not be suitable for a library research topic:*

1. Genetic counseling
2. The impact of the Tea Party on politics
3. The challenges of cybersecurity
4. What led to a recent tragedy, such as a natural disaster or mass murder
5. Tweeting or Instagramming as a marketing strategy
6. A Third World hot spot as described on the evening news
7. Reforming the financing of presidential election campaigns

Drawing on Your Interests

Let your interests guide your choice. A long-standing interest in basketball might suggest a paper on the pros and cons of expanding the number of teams in the National Basketball Association. An instructor's lecture might spark your interest in a historical event or person, an economic crisis, a scientific development, a sociological trend, a medical milestone, a political scandal, or the influences on an author. An argument with a friend might spur you to investigate latchkey children. A television documentary might arouse your curiosity about the changes in Inuit life style. A recent article or novel might inspire you to explore the occult or some taboo.

Be practical in selecting a topic or research question. Why not get a head start on a particular aspect of your major field by researching it now? Some management, marketing, or advertising strategy; the beginnings of current contract law; medical ethics—all of these topics, and many others, qualify. Think about your audience, the availability of information, and whether you can fit it into the guidelines for your paper.

To develop a focus for your paper, it's often helpful to brainstorm; skim online resources, encyclopedias, and other materials; and use the branching or clustering technique. If you're exploring the topic of child abuse, preparing a clustering diagram like the one in Figure 19.1 can help you decide how to narrow your topic as well as provide a rough map of areas to research. The more you brainstorm, the richer your map will be. Brainstorming often results in a series of questions, perhaps based on the writing strategies discussed in Chapters 8–16, that will help guide your research. Often it is helpful to state your main research question, followed by a series of related questions that elaborate on it. From our cluster example, a student wishing to explore the topic of psychological abuse might develop the following set of questions:

What is psychological abuse?
What long-term and short-term effects does it have on a child?

How can a child living at home be helped?
What psychological help is available for an adult who experienced
   childhood abuse?
What can be done to help victims of psychological abuse?
   Are there services to help limit the abuse?
Is family therapy an option?
   What is family therapy, and what does it do?
What therapies work best?
What do they do?
   How effective are they?

These questions make research easier. After all, the purpose of research is to answer questions. Later, as you examine source material, you will be seeking specific answers, not just randomly searching for information.

A quick search online or other sources may help focus your question or topic, determine possible directions for your research, or gain a broader context on the subject. Because Wikipedia is edited by users and can have inaccuracies, many faculty members do not want it used as a formal source; however, it can provide you with a quick general background on a number of topics. While they may not be later formal sources, skimming, or quickly reading, a number of the articles, blogs, and even discussions online can help you generate ideas. Often Wikipedia and other articles may have links to other information that can guide your search. If you have a more technical topic or issue, online encyclopedias, such as the *Encyclopedia of Life Sciences* or *International Encyclopedia of Linguistics* may help. Sometimes quickly skimming books, even their tables of

Figure 19.1   Clustering Diagram on Child Abuse.

contents, can offer ideas. Keep in mind the purpose of your first search. You are trying to help focus your topic, determine the different issues that you want to address, and gain some sense of the resources available on your topic. You are scouting the terrain. Move fast and cover a lot of initial area. You can always go back to something you found interesting.

More often than not, things won't fall neatly into place as you probe for a topic and then a focus. Don't be discouraged by false starts and blind alleys. Think of yourself as an explorer who will gradually become well-versed in your chosen topic.

FINDING YOUR TOPIC

- Make a list of your major interests that prompt questions.
- Identify issues or questions raised in class or the media.
- Brainstorm questions related to your initial question for focus.
- Do some initial readings around your topic to get an overview to focus your topic.

CASE HISTORY Nilofar Khanbhai was an undergraduate majoring in biology and considering a career in law or public health when she wrote the library research paper that is the sample MLA paper at the end of Chapter 20. The assignment was to write about a current issue or concern related to the student's major. Because the Ebola virus was a serious concern in the news and related to her interests in both law and public health, she decided to explore several options related to this issue: whether it was legal to bar individuals from other countries from entering the United States, whether it was appropriate to bring infected Americans home for treatment, whether the Centers for Disease Control and Prevention responded adequately, or how to control the spread of Ebola. Thinking about the issue, Nilofar concluded that a paper that had greater application to other possible outbreaks would be one that focused on the strategies for containing the outbreak: isolation and quarantine.

To establish a focus for her paper, Nilofar drafted a series of questions suggested by the writing strategies suggested in Chapters 8–16. Here are some of the questions she developed.

Could I *narrate* a history of Ebola and the attempts to contain it?
Could I *describe* the symptoms of the virus or the isolation units?
Could I *classify* the approaches to preventing the spread of infectious diseases?
Could I *compare* isolation and quarantine as an approach?

Could I explain the *process* involved in isolating a patient?
Could I *define* Ebola, isolation, and quarantine?
Could I identify the *causes* of the infection?
Could I explain the *effects* of isolation and quarantine?
Could I argue for or against isolation or quarantine as an adequate and appropriate measure to contain the disease?

These writing strategies can often help you narrow down a subject to a manageable topic.

For background reading concerning the controversy, Nilofar started by conducting a Google search and reading online newspaper articles on the issue. After getting a sense of the scope of the issue, Nilofar searched both a general database and a health-care database for articles and books on Ebola and effective containment strategies, with phrases like *Ebola, infectious disease control, medical quarantine,* and *medical isolation.* She found a book on Ebola and some articles that provided a more professional medical overview.

After reading the background material, Nilofar began to determine what she wanted to include in her paper. She came up with the following list:

1. The cause of Ebola and the history of its outbreak
2. Isolation as a treatment strategy
3. The reaction to isolation and the demand for quarantine
4. Quarantine as a treatment strategy
5. The legal implications and constraints on isolation and quarantine

On reflection, Nilofar concluded that despite her interest in law, topic 5 really was a different kind of issue and could possibly be a separate paper. From what she read, Nilofar began to expand her topic by using branching.

Isolation as a treatment strategy
- The history of isolation
- The effectiveness of isolation
- The process of isolation
- The costs of isolation

Discovering Your Sources

Once you have a topic, you're ready to see whether the library has the resources you'll need to complete the project. This step requires you to check additional reference tools and compile a working bibliography—a set of notes (electronic notes or cards) that list promising sources of information. This section discusses these reference tools and how to use them.

19.3

Conduct research using an online catalog, databases, Internet searches, and other sources.

Online Catalog

What It Is An online catalog lists all the books in the library, usually along with other holdings like magazines, newspapers, government documents, and electronic recordings. It may also provide additional information, such as whether a book has been checked out and, if so, the return date. Some catalogs even include the holdings of nearby libraries. Books are usually cataloged using Library of Congress call numbers, although some libraries use the Dewey decimal system.

Online catalogs vary from institution to institution. If you are not familiar with your system, be sure to ask your librarian. Because such systems work by matching the term or title you offer to its listing, it is very important to be careful of your spelling and try to experiment with lots of different terms. The phrase "shrinks" will not find you much if you are looking for works on "psychoanalysis," "Freud," "Freudian analysis," or "the unconscious." Computers cannot do the thinking for you.

Most systems let you conduct searches by key terms (those appearing in book titles and descriptions), author, title, and subject (based on the Library of Congress's cataloging system). Most systems let you select the kind of search by a menu or icons as in Figure 19.2. Searching may require you to view a series of screens having increasingly specific instructions, with the final screen providing information from a single book. Figure 19.3 illustrates a keyword search. Figure 19.4 shows the list of works discovered by the search, including the publication date; Figure 19.5 one specific work, including the call number to locate the book in your library stacks, an indication of the availability of the book, a brief description of the contents, and a list of subjects that could be used in additional searches.

Figure 19.2 The Online Catalog's opening screen allows you to select the type of search.

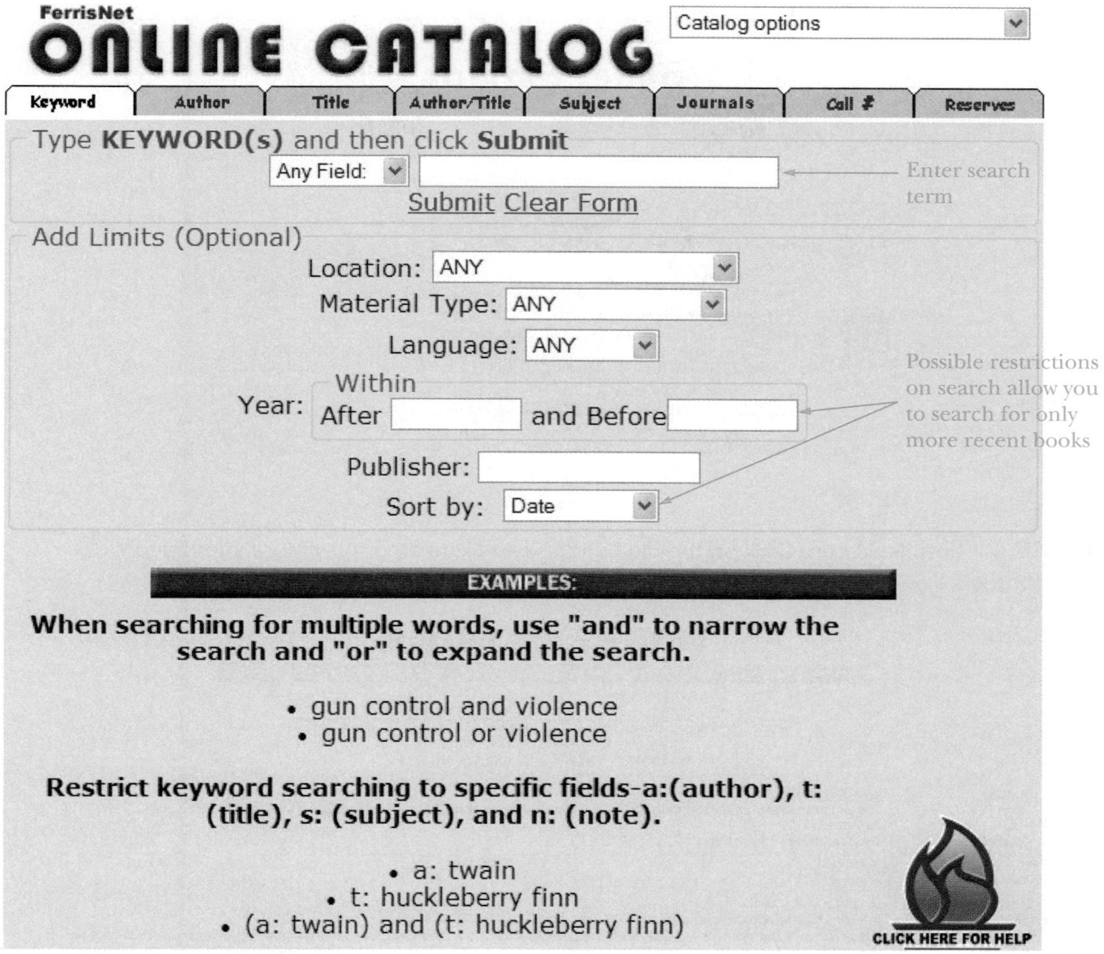

FerrisNet

ONLINE CATALOG

| Catalog options | ∨ |

| Keyword | Author | Title | Author/Title | Subject | Journals | Call # | Reserves |

Type **KEYWORD(s)** and then click **Submit**

| Any Field: ∨ | | ← —— Enter search term

Submit Clear Form

Add Limits (Optional)

Location: ANY ∨

Material Type: ANY ∨

Language: ANY ∨

Within
Year: After [ ] and Before [ ]

Possible restrictions on search allow you to search for only more recent books

Publisher: [ ]

Sort by: Date ∨

EXAMPLES:

When searching for multiple words, use "and" to narrow the search and "or" to expand the search.

- gun control and violence
- gun control or violence

Restrict keyword searching to specific fields-a:(author), t: (title), s: (subject), and n: (note).

- a: twain
- t: huckleberry finn
- (a: twain) and (t: huckleberry finn)

CLICK HERE FOR HELP

Figure 19.3   Keyword Search.
Software copyright Innovative Interfaces, Inc.

Often, a key term search (see Figure 19.4) can be the most helpful way to approach a topic. In this type of search, the computer checks the titles and descriptions of books for the key terms you enter and lists any that it finds. Different key terms will produce varying strings of publications, so it is a good idea to try different words or phrases for the same topic. For example, if you're searching for material on "electric cars," you might also try "electronic cars," "alternative fuels," and so on. Because such searches are very rapid, you can experiment with different combinations of terms to focus your search. If, for instance, you're asked to write a paper on some aspect of Japanese culture, you might investigate such combinations as "Japanese business," "Japan and education," and "Japanese feminists." Because key term searches allow you to use logical terms like *and, or, but,* and *not,* they are especially useful for narrowing a broad focus.

Buttons to move through the search program

Allows you to save selected records

History of your search

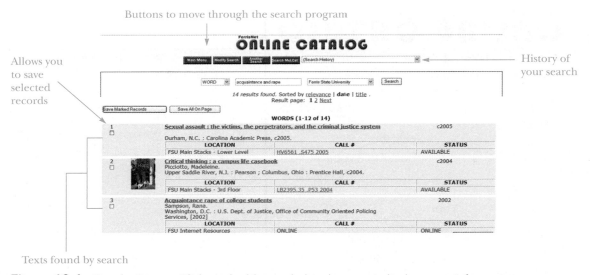

Texts found by search

Figure 19.4 Results Screen. Click on the blue underlined terms to display more information.
Software copyright Innovative Interfaces, Inc.

Details about the book

Figure 19.5 Detailed Search Results.
Software copyright Innovative Interfaces, Inc.

Obtaining the Books   Most researchers start with a key term search. Following the instructions in the paragraph on page 349, type in one or several terms, using the appropriate logical terms. Advanced search functions will allow you to limit the dates of your search if you are only looking for more recent texts.

When you have found a promising title, make a note of the relevant information. With some systems, this screen indicates whether the book is in the library or checked out and tells you how to proceed if you can't find it on the shelf.

If your terminal has a printer, use it to make a copy of each promising reference. Otherwise, record the following information in your electronic notes or on a note card:

Author(s)

Title

Chapter title and author(s), if applicable

Editor(s) and translator(s), as well as author(s) of any supplementary material

Total number of volumes (if more than one) and the number of the specific volume that you want to use

City of publication

Name of publisher

Date of publication

Also, copy the book's call number into your electronic notes on or in the upper left corner of the card.

Next, scan the books themselves. If your library stacks are closed, give the librarian a list of your call numbers and ask to see the books. If you can enter the stacks, locate the general areas where your books are shelved. Once you find your book, spend a few extra minutes browsing in the general area of each book; you may discover useful sources that you overlooked in the card catalog.

Skim each book's table of contents and any introductory material, such as a preface or introduction, to determine its scope and approach. Also check the index and note the pages with discussions that relate to your topic. Finally, thumb through portions that look promising. If the book won't help you, throw away the note card.

If a book is missing from the shelf and the computer hasn't indicated that someone has checked it out, then it's probably on reserve. Check at the circulation desk; if the book is on reserve, go to that section and examine it there. If someone has checked the book out and the due date is some time away, perhaps a library nearby will have a copy. Check with your librarian.

How to Use It   Follow the procedure given on pages 348–351 for computerized card catalogs, making any needed modifications.

EXERCISE   MyWritingLab

1. **Select five of the following subjects. Go to the online catalog and find one book about or by each. List each book's call number, author, title, publisher, and date of publication. Because subject headings may vary, investigate related categories, if necessary, to find an entry. To illustrate, if you find nothing under "mountaineering," check "mountain climbing" or "backpacking."**

1. The American workplace	**6.** Bill Gates
2. Campaign reform	**7.** Genetic research
3. Cancer research	**8.** Global warming
4. Children and divorce	**9.** HMOs
5. Fracking	**10.** Home schooling

11. The Internet and hacking
12. Colin Powell
13. Robotics

14. School vouchers
15. Oprah Winfrey

2. **Provide your instructor with a list of the books you found that appear useful for developing your paper's topic. For each book, furnish the information specified in Exercise 1, along with a brief note indicating why you think the book will be useful.**

Database Indexes

What They Are   Databases are computerized indexes of material in academic journals, magazines, newspapers, and other formats. They allow you to search a wide range of topics by keyword or subject, and many provide access to the full article online. Other times they identify the actual print version you are searching for and where you can locate it. In general, it is helpful to explore the available databases and the kind of information they make available. Often librarians offer sessions on the database, have handouts on the available databases and their usage, or can direct you to the database that will best serve your needs.

Perhaps the best place to start a search is with a general periodical database such as *First Search* or *Article First or WilsonSelect plus*. These databases provide access to listings of articles, arranged and subdivided by subject and keyword, that have appeared in over a thousand magazines and newspapers, including the entries in various other indexes. There are more specific databases for newspapers, for business, and for many other disciplines. Some databases such as *ERIC* (Educational Resources Information Center) and *Medline* (National Library of Medicine) give you access to citations of articles appearing in professional journals in a specific area. These articles, however, are usually aimed at a specialized audience and may be difficult to comprehend. Your library may have access to a number of different indexes, including ones to regional newspapers. Below are just a very few of the more general indexes.

Index	Uses
Article First	Good broad overview of journal and article publications
Business Newsbank	Access on articles specifically on business-related issues
Facts on File	Provides access to select databases that compile information rather than access articles. The Issues and Controversies Database can be a good place to get an overview of a topic or narrow your topic
General Reference Center Gold	Access to material on a broad range of topics in journals, magazines, and newspapers
Jstor	Provides access to academic articles on academic issues, especially useful for the humanities
Lexis-Nexis Academic Universe	Access to a range of articles in journals and magazines
Lexis-Nexis Newspapers	Access to information in newspapers
Literature Resources from Gale	Specific database directed to literature-related research

Index	Uses
Newsbank Retrospective	An index of older newspaper stories from 1970 to 1991
Readers Guide Retrospective	An index to older journal, magazine, and newspaper articles
Wilson Omnifile	Access to a large range of online articles
Wilson Business	Access to business-related articles in magazines and newspapers

While sometimes you can obtain the full article directly online, sometimes the database entry offers instead an abstract—a brief summary of the articles' main points. *A word of caution: Don't mistake an abstract for the full article; an abstract is a 200- to 300-word summary of a journal article and should not be used as a source. Always take notes on the full article.* Also, do not restrict your research to just articles available online.

Figure 19.6 is an example of a database screen that allows the user to select a specific subject area, which will make the databases for that area available. Unless you are prepared to use specialty information in an area, start by reviewing General and Multidisciplinary Resources.

Often the next screen offers you a choice of different databases. Many users find FirstSearch and Wilson Select Plus as useful places to start their research, but let your topic be your guide (Figure 19.7).

Keyword Search   Most databases allow you to search for a key term. Just follow the instructions for beginning the search and then enter your key term. If, for example, your topic is "teenage suicide," type "teenagers and suicide" onto the screen that's already showing and press the search or enter key. The computer will check titles and abstracts for the key terms and provide a list of the corresponding articles. Allow ample time to explore a number of possibilities. If you try several terms related to your topic, you will find a wider variety of articles that serve your purpose. Figure 19.8 is a sample database screen where users can indicate the term or terms they intend to search and,

Figure 19.6   Initial Library Screen. From this list of database topics, choose the database that best matches the subject of your research.
Used with permission of Ferris State University

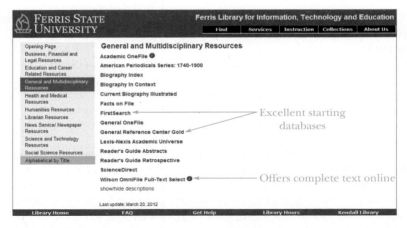

Figure 19.7 Second Library Screen. From this list of databases, you can choose those that are most likely to have resources you can use in your research papers.
Used with permission of Ferris State University

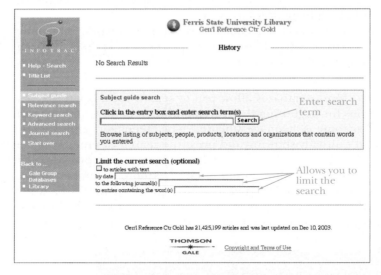

Figure 19.8 Search Screen for General Reference Center Gold.
From Gale. Infotrac Search Screen for General Reference Center Gold. © 2015, a part of Cengage Learning, Inc. Reproduced by permission. www.cengage.com/permissions. Also used by permission of Ferris State University.

if desired, select limits on the search. You would be well served by not limiting your search initially unless your teacher has placed certain restrictions on the dates of sources.

Subject Search   Because some periodical indexes, like *InfoTrac*, are organized around subject headings, it's a good idea to try a variety of subject terms because each will yield different articles. Often your keyword search results will suggest subject headings. If your entry matches a subject heading or you are referred to a cross-reference, the computer will use a series of screens to direct you to a list of articles.

Along the way, one of the screens may list subdivisions of the request being searched, as in the following example:

Acquaintance Rape, subdivisions of

—analysis	—prevention
—cases	—psychological aspects
—investigation	—research
—laws, regulations, etc.	—social aspects
—media coverage	—statistics
—moral and ethical aspects	—studying and teaching
—personal narratives	—usage

Such a list can uncover facets of your topic that you hadn't considered and that might enrich your final paper. For example, the subdivision "personal narratives" might contain an experience that would provide a powerful opening for the paper. Similarly, articles cataloged under "statistics" could provide information on the scope of the acquaintance rape problem.

Advanced Search   The final result of any search is a list of articles like the following one, obtained through General Reference Center Gold, for the search term "acquaintance rape":

The results for a search might look like the screen shot shown in Figure 19.9. Notice that several of the sources are available directly online by locating your cursor on the text choice and clicking.

This list shows that all three magazines are available in the library and that two articles are abstracted in the computer. (If the database provides the full text of an article, the notation "full text available" will appear after the citation.) The coded notation "Mag. Coll." indicates that the magazine is available on microfilm. The first two numbers and the letter in the code identify the number of the microfilm cassette. The remaining numbers indicate the microfilm page on which the article starts. The exact listings of your system may be somewhat different from what's shown here; the same kind of information, however, should be available.

Besides the previously mentioned specialized indexes, many others are available that you could use to supplement your search of general indexes. Here is a brief sampling of them:

Applied Science and Technology Index, 1958–date (indexed by subject)

Education Index, 1929–date (indexed by subject and author)

Humanities Index, 1974–date (indexed by subject and author)

International Index to Periodicals, 1907–1964 (indexed by subject and author; titled *Social Sciences and Humanities Index,* 1965–1974, and then separated into the *Humanities Index* and the *Social Sciences Index*)

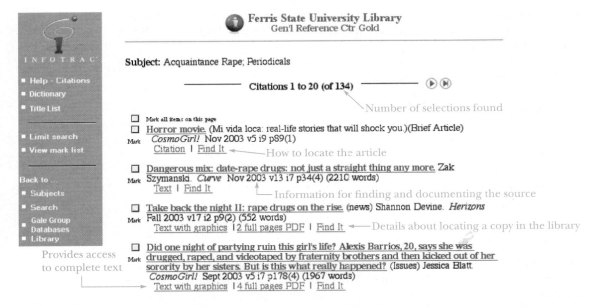

Figure 19.9 List of Results. Click on the blue underscored "Text" to see the complete article.
Used by permission of Ferris State University.

> *Social Sciences and Humanities Index,* 1965–1974 (indexed by subject and author)
>
> *Social Sciences Index,* 1975–date (indexed by subject and author)

All come in printed form, and most are also available on compact discs and online.

With periodical indexes, as with the online catalog, don't give up if a subject heading you're exploring yields few or no entries. Instead, explore related headings. For example, if your topic is teenage marriages, look also under "adolescence," "divorce," "teen pregnancies," and the like. Browse through the system and try a variety of options. Use this as an opportunity to gain different perspectives on your research project.

Obtaining the Articles If the article is available online, the database often allows you to mail the article to yourself or save the article to your computer. For references without the complete articles, print a copy of each promising reference you find. Otherwise, copy the following information into your notes.

> Author(s), if identified
> Title of article
> Name of periodical
> Volume or issue number (for professional and scholarly journals only)

Date of periodical

For newspapers, the edition name (city, metro) if more than one published, and section letter

The page range of the entire article

Name of database from which article was retrieved

URL or DOI of article, if applicable

Obtain printouts of whatever articles you can and check the topic sentences of paragraphs for essential points. Also, scan any accompanying abstracts or summaries. If an article appears useful, check to see whether it has a bibliography, which might include additional useful sources. Keep the notes for articles that seem promising—and any useful articles—and discard the others.

If the database does not indicate whether the library has the article and periodical, check the remaining references, including the ones from encyclopedia bibliographies, against the library's periodical catalog, often part of the online catalog, to see which periodicals are available and where they are located. Libraries frequently keep current issues in a periodical room or some other special section. Back issues of magazines are often kept on microfilm or bound into hardcover volumes and shelved. Most newspapers are on microfilm. Check the articles for which you don't have printouts in the same manner that you checked the others.

EXERCISE   *Select five of the following subjects and find one magazine article about   MyWritingLab each. Use at least three periodical indexes to locate the articles. List the author, if given; the title of the article; the name of the magazine; its date; the page range; and the name of the index used. Because subject categories may vary, investigate related categories, if necessary, to find an entry. To illustrate, if you find nothing under "bioengineered foods," check "genetically modified foods," or "bioaltered foods."*

1.	Animal rights	9.	Hedge funds
2.	Net neutrality	10.	Drones
3.	Paul Ryan	11.	Shaquille O'Neal
4.	Campaign finance reform	12.	Racial profiling
5.	Campus drinking	13.	Unemployment rate
6.	Corporate mergers	14.	Vegan
7.	Genetic screening	15.	X-ray astronomy
8.	Cyber warfare		

Searching the World Wide Web

The Internet includes a stupendous amount of information, much of it faulty. As a result, finding just the material you want can be difficult. To solve this problem, several *search engines* have been developed that can connect any search term or terms with potentially millions of sites that include the keywords. While studies have found that most students automatically use Google for searches, Figure 19.10 provides the addresses of several other search engines. Because the various search engines often select differently and produce different results, it's a good idea to use several engines while conducting your search.

Search Engine	Address
Google	www.google.com
Bing	www.bing.com
Yahoo	www.yahoo.com
Ask	www.ask.com

Figure 19.10 Popular Search Engines.

While each search engine works in a slightly different manner, they all provide similar sorts of information. Search engines often provide information that isn't useful. For that reason, you'll often want to narrow your search when you begin. Single terms such as "health," "cancer," or "crime" could give you a million possible sites; instead, you may want to search for "ovarian cancer" or even "ovarian cancer cures." Most search engines also let you add keywords that will further narrow what has already been found. Different words or phrases can produce different results, so try a variety of words for the same topic. It is important to be patient and scroll through several pages of search results. Often you might find a very helpful article only after scrolling through several pages of results.

You can scroll through the list of sites the engine has found. The sites are usually accompanied by a short description that may help you decide whether they are useful. If you select any highlighted words, the search engine will connect you to the selected Web page.

Evaluating Internet Material   Because anyone can post virtually anything on the Internet, it is crucial that you check the accuracy and validity of information you obtain from it. A source that sounds like a research center, for example, the Institute for Social Justice, could be a political or even a cult organization giving out one-sided or false information for its own purposes. While articles for professional journals are reviewed by experts to ensure that the information is reliable, no such safeguard exists on the Internet. Carelessly researched or ethically questionable material can and does appear. Here are some guidelines for checking the validity of an Internet source:

1. Is the source identified as a reputable professional organization, such as the American Cancer Society, a university like MIT, or a government agency like the Department of Justice? Keep in mind that anyone can use a professional-sounding name, so be alert.
2. Is there an identified author whose credentials you can check and who speaks with some authority? If there is no e-mail contact listed or you can't find another way to verify the contents of the Web site, don't use it.
3. Is the tone of the site professional? Does it maintain an objective stance and support its position with credible evidence?

4. Is the information consistent with the other material you have found? If the site disagrees with the standard information, does it offer adequate support for its claims?

5. Does the site explain how the data were obtained?

6. Does the site appear to misuse any data? For instance, is the sample too small? Are the claims pushed too far? Are the statistics biased?

Sometimes, of course, you may want to check out pages that present the views of individuals or organizations with strong but slanted positions to gain a better understanding of their thinking, but don't consider such pages to be reliable sources. When using the Internet, "Reader beware" is a prudent attitude.

E-Mail   You can use e-mail to ask knowledgeable people about your research topic and get swift answers to your questions. Use this approach, however, as a last resort since busy people have limited time. If you must contact experts, don't bother them with questions that you could easily answer by reading background material. Reserve e-mail for specific queries that defy answer after extensive research. Most search engines have clearly identified directories that allow you to look up an e-mail address if you know a person's name. Sometimes you can find the name of an expert through the Web pages of major universities. If you do get a response to your query, evaluate it carefully; an overburdened expert may dash off a quick response while doing something else.

Newsgroups   A newsgroup is a group of people who discuss a common interest by posting their responses to a common address for everyone to read. These discussions can be informal and often are not monitored; as a result, they leave something to be desired as a source for research. Still, your university system will likely give you access to newsgroups, so ask your computer center for an instruction sheet. A word of caution: Many newsgroups are intolerant of uninformed people intruding upon their conversation. Common netiquette (the etiquette of the Internet) calls for you to read what has already been written and to think before you write. Increasingly, online news stories or blogs are followed by a number of comments by those interested. While such discussions may offer ideas, remember that almost anyone can post comments without correction, so the comments may be very inaccurate.

Listservs   A listserv consists of numerous e-mail addresses that make up a mailing list of people interested in a particular topic. Once you sign up, everything posted to that listserv will be sent to your e-mail address. People who subscribe to three or four listservs may receive 30 or 40 e-mail messages every day. If you post a question on a listserv, you may get dozens of responses from professionals interested in the topic, and sorting out the validity of the different responses can be difficult. As with newsgroups, netiquette calls for you to acquire an understanding of your subject and follow the discussions on the listserv for some time before you post a question or a response. Your university computer professionals can probably supply you with instructions on how to find and sign up for a listserv. You can access a subject index of listservs at http://www.liszt.com.

FAQs Whenever you find a promising Web site, newsgroup, or listserv, you will often see a line for FAQs (frequently asked questions). It's a good idea to read the FAQs first since they may well answer your questions.

MyWritingLab **EXERCISE**

1. **Using an appropriate search engine, find information on each of the following topics:**
   a. the Vietnam War
   b. current crime statistics
   c. sexual harassment
   d. current government immigration policy

2. **Enter the name of a major university into a search engine and then search. You should find that university's home page. Try to access the university's library to find what books are available on a topic of your choice. You might try schools like Harvard, Duke, or Notre Dame.**

Creating an Annotated Bibliography

Your instructor may ask you to create an annotated bibliography, which is simply a bibliography following either the MLA (Chapter 20) or APA (Chapter 21) styles with the addition of a brief summary of the article or book and sometimes a critique. Scholars sometimes produce annotated bibliographies for publication to help other scholars have an overview of the research on a particular topic. Below is a sample entry for an annotated bibliography in MLA style.

> Anzaldua, Gloria. "La Conciencia De La Mestiza: Towards a New Consciousness." *Making Face, Making Soul/Haciendo Caras*, edited by Gloria Anzaldua, Aunt Lute Books, 1990, pp. 377–89.
>
> Gloria Anzaldua explores the concept of the mestiza, a borderlands figure pulled in multiple directions. Anzaldua narrates how this figure is simultaneously present in multiple spaces, having a foot in multiple cultures. The result of this experience, Anzaldua claims, is a tolerance for ambiguity and contradiction. Furthermore, the mestiza is here articulated as a powerful cultural figure, able to embody possibilities for change. However, there may be a danger in generalizing from one individual's experience and careful research on this cultural position would be necessary to determine its effect on those who may inhabit a space of multiple cultures.

Primary Research Findings

Besides relying on library materials, you may wish to use information obtained by conducting primary research. Chapter 22 provides detailed instructions for interviewing specialists, sending out questionnaires, and making direct observations. Before doing any type of primary research, always get your instructor's permission.

Adjusting Your Topic

After finishing your search for sources, you may need to adjust the scope and emphasis of your topic. If you start with "America's First Nuclear-Powered Submarine" but fail to turn up enough sources, you might expand your emphasis to

"America's First Nuclear-Powered Warships." On the other hand, if you're working with "America's First Nuclear-Powered Warships" and find yourself floundering in an ocean of sources, you might zero in on one type of vessel. Gathering evidence helps to develop your judgment about how many sources you need to do the job.

CASE HISTORY Once Nilofar Khanbhai had selected a focus for her topic, she began her research. Because of the contemporary nature of her topic, she began her search on the Internet using Google. She searched on a number of key terms including "Ebola," "Ebola prevention," "Ebola containment," "isolation," and "quarantine."

Next she moved to her campus database, where she started with Article First, where she similarly searched under "Ebola," "infectious disease control," "disease prevention," "isolation," and "quarantine." For more scientific articles, she searched a subject specific database: Health and Wellness Resource Center.

After she found a number of sources, Nilofar turned to the online catalog. First she searched using the key terms: "Ebola," "disease prevention," "infectious diseases," and "quarantine." She found additional subject words including "epidemiology-cases" and "communicable diseases—prevention" and also used those terms in a subject search.

Nilofar organized her search and then shared her list with a biology professor who was a specialist in infectious disease. He reviewed her sources and suggested a few additional sources. She also interviewed him, following the strategies in Chapter 22, about the university's policies on infectious disease control and its planned response to any incident of Ebola, but she determined as she began work on her paper that the information from this interview didn't fit her broader topic. She filed the interview away as something to use in a future paper.

A review of her sources demonstrated to Nilofar that she had sufficient information for her topic. One approach to thinking about a paper, her instructor indicated, was to pose a question and pose a tentative answer. Here is Nilofar's response.

Q. What are the most effective ways to control Ebola?
A. The research shows that careful isolation of infected individuals is the best way to control the disease. Quarantine, while a tempting solution, is hard to maintain and is less effective.

This answer gave Nilofar a direction and broad organization to her paper; it also served to guide her note-taking. She knew, of course, that as she did more research and took notes she might have to modify her tentative conclusion.

Taking Notes

19.4

Evaluate your sources, take notes using summary and paraphrase, and assemble a working bibliography.

To take notes, read your references carefully and record significant information. You might review or even expand your original research questions (pages 344–345) so that you can read with a better sense of purpose. Notes are the raw materials for your finished product, so develop them accurately.

Evaluating Your Sources

Evaluate your sources by considering these factors.

The Expertise of the Author Judge an author's expertise by examining his or her professional status. Say you're searching for information on some new cancer-treating drug. An article by the director of a national cancer research center would be a better bet than one by a staff writer for a magazine. Similarly, a historian's account of a national figure will probably have more balance and depth than a novelist's popularized account of that person's life. Gauging a writer's credentials is not difficult. Articles in periodicals often note authors' job titles along with their names. Some even supply thumbnail biographies. For a book, check its title page, preface, or introduction, and—if it's been left on—the dust jacket. Finally, notice whether the writer has other publications on this general subject. If your sources include two or more items by one person or if that person's name keeps cropping up as you take notes, you're probably dealing with an expert.

The Credibility of the Publication A book's credibility hinges on its approach and its reception by reviewers. Cast a cautious eye on books that take a popular rather than a scholarly approach. For research papers, scholarly treatments provide more solid fare. Weigh what reviewers said when a book first appeared. Two publications excerpt selected reviews and provide references to others. The *Book Review Digest* (1905–date) deals mainly with nontechnical works, while the *Technical Book Review Index* (1935–date) covers technical and scientific books. Turn first to the volume for the year the book came out. If you don't find any reviews, scan the next year's index. Often books published in the fall are not reviewed until the following year.

Periodical articles can also take a scholarly or popular tack. Editors of specialized journals and of some wide-circulation magazines—for example, *Scientific American* and *The Atlantic Monthly*—publish only in-depth, accurate articles. Most newsstand publications, however, popularize to some extent, and some deliberately strive for sensationalism. Popularizing may result in broad, general statements, skimpy details, and a sensational tone.

Don't automatically reject a source because the writer lacks expertise or offers a popularized treatment. Often, especially when writing about a current topic, you'll need to use material that falls short in some way. Remember, though, that you undertake research to become more knowledgeable than general readers are about a topic. When information in popular periodicals provides less than adequate coverage, candidly acknowledge the shortcomings.

Mechanics of Note Taking

There are many ways people effectively take notes: some use regular notebooks, others take notes with their computers or tablets, and many still use note cards. The goal in all these methods is the same. You need to make certain all your notes remain undividable, linked to their source, and will be easy to organize later. Table 19.1 presents some strategies.

Responding to Notes

As you take notes, reflect on your topic and try to come up with new ideas, see connections to other notes, and anticipate future research. Think of yourself as having a conversation with your sources, and jot down your responses on the

Table 19.1   Note-Taking Strategies

Medium	Taking Notes	Linking to Source	Organization
Computer or Tablet	Most people end up taking notes from an article on a single page. Separate notes on the page. Some people use a note-taking program that makes it easy to connect notes. Avoid cutting and pasting from the source and clearly indicate all quoted material with quotes.	Identify the article's bibliographical information on the top of the page. Next to each note indicate author's name, an abbreviation of the source name, and the information's page number.	Identify the subject of the note directly above the note. Later, it can be helpful to use the find function of your program to find all the related notes and group them together by subject on the same page.
Note Cards (4 × 6 cards)	Take one note per card. Staple two cards with the same note together. Be sure to mark quoted material with quotes.	Use a number linking to a bibliography with all the information. Identify author and abbreviated title on the bottom of the card. Always record page number of information.	Identify subject of the note card at the top for easy arrangement. Sometimes assign a number or color to major topics.
Notebook or Yellow Pad	In many ways similar to computers. Some people do organize their notebooks by topic and take notes accordingly.	Same as computers.	It can be difficult to try out different groupings using a notebook or yellow pad. Some people cut out the notes to rearrange them.

backs of your note cards or next to or beneath your computer notes in italics or other distinct fonts. Ask yourself these questions: Does this information agree with what I have learned so far? Does it suggest any new avenues to explore?

Does it leave me with questions about what's been said? Although it may take a few minutes to record your responses to a note, this type of analysis will help you write a paper that reflects *your* opinions, decisions, and evaluations, not one that smacks of notes merely patched together from different sources.

Types of Notes

A note can be a summary, paraphrase, or quotation. *Whenever you use any kind of note in your paper, give proper credit to your source. Failure to do so results in plagiarism—that is, literary theft—a serious offense even when committed unintentionally.* Pages 377–379 discuss plagiarism, and Chapters 20 and 21 explain proper documentation of sources. *Just as a note can be in these forms, the draft of your paper may also include a summary, paraphrase, or quotation.*

Summary   A summary condenses original material, presenting its core ideas *in your own words.* In order to write an effective summary, you must have a good grasp of the information, and this comprehension ensures that you are ready to use the material in your paper. You may include brief quotations if you enclose them in quotation marks. A properly written summary presents the main points in their original order without distorting their emphasis or meaning, and it omits supporting details and repetition. Summaries, then, serve up the heart of the matter.

Begin the summarizing process by asking yourself, "What points does the author make that have an important bearing on my topic and purpose?" To answer, note especially the topic sentences in the original, which often provide essential information. Copy the points in order; then condense and rewrite them in your own words. Figure 19.11 summarizes the Bertrand Russell passage that follows. We have underscored key points in the original.

Necessity for law

About a century and a half ago, there began a still-existing preference for impulsive actions over deliberate ones. Those responsible for this development believed that people are naturally good but institutions have perverted them. Actually, unfettered human nature breeds violence and brutality, and law is our only protection against anarchy. The law assumes the responsibility for revenge and settles disputes equitably. It frees people from the fear of being victimized by criminals and provides a means of catching them. Without it, civilization could not endure.

Russell, pp. 63–65

Figure 19.11   Summary.

Under the influence of the romantic movement, a process began about a hundred and fifty years ago, which has continued ever since—*a process of revaluing the traditional virtues,* placing some higher on the scale than before, and others lower. *The tendency has been to exalt impulse at the expense of deliberation.* The virtues that spring from the heart have come to be thought superior to those that are based upon reflection: a generous man is preferred to a man who is punctual in paying his debts. *Per contra,* deliberate sins are thought worse than impulsive sins: a hypocrite is more harshly condemned than a murderer. The upshot is that we tend to estimate virtues, not by their capacity for providing human happiness, but by their power of inspiring a personal liking for the possessors, and we are not apt to include among the qualities for which we like people, a habit of reflecting before making an important decision.

The men who started this movement were, in the main, gentle sentimentalists who imagined that, when the fetters of custom and law were removed, the *heart would be free to display its natural goodness. Human nature,* they thought, is good, but institutions have corrupted it; remove the institutions and we shall all become angels. *Unfortunately, the matter is not so simple as they thought.* Men who follow their impulses establish governments based on pogroms, clamour for war with foreign countries, and murder pacifists and Negroes. *Human nature unrestrained by law is violent and cruel.* In the London Zoo, the male baboons fought over the females until all the females were torn to pieces; human beings, left to the ungoverned impulse, would be no better. In ages that have had recent experience of anarchy, this has been obvious. All the great writers of the middle ages were passionate in their admiration of the law; it was the Thirty Years' War that led Grotius to become the first advocate of international law. *Law, respected and enforced, is in the long run the only alternative to violent and predatory anarchy;* and it is just as necessary to realize this now as it was in the time of Dante and Grotius.

What is the essence of law? On the one hand, it takes away from private citizens the right of revenge, which it confers upon the government. If a man steals your money, you must not steal it back, or thrash him, or shoot him; you must establish the facts before a neutral tribunal, which inflicts upon him such punishment as has seemed just to the disinterested legislators. On the other hand, *when two men have a dispute, the law provides a machinery for settling it,* again on principles laid down in advance by neutrals. The advantages of law are many. It diminishes the amount of private violence, and settles disagreements in a manner more nearly just than that which would result if the disputants fought it out by private war. *It makes it possible for men to work without being perpetually on the watch against bandits. When a crime has been committed it provides a skilled machine for discovering the criminal.*

Without law, the existence of civilized communities is impossible. In international law, there is as yet no effective law, for lack of an international police force capable of overpowering national armies, and it is daily becoming more evident that this defect must be remedied if civilization is to survive. Within single nations there is a dangerous tendency to think that moral indignation excuses the extra-legal punishment of criminals. In Germany an era of private murder (on the loftiest grounds) preceded and followed the victory of the Nazis. In fact, nine-tenths of what appeared as just indignation was sheer lust for cruelty; and this is equally true in other countries where mobs rob the law of its functions. In any civilized community, toleration of mob rule is the first step towards barbarism.

Bertrand Russell, "Respect for Law," *San Francisco Review,* Winter 1958, 63–65.

MyWritingLab **EXERCISE**

1. **Select two passages that your instructor approves from an essay in the Reader and prepare summaries for them.**
2. **Submit summaries of three pieces of information that you plan to use in writing your paper; also submit complete versions of the original.**

Paraphrase   To paraphrase is to restate material *in your own words* without attempting to condense it. Unlike a summary, a paraphrase allows you to present an essentially complete version of the original material. A note of caution, however: Don't copy the original source nearly verbatim, changing only a word here and there. To do so is to plagiarize. To avoid this offense, follow a read, think, and write-without-looking-at-the-original strategy when you take notes so that you concentrate on recording the information in your own words. Then verify the accuracy of your notes by checking them against the original source. Here is a sample passage; Figure 19.12 is its paraphrase.

> Over time, more and more of life has become subject to the controls of knowledge. However, this is never a one-way process. Scientific investigation is continually increasing our knowledge. But if we are to make good use of this knowledge, we must not only rid our minds of old, superseded beliefs and fragments of magic, but also recognize new superstitions for what they are. Both are generated by our wishes, our fears, and our feelings of helplessness in difficult situations.
>
> Margaret Mead, "New Superstitions for Old,"
> *A Way of Seeing*, New York: McCall, 1970. 266.

Combating Superstitions

As time has passed, knowledge has asserted its sway over larger and larger segments of human life. But the process cuts two ways. Science is forever adding to the storehouse of human knowledge. Before we can take proper advantage of its gifts, however, we must purge our minds of old and outmoded convictions, while recognizing the true nature of modern superstitions. Both stem from our desires, our apprehensions, and our sense of impotence under difficult circumstances.

Mead, p. 266

Figure 19.12   Paraphrase.

MyWritingLab **EXERCISE**   *Paraphrase a short passage from one of your textbooks, including this one. Submit a complete version of the passage with the assignment.*

Quotation   A quotation is a copy of original material. Since your paper should demonstrate that you've mastered your sources, don't rely extensively on quotations. You need practice in expressing yourself. As a general rule, avoid quotations except when

- the original displays special elegance or force
- you really need support from an authority
- you need to back up your interpretation of a passage from a literary work.

Paraphrasing a passage as well-written as the one below would rob it of much of its force.

> Man is himself, like the universe he inhabits, like the demoniacal stirring of the ooze from which he sprang, a tale of desolation. He walks in his mind from birth to death the long resounding shores of endless disillusionment. Finally, the commitment to life departs or turns to bitterness. But out of such desolation emerges the awful freedom to choose beyond the narrowly circumscribed circle that delimits the rational being.
>
> Loren Eiseley, *The Unexpected Universe*

Special rules govern the use of quotations. If, for clarity, you need to add an explanation or substitute a proper name for a personal pronoun, enclose the addition in *brackets*.

> The Declaration of Independence asserts that "the history of the present King of Great Britain [George III] is a history of repeated injuries and usurpations. . . ."

If your keyboard doesn't have brackets, insert them neatly with a dark pen.

Reproduce any grammatical or spelling errors in a source exactly as they appear in the original. To let your reader know that the original author, not you, made the mistake, insert the Latin word *sic* (meaning "thus") within brackets immediately after the error.

> As Wabash notes, "The threat to our enviroment [*sic*] comes from many directions."

If you're using the MLA documentation system and exclude an unneeded part of a quotation, show the omission with three spaced periods. Indicate omissions *within sentences* as follows:

> Writing in *The Age of Extremes*, Eric Hobsbawm observed, "What struck both the opponents of revolution and the revolutionists was that, after 1945, the primary form of revolutionary struggle . . . seemed to be guerilla warfare."

When an omission comes *at the end of a sentence* and what is actually quoted can also stand as a complete sentence, use an unspaced period followed by an ellipsis.

> In his second inaugural address, Lincoln voiced his hopes for the nation: "With malice toward none, with charity for all, with firmness in the right as God gives us to see the right, let us strive on to finish the work we are in. . . ."

Do the same when you drop *a whole sentence* within a quoted passage.

> According to newspaper columnist Grace Dunn, "Williamson's campaign will undoubtedly focus primarily on the legalized gambling issue because he hopes to capitalize on the strong opposition to it in his district. . . . Nonetheless, commentators all agree he faces an uphill fight in his attempt to unseat the incumbent."

Don't change or distort when you delete. Tampering like the following violates ethical standards:

Original passage: This film is poorly directed, and the acting uninspired; only the cameo appearance by Laurence Olivier makes it truly worth seeing.

Distorted version: This film is . . . truly worth seeing.

If the original passage you are quoting already includes ellipsis, place your own ellipsis in brackets [. . .] to distinguish your ellipsis from the one in the original. Some instructors may require you to enclose all ellipses in brackets. Follow your instructor's directions. *If you're using the APA documentation system, never enclose ellipsis within brackets.*

You can summarize or paraphrase original material but retain a few words or phrases to add vividness or keep a precise shade of meaning. Simply use quotation marks but no ellipsis.

> Presidential spokesperson Paula Plimpton notes that because of the "passionate advocacy" of its supporters, the push to roll back property taxes has been gaining momentum across the country.

When you copy a quotation onto a note card, put quotation marks at the beginning and the end so you won't mistake it for a paraphrase or a summary when you write the paper. If the quoted material starts on one page and ends on the next, use a slash mark (/) to show exactly where the shift comes. Then if you use only part of the quotation in your paper, you'll know whether to use one page number or two.

Don't expect to find a bonanza on every page you read. Sometimes one page will yield several notes, another page nothing. If you can't immediately gauge the value of some material, take it down. Useless information can be discarded later. Place a rubber band around your growing stack of note cards. Store them in a large envelope closed with a snap or string and labeled with your name and address. Submit them with your completed paper if your instructor requests.

CASE HISTORY Working bibliography in hand, Nilofar Khanbhai prepared her notes, organizing them in her laptop. Most of her notes were summaries of the source material. However, while her intent was to write most of the paper in her own language, because of the technical nature of the topic, she selected shorter quotations from authorities in the area. She was careful to mark the quotes as quotes in her notes to avoid confusion later.

As Nilofar took notes, a plan for her paper began to emerge. In the introduction, she would place the current effort to contain Ebola within the broader issue of infectious disease control; then she would explain the causes of Ebola and the narrative history of the recent epidemic. She would then explain isolation as a strategy and why it may be the most effective strategy, admit some of the concerns about isolation and the desire for a quarantine, and then explain why quarantine might not be an ideal response.

Organizing and Outlining

Next comes your formal outline, the blueprint that shows the divisions and subdivisions of your paper, the order of your ideas, and the relationships between ideas and supporting details. An outline is a tool that benefits both writer and reader.

A formal outline follows the pattern shown next:

19.5

Organize your notes to create an outline for a research paper.

```
I.
   A.
   B.
      1.
      2.
         a.
         b.
II.
```

You can see the significance of an item by its numeral, letter, or number designation and by its distance from the left margin; the farther it's indented, the less important it is. All items with the same designation have roughly the same importance.

Developing Your Outline

Developing an outline is an excellent way to think through your paper. It involves arranging material from various sources in an appropriate manner. Sorting and re-sorting your notes is a good way to proceed. First, determine the main divisions of your paper by checking the summarized notations at the tops of your notes, and then make one stack of cards for each division or organize a page of related computer notes. Next, review each stack or collection of notes carefully to determine further subdivisions and sort it into smaller stacks sections. Finally, use the stacks or sections to prepare your outline. Your word-processing program usually has an outline option that provides an outline format for you.

There are two types of formal outline: *topic* and *sentence.* A topic outline presents all entries as words, short phrases, or short clauses. A sentence outline presents them as complete sentences. To emphasize the relationships among elements, items of equal importance have parallel phrasing. Although neither is *the* preferred form, a sentence outline includes more details and also your attitude toward each idea. Many students first develop a topic outline, do additional research, and then polish and expand this version into a sentence outline. While it's easy to be sloppy in a topic outline, forming a sentence outline requires you to reach the kinds of conclusions that will be the backbone of your paper. The following segments of a topic and a sentence outline for a paper on tranquilizer dependence illustrate the difference between the two:

Topic Outline

```
  I.  The tranquilizer abuse problem
      A.  Reasons for the problem
          1.  Overpromotion
          2.  Overprescription
```

          3. Patient's misuse
             a. Dosage
             b. Length of usage
       B. Growth of the problem

Sentence Outline

     II. Tranquilizers are widely abused.
         A. Several factors account for the abuse of tranquilizers.
            1. Drug companies overpromote their product.
            2. Doctors often unnecessarily prescribe tranquilizers.
            3. Patients often do not follow their doctors' instructions.
               a. Some patients take more than prescribed doses.
               b. Some continue to use tranquilizers beyond the prescribed time.
         B. The problem of tranquilizer abuse appears to be growing.

Note that the items in the sentence outline are followed by periods, but those in the topic outline are not.

Keying Your Computer Notes or Note Cards to Your Outline

When your outline is finished, key your note cards or computer notes to it by writing at the top of each card or note the letters and numbers—such as IIA or IIIB2—for the appropriate outline category. Now arrange the cards into one stack, following the order shown in the outline, or move your computer notes into a new file in the order of the outline. If you use note cards, start with the top card in the stack and number all of them consecutively. If they later fall off the table or slide out of place, you can easily put them in order again. You might have a few stragglers left over when you complete this keying. Some of these may be worked into your paper as you write or revise it. With computer notes, resist the temptation to simply write the paper around your notes, which will produce a choppy effect. Instead, it is helpful to create an entirely new page to write the paper and draw on the notes when it meets your needs.

CASE HISTORY Organizing a first outline was easier for Nilofar because her notes were on her computer. She labeled the main points of her notes. This let her collect all her notes under related headings. Reviewing the headings of her notes, she then pulled those headings into a rough outline. She tried several possible patterns for her outline, because she could easily move topics until the logic of the paper seemed right.

Fighting Ebola with Isolation and Quarantine

Thesis statement: Isolation is effective for prevention during Ebola virus outbreaks, while quarantine's effect on prevention is counter-productive.

I. Several epidemics witnessed by people since 430 B.C.
   A. The definition of an epidemic
   B. Cases of and deaths from the worst Ebola outbreak in history
II. The origin and transmission of the Ebola virus
   A. Ebola virus transmitted from wild animals like bats
   B. The virus spreads through bodily fluids
III. History of the first Ebola outbreak
IV. The rise of isolation as a preventive method
   A. World Health Organization (WHO) 1977 guide
   B. Isolation effective during Ebola outbreak in1995
   C. Isolation could end the Ebola epidemic by January 2015
   D. Early-case isolation important to reduce transmission
V. Isolation units (IUs)
   A. General definition
   B. Design of U.S. isolation units
   C. Specialized protective gears for medical workers
VI. Maintenance and cost issues of isolation units
   A. General cost for treatment
   B. Cost of protective gear
   C. Additional costs for patients' waste disposal
   D. Hospitals' compensation
VII. Isolation's different meaning in politics and law
   A. Politicians support shutting off its border for West Africa
   B. Navarro College denied students from Ebola-hit countries
   C. Shutting off borders only brings fear and mistrust
VIII. History of quarantine
   A. Quarantine affects negatively by limiting freedom
   B. Quarantine only for significant asymptomatic transmission
   C. Quarantine may increase transmission
IX. Isolation proves more effective

This version of the outline is marked by nonparallel structure and inadequate attention to some points. Despite these weaknesses, it provided an adequate blueprint for the first draft of Nilofar's paper. You can see the final sentence outline and read the completed research paper starting on pages 401–413 in Chapter 20.

Ethical Issues

When you present the information you've gathered from a variety of sources, you'll want to proceed in an ethically responsible way. Asking and answering the following questions will help you do just that.

19.6

Write so that your research paper is ethical.

- Have I carefully researched my topic so that my conclusions are well-founded? Imagine the consequences if slipshod testing by an auto company led to the erroneous conclusion that the steering mechanism on one of its models met current safety standards.

- Have I adequately acknowledged any evidence that runs counter to the conclusions I draw? A paper that stresses the advantages of charter schools but deliberately avoids mentioning their disadvantages could be a form of deception.
- Have I properly documented my sources? Using someone else's words or ideas without giving proper credit is a form of academic dishonesty.
- Have I honestly represented the authority of my sources? If you read an article touting almond extract as a cure for cancer that was written by a practicing foot doctor, it would be dishonest to suggest that the article was written by a "prominent research scientist." Refer to someone as an "expert" only when that person's credentials warrant the label.
- Could my information have an undesirable effect on readers? If so, how can I address their concerns? A report describing a new antibiotic-resistant strain of tuberculosis might alarm some readers, and therefore the writer could provide appropriate reassurances of the limited risk to most people.

Writing Your Research Paper

19.7

Write a draft of your research paper, and include visuals to enhance your paper.

Some students think of a library research paper as a series of quotations, paraphrases, and summaries, one following the other throughout the paper. Not so. Without question, you use the material of others, but *you* select and organize it according to *your purpose. You* develop insights, and *you* draw conclusions about what you've read. You can best express your conclusions by setting your notes aside, stepping back to gain some perspective, and then expressing your sense of what you've learned. Many students find it helpful to write two or three pages on which they summarize what they want to say as well as whom they want to reach with their message and why. Like all forms of writing, research papers are written for some purpose and aimed at some audience.

DEVELOPING YOUR RESEARCH PAPER

- Identify audience and purpose.
- Brainstorm related questions.
- Research using available index.
- Narrow or adjust your topic based on initial research and reading.
- Identify key related material and take appropriate notes.
- Label notes by subject.
- Consider writing a quick draft without looking at notes to discover your direction.
- Create an outline.
- Connect notes to outline and organize notes.
- Begin writing based on outline.

Writing the First Draft

Your final research results will be expressed in a thesis. You've already drafted a tentative thesis, and now you'll probably refine or revise it to accommodate any changes in your perspective on the topic. Position the thesis in the introductory part of your paper unless you're analyzing a problem or recommending a solution; then you might hold back the thesis until later in the essay. If you do hold it back, state the problem clearly at the outset. Because of the paper's length, it's a good idea to reveal your organizational plan in your introductory section.

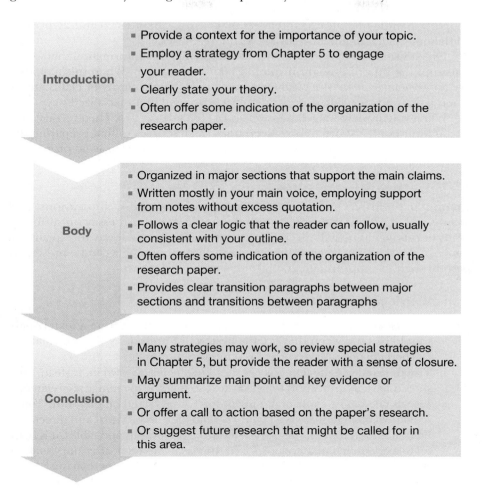

Introduction
- Provide a context for the importance of your topic.
- Employ a strategy from Chapter 5 to engage your reader.
- Clearly state your theory.
- Often offer some indication of the organization of the research paper.

Body
- Organized in major sections that support the main claims.
- Written mostly in your main voice, employing support from notes without excess quotation.
- Follows a clear logic that the reader can follow, usually consistent with your outline.
- Often offers some indication of the organization of the research paper.
- Provides clear transition paragraphs between major sections and transitions between paragraphs

Conclusion
- Many strategies may work, so review special strategies in Chapter 5, but provide the reader with a sense of closure.
- May summarize main point and key evidence or argument.
- Or offer a call to action based on the paper's research.
- Or suggest future research that might be called for in this area.

Write the paper section by section, following the divisions of your outline. But keep in mind that you're not locked into its pattern. If you see an opportunity to develop an important idea that you omitted from your outline, try it. If you discover that it might be better to introduce an item earlier than you intended, go ahead. Just be sure to check your organization later. As you write, think of yourself as supporting the conclusions you have reached with the appropriate material in your notes, not just as stringing these notes together. You, your argument, and your language should be in charge, not your sources. Some find that it can be helpful to put the sources aside, write the draft, and then go back to incorporate source material. Either way, you will then incorporate the material on your notes with your own assessments and with transitional elements that clarify your information and orient the reader. As you proceed, here again you'll use the writing strategies presented earlier in the book.

Because of this paper's length, you will probably need to connect its major sections with transitional paragraphs that pull together the material already covered and prepare the reader for what follows. Don't fret if the style bumps along or connections aren't always clear. These problems can be smoothed out when you revise. You will, of course, need to know how to document your sources properly, handle quotations, and avoid plagiarism. Chapters 20 and 21 present guidelines on documentation for MLA and APA styles.

On occasion you may want to include supplementary information that would interrupt the flow of thought if you placed it in the paper. When this happens, use an *explanatory note*.[1] A typical explanatory note might clarify or elaborate on a point, discuss some side issue, or define a term used in a specialized way.

When you finish writing, let this version sit for a day or two. Then revise it, just as you would with a shorter essay. Keep track of all sources so that preparing the bibliography will go smoothly. Check and recheck your paper to avoid plagiarism.

Using Images, Illustrations, and Graphs

Computer programs make it easy to import photographs, illustrations, and graphs into an essay and report. Visuals can be useful. An essay on different kinds of cats would be enhanced by pictures of cats. The best way to explain the bones in the skull is a labeled drawing. Complicated numbers can be presented best through the appropriate graphs or charts.

General Principles for Using Visuals

- **Use visuals only when they help.** Excess visuals detract from a text; visuals should be used when they are the best way of presenting the information. Clichéd clip art only detracts from important messages.
- **Visuals should fit the text.** Visuals shouldn't be just thrown in. Instead, they should have a connection to nearby text so that the meanings are related.
- **Visuals need to be explained.** Visuals don't always stand on their own. You need to explain to readers why they should look at the visual and direct their attention to what they should notice. With graphs and tables, it is helpful to explain first what to look for in the visual and then, after the visual, identify the major conclusion the readers could reach from the visual.
- **Visuals often need a title.** To direct the reader's attention, label all visuals. The title should tell the story of the visual.
- **Place visuals so they don't break up the text.** You want your page to be attractive but not distracting. Visuals need to be positioned so the page looks good but the flow of the text is not seriously interrupted.
- **Visuals should be honest.** It is important to represent the data fairly and not distort the image or graph to slant the information.

---

[1]This is an explanatory note. Position it at the bottom of the page, spaced four lines away from the main text. If more than one note occurs on a page, double space between them. If the note carries over to the next page, separate it from your text with a solid, full-length line. Put two spaces above the line and two spaces below it.

Pictures   The use of a scanner or digital camera makes it easy to import pictures, which can spice up the text. It is very easy to find images on the Internet related to your topic that you can download and incorporate into your paper. If you use pictures, make certain they are clear and simple. Readers shouldn't have to spend time trying to decipher the picture. Always document any image that comes from a source.

Tables   Including tables with columns and rows is an excellent way of comparing information such as the features of different computers, the quantity of sales, or even the quality of different employees. Make certain your table is clearly labeled. See Table 19.2 for an example.

Table 19.2 Use Different Classroom Media for Different Purposes

Features	Blackboard	Overhead	PowerPoint
Class Time Used	Extensive; text written out in class	Minimal; prepared before class	Minimal; prepared before class
Equipment Required	Usually in every classroom	In most classrooms or easily obtained	Limited by limited number of computers and screens
Information Presented	Text and hand-drawn images or low-resolution graphs	Text and images or graphs; variable resolutions	All text and visuals with good resolution
Flexibility in Classroom Environment	Plans can be easily changed; readily accepts new direction and student input	Limited flexibility: order can be varied between overheads; can write on blank overheads	Limited; hard to change order of presentation or enter new input

Pie Charts   Pie charts are an excellent way to present percentages or quantities of a whole. Figure 19.13 is a sample pie chart.

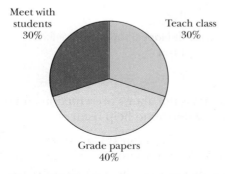

Figure 19.13   How Teachers Use Their Time.

Bar Graphs   Bar graphs can help you present and compare data that isn't a continuous trend, as Figure 19.14 shows.

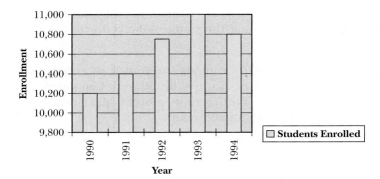

Figure 19.14   Student Enrollment Grows.

Line Graphs   Line graphs are an excellent way to show data that are continuous over time and show trends effectively. See Figure 19.15 for an example.

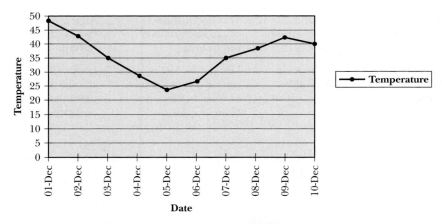

Figure 19.15   Temperatures at Noon Show Cold Spell.

Headers, Numbered Lists, and Bullets

Information in longer reports is not always presented in an unbroken stream of text. You can use a number of devices to help readers.

- **Bold headings and subheadings can guide the reader to different sections of the text.** When the sections of a longer report, or even a shorter business memo, can be broken into distinct sections, it can be helpful to label those sections with bold words or phrases that will direct the reader's attention. This text uses headings and subheadings, and so do some of the articles in the Reader.

- **Lists can be a useful way to present organized information.** Steps in a process, several recommendations, or the identification of important qualities can all be well represented by an indented list. The discussion questions in this text are all presented as numbered lists.
- **Bullets are used when listed information shouldn't be numbered because there is no implied sequence.** The recommendations for using visuals in this section are presented as a bulleted list. Lists and bullets should use parallelism, the same grammatical form.

Avoiding Plagiarism

Plagiarism occurs when a writer uses another person's material without properly acknowledging the debt. Sometimes plagiarism is deliberate, but often it happens because students simply don't understand what must be acknowledged and documented. Deliberate or not, plagiarism is absolutely unacceptable. *Any summary, paraphrase, or quotation you include in your paper must be documented as must statistics and graphics.* The only types of information escaping this requirement are those listed below:

19.8

Avoid plagiarism by integrating your sources with proper internal documentation.

1. *Common knowledge.* Common knowledge is information that most educated people would know. For instance, there's no need to document a statement that the Disney theme parks in California and Florida attract thousands of visitors each year. However, if you include precise daily, monthly, or yearly figures, then documentation is necessary.
2. *Your own conclusions.* As you write your paper, you'll incorporate your own conclusions at various points. (See the margin notes accompanying Nilofar Khanbhai's library research paper, page 411, for examples.) Such comments require no documentation. The same holds true for your own research. If you polled students on a campus issue, simply present the findings as your own.
3. *Facts found in many sources.* Facts such as the year of Shakespeare's death, the size of the 2001 national budget surplus, and the location of the Taj Mahal need not be documented. However, when there may be disputes about the facts in question (such as the size of the 2003 deficit) or when there may be some need to enforce the credibility of your figures, provide the source for your facts. If you are not certain that something is common knowledge, indicate your source.
4. *Standard terms.* Terms widely used in a particular field require no documentation. Examples include such computer terms as *mouse, CD-ROM,* and *download.*

Any piece of information not set off with quotation marks must be in your own words. Otherwise, even though you name your source, you plagiarize by stealing the original phrasing.

The following passages illustrate the improper and proper use of source material.

Original Passage

One might contend, of course, that our country's biological diversity is so great and the land is so developed—so criss-crossed with the works of man—that it will soon be hard to build a dam anywhere without endangering some species. But as we develop a national inventory of endangered species, we certainly can plan our *necessary* development so as to exterminate the smallest number possible.

James L. Buckley, "Three Cheers for the Snail Darter," *National Review*, September 14, 1979: 1144–45. Print.

■ Plagiarism

Our country's biological diversity is so great and the land is so developed that it will soon be hard to build a dam anywhere without endangering some species. But as we develop a national inventory of endangered species, we certainly can plan our necessary development so as to exterminate the smallest number possible.

This writer clearly plagiarizes. The absence of Buckley's name and the failure to enclose his words in quotation marks create the impression that this passage is the student's own work.

■ Plagiarism

Given the extensive diversity of species in America, development such as the construction of dams is likely to endanger some species, whether it is a rare plant, a species of frog, or a rare variety of fish. By creating a database of endangered species, however, we can facilitate a planning process that will place the minimum number of species at risk.

Although this writer uses original language, the absence of documentation suggests that these ideas are the student's without any recognition of Buckley's contribution. Despite the paraphrase, this is still plagiarism.

■ Plagiarism

Our country's biological diversity is so great and the land so developed that in the near future we may pose a threat to some creature whenever we construct a dam. By developing a national inventory of endangered species, however, we can plan necessary development so as to preserve as many species as possible (Buckley 1144).

This version credits the ideas to Buckley, but the student has plagiarized by failing to put quotation marks around the phrasing (underlined here) that was copied from the original. As a result, readers will think that the passage represents the student's own wording.

■ Proper Use of Original

> America has so many kinds of plants and animals, and it is so built up, that
> in the near future we may pose a threat to some living thing just by damming
> some waterway. If, however, we knew which of our nation's plants and animals
> were threatened, we could use this information to preserve as many species
> as we can (Buckley 1144).

This student has identified the author and used her own words. As a result, no plagiarism occurs.

Plagiarism is a serious offense because it robs the original writer of recognition. Students caught plagiarizing risk failure in the course or perhaps suspension from school. Whenever you are unsure whether material requires documentation, supply a reference.

Integrating and Synthesizing Sources

While the styles for documentation may vary, there are some principles you should follow. You should consistently seek to avoid plagiarism by indicating where you got information from even if you did not quote it. The following observations are related to the MLA format. You can signal the author before the information. For a more detailed account of summarizing and paraphrasing, see the section on note taking on pages 364–368.

19.9

Integrate and synthesize sources.

> According to Stephen Hawking,............. (75)

You may also place the source information after the information you got from the source by placing it in parentheses (Hawking 75).

If you paraphrased a section, you must be careful you did not directly quote large sections of the sentence. You can document paraphrases similar to other information, but it is important to clearly indicate where the paraphrase ends. Sometimes it is useful to signal that you are paraphrasing.

> To paraphrase Mark Twain,........... (32)

You are likely to have quotations in your paper. Quotes are always documented. Shorter quotes, less than five lines are marked by quotation marks. You may start by signaling the author of the quote. John Mayer argues that "........." (46). Or you may place the identifying information directly after the quote........... (Mayer 46).

Longer quotes are indented (five spaces for both MLA and APA) without quotation marks. Again, you should provide the identifying source information.

Refer to the appropriate chapter for the style you are using. Below is more detailed information on presenting quotes, using the MLA format for documentation and indentation.

■ Short Quotation

Ellen Goodman offers this further observation about writers who peddle formulas for achieving success through selfishness: "They are all Doctor Feelgoods, offering placebo prescriptions instead of strong medicine. They give us a way to live with ourselves, perhaps, but not a way to live with each other" (16).

■ Quotation within Short Quotation

The report further stated, "All great writing styles have their wellsprings in the personality of the writer. As Buffon said, 'The style is the man.'" (Duncan 49)

■ Quotation within Longer, Indented Quotation

Barbara Tuchman's *Proud Tower* presents a somewhat different view of the new conservative leaders:

> Besides riches, rank, broad acres, and ancient lineage, the new government also possessed, to the regret of the liberal opposition, and in the words of one of them, "an almost embarrassing wealth of talent and capacity." Secure in authority, resting comfortably on their electoral majority in the House of Commons and on a permanent majority in the House of Lords, of whom four-fifths were conservatives, they were in a position, admitted the same opponent, "of unassailable strength" (4).

Always provide some context for material that you quote. Various options exist. When you quote from a source for the first time, you might provide the author's full name and the source of the quotation, perhaps indicating the author's expertise as well. The passage just above omits the author's expertise; the passage below includes it.

> Writing in *Newsweek* magazine, Riena Gross, chief psychiatric social worker at Illinois Medical Center in Chicago, said, "Kids have no real sense that they belong anywhere or to anyone as they did ten or fifteen years ago. Parents have loosened the reins, and kids are kind of floundering" (74).

Or you might note the event prompting the quotation and then the author's name.

> Addressing a seminar at the University of Toronto, Dr. Joseph Pomeranz speculated that "acupuncture may work by activating a neural pain suppression mechanism in the brain" (324).

On other occasions, you might note only the author's full name and expertise.

> Economist Richard M. Cybert, president of Carnegie Mellon University, offers the following sad prediction about the steel industry's future: "It will never be as large an industry as it has been. There are a lot of plants that will never come back and many laborers that will never be rehired" (43).

After first citing an author's full name, use only the last name for subsequent references.

> In answering the objections of government agencies to the Freedom of Information Act, Wellford commented, "Increased citizen access should help citizens learn of governmental activities that weaken our First Amendment freedoms. Some administrative inconvenience isn't too large a price to pay for that" (137).

When quoting from a source with no author given, introduce the quotation with the name of the source.

> Commenting on the problems that law enforcement personnel have in coping with computer crime, *Credit and Financial Management* magazine pointed out, "A computer crime can be committed in three hundredths of a second, and the criminal can be thousands of miles from the 'scene,' using a telephone" ("Computer Crime" 43).

EXERCISE   *From the article "For Cops, Citizen Videos Bring Increased Scrutiny"*   MyWritingLab
(pages 524–528) summarize paragraphs 19–34 and create a paraphrase of paragraph 9. Assume the original source of USA Today *online edition. Page A1. Published 3/14/2011.*
Indicate if each of the following statements used in a paper that drew on a reading of "For Cops, Citizen Videos Bring Increased Scrutiny" is plagiarism or not and why.

1. Almost all phones include a video camera, allowing almost anyone to capture any event, including crimes of any kind, including poor conduct by the police.
2. Video has helped to resolve many instances of police misbehavior, but such images also can present a more varied account of officer behavior (Johnson A1).

3. A video of a beating that a University Maryland student received from a police officer received more than 200,000 hits on YouTube.
4. There are police officers who are concerned that the possibility of being video recorded while conducting their duty might cause them to hesitate when they need to act (Johnson A1).
5. The police in a few states have tried "to limit such recordings when they believe those recordings interfere with police actions" (Johnson A1).
6. According to the training officer for the Sheriff's office in Broward County, "her agency knows firsthand the power of video and has learned from it."

CASE HISTORY Using her outline and thesis statement as a guide, Nilofar prepared a first draft of her paper, following the MLA format required by her instructor. It didn't all come easily. In order to ensure an effective presentation, she checked her notes carefully to determine which material would provide the strongest support for her conclusions since she had much more material than she could use. She was careful to use her own words except when she was quoting. Given the technical nature of her topic, Nilofar took special pains to write using language her audience would understand and to avoid more technical medical terminology. To achieve smoothness, she tried to connect her major sections with transitions, aware that she could polish these connections when she revised the paper.

When she had completed the first draft, Nilofar set it aside for two days in order to distance herself from her writing. Then she returned to it and revised it carefully. Reading the paper from the perspective of a slightly skeptical critic, she looked for unsupported claims, questions that readers might have, sections that might be confusing or poorly organized, and weak transitions. Like most writers, Nilofar found sections that could be improved and places where she needed to make the language more appropriate for her audience. Next, she revised her initial topic outline and followed it when drafting the sentence outline that appears on pages 401–402. Nilofar then prepared the final draft of the paper itself, which begins on page 403. Direct your attention to its noteworthy features, which include italicized notations next to the paper indicating where Nilofar used the writing strategies discussed earlier in the text.

Preparing Your Finished Copy

19.10

Prepare a finished copy of your research paper.

Follow the revision guidelines in Chapter 4. In addition, verify that you have:

- included all key information
- clearly organized your material
- not overloaded your paper with quotations
- worked in your own observations
- put in-text documentation and source information in proper form

Prepare your final draft with a word-processing program. Be sure you have access to a laser or inkjet printer that produces dark, readable copy. Double-space throughout, including indented block quotations and the list of works you used to prepare the paper.

Two systems for formatting and documenting library research papers are in common use: the Modern Language Association (MLA) system, favored by many English and humanities instructors, and the American Psychological Association (APA) system, used by many social science and psychology instructors.

Writing Your Research Paper Checklist

Search Checklist

19.11

Use a checklist to plan your research paper from start to finish.

- Brainstorm to focus your topic.
- Get an overview by searching general references such as encyclopedias.
- Search your library for books.
    Use either key term or subject searches using a computer catalog.
    Copy or print out the call number that locates the book.
    Scan the books in your located section for unexpected finds.
- Search your periodical indexes and databases.
    Select an index or database that fits your topic.
    InfoTrac and Wilson Select are often useful starting indexes.
    Use either key term or subject searches.
    Use the headings you find to narrow or guide your search.
    Print or copy the title of the articles, the author, the magazine, the
        volume number, the page number, and the date.
    If you use a full text of an online article, be sure to copy the reference
        information.
    Find the hard copy, microfiche, or microfilm version of your article.
- Search the Internet.
    Use an appropriate search engine, such as Google or Yahoo.
    Try several combinations of terms or modify them to narrow a
        search.
    Assess the credibility of all Internet sources based on the source for
        the site, author, quality of the Web pages, consistency with other
        credible information.
    Be sure to copy or print the URL, DOI (digital object identifier),
        author (if any), and title (if any).

Taking Notes Checklist

- Evaluate your source by author's qualification, publication's credibility,
    and obvious bias.
- Take notes using cards, yellow pad, or computer file.
    Keep track of source and page number for each note.
    You may want to cross-reference notes with bibliography cards.
    Give a title to each note card that identifies the notes topic.
- Respond as you take notes with your own thoughts and observations.

- Consciously decide to summarize, paraphrase, or quote in your notes.
    If you paraphrase, it must be completely in your own words.
    If you quote, be sure to mark your quotes so you don't forget.
- Always consciously work to avoid plagiarism.
    Always carefully record your sources for notes.
    Do not simply change a few words in a paraphrase.
    Do not forget to mark quotes when you quote.
    Ask your teacher or a tutor if you are not sure of the rules.

Drafting Your Paper Checklist

- Take steps to integrate your information.
    Read over your notes.
    Possibly write a brief draft without looking at your notes.
- Write an outline.
    Determine the main divisions of your paper.
    Read note cards for subdivisions.
    Detail either a sentence or topic outline.
- Key your note cards to your outlines.
- Determine if you need to perform additional research.
- Draft your paper in sections.
    Work to keep the paper in your own voice.
    Don't get stuck on the introduction. Just write.
    Use your notes to support your claims but don't just cut and paste.
    Be sure to document as you write.
    Avoid plagiarism.
    Create deliberate transitions between sections.
    Go back and rework the introduction and conclusion.
    Carefully document using the material from the next chapter.

Revising Your Draft Checklist

- Do not be afraid to make extensive changes.
- Read and change the paper with an eye to your original purpose.
- Get feedback from other readers.
- Check for material that doesn't fit and needs to be cut.
- Check for holes that may require additional research and do it if needed.
- Check your notes to see that you didn't leave out something important.
- Check to see that the paper is easy to follow.
- Smooth your transitions and add transition paragraphs where needed.
- Make certain the draft is in a consistent voice.

CHAPTER 20
Documenting Sources: MLA Style

In this chapter, you will learn how to:

20.1 Prepare papers using the MLA system.

20.2 Prepare bibliographic references using the MLA style.

20.3 Follow MLA style to cite sources in your essay.

20.4 Integrate and cite quotations using the MLA style.

Visit MyWritingLab **to complete the writing assignments in this chapter and for more resources on MLA documentation style.**

In order to acknowledge and handle sources, you must know how to (1) prepare proper bibliographical references and (2) document sources within your text.

The kind of information included in bibliographical references depends on the type of source and the documentation system. Two most common systems are the Modern Language Association (MLA) system and the American Psychological Association (APA) system. There are other styles such as the Chicago Manual of Style that are used for other purposes. This chapter presents the MLA style. Chapter 21 presents the APA style. The MLA style is often used for papers in the humanities.

For more information, consult the *MLA Handbook*, 8th ed., 2016.

MLA System for Preparing Papers

- Number each page in the upper right corner, one-half inch from the top. Precede each page number with your last name.
- Starting one inch from the top of the first page, type your full name, the instructor's name, the course designation, and the date, all flush with the left margin.
- Double-space below the date, and center the title; then double-space before starting the first paragraph.
- Leave one-inch margins on all four sides except at the top of the first page. Indent the first line of each paragraph five spaces or one-half inch.

20.1

Prepare papers using the MLA system.

MLA

- The MLA system does not require a title page. If your instructor wants one, however, center (1) the title of the paper about two inches below the top of the sheet, (2) your name in the middle of the sheet, and (3) the instructor's name, course designation, and date about two inches from the bottom. Use capital and lowercase letters for everything. Repeat the title, again in capital and lowercase letters, on the first text page, centered about two inches from the top.
- Begin the bibliography on a new page that follows the text of the paper and give it the heading "Works Cited," without quotation marks. Center the heading on the page.
- List each bibliographic entry alphabetically according to the author's last name or, if no author is given, by the first significant word in the title. For a work with more than one author, alphabetize by the name that comes first.
- If there's more than one entry for an author, substitute three unspaced hyphens, followed by a period and a double space, for the author's name in the second and subsequent entries.
- Begin the first line of each entry at the left margin and indent subsequent lines five spaces.

Preparing Proper MLA Bibliographic References

20.2

Prepare bibliographic references using the MLA style.

The *MLA Handbook*, 8th edition, sets forth a concise set of guidelines to help you create your Works Cited list in the proper format. The following are the elements of a Works Cited entry, in the order in which they appear in the entry. Note that many sources will not contain all of these elements.

- **Author** can contain other identifying information, such as "editor," "director," or "translator." Each of these identifiers should be spelled out rather than abbreviated. Different rules apply to Works Cited entries with one author, two authors, and three or more authors.
- The **title of source** includes both the title and the subtitle.
- **Container** is the term that MLA uses for any type of print or electronic medium. A container may be a book, newspaper, journal, Website, film, email, podcast, lecture, and so on. One container can be nested inside a larger container. For example, a scholarly journal (the first container) may be found inside a larger container, such as the ProQuest academic database (the second container). When one container is nested inside another, both containers should be documented. Use a period to separate the two containers. Place the "inside" container first and the "outside" container second.
- **Other contributors** are people who played a role in creating or contributing to the source. Other contributions include, but are not limited to, "drawings by," and "translated by," and "adapted by."

- **Version** is the version you are citing (for example, the third edition of a textbook, or the city edition of a newspaper).
- **Number** refers to identifying numbers (for example, "vol. 14, no. 26"). Volume and issue numbers are commonly found in scholarly journals.
- **Date of publication** should be as specific as possible. For books, usually the year alone is sufficient; most books' copyright pages list a year of publication, but not a month or a day. Scholarly journals often provide a month and year of publication. Newspapers, Websites, and blog posts usually provide month, day, and year.
- **Location** refers to (1) page numbers in a print work and (2) a URL (uniform resource locater, or Web address) or DOI (digital object identifier) in an online source. MLA prefers DOIs over URLs because DOIs are more stable, while URLs can disappear overnight. Do not include "http://" or "https://" in URLs, but do include "www" if it is part of the URL. If an online source does not provide a publication date anywhere on the page, complete the Works Cited entry by specifying the date you accessed the URL.

The following blueprints will help you track the information you need and help you to create each entry in your MLA Works Cited list. Notice the punctuation following each element, and use the same punctuation in your entries. You can also visit the MLA's help center online at https://style.mla.org.

Works Cited Entry: Print Source

Author.	Block, Joel W.
Title of source.	"Sodom and Gomorrah: A Volcanic Disaster."
Title of container,	*Journal of Geological Education*,
Other contributors,	
Version,	
Number,	vol. 23, no. 5,
Publisher,	
Publication date,	1976,
Location.	pp. 74–77.

Works Cited Entry: Online Source

Author.	Meltzer, Martin I., et al.
Title of source.	"Estimating the Future Number of Cases in the Ebola Epidemic—Liberia and Sierra Leone, 2014–2015."
Title of first container,	*Centers for Disease Control and Prevention*,
Other contributors,	
Version,	
Number,	vol. 63, no. 3,
Publisher,	
Publication date,	16 Sept. 2014,
Location.	www.cdc.gov/mmwr/preview/mmwrhtml/su6303a1.htm.

Books

■ A Book with One Author

Wilk, Max. *Every Day's a Matinée.* W. W. Norton, 1975.

Spell out publishers' names in full. However, you may abbreviate publishers that are university presses. For example, Cambridge University Press may be abbreviated as "Cambridge UP."

■ A Book with Two Authors

List both authors in the format shown.

Duncan, Dayton, and Ken Burns. *Lewis and Clark.* Alfred A. Knopf, 1997.

■ A Book with Three or More Authors

List only the first author, followed by *et al.* (which means "and others").

Alder, Roger William, et al. *Mechanisms in Organic Chemistry.* John Wiley & Sons, 1971.

■ A Book with a Title That Includes Another Title

Set off the title of the mentioned work with quotation marks.

Tanner, John. *Anxiety in Eden: A Kierkegaardian Reading of "Paradise Lost."* Oxford UP, 1992.

■ A Book with Corporate or Association Authorship

Local Government Training. United Nations, Public Administration Division, 1968.

■ An Edition Other than the First

Turabian, Kate L. *A Manual for Writers of Term Papers, Theses, and Dissertations.* 6th ed., U of Chicago P, 1996.

■ A Book in Two or More Volumes

Bartram, Henry C. *The Cavalcade of America.* Alfred A. Knopf, 1959. 2 vols.

■ A Reprint of an Older Work

Matthiessen, F. O. *American Renaissance: Art and Expression in the Age of Emerson and Whitman.* 1941. Oxford UP, 1970.

■ A Book with an Editor Rather than an Author

Deetz, James, editor. *Man's Imprint from the Past: Readings in the Methods of Archaeology.* Little, Brown, 1971.

■ A Book with Both an Author and an Editor

Melville, Herman. *The Confidence Man.* Edited by Hershel Parker, W. W. Norton, 1971.

■ A Translation

Beauvoir, Simone de. *All Said and Done.* Translated by Patrick O'Brian, Putnam, 1974.

■ An Essay or Chapter in a Collection of Works by One Author

Woolf, Virginia. "The Lives of the Obscure." *The Common Reader, First Series,* Harcourt, 1925, pp. 111–18.

■ An Essay or Chapter in an Anthology

Angell, Roger. "On the Ball." *Subject and Strategy,* edited by Paul Eschholz and Alfred Rosa, St. Martin's Press, 1981, pp. 34–41.

Periodicals

Periodicals include newspapers, popular magazines, and specialized occupational and scholarly journals. The basic information for a periodical article includes the name of the article's author, name of the periodical, title of the article, date of publication, page range of the entire article, and, for scholarly journals and some magazines, the volume and issue number. Capitalize periodical titles.

■ An Article in a Scholarly Journal Consecutively Paged through the Entire Volume

Pfennig, David. "Kinship and Cannibalism." *Bioscience,* vol. 47, 1997, pp. 667–75.

■ An Article in a Scholarly Journal that Pages Each Issue Separately

Block, Joel W. "Sodom and Gomorrah: A Volcanic Disaster." *Journal of Geological Education,* vol. 23, no. 5, 1976, pp. 74–77.

■ An Unsigned Article in a Scholarly Journal

"Baby, It's Cold Inside." *Science,* vol. 276, 1997, pp. 537–38.

■ A Signed Article in an Occupational or Popular Magazine

Gopnik, Adam. "The Good Soldier." *The New Yorker,* 24 Nov. 1997, pp. 106–14.

■ An Unsigned Article in an Occupational or Popular Magazine

"Robot Productivity." *Production Engineering,* May 1982, pp. 52–55.

■ A Signed Article in a Daily Newspaper

Wade, Nicholas. "Germ Weapons: Deadly but Hard to Use." *The New York Times,* 26 Nov. 1997, natl. ed., pp. A13+.

■ An Unsigned Article in a Daily Newspaper

"The Arithmetic of Terrorism." *The Washington Post,* 14 Nov. 1997, p. A26.

Encyclopedia Articles

When documenting familiar works, such as the *Encyclopedia Americana,* the basic information for the MLA system includes the name of the article's author if known, the title of the article, the name of the encyclopedia, and the date of the edition.

Sobieszek, Robert A. "Photography." *World Book Encyclopedia,* 1991 ed.

The MLA system requires additional information when less familiar publications are documented.

Fears, J. Rufus. "Emperor's Cult." *Encyclopedia of Religion,* edited by Mircea Eliade, Macmillan, 1987, pp. 246-48. 16 vols.

For an anonymous article, the Works Cited entry begins with the article's title.

Government Documents

The basic information for a federal, state, or foreign government publication includes the name of the author, title of the publication, name of the government and agency issuing the publication, name of the printing or publishing group, if known, and date. When using a government as the author, arrange the government organizations from the largest entity to the smallest, as in the entry for *The Biology of Mental Disorders* below.

Carpenter, Russell D. *Defects in Hardened Timber.* Forest Service, United States Department of Agriculture, Government Printing Office, 1989.

Asbestos in the Home. Consumer Products Safety Commission, U.S. Environmental Protection Agency, Government Printing Office, 1989.

United States, Congress, Office of Technology Assessment. *The Biology of Mental Disorders.* Government Printing Office, 1992. 102nd Cong., 2nd session.

Other Sources

■ Book Reviews

Koenig, Rhoda. "Billy the Kid." Review of *Billy Bathgate,* by E. L. Doctorow. *New York,*
    20 Feb. 1989, pp. 20–21.

If the review is untitled, follow the above format but omit the missing element.

■ Published Interviews

Noriega, Manuel. "A Talk with Manuel Noriega." Interview by Felipe Hernandez. *News
    Report,* 20 Mar. 1997, pp. 28–30.

■ Personal Interviews

If you conducted the interview yourself, start with the name of the person interviewed and follow it with the kind of interview and the date conducted.

Newman, Paul. Personal interview. 18 May 2001.

■ Audiovisual Media

Frankenstein. Directed by James Whale, performances by Boris Karloff, John Boles, Colin
    Clive, and Mae Clarke, Universal, 1931.

If you are interested in the contribution of a particular person, start with that
person's name. Use the same model for videocassette and DVD recordings and
add release dates and distributors.

Whale, James, director. *Frankenstein.* Performances by Boris Karloff, John Boles, Colin
    Clive, and Mae Clarke, Universal, 1931.

Whale, James, director. *Frankenstein.* Performances by Boris Karloff, John Boles, Colin
    Clive, and Mae Clarke, Universal, 1931, Lion's Gate, 1999.

■ Television and Radio Programs

Washington Week in Review. Produced by S. Ducat. WKAR Television Network, East Lan-
    sing, MI, 6 Jan. 1995.

Use the following format when additional information is pertinent:

Peril at End House. By Agatha Christie, adapted by Clive Exton, directed by Renny Rye,
    produced by Brian Eastman. Performances by David Suchet and Hugh Fraser.
    Mystery, introduced by Diana Rigg, WKAR Television Network, East Lansing, MI,
    12 Aug. 1993.

■ Music and Sound Recordings

Smith, Bessie. *The World's Greatest Blues Singer*. Columbia, 1948.

Smith, Bessie. "Down Hearted Blues." *The World's Greatest Blues Singer*, Columbia, 1948.

■ CD-ROMs

Norman, J. L. "Barcelona." *Software Toolworks Multimedia Encyclopedia*, Grolier, 1996. Disc 1.

Online Sources

Often data from the Internet are incomplete, perhaps lacking an author, a title, or page or paragraph number. Include all the available, relevant information.

■ E-Books

The *MLA Handbook* makes no distinction between e-books read on an e-reader (such as an Amazon Kindle) and print books. However, if you read a book on a Website, be sure to include information about the container (for example, Project Gutenberg).

Defoe, Daniel. *Moll Flanders*. 1722. *Project Gutenberg*, www.gutenberg.org/files/370/370-h/370-h.htm.

Treat a chapter in an online book similar to a print chapter.

Free, Melissa. "The Doll's Dress Maker, the Doctor's Assistant, and the Limits of Difference." *Victorian Freaks: The Social Context of Freakery in Britain*, edited by Marlene Tromp, Ohio State UP, 2008, pp. 198-210, hdl.handle.net/1811/31838.

■ Periodicals on the World Wide Web

Periodicals online include specialized occupational and scholarly journals, popular magazines, newspapers, and newsletters. The basic information for a periodical includes the author's name, if known; the title of the article; the title of the periodical; the volume and issue numbers, if applicable; the date the article was published; the article's page numbers (if given); the online address (URL or DOI); and the date of retrieval if the online material is not dated.

Navarro, Mireya. "Women in Sports Cultivating New Playing Fields." *The New York Times*, 13 Feb. 2001, www.nytimes.com/2001/02/13/sports/13WOME.html?pagewanted=all.

"No Link Found in Violence, Videos." *Boston Globe*, 8 Aug. 2000, www.bostonglobe.com/news/2000/08/08/no-link-found-violence-videos.

Bouffard, Suzanne. "Learning from Our Students." *Harvard Education Letter,* vol. 31,

   no. 3, May/June 2015, hepg.org/hel-home/issues/31_3/helarticle/learning-

   from-our-students.

■ Editorials and Letters to the Editor

Indicate after the title that it is an editorial or a letter.

"Expanding Community College Access." Editorial. *The New York Times,* 15 Jan. 2015,

   www.nytimes.com/2015/01/15/opinion/expanding-community-college-access.

   html?_r=0.

■ Periodicals Accessed through an Online Library Service or Large Network Provider

Full-text articles are available online at libraries or at home through services such as LexisNexis, ProQuest Direct, Academic Search Complete, and
JSTOR. Cite the author's name, if known; the title of the article; the title of
the periodical; the volume and issue number; the date the article was published; the page numbers for the article (if the service identifies only the
initial page of the article, indicate the page followed by a plus sign: 132+);
and the URL or DOI.

   In the entry below, note that the Work Cited contains two containers: the
Journal of Modern Literature and the JSTOR academic database.

Cervetti, Nancy. "In the Breeches, Petticoats, and Pleasures of Orlando." *Journal of*

   Modern Literature, vol. 20, no. 2, Winter 1996, pp. 165-75. *JSTOR,* www.jstor.org/

   stable/3831473?seq=1#page_scan_tab_contents.

■ Encyclopedia Articles

The basic information for an encyclopedia article accessed through the Web includes the author's name, if known; title of the article; name of the encyclopedia; date of the edition; URL; and date of access (because online encyclopedias
are frequently updated).

Daniel, Ralph Thomas. "The History of Western Music." *Encyclopaedia Britannica*

   Online, 14 Apr. 2016, www.britannica.com/art/Western-music. Accessed

   2 Sept. 2016.

■ Government Documents

The basic information for a government document includes the name of the
author, if known; the title; the name of the government and agency issuing the
document; the publisher or printing group, if known; the date of publication;
the online address; and the date of access if the source does not indicate a publication date. When an organization is both author and publisher, begin with the
title and list the organization only as the publisher.

Alternatives to Incarceration. Georgia State, Probation Division of the Georgia
Department of Corrections, 1 July 1997, www.dcor.state.ga.us/AboutGDC/
Alternatives.

■ Web Sites

The basic information for a personal home page includes the name of its origi-
nator, if known; the title of the site in italics, if any (use *Home page* or other such
description if no title is given); the publisher or sponsor of the site; the date of
the latest update; and the date the material was retrieved from the site if the material cited does not have a publication date specified on the page.

"About Alzheimer's. Disease." *Alzheimer's Foundation of America (AFA)*, www.alzfdn.org/
AboutAlzheimers/definition.html. Accessed 4 Sept. 2016.

Mysterious Matters. Home page, mysteriousmatters.typepad.com. Accessed 6 Sept. 2016.

Social Media and E-Mail

■ Blogs

Cinelli, Bernardo. "Shale Gas Spreads to the South." *GE Global Research,* 13 Nov. 2014,
www.geglobalresearch.com/blog/shale-gas-spreads-south.

■ Facebook

NASA Johnson Space Center. "Nothing to Squirm About: Space Station Worms Help
Battle Muscle and Bone Loss." *Facebook*, 14 Jan. 2015.

■ Tweet

Costello, Carol. "Father of terror suspect #ChristopherLeeCornell says there's no way
his son plotted this attack on the U.S. Capitol by himself @CNN." 15 Jan. 2015,
9:04 AM, twitter.com/carolcnn/status/742353032822685696.

■ Listserv or Discussion Group

Graffeo, Clarissa. "Medical Comics." *International Association for the Fantastic in the Arts
Listserv,* 8 Jan. 2015, www.iafa-ls.com/med-com99887090765498.

■ E-Mail

Begin with the sender's name. Use the subject line of the email as the title.

Nicholson, Brad. "Casino Gambling." Email received by Jason Elridge, 2 Feb. 2010.

EXERCISE

1. **Using the MLA system, write a proper reference for each of the unstyled information sets that follow:**

    a. A book titled Gas Conditioning Fact Book. The book was published in 1962 by Dow Chemical Company in Midland, Michigan. No author is named.

    b. An unsigned article titled Booze Plays a Big Role in Car Crashes. The article was published in the November 28, 1997, state edition of the Detroit News. It appears on page 2 of section C.

    c. An essay written by C. Wright Mills and titled The Competitive Personality. The essay appeared in a collection of Mills's writings titled Power, Politics, and People. The collection was published in 1963 by Ballantine Books in New York. The book is edited and introduced by Irving Louis Horowitz. The essay appears on pages 263 through 273.

    d. An unsigned article titled Global Warming Fears on Rise. The article was published in the October 25, 1997, issue of Newswatch magazine. It appears on pages 29 to 31.

    e. A book written by Paul Theroux and titled The Kingdom by the Sea. The book was published in 1983 by the Houghton Mifflin Company in Boston.

    f. A book written by Kate Chopin and titled The Awakening. The book, edited by Margaret Culley, was published in 1976 by W. W. Norton and Company in New York.

    g. An article written by James E. Cooke and titled Alexander Hamilton. The article appears on pages 31 and 32 of the World Book Encyclopedia, Volume 9, published in 1996.

    h. An article written by Sarah McBride and titled Young Deadbeats Pose Problems for Credit-Card Issuers. The article was published in the November 28, 1997, Midwest edition of the Wall Street Journal. It appears on pages 1 and 6 of section B.

    i. A book written by Magdalena Dabrowski and Rudolph Leopold and titled Egon Schiele. The book was published in 1997 by the Yale University Press in New Haven, Connecticut.

    j. A book written by Jean Descola and titled A History of Spain. The book, translated by Elaine P. Halperin, was published in 1962 by Alfred A. Knopf in New York.

    k. An article written by John T. Flanagan and Raymond L. Grimer and titled Mexico in American Fiction to 1850. The article was published in 1940 in a journal called Hispania. It appears on pages 307 through 318. The volume number is 23.

    l. A United States government document titled Marine Fisheries Review. It was published by the National Marine Fisheries Service of the U.S. Department of Commerce in 1993 and is available from the Government Printing Office. No author is given.

    m. A book written by David Kahn and titled The Codebreakers. The second edition of the book was published in 1996 by Scribner's in New York.

    n. A book written by Joseph Blotner and titled Faulkner: A Biography. The book was published in two volumes in 1974 by Random House in New York.

    o. An article written by Calvin Tompkins and titled The Importance of Being Elitist. The article was published in the November 24, 1997, issue of the New Yorker. It appears on pages 58 through 69.

    p. A book written by Thomas Beer and titled Stephen Crane: A Study in American Letters. The book was published in 1923 and reprinted in 1972 by Octagon Books in New York.

    q. A review of a book written by Jacques Barzun and titled The Culture We Deserve. The review, by Beth Winona, appeared in the March 1989 issue of American Issues magazine and was titled Barzun and Culture. It appeared on pages 46 through 50.

    r. An interview of playwright Neil Simon. The interview was titled Neil Simon on the New York Theater and appeared in the September 3, 1997, issue of the Long Island News, on pages C4 and C5. The interviewer was Pearl Barnes.

    s. A film titled Casablanca. The film was directed by Michael Curtiz and starred Humphrey Bogart, Ingrid Bergman, Claude Rains, and Paul Henreid. It was released in 1942 by Warner Brothers.

    t. A television program titled Grizzly. It appeared on WNTR, New York, on February 3, 1997. The station is part of the CBS network.

    u. An online article with no author titled Robert Frost: A Reader Response Perspective. The article appears on the online journal Off the Wall and had a location of http://www.offthewall.com/articles/backdated_bin_RobertFrost_archive.html. The article is listed with the date May 8, 2003, but you found it on January 4, 2004.

    v. An article written by May Gottchalk and titled Reconsidering Dyslexia that you accessed through a database. The article was published in the May 24, 2002, issue of Education Matters, and you retrieved the article using Wilson Select on November 22, 2003, on the Ferris State University Library Web Database Access with the address http://library.ferris.edu/databaseframes.html.

    w. A personal page by Randy Cordial titled My Best Science Fiction Movies Ever. You found the web page on May 4, 2004, at http://www.cordial.com/bestscifi.htm.

2. **Prepare a proper MLA reference for each of the works you plan to use in writing your paper.**

3. **Prepare an annotated bibliography, explained on page 360, using MLA style for each of the works you have reviewed for your paper.**

Handling In-Text Citations

20.3

Follow MLA style to cite sources in your essay.

The MLA system uses notations that appear within the text and are set off by parentheses. The citation consists of the last name of the author and the page number of the publication in which the material originally appeared.

Basic Citation Form

■ Bibliographic Reference with One Author

Rothenberg, Randall. "Life in Cyburbia." *Esquire*, Feb. 1996, pp. 56–63.

■ Passage and Citation

A mania for the Internet has invaded . . . our poorest children have a stake in the Internet (Rothenberg 59).

Rothenberg states that a mania for the Internet . . . have a stake in the Internet (59).

■ Bibliographic Reference with Two Authors

Weider, Benjamin, and David Hapgood. *The Murder of Napoleon.* Congdon & Weed, 1982.

■ Passage and Citation

Four different autopsy reports were filed. . . . Nevertheless, cancer has become accepted as the cause (Weider and Hapgood 72).

■ Bibliographic Reference with Three or More Authors

If a source has more three or more authors use "*et al.,*" meaning "and others," for all but the first-named author.

Baugh, Albert C., et al. *A Literary History of England.* Appleton, 1948.

■ Passage and Citation

Although no one knows . . . writing plays together (Baugh et al. 573).

Authors with the Same Last Name

If your citations include authors with the same last name, use the initials of their first names to distinguish them.

■ Bibliographic Reference

Adler, Jerry. "Search for an Orange Thread." *Newsweek,* 16 June 1980, pp. 32–34.

Adler, William L. "The Agent Orange Controversy." *Detroit Free Press,* 18 Dec. 1979, state
    ed., p. B2.

■ Passage and Citation

As early as 1966, government . . . miscarriages, liver abscesses, and nerve damage
(J. Adler 32).

Separate Works by the Same Author

If your references include two or more works by the same author, add shortened forms of the titles to your in-text citation. Put shortened book titles in italics and use quotation marks around article and essay titles.

■ Bibliographic Reference

Mullin, Dennis. "After U.S. Troops Pull Out of Grenada." *U.S. News & World Report,*
    14 Nov. 1983, pp. 22–25.

- - -. "Why the Surprise Move in Grenada—and What Next." *U.S. News & World Report,* 7 Nov. 1983, pp. 31–34.

■ Passage and Citation

As the rangers evacuated students, . . . and free the governor (Mullin, "Why" 33).

Two Sources for the Same Citations

If two sources provide essentially the same information and you wish to mention both in one parenthetical citation, alphabetize them according to their authors' last names, list them with a semicolon between them, and position the citation as you would any other citation. Citations in MLA style do not need to be listed alphabetically.

■ Bibliographic Reference

Bryce, Bonnie. "The Controversy over Funding Community Colleges." *Detroit Free Press,* 13 Nov. 1988, state ed., pp. A4-A6.

Warshow, Harry. "Community College Funding Hits a Snag." *Grand Rapids Press,* 15 Nov. 1988, city ed., pp. A2-A3.

■ Passage and Citation

In contending that a 3% reduction in state funding, . . . enrollment was expected to jump by 15% during the next year (Warshow A2; Bryce A4).

Unsigned References

When you use a source for which no author is given, the in-text citation consists of all or part of the title, and the appropriate page numbers.

■ Bibliographic Reference

"Money and Classes." *The Progressive,* Oct. 1997, p. 10.

■ Passage and Citation

According to the General Accounting Office, repairing . . . many billions more ("Money" 10).

Citing Quotations

Set off quotations fewer than five lines long with quotation marks and run them into the text of the paper. For longer quotes (five lines or more), omit the quotation marks and indent the material five spaces (one-half inch) from the left margin. Double-space the typing. If you quote part or all of one paragraph, don't further indent the first line. If you quote two or more consecutive paragraphs, indent each one's first line three additional spaces.

20.4

Integrate and cite quotations using the MLA style.

Use single quotation marks for a quotation within a shorter quotation and double marks for a quotation within a longer, indented quotation. There are more detailed examples in Chapter 19. When the quotation is run into the text, position the citation as shown in the following examples.

■ Bibliographic Reference

Schapiro, Mark. "Children of a Lesser God." *Harper's Bazaar,* Apr. 1996, pp. 205+.

■ Passage and Citation

UN investigators who have studied the extent of child labor in developing countries estimate that "as many as 200 million children go to work rather than to school . . . making everything from clothing and shoes to handbags and carpets" (Schapiro 205).

With longer, indented quotations, skip one space after the end punctuation and type the reference in parentheses.

■ Bibliographic Reference

Newhouse, John. "The Diplomatic Round: A Freemasonry of Terrorism." *The New Yorker,* 8 July 1985, pp. 46–63.

■ Passage and Citation

One commentator offers this assessment of why foreign terrorist groups don't operate in this country:

> The reason that America has been spared so far, apparently, is that it is less vulnerable than Europe, especially to Middle Eastern extremists. Moving in and out of most European countries isn't difficult for non-Europeans; border controls are negligible. But American customs and immigration authorities, being hyper-alert to drug traffic, tend to pay attention to even marginally doubtful people, and a would-be terrorist . . . could come under surveillance for the wrong reason. (Newhouse 63)

Indirect Citations

In MLA style, if you use a quotation from person A that you obtained from a book or article written by person B or you paraphrase such a quotation, put "qtd. in" before the name of the publication's author in the parenthetical reference.

■ Bibliographic Reference

Klein, Joe. "Ready for Rudy." *New York,* 6 Mar. 1989, pp. 30–37.

■ Passage and Citation

Rudolph Giuliani favors the death penalty for "the murder of a law-enforcement officer, mass murder, a particularly heinous killing" but would impose it only "when there is certainty of guilt well beyond a reasonable doubt" (qtd. in Klein 37).

Authors Identified in Text

Sometimes you'll want to introduce a paraphrase, summary, or quotation with the name of its author. In this case, the page number may be positioned immediately after the name or follow the material cited.

■ Bibliographic Reference

Jacoby, Susan. "Waiting for the End: On Nursing Homes." *The New York Times Magazine,*
    31 Mar. 1974, city ed., pp. 80+.

■ Passage and Citation

Susan Jacoby (80) sums up the grim outlook of patients in bad nursing homes by noting that they are merely waiting to die.

Susan Jacoby sums up the grim outlook of patients in bad nursing homes by noting that they are merely waiting to die (80).

MyWritingLab   **EXERCISE**

1. *Using the MLA system, write a proper in-text citation for Exercise 1 on pages 395–396. The type of information (info only or quote) and page number in the original source are provided: a (info p. 222), and c (a quote p. 271), and g (info p. 31), i (info only p. 221), o (a partial quote on page 60, also use same author published a different year).*
    Assume that you have not used the author's name to introduce the material you cite. Where there are multiple pages in the reference, you can select the page or pages appropriate to your citation.
2. Using the MLA system, write a proper in-text citation for each of the bibliographic references you prepared for part 2 on page 396. Assume that you have not used the author's name to introduce the material you cite. Where there are multiple pages in the reference, you can select the page or pages appropriate to your citation.

SAMPLE

MLA STUDENT RESEARCH PAPER

Sentence Outline

Fighting Ebola with Isolation and Quarantine

Thesis statement: As the United States struggled to control the spread of Ebola, it considered two strategies: isolation and quarantine. Surprisingly, isolation turns out to be much more effective than quarantine for containing Ebola and was the approach recommended by experts and implemented by health organizations.

    I. To better constrain the disease, we need to understand the origin and means of communication of the Ebola virus.

        A. Ebola virus is transmitted from wild animals like bats and primates.

        B. The virus spreads through bodily fluids.

        C. The virus may also spread through contaminated needles and syringes.

   II. We need to consider the history of other Ebola outbreaks.

        A. The first case of Ebola virus was in Yambuku in 1976.

        B. The outbreak ended with no real preventive measures as workers fled their posts.

        C. Another Ebola outbreak in Nzara and Maridi in 1976 ended by means of identification and isolation.

 III. Isolation grew to be preferred as a preventive method.

        A. World Health Organization (WHO) published a guide in 1977 to control and prevent virus infections.

        B. The guide addressed isolation as a preventive method for virus outbreaks.

        C. Isolation proved effective during another Ebola outbreak in Kikwit in 1995.

        D. According to a study by Martin I. Meltzer et al., isolation could end the Ebola epidemic in Liberia and Sierra Leone by mid-January 2015.

        E. Alison P. Galvani, a professor of epidemiology, claims that early-case isolation is important to reduce transmission of virus.

  IV. Introduction of isolation units (IUs) for establishing isolation for patients is an important step.

        A. Isolation units are rooms or buildings that are located away from a hospital's main building.

States paper thesis

Sentence outline: Note the use of complete sentences throughout, use of periods following sections and subsection markers, and the use of indentation arrangement.

Continued from previous page

    B. Design of an isolation unit in the United States consists of negative air pressure, biosafety cabinets, and 20 air changes.

    C. Specialized protective gears are provided to medical workers.

    D. Protective gears for medical workers play an important role because they act as a barrier.

V. Maintenance and cost issues of isolation units can be costly.

    A. Treatment of Ebola-infected patients in isolation units at the University of Nebraska Medical Center averages $30,000 per day.

    B. Protective gears and respirators for medical workers at UC San Diego cost $1,100 apiece.

    C. There are additional costs for patients' waste disposal.

    D. Hospitals compensate for the low number of isolation units currently.

        1. Three hospital systems pooled resources to convert an intensive care unit (ICU) into an isolation unit.

        2. A shelter tent was utilized to create another isolation unit.

VI. Some believe quarantine will help contain the spread of Ebola.

    A. Quarantine involves isolating individuals exposed to the disease but not sick.

    B. Federal law justifies quarantine for several diseases.

    C. Politicians in New Jersey and other states instituted a policy of quarantine.

    D. Some politicians have called for restricting travel from countries with Ebola outbreaks.

    E. Navarro College denied international students from Ebola-hit countries.

VII. Quarantine can have negative consequences.

    A. Quarantine affects negatively on people and their families by limiting their freedom.

    B. Quarantine only works if there is significant asymptomatic transmission, which is not the case with Ebola.

    C. Quarantine may increase transmission of Ebola virus in unaffected people.

    D. Quarantine of countries may increase the distrust of government and decrease cooperation in fighting the spread of the disease.

    E. Quarantine can be costly, causing Governor Andrew M. Cuomo to recommend that medical workers treating Ebola patients monitor their health at home instead of utilizing means of quarantine.

VIII. Isolation proves to be more effective than quarantine during virus infection outbreaks.

Khanbhai 1

Nilofar Khanbhai

Professor von der Osten

English 250

December 24, 2016

Fighting Ebola with Isolation and Quarantine

Since 430 B.C. several epidemics have killed thousands or more people. The International Federation of Red Cross and Red Crescent Societies (IFRC) defines an epidemic as an "unusual increase in the number of cases of an infectious disease which already exists in a certain region or population" ("Biological"). Some historically important epidemics have included smallpox, Bubonic plague, yellow fever, severe acute respiratory syndrome (SARS), and Ebola. The year 2014 witnessed a severe case of Ebola outbreak with about 19,000 confirmed cases in Africa and four confirmed cases in the United States. Out of these cases, 7,400 deaths occurred in Africa, while one death occurred in the United States ("2014 Ebola"). These numbers bring us to an important question: How can we control the spread of this deadly disease? As the United States struggled to control the spread of Ebola, it considered two strategies: isolation and quarantine. Surprisingly, isolation turns out to be much more effective than quarantine for containing Ebola and was the approach recommended by experts and implemented by health organizations.

To understand how isolation and quarantine work, we first need to understand the origin of the Ebola virus and the means by which it is communicated. As the World Health Organization (WHO) reports, Ebola virus disease (EVD), also known as Ebola hemorrhagic fever, is caused by Zaire Ebola virus, and is transmitted to people by wild animals, specifically bats and mammals such as monkeys and apes. However, the main source of the Ebola virus is still unknown. This virus spreads to healthy people through bodily fluids like blood, sweat, urine, saliva,

1"

1/2"

1"

1"

1"

Khanbhai 2

feces, vomit, breast milk, and semen. It may also spread through objects like needles and syringes that were previously contaminated by infected patients. It is important to note that Ebola does not spread through water or air ("Ebola Virus").

According to Centers for Disease Control and Prevention (CDC), the first identified case of Ebola occurred in Yambuku, a small village in the Democratic Republic of Congo (DRC), and its surrounding areas in 1976 ("Outbreaks"). The first person was possibly infected from the blood of an animal that was butchered for food (Heymann). The virus immediately spread by personal contact and the use of contaminated needles and syringes in hospitals and clinics.

Also in 1976, another Ebola outbreak took place in Nzara and Maridi, Sudan. A total of 284 confirmed cases were confirmed; and out of these, 151 people died, leading to a mortality rate of 53 percent ("Outbreaks"). An international study team of WHO reported that the outbreak in Nzara originated with workers of a cotton factory, while the outbreak in Maridi was due to the transmission of the Ebola virus in a large and active hospital ("Ebola Hemorrhagic" 247). The Nzara outbreak was controlled by relying on two classic health principles: (1) early identification of symptoms such as fever, fatigue, headache, and chills, and (2) isolation of infected patients. Isolation requires infected individuals to be placed in a highly secure building or facility. Following these actions, the outbreak in Nzara diminished immediately.

Not long after the outbreaks, in 1977, the WHO released a guide for managing and controlling infections from hemorrhagic fever viruses like Marburg and Ebola. The guide included a list of preventive measures to avoid infection by direct spread of the virus. The primary preventive method was isolation. Isolation separates sick people with a contagious disease from people who are not sick. This method involves confining infected patients in a secure and separate building with a controlled environment, one

---

Margin annotations:

No author. Abbreviates the title

Transition that identifies narrative of how the disease was spread

Topic sentence identifying narrative of outbreak history

No author, so abbreviated title with page number

Identifies action that serves as cause

Transition sentence to section on response to Ebola

Defines isolation

Khanbhai 3

that only restricted workers such as trained doctors and nurses with protective gear are allowed to enter (Simpson 18).

Isolation procedures work to prevent the transmission of Ebola virus, which is rapid when not controlled. During another Ebola outbreak in Kikwit, DRC, patients were identified and isolated, and protective clothing was provided to health workers (Heymann). This method proved to be an extremely successful strategy in preventing the disease and ending the outbreak. Experts believe that isolation may be the key to controlling the Ebola epidemic that is currently raging through the African nations of Liberia and Sierra Leone. According to the article "Estimating the Future Number of Cases in the Ebola Epidemic – Liberia and Sierra Leone, 2014–2015," by Martin I. Meltzer et al., if approximately 70 percent of patients were placed in a safe and isolated household and community setting by late December 2014, the epidemic in Liberia and Sierra Leone could be contained and stopped by mid-January 2015. Clearly, prevention of the spread of Ebola needs to be an immediate priority in infected countries.

Data from several Ebola outbreaks suggest some clear steps that nations should take to isolate the infected patients. According to Michael Greenwood in his article "Lesson from Liberia: Targeted Patient Isolation Could Stem Ebola Epidemic," infected patients who are severely ill before the fifth day of their illness should be isolated by authorized officials. The Yale School of Public Health suggests this action to be the "most effective way to reduce the transmission of virus." Researchers modeled that isolating 75 percent of infected individuals within four days of symptom onset have "a high chance of eliminating the spread of disease" (Greenwood). Early response is important because as Alison P. Galvani, a professor of epidemiology, points out, "infectiousness increases greatly with disease progression" (Greenwood). In an article in *The Washington Post*, Dr. Harry Hull, a

---

Author and page

Provides an illustration of isolation and its effect on the spread of Ebola

Identifies source more fully and provides estimation of effect of isolation

Transition identifying a presentation of the isolation process

Identifies author and title of article

Establishes authority for Greenwood's claims

Khanbhai 4

disease epidemiologist, summarizes the main point that the key to success for eliminating Ebola is "early identification and isolation plus rapid tracing and monitoring of all contacts" (Hull).

How exactly is isolation achieved? Isolation techniques involve physically constructed areas as well as a set of procedures. Often, isolation units (IUs) are installed in hospitals or near the hospitals. Isolation units are rooms or buildings that are separated from the main hospital. Building an IU requires various design points that aid in reducing transmission of infectious diseases. The United States medical isolation facility consists of negative air pressure, which ensures air movement only from the hallway to the patient room and not in the opposite direction. The room is designed as an intensive care unit (ICU) so that patients with any degree of illness can be safely cared for. The units also have a biosafety cabinet for specimen processing. The rooms undergo 20 air changes per hour to rapidly remove infectious particles (Bloch).

The process of isolation includes many important procedures for preventing the spread of Ebola. Only a certain number of trained nursing staff are allowed to enter the premises of the IU to prevent the spread of virus to other people. Staff must wear protective clothing from head to toe, including gloves, gowns, visors, overshoes, and masks (Bloch). Disposable gear is immediately discarded in a large plastic bag and incinerated, whereas non-disposable gear is sterilized and laundered before reuse. Staff members handling patients are required to wash their hands with a disinfectant, such as sodium hypochlorite, phenol, iodophor, or formalin (Simpson 19–21). If a post-mortem procedure is carried out, pathologists wear protective gear and respirators. The corpse is wrapped in plastic sheeting that is soaked in disinfectant and then buried (Simpson 19–22).

The protective gear is a key factor in preventing transmission of the virus to health workers, as Ebola experts have discovered that advanced medical procedures like dialysis and

Khanbhai 5

respiratory intubation could create an aerosol and put health workers at high risk of contamination. Although aerosol is not the means of transmission, precaution must be taken by requiring hospital workers to wear protective gear (O'Donnell).

The cost and maintenance of isolation facilities and procedures is a challenge Dr. Jeffrey Gold, chancellor of the University of Nebraska Medical Center, says the cost of treating Ebola patients at the unit averaged $30,000 per day ("Hospitals"). Dr. Jay Doucet, director of emergency preparedness at the University of California at San Diego, states that the hoods and respirators that doctors and nurses wear cost about $1,100 apiece. While respirators and boots can be sanitized and reused, most of the other gear is thrown away after just one use. This means spending hundreds of dollars each time a worker enters the unit. Another expense is the cost of disposing of patients' waste. Dr. Doucet explains that "the law forbids the university from flushing the estimated 20 to 30 pounds of bodily fluids like diarrhea and vomit that other hospitals report Ebola patients generate daily." Additionally, all waste disposals need to be bagged, solidified, and autoclaved before disposal (Sisson 2).

Because isolation is the only strategy proven effective in fighting Ebola, it is essential that society address the challenges. Considering the high number of confirmed cases and number of deaths in Africa and other countries, we need thousands of IU's to contain the Ebola virus. Hospitals are trying to meet this high demand for IU's. For example, in Dallas, Texas, three hospital systems merged resources to create a treatment center in an empty ICU. In Kansas, a hospital built walls and hung plastic sheeting to create an isolation suite. A Western Shelter GK-1935 medical tent system became a pop-up isolation unit at Newark's University Hospital in New Jersey ("Hospitals"). Even though the hospitals are finding new ways to build more IU's, Dan Yamin, a postdoctoral associate at the Yale School of

---

Marginal annotations:

Author without page

Provides statistic for support

No author, so title and no page

Offers additional authority and qualifications

Author and page number documenting source for the information from Dr. Doucet

Identifies need to respond to problem

Offers one solution to problem

Offers second solution to problem

Khanbhai 6

Public Health states that in the absence of sufficient isolation units, "targeted isolation of those who are mostly responsible for transmission may be the most efficient way to contain Ebola" (Greenwood).

Transition to quarantine

Defines quarantine and distinguishes it from isolation

Indicates justification for quarantine

Provides illustration of quarantine for Ebola

Identifies quarantine laws that restrict access to the United States

Transition to section on problems of quarantine

Illustration of problem using a third-person narrative

There is a fine line between isolation and quarantine, which is another disease-control measure implemented by health officials and the federal government during outbreaks. Unlike isolation, quarantine "separates and restricts the movement of people who were exposed to a contagious disease to see if they become sick." People who undergo quarantine are not infected by the disease, but are mandated to quarantine based on their travel history and their exposure to diseases. Federal law authorizes quarantine for many diseases, including cholera, diphtheria, tuberculosis, plague, smallpox, yellow fever, SARS, and viral hemorrhagic fevers like Ebola and Marburg ("Legal"). Presently, New York, New Jersey, and Connecticut have declared automatic quarantine for medical workers who return from Ebola-hit regions like Africa (Wulfhorst and Morgan). Further, under section 361 of the Public Health Service Act, the U.S. Secretary of Health and Human Services is authorized to take measures to prevent the entry and spread of communicable diseases from foreign countries into the United States ("Legal"). Using this clause as justification, some American politicians have begun calling for the United States to shut its borders to West Africans (Wolfson). Some institutions have taken their own quarantine action. Navarro College, a two-year institution based in Texas, rejected international students from Ebola-hit countries (Stockdale).

Quarantine, even though an old practice, is controversial in respect to the social and psychological welfare of citizens and families, debates over its effectiveness, and economic costs. Quarantines can prove to be traumatic to the people who are quarantined and also to the individual's family. In October, Kaci Hickox, a nurse who treated Ebola patients in West Africa,

Khanbhai 7

was subjected to a 21-day incubation period of quarantine based on New Jersey policy to quarantine all individuals who have had contact with those infected with Ebola. Some suggest Hickox was placed in quarantine because she was running a fever (Robbins et al.). Hickox argued that she was asymptomatic when she returned to the United States, but was still mandated to undergo a quarantine procedure in Newark's University Hospital's Western Shelter GK-1935 medical tent, as the policy required. Hickox was outraged by this treatment and called her confinement "inhumane." Even though Hickox was healthy, she was isolated in a tent, where she had to "wear paper scrubs and use a port-a-potty-style toilet and could only see visitors through a plastic window." Governor Chris Christie of New Jersey terminated Hickox's quarantine after "she hadn't had any symptoms for 24 hours and had tested negative for Ebola" (Robbins et al.).

Additionally, experts claim that quarantines may not be very helpful for preventing the spread of Ebola. Troy Day et al. in their article "When Is Quarantine a Useful Control Strategy for Emerging Infectious Diseases?" state that quarantine is effective only in cases of significant asymptomatic transmission—in other words, only if a significant number of people carry a disease and are capable of transmitting it without exhibiting symptoms (479). Experts note that unlike SARS and the flu, Ebola is not easily spread by coughing or sneezing. Instead it requires direct contact with infected person's bodily fluids while he or she is "showing symptoms of disease" (Werner). Furthermore, quarantine may spread disease to quarantined persons. Dr. Harry F. Hull acknowledges the quarantine procedure that was put into action for the control of AIDS in 1980 and states that it was "counterproductive" and only increased the chances of AIDS transmission. Likewise, using quarantine in crowded slums in Liberia may have increased the spread of Ebola (Hull).

In-text citation for a source with three authors

Identifies another problem

Identifies more than three authors within the sentence

Page number

Comparison distinguishes Ebola from diseases where quarantine might have been used

Identifies possible negative effect of quarantine and illustrates with an example

Khanbhai 8

Similarly, experts claim that closing U.S. borders to West Africa would not stop Ebola from spreading outside Africa, but instead could worsen the outbreak in West Africa. Dr. Thomas Frieden, director of the Centers for Disease Control and Prevention (CDC), states that isolating communities stricken by Ebola "increases people's distrust of government, making them less likely to cooperate to help stop the spread of Ebola" (Wolfson). Moreover, Joanne Liu, the international president of Doctors Without Borders, argues that closing off borders only serves to "breed fear and unrest rather than contain the virus" (Wolfson). Thus, isolating Ebola-struck countries is not an answer for fighting a particular Ebola outbreak.

The costs of quarantine go beyond civil liberties and the unintended spread of disease. The costs of building and maintaining quarantine zones must also be considered. To reduce the high cost, Governor Andrew M. Cuomo declared that medical workers who had contact with Ebola patients but did not show symptoms of the disease would be allowed to remain at home. Cuomo emphasized that returning medical workers must monitor their health at homes to check whether they show any symptoms or not (Flegenheimer et al.). Although quarantines may not prove to be very effective, not everyone is anti-quarantine. Some believe that restricted quarantine measures can provide time to identify symptoms of Ebola, which may further prevent the spread of the virus.

In the absence of effective vaccines and therapeutics, the response to Ebola outbreaks has relied almost solely on the classic measures of communicable disease control: early identification of symptoms and isolation. Isolation, despite its costs, has proven effective in eliminating many epidemics and is currently the experts' best choice for managing Ebola. In contrast, quarantine may not be effective in Ebola outbreaks and raises

Identifies expert and authority for the position

Identifies source to make clear that this is not from an article authored by Frieden but rather the expert is cited in an article by Wolfson

Identifies conclusion

questions of civil liberties and even the unintended consequences of extending the disease, and may only be useful in a
carefully limited manner. Health officials are in agreement: The
best way to protect the United States from the disease is to end
the outbreak in West Africa by early identification of symptoms
and isolation.

Restates argument in brief

Restates thesis

Works Cited begins a new page

Works Cited

"Biological Hazards: Epidemics." *International Federation of Red Cross and Red Crescent Societies,* www.ifrc.org/en/what-we-do/disaster-management/about-disasters/definition-of-hazard/biological-hazards-epidemics. Accessed 20 Dec. 2016.

Bloch, Hannah. "Caring for the American Ebola Patients: Inside Emory's Isolation Unit." *National Public Radio,* 18 Aug. 2014, www.npr.org/sections/goatsandsoda/2014/08/18/340444100/caring-for-the-american-ebola-patients-inside-emorys-isolation-unit.

Day, Troy, et al. "When Is Quarantine a Useful Control Strategy for Emerging Infectious Diseases?" *American Journal of Epidemiology,* vol. 163, no. 5, 2005, pp. 479–85, aje.oxfordjournals.org/content/163/5/479.full.

"Ebola Haemorrhagic Fever in Sudan, 1976." *World Health Organization,* vol. 56, no. 2, 1978, pp. 247–54, www.ncbi.nlm.nih.gov/pmc/articles/PMC2395561.

"Ebola Virus Disease." *World Health Organization,* Jan. 2016, www.who.int/mediacentre/factsheets/fs103/en.

Flegenheimer, Matt, et al. "Under Pressure, Cuomo Says Ebola Quarantines Can Be Spent at Home." *The New York Times,* 26 Oct. 2014, www.nytimes.com/2014/10/27/nyregion/ebola-quarantine.html?_r=0.

Greenwood, Michael. "Lessons from Liberia: Targeted Patient Isolation Could Stem Ebola Epidemic." *Yale News,* 28 Oct. 2014,

Section of Web site, no author

Article with more than three authors in a journal with page numbers on the Web

Article without author but with page numbers on an organizational Web site

Article without author or page numbers on an organizational Web site

Newspaper article with three authors on the Web

Khanbhai 10

news.yale.edu/2014/10/28/lessons-liberia-targeted-patient-
isolation-could-stem-ebola-epidemic.

Heymann, David L. "Ebola: Learn From the Past." *Nature,* vol. 514,
no. 7522, 9 Oct. 2014, www.nature.com/news/ebola-learn-from-
the-past-1.16117.

"History of Quarantine." *Centers for Disease Control and Prevention*, 31 July 2014, www.cdc.gov/quarantine/historyquarantine.
html.

"Hospitals Improvise Ebola Defenses, At a Cost." *Fox News*, 19 Nov.
2014, www.foxnews.com/health/2014/11/19/hospitals-improvise-
ebola-defenses-at-cost.html.

Hull, Harry F. "Why Quarantines Won't Stop Ebola from Spreading in the U.S." *The Washington Post*, 3 Oct. 2014, www.
washingtonpost.com/posteverything/wp/2014/10/03/why-
quarantines-wont-stop-ebola-from-spreading-in-the-u-s/?utm_
term=.d8b8b2ee4b64.

"Legal Authorities for Isolation and Quarantine." *Centers for
Disease Control and Prevention*, 8 Oct. 2014, www.cdc.gov/
quarantine/aboutlawsregulationsquarantineisolation.html.

Meltzer, Martin I., et al. "Estimating the Future Number of
Cases in the Ebola Epidemic — Liberia and Sierra Leone,
2014–2015." *Centers for Disease Control and Prevention*, vol. 63,
no. 3, 16 Sept. 2014, www.cdc.gov/mmwr/preview/mmwrhtml/
su6303a1.htm.

O'Donnell, Noreen. "Ebola Experts: Advanced Medical Procedures
Could Add Risk." *National Broadcasting Company*, 15 Oct.
2014, www.necn.com/news/national-international/Ebola-
Experts-Questsion-Spread-Through-Aerosol-Method-
279148311.html.

"Outbreaks Chronology: Ebola Virus Disease." *Centers for Disease
Control and Prevention*, 14 Apr. 2016, www.cdc.gov/vhf/ebola/
outbreaks/history/chronology.html.

News article with
author on the Web

Article without author
on government Web
site

An article on an
online news network
site with a single
author

Article in an online
newspaper with three
authors

Robbins, Liz, et al. "Unapologetic, Christie Frees Nurse From Ebola Quarantine." *The New York Times*, 27 Oct. 2014, www.nytimes.com/2014/10/28/nyregion/nurse-in-newark-to-be-allowed-to-finish-ebola-quarantine-at-home-christie-says.html.

Simpson, D. I. H. "Isolation of the Patient." *Marburg and Ebola Virus Infections: A Guide for Their Diagnosis, Management, and Control*. 36th ed., Geneva, 1977, pp. 18–21.

Sisson, Paul. "Practice Paramount for UCSD Ebola Unit." *The San Diego Union-Tribune*, 31 Oct. 2014, www.sandiegouniontribune.com/news/2014/oct/31/ucsd-ebola-isolation-unit-drill-protective-gear.

Stockdale, Nicole. "Texas College Says It's Rejecting All International Students from Countries With Ebola." *The Dallas Morning News*, 15 Oct. 2014, dallasmorningviewsblog.dallasnews.com/2014/10/texas-college-says-its-rejecting-all-international-students-from-countries-with-ebola.html.

Werner, Erica. "Do Quarantines Actually Work? Experts Question Effectiveness." *Public Broadcasting Service (PBS) News Hour*, 30 Oct. 2014, www.pbs.org/newshour/rundown/quarantines-rarely-used-effectiveness-questioned.

Wolfson, Elijah. "Isolating Ebola-Affected Nations Could Worsen Outbreak, Experts Say." *Al Jazeera America*, 10 Oct. 2014, america.aljazeera.com/articles/2014/10/10/experts-isolatingebolaaffectednationscouldworsenoutbreak.html.

Wulfhorst, Ellen, and David Morgan. "Two U.S. States to Quarantine Health Workers Returning from Ebola Zones." *Reuters*, 24 Oct. 2014, www.reuters.com/article/us-health-ebola-newyork-idUSKCN0IC2CU20141024.

"2014 Ebola Outbreak in West Africa Case Counts." *Centers for Disease Control and Prevention*, 13 Apr. 2016, www.cdc.gov/vhf/ebola/outbreaks/2014-west-africa/case-counts.html.

A print book

Article on an online news site with a single author

An article on an online news service with two authors

21

Documenting Sources: APA Style

In this chapter, you will learn how to:

21.1 Prepare papers using the APA system.

21.2 Prepare bibliographic references using the APA style.

21.3 Follow APA style to cite sources in your essay.

21.4 Integrate and cite quotations using the APA style.

Visit MyWritingLab **to complete the writing assignments in this chapter and for more resources on APA documentation style.**

The American Psychological Association (APA) system is used by many social sciences, psychology, and many other academic disciplines. The APA is currently in its 6th edition.

To better meet the challenges of online publications, APA style now recommends that the unique work you are referencing in print and electronic form be identified by the digital object identifier (DOI), a unique identification sequence assigned by the International DOI Foundation. The DOI can often be found near the copyright notices of electronic journal articles or in some cases at the top of the first page of the article. When the DOI is used, there is no need to indicate the URL of the reference.

■ Sample

Mesmer-Magnus, J. R., & DeChurch, L. A. (2009). Information sharing and team performance: A meta-analysis. *Journal of Applied Psychology, 94*(2), 535–546. doi:10.1037/a0013773

Consult with your instructors on whether they wish you to employ the DOI with print and online sources when it is available.

APA System for Preparing Papers

- Number every page of the text in the upper right corner, starting with the title page. On the title page, about one-half inch from the top of the page (but use the header function of your word processing program), type the words "Running head," without quotation marks, flush with the left margin; then type a colon and a word or phrase that identifies the paper's topic in all capital letters. Running head: ABBREVIATED TITLE
- On all subsequent pages, type the abbreviated title (running head) in capital letters in the header flush to the left margin. ABBREVIATED TITLE
- The APA system requires a title page. However, the standard is for publication and not for the classroom. Consult your instructor on the format expected for the class. Many instructors expect the following: Center (1) the title of the paper about four inches from the top and (2) your name, two spaces below the title. About three-fourths of the way from the top, provide your institution's name or the course name, the name of your instructor if requested, and the date, typed double-spaced.
- The APA system includes a brief abstract that summarizes the main argument concisely. On the numbered page after the title page, center the word "Abstract." Then flush left, without an indent, include a brief summary of your research. For longer research papers you might add keywords. Indent, type *keywords:* using italics, then list the keywords that would help researchers find your article in a database.
- Repeat the title of the paper on the first text page, centered about one-and-a-half inches from the top and typed in capital and lowercase letters.
- Leave one-inch margins at the bottom and at both sides of each page. Indent the first line of each paragraph five spaces.
- Begin the bibliography on a new page that follows the text of the paper and give it the heading "References," without quotation marks. Center this heading on the page. Follow the alphabetizing and positioning guidelines for the MLA system except that if the listing includes more than one entry for an author, repeat the author's name.
- Begin the first line of each entry at the left margin and indent subsequent lines five spaces. In most word-processing programs, you can select "hanging indent" as a format option, under Format/Paragraph in Word, which will automatically provide the proper indentation for each entry. Double-space all entries.

21.1
Prepare papers using the APA system.

APA

Preparing Proper APA Bibliographic References

Books

The APA system uses initials rather than first and middle names for authors, editors, and translators.

21.2
Prepare bibliographic references using the APA style.

■ A Book with One Author

Wilk, M. (1975). *Every day's a matinée.* New York, NY: Norton.

■ A Book with Two Authors

Duncan, D., & Burns, K. (1997). *Lewis and Clark.* New York, NY: Knopf.

■ A Book with More than Three Authors

Alder, R. W., Finn, T., Bradley, M. A., & Li, A. W. (1971). *Mechanisms in organic chemistry.*
     New York, NY: Wiley.

The APA system gives up to and including six author or editor names in the reference list. Substitute "et al." for the seventh or more.

■ A Book with a Title That Includes Another Title

Words that would be italicized on their own should be set roman as part of an italicized title.

Tanner, J. (1992). *Anxiety in Eden: A Kierkegaardian reading of* Paradise Lost. Oxford,
     England: Oxford University Press.

■ A Book with Corporate or Association Authorship

United Nations, Public Administration Division. (1968). *Local government training.*
     New York, NY: Author.

When the author of the work is also the publisher, the APA system uses the word "Author" following the place of publication. If the work is published by another organization, its name replaces "Author."

■ An Edition Other than the First

Turabian, K. L. (1996). *A manual for writers of term papers, theses, and dissertations* (6th ed.).
     Chicago, IL: University of Chicago Press.

■ A Book in Two or More Volumes

Bartram, H. C. (1959). *The cavalcade of America* (Vols. 1–2). New York, NY: Knopf.

■ A Reprint of an Older Work

Matthiessen, F. O. (1970). *American renaissance: Art and expression in the age of Emerson and
     Whitman.* New York, NY: Oxford University Press. (Original work published 1941)

■ A Book with an Editor Rather than an Author

Deetz, J. (Ed.). (1971). *Man's imprint from the past: Readings in the methods of archaeology.*
     Boston, MA: Little, Brown.

■ A Book with Both an Author and an Editor

Melville, H. (1971). *The confidence man* H. Parker (Ed.). New York, NY: Norton. (Original
    work published 1857)

■ A Translation

Beauvoir, S. de. (1974). *All said and done* (P. O'Brian, Trans.). New York, NY: Putnam.
    (Original work published 1972)

■ An Essay or Chapter in a Collection of Works by One Author

Woolf, V. (1925). The lives of the obscure. In *The common reader, first series* (pp. 111–118).
    New York, NY: Harcourt Brace.

■ An Essay or Chapter in an Anthology

Angell, R. (1981). On the ball. In P. Eschholz & A. Rosa (Eds.), *Subject and strategy*
    (pp. 34–41). New York, NY: St. Martin's Press.

Periodicals

Periodicals include newspapers, popular magazines, and specialized occupational and scholarly journals. The basic information for a periodical article
includes the name of the article's author, the date of publication, the title of the
article, the name of the periodical, the page range of the entire article, and, for
scholarly journals, the volume number of the periodical.

■ An Article in a Scholarly Journal Consecutively Paged through the Entire
  Volume

Pfennig, D. (1997). Kinship and cannibalism. *Bioscience, 47,* 667–675.

■ An Article in a Scholarly Journal That Pages Each Issue Separately

Block, J. W. (1976). Sodom and Gomorrah: A volcanic disaster. *Journal of Geological Educa-
    tion, 23*(5), 74–77.

■ An Unsigned Article in a Scholarly Journal

Baby, it's cold inside. (1997). *Science, 276,* 537–538.

■ A Signed Article in an Occupational or Popular Magazine

Gopnik, A. (1997, November 24). The good soldier. *The New Yorker, 73,* 106–114.

■An Unsigned Article in an Occupational or Popular Magazine

Robot productivity. (1982, May). *Production Engineering, 29,* 52–55.

■A Signed Article in a Daily Newspaper

Wade, N. (1997, November 26). Germ weapons: Deadly but hard to use. *The New York Times,* pp. A13, A15.

■An Unsigned Article in a Daily Newspaper

The arithmetic of terrorism. (1997, November 14). *The Washington Post,* p. A26.

Encyclopedia Articles

The APA system requires publication information for all encyclopedia citations when documenting familiar works, such as the *Encyclopedia Americana.*

Fears, J. R. (1987). Emperor's cult. In *The encyclopedia of religion* (Vol. 5, pp. 101–102). New York, NY: Macmillan.

For an anonymous article, references for the APA system begin with the article's title. Position the publication date, within parentheses, after this title. The remaining format is identical to citations with an author.

Government Documents

The APA system includes the name of the author, the date of publication, and the place of publication and adds a cataloging code when one exists.

Carpenter, R. D. (1989). *Defects in hardened timber* (UCLC Publication No. 20504424). U.S. Department of Agriculture, Forest Service. Washington, DC: Government Printing Office.

U.S. Environmental Protection Agency, Consumer Products Safety Commission. (1989). *Asbestos in the home* (SUDOCS Report No. Y3.C76/3:2/A51/989). Washington, DC: Government Printing Office.

U.S. Congress, Office of Technology Assessment. (1992). *The biology of mental disorders* (SUDOCS Report No. Y3.T22/2:2/B57/10). Washington, DC: Government Printing Office.

Other Sources

■Book Reviews

Koenig, R. (1989, February 20). Billy the Kid [Review of the book *Billy Bathgate*]. *New York, 21,* 20–21.

If the review is untitled, follow the above format but omit the missing element.

■ Published Interviews

Hernandez, F. (1997, March 20). A talk with Manuel Noriega. *News Report, 15,* 28–30.

If the interview is untitled, follow the example above, omitting mention of a title.

■ Personal Interviews

For the APA system, a personal interview is considered personal correspondence and is not included in the References list. Instead, use an in-text parenthetical citation. Include the name of the person interviewed, the notation "personal communication," and the date: (Newman, personal communication, May 18, 2001).

■ Audiovisual Media

In the APA format, the citation begins with an individual's name and his or her contribution to the *motion picture* (use this term, not *film*). The country of origin (where it was made and released) is now required.

Whale, J. (Director). (1931). *Frankenstein* [Motion picture]. United States: Universal.

■ Television and Radio Programs

Ducat, S. (Producer). (1995, January 6). *Washington week in review* [Television broadcast]. Washington, DC: Public Broadcasting Service.

Use the following format when additional information is pertinent:

Exton, C. (Writer), & Rye, R. (Director). (1993). Peril at End House [Television series episode]. In B. Eastman (Producer), *Mystery.* Washington, DC: Public Broadcasting Service.

With the APA system, the name of the scriptwriter appears in the author's position, followed by the director. Any in-text references begin with the first name in the bibliographical reference (for example, Exton, 1993).

■ Music and Sound Recordings

The APA format requires identification of all formats, including a CD.

Smith, B. (1948). Down hearted blues. On *The world's greatest blues singer* [CD]. New York, NY: Columbia Records. (Original recording February 17, 1923)

Smith, B. (1997). *The essential Bessie Smith* [CD]. New York, NY: Columbia Records.

Recording dates, if different from the copyright year, follow the entry, enclosed in parentheses, with no final period.

■ CD-ROMs and Other Databases

Norman, J. L. (1996). Barcelona. In *Software toolworks multimedia encyclopedia* [CD-ROM].

Boston, MA: Grolier.

The APA *Manual* (6th ed.) takes the view that all aggregated databases are the same type of source, regardless of the format or manner of access (CD-ROM, library or university server, or online Web supplier). Follow the model above when you need to cite an entire CD-ROM (not a document from it). In a reference to information taken from a database (even a CD-ROM), give a "retrieval statement" containing the date you retrieved the document, article, or piece of data, as well as the full, correct name of the database. When you retrieve information from an online database, end the entry with a correct and complete URL for the specific document or version. In this case, the name of the database is omitted, unless this information will help in retrieval from a large or complex site. (See online models in the next section.)

Online Sources

The most recent edition of the *Publication Manual of the American Psychological Association* provides the APA's newest guidelines for documenting online sources. You can also consult the association's Web site for its most up-to-date information about citing electronic sources:

http://www.apastyle.org/elecref.html

Be sure to ask your instructor which format to follow and then use that format consistently. Often data from the Internet are incomplete, perhaps lacking an author, a title, or page or paragraph numbers. Include all the available information. The recommendation from the APA is that you cite document locations rather than home pages and that the referenced address actually works for that file. Remember, your goal is to allow your reader to find the source. Note the use of the DOI explained at the beginning of the section on APA References.

■ Books

Follow the general guidelines for a printed book and conclude with appropriate electronic source information, as modeled here, or use the DOI, if known.

Barrett, F. E. (1922). *Conception control and its effects on the individual and the nation.*

Retrieved from https://www.gutenberg.org/files/13906/13906-h/13906-h.htm

To cite part of an electronic book, place the part's title after the date of publication. The APA also cites a chapter or section identifier following the title of the complete document.

Free, M. (2008). The doll's dress maker, the doctor's assistant, and the limit of differ-

ence. In M. Tromp (Ed.), *Victorian freaks: The social context of freakery in Britain.*

Columbus, OH: Ohio State University Press, 2008. Retrieved from

http://www.wirbook.com/ebook/victorian-freaks.html

To cite a book on Kindle or another electronic book reader, you need to include the author, the date of publication, title, the e-book version, and either the DOI or the source of your book download.

Pinker, S. (1997). *How the mind works.* (Kindle DX version). Retrieved from

Amazon.com

■ Periodicals on the World Wide Web

The APA recommends using the models for print periodicals when document-ing online articles that do not vary from their printed versions. In such cases, add [Electronic version] after the title and before the period to complete the citation. When the electronic format alters the printed version (e.g., no pagination, added data or links), then cite as an online document, using a retrieval statement and the name of the database and/or the URL. APA guidelines ask for the identifica-tion of the server or the Web site in a retrieval statement only when it would be helpful in finding the source; for example, it is not necessary to state "Retrieved from the World Wide Web" since it is the most common access point to the Inter-net. If the DOI is available, that should be used instead of retrieval data.

Cervetti, N. (1996). In the breeches, petticoats, and pleasures of Orlando. *Journal of Mod-

ern Literature, 20*(2). Retrieved from http://www.indiana.edu/~iupress/journals/

mod-art2.html

Navarro, M. (2001, February 13). Women in sports cultivating new playing fields. *The

New York Times.* Retrieved from http://www.nytimes.com

No link found in violence, videos. (2000, August 8). *Boston Globe Online*, p. A14.

Retrieved from http://www.boston.com/dailyglobe2/no_li_nk_found_in_

violence_videos+.shtml

Oakes, J. (1999, January/February). Promotion or retention: Which one is social?

Harvard Education Letter. Retrieved from http://www.edletter.org/past/

issues/1999-jf/promotion.shtml

■ Periodicals Accessed through an Online Library Service or Large Network Provider

Increasingly, full-text articles are available online at libraries or at home through services such as LexisNexis, ProQuest Direct, and America Online. These ser-vices may or may not provide an online address for accessed material. In the APA documentation system, cite the author's name, if known; the date the article was published; the title of the article; the title of the periodical; and the page num-bers for the article, if available. Do not include the name of the database.

Clemetson, L. (2000, March 27). A ticket to private school. *Newsweek*. Retrieved from

> http://www.newsweek/com.icl/83469

APA style prefers that the URL that leads directly to the document file be provided, following the word *from*.

■ Encyclopedia Articles

The basic information for an encyclopedia article accessed through the World Wide Web includes the author's name, if known, the date of the edition, the title of the article, the name of the encyclopedia, and the online address.

Daniel, R. T. (1995). The history of Western music. In *Britannica online: Macropaedia*.

> Retrieved from http://www.eb.com:180/cgi-bin/g:DocF=macro/5004/45/0.html

■ Government Documents

The basic information for a government document includes the name of the author, if known, the date of publication, the title, a cataloging code if one is available, and the online address. If no author is given, begin by identifying the government agency as the author.

Probation Division of the Georgia Department of Corrections. (1997, July 1). *Alternatives*

> *to incarceration* (CSP Document No. 239875). Retrieved from http://www.harvard
> .edu/~innovat/aiga87.html

■ Web Sites

The APA *Manual* offers no specific guidelines for Web sites or personal home pages. We suggest that you use the following pattern, which conforms to general APA practice. Note that the APA system includes the date of the latest Web page revision, if known, in parentheses.

Lanthrop, O. (2000, May 28). Home page. Retrieved from http://www.cognivis.com

■ Social Media and E-Mail

Blogs and other social media should be cited only if they are retrievable by others.

Blog

Cinelli, B. (2014, November 11). Shale gas spreads to the south. [Blog post]. Retrieved

> from http://www.geglobalresearch.com/blog/shale-gas-spreads-south

Facebook

NASA.GOV. (2015, January 14). Nothing to squirm about: Space station worms help

> battle muscle and bone loss. [Facebook status update]. Retrieved from
> https://www.facebook.com/NASAJSC?fref=nf

Tweet

The Economist. (2015, January 20). Judging by the lack of economic news in Russia's

media, a crisis has arrived econ.st/1C/2yg [Tweet]. Retrieved from https//

twitter.com/TheEconomist/Status/55763214075903/805/photo/1.

■ Newsgroups, Electronic Mailing Lists, and E-Mail

The APA format treats e-mail as personal communications, which are cited in parentheses in the text only. Newsgroups, online forums, discussion groups, and electronic mailing lists that maintain archives can be cited in the References. With these electronic forms, indicate the author's full last name and initials (screen name if the name is not available); the exact posting date; the name of the thread or blog; a label in brackets describing the type of message, "Retrieved from" followed by the name of list if not in the URL; and the address for the archived message. Categories include Online forum comment (messages posted to newsgroups, online forums, or discussion group), Electronic mailing list message (a message on an electronic mailing List or Listserv), Web log message (for a blog post), and Video file (Video blog post).

Trehub, A. (2002, January 28). Re: The conscious access hypothesis [Online forum

comment]. Retrieved from University of Houston Psyche Discussion Forum:

http://listserv.uh.edu/cig-bin/wa?A2=psyche-b&F=&S=&P=2334

EXERCISE

MyWritingLab

1. **Using the information on the sources provided on pages 395–396, prepare an APA bibliographical reference for each source.**

2. **Prepare a proper APA reference for each of the works you plan to use in writing your paper.**

3. **Prepare an annotated bibliography, explained on page 360, using APA style for each of the works you have reviewed for your paper.**

Handling In-Text Citations

The APA system uses notations that appear within the text and are set off by parentheses. The system identifies the last name of the author or authors and the year of publication. A page number is provided in APA both with quotations and when the information is so specific that it is important to reference the specific page. The system is illustrated by the following examples.

21.3

Follow APA style to cite sources in your essay.

Basic Citation Form

■ Bibliographic Reference

Rothenberg, R. (1996, February). Life in cyburbia. *Esquire*, 56–63.

■ Passage and Citation

A mania for the Internet has invaded . . . our poorest children have a stake in the Internet (Rothenberg, 1996).

Rothenberg (1996) states that a mania for the Internet . . . have a stake in the Internet.

■ Bibliographic Reference

Weider, B., & Hapgood, D. (1982). *The murder of Napoleon.* New York, NY: Congdon.

■ Passage and Citation

Four different autopsy reports were filed…. Nevertheless, cancer has become accepted as the cause (Weider & Hapgood, 1982).

If a source has more than five authors, use "et al.," meaning "and others" for all but the first listed author.

■ Bibliographic Reference

Albert, M. S., Jones, K., Savage, C. R., Berkman, L., Seeman, T., Blazer, D., & Rowe, J. W. (1995). Predictors of cognitive change in older persons: MacArthur studies of successful aging. *Psychology and Aging,* 10(4), 578.

■ Passage and Citation

A longitudinal study… found education and activity levels to be predictors of cognitive change (Albert et al., 1995).

Authors with the Same Last Name

If your citations include authors with the same last name, use the initials of their first names to distinguish them.

■ Bibliographic Reference

Adler, J. (1980, June 16). Search for an orange thread. *Newsweek,* 32–34.

Adler, W. L. (1979, December, 18). The agent orange controversy. *Detroit Free Press,* state ed., p. B2.

■ Passage and Citation

As early as 1966, government . . . miscarriages, liver abscesses, and nerve damage (J. Adler, 1980).

Separate Works by the Same Author

For the APA system, use the conventional name–date–page number format.
(Note: Page numbers are not always needed.)

■ Bibliographic Reference

Mullin, D. (1983a, November 14). After U.S. troops pull out of Grenada. *US News &
World Report*, 22–25.

Mullin, D. (1983b, November 7). Why the surprise move in Grenada—and what next.
US News & World Report, 31–34.

■ Passage and Citation

As the rangers evacuated students, . . . and free the governor (Mullin, 1983b).

If the two works appeared in the same year, put an "a" or a "b," without quotes,
after the date to identify whether you are referring to the first or second entry
for that author in the bibliography, arranged alphabetically by title.

Two Sources for the Same Citations

If two sources provide essentially the same information and you wish to mention both in one parenthetical citation, alphabetize them according to their
authors' last names, list them with a semicolon between them, and position the
citation as you would any other citation.

■ Bibliographic Reference

Bryce, B. (1988, November 13). The controversy over funding community colleges.
Detroit Free Press, state ed., p. A4.

Warshow, H. (1988, November 15). Community college funding hits a snag. *Grand
Rapids Press*, city ed., p. A2.

■ Passage and Citation

In contending that a 3% reduction in stat funding . . . enrollment was expected to jump
by 15% during the next year (Bryce, 1988; Warshow, 1988).

Unsigned References

When you use a source for which no author is given, the in-text citation consists
of all or part of the title, the appropriate page numbers, and the date.

■ Bibliographic Reference

Money and Classes. (1997, October). *Progressive*, 10.

■ Passage and Citation

According to the General Accounting Office, repairing . . . many billions more ("Money and Classes," 1997).

Citing Quotations

21.4

Integrate and cite quotations using the APA style.

APA

Set off quotations fewer than forty words long with quotation marks and run them into the text of the paper. For longer quotes, omit the quotation marks and indent the material five spaces. Double-space the typing. If you quote part or all of one paragraph, don't further indent the first line. If you quote two or more consecutive paragraphs, indent each one's first line five additional spaces—except for the first paragraph in the quote which should not be additionally indented. Use single quotation marks for a quotation within a shorter quotation and double marks for a quotation within a longer, indented quotation. There are more detailed examples in Chapter 20, following MLA style.

When the quotation is run into the text, position the citation as shown in the following examples.

■ Bibliographic Reference

Schapiro, M. (1996, April). Children of a lesser god. *Harper's Bazaar*, 205+.

■ Passage and Citation

UN investigators who have studied the extent of child labor in developing countries estimate that "as many as 200 million children go to work rather than to school . . . making everything from clothing and shoes to handbags and carpets" (Schapiro, 1996, p. 205).

With longer, indented quotations, skip one space after the end punctuation and type the reference in parentheses.

■ Bibliographic Reference

Newhouse, J. (1985, July 8). The diplomatic round: A freemasonry of terrorism. *New Yorker*, 46–63.

■ Passage and Citation

One commentator offers this assessment of why foreign terrorist groups don't operate in this country:

The reason that America has been spared so far, apparently, is that it is less vulnerable than Europe, especially to Middle Eastern extremists. Moving in and out of most European countries isn't difficult for non-Europeans; border controls are negligible. But American customs and immigration authorities, being hyper-alert to drug traffic, tend to pay attention to even marginally doubtful people, and a would-be terrorist . . . could come under surveillance for the wrong reason. (Newhouse, 1985, p. 63)

Indirect Citations

In APA style, name the original work in the text and then give the secondary source in parentheses preceded by "as cited in."

■ Bibliographic Reference

Klein, J. (1989, March 6). Ready for Rudy. *New York*, 30–37.

■ Passage and Citation

Rudolph Giuliani favors the death penalty for "the murder of a law-enforcement officer, mass murder, a particularly heinous killing" but would impose it only "when there is certainty of guilt well beyond a reasonable doubt" (as cited in Klein, 1989, p. 37).

Authors Identified in Text

Sometimes you'll want to introduce a paraphrase, summary, or quotation with the name of its author. In this case, the page number may be positioned immediately after the name or follow the material cited.

■ Bibliographic Reference

Jacoby, S. (1974, March 31). Waiting for the end: On nursing homes. *New York Times Magazine*, city ed., 80+.

■ Passage and Citation

Susan Jacoby (1974, p. 80) sums up the grim outlook of patients in bad nursing homes by noting that they are merely waiting to die.

Susan Jacoby (1974) sums up the grim outlook of patients in bad nursing homes by noting that they are merely waiting to die (p. 80).

MyWritingLab   **EXERCISE**

1. *Using the APA system, write a proper in-text citation for Exercise 1 on page 423. The type of information (info only or quote) and page number in the original source are provided: a (info p. 222), c (a quote p. 271), g (info p. 31), i (info only p. 221), o (a partial quote on page 60, also use same author published a different year).*

    Assume that you have not used the author's name to introduce the material you cite. Where there are multiple pages in the reference, you can select the page or pages appropriate to your citation.

2. *Using the APA system, write a proper in-text citation for each of the bibliographic references you prepared for Exercise 2 on page 423. Assume that you have not used the author's name to introduce the material you cite. Where there are multiple pages in the reference, you can select the page or pages appropriate to your citation.*

SAMPLE

APA STUDENT RESEARCH PAPER

Running head with abbreviation of title.
Complete title

Student name
Name of the institution by instructor request. Instructors may ask instead for the name of the course and the name of the instructor.

Date by instructor request

Running head: HGTV: GLOBALLY SUCCESSFUL NETWORK   1

HGTV: Building Not Just Homes but a Globally Successful Network
Aubrey Cobb
University of Kentucky
November 14, 2014

Continues running head as an abbreviation of the title all capitalized

Centered identification of abstract

Abstract is flush left and double-spaced. It summarizes the paper

Because the paper is shorter and not for publication, no keywords are used

HGTV: GLOBALLY SUCCESSFUL NETWORK   2

Abstract

HGTV is a familiar television network owned by the conglomerate E. W. Scripps Company and is responsible for much of the increase in the conglomerate's profits. A review of the available business and news accounts of the network show that it owes its profitability and global outreach to a number of factors, including production in Canada to reduce costs, the use of the lower cost factors of reality TV, and the deliberate use of more universal themes and participants to break down global barriers. This paper reviews the data on HGTV's success and the reasons for that success.

HGTV: Building Not Just Homes but a Globally Successful Network
Introduction

Home & Garden Television (HGTV) is a television network with pro-gramming geared towards homeowners, renovators, people with an eye for design, and anyone seeking "do-it-yourself" inspiration. HGTV has combined the economic advantages of reality TV with the efficiency and cost-effectiveness of importing programming to achieve an inexpen-sively produced, incredibly successful television network. Due to the sim-plicity of its TV shows and the universality of its content, HGTV has been able to expand into a global brand without the issue of cultural barriers, also making it an easily exportable commodity.

Parent Company

HGTV is owned by the media conglomerate The E.W. Scripps Company ("E. W. Scripps Co (SSP) Company Profile," n.d.). The E.W. Scripps Company began as a print company that expanded into televi-sion and other venues (Carr, 2014). Due the recent decline in print sales, however, The Scripps Company moved its previously "print" content online and has ditched its print assets entirely (Carr, 2014). But this tran-sition to strictly Internet-based (aside from TV) content probably won't adversely affect The E.W. Scripps company; the company has other, much more profitable, business ventures to tend to.

The Scripps Company has its fingers in 19 different TV stations (10 ABC affiliates, 3 NBC affiliates, 5 Azteca affiliates, and 1 independent affiliate) ("E. W. Scripps Co [SSP] Company Profile," n.d.). These different media sources permeate all current media platforms: broadcast, online, smartphones, and tablets ("E. W. Scripps Co [SSP] Company Profile," n.d.). As a publicly held/traded company (Havens & Lotz, 2012), The Scripps Company makes a staggering 89% of the company's television revenue off of commercial spots ("E. W. Scripps Co [SSP] Company Profile," n.d.).

In 2007, The E.W. Scripps Company split into two separate companies; one took the name Scripps Network Interactive, and the other kept the original name of The E.W. Scripps Company (Anderson, 2013). Scripps Network Interactive calls itself a "lifestyle" company and it

Restatement of title cen-tered on the first page of the text

In response to the instructor's expectations, the student uses headers to guide the reader through the paper. Such use of headers is not required by the APA style

Thesis

Internal citation of an article without author without a date from an online news service

Internal citation of newspa-per article with date

When material is used from an earlier cited work within the document, both article and date are restated

Internal citation of a book with two authors

Transition in step of narra-tive of company

Article with author and date

HGTV: GLOBALLY SUCCESSFUL NETWORK   4

controls the company's cable and satellite networks ("Scripps to spin off cable, interactive companies," 2007). These networks include HGTV, Food Network, DIY Network, Fine Living Television Network, and Great American Country ("Scripps to spin off cable, interactive companies," 2007). It also controls Internet businesses such as HGTV.com and FoodNetwork.com, as well as Scripps' shopping services "Shopzilla" and "uSwitch" ("Scripps to spin off cable, interactive companies," 2007).

Online newspaper article with no author but publication date

Header identifying the section of definition of HGTV
Narrative of company history

HGTV as Part of a Conglomerate

HGTV was created in 1994 (Lubenski, 2005) as a place for do-it-yourselfers to congregate and bond over their desire to accomplish things around their homes by themselves. Twenty years after its introduction, HGTV now reaches 98 million homes in the United States alone (Anderson, 2013). Its online presence, HGTV.com, is reported to attract an average of 4 million unique visitors a day ("HGTV Rings in New Year with Highest-Ever Social Media Traffic," 2014). The growing popularity of the HGTV network has meant great things for the Scripps conglomerate as a whole.

Internal citation of online newspaper article with author

By definition, a conglomerate is a "company involved with many different products or services" (Havens & Lotz, 2012, p. 97). HGTV plays a pivotal role as part of the Scripps conglomeration because of the massive following the network's shows garner domestically and worldwide. HGTV alone was responsible for increasing Scripps Networks' profits by 7%–8% from 2013-2014 ("Financial Release," 2014). That is not including the Website, magazines, or other associated products.

Definition from a book source with two authors. Because it is a partial quote, the page number is given

Provides supporting data with supporting figure that includes source. Internal citation from a Web page

So what does this mean for HGTV as a network? Being a part of a major, publicly held conglomerate means that HGTV has responsibilities to the investors and stockholders, as well as advertisers and the government (Havens & Lotz, 2012). Having to satisfy so many people, HGTV could find itself in an expensive business model if it were following the traditional scripted form of creating television. Fortunately, HGTV has discovered the economic advantages of reality television and importing programming.

Continues definition

HGTV Taking Advantage of Cheap Production

HGTV has taken several steps to ensure the inexpensive nature of its TV shows stays as inexpensive as possible. HGTV utilizes the

Transition statement

HGTV: GLOBALLY SUCCESSFUL NETWORK   5

cheapest form of TV (reality TV), produces it in Canada, and imports it to
the United States, and the network is even smart enough to do all of the
"DIYing" in the shows at the expense of the homeowners.

Importing from Canada

Because HGTV is owned by a large conglomerate, it is broadcast
in several areas of the world. We will get to that later, but for now I
want to focus on North America. HGTV, although founded on U.S. soil,
has been increasingly popular in Canada. Not only is HGTV popular in
Canada, the majority of the shows that air around the world (especially
in the United States) are filmed and produced in Canada. Why? To put
it simply, *money*. To get around the high cost of production and staffing
in America, producers go across the border to Canada and pay for their
labor in Canadian dollars (Epstein, 2006). $1.00 of American money is
equivalent to $1.15 in Canadian dollars ("Daily Currency Converter").
While that conversion doesn't sound like much in that small an amount
of money, when millions of dollars are being spent, the $0.15 difference
can mean hundreds of thousands of dollars in savings.

Not only is the cash conversion saving networks money, the networks
also often receive additional discounts and subsidies from the countries
in which they're filming (Epstein, 2006). The specific province of Canada
in which a show is filmed can give up to an 18% rebate to the producers
for labor that comes from that province, and a tax credit awarded if "either
the director or the screenwriter and one of the two highest-paid actors are
Canadian" (Epstein, 2006, para. 3). All of these incentives are available
in an effort to attract networks to Canada, and for HGTV, it worked. This
outsourcing of jobs is becoming ever more popular, and was made possible
by conglomerates much like The Scripps Network (Havens & Lotz, 2012).

Since most of the shows that air on HGTV are turning into home-
renovation shows or home-buying shows, it is necessary for HGTV to
show homes that will attract and intrigue their viewers. One of the biggest benefits of filming in Canada is that the landscape is so similar to
the United States. It is almost impossible to tell a home on a Canadian
street from a home on a U.S. street. Since the HGTV Network has a base
in Canada, it has doubled up on savings by allowing 11 of its programs

Uses subheading consis-
tent with map

Online source with author
Provides supporting data
Cites Web page without
date

Provides supporting data

APA requires if there is no
page number, the para-
graph number of the online
source be indicated

In-text citation of online newspaper article with author

Header connected to map

Provides supporting explanation, causes for lower cost

Illustrates claims with an example

States cause for lower cost

Continues illustration

Final major header

Offers solution to problem

(more than any other cable network in the United States) to be produced in Canada, then importing them to the United States (Johnson, 2013).

Utilizing Reality TV's Inexpensive Nature

Everything that goes into filming a TV show costs money, and the more you can eliminate from the budget sheet, the better. Reality TV takes care of most of that. When filming a reality TV show, there is no need to rent studio space, no need for costume or set designs, no need for extensive scripts or hours of paying actors for rehearsal, and minimal cost associated with editing and post-production. HGTV has stars on every one of its shows who make up for the majority of the budget. The camera crew and lighting account for another portion. But HGTV has all but eliminated the need for much else.

Let's take a look at one of HGTV's most popular shows, *Property Brothers*, as an example of where HGTV is saving money. Two men, who are paid by HGTV, take *real* clients out to search for new homes that the brothers will then renovate for the buyers. The trick is, everything else is at the cost of the buyers. They pay for the new home, and they pay for the renovations. HGTV sits back and films it all with a small crew and makes a show out of it that attracts millions of viewers for HGTV each year.

HGTV has also utilized product placement within its shows to generate more profits. If we are still looking at *Property Brothers*, there are several examples of product placement. The brothers will mention by brand name the furniture brand, paint brand, stores they shop in, and even hardware brands for things like the kitchen faucets they put in. They do it in a way that appears organic (Havens & Lotz, 2012), however, and it comes off to the viewer as a suggestion of what they should buy for their own homes. It's clever and done almost seamlessly.

HGTV Breaking Down Cultural Barriers

Many networks face issues with exporting content, globalization of a product (Havens & Lotz, 2012) due to the cultural barriers that seem impossible to cross. Following the "reality TV" format can be an issue when it comes to exporting media if you aren't intending on selling just the format for a TV show. The simplicity of HGTV makes it easier than would typically be possible to export content. Home buying is universal.

Home renovation is universal. While the landscape of Canada may not be as familiar to someone watching in China as it is to us in the United States, the same issues occur with the homebuyers everywhere. DIYing, home buying, and home renovations do not depend on the culture to make sense; they are universally occurring things (Havens & Lotz, 2012).

Another advantage of filming in Canada is that some of the major cities (like Toronto) are so multicultural that many HGTV shows feature more races than just white people, which are typically the makeup of U.S. reality shows (Kane, 2014). Another popular show on HGTV, which was filmed in Canada, uses this fact to its advantage. The star of the show, Mike Holmes, reports that when his show features a Korean couple, for example, after the show airs he will receive fan letters from Korea telling him how funny he was (Kane, 2014). It really goes to show how far-reaching HGTV's success is; the network has transcended cultural boundaries.

Conclusion

HGTV has truly used all of the available techniques to make its shows inexpensive to produce, easy to export, and easy to offer up to advertisers for product placement. As part of a major conglomerate that has its fingers in several aspect of the media industry, HGTV is arguably one of the most successful endeavors that The Scripps Networks has invested in. The simplicity of the content is attractive to markets all around the globe, and the issues discussed on the shows are easily relatable for viewers almost everywhere.

Transition offering another solution to the problem

In-text citation of a blog post with an author

Offers an example as illustration

Provides summary of main argument for HGTV's global success

References

Anderson, S. (2013, December 10). Old-time media conglomerate E.W. Scripps injects itself with youth serum, acquires newsy for $35 million. *Startup Book*. Retrieved from http://startupbook.co/2013/12/10/old-time-media-conglomerate-e-w-scripps-injects-itself-with-youth-serum-by-acquiring-newsy-for-35-million/

Centered label of References

HGTV: GLOBALLY SUCCESSFUL NETWORK   9

Carr, D. (2014, August 10). Print is down, and now out. *The New York Times*. Retrieved from http://www.nytimes.com/2014/08/11/business/media/media-companies-spin-off-newspapers-to-uncertain-futures.html?src=me&_r=0

Daily Currency Converter. (n.d.). *Bank of Canada* [Web page]. Retrieved from http://www.bankofcanada.ca/rates/exchange/daily-converter/

Epstein, E. (2006, February 13). Why are so many movies shot in Canada? *Slate*. Retrieved from http://www.slate.com/articles/arts/the_hollywood_economist/2006/02/northern_expenditure.html

E. W. Scripps Co (SSP) Company Profile | Reuters.com. (n.d.). *Reuters*. Retrieved from http://www.reuters.com/finance/stocks/companyProfile?symbol=SSP

Financial Release. (2014, November 6). *Scripps Networks Interactive*. [Web page]. Retrieved from http://ir.scrippsnetworksinteractive.com/phoenix.zhtml?c=222475&p=irol-newsArticle&ID=1986659

Havens, T., & Lotz, A. (2012). *Understanding media industries*. New York, NY: Oxford University Press.

HGTV, a network devoted to view-it-yourselfers. (2002, December 8). *The Augustine Record*. Retrieved from http://staugustine.com/stories/120802/com_1175041.shtml

HGTV rings in new year with highest-ever social media traffic. (2014, January 3). *The Futon Critic* [Web page]. Retrieved from http://www.thefutoncritic.com/ratings/2014/01/03/hgtv-rings-in-new-year-with-highest-ever-social-media-traffic-139014/20140103hgtv01/

Johnson, K. (2013, November 7). Canada exports its home shows. *The Wall Street Journal*. Retrieved from http://online.wsj.com/articles/SB100014240527023045275045791716671606029080

Kane, L. (2014, August 22). How HGTV Canada built a specialty powerhouse and a global following. [Blog post]. Retrieved from http://holmesspot.blogspot.com/2014/08/tcanadas-global.html

Lubenski, C. (2005, May 8). The age of HGTV. *The San Diego Union-Tribune*. Retrieved from http://www.utsandiego.com/uniontrib/20050508/news_mz1hs08hgtv.html

Scripps to spin off cable, interactive companies. (2007, October 16). *Washington Business Journal*. Retrieved from http://www.bizjournals.com/washington/stories/2007/10/15/daily16.html?page=all

Part of a Web site

Article without author from an online news service

Online newspaper article without author

CHAPTER 22

Additional Research Strategies: Interviews, Questionnaires, Direct Observations

In this chapter, you will learn how to:

22.1 Identify the value of primary research.

22.2 Apply the general principles for primary research.

22.3 Conduct primary research ethically.

22.4 Prepare for and conduct interviews, and write a report based on interviews.

22.5 Develop and administer questionnaires, and write a report based on the data.

22.6 Conduct direct observations and write a report based on the observations.

Visit MyWritingLab **to complete the writing assignments in this chapter and for more resources on research.**

The library isn't the only source of information for research writing. Investigators also gather information through *primary research*, which includes such activities as consulting public records, performing experiments, conducting interviews, sending out questionnaires, and making direct observations of various kinds, including of media.

This chapter focuses on the latter three types, the most common primary research strategies.

The Value of Primary Research

What makes primary research so valuable? First, it allows individuals and organizations to collect recent information, often unavailable elsewhere, that precisely suits their needs. A company with a new product won't find articles on how customers react; such information simply doesn't exist. But a well-crafted questionnaire given to sample customers could suggest some answers and perhaps also some tips for improving the product. Similarly, someone wanting to

22.1
Identify the value of primary research.

gauge the success of an ongoing clothing drive by a local charitable organization might interview its director.

Even when published material exists, it may not contain desired information. Although numerous articles discuss student attitudes about required courses, you probably wouldn't find a report that explores student reaction to a new general education requirement at your school. You could, however, assemble this information by distributing a questionnaire. The findings might even contradict, and therefore cause you to question, the conclusions of others.

Primary research can also yield unexpected and significant information. Suppose you're investigating adult illiteracy, and you interview a professor with a specialty in this area of study. She explains the reasons why people who can't read resist help and supplies several relevant examples. Such information might not appear anywhere in print. Certainly the resulting report would carry more weight and elicit more interest than one without such insights.

You can integrate primary research into a report that consists largely of *secondary research*, the kind that depends on library materials. The student who wrote the sample MLA essay (p. 401) could have interviewed a biologist on campus about infectious diseases. The student who wrote the APA research paper on HGTV (p. 428) included some direct observations of actual TV shows but could have also expanded those observations. Often, however, writers detail the findings of primary research in separate reports. This would be the case if, for example, your employer asked you to interview users of a new computer system in order to determine their degree of satisfaction with it.

General Principles for Primary Research

22.2

Apply the general principles for primary research.

Primary research, like all research, requires well-formulated questions. Such questions must be specifically focused, contain clearly defined terms, and be answerable by the actual research. A vague, general question such as "What attitudes do Americans have about their government?" lacks the necessary precision and therefore can't be resolved. What kind(s) of attitudes? What level or branch of government? Which Americans? How would you gather their opinions? A more realistic question might be "According to the Mason College faculty, how adequate is the new congressional proposal for funding academic research in this country?" You could easily develop and distribute to faculty members a questionnaire addressing the different provisions of the proposal. In addition, you can't resolve ethical or philosophical questions through primary research. While you could use a questionnaire to determine student attitudes about the police using sobriety check lanes, such information won't decide the ethical issue of whether the police should use such check lanes.

For valid results, conduct your primary research in an impartial manner. Always aim to determine facts rather than to justify some belief you hold.

- First, **develop questions that have no built-in bias**. If you poll other students and ask them to tell you "how core-course teachers on this campus marked their papers unreasonably hard," those responding might falsify their answers to give you what you want. Instead, use neutral phrasing such as "Do you believe core-course teachers on this campus mark your papers fairly or unfairly? Explain."

- Second, **don't rely on atypical sources and situations for your data.** If you investigate the adequacy of parking space on campus, don't deliberately observe the parking lots on a day when some special event has flooded the campus with visitors. Careful readers will see what you have done and reject your findings.

Just as you avoid bias when gathering information, you should also report your results fairly.

- **Don't use inaccurate interpretations of your findings to make them agree with the conclusions you're after**. If you believe peer editing produces questionable results, don't claim that the students in a class you observed spent their time sneering at one another's work when in fact they offered constructive criticism.
- **Don't report conclusions that are unsupported by your actual research.** If you observe a large number of violent acts while watching Saturday cartoons, don't leap to the conclusion that the violence in the cartoons causes violent behavior in children. You simply don't have the evidence to support that assertion.
- **Don't cover up results that you don't like**. If your survey of teachers' marking practices shows that most of your respondents believe core-course instructors mark fairly, don't hide the fact because it doesn't match what you expected to discover. Instead, report your findings accurately and rethink your original position.

Ethical Issues

Today most people chuckle at an advertisement for a product recommended by "nine out of ten doctors." We recognize that the doctors were handpicked and don't represent an objective sample of adequate size. As a result, little harm occurs. With primary research, however, distorted investigating and reporting are sometimes hard to detect and can have significant consequences.

Say the officials of Anytown, USA, alarmed at a sharp rise in auto accidents caused by distracted drivers, schedule a special meeting attempting to ban cell phone calls by those driving within city limits. It would be unethical for a reporter opposed to the ban to write a supposedly objective feature article on the issue but include interviews only with people who share his views. Now suppose a presumably neutral group in the city of Lost Wages distributes a questionnaire to residents to gauge their reaction to a proposed gambling casino. It would be unethical to include a biased question such as "Should the city deprive its citizens of the revenue that a casino can provide?" Finally, imagine that a city manager, concerned by reports of motorists running the red light at a major intersection, gets the Department of Public Safety to investigate. A department employee conducts a 20-minute observation, then writes a report concluding that surveillance cameras are not needed there. Clearly, the employee has acted unethically in drawing a conclusion after such a limited observation. To help

22.3
Conduct primary research ethically.

ensure that your primary research reports are ethically responsible, ask and answer the following questions.

- Have I attempted to avoid bias in gathering and evaluating information?
- Are my data based on an adequate sample size? If not, have the limitations of the sample been clearly indicated?
- Is my information presented objectively and completely with no intentional effort to omit findings that run counter to my position?
- Are the people involved, whether I'm preparing an interview, questionnaire, or direct observation report, aware that they are part of a study and how the information will be used? Are they protected from harm that might result from their inclusion?
- Do I have permission to name in my report persons interviewed or observed?
- In an interview report, would the interviewee recognize and accept statements attributed to him or her?
- Have I noted any apparent bias in the interviewee?
- In a questionnaire report, have I avoided any biased questions?

Ethical Review of Primary Research

Many universities have ethical review panels that oversee all research that uses human and animal subjects to make certain that they are not harmed by the research. In some cases, some schools require studies that involve focus groups or interviews to be reviewed by the panel. If you are going to use primary research such as an interview or a survey, be sure to check with your teacher so that your study is consistent with your university's policies on research review.

Interviews

22.4

Prepare for and conduct interviews, and write a report based on interviews.

During an interview, questions are asked and answered. Some interviews amount to little more than brief, informal chats. Others, like those discussed here, may feature extended conversations, involve a series of questions, and require careful preparation. Interviewing an informed person provides you with firsthand answers to your queries, lets you ask follow-up questions, and gives you access to the most up-to-date thinking.

If you major in a business program, an instructor may require you to question a personnel manager about the company's employee relations program. If your field is social work, you might have to interview a case worker as part of your study of some kind of family problem. On the job, you might have to talk with prospective employees and then assess their suitability for a position in the company. Police officers routinely interview witnesses to accidents and crimes, and journalists do the same in pursuit of stories.

Choosing the Interviewee

Professional and technical personnel are a rich source of interview candidates. The faculty of any university can provide insights into a wide range of subjects. Doctors, pharmacists, and other health professionals can draw upon their expertise to help you, as can lawyers, engineers, researchers, corporation managers, and employees at every level of government—federal, state, and local.

Whom you interview depends, of course, on what you wish to know. For information on the safe disposal of high-level nuclear waste, you might consult a physics professor. If you want an expert view on the causes of homelessness, contact an authority such as a sociologist, who could provide objective information. If, however, you want to gain a sense of what it's like to be homeless, you might interview the manager of a shelter or (in a safe place) one or more homeless people. Interviews can be face to face, but you may also consider using a phone interview, employing Skype, using Chat, or even interacting via e-mail.

Preparing for the Interview

If you don't relish the thought of phoning to request an interview, keep in mind that most interviewees are eager to discuss their areas of expertise and are often flattered by the opportunity. The worst that can happen is a turndown, and in that event you can always find someone else in the same field.

Before you phone or use other media, review your own upcoming commitments and try to determine which ones you could reschedule if necessary. You may need to make an adjustment to accommodate the schedule of a busy person. When you call, indicate who you are, that you are requesting an interview, the subject of the interview, and how much time you'd like.

If the person agrees to meet with you, then ask when it would be convenient. Carefully record the time, day, and place of the interview, and if for any reason you need to cancel be sure to call well in advance. If you are using a phone interview or other medium, be sure to equally agree on the medium, contact information, and time in advance.

Before the interview, do as much background reading as possible. This reading will help you develop a list of key questions and avoid those with obvious and readily available answers. Write out your questions to help ensure that the interview will proceed smoothly.

Good questions permit elaboration and don't call for simple "yes" or "no" answers. To illustrate:

Poor:	Is it difficult to work with adult illiterates? (The obvious answer is "yes.")
Better:	What have you found most challenging about working with adult illiterates?

On the other hand, don't ask overly broad questions that can't be answered in a relatively brief interview.

Poor:	What's wrong with primary-school education?
Better:	Why do you think so many children have trouble learning to read?

Avoid questions that are biased and may insult the interviewee.

Poor:	Why do you bother to work with adult illiterates?
Better:	Why did you decide to work with adult illiterates?

Likewise, avoid questions that restrict the interviewee's options for answering.

Poor: What do you think accounts for the poor academic performance of so many American secondary-school students—too much TV watching or overly large classes?

Better: People often blame the poor academic performance of so many American students on too much TV watching or overly large classes. What importance do you attach to these factors? Do you think other factors contribute to the problem?

The number of questions you prepare depends on the length of the interview. It's a good idea to draft more questions than you think you'll have time to ask, then arrange them from most to least important. If the interviewee keeps to the schedule, you'll obtain your desired information. If the interviewee grants you extra time, your written follow-up will have even more substance.

Conducting the Interview

Naturally you'll want to arrive on time and to bring a notepad and a pen. Sometimes you can record an interview but only if you ask permission first. Because most people warm up slowly, you might start with one or two brief, general questions that provide you with useful background. Possibilities include "What is the nature of your specialty?" and "How long have you been employed in this field?"

Proceed by asking your most important questions first. If you believe that a question hasn't been answered or that an answer is incomplete, don't hesitate to ask follow-up questions.

As the interview unfolds, take notes but don't attempt to copy everything that's said. Instead, jot down key phrases and ideas that will serve as memory prompts. If you want to capture an essential explanation or some other important material in the interviewee's own words, ask the person to go slowly while you copy them down. When the interview is over, thank the person for talking to you. You may also offer to supply a copy of the finished report. Write a personal note thanking the person for his or her time. With the answers to your questions fresh in your mind, expand on your notes by filling in details, supplying necessary connections between points that were made, and noting your reactions.

Writing About the Interview

The project you're working on determines how to handle your interview information. If you're preparing a library research paper, include the material, suitably presented, at the appropriate spot and document it according to whatever system, MLA or APA, you're using.

Often, however, you'll be asked to prepare a separate report of the interview. Then, as with any other report, you'll need to organize and present the material in an effective order. Your topic, purpose, and audience will determine the arrangement you select. In any event, remember to establish the context for the report, identify the interviewee and his or her position, and present the information accurately.

STUDENT INTERVIEW REPORT

**Budget Cuts Affect State Police: An Interview
Report with Officer Robert Timmons**

Holly Swain

Confronted with a billion-dollar budget deficit, the state legislature and the governor have been forced to make sharp budget cuts. One of these cuts is the allocation to the state police. This decision has threatened the loss of some police jobs and aroused considerable controversy. How, many ask, will the police, who were already on a tight budget, be able to provide the public with adequate protection when they have even less money and fewer personnel?

When Trooper Robert Timmons, a state police officer based in Marywood County, first heard that the governor might call for police cutbacks, he didn't believe they would become a reality. Timmons thought the governor was just making "political noise." Actually, the state police head did at first propose cutting 350 jobs, Timmons's among them, to help meet a $19 million cutback. This proposal was rejected in favor of one that combined demotions, pay cuts, and the elimination of special programs. In addition, the amounts allotted for other purposes were also cut.

All of these actions, Timmons says, have had an unfortunate effect on the operations of the state police. As an example, he mentions a sergeant who was demoted to "accident reconstructionist," a job requiring him to review severe accidents and reconstruct what happened for the court. This demotion, Timmons says, has taken an excellent police officer out of the field, where he's most needed, and put him behind a desk.

Timmons notes several bad effects of cuts in the allocation for gasoline. Because of these cuts, troopers are expected to drive just 90 miles a night. Timmons thinks this limitation has a "direct effect on the public." A motorist stranded on a freeway might not be spotted and aided by a trooper who is unable to make another run through that territory. Late-night accidents might go undiscovered, with serious or fatal consequences for those involved. Many more speeders and drunk drivers will escape being caught.

As of now, Timmons says, there are only 3,000 state police, about 400 fewer than needed. Each year, 100 to 200 officers retire. These vacancies need to be filled, but according to Timmons, the state academy has

Continued on next page

Paragraph 1: establishes context for interview

Sentence 1, paragraph 2: identifies interviewee and his position

Remainder of report: presents information provided by interviewee

Continued from previous page

been closed for over a year. The personnel shortages that already exist and the cutbacks resulting from the state's budget troubles are making it harder and harder for the state police to do an adequate job of protecting the public.

Officer Timmons understands that the state government needs to control its spending. However, he believes that the present budget cutbacks for a department that is already understaffed are very unwise. "I feel the governor should have given the matter more thought," he says.

Questionnaires

22.5

Develop and administer questionnaires, and write a report based on the data.

A questionnaire consists essentially of a series of statements or questions to which recipients are asked to respond. Questionnaires help individuals and organizations determine what select groups of people think about particular products, services, issues, and personal matters. You yourself have probably completed a variety of questionnaires, including teacher evaluations and market surveys.

Questionnaires are used extensively both on campus and in the workplace. A social science instructor might ask you to prepare a survey that explores community reaction to a recently implemented curfew for teenagers. A business instructor might want you to survey a test-market group to determine its response to some new product. In fact, some marketing classes focus on survey techniques. But even if marketing isn't your specialty, learning how to construct questionnaires can serve you well in your career. If you work in the hotel, restaurant, or health service field, you could use a questionnaire to gauge customer satisfaction. The same holds true if you manage or own a small repair service. As a landscape specialist, you might survey the people in your community to learn what planting and maintenance services they desire. There are a number of survey tools available online, including Survey Monkey, that allow you to send people an electronic survey that is automatically tallied.

Developing the Questionnaire

When you develop a questionnaire, you need to target precisely what you want to know and what group you intend to survey. You could survey restaurant customers to determine their attitudes about the service and the quality of the food or to assess the types of food they prefer. Zero in on only one area of interest and then explore it with appropriate questions.

Begin the questionnaire with a clear explanation of what you intend to accomplish, and supply brief but clear instructions on how to respond to each part. Keep the questionnaire as short as possible, preferably no longer than a page or two. The longer the survey, the less likely that people will answer all the questions.

As you draw up your questions, take care to avoid these common errors:

1. Don't ask two questions in the same sentence. Their answers may be different.

   Unacceptable: Do you find that this year's Ford Taurus has better acceleration and fuel economy than last year's model?

   To correct this fault, use separate sentences.

   Better: Do you find that this year's Ford Taurus has better acceleration than last year's model?

   Better: Do you find that this year's Ford Taurus has better fuel economy than last year's model?

2. Don't include vague or ambiguous questions. Since people won't understand your intent, their answers may not reflect their beliefs.

   Unacceptable: Is assisted suicide a good idea?

   Better: Should assisted suicide be permitted for terminally ill patients?

3. Avoid biased questions. They might antagonize those who don't share your views and cause them not to complete the questionnaire.

   Unacceptable: Should Century City taxpayers continue to waste money on renovating the North Park Bridge?

   Better: Should Century City taxpayers spend an additional $100,000 to complete the North Park Bridge renovation?

Most questionnaire items fall into the categories that follow. The information you want determines which you choose. Often you'll need to include several or all of the categories in your questionnaire.

Two-Choice Items   Some items have two possible responses: yes/no, true/false, male/female.

Example: Do you plan to repaint your house during the summer months?

   ☐ yes
   ☐ no

Multiple-Choice Items   Often there are several possible responses to a questionnaire item. When you prepare this type of item, make sure that you include all significant choices and that the choices share some common ground. Don't ask if someone's primary vehicle is a subcompact, compact, full-size, or foreign car as size and place of manufacture are unrelated. To determine whether the vehicle is domestic or foreign, use a separate item.

Example: Check the income group that describes your combined family income.

   ☐ less than $9,999 a year
   ☐ $10,000–$19,999 a year

☐ $20,000–$29,999 a year
☐ $30,000–$39,999 a year
☐ $40,000–$50,000 a year
☐ over $50,000 a year

Checklists   Checklists allow respondents to mark more than one option. They can help you determine the range of factors that led to a decision.

Example: Please check any of the following factors that help explain why you decided not to re-enroll your child in Good Growth Private School:

☐ can no longer afford tuition
☐ moved
☐ dissatisfaction with child's progress
☐ disagree with school's educational approach
☐ conflict with teacher
☐ conflict with other staff
☐ child unhappy with school
☐ child had conflict with other children

Ranking Lists   Sometimes you may need to ask people to rank their preferences. This information will help you select the most suitable option from among several possibilities.

Example: Designating your first choice as "1," please rank your preferences in music from 1 through 5.

☐ classical
☐ country and western
☐ jazz
☐ rock and roll
☐ heavy metal
☐ rap

Using the responses to this item, the manager of a local radio station could broadcast the type of music that listeners clearly prefer.

Scale Items   When you are trying to determine the extent to which members of a group support or oppose some issue, using a scale can be helpful. Be sure to have people respond to a statement, *not* a question.

Example: Please circle the response that best reflects your feelings about the statement below.

SA = strongly agree, A = agree, N = no opinion, D = disagree, SD = strongly disagree

Women should be allowed to fly combat aircraft in time of war.

SA   A   N   D   SD

Open-Ended Items   When you want to gather ideas from other people, you might turn to open-ended items—those that don't limit the reader's response. If you do, keep such items narrow enough to be manageable. You should know, however, that readers are less likely to complete open-ended items and that they are difficult to sort and tally.

Example: Please list the three improvements that you would most like to see in Lowden's high school curriculum.

_____

_____

_____

_____

_____

_____

SAMPLE

STUDENT QUESTIONNAIRE

Survey on Public Smoking

Please take a few minutes to fill out this questionnaire. Your responses will help Bartram College ensure that its smoking policies are sensitive to the smoking habits and attitudes toward public smoking of Bartram College male smokers.

1. Do you smoke cigarettes? (check one) yes/no item
   _____ yes (If you checked yes, please go on to the next question.)
   _____ no (If you checked *no*, please go on to question 4.)

2. If you smoke, indicate how many cigarettes each day. (check one)   Multiple-choice item
   _____ less than half a pack
   _____ between a half and a whole pack
   _____ between one and two packs
   _____ more than two packs

3. If you smoke, what are you likely to do upon entering a public place with no posted smoking restrictions? (check one)
   _____ smoke freely
   _____ check to see whether your smoking is bothering others
   _____ ask others whether they would be bothered if you smoke
   _____ not smoke

Continued on next page

Continued from previous page

Checklist

4. Check the statements you believe are true.

_____ My health is at risk only if I am a smoker.

_____ Secondhand smoke contains the same ingredients as directly inhaled smoke.

_____ Secondhand smoke poses no health risk to nonsmokers.

_____ Secondhand smoke poses a health risk to nonsmokers.

_____ Secondhand smoke poses less of a health risk than directly inhaled smoke.

5. Please rate each of the statements below, using the following scale: SA = strongly agree, A = agree, N = no opinion, D = disagree, SD = strongly disagree.

Scale items

_____ There should be no restrictions on public smoking.

_____ Smoking should be prohibited in stores, banks, offices, and workshops.

_____ Smoking and nonsmoking sections in restaurants should be separated by a barrier that smoke cannot penetrate.

_____ Smokers and nonsmokers should have separate workplace lounges.

_____ All public smoking should be prohibited.

6. Please add one or two comments you might have regarding public smoking.

Open-ended item

_____

_____

_____

_____

_____

Testing and Administering the Questionnaire

When you have finished creating the questionnaire, ask several people to respond to the items and gauge their effectiveness. Are any items vague, ambiguous, biased, or otherwise faulty? If so, rewrite and retest them.

To ensure that you obtain an accurate assessment, make certain that you select an appropriate cross section of recipients. To illustrate, assume that you and many of your campus friends dislike early morning classes. You decide to draw up a questionnaire to sample the attitudes of other students. You suspect that many students share your dislike, and you plan to submit your findings to the college president for possible action. To obtain meaningful results, you'll have to sample a sizable group of students. Furthermore, this group will need to include representative numbers of first-year students, sophomores, juniors, and seniors because these classes may not share a uniform view. Failure to sample properly can call your results into question and cause the administration to disregard them. Proper sampling, on the other hand, pinpoints where dissatisfaction is greatest and suggests a possible response. Thus, if first-year students and sophomores register the most objections, the administration might decide to reduce the number of 100- and 200-level classes meeting at 8 a.m. Some sampling strategies, such as the use of Facebook as a tool to get results, can make it more difficult to get an adequate sample. When you are aware of weaknesses in your sampling, you can still use the data, but you must use it more carefully, clearly state the limitations of your sampling, and make certain you do not make claims that go beyond your sample population.

Totaling the Responses

When the recipients have finished marking the questionnaire, you will need to total the responses. Even without computer scoring, this job is easier than you might think. Simply prepare a table that lists the questionnaire items and the possible responses to each; then go through the questionnaire and add up the number of times each response is marked.

When you finish, turn your numbers into percentages, which provide an easier-to-understand comparison of the responses. Simply divide the number of times each possible response is checked by the total number of questionnaires and then multiply the result by 100.

Writing the Questionnaire Report

When you write your report, don't merely fill it with numbers and responses to the questionnaire items. Instead, look for patterns in the responses and try to draw conclusions from them. Follow the logical order of the conclusions you want to stress.

Typically, a report consists of two or three sections. The first, "Purpose and Scope," explains why the survey was performed, how many questionnaires were distributed and returned, and how the recipients were contacted. The second section, "Results," reports the conclusions that were drawn. Finally, if appropriate, a "Recommendations" section offers responses that seem warranted based on the survey findings.

SAMPLE

STUDENT QUESTIONNAIRE REPORT

Findings from Smoking Questionnaire Distributed to Bartram College Students

Kelly Reetz

Purpose and Scope of Survey

This survey was carried out to determine the smoking habits and attitudes toward public smoking of Bartram College's male students. The

Continued on next page

Provides background details on project, profile of respondents

Continued from previous page

assignment was one of my requirements for completing Public Health 201. Each of the 240 male students in Crandall Hall received a copy of the questionnaire in his mailbox, and 72 completed questionnaires were returned. This latter number equals 10 percent of the college's male student population and therefore can be considered a representative sample. Of those responding, 37, or 51 percent, were cigarette smokers. Thirty-five, or 49 percent, were nonsmokers. Of the smokers, all but 11 percent smoked over a pack of cigarettes a day.

Results of Survey

Smokers seemed fairly considerate of nonsmokers in public places. Only 16 percent said they would smoke freely. In fact, 51 percent said they wouldn't smoke at all. The remaining 33 percent indicated they would either look around to see whether they were bothering others or ask others whether they objected to cigarette smoke.

In general, respondents seemed aware that secondhand smoke poses a health risk. Seventy-six percent believe that such smoke contains the same ingredients as directly inhaled smoke, and an amazing 96 percent believe that anyone exposed to secondhand smoke may be at risk. Only 3 percent think no health risk is involved.

Opinions were strongly divided on the matter of banning all public smoking, with 79 percent strongly opposed and 21 percent strongly in favor. As might be expected, all of the smokers fell in the first group, but a surprising 51 percent of the nonsmokers did too. A sharp division was equally apparent between supporters and opponents of restaurant barriers, with 81 percent for or strongly for them and 19 percent against or strongly against them. In contrast to the findings on a smoking ban, all of the smokers favored barriers. Respondents overwhelmingly endorsed, 90 percent to 10 percent, prohibiting smoking in stores and banks and providing separate workplace lounges. Nobody registered a "no opinion" vote on any of the statements under item 5.

Responses to items 3 through 5 reveal an awareness among smokers of the dangers posed by secondhand cigarette smoke, a concern for the well-being of nonsmokers, and a willingness to accept restrictions, though not an outright ban, on public smoking. This attitude was consistent for both light and heavy smokers. For their part, about half the nonsmokers showed a tolerant attitude by supporting smoking restrictions but rejecting an outright ban.

Discusses responses to questionnaire item 3

Discusses responses to questionnaire item 4

Discusses responses to questionnaire item 5

Discusses patterns in responses to items 3–5

No smokers, but 71 percent of the nonsmokers, responded to the request to provide one or two additional comments. All of these comments dealt with how the respondents would act if bothered by someone else's smoke. Two-thirds said they would move to another spot, half of the remainder said they would ask the smoker to stop, and the other half said they would remain silent rather than risk an argument.

Discusses responses to item 6

Recommendations

As noted previously, this survey included only male students. To determine how its results compare with those for females, the same questionnaire should be administered to a similar group of female students.

Direct Observations

Often direct observation is the most effective means of answering research questions. If you want to know the extent and nature of violence in children's TV cartoons, watching a number of shows will tell you. Similarly, a researcher who seeks information about living conditions in an inner-city area can obtain it by visiting that locale. Such observations furnish firsthand answers to our questions. Notice that the material for observation can be very broad. Primary sources for study could include a review of the response of fans on a fan site, the letters of nineteenth-century women on Iowa farms, or the illustrations on cereal boxes.

In college and on the job, you may need to report your own observations. If you're majoring in business, an instructor might require a report on the work habits of employees at a small local company. If your field is biology, you might need to assess and report on the environmental health of a marsh, riverbank, or other ecological area. On the job, a factory superintendent might observe and then discuss in writing the particulars of some problem-plagued operation. Police officers routinely investigate and report on accidents, and waste-management specialists inspect and report on potential disposal sites.

The following suggestions will help you make your observations, record them, and then write your report.

22.6

Conduct direct observations and write a report based on the observations.

Preparing to Make the Observations

First, determine the purpose of your observations and keep the purpose firmly in mind as you proceed. Otherwise, you'll overlook important details and record less-than-helpful information. Obviously, observing a classroom to assess the interaction of students calls for a different set of notes than if you were observing the teacher's instructional style or the students' note-taking habits.

Next, establish the site or sites that will best supply you with the information you need. If you're trying to determine how college students interact in the classroom, then the time of day, kind of class, and types of students will all make a difference. You might have to visit more than one class in order to observe the different types of behavior.

If your observations will take place on private property or will involve an organized group such as a class or a legislative body, you'll need to obtain permission and to make an appointment. Also, you might want to supplement your observations with an interview. Ordinarily, the interview will take place after you make your observations so that you can ask about what you've seen. If technical information is needed in advance, the interview should precede the observations. However, you should have done research first so that you do not waste the expert's time and goodwill by asking about information that is reasonably available.

Because you'll probably be making a great many individual observations, try to develop a chart and a code for recording them. Suppose you're comparing the extent to which students interact with one another and with the instructor in remedial and nonremedial composition courses. After much thought, you might develop a chart like the one following:

Class Designation: Composition 100				
Minutes into observation when interaction occurred	Classroom location of interacting students	Number and sex of students	Subject of interaction	Length of interaction

With certain kinds of observations, using a chart will not be possible. In developing your code, you would undoubtedly use M = male and F = female to distinguish the sexes. To show the location of the interacting students, FC = front of class, MC = middle of class, and BC = back of class would probably work quite well. Coding the kinds of interaction presents a more difficult task. Here, after considering several possibilities, you might decide upon these symbols: CR = class related, SR = school related, SP = sports, D = dating, O = other matters. To save writing time, you'd probably want to use "min." for "minutes" and "sec." for "seconds" when recording the lengths of the interactions.

Making the Observations

If your visit involves a scheduled appointment, be sure to arrive on time and be ready to take notes. Select a location where you can observe without interfering. If you are observing people or animals, remember that they need to adjust to you before they will behave naturally.

Before you begin taking notes, record any pertinent general information. If you're observing a class, you might note the time it is meeting, its size, the name of the instructor, and whether he or she is present when you arrive. If you're observing an apartment, pertinent information would include the location and condition of the building, the time of the visit, and the general nature of the environment. Note also whether the landlord as well as the tenant knew you were coming: It is amazing how much cleanup landlords can carry out when they know an observer will soon arrive.

Don't feel as though you must take extensive notes. Do, however, record enough details to ensure that you won't forget any events, activities, or features that are important. If you have a chart and coding system, rely on it as much as possible when recording information. Refer to the chart at the bottom of this page for how the coded notes for part of a classroom visit might look.

If you haven't developed a chart, take enough notes so that you can produce a thorough report. Try to follow some note-taking pattern. When observing the condition of an apartment, you could proceed from room to room, jotting down observations such as "Front hallway, entranceway: paint peeling in large strips from wall, paint chips on floor. Hallway dark, bulb burned out. Linoleum curling up along sides. Cockroaches running along lower molding." Remain as objective as possible as you take notes. Record what you see, hear, and smell, and avoid loaded language. If you must record a subjective impression, identify it as such.

Ask questions if necessary, but rely primarily on what you observe, not what you're told. If the landlord of a run-down apartment you're visiting tells you that he's repainting the building but you see no signs that this is happening, ignore what he says or report it along with an appropriate cautionary comment. When you finish, thank the person(s) who made your observations possible or helped you in other ways.

When you leave the observation site, expand your notes by adding more details. Supply any needed connections and record your overall impressions. To illustrate, suppose you are expanding your notes on student interactions in a composition class. You might note that the greatest number of interactions occurred before and immediately after the instructor arrived, that all student–student interactions involved individuals seated together, that student–instructor interactions included students in all parts of the room, and that all the latter interactions were about subject-related matters. This information might stimulate interesting speculation concerning the student–student and student–teacher relationships in the class, causing you to conclude that the students were hesitant about having exchanges with the instructor. As you proceed, record only what you actually observed, not what you wanted or expected to observe.

Class Designation: Composition 100				
Minutes into observation when interaction occurred	Classroom location of interacting students	Number and sex of students	Subject of interaction	Length of interaction
0	FC	M-M	SP	1 min. 30 sec.
3	MC	F-F	D	Instructor arrived
5	FC, MC, BC	M-M-M-F-F	CR	3 min. 45 sec.
20	FC, MC	M-F-M	CR	1 min.

If upon reviewing your notes you find that you require more information, you may need to arrange a second or even a third visit to the observation site.

Writing the Report

Once your notes are in final form, you can start writing your report. On the job your employer may specify a certain form to follow. As a general rule, all such reports reflect their purposes, focus on relevant information, and remain objective.

Usually you begin by explaining the reason for the investigation, noting any preliminary arrangements that were made, and if appropriate, providing an overview of the observation site. Depending on the nature of the report, the primary means of organization may be as follows:

1. *Narration.* A report on the changing conduct of a child over a three-hour period in a day-care center would probably be organized by narration.
2. *Description.* A report assessing the tornado damage in a large urban area could present its details in spatial order.
3. *Classification.* A visit to a toxic-waste dump suspected of violating state regulations might produce a report classifying the types of waste improperly stored there.
4. *Point-by-point comparison.* If you're comparing two possible sites for a baseball stadium, shopping mall, or other structure, a point-by-point comparison will probably best suit your purpose.
5. *Cause and effect.* This pattern works well for reporting events whose effects are of special concern, such as the testing of a new siren intended to scare birds from an airport runway.
6. *Process.* This arrangement is indicated when readers will want to know step-by-step how some process—for example, a new test for determining the mineral content of water—is carried out.

Conclude the report by discussing the significance of the findings and making any other comments that seem justified.

SAMPLE

STUDENT OBSERVATION REPORT

Observations of an Inner-City Apartment Building

Caleb Thomas

Gives reason for visit, location of site

To fulfill part of the requirements for Social Service 321, I observed the housing conditions in an inner-city residential area. The building I selected is located in the city of Grand Mound, at the corner of Division Avenue and Hall Street, an area where most of the residents hold minimum-wage jobs or receive some form of public assistance.

I met the building supervisor, who had agreed to this visit, at 9:30 A.M. on Friday, April 13, 2001. The brick sides of the three-story apartment building appeared to be in good repair, but one second-story window was broken out and boarded up. Most windows had standard window shades, but a few were blocked with sheets or black plastic bags. Two had no coverings of any kind. Overall, the building's appearance was similar to that of several nearby apartment buildings.

Heavy traffic clogged Division Avenue at the time of my visit. Next to the apartment building stood three single-story wooden buildings housing an adult video store, a bar, and a novelty shop, all with boarded windows and peeling paint. Across the street, a single-story Goodwill store occupied the entire block. In front of it, three women in short skirts walked slowly back and forth, eyeing the cars that passed. Two men sat on crates, their backs to the building, drinking something out of paper bags.

The supervisor opened the unlocked metal door of the apartment building, and we went in. The hallway was lighted by a single dim bulb located on the wall toward the rear. Other bulbs along the wall and in two light fixtures hanging from the ceiling appeared burned out. Scraps of newspaper and chips of paint that had peeled from the ceiling and walls littered the floor. A strong urine-like smell pervaded the air.

Stating that he couldn't show me an occupied apartment because he "respected the privacy of the tenants," the supervisor took me to an unoccupied apartment on the first floor. He had trouble unlocking the wooden door; the key appeared to stick in the lock. The inside of the door had two bolt locks, one a few inches above the door handle and the other one near the floor. The door opened into a short hall with rooms off either side. Here, as in the building entrance, paint chips from the peeling walls and ceiling littered the floor. A battered socket on the wall held a single bulb, but when I flicked its switch, the bulb did not light. On the hall floor, linoleum curled at the edges. When I bent down to examine it more closely, several cockroaches scurried under the curl.

The first door on the right-hand side of the hall led into a 10-by-12-foot room that the supervisor identified as the living room. Here the walls had been recently painted—by a former tenant, the supervisor said—and a strong paint smell was still apparent. However, nothing else had been done to the rest of the room. The radiator was unshielded, several nail heads protruded from the stained and uncovered wooden floor, and the sagging ceiling had several long cracks. Plaster chips dotted the floor.

Continued on next page

Notes preliminary arrangements, provides overview of site location

Continues overview of site location

Describes building's hallway

Describes apartment hallway

Describes apartment living room

Continued from previous page

Describes apartment kitchen

A small kitchen was situated behind the living room. Again, linoleum floor covering curled from the baseboard, and cockroaches scurried for cover. The kitchen was furnished with a battered-looking gas stove, but there was no refrigerator (the supervisor said one was on order). The surface of the sink was chipped and had many brownish stains. When I turned on the faucet, a rusty brown stream of water spurted out. I asked for a sample to be tested for lead content, but the supervisor refused.

Describes apartment bathroom

The bathroom, located at the end of the hall, had no radiator. Its floor tiles, broken in a number of places, exposed a foot-long section of rotted wood. The toilet, with seat missing, would not flush when I tried it but simply made a hissing noise. A brown stain spread over the bottom of the bathtub and a large portion of its sides. The wall tiles around the tub bulged outward and appeared ready to collapse into the tub. The supervisor offered the observation that there had been "some trouble with the plumbing."

Describes apartment bedrooms

Two small bedrooms opened off the left side of the hall. Like the living room, both had unprotected radiators, uncovered wooden floors, and cracked ceilings. Walls were papered rather than painted, but long strips of the wallpaper were missing. In one bedroom, a piece of plasterboard hung on the wall as if covering a hole. The windows in both bedrooms were covered with sheets tacked to the wall.

When I had finished looking at the bedrooms, the supervisor quickly escorted me from the apartment and the building, declaring that he was too busy to show me any other vacant apartments. He also said he had no time to answer any questions.

Discusses significance of findings

Clearly, the building I visited fails to meet city housing code: The living conditions are not what most people would consider acceptable. A careful investigation, including a test of the water and of the paint for lead content, seems called for to determine whether this apartment constitutes a health risk.

Reader

The selections in this reader have been chosen to provide you with very different kinds of examples of writing, including newspaper articles, blog posts, traditional essays, and articles in more formal professional journals. They provide examples on which to model your own writing but also include ideas to spark discussion. In addition to the essays, you will find a range of materials to help you approach each reading:

- **Reading Strategies:** Strategies for reading essays that represent each writing strategy in the text (narration, illustration, process analysis, and so forth).
- **Reading Critically:** Approaches for reading material critically and becoming an effective critical thinker.
- **Reading as a Writer:** Ways to read as a writer so that you can learn techniques and uses of language from the examples.
- **Annotated Essays:** The first essay in each section provides annotations that walk you through the effective use of a writing strategy.
- **Discussion Questions:** These are intended to stimulate classroom discussion and prompt your own thinking.
- **Toward Key Insights:** These comments are meant to prompt you to broader reflection about the larger issues suggested by the essays.
- **Suggestions for Writing:** These writing prompts are intended to provide you with ideas for your own writing.
- **Using Multiple Strategies:** These appear with the last reading in each section, highlighting how writing usually uses more than one strategy. As you read each essay, you should note what strategies the writer used to think about and write about the topic. The "Using Multiple Strategies" comments model what you will want to note about each essay.

Most of all, these readings are selected to engage you, to get you thinking, and to help you grow as a writer.

Visit MyWritingLab **to complete the writing assignments.**

NARRATION ▬▬ ▬▬ ▬ ▬ ▬ ▬ ▬ ▬

Reading Strategies

1. Read the narrative rapidly to get a feel for the story and identify the main point.

2. Identify the main conflict that moves the story forward. Identify the major characters and what they may represent.

3. Read the narrative more slowly with the main point in mind. Keep an eye on how the narrative supports the main point.

Reading Critically

1. Consider if the narrative would seem different if told from another person's point of view. Consider that point of view.

2. Ask whether the narrative really supports the author's main point. Consider what other narratives could be told about the issue and determine whether they might undermine the writer's claims.

Reading as a Writer

1. Determine the setting, conflict, characters, and development of the narrative. You might want to outline the plot to determine how it was organized.

2. Notice any particularly effective movements in the plot. If you find a useful strategy, jot it down.

3. Observe how the writer used dialogue. Make a note of any especially effective uses.

JAMES ALEXANDER THOM

The Perfect Picture[1]

James Alexander Thom (born 1933) is a native of Gosport, Indiana, where his parents were physicians, and a graduate of Butler University. Before becoming a freelance writer in 1973, he worked as an editor for the Indianapolis Star *and the* Saturday Evening Post *and as a lecturer at Indiana University. He has authored one volume of essays and several historical novels, one of which,* Panther in the Sky, *earned the Best Novel Award from the Western Writers of America. His latest novel,* The Red Heart, *appeared in 1998. He is a contributor to many magazines. "The Perfect Picture" depicts an incident and an ethical dilemma that Thom experienced as a cub reporter.*

Introduction: notes time, locale, and cause of action; first-person point of view

1   It was early in the spring about 15 years ago—a day of pale sunlight and trees just beginning to bud. I was a young police reporter, driving to a scene I didn't want to see. A man, the police-dispatcher's broadcast said, had accidentally backed his pickup truck over his baby granddaughter in the driveway of the family home. It was a fatality.

Body: paragraphs 2–12; action begins

2   As I parked among police cars and TV-news cruisers, I saw a stocky white-haired man in cotton work clothes standing near a pickup. Cameras were

[1]Reprinted with permission from the August 1976 *Reader's Digest.* Copyright © 1976 by The Reader's Digest Assn., Inc.

trained on him, and reporters were sticking microphones in his face. Looking totally bewildered, he was trying to answer their questions. Mostly he was only moving his lips, blinking and choking up.

3   After a while the reporters gave up on him and followed the police into the small white house. I can still see in my mind's eye that devastated old man looking down at the place in the driveway where the child had been. Beside the house was a freshly spaded flower bed, and nearby a pile of dark, rich earth.

Time signal
Key event

4   "I was just backing up there to spread that good dirt," he said to me, though I had not asked him anything. "I didn't even know she was outdoors." He stretched his hand toward the flower bed, then let it flop to his side. He lapsed back into his thoughts, and I, like a good reporter, went into the house to find someone who could provide a recent photo of the toddler.

Dialogue

5   A few minutes later, with all the details in my notebook and a three-by-five studio portrait of the cherubic child tucked in my jacket pocket, I went toward the kitchen where the police had said the body was.

Time signal
Secondary event

6   I had brought a camera in with me—the big, bulky Speed Graphic which used to be the newspaper reporter's trademark. Everybody had drifted back out of the house together—family, police, reporters and photographers. Entering the kitchen, I came upon this scene:

7   On a Formica-topped table, backlighted by a frilly curtained window, lay the tiny body, wrapped in a clean white sheet. Somehow the grandfather had managed to stay away from the crowd. He was sitting on a chair beside the table, in profile to me and unaware of my presence, looking uncomprehendingly at the swaddled corpse.

Key event

8   The house was very quiet. A clock ticked. As I watched, the grandfather slowly leaned forward, curved his arms like parentheses around the head and feet of the little form, then pressed his face to the shroud and remained motionless.

Time signal

9   In that hushed moment I recognized the makings of a prize-winning news photograph. I appraised the light, adjusted the lens setting and distance, locked a bulb in the flashgun, raised the camera and composed the scene in the viewfinder.

10   Every element of the picture was perfect: the grandfather in his plain work clothes, his white hair backlighted by sunshine, the child's form wrapped in the sheet, the atmosphere of the simple home suggested by black iron trivets and World's Fair souvenir plates on the walls flanking the window. Outside, the police could be seen inspecting the fatal rear wheel of the pickup while the child's mother and father leaned in each other's arms.

11   I don't know how many seconds I stood there, unable to snap that shutter. I was keenly aware of the powerful story-telling value that photo would have, and my professional conscience told me to take it. Yet I couldn't make my hand fire that flashbulb and intrude on the poor man's island of grief.

Conflict

12   At length I lowered the camera and crept away, shaken with doubt about my suitability for the journalistic profession. Of course I never told the city editor or any fellow reporters about that missed opportunity for a perfect news picture.

Time signal
Action ends

13   Every day on the newscasts and in the papers, we see pictures of people in extreme conditions of grief and despair. Human suffering has become a spectator sport. And sometimes, as I'm watching news film, I remember that day.

14   I still feel right about what I did.

Conclusion: paragraphs 13 and 14; indirectly states point; notes writer's reaction

Discussion Questions

1. Thom notes in his opening paragraph that he is "driving to a scene I didn't want to see." How does this statement help explain what happens later?
2. The details, while providing the makings of a perfect picture, also highlight the horror of what has happened and through their impact on his sensitivity help influence Thom's decision. Do you think that Thom made the right decision? Why or why not?
3. When you are watching the news and see a reporter interviewing people who have just experienced a tragedy, how do you feel? Do you think the journalists are just doing their jobs, or are they exploiting people who are in pain?

Toward Key Insights

How have the media affected our sense of privacy?
Is their influence good or bad?
To answer these questions, consider the role of the newspaper photographer in "The Perfect Picture," TV crews at disasters, and talk shows built around very personal revelations.

Suggestion for Writing

Write a personal narrative that features a conflict over a choice between an advantageous and a morally satisfying decision. State your point directly or indirectly, and use time signals and dialogue as necessary.

DIANE GLANCY

Aunt Parnetta's Electric Blisters

Diane Glancy, a Cherokee currently living in Shawnee Mission, Kansas, taught Native American Literature and Creative Writing at Macalester College in Minnesota. She is the author of a number of collections of poetry and novels as well as a collection of nonfiction, The Dreams of a Broken Field. *She also created an award-winning independent film,* The Dome of Heaven.

> *Some stories can be told only in winter*
> *This is not one of them*
> *because the fridge is for Parnetta*
> *where it's always winter.*

1   Hey chekta! All this and now the refrigerator broke. Uncle Filo scratched the long gray hairs that hung in a tattered braid on his back. All that foot stomping and fancy dancing. Old warriors still at it.

2   "But when did it help?" Aunt Parnetta asked. The fridge ran all through the cold winter when she could have set the milk and eggs in the snow. The fish and

meat from the last hunt. The fridge had walked through the spring when she had her quilt and beading money. Now her penny jar was empty, and it was hot, and the glossy white box broke. The coffin! If Grandpa died, they could put him in it with his war ax and tomahawk. His old dog even. But how would she get a new fridge?

3   The repairman said he couldn't repair it. Whu chutah! Filo loaded his rifle and sent a bullet right through it. Well, he said, a man had to take revenge. Had to stand against civilization. He watched the summer sky for change as though the stars were white leaves across the hill. Would the stars fall? Would Filo have to rake them when cool weather came again? Filo coughed and scratched his shirt pocket as though something crawled deep within his breastbone. His heart maybe, if he ever found it. Aunt Parnetta stood at the sink, soaking the sheets before she washed them.

4   "Dern't nothin' we dude ever work?" Parnetta asked, poking the sheets with her stick.

5   "We bought that ferge back twenty yars," Filo told her. "And it nerlced since then."

6   "Weld, dernd," she answered. "Could have goned longer til the frost cohered us. Culb ha' set the milk ertside. But nowd. It weren't werk that far."

7   "Nope," Filo commented. "It weren't."

8   Parnetta looked at her beadwork. Her hands flopped at her sides. She couldn't have it done for a long time. She looked at the white patent-leathery box. Big enough for the both of them. For the cow if it died.

9   "Set it out in the backyard with the last one we had."

10   They drove to Tahlequah that afternoon, Filo's truck squirting dust and pinging rocks.

11   They parked in front of the hardware store on Muskogee Street. The regiments of stoves, fridges, washers, dryers, stood like white soldiers. The Yellow Hair Custer was there to command them. Little Big Horn. Whu chutah! The prices! Three hundred crackers.

12   "Some mord than thad," Filo surmised, his flannel shirt-collar tucked under itself, his braid sideways like a rattler on his back.

13   "Filo, I derrit think we shulb decide terday."

14   "No" the immediate answer stummed from his mouth like a roach from under the baseboard in the kitchen.

15   "We're just lookin'."

16   "Of course," said Custer.

17   They walked to the door leaving the stoves, washers, dryers, the televisions all blaring together, and the fridges lined up for battle.

18   Filo lifted his hand from the rattled truck.

19   "Surrender," Parnetta said. "Izend thad the way id always iz?"

20   The truck spurted and spattered and shook Filo and Aunt Parnetta before Filo got it backed into the street. The forward gear didn't buck as much as the backward.

21   When they got home, Filo took the back off tire fridge and looked at the motor. It could move a load of hay up the road if it had wheels. Could freeze half die fish in the pond. The minute coils, the twisting intestines of the fridge like the hog he butchered last winter, also with a bullet hole in its head.

22   "Nothin we dude nerks." Parnetta watched him from the kitchen window. "Everythin' against uz," she grumbled to herself.

23   Filo got his war feather from the shed, put it in his crooked braid. He stomped his feet, hooted. Filo, the medicine man, transcended to the spirit

world for the refrigerator. He shook each kink and bolt. The spirit of cold itself He whooped and warred in the yard for nearly half an hour.

24   "Not with a bullet hole in it." Parnetta shook her head and wiped the sweat from her face.

25   He got his wrench and hacksaw, the ax and hammer. It was dead now for sure. Parnetta knew it at the sink. It was the thing that would be buried in the backyard. "Like most of us libed," Aunt Parnetta talked to herself. "Filled with our own workings, not doint what we shulb."

26   Parnetta hung the sheets in the yard, white and square as the fridge itself.

27   The new refrigerator came in a delivery truck. It stood in the kitchen. Bought on time at a bargain. Cheapest in the store. Filo made sure of it. The interest over five years would be as much as the fridge. Aunt Parnetta tried to explain it to him. The men set the fridge where Parnetta instructed them. They adjusted and leveled the little hog feet. They gave Parnetta the packet of information, the guarantee. Then drove off in victory. The new smell of the gleaming white inside as though cleansed by cedar from the Keetowah fire.

28   Aunt Parnetta had Filo take her to the grocery store on the old road to Tahlequah. She loaded the cart with milk and butter. Frozen waffles. Orange juice. Anything that had to be kept cool. The fridge made noise, she thought, she would get used to it. But in the night, she heard the fridge. It seemed to fill her dreams. She had trouble going to sleep, even on the clean white sheets, and she had trouble staying asleep. The fridge was like a giant hog in the kitchen. Rutting and snorting all night. She got up once and unplugged it. Waking early the next morn to plug it in again before the milk and eggs got warm.

29   "That ferge bother yeu, Filo?" she asked.

30   "Nord."

31   Aunt Parnetta peeled her potatoes outside. She mended Filo's shirts under the shade tree. She didn't soak anything in the kitchen sink anymore, not even the sheets or Filo's socks. There were things she just had to endure, she grumped. That's the way it was.

32   When the grandchildren visited, she had them ran in the kitchen for whatever she needed. They picnicked on the old watermelon table in the backyard. She put up the old teepee for them to sleep in.

33   "Late in the summer fer that?" Filo quizzed her.

34   "Nert. It waz nert to get homesick for the summer that's leabing us like the childurn." She gratified him with her keen sense. Parnetta could think up anything for what she wanted to do.

35   Several nights Filo returned to their bed, with its geese-in-flight-over the-swamp pattern quilt, but Aunt Parnetta stayed in the teepee under the stars.

36   "We bined muried thurdy yars. Git in the house," Filo said one night under the white leaves of the stars.

37   "I can't sleep 'cause of that wild hog in the kitchen," Aunt Parnetta said. "I tald yeu that"

38   "Hey chelcta!" Filo answered her. "Why didn't yeu told me so I knowd whad yeu said." Filo covered the white box of the fridge with the geese quilt and an old Indian blanket he got from the shed. "Werd yeu stayed out thar all winder?"

39   "Til the beast we got in thar dies."

40   "Hawly gizard," Filo spurted. "Thard be anuther twendy yars!"

41   Aunt Parnetta was comforted by the bedroom that night. Old Filo's snore after he made his snorting love to her. The gray-and-blue-striped wallpaper with

its watermarks. The stovepipe curling up to the wall like a hog tail. The bureau dresser with a little doily and her hairbrush. Pictures by their grandchildren. A turquoise coyote and a ghostly figure the boy told her was Running Wind.

42   She fell into a light sleep where the white stars blew down from the sky, flapping like the white sheets on the line. She nudged Filo to get his rake. He turned sharply against her. Parnetta woke and sat on the edge of the bed.

43   "Yeu wand me to cuber the ferge wid something else?" Filo asked from his sleep.

44   "No," Aunt Parnetta answered him. "Nod unless id be the polar ice cap."

45   Now it was an old trip to Minnesota when she was a girl. Parnetta saw herself in a plaid shirt and braids. Had her hair been that dark? Now it was streaked with gray. Everything was like a child's drawing. Exaggerated. The way dreams were sometimes. A sun in the left corner of the picture. The trail of chimney smoke from the narrow house. It was cold. So cold that everything creaked. She heard cars running late into the night. Early mornings, steam growled out of the exhaust. The pane of window glass in the front door had been somewhere else. Old lettering showed up in the frost. Bones remembered, their aches in the cold. Teeth, their hurt. The way Parnetta remembered every bad thing that happened. She dwelled on it.

46   The cold place was shriveled to the small upright rectangle in her chest, holding the fish her grandson caught in the river. That's where the cold place was. Right inside her heart. No longer pumping like the blinker lights she saw in town. She was the Minnesota winter she remembered as a child. The electricity it took to keep her cold! The energy. The moon over her like a ceiling light. Stars were holes where the rain came in. The dripping buckets. All of them like Parnetta. The *hurrrrrrr* of the fridge. Off. On. All night. That white box. Wild boar! Think of it. She didn't always know why she was disgruntled. She just was. She saw herself as the fridge. A frozen fish stiff as a brick. The Great Spirit had her pegged. Could she find her heart, maybe, if she looked somewhere in her chest?

48   *Hurrrrrr. Rat-tat-at-rat. Hurrr.* The fridge came on again, and startled, she woke and teetered slightly on the edge of the bed while it growled.

49   But she was a stranger in this world. An Indian in a white man's land. "Even the ferge's whate," Parnetta told the Great Spirit.

50   Wasn't everybody a stranger and pilgrim?" The Great Spirit seemed to speak to her, or it was her own thoughts wandering in her head from her dreams.

51   "No," Parnetta insisted. Some people were at home on this earth, moving with ease. She would ask the Great Spirit more about it later. When he finally yanked the life out of her like the pin in a grenade.

52   Suddenly Parnetta realized that she was always moaning like the fridge. Maybe she irritated the Great Spirit like the white box irritated her. Did she sound that way to anyone else? Was that the Spirit's revenge? She was stuck with the cheapest box in the store. In fact, in her fears, wasn't it a white boar which would tear into the room and eat her soon as she got good and asleep?

53   Hadn't she seen the worst in things? Didn't she weigh herself in the winter with her coat on? Sometimes wrapped in the blanket also?

54   "Filo?" She turned to him. But he was out cold. Farther away than Minnesota.

55   "No. Just think about it, Parnetta," her thoughts seemed to say. The Spirit had blessed her life. But inside the white refrigerator of herself—inside the coils, an ice river surged. A glacier mowed its way across a continent. Everything

frozen for eons. In need of a Keetowah fire. Heat. The warmth of the Great Spirit. Filo was only a spark. He could not warm her. Even though he tried.

56   Maybe the Great Spirit had done her a favor. Hope like white sparks of stars glistened in her head. The electric blisters. *Temporary!* She could shut up. She belonged to the Spirit. He had just unplugged her a minute. Took his rifle right through her head.

57   The leaves growled and spewed white sparks in the sky. It was a volcano from the moon. Erupting in the heavens. Sending down its white sparks like the pinwheels Filo used to nail on trees. It was the bright sparks of the Keetowah fire, the holy bonfire from which smaller fires burned, spreading the purification of the Great Spirit into each house. Into each hard, old pinecone heart.

MyWritingLab ## Discussion Questions

1. Does this narrative have a stated or an unstated point? If it is stated, indicate where. If it is unstated, express it in your own words.
2. Having to buy a new refrigerator would not normally seem a matter for a narrative. What elements in this narrative make the purchase a part of a more important narrative?
3. In looking at possible new fridges in paragraphs 10–20, how does Diane Glancy use language to make the narrative about a larger conflict? What would you identify as that larger conflict?
4. Why does Aunt Parnetta seem unable to bear the new refrigerator? What is the significance of her response?
5. Narratives often use outward events to produce inner revelations. How does the new refrigerator lead to an inner revelation for Aunt Parnetta? What does she realize in the end?
6. This story uses unusual spellings to show the characters' dialect or manner of speaking, such as "Dern't nothin' we dude every work?" (paragraph 4). What are the examples of this dialect? How does it influence your perception of the main character? How does this dialect in contrast to the standard writing style of the narrative fit the theme of the narrative?
7. This narrative uses third-person point of view. How does this affect the narrative? How would the narrative change if it were told from the first-person point of view? Told by Parnetta? Told by Filo?

MyWritingLab ## Toward Key Insights

In what ways was Parnetta a stranger in this world and how did her self-identification in this way shape her experiences? More broadly, what are the ways we find ourselves at home or strangers in the world?

A small thing such as the noise of a new refrigerator leads Parnetta to a personal revelation. Why do small things often lead us toward inner discoveries?

MyWritingLab ## Suggestion for Writing

Write a narrative about a seemingly inconsequential event that led you to a personal revelation.

DAN GREENBURG

Sound and Fury

Dan Greenburg is a native of Chicago who holds a bachelor of fine arts from the University of Illinois and a master of fine arts from UCLA. A prolific writer, he has authored over 40 books, including such best sellers as How to Be a Jewish Mother, How to Make Yourself Miserable, How to Avoid Love and Marriage, *and a series of more than 24 children's books,* The Zack Files. *His articles have appeared in a wide and diverse range of popular magazines and been reprinted in many anthologies of humor and satire. He has been a guest on* The Today Show, Larry King Live, Late Night with David Letterman, *and other major TV talk shows. In this selection, Greenburg relates a situation in which soft words defused a potentially explosive situation.*

1   We carry around a lot of free-floating anger. What we do with it is what fascinates me.

2   My friend Lee Frank is a stand-up comedian who works regularly in New York comedy clubs. Not long ago I accompanied him to one of these places, where he was to be the late-night emcee and where I myself had once done a stand-up act in a gentler era.

3   The crowd that night was a typical weekend bunch—enthusiastic, hostile and drunk. A large contingent of inebriated young men from Long Island had decided that a comedian named Rusty who was currently on stage was the greatest thing since pop-top cans and began chanting his name after almost everything he said: "Rus-TEE! Rus-TEE!"

4   My friend Lee knew he had a tough act to follow.

5   Indeed, the moment Lee walked on stage, the inebriated young men from Long Island began chanting "Rus-TEE! Rus-TEE!" and didn't give him a chance. Poor Lee, the flop sweat running into his eyes, tried every trick he knew to win them over, and finally gave up.

6   When he left the stage I joined him at the bar in the back of the club to commiserate.

7   "You did the best you could," I told him.

8   "I don't know," he said, "I could have handled it better."

9   "How?"

10   "I don't know," he said.

11   As we spoke, the young men who'd given him such a tough time trickled into the bar area. One of them spotted Lee and observed to a companion that Lee might want to do something about their heckling.

12   Lee thought he heard the companion reply, "I'm down," a casual acknowledgment that he was willing to have a fistfight. Lee repeated their remarks to me and indicated that he, too, was "down."

13   Though slight of frame, Lee is a black belt in Tae Kwon Do, has had skirmishes with three-card monte con men in Times Square, and once even captured a robber-rapist. I am also slight of frame but have had no training in martial arts. I did have one fistfight in my adult life (with a movie producer), but as Lee's best friend, I assumed that I was "down" as well.

14   Considering that there were more than a dozen of them and only two of us, the period of time that might elapse between our being "down" and our being down seemed exceedingly brief.

15   The young man who'd made the remark drifted toward Lee.

16   The eyes of everyone in the bar shifted slightly and locked onto the two men like heat-seeking missiles. Fight-or-flight adrenaline and testosterone spurted into dozens of male cardiovascular systems. Safeties snapped off figurative weapons. Red warning lights lit up dozens of DEFCON systems; warheads were armed and aimed. In a moment this bar area might very well resemble a saloon in a B grade western.

17   "How ya doing?" said Lee, his voice flat as unleavened bread, trying to make up his mind whether to be friendly or hostile.

18   "Okay," said the guy, a pleasant-looking, clean-cut kid in his mid-20s.

19   I was fascinated by what was going on between the two of them, each feeling the other out in a neutral, unemotional, slightly bemused manner. I saw no hostility here, no xenophobic loathing, just two young males jockeying for position, going through the motions, doing the dance, willing to engage at the slightest provocation. I had seen my cat do this many times when a stranger strayed onto his turf.

20   And then I had a sudden flash of clarity: These guys could either rip each other's heads off now or they could share a beer, and both options would be equally acceptable to them.

21   I'd felt close to critical mass on many occasions myself. But here, feeling outside the action, I could see clearly that it had to do with the enormous reservoir of rage that we men carry around with us, rage that seethes just under the surface and is ready to be tapped in an instant, with or without just provocation.

22   "What're you in town for?" asked Lee casually.

23   The guy was watching Lee carefully, making minuscule adjustments on his sensing and triggering equipment.

24   "It's my birthday," said the guy.

25   Lee mulled over this information for a moment, still considering all his options. Then he made his decision.

26   "Happy birthday," said Lee finally, sticking out his hand.

27   The guy studied Lee's hand a moment. Then, deciding the gesture was sincere, he took the hand and shook it.

28   "Thanks," he said, and walked back to his buddies.

29   All over the room you could hear safeties snapping on, warheads being unarmed. The incident was over, and in a moment it was as if it had never happened.

30   I felt I had just witnessed in microcosm the mechanism that triggers most acts of aggression, from gang fights to international conflagrations. It was so simple: a minor act of provocation. A decision on how to interpret it. Whether or not to escalate. And, in this particular case, a peaceful outcome. What struck me was how absolutely arbitrarily it had all been decided.

Using Multiple Strategies

Narratives like Greenburg's essay often illustrate a point, in this case how we can decide to defuse anger rather than act on it. Greenburg uses several other strategies as well.

- Paragraph 21 explains the cause for what seem to be unnecessary conflicts in terms of a "reservoir of rage."

- The narrative also uses a contrast between the expected fight and the arming (in paragraph 16) and the alternative to conflict (in paragraph 29).

Discussion Questions

MyWritingLab

1. Discuss the appropriateness of Greenburg's title.
2. Does this essay have a stated or an unstated point? If it is stated, indicate where. If it is unstated, express it in your own words.
3. The expression "our being down" occurs twice in paragraph 14. Explain what it means in each instance.
4. Discuss the effectiveness of the figurative language in paragraph 16.
5. In paragraph 21 Greenburg credits "feeling outside the action" for helping him understand the rage involved in this situation as well as in others. Explain what he means.
6. How often do you think that the "equally acceptable" options mentioned in paragraph 20 occur in confrontations?

Toward Key Insights

MyWritingLab

What reasons can you give for the "free-floating anger" that Greenburg mentions at the outset of the essay?
How frequently and in what ways is this anger manifested?
What are some effective strategies for coping with this anger?

Suggestion for Writing

MyWritingLab

Write a narrative about a small incident that turned into a serious confrontation. Possible incidents might include an improper or reckless action of another driver, a minor disagreement with a friend or spouse, or a retaliation for an action at a sporting event. The outcome can be peaceful or otherwise.

DESCRIPTION

Reading Strategies

1. Identify a thesis statement (possibly first or last paragraph) and/or a statement of purpose. Read the essay with an anticipation of what the description is intended to accomplish.

2. Don't get lost in the details. Note, possibly writing in the margins, the overall impression or mood the description is evoking.

3. Decide how much of the description you need to remember. If the description is intended to create a mood, you may read quickly. If you are reading a description of rock formations for a geology class, you might want to take notes that organize the key features you need to remember under the appropriate headings.

4. Note if there is a pattern to the organization of the description. Recognizing the organizational pattern can make even dense writing easier to read.

Reading Critically

1. Identify the point of view of the description. The scene described might look very different from a different vantage point.

2. Look for how the details were selected. An emphasis on different details might have painted a very different picture.

3. Check to see if the conclusion of the essay really follows from the description. Just because a wilderness can be described as pristine doesn't mean that careful logging should be entirely banned.

Reading as a Writer

1. Identify and note down the organizational pattern if it is effective.

2. Jot down any phrases or sections that you find especially effective.

3. Examine the essay for word choice. Notice how the writer obtained the effects he or she did.

JOHN V. YOUNG

When the Full Moon Shines Its Magic over Monument Valley

John V. Young (1909–1999) was born in Oakland, California. After attending San Jose State Teachers College, he spent 12 years as a reporter and editor for several rural California newspapers, then held a series of personnel and public relations positions. In 1966, he became a full-time freelance writer, specializing in western travel pieces. His books include The Grand Canyon *(1969),* Ghost Towns of the Santa Cruz Mountains *(1979, 1984),* Hot Type and Pony Wire *(1980),* State Parks of New Mexico *(1984),* State Parks of Arizona *(1986), and* State Parks of Utah *(1989). His articles have appeared in* The New York Times *as well as in numerous travel publications. In the article that follows, he focuses on the sensations generated first by his surroundings and then by the moonrise.*

Title identifies dominant impression: magic

Introduction: paragraphs 1 and 2; identifies when, where, who, why

Touch impression

Sight impression Comparisons

Body: paragraphs 3–8 Fixed vantage point Sight impressions

Time signal

Sound impressions

Sight impressions

1   We were camped here in early spring, by one of those open-faced shelters that the Navajos have provided for tourists in this part of their vast tribal park on the Arizona–Utah border, 25 miles north of Kayenta. It was cool but pleasant, and we were alone, three men in a truck.

2   We were here for a purpose; to see the full moon rise over this most mysterious and lonely of scenic wonders, where fantastically eroded red and yellow sandstone shapes soar to the sky like a giant's chess pieces and where people—especially white strangers—come quickly to feel like pretty small change indeed.

3   Because all Navajo dwellings face east, our camp faced east—toward the rising sun and the rising moon and across a limitless expanse of tawny desert, that ancient sea, framed by the towering nearby twin pinnacles called The Mittens. We began to feel the magic even before the sun was fully down. It occurred when a diminutive wraith of a Navajo girl wearing a long, dark, velvet dress gleaming with silver ornaments drifted silently by, herding a flock of ghostly sheep to a waterhole somewhere. A bell on one of the rams tinkled faintly, and then its music was lost in the soft rustle of the night wind, leaving us with an impression that perhaps we had really seen nothing at all.

4   Just then, a large woolly dog appeared out of the gloom, seeming to materialize on the spot. It sat quietly on the edge of the glow from our campfire, its eyes shining like mirrors. It made no sound but when we offered food, it accepted the gift gravely and with much dignity. The dog then vanished again, probably to join the girl and her flock. We were not certain it was not part of the illusion.

Time signal
Sight impression
Comparison

5   As the sun disappeared entirely, the evening afterglow brush tipped all the spires and cliffs with magenta, deepening to purple, and the sand ripples stood out like miniature ocean waves in darkening shades of orange. Off to the east on the edge of the desert, a pale saffron glow told us the moon was about to rise behind a thin layer of clouds, slashed by the white contrail of an invisible jet airplane miles away.

Time signal
Sight impressions
Comparison
Sight impressions

6   We had our cameras on tripods and were fussing with light meters, making casual bets as to the exact place where the moon would first appear, when it happened—instant enchantment. Precisely between the twin spires of The Mittens, the enormous globe loomed suddenly, seeming as big as the sun itself, behind a coppery curtain on the rim of creation.

Sight impressions
Comparison
Vivid language

7   We were as totally unprepared for the great size of the moon as we were for its flaming color, nor could we have prepared ourselves for the improbable setting. We felt like the wizards of Stonehenge, commanding the planets to send their light through the magic orifices in line at the equinox. Had the Navajo medicine men contrived this for our benefit?

Sight impressions

Comparison

8   The massive disk of the moon seemed to rise very fast at first, an optical effect magnified by the crystalline air and the flatness of the landscape between us and the distant, ragged skyline. Then it seemed to pause for a moment, as if it were pinioned on one of the pinnacles or impaled on a sharply upthrusting rocky point. Its blazing light made inky shadows all around us, split by the brilliant wedge of the moon's path between the spires. The wind had stopped. There was not a sound anywhere, nor even a whisper. If a drum had sounded just then, it would not have been out of place, I suppose, but it would have frightened us half to death.

Sight impressions

Vivid language

Absent sound
impression

9   Before the moon had cleared the tops of The Mittens, the show was over and the magic was gone. A thin veil of clouds spread over the sky, ending the spell as suddenly as it had come upon us. It was as if the gods had decided that we had seen enough for mere mortals on one spring night, and I must confess it was something of a relief to find ourselves back on mundane earth again, with sand in our shoes and a chill in the air.

Conclusion: time
signal; renames
dominant impression

Notes writer's reaction

Touch impression

Discussion Questions

MyWritingLab

1. How does the last sentence in paragraph 7 ("Had the Navajo medicine men contrived this for our benefit?") relate to the purpose of the essay?
2. This description takes the form of a narrative. Where does the climax occur, and how does it affect the viewers?

Toward Key Insights

MyWritingLab

What makes certain experiences seem magical?
How important are such magical experiences, and how might they shape our perceptions of the everyday world?

MyWritingLab   ## Suggestion for Writing

Select a place you know well and describe it by conveying some dominant impression that emerges during daylight hours. Settle on an appropriate vantage point and either identify the impression or allow readers to determine it for themselves.

KESSLER BURNETT

Seaside Safari

Kessler Burnett is the editor of Chesapeake Life Magazine *and* Jewish Times of Baltimore. *Kessler is also responsible for the blog post* "Girls' Guide to the Eastern Shore." *This essay comes from the June 2009* Virginia Life.

1   Only a maniacal mind could have built this dock. The odd-sized planks erratically rise, fall, twist and wobble, reducing me to a high-wire act with each shaky step. The "net" below is but a soupy tidal flat, where an inattentive audience of fiddler crabs chaotically flit in and out of their dens, assuring me of a creepy landing place if my third-grade balance-beam skills fail to keep me dry. But the anticipation of finally entering the oyster watch house at dock's end commands my attention, and soon I am striding like an old salt toward my home away from home for the next 24 hours.

2   Like an arthritic spider, the nearly 100-year-old watch house rises above the marshlands of Smith Island, the second southernmost in Virginia's chain of 17 barrier islands that skirt the Atlantic seaboard. Propped on slanting stilts and covered in flaking asphalt shingles, the 400-square-foot structure is quaint from a distance. But to overnight guests such as I who haven't exercised their wilderness muscles in ages, the promise of a day (and night) without electricity or plumbing is admittedly a bit unnerving. While photographer Michael Bowles and I have come here for an authentic ecotourism experience, the original purpose of these shacks was purely business—Eastern Shore-style.

3   Common sights in this region during the nineteenth century, these wooden structures were constructed by watermen near their oyster beds, where they'd hole up for weeks on end, well-armed, guarding their harvests from poachers. With the invention of the outboard motor in the early 1900s, watermen could travel to and from the mainland at all hours with ease, thus ending the need for these overnight camps. Out of the estimated 100 watch houses that once dotted this expanse, today fewer than a dozen remain.

4   This particular watch house is the inspiration behind the overnight kayak excursions hosted by Southeast Expeditions, a Cape Charles-based eco-tour company owned by Dave Burden, our guide for the trip. The watch house weekends have become a popular venue for everything from bachelor parties to girlfriends' getaways to second honeymoons. Itineraries can be as rugged or as gentle as clients crave, with activities that range from shell hunting on the islands to tours of an aquaculture farm to dock-side Reiki administered by shipped-in masseuses to chef-prepared sunset suppers. "People who book this trip are looking for something unique," explains Dave, his shaggy, blond hair falling into his face as he lugs a cooler down the pier. "These are people who

want an adventure but don't want the same adventure that everybody else has. They want to feel like they've left their world behind for a completely different one."

5   And oh, what a different world this is. Pushing back the front door, scaly with peeling paint and rigged with a coat hanger as the knob, I enter an honest-to-goodness man cave. Cluttered with tools of an outdoorsman's trade—Deep Woods Off, lighter fluid, fishing books, kerosene lanterns, toilet paper rolls—it's an advanced study in testosterone. All four corners of the interior have dedicated themes (living room, dining room, kitchen, bedroom) that spill into one another. The prima donna in me is grateful for the few amenities: the clean, white bed on the lower bunk and the "bathroom," a closet-sized space with a plastic accordion shower door and a portable head, operated by a series of mysterious knobs and levers that I never fully master. While my idea of roughing it is using paper napkins at dinner, Michael is completely at home in these conditions. Raised in Zimbabwe, he has experienced countless safaris, paddled the hippo-laden Zambezi River and hunted crocodiles. Unwilling to be outdone by a man, I face my bathroom breaks with the same unfazed attitude as he and save my cringing for behind the accordion door.

6   While Michael and I map out our day with Southeast Expeditions' Bill Burnham, a guide and certified Virginia Master Naturalist, Dave cranks up the propane stove and prepares a wonderfully civilized lunch of grilled chicken atop mixed field greens and pine nuts. He promises that dinner, to be a surprise, will be equally elegant. In an instant, all concerns I've harbored about surviving this trip vanish. Sometimes the assurance of a good dinner is all the encouragement a girl needs to get through the day.

7   After a quick "kitchen" clean-up, Bill and I climb into a pair of kayaks tethered to the end of the dock and head for the white-sand beaches of Cobb's Island. Michael and Dave opt for the speed of the powerboat, and once their wake has rolled past, we are left to glide amid the wild, gentle rhythm of the salt marsh. Our paddles create a soft splash and gurgle as they cut into the still, murky water, but that is hardly the only sound: There is the buzz of crickets in the background, along with the sporadic chatter from clapper rails nesting deep within the spiky grasses. A pair of skimmers in flight paces our boats, their fire engine-red mandibles grazing the surface to scoop up to-go meals of shrimp and minnows.

8   Bill encourages me to keep an eye out for diamondback terrapins poking their heads above the grasses as well as for tiny marsh periwinkles that spend their days traveling up and down the cord grass blades, running to and from the tides. Taking a mental inventory, I realize that I've completely surrendered to my surroundings, grateful for the chance to float eye-level with a world that is too easily forgotten amid the clutter of worries that are eight delicious miles away on the mainland.

9   Although the turtles have chosen to remain hidden, the shells on Cobb's Island are a dime a dozen. As the four of us walk the scallop-hemmed shoreline, our heads bowed in shell-seeking mode, Dave explains how, due to waves, weather and tides, these islands live in a constant state of change, shifting shape by degrees every year. The billowy sand sinks like zoysia grass under my feet as we approach a handful of sandpipers erratically darting about. At the water's edge, we stand in silence, listening to the breaking waves toss shells against one another, producing a soulful, muted chime with each buffered collision. "That's one of my favorite sounds," says Dave with soft enthusiasm.

10   The peaceful moment is soon shattered with my inevitable inquiry regarding the island's dark side: sharks. Dave assures me that while nurse, sand and even small great white sharks have been sighted off the coast, they're rare. I take him at his word but inch a tad closer to his defensive tackle-sized frame as we head back to the boats.

11   Pushed homeward by the rush of the incoming tide, the effortless paddle back is a gentle luge ride through the curvy cuts. In no time, the drift delivers us back to the watch house, where our surprise, chef and local caterer Amy Brandt, has been ferried out to prepare dinner. While she whips up an entrée of Chesapeake Bay stew, a brothy concoction of red drum, scallops, clams and basmati rice, Michael and I move the dining room table out to the dock for an al fresco supper, complete with linens, a vase of lavender, candles and wine from Chatham Vineyards in nearby Machipongo. Dave mans the pot of steaming Cherrystone clams, which he serves with a plastic cup of Chardonnay for dipping, an unexpected twist that gives the bite-size bivalves a buttery flavor.

12   As the sun slides below the horizon, the lights from the Chesapeake Bay Bridge-Tunnel flicker in the distance, and the evening's ceiling is a glow-in-the-dark mosaic of planets and stars. After lingering over wine and a few hands of poker, we turn in, I on the bottom bunk, Amy in a cot, and Michael on the air mattress on the floor. As for Dave, he opts to sleep under the stars on the dock.

13   Dawn in the summertime marsh is like a newborn's shrill cry. Once it erupts, everyone in the house is up. The early light is intense and impatient, quickly illuminating every square inch of horizon as it reflects off the water's flat, calm surface. I wake to the sound of Michael climbing on the roof to grab a shot of the sunrise. He shouts an order to me to jump into a kayak for a photo op before the soft light loses it charm. Opening my eyes, my first thought is of Dave, who I fear has rolled off the dock and floated halfway to Bermuda by now. I peer out the window to see him safely asleep, wrapped in a dew-logged Mexican blanket like a human chimichanga.

14   After a short paddle, we pack up our belongings, load the kayaks into the boat, and make the 20-minute cruise back to the mainland. We share the waterway with cownose rays and pass old WWII submarine watchtowers and derelict hunting lodges on Mockhorn Island, where, in the 20th century, city swells came to shoot sage hens, ducks and geese. Staring at the clouds that dot the blue sky like pillowy snowball hydrangea, my thoughts begin the slow turn back toward reality, where deadlines, lawn care and my anemic 401K steal the spotlight from small wonders like periwinkles, the call of the curlew and the earthen hues of the marsh. I make all those requisite promises to myself that returning travelers conjure, about keeping the memories and holding on to the calm and all the revelations of self-growth. But this time, I will.

MyWritingLab   ## Discussion Questions

1. What strategies does the writer use to organize this essay? Why are these strategies used for the audience and purpose of the writing?
2. This is written explicitly as a work of travel writing. What details relate specifically to the travel interest of the piece? Who is its audience? If the writer were writing to botanists and ecologists interested in salt marshes, how would that change her description?

3. What impression is the writer trying to establish in the first paragraph? What descriptive details does the writer use to create that impression?
4. In paragraph 5, what details does the writer use to emphasize the impression of a "man cave?" Is it successful? Why or why not?
5. In paragraph 11, why does the writer spend so little space describing the trip back? Was that an appropriate decision for the essay?
6. In the conclusion, paragraph 14, how does the writer use description to sum up her final point?

Toward Key Insights   MyWritingLab

In what ways does the way we encounter our place influence our experience and subsequent description? The writer approaches this environment as a brief visitor. How would the experience and description be different, if she were moving in to live for a few years or if she were a waterman who made her living from the water?

Suggestion for Writing   MyWritingLab

Write an essay of a place you recently visited for a regional travel magazine. If you have the time, you might even take a weekend trip, taking notes in the process, to write your essay.

JOHN PHILLIP SANTOS

Back to the Future

John Phillips Santos was born and raised in San Antonio, Texas. He received a B.A. from the University of Notre Dame and an M.A. in English from St. Catherine's College at Oxford. He was the first Mexican-American Rhodes Scholar. He has written articles for The Los Angeles Times, The New York Times, *and* The San Antonio Express-News. *He is also author of* Places Left Unfinished at the Time of Creation. *This article appeared in the* Texas Monthly, *November 2010.*

1   Dawn near San Agustin Plaza, in downtown Laredo, my mother's birthplace, and the sun is beginning to singe the tips of the lanky cane along the Rio Grande. Already, an unshaded queue of Mexicanos, crossing over for day work or shopping, stretches well beyond the span of International Bridge #1, the city's oldest, also known as the Gateway to the Americas. And these are just the folks with visas. Uncounted others will have crossed the river surreptitiously under the protective cover of night. Still others could be waiting to cross, arduously hidden away under false truck beds or packed like cargo into crates, hoping luck is with their coyotes as they warily approach the checkpoint. Who knows?

2   Anything involving Mexico is bound to lead to mystery eventually, so it's not surprising that the question of the border and immigration is no exception. But the mystery here doesn't so much involve the border as it does the story of

migration itself. The deep subconscious of Mexican culture is full of mythic stories of ancestral migrations, captured in the ubiquitous images of footstep trails that appear in many of the earliest codices that have been preserved. The most important of these myths is the ancient story of the pilgrimage of the tribes who would become the Aztecs. Exhorted by their god Huitzilopochtli to leave their homeland of Aztlán in search of a new home, they uprooted and wandered for years before encountering the promised sign, an eagle standing on a cactus, devouring a serpent. There they founded Tenochtitlan, which later became Mexico City. Since then, it seems that every generation of Mexicanos, indigenous and mestizo, has been searching for a new homeland of great blessings, even if it should require a long journey to find it. It's an Exodus-like theme that you can trace from the oldest pictographic records of the indigenous world to the modern accounts of the undocumented people captured by the Border Patrol.

3   An hour passes, and the line barely moves, as the heat of the sun grows more unforgiving, minute by minute. I watch this scene from the balcony of an air-conditioned room in the Hotel La Posada, thinking how every one of those bobbing heads I see could be me. As with many other native Texans, immigration across this increasingly fractious border is a family legacy for me, and a personal issue. My mother's ancestors first came to the northern hinterlands of Nueva España that would eventually become North Mexico and South Texas sometime in the early 1600's, and later they were among the families who founded a constellation of villages along the river, including Laredo, in 1755. The U.S. Mexico border appeared well into their saga, like a haunting wraith of separation laid across lands already long settled by people of an emerging nation.

4   As an inheritor of this legacy, I can't count the times I've crossed the border—back and forth from Eagle Pass into Coahuila, from Laredo into Nuevo Laredo, from McAllen into Reynosa, from Brownsville to Matamoros, from Presidio to Ojinaga. On my father's side, my great-uncle Francisco Garcia crossed out of Coahuila at Piedras Negras, fleeing the turmoil of the revolution, sometime around 1914. He later recalled it as a quiet passing across a steel bridge that cost him a nickel, with no customs or border officers asking for papers. Now traffic is perpetually stalled at the bridges as agents scrutinize papers. Innumerable Border Patrol SUVs crisscross the highways and back roads of the region, often as helicopters hover overhead. Drones patrol the skies, seeking crossers who've avoided the patchwork cordons of agents, walls, and fences. Soon, we are promised, National Guard troops will arrive to establish forward operating bases to surveil the land, just as in Afghanistan.

5   Today's border is a landscape of ghosts, a geography populated with a host of specters from a long, fraught history, all the upheavals of the past five hundred years in our Texan patch of the New World. For decades, immigration policy has found it hard enough trying to close the border to the living. But it is truly powerless to detain the ghosts of the past. They continue to pass freely, some heading north, some heading south. No policing stratagem will ever capture them, nor can we ever fully know the magnetic force they exert upon us.

6   But what difference might it make if our immigration policy were shaped in full recognition of our complex past? The current debate has emerged from an extremely narrow spectrum of historical awareness. In a recent radio interview, Homeland Security Secretary and former Arizona governor Janet Napolitano

observed that "the border is a big and complicated place." By contrast, in the current tumult over immigration, the matter is often presented in the media as a simple choice between law and anarchy, between protecting American values and identity and abandoning them to a wave of immigrants from the south. Fueled by a spiraling whorl of fear and mistrust, the debate has reached the point that many hot-button issues come to, where they detach from reality and history and begin to create a new, self-justifying mythology.

7   I had come to the balcony at La Posada in Laredo to try and reattach to reality. In late summer, as the radios and televisions buzzed with discussions of racial profiling and birthright citizenship and amnesty, I set out from my home in San Antonio on a journey through South Texas, where the ghosts of history are as much a presence as the visions of the future. I went in search of those ghosts and in search of the living too, those who are telling another sort of story about migration that makes a full reckoning of the deep history of our contested, shared borderlands.

8   My first stop was the Kenedy Ranch Museum of South Texas, in Sarita, twenty miles south of Kingsville down U.S. 77. Encompassing 400,000 acres of former Spanish and Mexican land grant territories, the ranch has a uniquely South Texas mestizo legacy that began in the middle of the nineteenth century, when the founder, Mifflin Kenedy, an immigrant from Pennsylvania, married Petra Vela de Vidal, the daughter of one of the oldest Tejano families from that region. Along with the King Ranch, it's among the most legendary spreads of South Texas. But it's also home to one of my favorite museums. Installed in the Spanish Revival-style building in Sarita that once housed the ranch's business office, the Kenedy Ranch Museum's rooms are filled with artifacts and decked with bright historical murals, accompanied by a rigorous audio tour depicting the good, bad, and ugly of the past four centuries.

9   The director of this little-known gem of South Texas historical lore is border polymath Homero S. Vera. I first sought him out when I started inquiring into my family's place in the history of Nuevo Santander, the region of New Spain that included much of the Rio Grande Valley and the northern Mexican state of Tamaulipas. Formerly these lands were known only as *las tierras bárbaras de los infieles*, "the barbarous lands of the infidels."

10   Homero was raised on a ranch in Duval County in the 1950's, but it might as well have been the 1850's. Spanish was the family language. The Veras' rattlesnake-country rancho was the focus of family life. He hunted and trapped with uncles. The family made monthly trips into town for groceries and provisions. A committed ranchero by age five, Homero hated moving into Premont when his dad got a job as a mechanic in town.

11   Growing up this way gave Homero a powerful desire to help bring the early history of the region to a larger public. But his first chance didn't come until he was 44 years old, in 1997. After being laid off from a longtime job in a nearby Celanese chemical plant, he used his severance benefits to launch a monthly newsletter of South Texas history called *El Mesteño*, or "the Mustang," a reference to the wild horses that once roamed the coastal plains. During the seven years of its run, *El Mesteño* developed a loyal following, myself included. For anyone interested in the history of this region, it was a treasure trove. A typical issue might include features on the history of specific Hispano surnames of the region; analyses of founders' lives and early architectural styles; accounts of tequila-running routes to San Diego during the Prohibition era; recipes using local plants and herbs; traditional *dichos*, or "sayings," in the Valley;

perhaps even a profile of a visiting conjunto band—from Japan. The piquant rigor of these historical briefs quickly earned him the respect of such eminent Tejano historians as Andres Tijerina, Emilio Zamora, and Frank de la Teja and boosted circulation as high as two thousand before the journal quit publishing, in 2004.

12   I met Homero in his office at the museum. He was dressed in the denim shirt, jeans, and dusty work boots of a vaquero. A sofa was piled high with children's drawings of American Indian symbols from a recent school field trip. The walls were hung with a framed satellite photograph of the vast Kenedy Ranch and photos of local wildlife, including one of a white-throated caracara, a bird often called the Mexican eagle. Homero is a born corrector, and this photo occasioned his first correction of the afternoon.

13   "They say the caracara was actually the bird the Aztecs saw consuming the serpent over the cactus in the Valley of Mexico," he told me. "Somehow way back there, somebody switched the golden eagle in its place."

14   Homero is tall, husky, white-haired, fair-skinned, and hazel-eyed. He speaks quietly in a classic Valley manner, a gentle Texas drawl that still carries the hint of a Spanish accent. Explaining *El Mesteño*, he said, "I wanted to tell the story as it is, tell the facts as they are, so I began to focus on the stories of the ranches from the original Spanish land grants, beginning with the first surveys of the lands that were later settled, from Laredo to Corpus Christi. In schools, we were taught about the *Mayflower* and the pilgrims, but we were never taught about that."

15   The short version comes down to this, as Homero explained: The lands we now know as South Texas have always been a crossroads of undocumented immigrants, beginning with the indigenous peoples, then settlers from Spain, England and Ireland, Mexico and the United States, among many others. The museum's murals, painted in 2002 by Mexican-born Houston artist Daniel Lechón, reveal the story of how the intertwining destinies of all those nations played out in the hard-scrabble Rio Grande Valley.

16   We left the office and bumped down a long ranch road, through pastures where oaks mingled with sotol plants, to the house on the La Parra division, where Homero lives with his Mexican-born wife, Leticia, a schoolteacher. In the sitting room, with a ceiling fan keeping time and a repast of nilgai jerky and frosty Dos Equis before us, Homero reflected on the profound transformations in his beloved borderlands.

17   "The last five, ten years, the border has changed a lot, for the worse," he said. "And I don't know if it's going to get any better." He described how the experience of undocumented immigration has changed in his lifetime, from its origins in agricultural labor on the ranches of the region to an interval in the more and more complicated labor flows of globalization.

18   "The migration of the *indocumentados* is a business now," he said. "When I was growing up, they would come on their own, mostly rural people who would work on the ranches, gather one thousand dollars, two thousand dollars, and then it was '*Nos vemos el otro año*' ['See you next year']. It's very rare now to see one individual by himself; it's always a pack of people in the back of a truck or in the brush, a group of people led by a coyote, heading for North Carolina, Chicago, Houston."

19   He paused, his face suddenly looking resigned and wary. "Of course, we need some kind of legislation to allow these people to come here legally and live here and work here, but I don't know if that's gonna stop the violence, the trafficking. We need to eliminate the coyote, because the majority want to come and work the correct way." He grew quiet, with a worried look. "The drugs are

a different story." He told me how his wife had recently seen suspicious-looking black-uniformed individuals somewhere on the road between Riviera and Falfurrias, possibly narcos. The surging war among rival Mexican drug cartels just across the Rio Grande has introduced yet another confounding factor into the long history of migration in the borderlands. Homero never addressed this in *El Mesteño*, and he now wonders whether it isn't time to start up the journal again, to inform this new and disturbing chapter.

20   Night fell and we stepped out into the warm Sarita air. The sky was so limpid that the Milky Way glimmered like a band of pearly embers stretched across the sky. A shooting star tracked a path over us, an augur always regarded in my family as a greeting from the ancestors.

21   The next morning I set out for Laredo. All along the highways and farm-to-market roads—through Raymondville, La Gloria, Rio Grande City, and San Ygnacio—there were signs of the old agricultural way of life, verdant fields crowded with tall sugarcane stalks, others strewn with cantaloupes discarded during harvest. Abundant rain had left the land green, and flowers bloomed in every direction. Near Zapata, in the aftermath of the early-July flooding, the Rio Grande looked like a broad and tranquil inland sea.

22   But it was impossible to overlook the changes. I lost count of the number of Border Patrol SUVs I saw along those byways. Searching in San Isidro for the ruins of a Spanish stone *noria*, a well and aqueduct system, I drove through town and at one intersection saw a man on his knees, his hands cuffed behind his back, his head bowed, while two Border Patrol officers appeared to be finalizing papers for his detention.

23   The *noria* was Homero's idea. The previous night, before we turned in, we'd spent a few hours looking at artifacts from his private collection. First, a faded tricolor flag, dating from the 1820's, the era of a newly independent Mexican Republic. The insignia showed a Mexican eagle (not a golden eagle) with outstretched wings in the middle, clutching a snake in its beak, only this eagle also wore an imperial crown. The lettering read "Pva. De Texas, San Antonio de Bexar, Primera Brigada de Lanceros a Caballo." Next, a heraldic banner from an earlier era-red crossed staffs sewed onto a beige silk background, with an ornate rosy brocade border all around. Homero guessed it had probably hung from a standard carried in the vanguard of some eighteenth-century colonial regiment in Nueva España. Finally, he showed me several still-older documents. I looked closely at one, a printed mandate from the king of Spain issued on "24 de Junio, 1757" as an edict on the authority of Viceroy El Marques de las Amarillas, ordering the immediate and preemptive expulsion of all foreigners from the dominions of Nueva Espana, a hoary reminder of just how long the issue of illegal immigration has haunted these lands.

24   After this plunge into the continuum of deep South Texas time, I'd wondered aloud where it was still possible to see physical evidence of the Spanish colonial settlement in the borderlands. Farther north, in San Antonio, the missions have been restored and some have even been designated national park sites. But in South Texas, monuments from the past are harder to spot, hidden down dirt roads in small, forgotten towns. Homero had sent me to go looking for the *noria*.

25   I poked around San Isidro, trying to follow his directions, thinking about the past. Much of the current ardor over the border appears to assume that it has always existed. But rather than a divinely inscribed geographic demarcation that descended from the heavens all at once, the current border evolved slowly after its creation in the Treaty of Guadalupe Hidalgo, following the U.S.-Mexican War,

in 1848. First came a series of binational commissions made up of American and Mexican surveyors, astronomers, engineers, and cartographers, who didn't complete their work until 1857. Slowly the sometimes straight, sometimes crooked line of the border emerged out of these expeditions and negotiations, based partly on geodetic surveys, partly on stargazing, and partly on the dodgy cartographic testimony of a palimpsest of maps, which were often at odds with one another.

26 More than a century and a half later, the boundary still stands. In a time when the borders of "Old Europe" are being erased, the line along the Rio Grande has proved to be among the world's more stalwart partitions, taking its place on a recent BBC Mundo list of "*Los muros que no han caído*" ("The walls that have not fallen"). It's a doleful roll call, including Cyprus, Uzbekistan-Kyrgyzstan, the two Koreas, Botswana-Zimbabwe, and Israel-Palestine, among several others. By comparison with these, the Berlin Wall was an amateur act, a tenuous attempt to bifurcate a kindred nation on ideological terms. Last November I followed the celebrations for the twentieth anniversary of the fall of the Berlin Wall, and I wondered how Americans could feel such an upwelling of compassion for the reunification of a distant land without pausing to think about the wall being erected on their own southern border.

27 National security is a real concern, but in this history there's no denying the underlying cultural dynamic, with its generally unspoken assumptions about Texan and American identity. For instance, with Mexican Americans and other Latinos constituting 38 percent of all Texans, how much different would the reaction have been to the governor's openly talking about secession if his name were not Rick Perry but Ricardo Perez?

28 Things weren't always this way. After its official mapping was completed, the Texas-Mexico border remained porous, just as my Uncle Francisco found it, crossing from Piedras Negras to Eagle Pass in 1914, and indeed, the Border Patrol, created in 1915, didn't become a serious enforcement service until the Prohibition era. Moreover, tightened border security in response to undocumented immigration began in earnest only in the eighties. So, while rooted in a distant past that someone like Homero Verahas illuminated, immigration policy is really an issue of our times, our era of globalization.

29 Finally, after a long hunt, I found the *noria*. But the wide, deep well with a series of stone canals radiating out from the center had been left to go to seed. The sandstone and mortar construction was breaking down, and tires, old televisions, and other trash were piled up at the bottom of the stone cistern. This noble structure was being used as a dump.

30 Later that afternoon I arrived in Laredo and went straight to another museum. Nestled in the historic center, on the south side of San Agustin Plaza, the Museum of the Republic of the Rio Grande stands as yet another reminder of the complex history of the border region. In 1840, after the Texas Revolution, with borders still in dispute and disgruntled north Mexicans rejecting the centralist government in Mexico City, an insurgent movement led by General Antonio Canales created a new, independent republic encompassing north Mexico, present-day New Mexico, and the lands south of the Nueces River. The ill-starred Republic of the Rio Grande lasted only 293 days before it was brutally suppressed by the Mexican army, but the movement that sparked it smoldered for decades, inspiring periodic uprisings for independence in the Mexicano community of South Texas into the early twentieth century.

31 Housed in a sun-bleached sandstone hacienda that was the headquarters of the short-lived republic, the museum commemorates that period in a series of rooms arranged with historic home furnishings and vitrines exhibiting weaponry,

everyday objects, and documents from the movement. Standing before an array of maps that capture all the shifting borders of those times, Rick Villarreal, the former director of the museum, bemoaned how the story has been excluded from American history textbooks, dismissed as a Mexican intrigue. He quickly rehearsed the history of the movement and its links to the U.S.-Mexican War that soon followed, a war that, he noted, remains meaningful for Mexicanos.

32   "Mexican citizens always seem to have this idea that these lands were stolen by the United States," he said. "So they should have the right to come over, especially in the Southwest. They feel these lands were originally a part of Mexico, so 'Why should we recognize these Johnny-come-lately borders?' It all stems from that war, the U.S.-Mexican War. We're still feeling the repercussions."

33   If that sounds like 162-year-old sour grapes, consider that even Ulysses S. Grant, a veteran of the U.S.-Mexican War, recognized its injustice. The eighteenth president mused in his memoirs that the American Civil War, which erupted two decades later, could be seen as divine retribution for America's role in the war with Mexico. Grant wrote, "Nations, like individuals, are punished for their transgressions. We got our punishment in the most sanguinary and expensive war of modern times."

34   I thought about Grant's theory as I wandered around Laredo the next day. Are nations punished for their transgressions? How should we understand the current sanguinary episode unfolding across the river, the war among Mexican drug cartels vying for territory in the northern states? The day I arrived, there was a shoot-out in a barrio of Nuevo Laredo, with eight reported killed. But any such news is difficult to confirm. With newspaper and television journalists in Mexico unwilling to risk reporting such events, word spreads virally through Facebook, Twitter, and old-fashioned word of mouth. In the long saga of border conflicts affecting the experience of immigration, this one may be the gravest ever, the latest vexation laid over a tragedy, rooted in an enigma.

35   "I think the word is '*incertidumbre*,' right?" asked Maria Eugenia Guerra, an old friend and the founder and publisher of *LareDos*, an independent monthly news journal. I'd stopped into her busy downtown offices to hear the latest. "The uncertainty of it—we're in that." Guerra's ancestors (some of whom are mine as well) date back to the early 1600's in New Spain, and her family continues to own land in and near San Ygnacio, from the original *porciones*, as the Spanish land grants from the 1700's are widely known throughout South Texas. But for Guerra, along with so many other Laredoans, the widening impact of the narco war has changed everything.

36   "How will we end the violence?" she asked me. "We're so far away from what's really going to happen, and that's unknown to us, of course, but it has all the markings of a horrible era to come." She told me she had been considering something previously unimaginable—leaving Laredo, continuing the migration her ancestors began three hundred years ago.

37   "After centuries, I think—and I've never, ever thought this—but maybe my family should move north," she said. "Maybe this is the next northern migration."

38   Nearing twilight in Laredo, I returned to the museum for a few more snapshots. A small group of men were bringing in a load of crates, aluminum cases, and electrical cables, setting up light stands and arrays of what appeared to be scopes of some sort. I thought they were engineers or contractors working on a restoration project in the old building, but they turned out to be the seven members of the Laredo Paranormal Research Society (formerly, and more forebodingly, known as the Paranormal Entity Research Investigation League, or

P.E.R.I.L.), a cohort of ghost hunters, all of them law enforcement professionals by day. In other sites around Laredo, the society's hunters have caught "energy anomalies" in photographs of abandoned buildings, fleeting glimpses of a face in the dark doorway of an old hospital, and faint voices in cemeteries speaking English and Spanish.

39   They told me that there have been numerous reports of anomalous phenomena in the historic hacienda museum building. Mysterious orbs appear in tourist photographs, audio tour narrations spontaneously begin playing, and, spookiest of all, a crib made of heavy pecan wood was discovered rocking on its own. The night I found them, the investigators were setting up for a 72-hour surveillance, hoping to capture one of the local spirits in an infrared camera or a digital audio recording. I asked if they could discern the immigration status of their etheric quarry—and they replied only with skeptical looks.

40   I'm serious, I told them. We have this in common: We're all looking for ghosts.

Using Multiple Strategies

Descriptions can be made to create arguments, to illustrate a point, or to enrich a narration. In this case, Santos is using description to argue that the Mexicans have a long historical relationship to the Southwest. He uses several other strategies as well.

- The essay is organized as a narrative as the writer explores the traces of history, as in paragraphs 8 and 25.
- Some paragraphs (for example, paragraph 6) compare the complexity of the past with the ways the current immigration debate presents matters, a comparison that is followed through the essay, including comparisons of the past and present in paragraphs 27 and 28.
- Sometimes causes are given for current attitudes, as in paragraph 32.

MyWritingLab ## Discussion Questions

1. This is an essay that is not written primarily as a description but instead uses description to make its point. Where is description used in this essay? How does the inclusion of the descriptive details affect your reading of the essay?
2. How is the essay as a whole organized? How are the sections of description integrated into this larger organization?
3. In paragraphs 21 and 22, Santos contrasts two scenes. What are the differences in the two paragraphs and what point does Santos make by this contrast? Which of the two paragraphs seems to offer the more concrete description? In what ways does the contrast between a more general description and a more concrete description fit Santos' point?
4. In paragraph 39, Santos offers a description of unusual events very different from that in the rest of the essay. How does this description fit or not fit the essay? Is it effective?
5. The author indicates, "Today's border is a landscape of ghosts." Much of the essay tries to show us examples of the past in the present. What descriptive details in the essay evoke the past?

Toward Key Insights

Even abstract concepts like the challenges of immigration have very concrete and
describable elements. What is the relationship in this work between the more
general concepts and the detailed descriptions? What are examples of the way
other ideas or issues are realized in events and objects that can be described?
Everything has traces of its history that can be part of its description. What descriptive
details does Santos offer that show the history of this area in the Southwest? What
are some of the ways the ordinary objects or places in our life show a history?

Suggestions for Writing

1. Write about a place, such as the downtown area of a small city, that has a contrast between the new and the old and historical. Describe the scene so that the reader can see the contrast.
2. Take an idea or scene that has real-world examples that can be described and describe the event or scene so that the reader can understand how that scene demonstrates that idea.

PROCESS ANALYSIS ▬ ▬ ▬ ▬ ▬ ▬ ▬ ▬

Reading Strategies

1. Determine the reason you are reading the process essay. If it is to follow instructions, you will need to read in one way; if it is to understand a process, you will need to proceed differently.

2. If you are going to follow the instructions, read over the process first to get an understanding of the whole. Look for specific warnings or feedback you should consider. Get an idea of what the end result should look like. Gather any equipment you will need. Then follow the process step by step, checking after each step to make certain the results you are obtaining match those described in the process.

3. If you hope to understand the process, read first quickly to get an overview of the process. As you read through more slowly, it can be very helpful to take notes outlining the major steps of the process.

Reading Critically

1. Check to see if the process could be completed differently or more effectively. Are there any cautions that are not included in the essay that might be reasonable to observe?

2. If the writer is explaining a process, is there evidence that his or her account is correct? Check to see that there is good reason to believe the given account. Research could show that there are competing accounts.

Reading as a Writer

1. Observe how the writer uses verbs to indicate actions.

2. Notice how the writer gets from step to step in the process. If there is a strategy you could use, make note of it.

PERFECT HOME HVAC DESIGN.COM

Ground-Source-Heat-Pumps: Mother Earth Will Wrap You in Warmth

This selection is a web page posted by the company Perfect Home HVAC Design. Common to many web pages, there is no clear author. Dana Morley is the owner and chief designer for the company and has been a licensed HVAC contractor in Utah with 36 years of experience in HVAC. Since the web page has no clear author, its credibility depends on the professionalism of the site and company and the degree to which it is consistent with other web sites.

Ground-Source Heat Pumps

First paragraph lets reader know the relevance of website

1   If you are interested in installing an environmentally responsible heating, air conditioning and water heating system in your home, you have come to the right page.

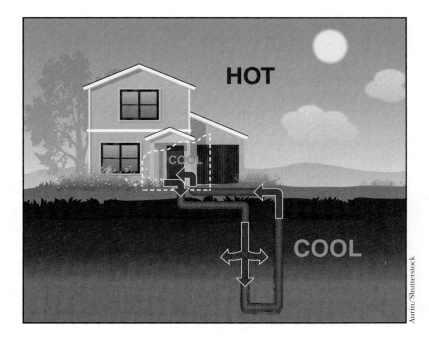

Image provides a clear visual overview of how technology works

2   Ground source heat pump systems are still rare mostly due to cost, but seem to be on the upswing each year due to increasing utility bills.

3   The Environmental Protection Agency (EPA) and the Department of Energy (DOE) have both listed the ground source heat pump systems as amongst the highest energy efficient and environmentally responsible home comfort and water heating systems available today.

4   The EPA has stated that geothermal technologies represent a major opportunity for reducing national energy use and pollution, while delivering comfort, reliability and savings to the homeowner.

5   The greatest heat storage facility available on Earth is the Earth itself. Temperatures below the surface of our planet remain virtually constant, whether it be winter, summer, spring, or fall. Ground source heat pumps tap into this stored energy to provide hot water, cooling and heating for homes. Residential applications are the subject here, but are certainly not the only viable options for use of a ground source heat pump system. Commercial or industrial structures can benefit from these types of systems as well.

Identifies importance of technology

Provides fundamental principles behind the process

Closed Loop GSHP System

6   A closed loop system can be installed horizontally under a lawn or garden area, driveway, or even under the home itself, anywhere that the required piping can be installed. The piping can also be installed vertically in shafts drilled for the piping. Your geothermal specialist will determine, after inspecting your site, which approach suits your application best. Factors he will be looking for are soil conditions, available space, installation economy, and the type of rock in the area.

Defines conditions for the process

7   Closed loop systems utilize water or an antifreeze solution circulating through plastic or copper piping installed beneath the earth's surface. During the heating season, the fluid is pumped through the loops, collecting heat from the ground and delivers the heat into the heat pump inside the building. During the summer, for cooling, the process is reversed. Heat is pulled from the residence and pumped out through the system loops to store the heat in the ground. Cool fluid returns to cool the residence.

Provides broader and more general steps of the process including materials and larger system

8   Inside, the heat pump is a package unit, which has a refrigerant loop, a water loop, a compressor, a reversing valve, and a heat exchanger. The transfer of heat actually takes place at the heat exchanger, which transfers the heat from the water into the refrigerant, or vice-versa, depending upon heating or cooling cycle.

Provides detailed account of key parts and the general process for the heat pump

9   In heating cycle, the water from outside passes past a refrigerant-filled heat exchanger. Heat transfers into the refrigerant and boils to become a vapor. The vapor is then compressed, causing it to become even hotter. Then the hot gas passes through the coil, where air is forced through the coil, picking up the heat and distributing it to the living space.

Provides more detailed example of heat pump

10   Once again, this process is reversed for cooling.

11   Not to confuse the issue, but some systems actually use the refrigerant to make a direct heat transfer outside with the ground. The process inside the heat pump is very similar to a split system air conditioner's process.

Offers an account of alternative

12   This process can also provide free hot water during the summer months, by passing the hot water collected during cooling mode through a water-to-water heat exchanger. A heat transfer takes place and the potable hot water is stored in a tank for use. This same process can deliver substantial hot water savings during the winter also.

Indicates alternative use in the process

13   A ground source heat pump system can be fitted to any residential project, new construction or retrofit, single-family or multi-family. For a retro-fit application, the existing ductwork from your former furnace or air handler can usually be used as the distribution system with minimal alterations.

Identifies conditions of establishment

14   Many geothermal companies work closely with a conventional heating and air conditioning company to provide the full package.

Open Loop Water Source Heat Pump Systems

15   Some residences have access to a pond or lake on their property. This is another good source for heat transfer from the piping system. An open loop water system can provide similar benefits of the closed loop system.

16   The operation is identical other than the loop piping system is placed directly on the bottom of the pond. The system pumps pull in water for the heating and cooling of the residence and then discharge the water directly back into the pond, into a return well, or into a leech field.

17   Installation of this type of system may require the approval of your local authorities. Due to the fact that open dispersal of the water back into the environment will mix with ground water, the authorities may wish to verify its source and cleanliness. It's easier to get approved beforehand than to backpedal for approvals.

18   Installation of geothermal, a ground source heat pump, or a water source heat pump is certainly not the most economical route to go for heating and cooling your home, on initial installation. But, the benefits abound. Manufacturers are offering rebates and special financing. Many utility companies offer rebates to help with installation. Both the homeowner and the builder should check into these programs when considering this type of system.

Benefits of a Ground Source Heat Pump

- Realize up to 50 percent savings on energy used to heat hot water.
- It can both heat and cool your home, and provide all of your hot water needs.
- Equipment size is very similar to a traditional forced air heating and air conditioning system.
- Energy consumption can be cut by 20 to 50 percent.
- Maintenance costs may be reduced.
- Underground piping carries a 50-year warranty.
- Systems are very quiet, both inside and out. No noisy compressors outside.
- No dangerous and unsightly outside fuel storage tanks are needed.
- Air inside the home is distributed more evenly. Hot and cold spots are gone.

A ground source heat pump does provide savings.

- Save money in operating and maintenance costs.
- Over time, the energy savings will exceed the installation costs. Make money on the deal! For the right system, your investment dollar may be recouped in only a few years.
- Rebates are available in most areas from local utility companies. Federal tax credits may also be available to help offset the initial installation costs.
- Heating efficiencies are as much as 70 percent higher than conventional. Cooling efficiencies are as much as 40 percent higher than conventional systems.

If that isn't enough to convince you to consider this type of system, think about our environment.

- There is no external venting into our atmosphere of harmful waste byproducts.
- Ground source heat pump systems that do use refrigerants are factory sealed, and seldom need recharging. Possibility of freon released to the atmosphere and damaging our ozone layer almost non-existent.
- Our natural resources are conserved.
- Fossil fuels are not burned.

Discussion Questions   MyWritingLab

1. What is the purpose of this process description? How does that purpose shape the way the web page is designed and the process is described?
2. Instead of simply providing a step-by-step presentation of the process, this website first describes the more general process and then provides more detailed steps for the process. Why did they do this? Is it effective?
3. Why is the illustration used to help account for this process? How helpful is it?
4. Why doesn't the website detail the process for cooling?
5. At the end of the website, it directly states the advantages of a geothermal system. Does this help or hinder the process account? Why or why not?

Toward Key Insights   MyWritingLab

How much do we know about the processes that strongly shape our life? Why don't many of us pay attention to such processes? What could be some advantages of our understanding these processes?

Many complete a college education without knowing how their car works, their homes are heated, or their wireless system functions. What if anything should an education teach people about their technological world? What should we be able to learn on our own? What does it take to learn about such processes?

Suggestions for Writing   MyWritingLab

1. Research a process that influences your life and the lives of others and design a possible website for that process, including the text and images that explain the process.
2. Take a very technical process that you understand and rewrite or revise that process so that it is available to a more general reader.

BETH WALD

Let's Get Vertical!

Beth Wald (born 1960) first felt the attraction of the mountains when, at age 16, she took a backpacking trip to Canada. A native of Minnesota, she studied botany and Russian at the University of Minnesota and then, in the mid-1980s, began a dual career as a freelance writer and photographer. Her career and her love of climbing have taken her around the world. Her articles have appeared in a variety of climbing and outdoor magazines, as have her photographs, which include environmental and cultural subjects as well as sports and travel. From 1988 to 1992, she was a contributing editor for Climbing Magazine. *In our selection, Wald acquaints potential recruits with the sport of rock climbing.*

1   Here I am, 400 feet up on the steep west face of Devil's Tower,[1] a tiny figure in a sea of petrified rock. I can't find enough footholds and handholds to keep climbing. My climbing partner anxiously looks up at me from his narrow ledge. I can see the silver sparkle of the climbing devices I've jammed into the crack every eight feet or so.

2   I study the last device I've placed, a half-inch aluminum wedge 12 feet below me. If I slip, it'll catch me, but only after a 24-foot fall, a real "screamer." It's too difficult to go back; I have to find a way up before my fingers get too tired. I must act quickly.

3   Finding a tiny opening in the crack, I jam two fingertips in, crimp them, pull hard, and kick my right foot onto a sloping knob, hoping it won't skid off. At the same time, I slap my right hand up to what looks like a good hold. To my horror, it's round and slippery.

4   My fingers start to slide. Panic rivets me for a second, but then a surge of adrenalin snaps me back into action. I scramble my feet higher, lunge with my left hand, and catch a wider crack. I manage to get a better grip just as my right hand pops off its slick hold. My feet find edges, and I regain my balance. Whipping a chock (wedge) off my harness, I slip it into the crack and clip my rope through a carabiner (oblong metal snaplink). After catching my breath, I start moving again, and the rest of the climb flows upward like a vertical dance.

The Challenges and Rewards

5   I've tried many sports, but I haven't found any to match the excitement of rock climbing. It's a unique world, with its own language, communities, controversies, heroes, villains, and devoted followers. I've lived in vans, tepees, tents, and caves; worked three jobs to save money for expenses; driven 24 hours to spend a weekend at a good rock; and lived on beans and rice for months at a time—all of this to be able to climb. What is it about scrambling up rocks that inspires such a passion? The answer is, no other sport offers so many challenges and so many rewards.

6   The physical challenges are obvious. You need flexibility, balance, and strength. But climbing is also a psychological game of defeating your fear, and it demands creative thinking. It's a bit like improvising a gymnastic routine 200 feet in the air while playing a game of chess.

7   Climbers visit some of the most spectacular places on earth and see them from a unique perspective—the top! Because the sport is so intense, friendships between climbers tend to be strong and enduring.

Anyone Can Climb

8   Kids playing in trees or on monkey bars know that climbing is a natural activity, but older people often have to relearn to trust their instincts. This isn't too hard, though. The ability to maintain self-control in difficult situations is the most important trait for a beginning climber to have. Panic is almost automatic when you run out of handholds 100 feet off the ground. The typical reaction is to freeze solid until you fall off. But with a little discipline, rational thinking, and/ or distraction tactics such as babbling to yourself, humming, or even screaming, fear can change to elation as you climb out of a tough spot.

9   Contrary to popular belief, you don't have to be superhumanly strong to climb. Self-confidence, agility, a good sense of balance, and determination will get you farther up the rock than bulging biceps. Once you've learned the basics, climbing itself will gradually make you stronger, though many dedicated climbers speed up the process by training at home or in the gym.

[1]A large, flat-topped rock formation, 876 feet high, in northeastern Wyoming.

10   Nonclimbers often ask, "How do the ropes get up there?" It's quite simple; the climbers bring them up as they climb. Most rock climbers today are "free climbers." In free climbing, the rope is used only for safety in case of a fall, *not* to help pull you up. (Climbing without a rope, called "free soloing," is a *very* dangerous activity practiced only by extremely experienced—and crazy—climbers.)

11   First, two climbers tie into opposite ends of a 150-foot-long nylon rope. Then one of them, the belayer, anchors himself or herself to a rock or tree. The other, the leader, starts to climb, occasionally stopping to jam a variety of aluminum wedges or other special gadgets, generically referred to as protection, into cracks in the rock. To each of these, he or she attaches a snaplink, called a carabiner, and clips the rope through. As the leader climbs, the belayer feeds out the rope, and it runs through the carabiners. If the leader falls, the belayer holds the rope, and the highest piece of protection catches the leader. The belayer uses special techniques and equipment to make it easy to stop falls.

12   When the leader reaches the end of a section of rock—called the pitch—and sets an anchor, he or she becomes the belayer. This person pulls up the slack of the rope as the other partner climbs and removes the protection. Once together again, they can either continue in the same manner or switch leaders. These worldwide techniques work on rock formations, cliffs, peaks, even buildings.

Rocks, Rocks Everywhere

13   Some of the best climbing cliffs in the country are in the Shawangunk Mountains, only two hours from New York City. Seneca Rocks in West Virginia draws climbers from Washington, D.C., and Pittsburgh, Pennsylvania. Chattanooga, Tennessee, has a fine cliff within the city limits. Most states in the U.S. and provinces in Canada offer at least one or two good climbing opportunities.

14   Even if there are no large cliffs or rock formations nearby, you can climb smaller rocks to practice techniques and get stronger. This is called bouldering. Many climbers who live in cities and towns have created climbing areas out of old stone walls and buildings. Ask someone at your local outdoor shop where you can go to start climbing.

Get a Helping Hand

15   There's no substitute for an expert teacher when it comes to learning basic techniques and safety procedures. One of the best (and least expensive) ways to learn climbing is to convince a veteran climber in your area to teach you. You can usually meet these types at the local crag or climbing shop.

16   As another option, many universities and colleges, some high schools, and some YMCAs have climbing clubs. Their main purpose is to introduce people to climbing and to teach the basics. Other clubs, such as the Appalachian Mountain Club in the eastern U.S. and the Mountaineers on the West Coast, also provide instruction. Ask at your outdoor shop for the names of clubs in your area.

17   If you live in a place completely lacking rocks and climbers, you can attend one of the fine climbing schools at the major climbing area closest to you. Magazines like *Climbing, Rock & Ice,* and *Outside* publish lists of these schools. Once you learn the basics, you're ready to get vertical.

18   In rock climbing, you can both lose yourself and find yourself. Life and all its troubles are reduced to figuring out the puzzle of the next section of cliff or forgotten in the challenge and delight of moving through vertical space. And learning how to control anxiety, how to piece together a difficult sequence of moves, and how to communicate with a partner are all skills that prove incredibly useful back on the ground!

MyWritingLab ## Discussion Questions

1. Discuss the effectiveness of Wald's title.
2. At the beginning of the essay, Wald notes that she is 400 feet up one side of Devil's Tower and positioned above her climbing partner. What do you think these statements accomplish?
3. In which paragraphs does Wald detail the actual process of climbing? What do the remaining paragraphs in the body of the essay accomplish?
4. Point out two places in the first four paragraphs where Wald cites reasons for her actions.
5. What attributes does Wald believe a rock climber must have? Refer to the essay when answering.
6. After reading this essay, are you ready to begin rock climbing? Does your answer stem from Wald's content, the manner of presentation, or both? Discuss.

MyWritingLab ## Toward Key Insights

What challenging activities appeal to you?
What level of risk are you willing to accept in an activity?
How do you account for your attitude about taking risks?

MyWritingLab ## Suggestion for Writing

Write a process paper in which you explain the attributes required and the steps involved in one of your recreational activities.

TANNER CHRISTENSEN

What Is the Creative Process?

Tanner Christensen works as a product designer for Facebook and lives in Palo Alto, CA. He is the creator of the iPad app "Brainbean" and the sole creator of a number of creativity apps such as "Prompts." Since 2008 he has maintained a blog called "Creative Something," where the following selection was posted.

1   How does a creative idea come to you? Where does it come from and why does it occur?

2   These are questions we—as humankind—have been asking for centuries, primarily because the process continues to mystify us. We can do a lot of incredible things, but we just can't quite figure out what's going on in our brains when we happen upon an idea that is novel or stumble into a solution for a problem.

3   For a very long time in the history of human thought, creativity *was* thought of as just that: mysticism, magic, incomprehensible.

4   The ancient Greeks used to believe that creativity was bestowed upon you from a higher, otherworldly being. If you were suitable for acting on an idea, the gods would grant it to you and expect you to follow through. Muses would visit you if you begged for their gifts.

5   The Romans believed that a creative muse was a spiritual guide that would visit those who were open to receiving them, in order to perform great work or feats.

6   Many people today still believe that creativity is granted through some divine power. Maybe creativity is an otherworldly gift, but for the sake of this article we'll focus solely on information that we can prove in one way or another.

7   So, in exploring the creative process we need to answer these questions: where do novel ideas come from, and (more interesting to explore, I think) where do the ideas reside once they make themselves known?

8   What we know today is that the brain works through connections of neural pathways.

9   You experience something (through any of your five senses) and networks in your body all react accordingly.

10   When those networks continuously become active, they create a type of "memory." And these memories are formed for many, many, many things, including things we don't consciously acknowledge (like the sound of a distant car horn in the city, or the chirping of a bird at the park, or the color of a stranger's shoes on the subway).

11   This all becomes extremely important for the creative process in a later step.

12   But the first step to the process has nothing to do with your experiences or knowledge. Instead, the first step to the process—believe it or not—is **intent.**

13   Imagine you're putting a puzzle together (a process we will relate to often while exploring that of creativity), and you have the box of pieces sitting out in front of you.

14   The first step to figuring out the puzzle is to want to solve the puzzle. That's the first step to creative thought as well, though the difference between the creative process and the process of putting a puzzle together is that, for creativity, you don't have to consciously have the intent.

15   It's enough to have an inkling of intent to have new ideas for the process to start, your subconscious can take care of the intent for you (and it undoubtedly will, if you let it).

16   We know this is true because the brain is making so many connections and continuously running through network processes on its own, even when we're asleep. So if you have a problem to solve, or a project you need to work on, or a deep desire to fulfill some creative need, you can count on your brain to naturally want to work on that.

17   So we have intent, we know that we're going to want to put the creative puzzle together in front of us, now what do we do?

18   The next step in the process is to **explore/gather**.

19   Like putting a puzzle together, we need to gather all of the pieces into one place. In this example the pieces of a puzzle are simply memories or our experiences with various objects or situations. Colors and shapes, sounds, movies, people we know, books we've read, food we've tasted, clothes we've tried on, relationships we've had, dreams we've dreamed, all count as pieces for our puzzle.

20   Your brain naturally sorts through pieces that may look like they fit and those that won't.

21   For creativity, our brains are naturally doing this gathering process already (again: by creating memories of things that we experience throughout our day). But we can add to the process by exploring, which is where real creative talent lies (identifying where pieces may be that we don't have already, or where unique pieces might fit even though they don't show up on the puzzle box that is our intent).

22   Maybe there are some additional pieces to our metaphorical puzzle under the table; have we checked there? Or maybe there are pieces that are more obvious about where they go than others; have we checked for those?

23   The first step to the creative process is intent (knowing we have a puzzle to solve and wanting to solve it), and the next is gathering information (or the individual pieces that may be part of the puzzle) and exploring (looking for pieces that might be missing or could help put the puzzle together more effectively).

24   What happens next is the part that creatives love most: action.

25   Now that you have intent and pieces to work with, you have to start putting pieces together; physically seeing where things fit together and where they don't. This is the step of **connecting/experimenting**.

26   Often during this phase of the process you'll start seeing things that don't work and things that absolutely will. You'll notice when there are gaping holes in what you have and what you hope to end up with (maybe some pieces went missing or maybe you need to find substitutes).

27   The purpose of this phase isn't to critique, however, which many people mistakenly do while trying to create.

28   You can't accurately critique a painting that is only half-way done; that's not fair to what the final painting could be.

29   This is true of ideas as well. Until an idea is more fully flushed out, you may be doing yourself a disservice to try and critique it. So, like putting a puzzle together, don't step back from what you're working on until you're closer to the end and sure it's either what you were hoping for or too far off.

30   Once you have started to **create** something from all of the experimentation and seeing where various pieces can go, you can finally step back and do the last step of the process: **evaluate.**

31   Without evaluation, your brain doesn't know whether it's on the right track or not. And how could you anyway? If you don't take time to evaluate a mostly-complete idea that's like putting a puzzle together blindfolded: how do you know if you've done it well or not?

32   The real magic to all of this is that it's a process that occurs so often in our subconscious, without us having to do anything at all.

33   If we're providing the right materials for our mind to pull from (i.e., all of the right pieces for any particular puzzle), it will often do much of the work for us. Which is why ideas seem to "strike us" when we're least expecting them.

34   So, **to recap:**

35   Where do ideas come from? Our experiences and knowledge. *Creative* ideas are the result of a broad intent and a lot of connecting/experimenting on the part of your subconscious. Our brains *want* to come up with original thoughts; we simply have to get out of the way.

36   And where do ideas actually exist? As romantic as it sounds: in us. In our neural networks, which are formed and strengthened by our experiences and thoughts.

37   That's it!

38   In conclusion: if I had to give you one tidbit of advice on how to improve your own creative process, it would be this: make sure you have a lot of varied experiences and knowledge for your subconscious to utilize, then get out of its way (read that carefully–it means: stop thinking about the project or problem).

39   Your brain will run through the process on its own and before you know it you'll have some insight into what action you need to take in order to make that creative idea a reality.

40   And that, in an extremely large nutshell, is the creative process.

Using Multiple Strategies

Often processes are used as a way of defining something. Presenting the creative process defines creativity.

- Paragraphs 13 and 14 compare the creative process with solving a puzzle, an analogy.

- The writer uses an explanation of the brain's processes, as in paragraph 16, as causes of the creative process and to explain the creative process.

Discussion Questions

MyWritingLab

1. The essay starts by describing earlier ways of accounting for creativity. Why is this description important to the purpose of the essay? Is it helpful for the reader?
2. Instead of offering very specific and concrete steps, how does this essay explain the steps in the process of creativity? Why does the writer present those steps in this way?
3. What strategies does this writer use to make something more abstract like the steps of creativity clear and understandable for the reader? Did you find these strategies helpful?
4. Why does the writer recap such a short account of the creative process? What final point does he want to make about the creative process? Does this final advice fit or not fit the rest of the essay?
5. This essay was posted on a blog rather than published in a more formal, academic publication. In what ways does the writing seem fitted to a blog format? What would have to be changed to make it more suitable for more formal publications?

Toward Key Insights

MyWritingLab

The author makes clear in several places that for the creative process to be effective it needs to be something the brain does unconsciously. Often, though, writers detail processes we need to do unconsciously. What might be the advantages of explaining the steps of an otherwise unconscious process? What are some other processes that in the end we need to do unconsciously to do them effectively but may benefit from being explained?

Suggestion for Writing

MyWritingLab

Take a more abstract process such as reading, making casual conversation, or solving complex problems and write an essay or blog post on the steps for this process to be effective.

ILLUSTRATION ▬▬ ▬▬ ▬▬ ▬▬ ▬▬ ▬▬ ▬▬

Reading Strategies

1. Read the introductory and concluding paragraphs quickly to determine the thesis for the illustration. Then read the essay quickly to get the main point of the essay. Jot down the key points of the illustration.

2. Determine, based on your own purpose for reading and the level of the essay, if it is necessary to read the essay more carefully.

3. If a more careful reading is warranted, read slowly, noticing and jotting down any key details of the illustration that make a more general point.

Reading Critically

1. Test whether the illustration really demonstrates the main point.

2. Determine whether the illustrations are typical or atypical.

3. Test the point by seeing if there are illustrations that would illuminate a different position.

Reading as a Writer

1. Identify and evaluate the kinds of examples used in the illustration.

2. Notice the strategies used to link the illustrations to a main point.

3. Identify and evaluate how the illustrations were organized (as short narratives, as descriptions) and jot down any strategies you found useful.

LEXI KROCK

| Title identifies topic |

Accidental Discoveries

Lexi Krock received her B.A. in Russian, French, and English literature from Reed College. She served as associate producer and producer at Nova ScienceNow *at WGBH PBS in Boston. She has been a part of a number of journalism teams that have won awards that included the Pulitzer and Peabody. She has gone on to the* New York Times, *where she is now Special Projects Editor of Interactive News under the name Lexi Mainland. The essay below was posted on the PBS Nova Web site on February 27, 2001.*

1   From the chance discovery of quinine as a malaria treatment in the 17th century to Alexander Fleming's accidental encounter with penicillium mold in 1928, some of medicine's most important advances have occurred through serendipity. Read about seven of them here.

Fortuitous Accidents

| Attracts reader attention through vivid contrast of harmful and helpful accidents |

2   Accidents in medicine: The idea sends chills down your spine as you conjure up thoughts of misdiagnoses, mistakenly prescribed drugs, and wrongly amputated limbs. Yet while accidents in the examining room or on the operating table can be regrettable, even tragic, those that occur in the laboratory

Illustration   **491**

can sometimes lead to spectacular advances, life-saving treatments, and Nobel Prizes.

3   A seemingly insignificant finding by one researcher leads to a breakthrough discovery by another; a physician methodically pursuing the answer to a medical conundrum over many years suddenly has a "Eureka" moment; a scientist who chooses to study a contaminant in his culture rather than tossing it out stumbles upon something entirely new. Consider the following historic cases:

Quinine

4   The story behind the chance discovery of the anti-malarial drug quinine may be more legend than fact, but it is nevertheless a story worthy of note. The account that has gained the most currency credits a South American Indian with being the first to find a medical application for quinine. According to legend, the man unwittingly ingested quinine while suffering a malarial fever in a jungle high in the Andes. Needing desperately to quench his thirst, he drank his fill from a small, bitter-tasting pool of water. Nearby stood one or more varieties of cinchona, which grows from Colombia to Bolivia on humid slopes above 5,000 feet. The bark of the cinchona, which the indigenous people knew as *quina-quina*, was thought to be poisonous. But when this man's fever miraculously abated, he brought news of the medicinal tree back to his tribe, which began to use its bark to treat malaria.

5   Since the first officially noted use of quinine to fight malaria occurred in a community of Jesuit missionaries in Lima, Peru in 1630, historians have surmised that Indian tribes taught the missionaries how to extract the chemical quinine from cinchona bark. In any case, the Jesuits' use of quinine as a malaria medication was the first documented use of a chemical compound to successfully treat an infectious disease. To this day, quinine-based anti-malarials are widely used as effective treatments against the growth and reproduction of malarial parasites in humans.

Smallpox Vaccination

6   In 1796, Edward Jenner, a British scientist and surgeon, had a brainstorm that ultimately led to the development of the first vaccine. A young milkmaid had told him how people who contracted cowpox, a harmless disease easily picked up during contact with cows, never got smallpox, a deadly scourge.

7   With this in mind, Jenner took samples from the open cowpox sores on the hands of a young dairymaid named Sarah Nelmes and inoculated eight-year-old James Phipps with pus he extracted from Nelmes' sores. (Experimenting on a child would be anathema today, but this was the 18th century.) The boy developed a slight fever and a few lesions but remained for the most part unscathed. A few months later, Jenner gave the boy another injection, this one containing smallpox. James failed to develop the disease, and the idea behind the modern vaccine was born.

8   Though doctors and scientists would not begin to understand the biological basis of immunity for at least 50 years after Jenner's first inoculation, the technique of vaccinating against smallpox using the human strain of cowpox soon became a common and effective practice worldwide.

Uses header to guide reader to major discoveries

Identifies the use of narratives as an illustration device. Identifies as well the probable value of a legendary though not necessarily factual story

Presents narrative of accidental discovery and result

Identifies date, person, and discovery to be explained in narrative

Presents narrative establishing accidental results

X-Rays

9   X-rays have become an important tool for medical diagnoses, but their discovery in 1895 by the German physicist Wilhelm Conrad Röntgen had little to do with medical experimentation. Röntgen was studying cathode rays, the phosphorescent stream of electrons used today in everything from televisions to fluorescent light bulbs. One earlier scientist had found that cathode rays can penetrate thin pieces of metal, while another showed that these rays could light up a fluorescent screen placed an inch or two away from a thin aluminum "window" in the glass tube.

10   Röntgen wanted to determine if he could see cathode rays escaping from a glass tube completely covered with black cardboard. While performing this experiment, Röntgen noticed that a glow appeared in his darkened laboratory several feet away from his cardboard-covered glass tube. At first he thought a tear in the paper sheathing was allowing light from the high-voltage coil inside the cathode-ray tube to escape. But he soon realized he had happened upon something entirely different. Rays of light were passing right through the thick paper and appearing on a fluorescent screen over a yard away.

11   Röntgen found that this new ray, which had many characteristics different from the cathode ray he had been studying, could penetrate solids and even record the image of a human skeleton on a photographic negative. In 1901, the first year of the Nobel Prize, Röntgen won for his accidental discovery of what he called the "X-ray," which physicians worldwide soon adopted as a standard medical tool.

Allergy

12   Charles Robert Richet, a French physiologist, made several experiments testing the reaction of dogs exposed to poison from the tentacles of sea anemones. Some of the dogs died from allergic shock, but others survived their reactions and made full recoveries. Weeks later, because the recovered dogs seemed completely normal, Richet wasted no time in reusing them for more experiments. They were given another dose of anemone poison, this time much smaller than before. The first time the dogs' allergic symptoms, including vomiting, shock, loss of consciousness, and in some cases death, had taken several days to fully develop. But this time the dogs suffered such serious symptoms just minutes after Richet administered the poison.

13   Though Richet was puzzled by what had happened, he realized he could not disregard the unexpected result of his experiment. Later, he noted that his eventual conclusions about the dogs' affliction were "not at all the result of deep thinking, but of a simple observation, almost accidental; so that I have had no other merit than that of not refusing to see the facts which presented themselves before me, completely evident."

14   Richet's conclusions from his findings came to form the theoretical basis of the medical study and treatment of allergies. He eventually proved that there was a physiological state called anaphylaxis that was the antithesis of prophylaxis: When an allergic subject is exposed to an allergen a second time, he or she is even more sensitive to its effects than the first time. Instead of building immunity to the substance through exposure (prophylaxis), the allergic subject's immunity becomes greatly reduced.

15   In 1913, Richet received the Nobel Prize for his discovery and articulation of diseases of allergy.

Illustration **493**

Insulin

16   Frederick G. Banting, a young Canadian doctor, and Professor John J. R. MacLeod of the University of Toronto shared a Nobel Prize in 1923 for their isolation and clinical use of insulin against diabetes. Their work with insulin followed from the chance discovery of the link between the pancreas and blood-sugar levels by two other doctors on the other side of the Atlantic decades earlier.

17   In 1889, German physicians Joseph von Mering and Oscar Minkowski removed the pancreas from a healthy dog in order to study the role of the pancreas in digestion. Several days after the dog's pancreas was removed, the doctors happened to notice a swarm of flies feeding on a puddle of the dog's urine. On testing the urine to determine the cause of the flies' attraction, the doctors realized that the dog was secreting sugar in its urine, a sign of diabetes. Because the dog had been healthy prior to the surgery, the doctors knew that they had created its diabetic condition by removing its pancreas and thus understood for the first time the relationship between the pancreas and diabetes.

18   With more tests, von Mering and Minkowski concluded that a healthy pancreas must secrete a substance that controls the metabolism of sugar in the body. Though many scientists tried in vain to isolate the particular substance released by the pancreas after the Germans' accidental discovery, it was Banting and MacLeod who established that the mysterious substance was insulin and began to put it to use as the first truly valuable means of controlling diabetes.

Pap Smear

19   Dr. George Nicholas Papanicolaou's chance observation, while doing a genetic study, of cancer cells on a slide containing a specimen from a woman's uterus spawned the routine use of the so-called "Pap smear," a simple test that has saved millions of women from the ravages of uterine cancer.

20   In 1923, Papanicolaou undertook a study of vaginal fluid in women, in hopes of observing cellular changes over the course of a menstrual cycle. In female guinea pigs, Papanicolaou had already noticed cell transformation and wanted to corroborate the phenomenon in human females. It happened that one of Papanicolaou's human subjects was suffering from uterine cancer.

21   Upon examination of a slide made from a smear of the patient's vaginal fluid, Papanicolaou was astonished to discover that abnormal cancer cells could be plainly observed under a microscope. "The first observation of cancer cells in the smear of the uterine cervix," he later wrote, "gave me one of the greatest thrills I ever experienced during my scientific career." Papanicolaou quickly realized that doctors could administer a simple test to gather a sample of vaginal fluid and test it for early signs of uterine and other cancers.

Penicillin

22   The identification of penicillium mold by Dr. Alexander Fleming in 1928 is one of the best-known stories of medical discovery, not only because of its accidental nature, but also because penicillin has remained one of the most important and useful drugs in our arsenal, and its discovery triggered invaluable research into a range of other invaluable antibiotic drugs.

23   While researching the flu in the summer of 1928, Dr. Fleming noticed that some mold had contaminated a flu culture in one of his petri dishes. Instead of

---

Marginal annotations:

Identifies researchers, historical context, and the topic of illustration

Continues the practice of identifying the role of earlier discoveries

Explains as a narrative the process of the accidental discovery

Explains the cause-and-effect mechanism that shows the importance of their discovery

Identifies researcher, the accidental circumstances of the discovery, and the results of the discovery, including the importance of the results

Provides a narrative of the process that leads to the discovery

Uses a quote to confirm the eureka moment of discovery

Identifies the recognition of the statement of results

Provides historical context and the role of the example as an illustration of discovery; also states the importance of the discovery

Identifies the accidental event as part of the narrative

throwing out the ruined dish, he decided to examine the moldy sample more closely.

24   Fleming had reaped the benefits of taking time to scrutinize contaminated samples before. In 1922, Fleming had accidentally shed one of his own tears into a bacteria sample and noticed that the spot where the tear had fallen was free of the bacteria that grew all around it. This discovery peaked his curiosity. After conducting some tests, he concluded that tears contain an antibiotic-like enzyme that could stave off minor bacterial growth.

25   Six years later, the mold Fleming observed in his petri dish reminded him of this first experience with a contaminated sample. The area surrounding the mold growing in the dish was clear, which told Fleming that the mold was lethal to the potent staphylococcus bacteria in the dish. Later he noted, "But for the previous experience, I would have thrown the plate away, as many bacteriologists have done before."

26   Instead, Fleming took the time to isolate the mold, eventually categorizing it as belonging to the genus *penicillium*. After many tests, Fleming realized that he had discovered a non-toxic antibiotic substance capable of killing many of the bacteria that cause minor and severe infections in humans and other animals. His work, which has saved countless lives, won him the Nobel Prize in 1945.

Keep That Mind Open

27   For all you would-be Nobel Prize-winners, remember the one trait that tied all these lucky strikers together: openmindedness. As the American physicist Joseph Henry once noted, "The seeds of great discoveries are constantly floating around us, but they only take root in minds well prepared to receive them."

MyWritingLab   ## Discussion Questions

1. Rather than using only a few examples, the writer chose to use seven very common medical examples. How do the choices of examples and the number of examples help illustrate the main point about accidental discoveries?

2. Why in paragraph 2 does the writer speak of medical accidents that are harmful? How is the contrast with the rest of the work helpful to the point of the essay?

3. The writer tends to follow the same pattern with each illustration. What is that pattern and how does it help the reader follow the author's illustration?

4. In paragraph 3 the writer points to the role of previous discoveries. Where else in the essay does the writer point to such discoveries and their role in an accidental discovery? How does this strategy affect the coherence of the essay?

5. How does the conclusion, paragraph 27, differ from the rest of the essay? Why might the writer have chosen to end in this fashion? Is the conclusion effective?

6. This essay talks about scientific discovery for a lay audience. How has the writer adjusted the language about the science to meet the needs of the average reader? Where do you find the language appropriate and where inappropriate?

Margin annotations:

Connects this with other accidental discoveries to highlight role of such discoveries by Fleming

Continues the narrative of process of discovery

Uses the quote to identify the value that led to this accidental discovery

Identifies the results of the discovery

New type of heading indicates an end of the examples and an appeal to the reader

Conclusion offers advice to reader

Illustration   **495**

Toward Key Insights

MyWritingLab

Illustrations provide an example to demonstrate a main point. This illustration focuses on accidental discoveries and on the role of chance. But these discoveries also depended on the knowledge and training of the discoverers. How could these examples also be used to demonstrate not the role of accidental discovery but rather the role of effective preparation to make discoveries?

One statistical problem is that we can often fixate on a few successes and forget all the failures. People who hit the jackpot at a casino may forget that they lost much more money than they won. How would the above illustration look if we considered all the accidents that prevented real discoveries, led down blind alleys, or resulted in real harm?

Suggestions for Writing

MyWritingLab

1. Make notes on the role of chance in your own educational, career, or life choices and interview others about how chance affected their lives. Write an essay on the role of chance in our lives.
2. Interview scientists, artists, or writers on your campus or do library or Internet research to write an illustration on the secrets of successful discovery or creation.
3. Based on your own experience, interviews, or research, write an essay illustrating how lack of readiness or preparation can lead to missed opportunities.

JUDITH NEWMAN

If You're Happy and You Know It, Must I Know, Too?

Judith Newman is a freelance writer who has appeared in Mademoiselle, The Wall Street Journal, National Geographic, Vogue, Vanity Fair, *and other publications. She is contributing editor for* Allure. *Recently she published* You Make Me Feel Like an Unnatural Woman: Diary of New Old Mother. *This selection occurs in the October 21, 2011, online version of* The New York Times.

1   Mary Lou DiNardo checked three times to make sure: was that a smiley face at the end of the latest e-mail from her most dour client?

2   A West Coast real estate executive, he had an M.B.A. from a prestigious university and was "a very intellectual, serious man," said Ms. DiNardo, president of TK/PR, a public relations firm. "I've been dealing with him for seven years. All of a sudden, while we're discussing problems with a vendor, he's signing off with these smiling or winking faces. I mean, this is a guy who I don't think I've seen with a smile on his *actual* face."

3   Ms. DiNardo joins the ranks of professionals who have found themselves on the receiving end of smileys, winks and LOL's, as the emoticon has rather suddenly migrated from the e-mails and texts of teenagers (and perhaps the more

frothy adults) to the correspondence of business people who pride themselves on their gravitas.

4   "Oh, no question, I've been sending and receiving them more often," said Martha Heller, president of Heller Search Associates, a search firm for technology executives for Fortune 500 companies. "Generally I'll use a smiley or a wink when I'm indicating that my previous comment was meant to be a joke. Like, I hired a guy who's head of sales and marketing to launch my company into the wonderful world of social media, and I sent him a note—'I hear there's this thing called Twitter'—and I added the smiley so he knew I wasn't that clueless."

5   Lisa M. Bates, an assistant professor of epidemiology at Columbia, has lately embraced the smiley—as have her academic colleagues, albeit "sparingly and strategically," she said. "Basically, I'm often sarcastic and in a hurry, and a well-planted smiley face can take the edge off and avoid misunderstanding," Dr. Bates wrote in an e-mail. "I figure they have saved me some grief from misconstrued tone many times."

6   Emoticons can produce another layer of confusion, however: they don't always read the same way across different technical interfaces. "In the text function of my BlackBerry there is a sidebar menu of emoticons (how ridiculous is that?) that shows the yellow smiley faces, except they are also crying and raging, and winking and blowing kisses, etc.," Dr. Bates wrote. "I sent a fairly new acquaintance a 'big hug' emoticon—which, for the record, was ironic. But anyway, on his iPhone it came up with the symbols, not the smiley face, which don't look anything like a big hug. From his perspective they look like a view of, er, splayed lady parts: ({|)." He then ran around his lab showing colleagues excitedly what I had just sent him. Half (mostly men) concurred with his interpretation, and the others (mostly women) didn't and probably thought he was kind of a desperate perv."

7   These little misinterpretations aside, recent adoptees like Dr. Bates and Ms. Heller said that emoticons not only signal intention in a medium where it's notoriously hard to read tone, they also denote a special congenial relationship between sender and recipient. "I see it as a relationship-building exercise," Ms. Heller said.

8   Students of digital communication see the emerging acceptance of whimsical signifiers as inevitable, if not always desirable. "They're part of the degradation of writing skills—grammar, syntax, sentence structure, even penmanship—that come with digital technology," said Bill Lancaster, a lecturer in communications at Northeastern University in Boston. "Certainly I understand the need for clarity. But language, used properly, is clear on its own."

9   Perhaps it's no surprise, then, that writers and teachers of writing are among the last emoticon holdouts. "I am deeply offended by them," said Maria McErlane, a British journalist, actress and radio personality on BBC Radio 2. "If anybody on Facebook sends me a message with a little smiley-frowny face or a little sunshine with glasses on them, I will de-friend them. I also de-friend for OMG and LOL. They get no second chance. I find it lazy. Are your words not enough? To use a little picture with sunglasses on it to let you know how you're feeling is beyond ridiculous."

10   Another harsh critic is Michele Farinet, a parent coordinator in an elementary school in Manhattan who spends much of her days answering and responding to e-mails of the (largely professional) body of parents. The whole subject touches a raw nerve.

Illustration   **497**

11   "To me, it's like bad moviemaking, where as soon as Dad grabs the puppy, the shot immediately goes to Junior's teary face—like the director does not trust the audience to have an appropriately developed emotion by itself," Ms. Farinet wrote in an e-mail. "That's what emoticons do. PLEASE don't 'show' me that I should be happy-faced or sad-faced or that you are sad-faced or happy-faced."

12   "Can you imagine," wrote Ms. Farinet, "reading the end of 'The Great Gatsby' like that?: So we beat on, boats against the current, borne back ceaselessly into the past:-("

Discussion Questions
MyWritingLab

1. What would you identify as the thesis statement in this essay? What if anything in the essay doesn't fit this thesis statement?
2. How do paragraphs 8–12 fit or not fit the thrust of the essay? Why do you think the writer included these paragraphs? Is this approach effective to her main point?
3. One strategy in a conclusion is to end with some slight humor that makes your point. What point do you think the writer was making with the conclusion on paragraph 12? Is it effective?
4. Instead of using one more detailed example, the author used several shorter examples? Why was it important to use shorter examples? Were they effective?
5. What do you see as the level of diction or language style of this essay? Why did the author select that level of diction?

Toward Key Insights
MyWritingLab

With text messaging and twitter, people are actually writing more than they did when depending on the phone as a principle means of communication. In what ways are new media changing how we communicate with each other? What are the advantages and challenges of these changes?

Often as people change the way they communicate, there are different attitudes that develop about the available tools and styles of communication. What are the different ways people are responding to some of the social networking styles of communication?

Suggestions for Writing
MyWritingLab

1. Collect writing samples from social media communication such as texting or Facebook and write a paper illustrating how language is used in such communication.
2. There are always differing reactions to any new technology or style of communication. Interview several different people about social media as a form of communication and write a paper illustrating how people adapt to changing media for communication.

CATHERINE STEINER ADAIR

The Revolution in the Living Room

Catherine Steiner-Adair, Ed.D., is a practicing clinical psychologist and educational consultant. She is a research associate in the Department of Psychiatry at Harvard Medical School. She posts blogs on family life and has published two books. This article is from the first chapter of her recent book, The Big Disconnect: Protecting Childhood and Family Relationships in the Digital Age *(2013).*

1   John is distraught because his marriage and family are disintegrating. A flashpoint is the invasive presence that online time, social networking, texting, and the like have in their lives. His wife has a long commute to her job and she routinely communicates by text with him and their two children, eight and fourteen years old. This includes when she is home and they are all in the house. She's a tech enthusiast; she enjoys bringing the newest gadgets home and isn't bothered by the time the children spend on them. John prefers face-to-face conversation, or phone calls—voice contact. They fight over whether access to all this tech is hurting their children. The emotional disconnect between the two of them is acted out and amplified through their battles over technology.

2   John worries about his children and the way their online diversions, texting, and social networking have become the default mode for their attention. Car rides used to include conversation or quiet time with them. No more. Wherever they go his children are either fighting over who has the digital tablet or they are plugged in and oblivious. On their last trip, he recalls, their son texted constantly on his phone; the family also had a handheld digital movie player. "So they're watching a movie, but all their heads are down like this [he looks down at his lap], and they're playing games, too, doing some idiotic thing like putting cubes into a box or making a car jump over and over." Back home, what used to be old-fashioned downtime before dinner to hang out as a family, swap stories from the day, and make small talk has vanished. The kids stay in their rooms with their laptops until dinner is ready. Or they come to the table with screens to continue "looking up stuff—you know, looking up shoes or looking up music."

3   "You know, it's almost like nervously filling the time with a passive activity, like biting your nails," he says. "Instead of biting their nails, people are texting people and Googling them. And young people being the way they are, I mean, what information are they really exchanging? *Hey? Huh? Hey, yeah. What you doing? So bored.*" How can that be meaningful? he wonders. What is the quality of all this connection?

4   John is also disturbed by what he sees in the broader social context and the reflection of that in his children s friendships. "There's a social weirdness to it," he says of the way people continue to text or take calls even when they're engaged in face-to-face conversations. "That's what I see in my children, in their relationships. . . , My son has had a friend come over for a playdate, and my son is, like, skateboarding, and his friend is just standing there texting, right? " He feels defeated in his efforts to rein in his kids' media usage or to reconcile with the digital makeover of his family. "Yeah, I mean, we're sort of stuck with it, is the problem. I guess that's really the very crux of it. Because the society's all wired around it now."

Illustration **499**

5   Everywhere I go, from parent conferences to kitchen table conversations, a similar mix of confusion and clarity characterizes the concern about tech and family.

6   "When you have very busy lives, your relationships become completely utilitarian and nagging," says Helene, reflecting on life with her husband and two teenage children. She rattles off the to-do list of deadlines and scheduling that dominates their conversations: homework, camp application deadlines, games, sports, concerts, practice, the family social calendar. "It's like were this little business, and we just interact, so if you want to have any kind of connection otherwise, you send the YouTube video, send the text . . . we never talk directly, we never look each other in the eye anymore."

7   Another mother tells me of her dawning awareness that something fundamental is changing about family life, echoing the overwhelming sense of unease so many parents share: "I have this feeling that we're all just camped out in the house on these different screens, and I feel like there's been this deterioration of connection, and I don't know how," she says.

8   I know that feeling as a parent, too. I remember this eerie feeling that our family's way of being a family felt like it was slipping away as our home computer began to dominate our children's time and attention. The dynamic shifted beyond what I had anticipated as normal adolescent behavior, especially during our son Daniel's teen years, as he spent more and more time on computer games and online socializing. He was in that first generation of digital natives, those children of the early 1980s who grew up around bulky home computers, floppy disks, and loaf-size mobile phones used almost exclusively by their parents and mostly just for work. These were the kids who were in elementary school when the first wave of computers hit the classroom. It was easy for us to set limits on TV (none during the school week) and to set clear limits on the weekends. But like so many of his peers, Daniel entered adolescence fully computer literate, his intellect wired for upgrades, his appetite eager for mastering games. Suddenly his after-school social life shifted to a new playing field: computer games. Homework called for screen time, too, and exploratory research on the Internet. So we said yes to a computer, then yes, however hesitantly at times, to new tech, updates, and more computer games when it seemed they were the new requirement for a teenager to stay connected with his friends. On the one hand, his home computer transformed Daniel's academic life in ways that excited all of us. His success in the screen world of wizardry and warfare transformed his social life in ways that thrilled him and us. One wave after another, tech swept through the home front. Our son's feelings about it were predictable: he loved it. But we were conflicted. It was fun watching him have great experiences. Not so much having to argue or negotiate constantly with him over screen time or game choices. And then feeling: *this is invading my family and eating my son alive and I dont like it.* Even when his grades and behavior were fine, and he was fine, something about that computer's gravitational pull just didn't feel right.

9   Another experience that focused the evolving and unsettling picture for me arose not at home but one afternoon in Washington, D.C. My husband, Fred, and I were visiting Arlington National Cemetery across the river in Virginia. Walking through the grounds that still vibrate with the pain and sacrifice of war, we noticed that no matter where we went people were talking on their cell phones with no regard for the people around them or for their own privacy. A family of several generations hovered at one stone and right next to them a man was arguing and swearing to someone on the phone. Parents knelt quietly

at a specific gravesite while their kids were texting and laughing on their phones. The solemn surroundings invited quiet reflection, or at least quiet respect for the place where so many are buried. But quiet respect was no longer the norm.

10   We eventually stopped for a bite to eat at a bustling street café where, at the table across from us, sat a teenage girl, maybe sixteen or so, with a middle-aged woman who appeared to be her mother. Through the entire meal the girl said only about three sentences to the woman just inches away and her comments were brief and perfunctory. The rest of the time she looked steadily down, texting on the smartphone on her lap under the table. A noticeable silence defined the space between the two, the woman glancing at the girl periodically with a hopeful look, while the girl maintained eye contact only with the tiny screen on her lap, continuing her lively texting. It was disturbing to see. There they sat together, but not really. It felt sadly familiar. It was the quintessential family portrait of the Digital Age of Disconnection.

11   In my work, both as a therapist and school consultant, in the context of our relationship with tech I am always struck by the one eternal and incontrovertible truth about families: children need their parents' time and attention and families thrive when parents have strong, healthy relationships with their children and children are attuned to the family milieu. But this reality can be so easily lost when we are lured away by the siren call of the virtual world.

Using Multiple Strategies

This illustration uses multiple strategies as part of a longer argument about how families need to respond to digital distractions.

- Illustrations often use examples to illustrate, and as in this case illustrations are often short narratives as in paragraphs 2 and 8, 9 and 10.
- Narratives usually use illustration and description, as in paragraph 10.
- The writer uses comparison, as in paragraph 2 to contrast family interaction in the virtual age with earlier patterns of interaction.

MyWritingLab ## Discussion Questions

1. This is a selection from a chapter in a full book. What would you see as the thesis statement of this selection? Where is it stated most explicitly?
2. This selection uses multiple examples. Why might this be a reasonable choice for the writer? Are the examples effective and believable? Why or why not?
3. Do you think the examples the writer chooses are representative, or did she leave out examples that would contradict her point? Is her illustration ethical?
4. In several paragraphs, such as 4, 6, and 7, the writer quotes ordinary individuals using informal everyday speech rather than more academic language. Why might she have made that choice? What is the effect on the passage?
5. Paragraph 8 offers a longer narrative example. What point does this example make? Why was a longer narrative needed here to make that point?
6. Do the examples support the conclusions in paragraph 11? Why or why not?

Toward Key Insights

Often we try to use illustration to show an effect: whether our digital age is changing the family, television is encouraging violence, or large class size interferes
with learning. However, examples do not really demonstrate that the effects
actually follow the suggested causes. Does this author really prove that the
digital age is having a negative impact on family life? What might be some
counter-examples? In general, what problems do you see in trying to argue for
an effect from examples in illustration?

Suggestions for Writing

1. "The Revolution in the Living Room" suggests the negative impact digital
   devices may have on family life. Write a paper illustrating the ways that digital
   devices can enhance family life.
2. Make your own observations about the digital age and collect your examples
   on its impacts on family life, friendship interaction, or classroom life. Write a
   paper that illustrates your conclusion.

CLASSIFICATION

Reading Strategies

1. Identify your purpose for reading the essay and the writer's purpose for the
classification. This will determine how carefully you will need to read the selection.

2. Do not lose the big picture. Identify what is being classified—types of cars, kinds
of dates—and why it is being classified.

3. Notice each of the major categories and the distinctive characteristics of each
category. When this material is important to you, it can be very useful to make a table
that identifies each major classification and identifies the distinctive features of each
category. When carefully organized, such a table can be very helpful.

Reading Critically

1. Determine if there is reasonable evidence for the classification system or if the
system is arbitrary.

2. Try to come up with an alternative classification system.

3. Check to see if the categories of the classification are clear or overlap.

4. Determine whether the defining features are distinct enough to clearly apply the
system.

5. Try applying the system. Does it work?

Reading as a Writer

1. Identify how the essay establishes the characteristics of the classification system.

2. Often the transition sentences in a classification essay are awkward. Examine the
transition sentences and evaluate the effectiveness of the transitions.

BERNICE MCCARTHY

A Tale of Four Learners

Bernice McCarthy, Ph.D., earned her doctorate in education and learning theory from Northwestern University. She founded About Learning, Inc., a consulting firm on educational theory and research. She has published a number of articles and presented workshops at major institutions. In this essay, she classifies learners based on the 4MAT System® she created.

1   A young man at a midwestern middle school said of his social studies teacher, "She doesn't label us, and she helps us do all kinds of things." That student expressed very simply my evolving understanding of style since I created the 4MAT System in 1979. The way one perceives reality and reacts to it forms a pattern over time. This pattern comes to dominate the way one integrates ideas, skills, and information about people and the way one adapts knowledge and forms meaning.

2   But to learn successfully, a student also needs expertise in other learning styles; together these styles form a natural cycle of learning. That middle school teacher apparently honored the unique style that each student brought to her classroom, while helping each one do some stretching and master all the ways of learning.

3   Following are true stories about four types of learners. They illustrate how students with different learning styles experience school and why we must create opportunities for diverse learning experiences for every child.

4   Linda was in 6th grade when she hit the wall in math. She had loved school up until then. Her teachers and classmates agreed that her poetry was quite good, and her poems often appeared in local publications. But math was a problem. She couldn't connect it to anything—she simply could not see the patterns. Her teachers were not pleased with her and she longed to please them.

5   Linda went on to college, and when she was a junior, a new professor arrived on campus. The day before Linda's statistics class began, she met him in the hallway. He said, "Oh, you're Linda; I've been reading your poetry. You are going to do very well in statistics."

6   She looked at him in amazement. "How can you say that? I have such difficulty in all my math classes."

7   He smiled and answered, "I can tell from your poetry that you understand symmetry. Statistics is about symmetry. As a matter of fact, statistics is the poetry of math." Linda went on to earn an A in that class. Her professor had connected statistics to her life and showed her the patterns (McCarthy 1996).

8   Linda is a Type 1 learner—the highly imaginative student who favors feeling and reflecting. These learners

9   ■ are at home with their feelings, people-oriented, outstanding observers of people, great listeners and nurturers, and committed to making the world a better place.

10   ■ prefer to learn by talking about experiences; listening and watching quietly, then responding to others and discussing ideas; asking questions; brainstorming; and examining relationships. They work well in groups or teams but also enjoy reading quietly.

11   ■ experience difficulty with long verbal explanations, with giving oral presentations, and with memorizing large chunks of abstract information.

They dislike confusion or conflict, environments where mistakes are openly criticized, or where they cannot discuss their perceptions.

12   ■ have a cognitive style that puts perception before judgment, subjective knowledge before objective facts, and reflection before action. They prefer to make decisions based on feeling, are visual/auditory/kinesthetic, and experiential before conceptual.

13   As a Type 1 learner, Linda needed to connect math to her real life, to know why it was useful as a way of thinking and a way of formulating problems and solutions. She also needed her teachers to believe in her and to spend time with and nurture her.

                                                       Completes example

14   Marcus was in 1st grade, and he loved school. Everything he longed for was present there—the teacher's loving interest, the thrill of deciphering the symbols that meant things, the things he could touch and feel, the addition problems that the teacher wrote on the chalkboard. He could always see the answers. His excitement was like that of the basketball player who knows that if he can just get his hands on the ball, he can sink it. Each question became an exciting foray into even more questions. And as his reading improved rapidly, he could not get enough of books. He welcomed the words and ideas of each new writer. He felt confident; he knew he belonged (McCarthy 1996).

                                                       Example of second type

15   Marcus is a Type 2 learner—the analytic student who favors reflecting and thinking. These learners

                                                       Defines second type of learner

16   ■ have a knowledge-oriented style; are outstanding at conceptualizing material; analyze and classify their experiences and organize ideas; are highly organized and at home with details and data; are good at step-by-step tasks; are fascinated with structure; believe in their ability to understand; and are committed to making the world more lucid.

                                                       Identifies characteristics of second type

17   ■ prefer to learn through lectures and objective explanations, by working independently and systematically, and by reading and exchanging ideas.

18   ■ experience difficulty in noisy, high-activity environments, ambiguous situations, and working in groups. They also have trouble with open-ended assignments, as well as with presentations, role-playing, and nonsequential instructions. They have difficulty talking about feelings as well.

19   ■ have a cognitive style that is objective thinking, reflection before action, impersonal, auditory/visual/kinesthetic, conceptual over experiential. They tend to make judgments first, then support them with their perceptions.

20   As a Type 2 learner, Marcus found school an absolute joy. Testing, so frightening to Linda, was a tonic for him, a chance to prove he could do it. Because he was naturally verbal and school is mostly a verbal challenge, he was—and continues to be—successful.

                                                       Completes example

21   When Jimmy was in 2nd grade he did not like to read, and that made school difficult. He did enjoy having others read to him, and his younger brother, a 1st grader, read him stories every night. Jimmy did excel in math and art. He loved to work alone on projects and never wanted help. When he was asked to illustrate a story or build something to depict a math concept, he approached the task excitedly. He was happiest when he could solve a problem by creating a three-dimensional solution.

                                                       Example of third type

22   Unfortunately, Jimmy had a rigid teacher whose timing was always different from his own. Jimmy either finished too fast or took too long when he got really interested in a project. Once his teacher said in exasperation, "I didn't say you had to do your best work, Jimmy, just get it done!" When Jimmy's family bought a new VCR, they read the directions aloud to figure out how it worked.

Jimmy stepped up and simply made it work. His reading problem continued into 3rd grade when he caught up with the others, but he never let it get him down—he was simply too busy doing other kinds of things (McCarthy 1996).

Defines third type of learner

23   Jimmy is a Type 3 learner—the common-sense learner who favors thinking and doing. These learners

Identifies characteristics of third type

24   ■ are great problem solvers and are drawn to how things work. They are at home with tasks and deadlines, are productive and committed to making the world work better, and they believe in their ability to get the job done. They are also active and need opportunities to move around.

25   ■ prefer to learn through active problem solving; step-by-step procedures; touching, manipulating, and constructing; demonstrations; experimentation and tinkering; and competition.

26   ■ experience difficulty when reading is the primary means of learning and whenever they cannot physically test what they are told. They have trouble with verbal complexity, paradoxes or unclear choices, subtle relationships, and open-ended academic tasks. They also have difficulty expressing feelings.

27   ■ have a cognitive style that features objective thinking and facts over ideas, action before reflection, and judgment before perception. Their style is impersonal and kinesthetic/auditory/visual.

Completes example

28   As a Type 3 learner, Jimmy needed to work things out in his own way, to create unique solutions to problems, and, most of all, to show what he learned by doing something concrete with it. His verbal skills did not kick in until well into the 3rd grade. Although this is not unusual with highly spatial learners, teachers treated it as an aberration. School was simply too regimented and too verbal for Jimmy. What saved him was his focus on his own learning.

Example of fourth type of learner

29   When Leah was a high school freshman, she liked her new friends and some of her teachers. But she had a fierce need to learn, and school was not nearly exciting enough for her. She found so much of it deadening—memorizing endless facts that were totally irrelevant to her life. Leah had a wonderful spontaneity, and when it took hold of her, she focused so intensely that time became meaningless. Her teachers came to regard this spontaneity as a liability that was taking her away from the things she needed to know.

30   At first Leah persevered. Instead of preparing a juvenile justice report based on her social studies text, she asked to be allowed to go to juvenile court and see for herself, and then present her findings in a skit. Her teachers seldom agreed to her proposals, and after a while Leah stopped trying. She had natural leadership talent, which she expressed through her extra-curricular activities—the one part of school she came to love. She graduated, but has believed ever since then that real learning does not happen in school (McCarthy 1996).

Defines fourth type

31   Leah is a Type 4 learner—the dynamic learner who favors creating and acting. These learners

Identifies characteristics of fourth type

32   ■ are proud of their subjectivity, at home with ambiguity and change, and great risk takers and entrepreneurs. They act to extend and enrich their experiences and to challenge the boundaries of their worlds for the sake of growth and renewal, and they believe in their ability to influence what happens. They initiate learning by looking for unique aspects of the information to learn and they sustain learning through trial and error.

33   ■ prefer to learn by self-discovery, talking, convincing others, looking for creative solutions to problems, and engaging in free flights of ideas. They

also like to work independently and tackle open-ended academic tasks with lots of options, paradox, or subtle relationships. Their interpersonal skills are good.

34   ■ experience difficulty with rigid routines when they are not allowed to question. They also have trouble with visual complexity, methodical tasks, time management, and absolutes.

35   ■ have a cognitive style that is perception first with slight attention to judgment, subjective, relational, action-oriented, kinesthetic/auditory/visual, and experiential over conceptual.

36   Leah found learning for school's sake incomprehensible. As in Jimmy's case, doing was crucial to her approach. She preferred interviewing over reading, going to court to see for herself, exploring instead of hearing how others see things.

Complete examples

37   In any classroom, Linda, Marcus, Jimmy, Leah, and their many shades and varieties sit before the teacher—challenging and waiting to be challenged. The frustrating question is: why are some learners honored in our schools and others ignored, discouraged, or even frowned upon? Why did Marcus fare so well, while Linda, Jimmy, and Leah struggled to be accepted?

Raises question essay answers

38   In my definition of learning, the learner makes meaning by moving through a natural cycle—a movement from feeling to reflecting to thinking and, finally, to acting. This cycle results from the interplay of two separate dimensions—perceiving and processing (Kolb 1984).

Explains learning processes that result in learning types

39   In perceiving, we take in what happens to us by (1) feeling, as we grasp our experience, and then by (2) thinking, as we begin to separate ourselves from the experience and name and classify it. The resulting concepts become our way of interpreting our world (Kegan 1982).

40   We also process experiences in two ways: by (1) reflecting on them, and then by (2) acting on those reflections. We also try things; we tinker.

41   The places in this cycle that we find most comfortable—where we function with natural ease and grace—are our learning preferences or styles, the "spins" we put on learning.

42   Unfortunately, schools tend to honor only one aspect of perceiving—thinking. This is very tough on kids whose approach to learning is predominately feeling. Linda and Leah, like many other Type 1 and 4 learners—both male and female—are naturals on the feeling end of experience. Jimmy and Marcus, the Type 2 and 3 learners, favor the thinking end.

Answers question about schools and learning style

43   As with feeling and thinking, reflecting and acting need to be in balance. But our schools favor reflecting. Marcus excelled at that, while both Jimmy and Leah needed to act. The lack of hands-on learning created difficulties for both of them.

Explains use of learning styles

44   Even as I define styles in my work, I caution that we must be wary of labels. Over time, and with experience, practice, and encouragement, students become comfortable with learning styles that aren't naturally their own. Successful learners, in fact, develop multiple styles.

Qualifies use of classification system

45   The 4MAT framework is designed to help students gain expertise in every learning style. We design lesson units as cycles built around core concepts, each of which incorporates experiencing (Type 1), conceptualizing (Type 2), applying (Type 3), and creating (Type 4). The styles answer the questions:

Demonstrates use of classification

46   ■ Why do I need to know this? (the personal meaning of Type 1)
    ■ What exactly is this content or skill? (the conceptual understanding of Type 2)

- How will I use this in my life? (the real-life skills of Type 3)
- If I do use this, what possibilities will it create? (the unique adaptations of Type 4)

47   Had the teachers of Linda, Marcus, Jimmy, and Leah used the entire cycle of learning styles, including those areas in which each student needed to stretch, all four students would have acquired expertise in all facets of the cycle. They would have made personal connections to the learning, examined expert knowledge, used what they were learning to solve problems, and come up with new ways to apply the learning—both personally and in the world at large. (As it happened, the students learned to do these things on their own.)

48   In addressing the various learning styles, the 4MAT System also incorporates elements of brain research—in particular, the different ways that the right and left hemispheres of the cerebral cortex process information (Benson 1985, McCarthy 1981 and 1987, Sylvester 1995, Wittrock 1985). I call these contrasting mental operations the Left and Right Modes.

Explains classification system with brain research

49   The Left Mode is analytical and knows those things we can describe with precision. It examines cause and effect, breaks things down into parts and categorizes them, seeks and uses language and symbols, abstracts experience for comprehension, generates theory, and creates models. It is sequential and works in time.

50   The Right Mode knows more than it can tell, filling in gaps and imagining. It is intuitive. It senses feelings; forms images and mental combinations; and seeks and uses patterns, relationships, and connections. It manipulates form, distance, and space.

51   Excellence and higher-order thinking demand that we honor both sides of the brain, teaching interactively with hands-on, real-life, messy problem solving. Learners speak in words, signs, symbols, movement, and through music. The more voices students master, the more new learning they will do. Unfortunately, however, teachers persist in lecturing and using logical, sequential problem solving most of the time.

Demonstrates use of classification in assessing

52   In assessing student performance, traditional methods work fairly well for Type 2 learners, who like to prove themselves, and Type 3 learners, who do well on tests in general. Traditional testing doesn't work as well for Types 1 and 4, however. Type 1 learners have difficulty in formal testing situations, especially when tests are timed and call for precise answers. Type 4 learners have trouble doing things by the book and with absolutes and rigid routines when they are not allowed to ask questions.

53   Further, students change roles as they move through the learning cycle. Tests that require students to recall facts obviously do not reflect the subtlety of these changes.

54   We need assessment tools that help us understand the whole person. We must assess the students' ability to picture the concept, to experiment with the idea, to combine skills in order to solve complex problems, to edit and refine their work, and to adapt and integrate learning. We need to know how students are connecting information to their own experiences, how they are blending expert knowledge with their own, and how creative they are. We also need some way of measuring how students reflect on material, conceptualize, and represent what they have learned through various kinds of performances.

55   Successful learning is a continuous, cyclical, lifelong process of differentiating and integrating these personal modes of adaptation. Teachers do not

need to label learners according to their style; they need to help them work for balance and wholeness. Leah needs to learn the ways of Marcus; Jimmy needs Linda's ways. And all learners need encouragement to grow.

56   Learning is both reflective and active, verbal and nonverbal, concrete and abstract, head and heart. The teacher must use many instructional methods that are personally meaningful to each student. The more students can travel the cycle, the better they can move to higher-order thinking.

57   As a final note, what became of the students I described earlier? Linda directs the management division of a major human resources consulting firm. Marcus, a former professor of statistics at a prestigious university, is now president of a research firm. Jimmy will be a senior in high school this fall. He scored 100 percent on the Illinois State Math Achievement Test and achieved cum laude in the International Latin Exam. He also had his art portfolio favorably reviewed by the Art Institute of Chicago. And Leah? Leah is a pseudonym for the author of this article.

Conclusion restates introduction and thesis in a more developed way

Completes examples by demonstrating the success of each student

References

Benson, David Frank. "Language in the Left Hemisphere." The Dual Brain: Hemispheric Specialization in Humans. Ed. David Frank Benson and Eran Zaidel. New York: Guilford, 1985. Print.

Kegan, Robert. The Evolving Self: Problems and Process in Human Development. Cambridge, MA: Harvard UP, 1982. Print.

Kolb, David A. Experiential Learning: Experience as the Source of Learning and Development. Englewood Cliffs, NJ: Prentice-Hall, 1984. Print.

McCarthy, Bernice. The 4MAT System: Teaching to Learning Styles with Right/Left Mode Techniques. Barrington, IL: Excel, Inc., 1981, 1987. Print.

McCarthy, Bernice. About Learning. Barrington, IL: Excel, Inc., 1996. Print.

Sylvester, Robert. A Celebration of Neurons: An Educator's Guide to the Human Brain. Alexandria, VA: ASCD, 1995. Print.

Wittrock, Merlin C. "Education and Recent Neuropsychological and Cognitive Research." The Dual Brain: Hemispheric Specialization in Humans. Ed. D. F. Benson and E. Zaidel. New York: Guilford, 1985. Print.

Discussion Questions

MyWritingLab

1. The author starts with an example of praise for a teacher who did not "label" her students but then goes on to classify learning styles. Is this a contradiction?
2. With each type of learning style, the author follows the same pattern. What is the pattern that she uses and is it effective?
3. In paragraphs 4, 22, and 30, the author identifies the problems three out of the four sample students had in school. Why does she do this? Is it effective?
4. After discussing the four learning styles, the author discusses in paragraphs 38–43 what she identifies as the learning cycle. How do the different learning styles fit together into a learning cycle and how is the idea of the learning cycle important in relation to the classification system?

5. It could be easy to imagine someone who has qualities of more than one learning style. Is this a problem for the writer's classification of learning styles?

6. In the conclusion the author informs us of the successes of her four example students. How is this conclusion important to the essay?

MyWritingLab ## Toward Key Insights

Try to match yourself to the four learning styles. Does one learning style seem most like you? What does your response say about the classification system?

What learning styles seem to dominate in most of your classes? What effects does this seem to have on the learning success of students? Do people who have different learning styles have difficulty adjusting to the dominant learning style of educational institutions?

MyWritingLab ## Suggestion for Writing

Write an essay classifying teaching styles, including the different kinds of activities involved in the classroom and the different kinds of assessment.

CAMPUS EXPLORER

Different Types of Distance Learning: The Four General Categories for Online Programs

This selection is from the "Campus Explorer" web site, which is managed as a free service to help students, parents, and high school counselors select the best college education opportunity.

1   Distance learning has evolved greatly since the days of correspondence learning in which the student would receive course materials including textbooks and other course materials through the mail. Students would then work completely at their own pace, finishing the course according to their work and life schedule. Although correspondence courses still exist, they are quickly being replaced by online courses, which offer instruction from teachers, interaction with other students, and a forum for feedback.

2   There are a number of advantages to the new formats of distance learning, such as making permanent professional contacts, a greater amount of teacher support, and a multimedia educational experience. With the advent and improvements on computer, digital, and Internet technology, the shift from the traditional classroom experience to online or distance learning only seems natural.

This is especially true for programs that traditionally require large amounts of reading and written assignments, such as business administration and management, human resources management and services, finance, and accounting.

3   There are a variety of ways to structure distance learning courses. The format depends on the purpose of the online course. Are you seeking an online degree and taking a full online course load? Or are you supplementing your on-campus curriculum with online classes? Or perhaps your school has an overload of courses and requires that you take an online course. Whatever the reason, it is important to know which type of distance learning course you are taking so you can understand the time and travel requirements that will be expected of you.

Synchronous vs. Asynchronous Distance Learning

4   The four types of distance learning fall under the categories of either synchronous or asynchronous. Synchronous literally means "at the same time," while asynchronous means "not at the same time." Synchronous distance learning involves live communication either through sitting in a classroom, chatting online, or teleconferencing. Asynchronous distance learning usually has a set of weekly deadlines, but otherwise allows students to work at their own pace. Students have more interaction with their peers and deliver correspondence through online bulletin boards. This type of learning might get tedious for some because they are usually only receiving the information through text medium; however, some asynchronous classes involve video or audio supplements.

5   Synchronous learning is less flexible and disrupts the student's life to a greater extent. It is, however, the most popular form of college distance learning and continuing education programs, as it facilitates a greater amount of interaction between students and professors.

6   Some classes that do well in a synchronous format include those degree programs that highlight communication, such as general psychology, nursing, general education, and counseling psychology. Those programs that weigh more heavily on projects and assignments thrive in an asynchronous format because they provide the students with more time to focus on their work. A few degrees that work well in this format include marketing, healthcare administration, legal assistant or paralegal, educational/instructional media design, and advertising.

Open-Schedule Online Courses

7   With open-schedule online courses, students are allotted the greatest amount of freedom. This is an asynchronous form of learning in which students are provided Internet-based textbooks, mailing lists, email, and bulletin boards to complete their coursework. At the beginning of classes, the student is provided a set of deadlines, but is allowed to work at his or her own pace as long as the work is turned in by the deadline. This type of learning is great for students who work well independently and those who do not procrastinate.

Hybrid Distance Learning

8   Hybrid courses combine synchronous and asynchronous learning to create a structure in which the student is required to meet at a specific time in a classroom or Internet chat room. However, students are allowed to complete assignments on their own time and may pass them in through an online forum. This

option is sometimes offered when a university lacks adequate space to accommodate all its course loads.

Computer-Based Distance Learning

9   The main difference between computer-based learning and hybrid learning is that students are not allowed an open schedule. They are required to meet in a specific computer lab or in a classroom at a designated time each week.

Fixed-Time Online Courses

10   The most common type of distance learning today is fixed-time courses. As the title states, these courses are strictly online, but students are required to login to their online learning site at a specific time. Although the course is completely online, the format remains synchronous because mandatory live chats are often required.

MyWritingLab ## Discussion Questions

1. Who is the identified audience for this classification and how does that influence the writing? How might the writing differ if the selection were written for college faculty?
2. Paragraph 4 explains the difference between asynchronous and synchronous courses. Why is this distinction important for the writer? How is it helpful for the reader?
3. This selection is written for the web as an introduction. How has that fact influenced the writing? What additional material would have made this classification more helpful to you as a student?
4. Is this classification helpful? Why or why not? How else might online courses be classified?

MyWritingLab ## Toward Key Insights

Classification systems can take many forms. A writer could have classified online courses based on the ways they involved the student, distinguishing teacher-directed courses with videotaped lectures from student-driven courses that use discussion boards to explore course concepts. What should determine how things are classified? What kinds of classifications seem more fixed (e.g., biological categories) and which are more subject to variation? What creates this difference in the flexibility of a classification system?

MyWritingLab ## Suggestions for Writing

1. Write a blog post offering a different classification for online courses that could be useful to college students taking such a course.
2. Just as online courses can be classified, so can face-to-face courses that meet in the classroom. Write a classification of classroom courses that could be useful to incoming first-year students.

ALINA VRABIE

What Kind of Procrastinator Are You?

Alina Vrabie studied journalism at Seneca College of Applied Arts and Technology and has a B.A. in professional writing and film from York University. She has taught ESL in Nicaragua; worked as a reporter, producer, and music programmer for a radio station; and is a content writer for Sandglaz, an online site, where this post originally appeared. She lives in Toronto, Canada, and loves to travel.

1   Procrastination is productivity's arch-nemesis.

2   About 20% of adults in the United States are chronic procrastinators, according to research by psychology professor Joseph Ferrari.

3   Other research suggests that 80% to 95% of college students procrastinate, especially when it comes to their coursework.

4   There's no doubt that procrastination is a universal problem. We can all relate to how it feels to endlessly put off tasks. That's because our brains are actually wired for it. Procrastination is a battle between our limbic system (the unconscious and automatic part of the brain that makes you pull away your hand from fire) and the prefrontal cortex (the voice of reason and the planner).

5   When you are confronted with a task that you don't necessarily like, your limbic system and your prefrontal cortex will fight with each other. Pretty often, it's the limbic system that wins. That's when you decide to leave for tomorrow what you can do today.

6   Procrastination makes us feel really bad about ourselves—feelings of guilt and self-doubt—and the more you procrastinate, the worse you feel. But that's not all. A recent study by Dr. Ferrari, the psychology professor we mentioned above, suggests that procrastination also predicts lower salaries and a higher likelihood of unemployment. It also predicts other problems such as neglecting your health and failing to save for retirement. Overall, a long-term habit of procrastination can have dire consequences on your well-being.

7   Procrastination doesn't only mean missing deadlines and abandoning tasks. Many chronic procrastinators meet deadlines by completing work at the eleventh hour, but fail to achieve their full potential by rushing the task.

8   If you're looking to turn around your procrastinating habit, then it's important to understand why you leave tasks until the last possible minute. What type of procrastinator are you?

The Thrill-Seeker

9   If you're a Thrill-Seeker, then you procrastinate because you actually get a rush from completing things last minute. You feel that you thrive under pressure and you love the adrenaline you get from handing in work in the last possible minute. But are you accomplishing your full potential when you're spending so little time on your projects?

The Avoider

10   The Avoider runs away from the discomfort of going through with a task that either is unpleasant or has high stakes. Avoiders are almost always too

focused on what others might think. They run away from fear of failure or sometimes even fear of success.

11   They would much rather have others think that they lack effort rather than ability. They often try to make themselves feel better by running away from the task and not putting in any effort. Does *"I wasn't even trying"* sound familiar?

The Indecisive Procrastinator

12   Indecisive Procrastinators simply can't make a decision. Usually, this is a result of the fear they will be blamed for a negative outcome. This type of procrastinator runs away from responsibility. After all, if they're not making a decision, the result won't be their fault.

The Perfectionist

13   Perfectionists set such high standards for themselves that they become overwhelmed. This type of procrastinator might even get started on work, which the other kinds of procrastinators usually have a hard time doing, but they fail to finish when they can't meet the unrealistic expectations they set for themselves.

14   Because they can't do something perfectly, then nothing gets done at all. Cue cycle of anxiety and shame.

The Busy Procrastinator

15   Busy procrastinators are just too busy to actually get down to the bottom of their to-do list. Everything seems equally important and they can't decide what to do first. Choosing only one task would mean that the others won't get done. Just like in the case of the Perfectionist, the Busy Procrastinator might actually start some of her work, but will fail to finish it. What this type of procrastinator needs is a big dose of prioritizing.

Using Multiple Strategies

The classification of procrastination here helps readers identify their own process of procrastination to allow them to take steps to change. Classification can also use other strategies.

- Paragraphs 4–7 uses a cause/effect approach to identify the cause of procrastination. Each type of procrastinator is then explained based on its cause.
- Paragraph 7 offers a partial definition of procrastination.

MyWritingLab ## Discussion Questions

1. Before initiating the classification, the author explains in paragraphs 1–5 the scope and possible explanation for procrastination. Why start this way? How does this beginning influence the reading of the rest of the essay?
2. What is the purpose of paragraphs 6 and 7? To what extent are these paragraphs effective or ineffective in serving their purpose?
3. Why does the writer directly address the reader in paragraph 8? How does that likely influence the way readers read the rest of the blog?

4. The blog suggests five types of procrastinators. How effective is this classification system? Are there reasons for procrastinating that the author has left out? Do any of the categories overlap?

5. This selection was an online blog. How has that affected the writing of the blog? If this were to be developed as a more formal essay for a professional journal, what changes would be necessary?

Toward Key Insights

MyWritingLab

Often we present personal characteristics such as "procrastination," "laziness," or "sloppiness" as broad moral evaluations. The essay demonstrates that many such characteristics have broader causes, which in turn can be related to different specific underlying causes. There may be many reasons for being a bad speller or poor proofreader. What are some general personality traits that might merit a more careful analysis? How might different causes or motives for these traits produce a classification system?

Suggestions for Writing

MyWritingLab

1. Interview students about their reasons for procrastination. Based on this research, and using the results of the interviews as examples for support, write your own classification of procrastination.

2. Research a general personality trait such as laziness or sloppiness or perfectionism, possibly also interviewing those with the trait, and write a classification that distinguishes the different reasons and/or characteristics of the trait.

COMPARISON

Reading Strategies

1. Identify your purpose for reading the comparison and the author's purpose for the comparison. Determine how carefully you need to read the comparison.

2. Identify the items that are being compared.

3. Identify the pattern of organization (point by point or block) that is used in the comparison.

4. Read carefully to establish the points of similarities and differences. When the information might be necessary for future purposes, it can be helpful to create a table that matches similarities and differences.

Reading Critically

1. Test to see if there are any biases guiding the comparison. Does the writer show any preference or prejudice?

2. Determine if the accounts of similarities and differences are accurate or whether they are exaggerated.

3. Test to see if there are other similarities or differences that can be established. Are the items more alike or more different than the author tries to suggest?

Reading as a Writer

1. Examine how the author organized the essay. Was the organization effective in guiding the reader through the essay? Note what organizational pattern was most effective.

2. Notice the sentences that the writer uses for transitions. Jot down any useful techniques.

3. Observe how much detail was used to substantiate the comparison.

BRUCE CATTON

Grant and Lee: A Study in Contrasts

Bruce Catton (1899–1978) was a nationally recognized expert on the Civil War. Born in Petoskey, Michigan, he attended Oberlin College, then worked as a reporter for several large newspapers. Between 1942 and 1948, he held several positions in the U.S. government and then became an editor of American Heritage *magazine. His first book on the Civil War,* Mr. Lincoln's Army, *appeared in 1951 and was followed by* Glory Road *(1952) and* A Stillness at Appomattox *(1953). This last book won the Pulitzer Prize and the National Book Award and established Catton's reputation as a Civil War historian. In the years that followed, Catton continued to write books on the Civil War. In 1972 he published the autobiographical* Waiting for the Morning Train *and in 1974* Michigan: A Bicentennial History. *In our selection, Catton points out differences as well as similarities in the two foremost adversaries of the Civil War.*

Title sets up differences	(margin note)

1   When Ulysses S. Grant and Robert E. Lee met in the parlor of a modest house at Appomattox Court House, Virginia, on April 9, 1865, to work out the terms for the surrender of Lee's Army of Northern Virginia, a great chapter in American life came to a close, and a great new chapter began.

2   These men were bringing the Civil War to its virtual finish. To be sure, other armies had yet to surrender, and for a few days the fugitive Confederate government would struggle desperately and vainly, trying to find some way to go on living now that its chief support was gone. But in effect it was all over when Grant and Lee signed the papers. And the little room where they wrote out the terms was the scene of one of the poignant, dramatic contrasts in American history.

3   They were two strong men, these oddly different generals, and they represented the strengths of two conflicting currents that, through them, had come into final collision.

4   Back of Robert E. Lee was the notion that the old aristocratic concept might somehow survive and be dominant in American life.

5   Lee was tidewater Virginia, and in his background were family, culture, and tradition . . . the age of chivalry transplanted to a New World which was making its own legends and its own myths. He embodied a way of life that had come down through the age of knighthood and the English country squire. America was a land that was beginning all over again, dedicated to nothing much more complicated than the rather hazy belief that all men had equal rights and should have an equal chance in the world. In such a land Lee stood for the feeling that it was somehow of advantage to human society to have a pronounced inequality in the social structure. There should be a leisure class, backed by ownership

Margin notes:

Introduction: paragraphs 1–3; background; significance of following contrasts

Body: paragraph 4 to first part, paragraph 16; alternating pattern throughout

First difference paragraphs 4–6; Lee's background, character

of land; in turn, society itself should be keyed to the land as the chief source of wealth and influence. It would bring forth (according to this ideal) a class of men with a strong sense of obligation to the community; men who lived not to gain advantage for themselves, but to meet the solemn obligations which had been laid on them by the very fact that they were privileged. From them the country would get its leadership; to them it could look for the higher values—of thought, of conduct, or personal deportment—to give it strength and virtue.

6   Lee embodied the noblest elements of this aristocratic ideal. Through him, the landed nobility justified itself. For four years, the Southern states had fought a desperate war to uphold the ideals for which Lee stood. In the end, it almost seemed as if the Confederacy fought for Lee; as if he himself was the Confederacy . . . the best thing that the way of life for which the Confederacy stood could ever have to offer. He had passed into legend before Appomattox. Thousands of tired, underfed, poorly clothed Confederate soldiers, long since past the simple enthusiasm of the early days of the struggle, somehow considered Lee the symbol of everything for which they had been willing to die. But they could not quite put this feeling into words. If the Lost Cause, sanctified by so much heroism and so many deaths, had a living justification, its justification was General Lee.

7   Grant, the son of a tanner on the Western frontier, was everything Lee was not. He had come up the hard way and embodied nothing in particular except the eternal toughness and sinewy fiber of the men who grew up beyond the mountains. He was one of a body of men who owed reverence and obeisance to no one, who were self-reliant to a fault, who cared hardly anything for the past but who had a sharp eye for the future.

Paragraphs 7–9: Grant's background, character

8   These frontier men were the precise opposites of the tidewater aristocrats. Back of them, in the great surge that had taken people over the Alleghenies and into the opening Western country, there was a deep, implicit dissatisfaction with a past that had settled into grooves. They stood for democracy not from any reasoned conclusion about the proper ordering of human society, but simply because they had grown up in the middle of democracy and knew how it worked. Their society might have privileges, but they would be privileges each man had won for himself. Forms and patterns meant nothing. No man was born to anything, except perhaps to a chance to show how far he could rise. Life was competition.

9   Yet along with this feeling had come a deep sense of belonging to a national community. The Westerner who developed a farm, opened a shop, or set up in business as a trader could hope to prosper only as his own community prospered—and his community ran from the Atlantic to the Pacific and from Canada down to Mexico. If the land was settled, with towns and highways and accessible markets, he could better himself. He saw his fate in terms of the nation's own destiny. As its horizons expanded, so did his. He had, in other words, an acute dollars-and-cents stake in the continued growth and development of his country.

10   And that, perhaps, is where the contrast between Grant and Lee becomes most striking. The Virginia aristocrat, inevitably, saw himself in relation to his own region. He lived in a static society which could endure almost anything except change. Instinctively, first loyalty would go to the locality in which that society existed. He would fight to the limit of endurance to defend it, because in defending it he was defending everything that gave his own life its deepest meaning.

Second difference: Lee's loyalty

Grant's loyalty

11   The Westerner, on the other hand, would fight with an equal tenacity for the broader concept of society. He fought so because everything he lived by was tied to growth, expansion, and a constantly widening horizon. What he lived by would survive or fall with the nation itself. He could not possibly stand by unmoved in the face of an attempt to destroy the Union. He would combat it with everything he had, because he could only see it as an effort to cut the ground out from under his feet.

Summary of significant differences

12   So Grant and Lee were in complete contrast, representing two diametrically opposed elements in American life. Grant was the modern man emerging; beyond him, ready to come on the stage, was the great age of steel and machinery, of crowded cities and a restless burgeoning vitality. Lee might have ridden down from the old age of chivalry, lance in hand, silken banner fluttering over his head. Each man was the perfect champion of his cause, drawing both his strengths and his weaknesses from the people he led.

Transition paragraph signals switch to similarities

13   Yet it was not all contrast, after all. Different as they were—in background, in personality, in underlying aspiration—these two great soldiers had much in common. Under everything else, they were marvelous fighters. Furthermore, their fighting qualities were really very much alike.

First similarity

14   Each man had, to begin with, the great virtue of utter tenacity and fidelity. Grant fought his way down the Mississippi Valley in spite of acute personal discouragement and profound military handicaps. Lee hung on in the trenches at Petersburg after hope itself had died. In each man there was an indomitable quality . . . the born fighter's refusal to give up as long as he can still remain on his feet and lift his two fists.

Second similarity

15   Daring and resourcefulness they had, too; the ability to think faster and move faster than the enemy. These were the qualities which gave Lee the dazzling campaigns of Second Manassas and Chancellorsville and won Vicksburg for Grant.

Third similarity; notes order of climax

Conclusion: significance of the meeting

16   Lastly, and perhaps greatest of all, there was the ability, at the end, to turn quickly from war to peace once the fighting was over. Out of the way these two men behaved at Appomattox came the possibility of a peace of reconciliation. It was a possibility not wholly realized, in the years to come, but which did, in the end, help the two sections to become one nation again . . . after a war whose bitterness might have seemed to make such a reunion wholly impossible. No part of either man's life became him more than the part he played in this brief meeting in the McLean house at Appomattox. Their behavior there put all succeeding generations of Americans in their debt. Two great Americans, Grant and Lee—very different, yet under everything very much alike. Their encounter at Appomattox was one of the great moments of American history.

MyWritingLab   ## Discussion Questions

1. Where is Catton's thesis statement?
2. Summarize the way of life that Lee stood for, and then do the same for Grant.
3. Why do the differences between Grant and Lee receive more extended treatment than the similarities? Why are the similarities discussed last?
4. How would you characterize Catton's attitude toward the two men? Refer to specific parts of the essay when answering.

Toward Key Insights

To what extent does modern society reflect the values embodied by Grant and Lee?

How would you characterize the upper class in the United States today? Does it consist of leisured individuals who own extensive property, as Lee did, or does it have other characteristics? Are its values the same as Lee's? If not, how are they different?

If Grant was typical of the "self-reliant" non-aristocrat, how is his contemporary counterpart similar to and different from him?

Suggestion for Writing

Write an essay comparing two past or present political or military figures—perhaps Abraham Lincoln and Jefferson Davis or Dwight Eisenhower and Erwin Rommel. Try for a balanced treatment and select an appropriate organization.

CHRIS LEE

Invasion of the Bodybuilders

Chris Lee is currently the senior entertainment writer for Newsweek. *Earlier he was Entertainment and culture reporter for the* Los Angeles Times. *He has extensive articles to his credit in a number of publications and regularly tweets. This selection appeared in* Newsweek *in 2011.*

1   Macho men are back with a vengeance—and they're making the U.S.A. feel good again.

2   It's easy to mistake this summer's behemoth leading men for overactive gym rats. Actor-model Jason Momoa packed on 30 pounds to his runway-ready frame to revive Conan the Barbarian. Chris Evans endured months of nausea-inducing workouts to bulk up for Captain America: The First Avenger. Even Ryan Reynolds got into the game, undergoing a radical pectoral transformation for The Green Lantern.

3   They're hardly alone in favoring bench presses over Brechtian technique for their close-ups. The multiplex exploded in April with the arrival of Fast Five, a shoot-'em-up heist film that showcases the musculature of Vin Diesel and Dwayne "The Rock" Johnson during their rampage across Rio de Janeiro. The following week, the comic-book adaptation Thor featured Chris Hemsworth as the Asgardian god of thunder with biceps the size of canned hams.

4   But even while guys chugging Muscle Milk seem to have the cultural zeitgeist in a headlock, a war is brewing between the he-men and action moviedom's 98-pound weaklings. A new crop of machismo-challenged heroes—call them the "emo" super-dudes—is headed for screens next year. Spider-Man's franchise reboot rests on the shoulders of waifish actor Andrew Garfield, best known as a nerd in The Social Network. Brooding British thespian Henry Cavill (famous to Showtime fans of The Tudors) is on tap as the new Superman. And Hollywood's

reigning Sensitive Male, Mark Ruffalo, will portray none other than the Incredible Hulk in Marvel's The Avengers. What could his Hulk possibly smash?

5   Every generation gets the idol it deserves, as the conventional wisdom goes, with marquee actors often standing in as avatars for the collective imagination. Thanks to his Charles Atlas physique and Brylcreemed hair, Adventures of Superman star George Reeves became the television embodiment of Cold War-era American idealism. At the other end of the spectrum, surging with steroids and excess testosterone, Arnold Schwarzenegger and Sylvester Stallone became touchstones of excess in the '80s. (The Governator recently became a symbol of excess again for reasons unrelated to the size of his quads.)

6   It wasn't long ago that superheroes were swathed in Prada suits in sizes much smaller than XXXL. Tobey Maguire and Robert Downey Jr. weren't initially known as action stars, and still managed to translate their brooding shtick into box-office gold.

7   But in 2011, at a time of global economic uncertainty and with the U.S. embroiled in three wars, the pendulum has swung the other way. Today's alpha males are signaling a cultural shift: a "might equals right" moment. "There is a huge vogue for these heroes at the moment," says movie historian David Thomson, author of The New Biographical Dictionary of Film. "The country is very insecure about an awful lot of things. And wanting to watch guys with buffed-up egos and bodies, the toughest guys in the world—it could be a response to that."

8   As Captain America screenwriter Stephen McFeely sees it, "There's little tolerance for guys in fake-muscle suits—people know the difference. We want to know our actors might be able to kick our asses."

9   Movie studios didn't magically decide that size matters. To hear it from Fast Five producer Neal Moritz, the current crop of musclebound stars surfaced only after the number of actors who could actually act while, say, firing a machine gun and running through a jungle had dwindled dramatically. "Hollywood has always looked for macho guys to be in big action films," said Moritz. "The problem is they aren't the ones who spend time studying drama and becoming great actors. But now we do have actors like Vin Diesel and The Rock, guys who have incredible charisma and can run and jump and fight—and as an audience, we're going to believe the things they're doing."

10   Acclaimed Irish actor Michael Fassbender can speak to both sides of the divide. He bulked up to portray a Spartan warrior in the 2007 action epic 300—a seminal work in the macho-cinema canon—and slimmed down to play Magneto, a super-mutant whose mind is his real weapon, in this summer's X-Men: First Class.

11   Fassbender explained that onscreen assets are never flaunted without merit. "It's whatever goes for the character," he said. "In 300, these guys are carrying copper shields and doing battle for, like, eight hours. Magneto's thing is manipulating metal. He doesn't need those muscles."

12   Still, other heroes bank on their chiseled masculinity. Director Kenneth Branagh saw hundreds of potential Thors before hiring Hemsworth, who packed on so much mass for the role that he initially couldn't fit into his costume. Discussing what he looked for in his leading man, Branagh could be describing the trend that has given macho men a temporary leg up on emo boys.

13   "We wanted an old-fashioned leading man," the director said. "A good-looking lad you're happy to watch think. An oak-tree presence. Someone who really occupies the space."

Discussion Questions

MyWritingLab

1. This essay clearly uses an informal style of writing. What are some examples of the informal style of the essay? Why did the author use this style? Is the style effective? Why or why not?
2. This article does not follow a traditional structure of a comparison essay. What are the major comparisons in the essay? Why doesn't the author follow a straightforward organizational pattern for a comparison? Does the comparison work? Why or why not?
3. What is the thesis of this paper? Where in the article does the author directly state this thesis?
4. The author uses a number of quotes from people in the movie business. How do the quotes affect the article? Could the article be as effective without those quotes? Why or why not?

Toward Key Insights

MyWritingLab

The author states that "Every generation gets the idol it deserves, as the conventional wisdom goes, with marquee actors often standing in as avatars for the collective imagination." To what extent is or isn't it true that we get the idols we deserve that reflect the "collective imagination?" Why might this occur? What are some examples of this?

The author also suggests that different historical periods face different kinds of concerns, and that in some ways our heroes may be the response to that. In what ways might or might not different historical periods call for different kinds of heroes?

Suggestions for Writing

MyWritingLab

1. This article does not offer a complete point-by-point comparison. Examine carefully the heroes evoked by the author and then write a more complete comparison between muscular macho heroes and "emo super-dudes." You might want to focus specifically between a hero like Spiderman and a hero like Thor, both adaptations to the movies from comics.
2. Identify a point of comparison in movies or television—it could be how fathers are represented in two historical periods or different types of leading women—and then explore several examples and write a comparison on the topic to make your point.

JANE GRAHAM

Are Video Games Now More Sophisticated than Cinema?

Jane Graham currently lives in Glasgow, Scotland, where she works as a freelance journalist. She has written for The Belfast Telegraph, The Scotsman, Uncut, *and other works. This selection was posted on* The Guardian *in 2011.*

1   The appearance of pioneering new adventure game LA Noire has reignited a debate among gamers and film lovers which has been bubbling under for years. Not least for *Guardian* columnist Charlie Brooker, who asserted last week that video games display an intelligence and imagination well beyond the majority of contemporary cinema. Gaming's huge commercial success, he argued, is "the equivalent of films of the intelligence and quality *of 2001: A Space Odyssey* and *The Maltese Falcon* not just being released to great fanfare in 2011, but actually going on to smash box office records."

2   It's likely the gaming community stood up and cheered this assessment when it appeared – that was certainly the sentiment expressed by a huge number of those who commented online. At the same time, film fans were moved to defend their passion for cinema. Many agree that the studios are spewing out too many knucklehead superhero movies, cliché-ridden genre pics and feeble-minded multi-sequels, but still firmly believe that cinema refreshes the parts that even the best games in the world can't reach.

3   Hollywood has long regarded itself as the billion-dollar big daddy of the image entertainment world. It has the glamour, the iconography, the big brands, the A-listers and lots of cold, hard cash. In 2010, the US box office was worth $10.6bn. But for a supposed subculture, the gaming industry is just as impressive a market player, if not more so—outshining the movie moguls with an estimated annual revenue of around $18.6bn in the United States last year. The biggest hit of 2010, Call of Duty: Black Ops, has already grossed more than $1bn for its publisher Activision—fewer than 10 films released in the last decade can claim the same. The gaming industry is no longer the snot-nosed little punk of the entertainment world—little wonder fans and creators alike are calling for serious critical recognition of the medium.

4   "There's an element of self-justification going on in gaming right now," says Raymond Boyle, professor of communications at Glasgow University's Centre for Cultural Policy Research. "As industries emerge and prove their commercial worth and their influence on policy makers, they want people to accept that they're not just a sausage factory; that there's an integrity and an art to what they do. They begin to crave acceptance, a place at the broader cultural table. The Nintendo generation has grown up, and they resent the general perception of a gamer as a spotty, geeky teenager."

5   Brooker is clearly not alone in believing that, with the atmospheric crime thriller LA Noire, publisher Rockstar has succeeded in not just competing with mainstream Hollywood qualitatively, but "embarrassing" it. But are the console-centric lobby overplaying their hand, overlooking those elements of film which, in artistic terms, video games cannot match? Geoff Andrew, head of film programme at BFI Southbank, thinks so. "It's sadly true that quite a lot of recent Hollywood product has descended to the level of a game, simply providing one exciting graphic set piece after the other," he says. "But if you look at the wider picture, you find films which are not just about producing excitement, but making people think in new ways about the world they live in, asking how the story relates to them, what the authors are trying to tell them, or what questions they're asking."

6   As Andrew sees it, the equation is simple, and its implications unequivocal. Turning a film into a game necessitates "reducing" it, while transforming a game into a film requires "fleshing it out." Says Andrew: "Hitchcock knew how to push buttons; his idea of 'pure cinema' was about frightening us. But he also went beyond that, which is why a film like *Vertigo* has a sense of mystery and

poetry. We're trying to understand why this guy is so obsessed with recreating someone he thinks is dead, not just how he can do it, which is what the game would be about."

7   "Think of a film like *The White Ribbon*—it's quite impossible to think of that as a game. If it was, it would probably be a whodunnit. Or something worse, a game where you kill people off. But its whole resonance comes from its political meaning, its historical associations, the ambiguity and psychological complexity of it. You couldn't find that in a game."

8   The argument that gaming is a uniquely immersive experience is a relatively old one, but it's gained kudos as games such as Heavy Rain and LA Noire have got smarter, demanding both intellectual and emotional intelligence. (Though let's not get carried away: LA Noire's instruction manual includes hints such as: "A person who is lying may often avoid direct eye contact." Duh.)

9   But while seasoned players such as Martin Neill, CEO of online software retail developer AirPOS, insist that LA Noire presents an "augmented reality" that's so absorbing it "messes with your brain," some argue that the cinema environment, alongside the element of personal abdication involved, makes film the more consuming medium.

10   "The notion that we need to control something in order for it to be immersive is wrong," says Professor Christine Geraghty, editor of the *Journal of British Cinema and Television*. "Going into a big dark room and sitting in front of a huge screen, amongst an audience but also alone—they're such important parts of cinema's immersive quality. You need to have the pace set for you, maybe be forced to slow down or hurtled along at breakneck speed, to really experience the build of the film towards a climax, the release of tension or the moment of horror. Cinema is unique in that way—we may need to be won over by the film, but we don't have to be won over by the form itself. We go in with a willingness to surrender."

11   This voluntary disarmament, the artistic equivalent of what Boyle likens to "being on a plane and putting your life into the hands of a pilot," is a crucial aspect of cinema's power, particularly if we are in the hands of a master film-maker of the commercial idiom, such as Christopher Nolan, who can combine mainstream flash and nudge us not just to think, which games such as LA Noire or Portal 2 can certainly do, but to reflect over time. Nolan's dark, difficult *Inception* is also the 25th highest-grossing film of all time, a poke in the eye for those who contend that smart, challenging films don't make big money any more.

12   "Nolan has always been interested in puzzle films, which have a game-like process," says Andrew. "You have to follow clues and engage intellectually. But his films work on a much deeper level than just solving puzzles. *Inception*, *Memento*, and *Insomnia* are really about people gaining power over others by taking control of the narrative, by spinning a more persuasive story."

13   The gamers see the issue differently. "*Inception* takes you on a ride," says Neill. "With LA Noire you decide which way to go. It's all about the endgame. Your aim is to get to the next level and move up to a bigger challenge. Every tiny thing you do, every turn you take on the road, what you ask your witnesses, what clues you think are important—everything is a test of your ability to make a quick decision, and get it right."

14   This thrust is at the heart of the pleasure of interactive gaming, but it might also mark its aesthetic limitations. Even with the emotional backstory LA Noire provides for your war-veteran-turned-cop character, the bottom line is that he is essentially your puppet, and every time you put him on pause, leaving him

standing gazing pointlessly at a fish-head ("Not every clue is relevant to your investigation"), you're reminded he has no life of his own. He is there to help you find the answer and tie up the case.

15   Not only does this hinder your chances of connecting emotionally with him, it also reminds you that gaming is goal-orientated; every "scene" has a function. There's certainly no room for individually inspired whimsy, like the "Royale with cheese" chitchat in Tarantino's *Pulp Fiction*, or the beguiling, limb-bending dance Johnny Depp unexpectedly launches into in Tim Burton's *Alice in Wonderland* (the, ahem, sixth highest-grossing film of all time). They just don't have a place in such a strictly target-driven environment.

16   Similarly, the need for games to possess a universal language which must be understood by millions of users worldwide necessitates a reliance on traditional conventions and a rejection of ambiguity. Characters and plot must conform to "game sense"; if they confuse or challenge too much, they simply won't be readable enough to fulfill their role. "It's interesting that LA Noire, this breakthrough game, has chosen to ape film noir," says Geraghty. "Noir is a very stylized genre which very quickly became prone to cliché. It became very coded, a series of symbols—certain kinds of hats, clothes, weapons, women."

17   "We recently revived *The Big Sleep*, a classic film noir, at the BFI," says Andrew. "It has a very strong, eventful narrative, but that's not the joy of the film. It's not just a thriller, it's also a love story and a comedy. And that sheer chemistry between Bogart and Bacall—that's something you could never get in a game."

Using Multiple Strategies

Jane Graham uses the comparison here to create an argument that cinema may be more sophisticated than video games. The author also uses other strategies:

- Paragraph 4 offers a cause for why the video game industry begins to stress the quality of video games.
- Paragraphs 10 and 11 use description to capture the cinema experience.
- The comparison uses specific video games and movies to illustrate its points.

MyWritingLab ## Discussion Questions

1. What point is the author trying to make about video games and cinema? How has her conclusion shaped her comparison?
2. What organizational strategy does the writer apply, block or point-by-point comparison? Why does this strategy fit the essay?
3. What is the main point of the comparison in paragraphs 12 and 13? How does this comparison fit the rest of the essay?
4. Does the writer give greater detail about the experience of video games or cinema? How does this choice affect the comparison? Is this representation ethical?
5. How does the writer use authorities in this essay? In what ways do they contribute or distract from the comparison?
6. What does the writer accomplish by the conclusion, paragraph 17? Is it a fair way to end the essay?

Toward Key Insights

Today many works appear in many media platforms: books, movies, video games, and TV series. Not surprisingly, there have been many attempts to compare media. The challenge in such comparisons is that the media are different enough that the comparison may vary depending on the media that is given priority. How might the comparisons differ depending on whether we gave the privilege to books, movies, television, or video games?

Suggestions for Writing

1. Write your own comparison of cinema and video games to be posted on a blog.
2. Write a comparison of any two types of media: books and movies; movies and television; movies and video games.
3. Write a review to be posted on an entertainment Web site that compares two media versions of the same work, such as the comic book and movie, or the movie and video game.

CAUSE AND EFFECT

Reading Strategies

1. Identify the main event that is trying to be explained or the event whose effects are being studied.

2. Determine whether the writer is identifying a chain of causes that yield a result or is considering multiple causes for the same event.

3. Be careful. In more sophisticated academic writing, authors often look at several causes that they try to show are not the real explanation. Only after ruling out some key explanations do they offer the explanation that they think is most plausible.

4. It can be helpful to make a diagram showing the connection between the causes and the effects.

Reading Critically

1. Evaluate the evidence the writer gives for the relationship between cause and effect. How does he or she prove that the cause(s) have the effect(s) in question?

2. Try to determine if there could be other causes or effects that the writer hasn't mentioned.

3. Writers often confuse "correlation" for causation. Just because something happens before or around another event doesn't mean that it is the cause of the event. Just because George W. Bush was president when the terrorists attacked the World Trade Centers does not mean that his presidency was in any way a cause of the attack. Does the writer confuse correlation and causation?

Reading as a Writer

1.   Note how the writer organizes the causes and effects to keep them clear and distinct.

2.   Observe what devices the writer uses to demonstrate the connection between the causes and the effects.

3.   Examine how the writer pulls his or her ideas together in the conclusion.

KEVIN JOHNSON

For Cops, Citizen Videos Bring Increased Scrutiny. Are Incidents Caught on Tape Hindering Officers?

Kevin Johnson is a reporter for USA Today, *where he covers justice and national law enforcement issues. This selection came from the October 14, 2010, print edition of* USA Today.

1   TALLAHASSEE—Diop Kamau's home in a leafy, gated community just north of town is not easy to find—for good reason. For more than two decades, the 52-year-old former Hawthorne, Calif., police officer has made a living embarrassing cops with a video camera.

2   Stung by the rough treatment of his father during a 1987 traffic stop by another California department, Kamau turned to a second career recording police across the country in compromising—often abusive—encounters with the public.

3   Some of the controversial videos made using hidden microphones and cameras found their way to network and cable television, exposing police to deserved criticism. Mostly, the videos helped launch a new generation of public accountability for local law enforcement. One of Kamau's most effective weapons is a battered 1968 Chevrolet Impala, wired with microphones and cameras, that Kamau, who is black, drives to test the racial profiling tendencies of local police on behalf of paying clients.

4   "Frankly, there are a lot of people with badges and guns who don't like me very much," Kamau says, motioning to the network of surveillance cameras that protect his home from unwanted visitors. "I step on a lot of toes."

5   Starting with the grainy images first broadcast by Kamau and other pioneer citizen watchdogs—notably the 1991 beating of Rodney King in Los Angeles, shot by a nearby resident—the public surveillance of cops has exploded to potentially include anyone with a cellphone.

6   The videos are so ubiquitous that analysts and police debate whether they are serving the public interest—or undermining public trust in law enforcement and even putting officers' lives in jeopardy. The videos are subjecting officers' actions in public places to new scrutiny and changing the way accusations against cops play out in court. In some communities, police are fighting back by enforcing laws that limit such recordings. Other departments are seeking new training for officers to prepare for the ever-present surveillance on the street.

7 Just about every day, it seems, there is fresh video of cops engaged in controversial actions: Police slamming an unarmed man to the street in Denver. A college student thrashed by officers with batons during a University Maryland basketball victory celebration. An Oakland transit officer fatally shooting an unarmed man on a train platform.

 "There is no city not at risk of a video showing an officer doing something wrong," says San Jose Police Chief Rob Davis, president of the Major Cities Chiefs Association, a coalition representing the 56 largest cities in the USA. "The question, when one of these videos do surface, is what we do about it."

8 In Illinois, Maryland and Massachusetts, some police have responded by trying to limit such recordings when they believe those recordings interfere with police actions.

9 In Maryland, motorcyclist Anthony Graber was charged with felony violations of Maryland's wiretapping law for recording a March 5 encounter with a gun-brandishing state trooper during a traffic stop. The law requires both parties to consent to the recording of a private conversation. Graber faced a maximum 16-year prison sentence if convicted until Harford County Circuit Court Judge Emory Pitt threw out the case Sept. 27, saying, "Those of us who are public officials and are entrusted with the power of the state are ultimately accountable to the public."

10 Some departments have sought training for officers to prepare them for increased surveillance of police activity.

11 "All of our people should be conducting themselves like they are being recorded all the time," says Lt. Robin Larson, who oversees training for the 3,200-officer Broward County, Fla., Sheriff's Office, which once hired Kamau to help prepare new cadets by making them aware their actions could be taped and transmitted.

12 Some police believe videotaping officers poses broad risks that reach beyond Internet embarrassments: It could cause officers to hesitate in life-threatening situations.

13 "The proliferation of cheap video equipment is presenting a whole new dynamic for law enforcement," says Jim Pasco, executive director of the Fraternal Order of Police, the nation's largest police union. "It has had a chilling effect on some officers who are now afraid to act for fear of retribution by video. This has become a serious safety issue. I'm afraid something terrible will happen."

14 Kamau and others argue terrible things already have occurred to victims of officer abuse, and video has brought some of the most brutal cases to the public's attention. Video also has helped narrow the "credibility gap" between police and their accusers, civil rights lawyer John Burris says.

15 "It used to be that the police officer always got the benefit of the doubt," says Burris, who represented Rodney King in a civil lawsuit against the city of Los Angeles related to his videotaped beating by white Los Angeles police officers. Television broadcasts of the infamous tape, one of the first to show the power of citizen videos of police actions, prompted widespread public outrage.

16 "The camera, increasingly, is offering a shock to the consciousness," Burris says.

17 To ignore the effect of video on police credibility, Kamau says, is "like disregarding the influence of the Internet on political campaigns."

18 "Things are changing dramatically," he says, "and police are not prepared for it."

Marginal annotations:

- Example of videos
- Raises questions
- Identifies effect 1
- Details effect 1 with example
- Effect 2
- Effect 2 detailed example
- Effect 3
- Effect 3 detailed
- Transition Effect 4
- Effect 5
- Effect 4 Detailed example

Video Helps Explain Officer's Actions

19   Video has helped to resolve many cases of police misconduct, but such images also can present a more complex account of officer behavior.

20   Former Oakland transit cop Johannes Mehserle is in jail awaiting sentencing on Nov. 5 in connection with the fatal shooting of Oscar Grant largely because the incident was captured on video.

21   Yet video also is the reason, defense attorney Michael Rains says, that Mehserle was convicted July 8 of the lesser offense of involuntary manslaughter after he was charged with murdering the unarmed, 22-year-old train passenger.

22   The criminal allegations followed transit officers' response to reports of fighting aboard a Bay Area Rapid Transit (BART) train in the early morning hours of New Year's Day 2009.

23   Grant was among a group pulled off the train at a local stop, according to court documents. Mehserle and another officer had detained the group, the documents state, when Mehserle shot the unarmed Grant while the man's hands were cuffed behind his back in a scene captured by bystanders on cellphone and video cameras. The images of the shooting involving a white officer and a black victim quickly hit the Internet, where they prompted violent protests in Oakland and instant comparisons to the Rodney King case.

24   "The King video went viral pretty quickly for back then," says Burris, who also represents the Grant family. "But this went as fast as anything could go. The outrage came much quicker."

25   State prosecutors charged Mehserle with murder, and the case—because of its notoriety and local unrest—was moved to Los Angeles.

26   Defense attorney Rains concedes the raw video initially had a "shocking effect" on jurors.

27   "I tried to prepare them for it," he says. "I guess you don't get oblivious to seeing something like that."

28   What did help Mehserle's case, Rains says, is that more than one video showed what happened that morning; six were introduced at trial. Taken together, Rains argued, the videos captured several angles and supported his client's claim that he meant to draw a stun gun but mistakenly pulled his .40-caliber handgun.

29   Rains says his client's hand movements recorded on some of the videos were consistent with attempts to open the snap of the holster of his stun gun.

30   "His body was doing things as if to draw and fire the Taser, not the gun," Rains says.

31   More video, Rains says, shows Mehserle's "compelling" reaction after the shooting.

32   "The video shows him throwing his hands to his head in shock," Rains says. "It was a terrible thing to happen. It was a tragedy it did." But the attorney says he was "very, very happy to have this video."

33   Although Burris does not agree with the jury's apparent interpretation of the videos (jurors have not spoken publicly about their decision), he also is happy they exist.

34   "Without the videos, there would have been no prosecution," he says. "It meant everything."

A "Profound Effect" on Officers' Actions

35   David Allred, a former Justice Department official who prosecuted police misconduct cases for more than 30 years, says the proliferation of video in police cases is likely to have "a profound effect" on the long-term behavior of officers.

36   "If you're prosecuting a case and you can find video to support it, it's just terrific," Allred says. "But often it's terrific for the police, as well, because it can just as easily exonerate officers."

37   "The real impact, I think, is on what officers will do if they think they are being photographed."

38   One of the most-viewed incidents—more than 200,000 views on YouTube—is a March encounter between a University of Maryland student and Prince George's County, Md., police officers during a celebration of a Maryland basketball victory.

39   A video shows senior Jack McKenna approaching officers, who began pummeling him with batons. A police report alleged that McKenna had provoked the encounter by striking mounted officers and their horses, contrary to what is shown in the video.

40   Three officers have been suspended and the case remains under investigation by Prince George's County and the Justice Department.

41   In August, the city of Denver's public safety manager resigned and two officers were reassigned after questions surfaced about police conduct in at least two incidents captured on video. The incidents, which remain under investigation by Denver police, include an April 2009 encounter between police and two pedestrians, one of whom is shown being violently wrestled to the street.

42   The encounter was recorded by a security camera mounted on a light pole and later landed the alleged victims on network morning news programs.

43   "At this point, officers need to be constantly reminded that the potential for them to be on video or to be photographed is extraordinarily high," Pasco says.

"It Embarrassed Us"

44   Larson, the Broward County Sheriff's Office training officer, says her agency knows firsthand the power of video and has learned from it.

45   The lesson was delivered about three years ago by Kamau. While working for his private investigative firm policeabuse.com and a client, the former cop walked into one of the agency's reception areas with a hidden camera and found immediate problems with the way officers and employees dealt with the public. Kamau says police routinely provided incorrect information to people or couldn't answer basic questions about department policy, such as how to file a complaint against police.

46   "It embarrassed us," Larson says, adding the video found its way to local television.

47   Larson says the incident "sparked a lot of activity" within the agency, leading to changes in public reception area staffing, including retraining. Police officials also invited Kamau to help train new cadets.

48   "Even though he could be viewed as the enemy, we were open to learning from the experience," she says. "If we screwed up, give us your thoughts on how we can make it better."

49   Kamau, who helps clients resolve their grievances with police, says he counsels many of them to arm themselves with cameras to support their cases.

50   "Video is making victims more credible," Kamau says. "If Rodney King would have tried to tell his story without video, nobody would have believed it."

Transition to next effect

Repeats earlier effects as part of transition

Statement of new effect 6

Causal sequence to effect 6; Initial event

Reaction to event

Effect based on event

New incident as an example and its effect

Effect 6; broad effect of being videotaped

New example

Effect from above example

How example resulted in effect 6

Broad statement of overall effect

MyWritingLab # Discussion Questions

1. What are the major effects the writer suggests the videoing of police officers is having? Given the number of effects discussed, how does the writer organize the essay? Why is or isn't this organizational structure effective?
2. In the beginning of the essay, the writer focuses on the experience of one person who engages in videotaping police. Why does the writer start with this one individual? How does it affect the overall essay?
3. The writer uses different examples for the different effects and uses quotes. Why does the writer use this approach? How effective is the approach for the reader?
4. Because this essay is a newspaper article from *USA Today*, it uses a number of shorter paragraphs. Why is this style common in newspapers? How does it affect the reading of the essay?
5. Overall, do you think the writer believes the increased videoing of police is socially beneficial or not? Should the writer have been completely balanced between harmful and beneficial consequences or presented the effects that seem most common? What counts as fairness in writing in this context?

MyWritingLab # Toward Key Insights

Even simple technological changes can have profound effects. While often we may overlook those effects, careful observations can begin to identify the impact of a technology on our lives. What technologies do you think have been introduced in your lifetime that has had an effect? What do you think are the effects of that technology?

Often we oversimplify the world and look at new technologies or practices as either good or bad. This essay makes clear that even when a technology has mostly beneficial effects, it can have negative effects as well. Where do you see technologies or social practices that many tend to see as good or ill that actually have a complex range of positive and negative consequences?

MyWritingLab # Suggestions for Writing

1. Identify a technology or social practice that has been introduced in your lifetime and identify the effects of that technology or practice on our lives.
2. Interview several teachers on the impact of new technologies and software, such as YouTube, on teaching, positive and negative. Write a paper to new teachers helping them understand the consequences of the technology. You might focus on a single technology or practice, such as Facebook, or you may broaden your focus to include something general like social media.

CAROLINE KNAPP

Why We Keep Stuff: If You Want to Understand People, Take a Look at What They Hang on To

Caroline Knapp, a humane and thoughtful writer, died at the age of 42 in 2002. She worked for the Phoenix newspapers as staff writer, editor, and contributing columnist. This essay is taken from The Merry Recluse: A Life in Essay—*a collection of some of the best of Knapp's writing.*

1   Stuff, stuff, I am surrounded by stuff. Stuff I don't need, stuff I don't use, but stuff I feel compelled to keep. Here in my office, as I write this, I am drowning in a sea of stuff.

2   There is the stuff of procrastination—piles of letters I should answer, manuscripts I should return, memos I should file away.

3   There is the stuff of daily business—interoffice communications in one heap here, this form and that form in that heap there, bills in yet another.

4   But mostly, there is the more generalized stuff, the stuff we all hold on to for inexplicable reasons—the stuff, in other words, of which stuff is made. Old catalogs of stuff I *might* want to order someday. Old magazines I *might* want to read, or reread. Unsolicited freelance articles I *might* want to publish. And even more useless stuff, stuff with no discernible purpose or future value.

5   On one corner of a shelf hangs a bunch of ribbons, saved over the years from various packages. On another, a pile of old letters from readers that I'll no doubt never open again and never answer. On my desk, a Rolodex crammed with numbers I'll never call (the National Association of Theater Operators? The Detroit office of the National Transportation Union? *Huh?*). In one corner, I even have a pile of envelopes containing transaction slips from the automatic teller machine that date all the way back to February 1988. That's more than three years of bank slips—stuff, pure and simple.

6   Yet in an odd way, a lot of the stuff has meaning. Granted, the significance of a pile of old ribbons may be minimal, but I think the things that people choose to hang on to, and the ways they hang on to them, are quite telling—small testimonies to the ways people organize their lives on both external and internal levels. Want to understand people a little more clearly? Look through their stuff.

. . .

7   Several years ago, as I was preparing to move out of an apartment I'd lived in for four years, I undertook my first major purge of stuff, which provided an excellent lesson in the nature of the beast. Historically, I've been a relentless pack rat, the sort of person who keeps vast numbers of relics and mementos in vast numbers of boxes around the house—ticket stubs to concerts and movies; store receipts for goods and clothing I'd long ago stopped thinking about returning; letters from people I'd long ago lost track of; even old shoes. But moving out of that particular apartment was a big step—I was leaving a place where I'd lived alone (with plenty of room for stuff) and into a new apartment—and presumably, a new life—with a man (who had much less room for stuff).

8   Accordingly, the purge was more than a logistical necessity; it also had a certain psychological value. Sure, it made sense to get rid of a lot of it: I didn't

really need to hang on to that broken toaster-oven, or that tattered coat I'd stopped wearing years before. I didn't need to save the letter of acceptance from the graduate school I'd long ago decided not to attend. I didn't need the three boxes of back issues of Gourmet magazine. But divesting myself of all that stuff meant much more than whittling down my possessions to a manageable degree.

9   At one point, I remember going through a dresser in which I kept several pairs of jeans that I'd worn during a long and protracted struggle with anorexia. They were tiny jeans in tiny, skeletal sizes, jean with bad associations, jeans with no place in the life of someone who was trying to launch into a healthier way of living. But I'd held on to them for years and, in doing so, had held on to a set of possibilities: that I might one day need those tiny, cigarette-legged jeans again; that I might one day fit into them; and accordingly, that what I felt to be my "recovery" from anorexia might be tenuous at best, false at worst.

10   The message hidden away in that dresser drawer had to do with fear, and, needless to say, throwing out the clothes from that earlier time was an enormously healthy move: it was part of an effort to say good-bye to a person I used to be.

11   And so it is with most of our stuff: the things we keep stored away in our closets and shelves often mirror the things we hold on to inside: fears, memories, dreams, false perceptions. A good deal of that stuff in my office, for example, speaks to an abiding terror of screwing up, a fear that I might actually *need* one of those articles from one of those old magazines, or one of those old phone numbers from the Rolodex, or one of those memos or letters or whatever.

12   Lurking behind the automatic-teller-machine slips? My relentless fear of finance, and the accompanying conviction that as soon as I toss them all out, the bank will call and inform me that some huge deposit I could once verify has disappeared. Even the pile of ribbons on the shelf reflects some vague anxiety, a (comparatively minor and obsessive) worry—that one of these days, I'll have a present to wrap and (gasp) there'll be no ribbon at hand to tie it up. My mother keeps a huge basket at home filled with nothing but rubber bands, and I'm sure she holds on to it for the same reasons: it speaks to an absolute certainty on her part that the moment she throws them away, she'll find herself in desperate need of an elastic.

13   We might need it. We might miss it. It might come back in style and we might want to wear it again. If getting rid of stuff is hard, it's because it feels like cutting off options. Or sides of ourselves. Or pieces of our history. And, the actual value of holding on to stuff notwithstanding, those things can be unsettling to give up. The movie and ticket stubs I'd kept stored away for years in my old apartment, for example, reflected good times, happy moments in relationships that I didn't want to forget; the ragged coat was a piece of clothing I'd felt pretty in, a feeling I didn't want to lose; the *Gourmet* magazines held out hopes for my (then sorely lacking) kitchen skills. Even the broken toaster-oven contained a memory—I'd bought it almost a decade earlier, with a man I'd been involved with, during a very happy year we'd lived together.

14   The trick, I suppose, is to learn to manage stuff, the same way you learn to manage fears and feelings. To throw a little logic into the heaps of stuff. To think a little rationally. Would the world really come crashing down if I tossed out some crucial phone number? Would my personal history really get tossed into the trash along with my mementos? Would I die, or even suffer a mite, without all those ribbons?

15   No, probably not. But I think I'll keep holding on to those bank slips . . . just in case.

Discussion Questions

1. What is the value of a personal reflective essay such as this one for writer and reader?
2. What is the real thesis of this essay and where is it located?
3. What role do the several paragraphs detailing the kinds of clutter the author has failed to discard play in the full essay? Why did she spend so much time describing her stuff?
4. What does the author see as the dominant cause for why people fail to discard things? How does the more general cause relate to many other more specific causes?
5. In what ways does this writer sustain a personal and even intimate tone with her readers? Is this effective?
6. How do the final two paragraphs fit the essay?

Toward Key Insights

This essay provides an excellent example of a personal reflective essay. As a result, the author's discussion of why we keep certain things is not scientific. What might be the advantages of this kind of essay over a psychological study of why people retain certain items? What are some weaknesses of this kind of writing?

In the personal reflective essay, writers share with their readers more personal elements of their thoughts and lives, such as Caroline Knapp's discussion of her past struggle with anorexia. How do such intimate revelations affect readers and their relationship with the text?

Suggestion for Writing

Write a personal reflective essay to explain what you think cause some personal behaviors or emotional states, such as procrastination or impulse shopping, for readers who may share those behaviors.

DAVID DOBBS

Beautiful Brains

David Dobbs is a freelance journalist who writes about science, medicine, and culture for the New York Times, National Geographic, Wired, *and* Scientific American. *He is the author of the book* Reef Madness: Charles Darwin, Alexander Agazzi, and the Meaning of Coral. *"Beautiful Brains" was published in* National Geographic *in 2011.*

Moody. Impulsive. Maddening. Why do teenagers act the way they do? Viewed through the eyes of evolution, their most exasperating traits may be the key to success as adults.

1   Although you know your teenager takes some chances, it can be a shock to hear about them.

2   One fine May morning not long ago my oldest son, 17 at the time, phoned to tell me that he had just spent a couple hours at the state police barracks. Apparently he had been driving "a little fast." What, I asked, was "a little fast"? Turns out this product of my genes and loving care, the boy-man I had swaddled, coddled, cooed at, and then pushed and pulled to the brink of manhood, had been flying down the highway at 113 miles an hour.

3   "That's more than a little fast," I said.

4   He agreed. In fact, he sounded somber and contrite. He did not object when I told him he'd have to pay the fines and probably for a lawyer. He did not argue when I pointed out that if anything happens at that speed—a dog in the road, a blown tire, a sneeze—he dies. He was in fact almost irritatingly reasonable. He even proffered that the cop did the right thing in stopping him, for, as he put it, "We can't all go around doing 113."

5   He did, however, object to one thing. He didn't like it that one of the several citations he received was for reckless driving.

6   "Well," I huffed, sensing an opportunity to finally yell at him, "what would you call it?"

7   "It's just not accurate," he said calmly. " 'Reckless' sounds like you're not paying attention. But I was. I made a deliberate point of doing this on an empty stretch of dry interstate, in broad daylight, with good sight lines and no traffic. I mean, I wasn't just gunning the thing. I was driving."

8   "I guess that's what I want you to know. If it makes you feel any better, I was really focused."

9   Actually, it did make me feel better. That bothered me, for I didn't understand why. Now I do.

10   My son's high-speed adventure raised the question long asked by people who have pondered the class of humans we call teenagers: What on Earth was he doing? Parents often phrase this question more colorfully. Scientists put it more coolly. They ask, What can explain this behavior? But even that is just another way of wondering, What is wrong with these kids? Why do they act this way? The question passes judgment even as it inquires.

11   Through the ages, most answers have cited dark forces that uniquely affect the teen. Aristotle concluded more than 2,300 years ago that "the young are heated by Nature as drunken men by wine." A shepherd in William Shakespeare's *The Winter's Tale* wishes "there were no age between ten and three-and-twenty, or that youth would sleep out the rest; for there is nothing in the between but getting wenches with child, wronging the ancientry, stealing, fighting." His lament colors most modern scientific inquiries as well. G. Stanley Hall, who formalized adolescent studies with his 1904 *Adolescence: Its Psychology and Its Relations to Physiology, Anthropology, Sociology, Sex, Crime, Religion, and Education*, believed this period of "storm and stress" replicated earlier, less civilized stages of human development. Freud saw adolescence as an expression of torturous psychosexual conflict; Erik Erikson, as the most tumultuous of life's several identity crises. Adolescence: always a problem.

12   Such thinking carried into the late 20th century, when researchers developed brain-imaging technology that enabled them to see the teen brain in enough detail to track both its physical development and its patterns of activity. These imaging tools offered a new way to ask the same question—What's wrong with these kids?—and revealed an answer that surprised almost everyone. Our

brains, it turned out, take much longer to develop than we had thought. This revelation suggested both a simplistic, unflattering explanation for teens' maddening behavior—and a more complex, affirmative explanation as well.

13   The first full series of scans of the developing adolescent brain—a National Institutes of Health (NIH) project that studied over a hundred young people as they grew up during the 1990s—showed that our brains undergo a massive reorganization between our 12th and 25th years. The brain doesn't actually grow very much during this period. It has already reached 90 percent of its full size by the time a person is six, and a thickening skull accounts for most head growth afterward. But as we move through adolescence, the brain undergoes extensive remodeling, resembling a network and wiring upgrade.

14   For starters, the brain's axons—the long nerve fibers that neurons use to send signals to other neurons—become gradually more insulated with a fatty substance called myelin (the brain's white matter), eventually boosting the axons' transmission speed up to a hundred times. Meanwhile, dendrites, the branchlike extensions that neurons use to receive signals from nearby axons, grow twiggier, and the most heavily used synapses—the little chemical junctures across which axons and dendrites pass notes—grow richer and stronger. At the same time, synapses that see little use begin to wither. This synaptic pruning, as it is called, causes the brain's cortex—the outer layer of gray matter where we do much of our conscious and complicated thinking—to become thinner but more efficient. Taken together, these changes make the entire brain a much faster and more sophisticated organ.

15   This process of maturation, once thought to be largely finished by elementary school, continues throughout adolescence. Imaging work done since the 1990s shows that these physical changes move in a slow wave from the brain's rear to its front, from areas close to the brain stem that look after older and more behaviorally basic functions, such as vision, movement, and fundamental processing, to the evolutionarily newer and more complicated thinking areas up front. The corpus callosum, which connects the brain's left and right hemispheres and carries traffic essential to many advanced brain functions, steadily thickens. Stronger links also develop between the hippocampus, a sort of memory directory, and frontal areas that set goals and weigh different agendas; as a result, we get better at integrating memory and experience into our decisions. At the same time, the frontal areas develop greater speed and richer connections, allowing us to generate and weigh far more variables and agendas than before.

16   When this development proceeds normally, we get better at balancing impulse, desire, goals, self-interest, rules, ethics, and even altruism, generating behavior that is more complex and, sometimes at least, more sensible. But at times, and especially at first, the brain does this work clumsily. It's hard to get all those new cogs to mesh.

17   Beatriz Luna, a University of Pittsburgh professor of psychiatry who uses neuro-imaging to study the teen brain, used a simple test that illustrates this learning curve. Luna scanned the brains of children, teens, and twentysomethings while they performed an anti-saccade task, a sort of eyes-only video game where you have to stop yourself from looking at a suddenly appearing light. You view a screen on which the red crosshairs at the center occasionally disappear just as a light flickers elsewhere on the screen. Your instructions are to not look at the light and instead to look in the opposite direction. A sensor detects any eye movement. It's a tough assignment, since flickering lights naturally

draw our attention. To succeed, you must override both a normal impulse to attend to new information and curiosity about something forbidden. Brain geeks call this response inhibition.

18   Ten-year-olds stink at it, failing about 45 percent of the time. Teens do much better. In fact, by age 15 they can score as well as adults if they're motivated, resisting temptation about 70 to 80 percent of the time. What Luna found most interesting, however, was not those scores. It was the brain scans she took while people took the test. Compared with adults, teens tended to make less use of brain regions that monitor performance, spot errors, plan, and stay focused—areas the adults seemed to bring online automatically. This let the adults use a variety of brain resources and better resist temptation, while the teens used those areas less often and more readily gave in to the impulse to look at the flickering light—just as they're more likely to look away from the road to read a text message.

19   If offered an extra reward, however, teens showed they could push those executive regions to work harder, improving their scores. And by age 20, their brains respond to this task much as the adults' do. Luna suspects the improvement comes as richer networks and faster connections make the executive region more effective.

20   These studies help explain why teens behave with such vexing inconsistency: beguiling at breakfast, disgusting at dinner; masterful on Monday, sleepwalking on Saturday. Along with lacking experience generally, they're still learning to use their brain's new networks. Stress, fatigue, or challenges can cause a misfire. Abigail Baird, a Vassar psychologist who studies teens, calls this neural gawkiness—an equivalent to the physical awkwardness teens sometimes display while mastering their growing bodies.

21   The slow and uneven developmental arc revealed by these imaging studies offers an alluringly pithy explanation for why teens may do stupid things like drive at 113 miles an hour, aggrieve their ancientry, and get people (or get gotten) with child: They act that way because their brains aren't done! You can see it right there in the scans!

22   This view, as titles from the explosion of scientific papers and popular articles about the "teen brain" put it, presents adolescents as "works in progress" whose "immature brains" lead some to question whether they are in a state "akin to mental retardation."

23   The story you're reading right now, however, tells a different scientific tale about the teen brain. Over the past five years or so, even as the work-in-progress story spread into our culture, the discipline of adolescent brain studies learned to do some more-complex thinking of its own. A few researchers began to view recent brain and genetic findings in a brighter, more flattering light, one distinctly colored by evolutionary theory. The resulting account of the adolescent brain—call it the adaptive-adolescent story—casts the teen less as a rough draft than as an exquisitely sensitive, highly adaptable creature wired almost perfectly for the job of moving from the safety of home into the complicated world outside.

24   This view will likely sit better with teens. More important, it sits better with biology's most fundamental principle, that of natural selection. Selection is hell on dysfunctional traits. If adolescence is essentially a collection of them—angst, idiocy, and haste; impulsiveness, selfishness, and reckless bumbling—then how did those traits survive selection? They couldn't—not if they were the period's most fundamental or consequential features.

25   The answer is that those troublesome traits don't really characterize adolescence; they're just what we notice most because they annoy us or put our children in danger. As B. J. Casey, a neuroscientist at Weill Cornell Medical College who has spent nearly a decade applying brain and genetic studies to our understanding of adolescence, puts it, "We're so used to seeing adolescence as a problem. But the more we learn about what really makes this period unique, the more adolescence starts to seem like a highly functional, even adaptive period. It's exactly what you'd need to do the things you have to do then."

26   To see past the distracting, dopey teenager and glimpse the adaptive adolescent within, we should look not at specific, sometimes startling, behaviors, such as skateboarding down stairways or dating fast company, but at the broader traits that underlie those acts.

27   Let's start with the teen's love of the thrill. We all like new and exciting things, but we never value them more highly than we do during adolescence. Here we hit a high in what behavioral scientists call sensation seeking: the hunt for the neural buzz, the jolt of the unusual or unexpected.

28   Seeking sensation isn't necessarily impulsive. You might plan a sensation-seeking experience—a skydive or a fast drive—quite deliberately, as my son did. Impulsivity generally drops throughout life, starting at about age 10, but this love of the thrill peaks at around age 15. And although sensation seeking can lead to dangerous behaviors, it can also generate positive ones: The urge to meet more people, for instance, can create a wider circle of friends, which generally makes us healthier, happier, safer, and more successful.

29   This upside probably explains why an openness to the new, though it can sometimes kill the cat, remains a highlight of adolescent development. A love of novelty leads directly to useful experience. More broadly, the hunt for sensation provides the inspiration needed to "get you out of the house" and into new terrain, as Jay Giedd, a pioneering researcher in teen brain development at NIH, puts it.

30   Also peaking during adolescence (and perhaps aggrieving the ancientry the most) is risk-taking. We court risk more avidly as teens than at any other time. This shows reliably in the lab, where teens take more chances in controlled experiments involving everything from card games to simulated driving. And it shows in real life, where the period from roughly 15 to 25 brings peaks in all sorts of risky ventures and ugly outcomes. This age group dies of accidents of almost every sort (other than work accidents) at high rates. Most long-term drug or alcohol abuse starts during adolescence, and even people who later drink responsibly often drink too much as teens. Especially in cultures where teenage driving is common, this takes a gory toll: In the United States, one in three teen deaths is from car crashes, many involving alcohol.

31   Are these kids just being stupid? That's the conventional explanation: They're not thinking, or by the work-in-progress model, their puny developing brains fail them.

32   Yet these explanations don't hold up. As Laurence Steinberg, a developmental psychologist specializing in adolescence at Temple University, points out, even 14- to 17-year-olds—the biggest risk takers—use the same basic cognitive strategies that adults do, and they usually reason their way through problems just as well as adults. Contrary to popular belief, they also fully recognize they're mortal. And, like adults, says Steinberg, "teens actually overestimate risk."

33   So if teens think as well as adults do and recognize risk just as well, why do they take more chances? Here, as elsewhere, the problem lies less in what teens

lack compared with adults than in what they have more of. Teens take more risks not because they don't understand the dangers but because they weigh risk versus reward differently: In situations where risk can get them something they want, they value the reward more heavily than adults do.

34   A video game Steinberg uses draws this out nicely. In the game, you try to drive across town in as little time as possible. Along the way you encounter several traffic lights. As in real life, the traffic lights sometimes turn from green to yellow as you approach them, forcing a quick go-or-stop decision. You save time—and score more points—if you drive through before the light turns red. But if you try to drive through the red and don't beat it, you lose even more time than you would have if you had stopped for it. Thus the game rewards you for taking a certain amount of risk but punishes you for taking too much.

35   When teens drive the course alone, in what Steinberg calls the emotionally "cool" situation of an empty room, they take risks at about the same rates that adults do. Add stakes that the teen cares about, however, and the situation changes. In this case Steinberg added friends: When he brought a teen's friends into the room to watch, the teen would take twice as many risks, trying to gun it through lights he'd stopped for before. The adults, meanwhile, drove no differently with a friend watching.

36   To Steinberg, this shows clearly that risk-taking rises not from puny thinking but from a higher regard for reward.

37   "They didn't take more chances because they suddenly downgraded the risk," says Steinberg. "They did so because they gave more weight to the payoff."

38   Researchers such as Steinberg and Casey believe this risk-friendly weighing of cost versus reward has been selected for because, over the course of human evolution, the willingness to take risks during this period of life has granted an adaptive edge. Succeeding often requires moving out of the home and into less secure situations. "The more you seek novelty and take risks," says Baird, "the better you do." This responsiveness to reward thus works like the desire for new sensation: It gets you out of the house and into new turf.

39   As Steinberg's driving game suggests, teens respond strongly to social rewards. Physiology and evolutionary theory alike offer explanations for this tendency. Physiologically, adolescence brings a peak in the brain's sensitivity to dopamine, a neurotransmitter that appears to prime and fire reward circuits and aids in learning patterns and making decisions. This helps explain the teen's quickness of learning and extraordinary receptivity to reward—and his keen, sometimes melodramatic reaction to success as well as defeat.

40   The teen brain is similarly attuned to oxytocin, another neural hormone, which (among other things) makes social connections in particular more rewarding. The neural networks and dynamics associated with general reward and social interactions overlap heavily. Engage one, and you often engage the other. Engage them during adolescence, and you light a fire.

41   This helps explain another trait that marks adolescence: Teens prefer the company of those their own age more than ever before or after. At one level, this passion for same-age peers merely expresses in the social realm the teen's general attraction to novelty: Teens offer teens far more novelty than familiar old family does.

42   Yet teens gravitate toward peers for another, more powerful reason: to invest in the future rather than the past. We enter a world made by our parents. But we will live most of our lives, and prosper (or not) in a world run and remade by our peers. Knowing, understanding, and building relationships with them bears

critically on success. Socially savvy rats or monkeys, for instance, generally get the best nesting areas or territories, the most food and water, more allies, and more sex with better and fitter mates. And no species is more intricately and deeply social than humans are.

43   This supremely human characteristic makes peer relations not a sideshow but the main show. Some brain-scan studies, in fact, suggest that our brains react to peer exclusion much as they respond to threats to physical health or food supply. At a neural level, in other words, we perceive social rejection as a threat to existence. Knowing this might make it easier to abide the hysteria of a 13-year-old deceived by a friend or the gloom of a 15-year-old not invited to a party. These people! we lament. They react to social ups and downs as if their fates depended upon them! They're right. They do.

44   Excitement, novelty, risk, the company of peers. These traits may seem to add up to nothing more than doing foolish new stuff with friends. Look deeper, however, and you see that these traits that define adolescence make us more adaptive, both as individuals and as a species. That's doubtless why these traits, broadly defined, seem to show themselves in virtually all human cultures, modern or tribal. They may concentrate and express themselves more starkly in modern Western cultures, in which teens spend so much time with each other. But anthropologists have found that virtually all the world's cultures recognize adolescence as a distinct period in which adolescents prefer novelty, excitement, and peers. This near-universal recognition sinks the notion that it's a cultural construct.

45   Culture clearly shapes adolescence. It influences its expression and possibly its length. It can magnify its manifestations. Yet culture does not create adolescence. The period's uniqueness rises from genes and developmental processes that have been selected for over thousands of generations because they play an amplified role during this key transitional period: producing a creature optimally primed to leave a safe home and move into unfamiliar territory.

46   The move outward from home is the most difficult thing that humans do, as well as the most critical—not just for individuals but for a species that has shown an unmatched ability to master challenging new environments. In scientific terms, teenagers can be a pain in the ass. But they are quite possibly the most fully, crucially adaptive human beings around. Without them, humanity might not have so readily spread across the globe.

47   This adaptive-adolescence view, however accurate, can be tricky to come to terms with—the more so for parents dealing with teens in their most trying, contrary, or flat-out scary moments. It's reassuring to recast worrisome aspects as signs of an organism learning how to negotiate its surroundings. But natural selection swings a sharp edge, and the teen's sloppier moments can bring unbearable consequences. We may not run the risk of being killed in ritualistic battles or being eaten by leopards, but drugs, drinking, driving, and crime take a mighty toll. My son lives, and thrives, sans car, at college. Some of his high school friends, however, died during their driving experiments. Our children wield their adaptive plasticity amid small but horrific risks.

48   We parents, of course, often stumble too, as we try to walk the blurry line between helping and hindering our kids as they adapt to adulthood. The United States spends about a billion dollars a year on programs to counsel adolescents on violence, gangs, suicide, sex, substance abuse, and other potential pitfalls. Few of them work.

49   Yet we can and do help. We can ward off some of the world's worst hazards and nudge adolescents toward appropriate responses to the rest. Studies show that when parents engage and guide their teens with a light but steady hand, staying connected but allowing independence, their kids generally do much better in life. Adolescents want to learn primarily, but not entirely, from their friends. At some level and at some times (and it's the parent's job to spot when), the teen recognizes that the parent can offer certain kernels of wisdom—knowledge valued not because it comes from parental authority but because it comes from the parent's own struggles to learn how the world turns. The teen rightly perceives that she must understand not just her parents' world but also the one she is entering. Yet if allowed to, she can appreciate that her parents once faced the same problems and may remember a few things worth knowing.

50   Meanwhile, in times of doubt, take inspiration in one last distinction of the teen brain—a final key to both its clumsiness and its remarkable adaptability. This is the prolonged plasticity of those late-developing frontal areas as they slowly mature. As noted earlier, these areas are the last to lay down the fatty myelin insulation—the brain's white matter—that speeds transmission. And at first glance this seems like bad news: If we need these areas for the complex task of entering the world, why aren't they running at full speed when the challenges are most daunting?

51   The answer is that speed comes at the price of flexibility. While a myelin coating greatly accelerates an axon's bandwidth, it also inhibits the growth of new branches from the axon. According to Douglas Fields, an NIH neuroscientist who has spent years studying myelin, "This makes the period when a brain area lays down myelin a sort of crucial period of learning—the wiring is getting upgraded, but once that's done, it's harder to change."

52   The window in which experience can best rewire those connections is highly specific to each brain area. Thus the brain's language centers acquire their insulation most heavily in the first 13 years, when a child is learning language. The completed insulation consolidates those gains—but makes further gains, such as second languages, far harder to come by.

53   So it is with the forebrain's myelination during the late teens and early 20s. This delayed completion—a withholding of readiness—heightens flexibility just as we confront and enter the world that we will face as adults.

54   This long, slow, back-to-front developmental wave, completed only in the mid-20s, appears to be a uniquely human adaptation. It may be one of our most consequential. It can seem a bit crazy that we humans don't wise up a bit earlier in life. But if we smartened up sooner, we'd end up dumber.

Using Multiple Strategies

David Dobbs uses cause and effect to create an argument that changes our minds about the brains of adolescents. To accomplish this task, he uses other strategies as well as the dominant emphasis on cause and effect.

- Paragraphs 1–9 present a narrative about his son's behavior to hook the reader and demonstrate the behavior he will explain.
- To discuss causes, writers often have to explain the steps in a process. Paragraphs 13–16 demonstrate the use of process to explain causes. To report science, writers also need to explain the process of experiments, as in paragraphs 17 and 34.

- Since the writer uses technical terms about the brain, he offers definitions, as in paragraph 14. This definition also describes the brain.
- The writer often compares teens and adults, as in paragraph 18, to highlight the differences that are a concern for many adults.

Discussion Questions MyWritingLab

1. What causes does the writer give for risky teenage behaviors? How does the writer organize the explanation? Is it effective?
2. Paragraphs 2–9 provide a personal example before the writer moves forward with a fairly complex explanation. Why does the writer start that way? Where else in the essay does the writer refer back to this incident? How does this example then function overall in this essay?
3. What does paragraph 11 contribute to the article? Why is or isn't it important?
4. This article was published in *National Geographic,* which is for a more general audience; yet it addresses some complex issues. What strategies does the writer use to help explain complex causes in a way that will be comprehensible and engaging for its readers?
5. What does the conclusion, paragraph 54, add to the article? What does it accomplish as a conclusion? How does it change the reader's perception of teen risky behavior and the reasons behind that behavior?

Toward Key Insights MyWritingLab

There is an increasing tendency to explain human behavior in terms of what we know about the brain or evolution. In this article, is the use of such explanations helpful for the readers? How? Does discussing our experiences, such as grief or love, in terms of brain chemistry cheapen the experience (as some suggest) or provide new insights that can aid us in understanding ourselves? What other behaviors or experiences might benefit from such explanations?

Suggestions for Writing MyWritingLab

1. Based on your experience, write an essay explaining the causes you have seen for teen risky behavior (other than those specified in the essay).
2. Take an observed human behavior or experience—altruism, lying, grief, rage, and so on. Research the behavior and write an essay explaining it.

DEFINITION

Reading Strategies

1. Clearly identify the term being defined.
2. Mark as you read the characteristics that are part of the defining characteristic of the concept. It can help to make a list of these defining characteristics.
3. Note specifically what the term being defined is *not* supposed to mean.

4. Observe any analogies, similes, or metaphors, noting specifically what the concept is suppose to be like.

5. Try to see if you can apply the concept.

Reading Critically

1. Check to see if the definition matches your intuition.

2. Determine if the definition is too narrow. If a person defines literature as works of fiction, the definition could leave out poetry.

3. Determine by applying the definition if it is too broad. If a person defines literature as works of writing, the definition would include phone books—a clearly unintended consequence of the definition.

4. Test if there are other available or possible definitions.

Reading as a Writer

1. Notice how the writer uses the introduction to explain the importance of the concept and the definition.

2. Identify the key strategies the writer uses to construct a definition—stating the defining characteristics, providing examples, indicating that to which the term does not apply.

3. Observe how the writer limits the definition so that it is not overapplied.

4. If the writer employs analogy, simile, or metaphor, determine how the device works in the context of the definition.

MARC ZWELLING

The Blended Economy

Marc Zwelling graduated with a BS degree in journalism from Northwestern University in 1968. After graduating, he worked for Canadian Press, the Toronto Telegram, *and as public relations official for the United Steelworkers of America. He is currently president of Vector Research and Development, Inc., and conducts opinion surveys and completes feasibility studies. He has facilitated numerous workshops and written extensively about future trends. In this selection, he examines the changing nature of the business marketplace.*

1   The traditional way to innovate is to carve a specialized niche. Some building contractors specialize in renovating nineteenth-century homes. Lawyers practice trade law, criminal law, family law, labor law, immigration, copyright, or libel. Doctors can be ear-nose-throat specialists, gerontologists, or pediatricians. Specialization is efficient; specialists do their jobs faster because they know them better than non-specialists. And a niche is usually more profitable than the mass market from which someone sliced it. The trouble with a niche is that when competitors recognize it's profitable they rush in.

2   Blending is the opposite of specialization. Instead of burrowing deeper into a field or product to specialize, blending creates a new market category. The secret in the technique is to unite different, not similar, ideas, products, or services. Minivans and sport-utility vehicles, for example, grew from blending cars and trucks, creating whole new categories of consumer vehicles.

Identifies contrasting approach for comparison

Provides a short definition

3   Companies can continually generate new ideas by blending. Most new products today are simply extrapolations of successful products, such as a faster microprocessor, a cheaper airline ticket, a smaller camera, and so on. These innovations eventually run out of possibilities. Blending different ideas instead produces limitless new directions for innovative products.

4   A food company searching for a new product for kids might think of blending different items from a list of opposites like "frozen or unfrozen," "milk or cola," "peanut butter or peanuts," "salad or soup." Perhaps kids who love peanuts would savor them in a soup. And perhaps a cola could be frozen so it would stay cold longer, requiring no ice. The ideas may prove impractical, nonsensical, or just plain awful, but the point is to generate more ideas because they can lead to practical products.

5   Blending also operates within social and economic trends. For instance, barriers are falling between work and leisure, devastating some retail clothing chains and department stores as employees don the same outfits at home and the office.

6   In the job market, there is vast potential to create opportunities by combining apparently unrelated occupations. Consider the number of specialists you must work with to buy or sell a house: There is a real estate agent, the loan officer, the building inspector, an insurance agent, and the mover. One specialist hands you off to another. The blending opportunity here is for, perhaps, a "home transitions" professional who can manage all these different steps.

Some employees may have over-specialized. Specialization narrows a worker's opportunities in a slowly growing economy and causes bottlenecks in a booming economy. Blending avoids these problems.

7   *The New York Times* recently reported unprecedented growth in the new profession of legal nurse consultant. From none a decade ago, there are more than 4,000 in America today. Blending the skills of nurses and lawyers, legal nurse consultants help lawyers in medical-related lawsuits. Blending professions is not the same as stacking one university degree on another. The legal nurse consultant is still a nurse, not a lawyer. Nurses learn enough law in training institutes to become legal nurse consultants.

8   Another example of a blended career opportunity might be an ergonomic architect—a designer and engineer with special training in child development to make safer houses for families with small children.

9   Try mixing and matching completely dissimilar occupations, such as carpenter, receptionist, software writer, investment adviser, security guard, dentist, chemical engineer, lifeguard, teacher, embalmer, chef, hairstylist, pharmacist, actor.

10   A list like this may yield few blended jobs in the literal sense, but it triggers thinking about ways to add value to products and services and differentiate businesses in super-competitive markets. For instance, a funeral home could offer caskets carved by its own carpenters. A supermarket could build customer loyalty if its meat cutters demonstrate cooking techniques. A chef with pharmaceutical training or a pharmacist with cooking skills could help customers create healthier meals using herbs and other natural supplements.

11   Career blending is most likely to develop among entrepreneurs, as attempts to blend work in traditional settings have historically met with resistance: Unions protest that management wants to make one employee do two jobs for one worker's pay. Management says unions obstruct change and efficiency.

Examples to illustrate the definition

Offers a second comparison to define the term "blending"

Provides examples

Identifies advantage of concept

Offers a different example

Offers another example

Explains advantage of blending

Another example

Illustrates the process of blending

Identifies limitations of the concept

Repeats advantage of
"blending" based on
effect

12   Indeed, most fields resist merging and consolidating because of tradition. But since nobody can predict what the market will bear, the greater the number of innovations you can generate in products, services, and careers, the greater your chance of success.

Discussion Questions

1. In the first two paragraphs, the author contrasts blending with specialization. What might be his reason for such an approach?
2. What techniques does the writer use to define blends? How effective are those approaches?
3. What examples of blends were most effective, which least effective, and why?

Toward Key Insights

Often we are trapped in our thinking by established categories. How can blending help break us out of those established categories?

Suggestion for Writing

Create a blend of your own, perhaps even creating a new word for the blend just as brunch is a blend of breakfast and lunch. Write a short paper defining your blend.

MARTI BERCAW

Krumping

Marti Bercaw is a writer and video journalist at Social, *an online journal from which this article was taken. She loves dance and frequently writes about that topic. Other articles include "Celebrate Michael Jackson's Life and Music at University City Walk!" and "The Jabbawockeez: America's 1st Best Dance Crew."*

1   On the 3rd Saturday of every month Tommy the Clown and Debbie Allen have a "Battle" that hundreds of L.A. kids join. It is a Clowning Krumping dance war of the creative kind, organized by 2 dedicated adults who love dance, love kids and understand the power of expression through dance.

2   The location is the Debbie Allen Dance Academy in Culver City and the stage is a quasi-boxing ring set up in a huge studio. 500 chairs and standing-room-only space is filled to capacity by the time the show starts . . . and what a show it is!

3   Tommy the Clown serves as the Master of Ceremonies and referee with a whistle. Larry the Clown is the DJ who supplies a powerful mix of music. Ani Dizon, Tommy's manager, coordinates the whole event and process. Lil Tommy, Tommy's brother, is there to help when he is not traveling the world performing Clown and Krump Dance with his crew, and he teaches Clowning classes at D.A.D.A., too.

4   On stage, two girl-to-girl or boy-to-boy dancers challenge each other in a series of rounds. One opponent sits while the other performs.

5   Individual dancers "call each other out" as well as the members of a crew but it's always one performer at a time. Dancers have been as young as 4 with no limit on the high end. Everyone, even Grandparents, are welcome to battle onstage but teenagers are in the majority.

6   The audience is made up of kids, parents, grandparents and friends. The challenging dance crew changes every month, unless there is a rematch, and goes up against the current winning crew who holds onto the gold embellished championship belt until it passes to the next winner. There are cash prizes as well. The audience votes by applause at the end of each battle. Battle scores are tallied to determine the winning crew.

7   Sometimes it's clear who has won and sometimes they have to rely on an applause meter to determine the winner. It's a tough call because all the dancers are brilliant at freestyle . . . that's what it's all about.

About Krump

8   "Clowning" is movement invented by Tommy the Clown who developed the strange, stilted, goofy and erratic motion to entertain audiences as a clown at parties and local events around Los Angeles from as far back as 1992. Needless to say, it caught on in a big way.

9   Street dance has an evolutionary life of its own and its very nature demands constant adaptation and change. What was once "Clowning" evolved to "Krump Dance" or Krumping. As Tommy put it, "Krumping is the dark side of Clowning." In homage to the clown, some dancers paint designs on half their face.

10   The first time I saw "Clowning/Krumping" was five years ago. Over time, it has spread to other cities in the U.S., Europe and Asia. "Rize," a documentary by David Lachappelle, permanently writes "Clowning" and "Krumping" into the pop history record. It will read that this dance was born in South Central Los Angeles beginning in the last decade of the century and was performed by inner city kids who, as the third generation who's offered hip hop, were hungry for something new. They made it happen.

Krump Described

11   Krumping incorporates extreme, almost impossible freestyle body motion, coordination and rhythm. Basics include chest popping, a Charlie Chaplin-esque, comic, stumbling, staccato stride and toe dance, feet that turn out, feet that turn in, arms that go wide in a ranting wave, the body jerking up and down, prancing, the torso bent from the waist that circles around the hips 360 degrees, raised arms that wrap over and around the body, the neck and head jutting forward, the mouth chattering as if in a real or silent monologue. The dance is frenzied and rapid, displaying a set of attitudes running the gamut from hostile to aggressive to seductive to comical and back again. Girls can be as good as the guys but there are fewer who compete. Their attitude can include more sexual, bump and grind elements with a flamboyant, exaggerated edge or they can have an attitude that is hard and aggressive, just like their male counterparts.

12   Krumping is not hip hop, though it uses the music and springs from the same mold. For now, it seems to stand alone as a pure urban expression.

13   It isn't pretty and it offers no apology because it tells a vivid story about being young in a hostile and dangerous world run amok. The dancer can shift from malevolent character to clown in a flash like what comes at you as you surf

channels on a TV. Click, click. Life turns on a dime at the push of a button in today's world. We see the reflection in Krumping.

14   Debbie Allen and Tommy the Clown do Los Angeles a great service by providing and supporting the monthly "Battles." It is true that kids who would otherwise be involved with gangs or get into other trouble are given a creative alternative. But it is also true that these kids are already gifted, articulate about their medium and highly motivated to achieve excellence.

15   In exchange for the chance to perform, the "Clowns and Krumpers" offer everyone who cares about dance or the creation of dance form or the poetry of rap, or the embodied voice of our American culture a chance to witness art in the making.

MyWritingLab ## Discussion Questions

1. What is the writer's overall purpose in writing this essay? Where is that purpose most evident?
2. Why does the author start the essay with a brief account of a specific competition?
3. What are some distinguishing features that help define Krumping?
4. The original online article had links to video clips of a Krumping competition. Where, if at all, would such video clips be helpful and why? Where would they not be needed and why?
5. In the end, the author identifies some positive features of Krumping. What impact do paragraphs 14 and 15 have on the reader?

MyWritingLab ## Toward Key Insights

Increasingly, texts are being placed online where they can be supplemented by pictures as well as video and audio clips. To what extent does textual content like a definition need to stand on its own and to what extent can it depend on Web-based support material? You might want to consider the above essay as an example.

Cultural phenomenon like music and dance are especially hard to define. What are some of the challenges of defining things like Hip-Hop, Krumping, Breaking, and other similar phenomenon?

MyWritingLab ## Suggestion for Writing

Take a contemporary movement such as Hip-Hop and, following the example of Marti Bercaw, write a definition paper explaining the movement.

JUDITH SILLS

The Power of No

Judith Sills, Ph.D. is a media psychologist and consultant who received her degree in personality and social psychology from the New School of Social Research. She is the author of Excess Baggage: Getting Out of Your Own Way. *She is a frequent contributor to* Psychology Today, *which published this selection in 2013. She lives in Philadelphia, Pennsylvania, where she maintains a private practice.*

Wielded wisely, *No* is an instrument of integrity and a shield against exploitation. It often takes courage to say. It is hard to receive. But setting limits sets us free.

1   There comes a moment when you say "Don't call me," and you finally mean it; when you return the charming gift because you forced yourself to acknowledge its invisible strings; when you turn down the friend's request for a helping hand, the colleague's plea for immediate advice, even the teenage son's expectation that dinner will appear before him—all because you have goals of your own from which you refuse to be deflected. Whether trivial or tormenting, each of these moments is an exercise in that poorly understood power, namely, the power of *No.*

2   There's a lot of talk, and a lot to be said, for the power of *Yes. Yes* supports risk-taking, courage, and an open-hearted approach to life whose grace cannot be minimized. But *No*—a metal grate that slams shut the window between one's self and the influence of others—is rarely celebrated. It's a hidden power because it is both easily misunderstood and difficult to engage.

3   It's likely that we are unaware of the surge of strength we draw from *No* because, in part, it is easily confused with negativity. Either can involve a turning away, a shake of the head, or a firm refusal. But they are distinctly different psychological states.

4   Negativity is a chronic attitude, a pair of emotional glasses through which some people get a cloudy view of the world. Negativity expresses itself in a whining perfectionism, a petulant discontent, or risk-averse naysaying. It's an energy sapper. Negative people may douse the enthusiasm of others, but rarely inspire them to action. Negativity certainly ensures that you will not be pleased. You will also not be powerful.

5   Where negativity is an ongoing attitude, *No* is a moment of clear choice. It announces, however indirectly, something affirmative about you. "I will not sign"—because that is not my truth. "I will not join your committee, help with your kids, review your project"—because I am committed to some important project of my own. "Count me out"—because I'm not comfortable, not in agreement, not on the bandwagon. "No, thank you"—because you might feel hurt if I turn down your invitation, but my needs take priority.

6   The *No* that is an affirmation of self implicitly acknowledges personal responsibility. It says that while each of us interacts with others, and loves, respects, and values those relationships, we do not and cannot allow ourselves always to be influenced by them. The strength we draw from saying *No* is that it underscores this hard truth of maturity: The buck stops here.

7   *No* is both the tool and the barrier by which we establish and maintain the distinct perimeter of the self. *No* says, "This is who I am; this is what I value; this is what I will and will not do; this is how I will choose to act." We love others, give to others, cooperate with others, and please others, but we are, always and at the core, distinct and separate selves. We need *No* to carve and support that space.

8   *No* recognizes that we are the agents of our own limits. For most of us, this self-in-charge-and-wholly-responsible is a powerful, lonely, and very adult awareness. We approach it two steps forward and one giant retreat—giving in to the beloved, to the bully, to our own urges for another drink or an unnecessary purchase. The closer we get to manning the barricade of self-set limits, the stronger we are. That strength requires the power of *No.*

9   *No* has two faces: the one we turn toward ourselves and the one that creates boundaries between ourselves and others. The struggle to strengthen our internal *No*, the one we address to our own self-destructive impulses, is the struggle with which we are most familiar. That *No* controls our vent of rage on the road and our urge for the cigarette. We call that *No* "self-discipline."

10   The *No* we direct toward ourselves comes from an internal self-governor whose job is to contain our urges and manage our priorities within an iron fist of reason. All our lives we may work on refining that self-governor, tweaking it, building it, shoring it up. The huge rewards of our governor's developing ability to say *No*—not too rigidly, but often enough and wisely, too—are productivity and peace of mind. The power of *No* is in that payoff.

11   The *No* we are able to say to others also evolves through life, beginning with the primitive *Nos* of our childhood. Anyone who has ever tried to put a 2-year-old into a car seat has real-life evidence. As the 2-year-old begins to differentiate himself—his will, his wishes—from those of Mom, he hurls one loud, endless cry: NOOOOOOOO. *No*, I won't put on those socks, won't eat that mush, won't leave the park! That primordial, powerful *No* is the original assertion of the self against the other. For the rest of our days we are challenged to find the proper, effective way to draw that line.

Line in the Sand

12   How much *No* is too much? Who turns down a needy friend to tend one's own garden? Where is the line between self actualized and selfish? Who refuses to lend support to the modest effort of a group of friends? What is the boundary between important principles and stubborn oppositionalism?

13   As a general guideline, five situations benefit from increasing strength to say *No*.

14   **When it keeps you true to your principles and values.** It's a beautiful thing—emotionally, spiritually, and even professionally—to be generous, to be supportive. But, as sociologists Roger Mayer, James Davis, and F. David Schoorman point out in their classic studies of organizations, integrity is as essential as benevolence in establishing interpersonal trust. It is a requirement for effectiveness.

15   Jack, for example, has always cherished his role as the go-to guy for his buddies. "Jack has your back" has been his proud mantra since high school. So when a close, married friend began an affair, Jack maintained a discreet silence. However, when that close friend asked Jack for the loan of his vacation home as a convenient site for the clandestine relationship, Jack wrestled with his conscience. He wanted to continue to be seen as a great guy, but he found himself uncomfortable being part of a deception, however secondhand. In the end, he said just that, as he turned his friend down.

16   Jack's *No* dinged the friendship a bit and violated an unspoken male code, at least among Jack's peers. Still, if being liked by others is often a by-product of saying *Yes*, liking yourself sometimes comes only from saying *No*.

17   **When it protects you from cheerful exploitation by others.** It's remarkable how much some people will ask of you, even demand from you, things for which you yourself wouldn't dream of asking. Protect yourself best from the many who feel entitled to ask by being strong enough to say a firm, clear, calm *No*.

18   Take a classic school and office scenario: A happy, popular, slacker colleague asks again to borrow his worker bee teammate's careful notes. Mr. Worker Bee resents being used, but can't think of a good reason to refuse. So he acquiesces. Gets asked again. Resents more. Can't think of a good reason to say *No*, so he gives in. And so the cycle goes.

19   Finally, paying attention to his own feeling of being taken advantage of—instead of focusing on finding a reason acceptable to the cheerful exploiter—Worker Bee turns Mr. Popular down. Scraping up his backbone, Mr. Worker Bee simply says, "*No*, I'm not comfortable with that."

20   His *No* earns him a chilly reception in the company cafeteria for a week or two. It isn't a pleasant time, but it passes. In its wake, Mr. Worker Bee will find a new safety. *No* is a necessary life shield against the charming users who sniff out softies. It turns out nice guys can say *No*.

21   **When it keeps you focused on your own goals.** When her boss criticized her for the second time as a "Chatty Cathy" whose work was late because she wasted too much time talking, Amy felt hurt and unfairly evaluated. Was it her fault that people loved to stop by her cubicle? How was she supposed to turn away Marsha, whose aging mother presented so many problems, or Jim, who wanted her thoughts on the best way to proceed with their clients? Her colleagues needed her support; cutting them short would hurt their feelings and her relationships.

22   Amy clearly needs the power of *No*. Why? Because, loving and being interested in them as she is, Amy is losing sight of her own responsibilities, her own agenda. *No* is a necessary tool to keep your goals in mind. Frankly, meeting your own goals is what you are being paid for and what will pay off. We all need *No* to do our job instead of someone else's.

23   **When it protects you from abuse by others.** Sadly, our most important relationships often invite our ugliest communications. In part that's because the people closest to us arouse our strongest emotions, and in part it's because they are the people we fear losing the most. Fear can sap the strength we need to say *No*, just when we need that power most.

24   A mean adult daughter is a case in point. Isabelle would insist that she loves her mother, but she also finds her irritating, offering the grandchildren too many snacks, giving Isabelle useless, anxiety-driven advice about health, bad weather, or spending. When Isabelle gets irritated, she snaps. She's rude ("Shut up!"), insulting ("Trying to make my kids fat like you, Mom?"), or just downright mean (derisive and contemptuous dismissal). Her frequent assaults hurt Mom deeply, and Mom complains bitterly and often to other family members about Isabelle's treatment.

25   Despite the support of her family, Mom never draws a line with Isabelle herself. She has yet to pull herself up and say, "Do not speak to me like that." She feels unable to because, quite simply, "This is my daughter. If I tell her she's not allowed to speak a certain way, she is quite capable of not speaking to me at all. I just can't risk it." Stripped of the power of *No*, we leave ourselves vulnerable to verbal assault.

26   **When you need the strength to change course.** The invitations are in the mail, but the impending marriage is a mistake. The job looks good to the rest of the world, but it's making you sick in the morning. Your family has sacrificed to pay the tuition, but law school feels like a poor fit. When you find yourself going down the wrong road, *No* is the power necessary to turn yourself around.

27   The obstacles to this potent *No* are twofold: First, of course, you have to be able to tolerate acknowledging, if only to yourself, that you made a mistake. So many of us would rather be right than happy. We will continue blindly down the wrong path because we simply can't bring ourselves to read the road signs. Most of the time, though, we know when we need to draw the line.

28   The problem is getting ourselves to do it. Accessing your own power requires overcoming one huge obstacle: the cost of dishing out *No*.

Dishing It Out

29   Simply, *No* is not a warm send. It's tough to deliver, in large part because we have a gut sense of how it will be received—not well.

30   Neuroscience supports our hunch that *No* is going to register far more harshly than we may have intended. The human brain is hardwired to respond to *No* more quickly, more intensely, and more persistently than to a positive signal. *No* is stronger than *Yes*.

31   The brain's so-called negativity bias, first described by psychologist Roy F. Baumeister, Ph.D., of Florida State University, explains why negative experiences have a more enduring impact on emotion than positive events of equal intensity. The brain reacts pleasantly to positive stimuli but wildly painfully to negative stimuli. *No* matter how you gift-wrap it, *No* is a negative event. This holds true whether we are discussing financial matters (we are far more upset by losing a chunk of money than we are pleased by gaining an equal amount), interpersonal events (negative first impressions are difficult to overcome), or personal information (negative job feedback has a much more profound effect than positive information).

32   John Cacioppo, Ph.D., and colleagues at the University of Chicago actually measured the electrical output of the cerebral cortex to demonstrate that, across a variety of situations, negative information leads to a swift and outsize surge in activity. One hurt lingers longer than one compliment. Nevertheless, the ability to rapidly detect bad news and weight it so heavily, Cacioppo says, evolved for a very positive reason—to keep us out of harm's way.

33   And *No* hurts.

34   Whether reasonably required ("I can't lend my car because I'm not insured for other drivers"), tactfully couched ("Yours is the best banana bread ever, but my doctor has me on a special diet") or firmly asserted ("Thank you for asking, but I am already committed this weekend"), the receiver hears *No*. And feels bad.

35   Perhaps we intuitively grasp this brain bias, this neurological oversensitivity to *No* and for this reason alone are very reluctant to trigger that powerful reaction in others. Too, whether we sense the brain's negativity bias, many of us hesitate to deliver a *No* because of the real interpersonal damage it may do. *No* is not generally a way to win friends.

36   While we are not all equally vulnerable, some of us find the sting of displeasing others absolutely intolerable. We popularly refer to these people as "pleasers," and you probably know the degree to which you are one.

37   Pleasers are so relationship-oriented that they will automatically say what someone else wants to hear, agree with someone else's ideas, or bow to another's agenda without hesitation. A pleaser is frequently socially perceived as "nice," is usually well liked, and often feels taken advantage of, underappreciated, and uncertain in her decision making. It's not an even trade-off; when you cannot say *No* to others, you disappear.

38   There's a third cost to *No* that causes many of us to pull back: *No* can lead to conflict. That's a path few of us wish to take if it can be avoided.

39   You may hesitate to say *No* because the challenge you anticipate from others has merit. The line between selfish and necessary self-interest is not always clear. You want to turn down an invitation because you don't like parties. Your friend really wants your support. She will vigorously object, and you envision her making some good points. That makes *No* tough.

40   But face it: Some people will fight your *No* regardless of the issue. Such folks take others' boundaries as a personal affront. They challenge you, press you to justify yourself. It is a character style, and a successful one in many circumstances. ("Don't take *No* for an answer" is probably the best sales technique of all.) Set up a fence and this parent, spouse, colleague, or friend sees a barrier erected for the sole purpose of testing his ability to knock it down. Your *No* is his call to arms; most of us hesitate before we go into battle. It's easy to decide it's just not worth it.

41   Finally, it may be tough to dish out a *No* because you can see the hurt it inflicts. Even reflected pain—a wounded look, tears, slumped disappointment—is difficult to bear. That's a *No* we want to avoid—sometimes when we shouldn't.

42   All of these may be good reasons why we find *No* tough to dish out. Tough, but absolutely necessary. Because in the big picture, bottom line, we need to stick up for ourselves. *No* is the weapon we bring to the party.

Sing Out, Louise

43   There's *No* free lunch. If you are a person who is naturally open-hearted and generous, *No* can be an unnatural stretch. If you are one of those who really longs to be liked, it's more than a stretch. It's a cringe. Unfamiliar, uncomfortable but very, very necessary, because constant, craven *Yes* carves little slices from you, while *No* is a rock and a shield. Therein lies its power.

44   Organizational psychologist Adam Grant, author of *Give and Take* and a professor at the University of Pennsylvania's Wharton School, outs the many professional rewards and successes that accrue to generous givers. Still, Grant emphasizes that "the ability to say *No* is one of the most important skills one can have, particularly for givers."

45   Grant points to the power of *No* as necessary to carve time for one's own goals and agenda. Without it, other people dictate your schedule and limit your accomplishments. Says Grant, "Saying *No* is especially huge in establishing a work/life balance. Without that ability, work will cannibalize your life."

46   *No* also makes other people respect you and your time more, Grant notes. "When you are able to say *No*, people are careful to come to you with only meaningful requests, rather than simply asking for any help you might be able to give."

47   *No* makes your *Yes* more meaningful, or as Grant puts it, "It makes you more of a specialist, rather than a generalist in what you give to others." When we say *Yes* thoughtfully, because we are giving in our area of expertise, rather than saying *Yes* out of a need to be liked, we are far more apt to feel satisfied by giving.

48   *No* pays off in the personal arena as well as the professional one. It's exhilarating to feel in charge of one's self, to be the boundary setter and the decider. There's a bonus in energy and self-confidence.

49   Too, *No* tests the health and equity of your closest relationships. If you feel you cannot say *No*, at least to some things, some of the time, then you are not being loved—you are being controlled.

50   Finally, and perhaps most important, personal integrity requires the power of *No*. The ability to say *No* is an essential element of one's moral compass. Without it, we are merely agreeable pleasers, the Pillsbury doughboys of morals and values. Whatever the cost or quake involved when you deliver a *No*, backbone is defined by your ability to say it.

Using Multiple Strategies

Effective definitions often use many strategies. This essay is no exception; as Judith Sills writes to redefine our concept of "No" so that we see it as more positive, she uses the following strategy.

- She uses comparison to distinguish "No" from "Negativity" in paragraphs 4 and 5, and to compare inner and outer "No" in paragraph 9. Definitions often use comparisons to distinguish one thing from others.
- Judith helps define "No" in paragraph 16, and other paragraphs, explaining the effect of saying "No." Paragraphs 45–50 present the beneficial effects of "No" to again define its effects and make the argument for employing "No." Paragraphs 35 and 36 explain the causes of our reaction to negative responses.
- Judith illustrates each point with a narrative example as in paragraph 18.

MyWritingLab ## Discussion Questions

1. What is the author trying to accomplish in re-defining "No" in this essay? Do the organization and content fit this purpose? Why, how, or why not?
2. This article starts by distinguishing "No" from "Negativity." What is the difference? Why does the author make this distinction? How does the author define "No" as a positive?
3. How does the indication of where "No" would be useful (with specific examples) help in the definition? Why might the writer have chosen to include this discussion?
4. In paragraphs 39–42, the author details the reason "No" is painful for us, including information from brain research. What does this section contribute to the definition and how does it help the writer achieve her purpose?
5. How do paragraphs 43–50 contribute to the writer's re-definition of "No?" Is this section an effective way to end this essay?

MyWritingLab ## Toward Key Insights

Words like "No" are ones we take for granted but can have powerful impacts on our lives. What attitudes did you have about "No" before reading this essay and how has this essay changed those attitudes (if at all)? What did it take to change your view of "No," if it did change? What do your responses suggest about the ways in which simple words with a big impact can be re-defined?

What other significant words or phrases might be re-defined? Why might this process of re-defining be difficult?

MyWritingLab ## Suggestions for Writing

1. Identify a common word or phrase like "yes" or "novice" that you believe could be re-defined. Write an article helping readers see the word in a new way.
2. Identify something you think is undervalued because of how it is perceived and write for an audience that is likely to undervalue it to help them re-conceive the object or activity. For example, you might re-define items like "hip-hop," "roller derby," or "professional wrestling."

ARGUMENT ▬ ▬ ▬ ▬ ▬ ▬ ▬ ▬

Reading Strategies

    1. Identify the background of the author if possible. Does the author bring any expertise or experience that helps make the argument more credible?

    2. Read the introduction and conclusion to gain a sense of the thesis and main points of the argument.

    3. Read the argument quickly to gain an overall sense of the major points of the essay and an understanding of the organizational pattern.

    4. Look for the organizational pattern of the essay and keep an eye out for transition sentences. Often an author argues by first presenting the viewpoint of several other authors, then pointing out limitations of those views, then presenting his or her own position and offering support, and finally admitting possible limitations and problems with the author's position (possibly answering these objections). This pattern often confuses readers.

    5. Read carefully to identify the major claims of the argument, the reasons for the author's position, and any evidence presented for any of the claims. It can be very helpful to outline an argument, making a special note of the major reasons and evidence for the claim. Note the author's approach. Is the argument mostly deductive or inductive? Does the author try to show the negative consequences of opposing views? Does the author base the argument on authority?

Reading Critically

    1. Check to see if the author demonstrates any overt bias.

    2. Test to determine if the reasons given really support the author's thesis.

    3. Test to see if the evidence is adequate. Does the evidence support the claims? Is the source of the evidence trustworthy and unbiased? Is the evidence extensive or scanty? Could contrary evidence be offered?

    4. Check the essay for informal fallacies.

    5. Try to offer objections to the author's claims. Write objections in the margins or on a separate piece of paper.

    6. See if you can formulate alternative conclusions to those proposed by the author.

    7. Try to formulate reasons and concerns that the author may have neglected.

    8. Read essays that present other viewpoints and compare.

Reading as a Writer

    1. Note the organizational pattern of the argument. Identify how you might use the pattern in your arguments.

    2. Examine how the writer connects the reasons with the major thesis.

    3. Identify how the evidence is presented and connected as support.

    4. Notice any effective word choice that helps cement the emotional argument.

    5. Evaluate how the author establishes tone and ethos.

    6. Examine how the author answers possible objections.

PATRICK MOORE

Going Nuclear

Patrick Moore was born in 1947, received a Ph.D. in ecology from the university of British Columbia and served as an environmental activist with Greenpeace from 1971–1986. Since then, he has taken very different views from Greenpeace, suggesting that global warming may not be man made and that nuclear power is an important environmental solution. He is co-founder and chief scientist for the consulting firm of Greenspirit Strategies. He is also a paid lobbyist for the Nuclear Energy Institute. One question readers need to consider is whether his history and current affiliations should influence how his article is evaluated. "Going Nuclear" appeared as an opinion piece in the Sunday edition of the Washington Post, *April 16, 2006.*

Establishes credibility for audience	1 In the early 1970s when I helped found Greenpeace, I believed that nuclear energy was synonymous with nuclear holocaust, as did most of my compatriots. That's the conviction that inspired Greenpeace's first voyage up the spectacular rocky northwest coast to protest the testing of U.S. hydrogen bombs in Alaska's Aleutian Islands. Thirty years on, my views have changed, and the rest of the environmental movement needs to update its views, too, because nuclear energy may just be the energy source that can save our planet from another possible disaster: catastrophic climate change.

Establishes credibility for audience

Defines audience for argument

States thesis

In the early 1970s when I helped found Greenpeace, I believed that nuclear energy was synonymous with nuclear holocaust, as did most of my compatriots. That's the conviction that inspired Greenpeace's first voyage up the spectacular rocky northwest coast to protest the testing of U.S. hydrogen bombs in Alaska's Aleutian Islands. Thirty years on, my views have changed, and the rest of the environmental movement needs to update its views, too, because nuclear energy may just be the energy source that can save our planet from another possible disaster: catastrophic climate change.

Identifies problem with evidence

2   Look at it this way: More than 600 coal-fired electric plants in the United States produce 36 percent of U.S. emissions—or nearly 10 percent of global emissions—of CO_2, the primary greenhouse gas responsible for climate change. Nuclear energy is the only large-scale, cost-effective energy source that can reduce these emissions while continuing to satisfy a growing demand for power. And these days it can do so safely.

Offers answer to problem

3   I say that guardedly, of course, just days after Iranian President Mahmoud Ahmadinejad announced that his country had enriched uranium. "The nuclear technology is only for the purpose of peace and nothing else," he said. But there is widespread speculation that, even though the process is ostensibly dedicated to producing electricity, it is in fact a cover for building nuclear weapons.

Acknowledges criticism

4   And although I don't want to underestimate the very real dangers of nuclear technology in the hands of rogue states, we cannot simply ban every technology that is dangerous. That was the all-or-nothing mentality at the height of the Cold War, when anything nuclear seemed to spell doom for humanity and the environment. In 1979, Jane Fonda and Jack Lemmon produced a frisson of fear with their starring roles in "The China Syndrome," a fictional evocation of nuclear disaster in which a reactor meltdown threatens a city's survival. Less than two weeks after the blockbuster film opened, a reactor core meltdown at Pennsylvania's Three Mile Island nuclear power plant sent shivers of very real anguish throughout the country.

Answers objection with claim that can be tested by reader

5   What nobody noticed at the time, though, was that Three Mile Island was in fact a success story: The concrete containment structure did just what it was designed to do—prevent radiation from escaping into the environment. And although the reactor itself was crippled, there was no injury or death among nuclear workers or nearby residents. Three Mile Island was the only serious accident in the history of nuclear energy generation in the United States, but it was

enough to scare us away from further developing the technology: There hasn't been a nuclear plant ordered up since then.

6   Today, there are 103 nuclear reactors quietly delivering just 20 percent of America's electricity. Eighty percent of the people living within 10 miles of these plants approve of them (that's not including the nuclear workers). Although I don't live near a nuclear plant, I am now squarely in their camp.

Offers evidence of public support

7   And I am not alone among seasoned environmental activists in changing my mind on this subject. British atmospheric scientist James Lovelock, father of the Gaia theory, believes that nuclear energy is the only way to avoid catastrophic climate change. Stewart Brand, founder of the "Whole Earth Catalog," says the environmental movement must embrace nuclear energy to wean ourselves from fossil fuels. On occasion, such opinions have been met with excommunication from the anti-nuclear priesthood: The late British Bishop Hugh Montefiore, founder and director of Friends of the Earth, was forced to resign from the group's board after he wrote a pro-nuclear article in a church newsletter.

Cites an authority recognizable by possible readers

8   There are signs of a new willingness to listen, though, even among the staunchest anti-nuclear campaigners. When I attended the Kyoto climate meeting in Montreal last December, I spoke to a packed house on the question of a sustainable energy future. I argued that the only way to reduce fossil fuel emissions from electrical production is through an aggressive program of renewable energy sources (hydroelectric, geothermal heat pumps, wind, etc.) plus nuclear. The Greenpeace spokesperson was first at the mike for the question period, and I expected a tongue-lashing. Instead, he began by saying he agreed with much of what I said—not the nuclear bit, of course, but there was a clear feeling that all options must be explored.

9   Here's why: Wind and solar power have their place, but because they are intermittent and unpredictable they simply can't replace big baseload plants such as coal, nuclear and hydroelectric. Natural gas, a fossil fuel, is too expensive already, and its price is too volatile to risk building big baseload plants. Given that hydroelectric resources are built pretty much to capacity, nuclear is, by elimination, the only viable substitute for coal. It's that simple.

Demonstrates limitations with alternatives

10   That's not to say that there aren't real problems—as well as various myths—associated with nuclear energy. Each concern deserves careful consideration:

Structures essay to answer objections

11   *Nuclear energy is expensive.* It is in fact one of the least expensive energy sources. In 2004, the average cost of producing nuclear energy in the United States was less than two cents per kilowatt-hour, comparable with coal and hydroelectric. Advances in technology will bring the cost down further in the future.

States objection

Provides evidence to counter objection

12   *Nuclear plants are not safe.* Although Three Mile Island was a success story, the accident at Chernobyl, 20 years ago this month, was not. But Chernobyl was an accident waiting to happen. This early model of Soviet reactor had no containment vessel, was an inherently bad design and its operators literally blew it up. The multi-agency U.N. Chernobyl Forum reported last year that 56 deaths could be directly attributed to the accident, most of those from radiation or burns suffered while fighting the fire. Tragic as those deaths were, they pale in comparison to the more than 5,000 coal-mining deaths that occur worldwide every year. No one has died of a radiation-related accident in the history of the U.S. civilian nuclear reactor program. (And although hundreds of uranium mine workers did die from radiation exposure underground in the early years of that industry, that problem was long ago corrected.)

Identifies objections

13   *Nuclear waste will be dangerous for thousands of years.* Within 40 years, used fuel has less than one-thousandth of the radioactivity it had when it was removed

Uses evidence to place risk in perspective

from the reactor. And it is incorrect to call it waste, because 95 percent of the potential energy is still contained in the used fuel after the first cycle. Now that the United States has removed the ban on recycling used fuel, it will be possible to use that energy and to greatly reduce the amount of waste that needs treatment and disposal. Last month, Japan joined France, Britain and Russia in the nuclear-fuel-recycling business. The United States will not be far behind.

14   *Nuclear reactors are vulnerable to terrorist attack.* The six-feet-thick reinforced concrete containment vessel protects the contents from the outside as well as the inside. And even if a jumbo jet did crash into a reactor and breach the containment, the reactor would not explode. There are many types of facilities that are far more vulnerable, including liquid natural gas plants, chemical plants and numerous political targets.

15   *Nuclear fuel can be diverted to make nuclear weapons.* This is the most serious issue associated with nuclear energy and the most difficult to address, as the example of Iran shows. But just because nuclear technology can be put to evil purposes is not an argument to ban its use.

16   Over the past 20 years, one of the simplest tools—the machete—has been used to kill more than a million people in Africa, far more than were killed in the Hiroshima and Nagasaki nuclear bombings combined. What are car bombs made of? Diesel oil, fertilizer and cars. If we banned everything that can be used to kill people, we would never have harnessed fire.

17   The only practical approach to the issue of nuclear weapons proliferation is to put it higher on the international agenda and to use diplomacy and, where necessary, force to prevent countries or terrorists from using nuclear materials for destructive ends. And new technologies such as the reprocessing system recently introduced in Japan (in which the plutonium is never separated from the uranium) can make it much more difficult for terrorists or rogue states to use civilian materials to manufacture weapons.

18   The 600-plus coal-fired plants emit nearly 2 billion tons of CO_2 annually—the equivalent of the exhaust from about 300 million automobiles. In addition, the Clean Air Council reports that coal plants are responsible for 64 percent of sulfur dioxide emissions, 26 percent of nitrous oxides and 33 percent of mercury emissions. These pollutants are eroding the health of our environment, producing acid rain, smog, respiratory illness and mercury contamination.

19   Meanwhile, the 103 nuclear plants operating in the United States effectively avoid the release of 700 million tons of CO_2 emissions annually—the equivalent of the exhaust from more than 100 million automobiles. Imagine if the ratio of coal to nuclear were reversed so that only 20 percent of our electricity was generated from coal and 60 percent from nuclear. This would go a long way toward cleaning the air and reducing greenhouse gas emissions. Every responsible environmentalist should support a move in that direction.

MyWritingLab

Discussion Questions

1. In paragraph 1, the introduction, the author identifies his role in Greenpeace and his initial opposition to nuclear power before he states his current support for nuclear power. Why does the author start in this way, and is it effective?
2. Should the fact that the author is clearly paid to support nuclear power by the nuclear industry have any bearing on how readers evaluate his argument?

3. Who is the target audience for this argument? Why did the writer choose this target audience? What particular parts of the argument are used specifically for that audience?
4. The author attempts to answer common "myths" about nuclear power. Why does he employ this strategy? Why is or isn't his approach effective with his readers?
5. The author's argument is that nuclear power is the best answer to global warming. What could he do to strengthen this argument?

Toward Key Insights

MyWritingLab

Often we face not the best possible answer but rather the least undesirable option. Consider the ways that in this and other situations we may face such unfortunate choices.

The discussion of nuclear power often comes down to an assessment of risk. How much risk is there? How can risk be evaluated in determining whether we should expand the number of nuclear power plants?

Suggestions for Writing

MyWritingLab

1. Focusing on the core point of this essay, do additional research and write an argument either supporting or opposing the use of nuclear power as a solution to global warming.
2. Take one of the myths he discusses, do additional research, and write a paper arguing for or against that point, such as whether or not nuclear power is expensive.
3. If you oppose nuclear power, write to environmentalists countering this author's argument that nuclear power is the answer to environmental problems.
4. If you support nuclear power, do additional research and write an article specifically to an audience opposed to nuclear power because of the risks involved and who are not strong environmentalists otherwise.

ALEXIS ROWELL

Ten Reasons Why New Nuclear Was a Mistake—Even Before Fukushima

Alexis Rowell was born in 1965. He was for a time a BBC Journalist. He was the founder of the consulting group cuttingthecarbon and was elected member of Camden Council in 2006. He has been appointed to be Camden Eco Champion and is Chair of the council's All-party Sustainability Task Force. He is author of Communities, Councils & a Low Carbon Future. *The article below was posted on March 15, 2011, on the website Transition Culture: an Evolving Exploration into the Head, Heart, and Hands of Energy Descent.*

1   It's hardly a surprise that building nuclear power stations on seismic fault lines, as Japan has done, turns out to be a foolish thing. In the pause for

reflection about the safety of nuclear power that the Fukushima disaster is bound to create, here are ten reasons why it's a mistake to build a new round of nuclear power stations in the UK.

Nuclear Power Is Too Expensive

2   Nuclear has always been an expensive white elephant. UK taxpayers currently subsidise nuclear directly to the tune of more than £1bn per year.[1] But the indirect subsidies such as decommissioning and insurance are far greater.

3   The cost of decommissioning old nuclear in the UK is now estimated to be at least £73bn.[2] Surely anyone wishing to provide new nuclear should have to put that sort of sum into an up-front clean-up fund. But of course they won't. They can't possibly afford to.

4   If there's a nuclear accident in the UK, then who will pay? An insurance company? Not a hope. Existing UK reactors are insured to the tune of £140m each, which the government is talking about increasing to £1.2bn, but that's still nothing like enough to cover a serious accident like Fukushima or Three Mile Island or Chernobyl.[3]

5   Nuclear power is uninsurable. It's too risky and the potential payouts are too big. The government, meaning the UK taxpayer, will have to pay as we did to bail out the banks. The free market will never bear the true costs of nuclear.

6   A report published by the US Union of Concerned Scientists last month said nuclear power had never operated in the United States without public subsidies.[4] The existence of an Office of Nuclear Development at the Department of Energy and Climate Change (DECC) makes a mockery of Chris Huhne's claim that no public money will be spent on new nuclear.[5]

7   Only two atomic power stations are under construction in Western Europe: one in France and one in Finland. The Finnish reactor, which was supposed to be the first of a new generation of "safe" and "affordable" units, has been subsidised by the French nuclear industry (and therefore the French state) as a loss leader in the hope that it will spark a new nuclear building boom. When the decision was announced Standard & Poor instantly downgraded to "negative" the stock of the Finnish utility commissioning the reactor. The project has been plagued with cost overruns and delays (it was due to open in 2009), is under investigation by the Finnish nuclear safety regulator STUK and is probably the single best reason why new nuclear is a mistake.[6]

New Nuclear Power Stations Won't Be Ready in Time

8   According to the 2007 Energy White Paper the earliest the first new nuclear power station could possibly be ready is 2020.[7] Chris Huhne occasionally says it might be possible by 2018 but most observers disagree. However we need to replace 40% of our energy generation by 2015 because old nuclear and coal-fired plants are set to close. New nuclear will come too late.

[1] www.psiru.org/reports/2008-03-E-nuclearsubsidies.doc
[2] http://news.bbc.co.uk/1/hi/business/4859980.stm
  http://www.guardian.co.uk/environment/2008/jan/30/nuclearpower.energy
[3] http://www.decc.gov.uk/en/content/cms/news/pn11_007/pn11_007.aspx
[4] Koplow, D. (2011). http://www.ucsusa.org/assets/documents/nuclear_power/nuclear_subsidies_report.pdf
[5] www.decc.gov.uk/en/content/cms/what_we_do/uk_supply/energy_mix/nuclear/new/office/office.aspx
[6] Thomas, S. (2010). "The Economics of Nuclear Power: An Update." http://boell.org/downloads/Thomas_UK_web.pdf
[7] http://www.decc.gov.uk/en/content/cms/legislation/white_papers/white_paper_07/white_paper_07.aspx

Nuclear Does Not and Will Not Safeguard Our Energy Security

9   Nuclear power currently provides 18% of our electricity but only about 1% of our total energy needs.[8] Three quarters of the UK's primary energy demand comes from gas and oil.[9] Gas is used for most of our space heating and hot water. Oil is used for virtually all forms of transport. Indeed the vast majority of our oil and gas consumption is for purposes other than producing electricity. Nuclear power cannot replace that energy, while gas and oil deliveries are threatened by tightening supply (peak oil) and political instability. A 2008 Sussex University study concluded: "we are not convinced that there is a strong security case for new nuclear, especially if the costs and risks of strategies that include new nuclear are considered alongside those of strategies that do not."[10]

Nuclear Power Is Not Green

10   Mining uranium requires fossils fuels. So does building a nuclear power station. And so does trying to dispose of radioactive waste. Over its lifecycle a nuclear power station produces as much carbon dioxide as a gas-fired power station.[11] Better than oil or coal but not carbon-free. And it will get worse. In the not too distant future uranium will become so hard to mine that it will require more fossil fuels to extract it than the energy that will be produced from it.[12]

Nuclear Power Will Do Little to Reduce Our Carbon Emissions

11   Even if Britain built ten new reactors, nuclear power would only deliver a 4% cut in carbon emissions some time after 2025.[13] But that's too late. We need the carbon reductions now. We'd do better to ban standby buttons on electrical appliances than to develop new nuclear power.

Nuclear Power Stations Are Inefficient

12   We really need to stop producing electricity in huge power stations hundreds of miles away which waste 60% of the energy they produce as heat through cooling towers and another 7–9% in transmission losses across the national grid. If we produce energy locally and use Combined Heat and Power (CHP), then we can reach efficiencies of 80–90%.[14] Nuclear cannot and never has been made to work with CHP because to distribute the heat you need residents or businesses to be close by. But how many people want to live near a nuclear power station?

Plane Crashes Are a Risk to Nuclear Power Stations

13   In February 2011 a Loughborough University aviation expert suggested the chance of a plane crashing into a UK reactor was 20% higher than official estimates and The Guardian reported that a Health & Safety Executive internal

---

[8]http://www.decc.gov.uk/en/content/cms/what_we_do/uk_supply/energy_mix; http://www.decc.gov.uk/assets/decc/Statistics/publications/dukes/348-dukes-2010-printed.pdf
[9]http://www.oilandgasuk.co.uk/economics.cfm
[10]Watson, J. & Scott, A. "New Nuclear Power in the UK: A Strategy for Energy Security?" http://www.sussex.ac.uk/Users/prpp4/Supergen_Nuclear_and_Security.pdf
[11]Van Leeuwen, J. & Smith, P. (2008). "Nuclear power the energy balance." http://www.stormsmith.nl/
[12]http://en.wikipedia.org/wiki/Peak_uranium
[13]http://www.greenpeace.org.uk/climate/nuclear-power
[14]http://en.wikipedia.org/wiki/Cogeneration

report had admitted that a crash could trigger "significant radiological re-leases."[15] Finally, if you can fly a plane into the Twin Towers, then you can certainly fly one into a nuclear power station.

Nuclear Power Kills

14   Miscarriage rates by women living near the Sellafield nuclear reprocessing facility are higher than would be expected.[16] Billions of fish are killed every year when they get trapped in the cooling water intake pipes of nuclear reactors.[17]

It's a Myth that Renewables Cannot Provide Baseload

15   There has never been a day on record when the wind has not blown some-where in the UK. The point about baseload is that what you need is enough peo-ple in enough places producing electricity. The more you decentralise electricity generation the more secure the baseload becomes. The same principle holds for investing in shares—it's much more risky to invest everything in a couple of big companies than it is to invest in a basket of shares that reflect all aspects of the market. The real reason why proponents of nuclear are obliged to talk about baseload is that it's uneconomic to do much with atomic reactors other than run them continuously, whether or not the energy is needed. And in the UK that has usually meant prioritising nuclear over available wind energy.

Global Expansion Could Lead to New Nuclear Security Risks

16   In February 2011 the Royal Society launched an inquiry into nuclear non-proliferation saying that a global expansion of nuclear power "could lead to the wider proliferation of nuclear weapons, as well as creating new nuclear security risks," which could "impact on international progress towards nuclear disarma-ment."[18] Look at the problems the international community is having with the Iranian nuclear power programme. Many observers believe the US and Israel re-cently collaborated on a cyber sabotage project to slow the Iranian development up and prevent it from developing atomic weapons.[19]

And We Still Have No Idea What to Do with Nuclear Waste

17   All those arguments against new nuclear and not one of them was about nuclear waste. The 2003 Energy White Paper said one of the reasons why the then government wasn't proposing new nuclear was because there were "impor-tant issues of nuclear waste to be resolved." Have they been? No.

18   There are perfectly good non-nuclear solutions but they all require a lot more government intervention than the coalition government seems prepared to contemplate. They are:

1) Energy Efficiency

19   As it stands, the government's Green Deal—under which householders can borrow funds for energy efficiency measures to be repaid out of energy bill

[15]http://www.guardian.co.uk/environment/2011/feb/21/nuclear-risk-plane-crashes
[16]Jones, K. & Wheater, A. (1989). "Obstetric outcomes in West Cumberland Hospital: is there a risk from Sellafield?" http://www.ncbi.nlm.nih.gov/pmc/articles/PMC1292295/
[17]Speight, M. & Henderson, P. (2010). *Marine Ecology—Concepts and Applications.* p. 186
[18]http://royalsociety.org/nonproliferation/
[19]http://www.reuters.com/article/2011/02/07/us-nuclear-iran-idUSTRE71622Z20110207

savings—is set to be a completely inadequate sticking plaster solution. It feels like the government has decided that existing buildings are too difficult to deal with seriously which is why they're so gung-ho about new nuclear—to fuel electric radiators the energy from which will then be wasted through leaky windows, walls, roofs and floors. The only way to create genuinely low energy buildings is by using Passivhaus design.[20] Asking the UK's building sector to refurbish buildings using a proper engineering standard will be a challenge, but it is at least a coherent approach. Unlike new nuclear and the Green Deal.

2) Renewables (and possibly combined heat & power in urban areas if we can find enough non-fossil fuels to run it)

20   Nuclear has taken up a huge amount of civil servant time over the last few years. That's time that could have been spent on renewables. Britain has by far the most potential for wind and tidal power in Europe because of our geography. 40% of Europe's wind passes through these isles.[21] Yet in 2010 we produced just 3.2% of our electricity from wind. Germany obtained 9.4% of its electricity from wind in 2010, Spain generated 14.4% and Denmark managed a whopping 24%.[22]

21   The reason the Danes are so far ahead on wind is because they learnt the right lessons from the oil shocks of the 1970s and started planning for a renewably-powered future back then. The UK, by contrast, was blinded by the discovery of North Sea Oil.

3) Tradable Energy Quotas (TEQs)

22   Tradable Energy Quotas (TEQs) are a way of using the market to reduce fossil fuel energy consumption.[23] Every adult is given an equal free entitlement of TEQs units each week. Other energy users (government, industry etc.) bid for their units at a weekly auction. If you use less than your entitlement, you can sell your surplus. If you need more, you can buy them. All trading takes place at a single national price, which will rise and fall in line with demand. When you buy energy, such as petrol for your car or electricity for your household, units corresponding to the amount of energy you have bought are deducted from your TEQs account, in addition to your money payment. The total number of units available in the country is set out in the TEQs Budget, which goes down each year.

23   *There are greener, cheaper, more secure, quicker to install, safer alternatives to new nuclear so don't let yourself be persuaded that it's the only solution. It's not.*

Discussion Questions

MyWritingLab

1. The writer offers ten reasons against nuclear power and organizes them with bold headers. What might be his rhetorical reason for organizing them in this way? Is it effective?
2. The writer spends the most time arguing that nuclear power is too expensive rather than unsafe. Why might he have chosen to focus on that concern? Is that

[20]http://www.cuttingthecarbon.co.uk/home/passivhaus-standard
[21]http://www.energysavingtrust.org.uk/Generate-your-own-energy/Wind-Turbines
[22]http://ewea.org/fileadmin/ewea_documents/documents/statistics/EWEA_Annual_Statistics_2010.pdf
[23]http://www.teqs.net

rhetorically appropriate if his goal is to persuade his readers to oppose nuclear power?

3. In paragraph 12, the writer makes a very technical point about efficiency. What did you understand might be the writer's point here? How could this paragraph be rewritten to be more effective for less knowledgeable readers?

4. In rejecting nuclear power, is it important for the writer to suggest other alternatives? Is his argument for alternatives effective? How effective is his evidence in paragraph 20 for the potential of wind industry?

5. The article documents its sources and presents them in footnotes. To what extent, if at all, does this strengthen or weaken the argument of the article? Why?

MyWritingLab ## Toward Key Insights

Increasingly arguments are carried out through blogs rather than newspaper opinion pages. This article was a blog. How might writing for a blog differ from writing for a print media, and in what ways is it the same?

The article is written about England's nuclear program to an English audience. England faces different challenges from the United States; for example, it is much more populated and does not have any extremely remote areas. England's economy is also different from that of the United States. To what extent are or aren't the arguments applicable to other countries such as the United States that may face different situations?

MyWritingLab ## Suggestions for Writing

1. Identify one key issue raised by the article, such as whether nuclear power is too expensive or whether nuclear power is too inefficient, and then research the topic and write an argument about it.

2. Research the safety of nuclear power and write an argument on whether nuclear power is or is not safe.

3. Having read both articles in the Reader, do additional research and write an argument to concerned American readers on whether or not America should support the construction of new nuclear power plants to meet our energy needs.

CHRIS WILSON

Why Keystone Pipeline Is a Bad Idea for Texas

(The Dallas Morning News, 27 September 2011)

Chris Wilson is a 20-year environmental activist. She has a dual degree in chemical engineering and biochemistry. She has worked as a process control engineer for Union Carbide and Asea Brown Boveri. She is a member of STOP (Stop Tarsands Oil Pipelines).

1   The Keystone XL pipeline would carry oil, but the problem it would create for Texas is actually in regard to another liquid: our state's water supply.

2   If allowed, the proposed Keystone XL pipeline would carry 830,000 barrels a day of Alberta oil-sands crude 1,700 miles, through six states, to Texas Gulf Coast refineries. That's twice the length of the Alaska Pipeline.

3   Texas would be home to the longest span of the Keystone project, and that puts our state at the biggest risk. Crude removed from Canada's oil sands (also known as tar sands) is different from conventional Texas crude. When mined, oil-sand crude looks like asphalt. To transport it, the resource would have to be liquefied, heated to a high temperature, and treated with a toxic additive before it could be pumped through high-pressure pipes. That additive includes heavy metals, such as arsenic and lead, and carcinogens, such as benzene. Oil-sand crude is acidic and highly corrosive, especially in the high-temperature, high-pressure environment of a pipeline.

3   TransCanada, the company behind the proposal, predicted its existing Keystone 1 pipeline would leak once every seven years. It leaked 12 times in the first year. The largest of those spills, in North Dakota, was a six-story gusher spewing 21,000 gallons of oil-sands crude. On June 3 of this year, the U.S. Department of Transportation's Pipeline and Hazardous Materials Safety office determined that the Keystone pipeline was an "imminent threat to life, property, and the environment."

4   TransCanada proposes to build a 36-inch, thin-wall pipe that would operate at higher maximum pressure and temperature than is permitted under existing regulations. TransCanada says it will comply with many special conditions for the pipeline, yet most of those conditions are standard pipeline requirements and not specific to oil-sands crude.

5   In June, the head of the federal pipeline safety agency, Cynthia Quarterman, told Congress that the U.S. pipeline system was not designed with oil-sands crude in mind, that safety regulations were not written to address its unique risks, and that the agency had not yet studied the issue or been involved in the State Department's environmental review of Keystone XL.

6   That's not the only thing the State Department missed. The environmental review acknowledges the serious risks that oil-sands crude spills pose to water resources. However, the State Department limited consideration of effects only to "sole source" aquifers, while an oil-sands crude spill could contaminate all water sources. The State Department also has said that Keystone XL could leak as much as 1.7 million gallons per day without setting off the automatic leak-detection system. Finally, federal officials ignored the fact that Texas is experiencing an extreme drought.

7   In Texas, Keystone XL would cross over the Carrizo-Wilcox Aquifer, the state's third largest and the water supply for 60 counties and up to 12 million Texans, including those in the Dallas-Fort Worth area. The State Department ignored those facts, limiting its impact analysis to major water bodies within 10 miles of the proposed pipeline and municipal and private wells within one mile of the pipeline.

8   In June 2010, when the Enbridge Energy oil spill dropped 840,000 gallons of hazardous oil-sands crude into the Kalamazoo River in Michigan, the damage spread 40 miles. People downstream are sick; many people fell ill from exposure to toxic oil-sands vapors. We can't allow that to happen here.

9   Texans can live without the Alberta oil-sands oil, but we can't live without clean water and our health.

MyWritingLab   ## Discussion Questions

1. Written as an editorial for the *Dallas Morning News*, this argument, like many arguments, targets a specific and local audience. In what ways has the writer shaped her argument to meet the needs of her particular audience?
2. The writer is a part of an organization dedicated to stopping the Keystone Pipeline. In what ways should that fact influence or not influence our reading of the argument?
3. What evidence does the writer use to argue that the pipeline poses an environmental risk? In what ways is or isn't the evidence persuasive?
4. In what ways does this writer use authorities to help make her argument?
5. Is the example of the Kalamazoo River spill an effective addition to the argument? Why or why not?
6. The reader uses the conclusion to echo the introduction. Why might have the writer used this strategy? To what extent is or isn't it an effective strategy?

MyWritingLab   ## Toward Key Insights

Often people who may not be concerned about a larger issue (such as enhancing American education or protecting the environment) will have a greater interest when those issues are shown to be local issues that affect them. Why might this be the case? What does that suggest about how writers can argue effectively on larger global or national policy issues?

MyWritingLab   ## Suggestions for Writing

1. Identify a large-scale issue that might be important to you, such as climate change, the cost of education, or the right to bear arms. Research the issue and write an editorial detailing the local concerns about the matter for a large newspaper in your area.
2. Read the following article on the Keystone Pipeline (titled "Keystone Pipeline Foes Should Face Reality"), do additional research, and then write a more detailed article on the issue.
3. Research an issue of environmental dispute such as fracking or climate change. Write an argument supporting your position.

CHRISTOPHER R. KNITTEL

Keystone Pipeline Foes Should Face Reality

Christopher Knittel is the co-director of the Center for Energy and Environmental Policy Research at MIT. He is a professor of energy economics at the Sloan School of Management. He is the associate editor of a number of academic journals and has published research in a wide range of academic journals including The American Economic

Review *and* The Energy Journal. *He publishes essays for the more general reader in* journals *such as* Cognoscenti *and* Bloomberg News, *which posted this essay in 2013.*

1   Opponents of the Keystone XL oil pipeline warn of its potentially cata-strophic consequences. Building it, climate scientist James Hansen says, would mean "game over" for the climate.

2   *New York Times* columnist Thomas Friedman hopes that, if it's given a green light, "Bill McKibben and his 350.org coalition go crazy." And he means "chain-themselves-to-the-White-House-fence-stop-traffic-at-the-Capitol kind of crazy."

3   Are they all just crying wolf and using Keystone XL as a proxy battle against oil?

4   I hope so, because the economics behind laying a pipeline from Alberta, Canada, to the U.S. Gulf Coast would make it difficult for the pipeline to have any effect on greenhouse-gas emissions. I trust that if opponents dug a little deeper into the issues and the market for oil, they would agree–at least privately.

5   Three things would need to be true for Keystone to lead to more emissions. Otherwise, the pipeline could actually reduce them.

6   First, in the absence of this pipeline, Canada would need to not build an alternative one (and not use rail) to transport crude from the Alberta tar sands. Two western-route pipeline proposals exist: one would lead from the tar sands to southern British Columbia; the other would take a more northern route. Apipeline to eastern Canada has also been discussed.

7   Perhaps environmentalists believe that if they win the fight against Keystone, they would have the momentum to defeat all three Canadian alternatives as well. But let's calculate how much such a pipeline is worth to tar-sands producers, a major Canadian industry. Considering that just more than 1.6 million barrels of tar-sands crude is extracted each day, and that a pipeline would add roughly $20 a barrel to the price of that oil (without a pipeline, tar-sands crude has to be sold at a discount), a pipeline would bring producers $32 million a day. That is a very large incentive to get pipes in the ground. Good luck stopping them.

8   Second, Keystone's existence would have to cause a significant increase in production from the tar sands. The question here is, would that extra $20 a bar-rel cause producers to extract a lot more crude? Normally, when the price of something rises, the amount companies are willing to produce also increases. In the case of oil, however, this supply response is often fairly small. So any produc-tion increase in response to Keystone would probably be minimal.

9   Finally, the oil displaced by crude from the pipeline would need to be cleaner than what comes from the tar sands. We've all heard how dirty tar-sands crude is. Measured throughout the well-to-wheels life of the oil, greenhouse-gas emissions from tar-sands crude are 14 percent to 20 percent greater than those from the average type of oil used in the United States. What really matters, how-ever, are the emissions from the kind of oil that tar-sands crude would replace.

10   There is good reason to think that the tar-sands oil would displace addi-tional extra-heavy oil coming from Venezuela. If this is the case, tar sands might actually be good for the climate. A recent Cambridge Energy Research Associ-ates study found that gasoline refined from the average tar-sands crude sold to the United States is actually cleaner than that refined from either Venezuelan Petrozuata oil or California Kern River oil. There is no tar-sands oil dirtier than Venezuelan Petrozuata oil.

11   It may very well be that any additional tar-sands oil brought to the United States via Keystone XL—again, assuming there is additional oil—would be significantly dirtier than what is sold to the United States now. But this possibility is what the debate should focus on, not unsubstantiated talk of doom and gloom.

12   Maybe the opponents of Keystone XL understand all of this and oppose the pipeline merely for symbolic reasons. Maybe the politics of climate change require hyperbole. My hope, however, is that policy will be driven by facts.

MyWritingLab Discussion Questions

1. What specific issue is this writer addressing? Does this focus strengthen or weaken the writer's argument? Why?
2. What is the strongest argument in support of the writer's thesis? Which do you think is the weakest? Why?
3. This writer is a professor of energy economics. In what ways should the writer's credentials influence or not influence our response to his argument?
4. What argument is the writer making in paragraph 7? Is that argument effective?
5. Compare this argument with that found in "Why Keystone Pipeline Is a Bad Idea for Texas." Which argument did you find more effective and why? Could both essays be right, or do they disagree in some fundamental way?
6. How does the writer represent those he is opposing in paragraphs 1, 2, 3, 4, 11, and 12? What kind of contrast between himself and those he opposes is he trying to establish? Is this approach effective? Is it ethical?

MyWritingLab Toward Key Insights

What may seem like a larger issue can resolve into smaller issues. The issue of the construction of the Keystone Pipeline can resolve into the effects on the climate, the risks of the pipeline itself, the impact on employment, the impact on U.S. energy independence, and so on. In general, focusing on a specific piece of an argument—such whether a border fence to restrict illegal immigration is feasible—allows for a more detailed coverage of that issue but can be accused of not looking at the other issues. How would you weight the strengths and challenges of such focused arguments?

MyWritingLab Suggestions for Writing

1. Choose an important social issue, such as climate change, fracking, immigration, or another topic. Research the topic, identify a key piece of the big picture, and then write a detailed argument specifying your position on that issue.
2. Research the issue of the Keystone Pipeline and write an argument on the more general question of whether building it is a good idea. Alternatively, focus on a more specific question such as whether it will create jobs, increase the risk of oil spills, or have an impact on the climate.

3. Conduct research and write an argument disagreeing either with this essay or with "Why Keystone Pipeline is a Bad Idea for Texas." Your argument should summarize the argument you are rejecting and provide the reasons and evidence that are the basis for your disagreement.

JONATHAN ZIMMERMAN

When Teachers Talk Out of School

Jonathan Zimmerman is Professor of History and Education as well as Department Chair at New York University. He received his M.A. and Ph.D. from John Hopkins University. He was also a Peace Core volunteer and a high school teacher. He is the author of Small Wonder: The Little Red Schoolhouse in History and Memory *as well as other books and articles. This selection is from June 3, 2011,* The New York Times.

1   In 1927, a schoolteacher in Secaucus, N.J., named Helen Clark lost her teaching license. The reason? Somebody had seen her smoking cigarettes after school hours. In communities across the United States, that was a ground for dismissal. So was card-playing, dancing and failure to attend church. Even after Prohibition ended, teachers could be dismissed for drinking or frequenting a place where liquor was served.

2   Today, teachers can be suspended, and even fired, for what they write on Facebook.

3   Just ask Christine Rubino, the New York City math teacher who may soon be dismissed for posting angry messages about her students. Last June, just before summer vacation began, a Harlem schoolgirl drowned during a field trip to a beach. Ms. Rubino had nothing to do with that incident, but the following afternoon, she typed a quick note on Facebook about a particularly rowdy group of Brooklyn fifth graders in her charge.

4   "After today, I'm thinking the beach is a good trip for my class," she wrote. "I hate their guts."

5   One of Ms. Rubino's Facebook friends then asked, "Wouldn't you throw a life jacket to little Kwami?"

6   "No, I wouldn't for a million dollars," Ms. Rubino replied. She was pulled from the classroom in February and faced termination hearings; the case is now with an arbitrator.

7   Ms. Rubino's online outburst was only the latest example of its kind. In April, a first-grade teacher in Paterson, N.J., was suspended for writing on her Facebook page that she felt like a "warden" overseeing "future criminals." In February, a high school English teacher in suburban Philadelphia was suspended for a blog entry calling her students "rude, disengaged, lazy whiners;" in another post, she imagined writing "frightfully dim" or "dresses like a street-walker" on their report cards.

8   Such teachers have become minor Internet celebrities, lauded by their fans for exposing students' insolent manners and desultory work habits. Their backers also say that teachers' freedom of speech is imperiled when we penalize their out-of-school remarks.

9   But these defenders have it backward. The truly scary restrictions on teacher speech lie inside the schoolhouse walls, not beyond them. And by supporting

teachers' right to rant against students online, we devalue their status as professionals and actually make it harder to protect real academic freedom in the classroom.

10   Last October, a federal appeals court upheld the dismissal of an Ohio high-school teacher who had asked students to report about books that had been banned from schools and libraries. The exercise wasn't in the official curriculum, and parents had complained about their children reading some of the banned books.

11   Three years before that, the courts allowed an Indiana school board to fire a teacher who told her students that she had honked her car horn in support of a rally against the war in Iraq. The reason was the same: she had deviated from the "approved" curriculum.

12   Meanwhile, in Wisconsin and elsewhere, state legislatures are moving to restrict or eliminate teachers' collective bargaining rights. That means unions will have a more difficult time defending teachers' freedom of speech.

13   So the rest of us need to make a fresh case for why teachers should have this freedom. And the answer starts, paradoxically, with the limits they should impose on themselves.

14   All professionals restrict their own speech, after all, reflecting the special purposes and responsibilities of their occupations. A psychologist should not discuss his patients' darkest secrets on a crowded train, which would violate the trust and confidence they have placed in him. A lawyer should not disparage her clients publicly, because her job is to represent them to the best of her ability.

15   And a teacher should not lob gratuitous barbs at her students, which contradicts her own professional duty: to teach the skills and habits of democracy. Yes, teachers have a responsibility to transmit the topics and principles of the prescribed curriculum. But they also need to teach democratic capacities—including reason, debate and tolerance—so our children learn to think on their own.

16   Teachers won't be able to model those skills if our schools and courts continue to muzzle them. But the same democratic imperative also demands that teachers responsibly restrict what they say, just as other professionals do.

17   A similar sense of restraint is needed in class as well: although I would fully support a teacher's right to voice an anti-war view, I would not want her to tell the class that it is the only appropriate view. That's indoctrination, not education, and it inhibits the critical thinking skills that democracy demands.

18   Outside school, meanwhile, teachers must also avoid public language that mocks, demeans or disparages the children they instruct. Cruel blog posts about lazy or disobedient students echo the snarky smackdown culture of cable TV talk shows. And they're anathema to a truly democratic dialogue.

Using Multiple Strategies

Argument writing often uses additional strategies, including shorter arguments, to make its point.

- In paragraphs 3–7, the writer uses a narrative to illustrate the issue he is addressing.

- In paragraph 8, the writer establishes a comparison between out-of-classroom speech and in-the-classroom speech. Paragraph 14 compares teachers with other professionals.
- Paragraph 15 defines a teacher's duties.
- Arguments often point out effects to show an undesirable outcome of something being argued against. Zimmerman does this in paragraphs 9 and 17.

Discussion Questions
MyWritingLab

1. This is an argument about values. What are the reasons the author offers for his position? Are those reasons effective or not?
2. Much of the discussion on this issue revolves around questions of value. What kinds of evidence, if any, might be used to strengthen the claims in the essay?
3. What is the purpose of paragraphs 10–12 in relation to the writer's main argument? What audiences might it address? Is this approach effective?
4. In the conclusion, the author associates negative comments through social media with a "snarky smackdown culture." Why does he make this comparison in the conclusion? Is it effective?
5. This essay was originally an opinion piece in *The New York Times?* How do you anticipate different audiences would respond to the article: teachers, parents, school administrators, or other professionals?

Toward Key Insights
MyWritingLab

Little on the Web is really private, whether on Facebook, e-mail, or a semiprivate blog. In a flash, any posting can be very public. How then should we balance our free speech rights and the possible consequences of our comments on such a media? There have been cases of cyberbullying and online slander that harms a person's reputation. How would you balance free speech with a person's responsibility for what he or she claims?

Employers increasingly have a concern about a person's out of work behavior. Some companies do not allow employees to smoke off the job, test for it, and fire employees who do not comply. Employees who maintain blogs that express views that the company feels may reflect negatively on the employee and the company may be fired. How much say should any employer, including public employers such as public schools, have over an individual's life?

Suggestions for Writing
MyWritingLab

1. Write to your school board arguing either for or against a policy that would suspend any teacher who makes negative comments about students generally or specifically or about the school itself in any medium that becomes public.
2. Write to your school board arguing either for or against a policy that would suspend any student who made very negative and untrue comments about either teachers or other students in any medium that becomes public.

3. More generally, further research this issue, and write an argument for or against the restriction of the private speech of individuals by their employer or by their professional organization.

TODD PETTIGREW

Protecting Free Speech for Teachers in a Social Media World

Todd Pettigrew is an associate professor of English at Cape Breton University, Canada. He earned his Ph.D. from the University of Waterloo and primarily focuses his research on early modern literature and culture, especially drama and medical history. He posts frequently on educational issues on Maclean's online, the source of this argument.

1   Florida teacher Jerry Buell has been suspended from teaching after posting controversial comments on his Facebook page. The American history teacher was angered by a TV news report on the legalization of gay marriage in New York, according to Fox News. "I almost threw up," he wrote in a post. "If they want to call it a union, go ahead. But don't insult a man and woman's marriage by throwing it in the same cesspool of whatever. God will not be mocked. When did this sin become acceptable?"

2   School district officials say that Buell has crossed a line, that teachers are bound by special codes of ethics, and that a Facebook page is a public forum.

3   Nonsense. Readers of this space will know that I am an outspoken advocate for the rights of gays and lesbians. (This post, for example.) And I hasten to point out that Buell's statements are, in my judgment, stupid and mean-spirited. But he has the right to make them.

4   A Facebook page is a personal expression of one's own particular tastes and attitudes. Indeed, it is hard to think of any mode of communication more centered on an individual. Buell was describing his revulsion toward love unlike his own; he did not claim to be speaking for the Lake County School District, or for Mount Dora High School or for anyone else.

5   I have sympathy with those who believe a gay student may now be uncomfortable in this guy's class.

6   But if the standard is whether someone could potentially be uncomfortable, that's casting much too wide a net. If that standard holds, it could be used to restrict the expression of almost any comment on any controversial issue. Suppose, for instance, Buell had said the reverse. Suppose he had celebrated the gay marriage legislation in New York. Would some devout Christians feel uncomfortable in his class?

7   Probably. The question must not be what a student heard about what a teacher said on the Internet. The test must be: how does that teacher comport himself in class? If he's worth his salary, he should take special care to make sure that when controversial issues come up, he presents all sides fairly. I myself am a committed atheist, but when religious questions come up—as they often do in literary studies—I try to ensure that the discussion is appropriately balanced.

8   In cases like Jerry Buell's, people are quick to point out that there are limits to free speech; of course there are. But in a free society those limits have to be clearly defined and enforced only when absolutely necessary. If being wrong on Facebook is a crime, who among us is safe?

9   As long as he's keeping his opinion to himself in class, Jerry Buell should keep his job.

Discussion Questions

MyWritingLab

1. What is the main argument the writer offers to support free speech by teachers on the Internet? Is it convincing?
2. Why does the writer disclose his own position on highly charged issues in paragraphs 3 and 7? In what ways does this disclosure help or harm his argument?
3. In paragraph 8, the writer admits that there are limits to free speech. Why does he admit to such limits? Is his answer to his own observation about the limits to free speech convincing? Why or why not?
4. This essay argues about one particular case. How broadly does the argument apply? Does it also apply to teachers who post negative comments about students on their Facebook page? What about other social media such as Twitter or a blog?
5. In the conclusion, the writer makes a sharp distinction between class and out of class conduct. Is this distinction appropriate or, as Andrew Zimmerman suggests in "When Teachers Talk Out of School," do teachers also have a responsibility in their out-of-class communication to serve as role models?

Toward Key Insights

MyWritingLab

1. We may easily point to the protection of free speech in the U.S. Constitution. But this protection only restricts the government's ability to restrain speech. In reality, there are many restrictions on speech, including limits on obscenity, on advocating violence, on supporting terrorist organizations, and more. Employers similarly have the power to dismiss employees for speech that they believe harms the employer's interests. What types of speech do you think should be protected and why? What kinds of speech should not be protected and why?
2. The writer seems to assume a model of education in which teachers should keep their opinions out of the classroom and represent most sides. Yet we would not expect teachers to defend slavery in a history class or argue for the disadvantages of reading literature in an English class. To what extent should or shouldn't teachers be able to express their opinion in the classroom? Explain.

Suggestions for Writing

MyWritingLab

1. Write to your local newspaper or a blog entry on whether or not and to what extent teachers have a right to post unpopular or controversial positions on social media.

2. Write to your school paper about whether or not it is appropriate for teachers to express their personal opinions on controversial issues such as politics or religion in class.

3. Research the constitutional protection on free speech. Develop an argument on where you think free speech needs to be protected or limited. For example, should someone be able to be arrested for posting blogs defending or even encouraging eco-terrorism?

Handbook

Sentence Elements

Learning the parts of English sentences won't in itself improve your writing, but it will equip you to handle errors at the sentence level. Before you can identify and correct unwarranted shifts from past to present time, for example, you need to know about verbs and their tenses. Similarly, recognizing and correcting pronoun case errors requires a knowledge of what pronouns are and how they are used. In this section, we first cover subjects and predicates, then complements, appositives, and the parts of speech, and, finally, phrases and clauses.

Visit MyWritingLab **to complete the writing assignments in this chapter and for more resources on sentences.**

Subjects and Predicates

The subject of a sentence tells who or what it is about. A *simple subject* consists of a noun or a noun substitute. A *complete subject* consists of a simple subject plus any words that limit or describe it.

The predicate tells something about the subject and completes the thought of the sentence. A *simple predicate* consists of one or more verbs (words that show action or existence); a *complete predicate* includes any associated words also. In the following examples, the simple subjects are underlined once and the simple predicates twice. The subjects and predicates are separated with slash marks.

> <u>William</u>/<u>laughed.</u>
> <u>Sarah</u>/<u>painted</u> the kitchen.
> The <u>student</u> over there in the corner/<u>is majoring</u> in art.

Complex subjects can be very long; it is helpful to be able to pick the simple subject out of a complex subject.

sent

The <u>storms</u> in March, which dropped a record rainfall in a week's time,/ <u>resulted</u> in fierce floods.

A sentence can have a compound subject (two or more separate subjects), a compound predicate (two or more separate predicates), or both.

The <u>elephants</u> and their <u>trainer</u>/<u>bowed</u> to the audience and <u>left</u> the ring.

Sentences that ask questions don't follow the usual simple subject–simple predicate order. Instead, the word order may be changed slightly.

<u>Is</u>/<u>Angela</u>/ an experienced mountain climber?

<u>Has</u>/<u>a package</u>/ arrived yet for me?

When <u>will</u>/<u>we</u>/ be allowed to park on campus?

Sometimes certain types of phrases and clauses can fall between the subject and the predicate. These should not be confused with the subject. They are usually easy to detect since they can be moved elsewhere in the sentence. The subject is underlined.

<u>My dog</u>/, *since he has gotten old*, simply lies around the house.

<u>My dog</u>/simply lies around the house *since he has gotten old*.

Sometimes a phrase that is not part of the subject can introduce the sentence. This phrase can also usually be moved.

After we have repaired the rock wall,/<u>we</u>/will begin to plant the new flowers.

<u>We</u>/will begin to plant the new flowers *after we have repaired the rock wall*.

MyWritingLab   **EXERCISE**   *Place a slash mark between the complete subject and the complete predicate; then underline the simple subject once and the verb(s) twice. If a subject comes between an auxiliary verb and the main verb, set it off with two slash marks. If a phrase that is not the subject comes between the subject and the predicate, set it off with two slash marks.*

1. New Orleans has gradually been restored since Hurricane Katrina.
2. Marco started his network security business while he was still in college.
3. The cup of coffee on the counter is mine.
4. Do you know how to design a Web page?
5. The construction students, despite the steady rain, went outside to complete their surveying field experience.
6. Because of the severe drought, the forest service has banned campfires in the area.

Complements

A complement is a word or word group that forms part of the predicate and helps complete the meaning of the sentence. Anything that comes after the verb is usually a complement. There are many kinds of complements, including phrases and clauses, that will be reviewed later in this chapter. Four common complements of traditional grammar are direct objects, indirect objects, subject complements, and object complements.

A *direct object* names whatever receives, or results from, the action of a verb.

Hilary painted a *picture*. (Direct object results from action of verb *painted*.)

They took *coffee* and *sandwiches* to the picnic. (Direct objects receive action of verb *took*.)

An *indirect object* identifies someone or something that receives whatever is named by the direct object.

Doris lent *me* her calculator. (Indirect object *me* receives *calculator*, the direct object.)

Will and Al bought their *boat* new sails. (Indirect object *boat* receives *sails*, the direct object.)

An indirect object can be converted to a prepositional phrase that begins with *to* or *for* and follows the direct object.

Doris lent her calculator *to me*.

Will and Al bought new sails *for their boat*.

A *subject complement* follows a linking verb—one that indicates existence rather than action. It renames or describes the subject.

Desmond is a *carpenter*. (Complement *carpenter* renames subject *Desmond*.)

An *object complement* follows a direct object and renames or describes it. The following are two examples.

The council named Donna *treasurer*. (Object complement *treasurer* renames direct object *Donna*.)

The audience thought the play *silly*. (Object complement *silly* describes direct object *play*.)

If a word is an object complement, you can form a short test sentence using *is*. The following are two examples.

Donna is *treasurer*.

The play is *silly*.

Appositives

An appositive is a noun or word group serving as a noun that follows another noun or noun substitute and expands its meaning. Appositives may be restrictive or nonrestrictive. Restrictive appositives distinguish whatever they modify from other items in the same class. They are written without commas.

My sister *Heidi* is a professional golfer. (Appositive *Heidi* distinguishes her from other sisters.)

Nonrestrictive appositives provide more information about whatever they modify. This sort of appositive is set off by a pair of commas except at the end of a sentence; then it is preceded by a single comma.

Todd plans to major in paleontology, *the study of fossils*. (Appositive defines *paleontology*.)

noun   MyWritingLab   **EXERCISE**   *Identify each italicized item as a direct object (DO), an indirect object (IO), a subject complement (SC), an object complement (OC), or an appositive (AP).*

1. The critics considered the movie *a masterpiece.*
2. Calculus can be too *abstract* for some students.
3. Jasmine completed her research *paper* two weeks ahead of the due date.
4. My father, a committed perfectionist, taught *me* **the value of a job done well.**
5. Our chemistry professor handed us *the chemicals* and *flask* we needed for the assigned lab.
6. Mr. Hanley offered *me* a job.

Parts of Speech

Traditional English grammar classifies words into eight parts of speech: *nouns, pronouns, verbs, adjectives, adverbs, prepositions, conjunctions,* and *interjections.* This section discusses these categories as well as verbals, phrases, and clauses, which also serve as parts of speech.

It is important to recognize that words that may look like one part of speech can function as another part of speech. For example, the verb *swim* can function as a noun. *Swimming* is good for your health. To identify a word as a part of speech is to identify how it functions in a sentence.

Traditional grammar defined nouns as words that name persons, places, things, conditions, ideas, or qualities. Most nouns can take a plural (book, books), possessive (Andy, Andy's), or article (bench, the bench).

Proper Nouns

Some nouns, called *proper nouns,* identify one-of-a-kind items like the following and are commonly capitalized.

France	New Years
Pacific Ocean	Wyandotte Corporation
Pulitzer Prize	World Series

Common Nouns

Common nouns name general classes or categories of items. Some common nouns are *abstract* and name a condition, idea, or quality that we can't experience with our five senses. *Abstract nouns* often cannot accept the plural; we cannot usually say we have *envys. Concrete nouns* identify something that we can experience with one or more of our senses and usually have plural forms.

Abstract Nouns	**Concrete Nouns**
arrogance	man
fear	bicycle
liberalism	desk

pro

Count and Non-Count Nouns

Most nouns identify things we can count and such nouns usually can take the plural form: *three bananas, a book, two children*. Some nouns, including many abstract nouns, cannot accept a plural: *coffee, water, bread*.

EXERCISE   *Identify the nouns in the following sentences. Indicate if they are proper nouns (PN) or common nouns (CN), count nouns (count) non-count nouns (non-count), or collective nouns (coll). Clearly, a noun can belong to more than one category.*

MyWritingLab

1. The jury deliberated for days but was unable to reach a verdict.
2. Americans want to be secure from terrorist attacks without surrendering their fundamental liberties.
3. Many consumers prefer to catch up on their favorite shows using services such as Netflix or Hulu.
4. When engaged in strenuous exercise, you should drink plenty of water to keep your body hydrated.
5. The southern coast of Alaska can be warmer in February than much of the Midwest.

Pronouns

Pronouns are a special class of words that can fit the place of nouns in a sentence and sometimes can be seen as taking the place of a noun in a sentence. Pronouns can help you avoid the awkward repetition of nouns.

Personal Pronouns   Personal pronouns refer to identifiable persons or things. Personal pronouns have different cases. The subjective case is used when the pronoun serves as the subject of the sentence or clause. *I helped Steve.* The objective case is used when the pronoun is the object of a verb or preposition. *Steve helped **me**. We spoke about **him**.* The possessive case shows possession or ownership. *That is **my** briefcase. My, your, our,* and *their* always precede nouns, as in *their car. Mine, hers, ours, yours,* and *theirs* do not precede nouns, as in *That book is mine. His* and *its* may or may not precede nouns.

	Subjective	**Objective**	**Possessive**
Singular			
First person	I	me	my, mine
Second person	you	you	your, yours
Third person	he, she, it	him, her, it	his, her, hers, its
Plural			
First person	we	us	our, ours
Second person	you	you	your, yours
Third person	they	them	their, theirs

Relative Pronouns   A relative pronoun relates a dependent clause—a word group that has a subject and a predicate but cannot function as an independent sentence—to a noun or pronoun, called an antecedent, in the main part of the sentence.

The relative pronouns include the following:

who   whose   what   whoever   whichever
whom   which   that   whomever   whatever

Who in its various forms refers to people, *which* to things, and *that* to either people or things.

Mary Beth Cartwright, *who* was arrested last week for fraud, was Evansville's "Model Citizen" two years ago. (The antecedent of *who* is *Mary Beth Cartwright.*)

He took the electric razor, *which* needed a new cutting head, to the repair shop. (The antecedent of *which* is *electric razor.*)

David Bullock is someone *whom* we should definitely hire. (The antecedent of *whom* is *someone.*)

Montreal is a city *that* I've always wanted to visit. (The antecedent of *that* is *city.*)

Which typically introduces nonrestrictive clauses; that is, clauses that provide more information about whatever they modify (see page 624).

The palace, *which* was in bad condition a century ago, is finally going to be restored. (Clause adds information about palace.)

That is typically used in other situations, especially to introduce restrictive clauses: those that distinguish the things they modify from others in the same class (see page 624).

The used car *that* I bought last week at Honest Bill's has already broken down twice. (Clause distinguishes writer's used car from others.)

Pages 607-608 explain the use of *who* and *whom.*

Interrogative Pronouns   Interrogative pronouns introduce questions. All of the relative pronouns except *that* also function as interrogative pronouns.

who   which   whoever   whichever
whom   what   whomever   whatever
whose

What is the matter?

Who asked you?

Whatever do you mean?

When *what, which,* and *whose* are followed by nouns, they act as adjectives, not pronouns.

Which movie should we see?

Demonstrative Pronouns   As their name suggests, demonstrative pronouns point things out. There are four such pronouns.

this   these
that   those

This and its plural *these* identify recent or nearby things.

> *This* is the play to see.
>
> *These* are the times that try men's souls.

That and its plural *those* identify less recent or more distant things.

> *That* is Mary's house across the road.
>
> *Those* were very good peaches you had for sale last week.

Reflexive and Intensive Pronouns   A reflexive pronoun is used when the pronoun refers back to a noun in the same clause. An intensive pronoun lends emphasis to a noun or pronoun. The two sets of pronouns are identical.

myself	herself	ourselves
yourself	itself	yourselves
himself	oneself	themselves

> My father cut *himself* while shaving. (reflexive pronoun)
>
> The president *himself* has asked me to undertake this mission. (intensive pronoun)

Don't substitute a reflexive pronoun for a personal pronoun.

Faulty	*Jill* and *myself* are going to a movie.
Revision	*Jill* and *I* are going to a movie.
Faulty	Give the tickets to *John* and *myself*.
Revision	Give the tickets to *John* and *me*.

Sometimes you'll hear people say things like "He made it *hisself*," "They're only fooling *theirself*," or "They bought *theirselves* sodas." Such forms are nonstandard. Say "himself" and "themselves" instead.

Indefinite Pronouns   These pronouns refer to unidentified persons, places, or things. One group of indefinite pronouns consistently acts as pronouns.

anybody	everything	one
anyone	nobody	somebody
anything	no one	someone
everybody	nothing	something
everyone		

A second group may function as either pronouns or adjectives.

all	any	most	few	much
another	each	either	many	neither

Here are some examples:

> *Everyone* is welcome. (indefinite pronoun)
>
> *Many* are called, but *few* are chosen. (indefinite pronouns)
>
> *Many* men but only a *few* women attend the Air Force Academy. (adjectives)

Pages 601–603 discuss indefinite pronouns as antecedents.

Reciprocal Pronouns   The two reciprocal pronouns show an interchange of action between two or more parties. *Each other* is used when two parties interact, *one another* when three or more do.

> Pam and Patty accidentally gave *each other* the same thing for Christmas. (two persons)
>
> The members of the football team joyfully embraced *one another* after their victory. (more than two persons)

MyWritingLab   **EXERCISE**   *Identify each pronoun in the following sentences and indicate its type (personal, relative, interrogative, demonstrative, reflexive, intensive, indefinite, reciprocal). If it is a personal pronoun, indicate if it is in the subjective (S), objective (O), or possessive (P) case.*

1. Who knows which of these rental boats is mine?
2. Often employers do not fully know what they can reasonably expect from their employees.
3. Which fraternity did he say he was considering joining?
4. Fred has been looking for someone who can design a Web site for his part-time cleaning business.
5. This is the kind of day that I really enjoy.
6. I myself have had difficulty remembering to check my e-mail each day without a note on my smart phone to remind me.

Verbs

A verb indicates action or existence. Main verbs fall into two classes: *action verbs* and *linking verbs*. A very different type of verb is the *auxiliary* (or *helping*) verb, which adds specific kinds of meaning to the main verb.

Action Verbs   As its name suggests, an action verb expresses action. Some action verbs are transitive, others intransitive. A *transitive* verb has a direct object that receives or results from the action and rounds out the meaning of the sentence.

> The photographer *took* the picture.

Without the direct object, this sentence would not express a complete thought. In contrast, an *intransitive* verb requires no direct object to complete the meaning of the sentence.

> Lee Ann *gasped* loudly.
>
> Little Tommy Tucker *sings* for his supper.

Many action verbs can play both transitive and intransitive roles, depending on the sentences they are used in.

> Kari *rode* her bicycle into town. (transitive verb)
>
> Karl *rode* in the front seat of the car. (intransitive verb)

Linking Verbs   A linking verb shows existence or a state of affairs such as taste rather than action. Linking verbs are often followed by subject complements that reflect back on the subject of the sentence.

vbs

Ms. Davis *is* our new director. (Complement *director* renames subject
Ms. Davis.)

The soup *was* lukewarm. (Complement *lukewarm* describes subject *soup.*)

The most common linking verbs are forms of the verb *to be (is, are, am, was, were,
be, being, been.)* Likewise, verbs such as *seem, become, appear, remain, feel, look, smell,
sound,* and *taste* function as linking verbs when they do not indicate actual physical action. In such cases, they are followed by adjectives (see pages 583–585).
Here is an example:

Harry looked *angry.*

When such verbs do indicate physical action, they function as action verbs and
are followed by adverbs (see pages 585–586).

Harry looked *angrily* at the referee.

Auxiliary Verbs Auxiliary (helping) verbs accompany action or linking verbs
and provide information about time, possibility, or obligation, or establish the
passive. *Have, be,* and *do* can function as both auxiliary and main verbs.

The auxiliary verbs *have (has, had)* and *be (is, are, was, were)* can provide information about time.

Carol has repaired your computer.

Carol is reformatting your hard drive.

The auxiliary verb *do* is inserted to form the negative or a question when there
is no other auxiliary.

Ellen *did* not resign.

Did Ellen resign?

Auxiliary verbs called modals show time, obligation, possibility, or ability:
shall, should, will, would, can, could, may, might. With questions, the auxiliary verb
is often moved to the front.

Will Ellen *resign?*

EXERCISE *Identify each verb or auxiliary in the following sentences and indicate
whether it is a main verb (MV) or auxiliary (AUX).*

My WritingLab

1. The heavy rain flooded several streets and left many motorists stranded in
   their cars.
2. We should be considering ways that we can improve the quality of our lives.
3. Did you check the rates for phone calls and text messages once we cross into
   Canada?
4. The full moon tonight will be beautiful, but it also may make it harder to see the
   meteor shower.
5. With genetic screening, we can identify individuals who are at higher risk for many
   serious diseases.
6. The cost of college has been steadily rising over the last decade.

Tense Verbs change form to show distinctions in time. Every main verb has
two basic tenses: present and past.

The *present tense* shows present condition and general or habitual action, indicates permanent truths, tells about past events in the historical present, and sometimes denotes action at some definite future time.

Verbs in the present tense must agree with their subjects. If the subject of a verb is a singular noun or pronoun (*he, she, it*), add *s* or *es* (if the word ends with an *s* or *ch* sound, as in *talks* or *teaches*). If the subject is plural or a second-person pronoun (*you*), the verb takes no ending (*talk, teach*).

The past tense shows that a condition existed or an action was completed in the past. This verb tense leaves the time indefinite, but surrounding words may specify it. Most verbs are regular and form the past tense by adding *-ed:talk, talked*. Some verbs are irregular and form the past by changing the vowel: *stand, stood*. A very few verbs do not change forms at all in creating the past: *set, set*.

Past Participle   In addition to the basic tenses, there is a *past participle* form of the main verb that is used to form the perfect form of the verb phrase and the passive voice. For most verbs, the past participle form is identical with the past tense in form.

Present	Past	Past Participle
talk	talk**ed**	talk**ed**
stand	st**oo**d	st**oo**d
set	set	set

Some verbs have different past forms and past participles. This can often lead to errors where less experienced writers often use the regular past (*He has **swam** this river before*) when the past participle form is required (*he has **swum** this river before*). Similarly, "he broke the window" but "he has broken the window"; "he flew his plane" but "he has flown recently."

Time and Verb Forms

In addition to the tenses in English, many other forms of the verb express time.

Future Time   *Future time* is frequently indicated by the auxiliary modals *shall* or *will* with the present tense form of the verb.

You *will feel* better after a good night's sleep. (future condition)

Perfect Verb Forms   The perfect form of a verb is formed by a form of the auxiliary verb *have* and the past participle of the verb.

The *present perfect* tense is formed with *has* or *have* and the past participle of the main verb. It shows that a past condition or action, or its effect, continues until the present time.

Juanita *has driven* a United Parcel Service truck for five years. (Action continues until present.)

The *past perfect* tense combines *had* and the past participle of the main verb. It refers to a past condition or action that was completed before another past condition or action.

He *had been* in the army two years when the war ended. (Past perfect condition occurred first.)

The *future perfect* tense is formed from the verbs *shall have* or *will have* plus the past participle of the main verb. It shows that a condition or an action will have been completed at some time in the future. Surrounding words specify time.

Our sales manager *will have been* with the company 10 years next July. (Condition will end.)

Progressive Verb Forms   Each verb form, including the basic tenses, has a *progressive form* that indicates action in progress. The progressive is always indicated by some form of the verb *to be* followed by a present participle (or progressive), a verb that ends in *-ing*. "I am running." "He was running." "He had been running." "He will be running."

Pages 610–611 discuss unwarranted shifts in tense and their correction.

An easy way to identify the form of the verb phrase is to use the following formula.

(modal) + (have + en/ed) + (be + ing) + main verb
        Perfect   *Progressive*

Simply read the first available tense. If the modal is *will*, then that designates future time. Then if *have, has,* or *had* is present, the verb phrase is *perfect.* If a form of *be* is present and the main verb ends with *ing,* then the verb phrase is progressive.

will   have   been   living
Future   *Perfect*   *Progressive*

Usage   While most students use regular tenses and the progressive accurately, many less experienced writers do not always use the perfect verb form where appropriate. This is acceptable in informal writing; it is not acceptable for most formal writing.

Not acceptable Jim *studied* accounting for the last three years. (This suggests that the action is over and done with.)

Acceptable Jim *has studied* accounting for the last three years. (The present perfect verb form shows that the action comes right up to the present and may not be finished yet.)

Voice   Transitive verbs have two voices: active and passive. A verb is in the *active voice* when the subject carries out the action named by the verb.

Barry *planned* a picnic. (Subject *Barry* performs action.)

A verb is in the *passive voice* when the subject receives the action. The performer may be identified in an accompanying phrase or go unmentioned.

A picnic *was planned* by Barry. (The phrase *by Barry* identifies the performer.)
The picnic *was cancelled.* (The performer goes unmentioned.)

A passive construction always uses a form of *to be* and the past participle of an action verb. Like other constructions, the passive may show past, present, or future time.

vbs

Amy *is paid* handsomely for her investment advice. (present tense)

I *was warned* by a sound truck that a tornado was nearby. (past tense)

I *will be sent* to Ghana soon by the Peace Corps. (future tense)

Technical and scientific writing commonly uses the passive voice to explain processes since it focuses on the objective observation or the action rather than the agent who can vary and should be irrelevant to the result. Other kinds of writing, however, avoid the passive voice except when it is desirable to not identify the one performing the action or when the action is more significant than the actor. In Chapter 6, see pages 115–116 for more information on usage.

MyWritingLab   **EXERCISE**   *Identify each verb group in the following sentences, indicate its form (present, past, future, present perfect, past perfect, future perfect, and any of the progressive forms), and note any use of the passive voice.*

1. Devon broke his leg when he was thrown from his horse.
2. Deidra has managed our money for the last several years.
3. *Bright Eyes* is touring across Europe this year.
4. GTE Electric will have repaired the damage to the transformer before dinnertime.
5. Transfer credits will be evaluated within a week after a transcript has been received.
6. Maria has been acting in Shakespeare plays every summer since she first moved to Michigan.

Mood   The mood of a verb shows whether the writer regards a statement as a

1. fact
2. command or request
3. wish, possibility, condition contrary to fact, or the like.

English has three moods: the indicative, imperative, and subjunctive.

A sentence in the *indicative mood* states a real or supposed fact or asks a question.

Nancy *graduates* from high school tomorrow.

We *lived* in Oakmont when Rachel was born.

A sentence in the *imperative mood* delivers a command or makes a request.

Leave the room immediately! (command)

Please *turn* the music down. (request)

The subject of a sentence in the imperative mood is always *you*. Although ordinarily unstated, the subject sometimes appears in the sentence.

You leave the room immediately!

The *subjunctive mood* is used

1. in *if, as if,* and *as though* clauses to express a wish, a possibility, or an action or a condition contrary to fact
2. in *that* clauses expressing orders, demands, requests, resolutions, proposals, or motions

3. with modal auxiliaries to express wishes, probability, possibility, permission, requirements, recommendations, suggestions, and conditions contrary to fact.

To express a present or future wish, possibility, condition or action in an *if*, *as if*, or *as though* clause, use *were* with any personal pronoun or noun serving as the subject of the clause.

If only Stan *were* less gullible! (present wish contrary to fact)

Even if Kay *were* to explain, Mary wouldn't believe her. (future possibility)

Arthur is behaving as if he *were* a millionaire (present condition contrary to fact)

To express a wish, possibility, or condition contrary to past facts, use *had been* or *had* plus the past participle of an action verb.

If the engine *had been lubricated*, the bearing wouldn't have burned out. (past condition contrary to fact)

EXERCISE   *For each of the following sentences, identify the mood as indicative (IND), imperative (IMP), or subjunctive (SUB):*   MyWritingLab

1. See your doctor before starting a strenuous exercise program.
2. The tired runner staggered across the finish line.
3. These new cell phones should prove very popular.
4. Let me know what you think of this novel.
5. Hang gliding is a great sport for anyone unafraid of heights.
6. If you practiced more, you could become an outstanding pianist.

Adjectives

An adjective *modifies* a noun or pronoun by describing it, limiting it, or otherwise making its meaning more exact.

The *brass* candlestick stood next to the *fragile* vase. (*Brass* modifies *candlestick*, and *fragile* modifies *vase*.)

The cat is *long-haired* and *sleek*. (*Long-haired* and *sleek* modify *cat*.)

Common Adjectives   Most adjectives use the standard form of adjectives. Two or more adjectives may modify the same noun or pronoun.

He applied *clear* lacquer to the tabletop.

The *slim, sophisticated* model glided onto the runway.

The child was *active, happy*, and *polite*.

Proper Adjectives   A proper adjective is derived from a proper noun and is always capitalized.

The *American* principles of democracy have encouraged many living under tyranny.

Comparison with Adjectives   Adjectives can be used to show comparison. When two things are compared, shorter adjectives usually add *-er* and longer adjectives add *more*. When three or more things are compared, shorter adjectives usually add *-est* and longer ones add *most*.

> John is *taller* than Pete. (short adjective comparing two things)
> Sandra seems *more engaged* than Jill today. (long adjective comparing two things)
> John is the *tallest* of the three brothers. (short adjective comparing three things)
> Sandra is the *most engaged* student in the class. (longer adjective comparing more than three things)

Some adjectives, like the examples below, have irregular forms for comparisons.

> good—better—best
> bad—worse—worst

Don't use the *-est* form of the shorter adjective to compare just two things.

> *Faulty*   This is the *smallest* of the two castles.

Instead, use the *-er* form.

> *Revision*   This is the *smaller* of the two castles.

Determiners   There is a category of words that are sometimes classified with adjectives that limit the noun or pronoun but do not name a quality or characteristic of the noun or pronoun.

> *Three* sailboats raced around the island.

While we know how many sailboats are involved, there is no descriptive content added to the concept of sailboats.

There are many different kinds of determiners.

Determiners	Name
a, an	Indefinite article
the	Definite article
this, that, these, those	Demonstrative
one, two, three, four, five	Cardinal number
first, second, third, fourth	Ordinal number
my, our, your, his, her, hers, its, their	Possessive pronoun
some, any, no, every, another, enough, either, neither, all, both, each, less, other, many, more, most, few, several	Indefinite pronoun
Tom's, Mary's	Possessive noun
which, whose	Interrogative or relative determiner depending on use

The most common determiners are the indefinite article *a/an* and the definite article *the*.

EXERCISE *Identify the adjectives and determiners in the following sentences.*

1. The climbers seemed very tiny as they rappelled down the sheer cliff.
2. Janine's paper offered an insightful and well-supported argument.
3. Fresh grapefruit juice can be a tart but tasty breakfast beverage.
4. The stormy sea fiercely battered the frightfully frail boats tethered to the bucking docks.
5. Many contemporary homes employ an open-concept design where there are fewer walls dividing rooms than in earlier homes.
6. An online class can offer students greater flexibility in their schedules but less personal contact with their instructors.

Adverbs

An adverb modifies a verb, an adjective, another adverb, or a whole sentence. Adverbs generally answer questions such as "How?" "When?" "Where?" "How often?" and "To what extent?"

The floodwaters receded *very* slowly. (Adverb modifies adverb and answers the question "How?")

My sister will visit me *tomorrow*. (Adverb modifies verb and answers the question "When?")

The coach walked *away* from the bench. (Adverb modifies verb and answers the question "Where?")

The tire is *too* worn to be safe. (Adverb modifies adjective and answers the question "To what extent?")

The teller is *frequently* late for work. (Adverb modifies adjective and answers the question "How often?")

Formation of Adverbs   Most adverbs are formed by adding *-ly* to adjectives.

The wind is *restless*. (*Restless* is an adjective modifying *wind*.)
He walked *restlessly* around the room. (*Restlessly* is an adverb modifying *walked*.)

Many common adverbs, however (*almost, never, quite, soon, then, there, and too*), lack *-ly* endings.

I *soon* realized that pleasing my boss was impossible.
This movie is *too* gruesome for my taste.

Furthermore, some words such as *better, early, late, hard, little, near, only, straight,* and *wrong* do double duty as either adjectives or adverbs.

We must have taken a *wrong* turn. (*Wrong* is an adjective modifying the noun *turn*.)

Where did I go *wrong*? (*Wrong* is an adverb modifying the verb *go*.)

Comparison with Adverbs   Like adjectives, adverbs can show comparison. When two things are compared, adverbs add *more*. When three or more things are compared, *most* is used.

Harold works *more* efficiently than Don. (adverb comparing two people)

prep

Of all the people in the shop, Harold works the *most* efficiently. (adverb comparing more than two people)

Some adverbs, like some adjectives, use irregular forms for comparisons.

well—better—best

much—more—most

MyWritingLab   **EXERCISE**   *Identify the adverbs in the following sentences:*

1. Three friends slowly but steadily hiked up the mountain trail.
2. While print media often carefully report yesterday's news, online media hastily follow what is happening today.
3. While the screenplay was exceptionally well written, the movie itself was poorly directed and badly miscast.
4. Last winter was so very cold that many foolishly began to wish for climate change.
5. The aerobics instructor's music was too loud for most of her students, but no one really wanted to tell her.

Prepositions

A preposition links its object—a noun or noun substitute—to some other word in the sentence and shows a relationship between them. The relationship is often one of location, time, means, or reason or purpose. The word group containing the preposition and its object makes up a prepositional phrase.

The new insulation *in* the attic keeps my house much warmer now. (Preposition *in* links object *attic* to *insulation* and shows location.)

We have postponed the meeting *until* tomorrow. (Preposition *until* links object *tomorrow* to *postponed* and shows time.)

The tourists traveled *by* automobile. (Preposition *by* links object *automobile* to *traveled* and shows means.)

Warren swims *for* exercise. (Preposition *for* links object *exercise* to *swims* and shows reason or purpose.)

While most prepositions are one word, such as "up," there are a few that consist of more than one word, such as "by reason of" and "instead of."

MyWritingLab   **EXERCISE**   *Identify the prepositions (P) and their objects (O) in the following sentences:*

1. Angela searched her house for a book of poems by Rilke.
2. Last summer Sandy paddled around Isle Royale in a sea kayak.
3. Despite the advice of her financial planner, Joanna paid the remaining principal on her mortgage rather than investing her inheritance in stocks and bonds.
4. Tanisha had waited for several months before she learned that she had been accepted into law school at New York University.
5. In his paper on cloning, James cut through the confusion about the topic and clearly presented the arguments for each side of the issue.

Conjunctions

Conjunctions serve as connectors, linking parts of sentences or whole sentences. These connectors fall into three groups: coordinating conjunctions, subordinating conjunctions, and conjunctive adverbs.

Coordinating Conjunctions   Coordinating conjunctions connect terms of equal grammatical importance: words, word groups, and simple sentences. These conjunctions can occur singly *(and, but, or, nor, for, yet, so)* or in pairs called correlative conjunctions *(either—or, neither—nor, both—and, and not only—but also)*. The elements that follow correlative conjunctions must be parallel; that is, have the same grammatical form.

> Tom *and* his cousin are opening a coffee shop. (Coordinating conjunction connects nouns.)
>
> Shall I serve the tea in the living room *or* on the veranda? (Coordinating conjunction connects phrases.)
>
> I am going to Europe this summer, *but* Marjorie is staying home. (Coordinating conjunction connects simple sentences.)
>
> Amy *not only* teaches English *but also* writes novels. (Correlative conjunctions connect parallel predicates.)
>
> You can study nursing *either* at Ferris State University *or* at DeWitt College. (Correlative conjunctions connect parallel phrases.)
>
> Friendship is *both* pleasure *and* pain. (Correlative conjunctions connect parallel nouns.)

Subordinating Conjunctions   Like relative pronouns, subordinating conjunctions introduce subordinate clauses, relating them to independent clauses, which can stand alone as complete sentences. Examples of subordinating conjunctions include *because, as if, even though, since, so that, whereas,* and *whenever.*

> I enjoyed the TV program *because* it was so well acted. (Conjunction connects *it was so well acted* to rest of sentence.)
>
> *Whenever* you're ready, we can begin dinner. (Conjunction connects *you're ready* to rest of sentence.)

Conjunctive Adverbs   These connectors resemble both conjunctions and adverbs. Like conjunctions, they serve as linking devices between elements of equal rank. Like adverbs, they function as modifiers, showing such things as similarity, contrast, result or effect, addition, emphasis, time, and example.

> The job will require you to travel a great deal; *however*, the salary is excellent.
>
> Sean cares nothing for clothes; *in fact*, all of his socks have holes in their toes.

inter

The following list groups the most common conjunctive adverbs according to function:

Similarity: likewise, similarly

Contrast: however, nevertheless, on the contrary, on the other hand, otherwise

Result or effect: accordingly, as a result, consequently, hence, therefore, thus

Addition: also, furthermore, in addition, in the first place, moreover

Emphasis or clarity: in fact, in other words, indeed, that is

Time: afterward, later, meanwhile, subsequently

Example: for example, for instance, to illustrate

Conjunctive adverbs should not be confused with coordinating conjunctions. Unlike conjunctions and more like adverbs, conjunctive adverbs can move, often to create a specific emphasis.

The job will require you to travel a great deal; the salary, *however,* is excellent.

The job will require you to travel a great deal; *however,* the salary is excellent.

Because conjunctive adverbs can move, the second independent clause must be treated as a complete sentence and either be joined to the previous independent clause with a semicolon or be separated by a period.

Interjections

An interjection is an exclamatory word used to gain attention or to express strong feeling. It has no grammatical connection to the rest of the sentence. An interjection is followed by an exclamation point or a comma.

Hey! Watch how you're driving! (strong interjection)

Oh, is the party over already? (mild interjection)

MyWritingLab   **EXERCISE**   *Identify the coordinating conjunctions (CC), subordinating conjunctions (SC), conjunctive adverbs (CA), and interjections (I) in the following sentences:*

1. There is evidence that the polar ice caps are receding; however, scientists do not yet know the probable impact of this event.
2. Neither term limits nor campaign reform will take money out of politics.
3. Since there has been an increase in the alligator population, some lawmakers think the ban on alligator hide products should be lifted.
4. Rats! My computer ate my report.
5. Most companies work hard to secure their Internet sites, but hackers can usually find their way around these safeguards.

Phrases and Clauses

Phrases

A phrase is a group of words that lacks a subject and a predicate and serves as a single part of speech. This section discusses four basic kinds of phrase: *prepositional*, *participial*, *gerund*, and *infinitive*. The last three are based on participles, gerunds, and infinitives, which are verb forms known as verbals. A fifth type of phrase, the verb phrase, consists of sets of two or more verbs (*has fixed, had been sick, will have been selected*, and the like).

Prepositional Phrases   A prepositional phrase consists of a preposition, one or more objects, and any associated words. These phrases serve as adjectives or adverbs.

> The picture *over the mantel* was my mother's. (prepositional phrase as adjective)
>
> He bought ice skates *for himself.* (prepositional phrase as adverb modifying verb)
>
> The toddler was afraid *of the dog.* (prepositional phrase as adverb modifying adjective)
>
> Our visitors arrived late *in the day.* (prepositional phrase as adverb modifying another adverb)

Frequently, prepositional phrases occur in series. Sometimes they form chains in which each phrase modifies the object of the preceding phrase. At other times, some or all of the phrases may modify the verb or verb phrase.

> John works *in a clothing store/on Main Street/ during the summer.*

Here the first and third phrases serve as adverbs modifying the verb *works* and answering the questions "Where?" and "When?" while the second phrase serves as an adjective modifying *store* and answering the question "Where?"

On occasion, especially in questions, a preposition may be separated from its object, making the phrase difficult to find.

> Dr. Perry is the person *whom* I've been looking *for.*
>
> *What* are you shouting *about?*

Participial Phrases   A participial phrase consists of a participle plus associated words. Participles are verb forms that, when used in participial phrases, function as adjectives or adverbs. A present participle ends in *-ing* and indicates an action currently being carried out. A past participle ends in *-ed, -en, -e, -n, -d,* or *-t* and indicates some past action.

> The chef *preparing dinner* trained in France. (present participial phrase as adjective)
>
> The background, *sketched in lightly,* accented the features of the woman in the painting. (past participial phrase as adjective)
>
> She left *whistling a jolly melody.* (present participial phrase as adverb)

A perfect participial phrase consists of *having* or *having been* plus a past participle and any associated words. Like a past participial phrase, it indicates a past action.

> *Having alerted the townspeople about the tornado*, the sound truck returned to the city garage. (perfect participial phrase)
> *Having been alerted to the tornado*, the townspeople sought shelter in their basements. (perfect participial phrase)

Some participial phrases that modify persons or things distinguish them from others in the same class. These phrases are written without commas. Other phrases provide more information about the persons or things they modify and are set off with commas.

> The man *fixing my car* is a master mechanic. (Phrase distinguishes man fixing car from others.)
> Mr. Welsh, *fatigued by the tennis game*, rested in the shade. (Phrase provides more information about Mr. Welsh.)

Gerund Phrases   A gerund phrase consists of a gerund and the words associated with it. Like present participles, gerunds are verb forms that end in *-ing*. Unlike participles, though, they function as nouns rather than as adjectives or adverbs.

> Kathryn's hobby is *collecting stamps*. (gerund phrase as subject complement)
> Kathryn's hobby, *collecting stamps*, has made her many friends. (gerund phrase as appositive)
> He devoted every spare moment to *overhauling the car*. (gerund phrase as object of preposition.)

Infinitive Phrases   An infinitive phrase consists of the present principal part of a verb preceded by *to (to fix, to eat)*, together with any accompanying words. These phrases serve as adjectives, adverbs, and nouns.

> This looks like a good place *to plant the shrub*. (infinitive phrase as adjective)
> Lenore worked *to earn money for college*. (infinitive phrase as adverb)
> My goal is *to have my own business some day*. (infinitive phrase as noun)

Gerunds can often be substituted for infinitives and vice versa.

> *To repair this fender* will cost two hundred dollars. (infinitive phrase as subject)
> *Repairing this fender* will cost two hundred dollars. (gerund phrase as subject)
> At times the *to* in an infinitive is omitted following verbs such as *make, dare, let,* and *help.*
> Kristin didn't dare *(to) move* a muscle.
> The psychiatrist helped me *(to) overcome* my fear of flying.